THE LIFE OF ELIZABETH BARRETT BROWNING

Elizabeth Barrett Browning

THE LIFE OF
Elizabeth Barrett Browning

BY GARDNER B. TAPLIN

New Haven: YALE UNIVERSITY PRESS, 1957

© *1957 by Yale University Press, Inc.*
Printed in the United States of America by
Vail-Ballou Press, Inc., Binghamton, N.Y.
All rights reserved. This book may not be
reproduced, in whole or in part, in any form
(except by reviewers for the public press),
without written permission from the publishers.
Library of Congress catalog card number: 57-6344

To *H. G. T.* and *H. B. T.*
who have shared in the making of this book

PREFACE

THE AIM of this volume is to present a full-length biography of Elizabeth Barrett Browning based on original sources. My first impulse to write the book may be traced to a remark by Howard Mumford Jones in his course on Victorian literature at Harvard that there was no complete and authoritative treatment of Mrs. Browning's life and works and that in view of the great influence she had upon her age, a comprehensive study was needed. During the academic years 1948–49 and 1953–54 I traveled in England and Italy gathering materials and visiting many of the places associated with the Barrett family and the Brownings: Coxhoe, Ledbury, Sidmouth, Torquay, and London; Pisa, Florence, Bagni di Lucca, Siena, and Rome. I have also examined manuscripts of her poems, unpublished letters in private and public collections on both sides of the Atlantic, and many of the volumes she owned, in the margins of which she jotted down her comments.

The letters to H. S. Boyd, which give for the first time a detailed picture of the early period of her life, appeared only last year, in a volume edited by Barbara McCarthy. Portions of the correspondence from Elizabeth Barrett to Miss Mitford were brought out two years ago by Betty Miller. The letters to her brother George are to be published within a few months by the University of Illinois Press. But it is a curious fact that although the sesquicentennial of her birth is being observed this year (1956), hundreds of her most interesting letters have not yet been published. The 113 letters—most of them long and intimate—which she wrote to her sister Arabel over a period of 22 years, the 121 letters to her American friend in Italy, Mrs. Eckley, large parts of the extensive correspondence to her sister Henrietta and her close friend Miss Mitford, and much that she wrote to Mrs. Jameson, Kenyon, and Mrs. Martin may be seen only in manuscript. And in spite of all that has been written on the Brownings, earlier biographers and critics have made almost no use of this mass of primary material.

The present owners of all of Mrs. Browning's manuscripts of which I have knowledge have sent me information or granted me access to their holdings without restriction. It has therefore been my good fortune to see almost every letter which Mrs. Browning is known to have written, except for a portion of her correspondence to Isa Blagden and to Sarianna Browning, both sets of which seem mostly to have disappeared after the Sotheby sale of the Browning collections in 1913.

Since this book is based on so much fresh material, I have been able to offer several new points of view. For example, the hitherto unpublished portions of Mrs. Browning's letters to her sister Henrietta make it clear that the Barrett family's principal objection to her marriage with Browning was the fact that he was dependent upon his wife's income. They also emphasize her long-continued bitterness and despair because of her father's unrelenting attitude after her marriage. Her letters to Arabel Barrett present hundreds of new details about the Brownings' family life in Italy and Mrs. Browning's literary career.

Elizabeth Barrett once wrote her suitor, "I, for my part, value letters (to talk literature) as the most vital part of biography." Insofar as possible, I have given the story of her life as she herself told it; in this way all aspects of the subject can be documented, for she wrote about herself fully from early childhood until the last few weeks before her death. To the Brownings' many admirers who have felt that because of the intimate and personal qualities of the love letters, it was a sacrilege for the Brownings' son to arrange for their publication, I would again cite the words of Elizabeth Barrett in support of my belief that she would have approved. "If the secrets of our daily lives and inner souls may instruct other surviving souls," she wrote, "let them be open to men hereafter, even as they are to God now."

In the autumn of 1948 when I was in Italy, I learned that Dorothy Hewlett was also preparing a biography of Mrs. Browning. The following spring I saw Miss Hewlett in London, and we then agreed upon a division of labor. Her volume, which was published in 1952, was to be mainly biographical, while mine was to

Preface

be primarily a discussion of the poetry and of the development of Mrs. Browning's reputation. These last few years, however, I have found so much new biographical information in Mrs. Browning's unpublished letters that I have written a fuller biography than I had originally planned.

In the texts of letters reproduced here, I have retained Mrs. Browning's characteristic punctuation of two dots, which often have the force of a dash. In the Bibliography the check list of Mrs. Browning's publications supplements the bibliography published by T. J. Wise in 1918; to this list I have added 18 items of Mrs. Browning's contributions to periodicals which are not in Wise. Since the Wise bibliography was a limited edition of 100 copies and is available in only a few libraries, I have also included for the reader's convenience all of Mrs. Browning's contributions to periodicals listed by Wise. Miss Hewlett at the end of her biography (pp. 385-8) lists the main books of reference. In general I have indicated the sources of all material except a few books which have long been familiar to students of the Brownings. Whenever a source for a quotation is not given, the reader may assume that the quotation comes from Mrs. Browning's letters to Horne (1877), her letters edited by Kenyon (1897), the love letters which Browning and Elizabeth Barrett wrote to each other (1899), and Mrs. Browning's letters to Henrietta edited by Huxley (1929). Most of the quotations in Chapters 9 and 10 have been taken from the love letters.

For the many courtesies which I have received I wish to express thanks to the officials and attendants of the three libraries where I wrote this book: the British Museum, the Harvard College Library, and the Boston Public Library—as well as to the director of the Houghton Library at Harvard for permission to quote from its Browning manuscripts. I am much indebted to the Wellesley College Library for permission to publish from Mrs. Browning's letters, and particularly to Research Librarian Hannah D. French, who has helped me in countless ways.

I also record my gratitude to the following persons and institutions: Dr. John D. Gordan, Curator of the Henry W. and Albert A. Berg Collection in the New York Public Library, for permission to publish from Mrs. Browning's manuscripts; the Keeper of Manuscripts, New York Public Library, for permission to publish part of a letter from Elizabeth Barrett to E. H. Barker, in the A. W. Anthony Collection of the Manuscript Division; Arthur A. Houghton, Jr., for bringing his valuable Browning collection to New York so that I might examine it in the summer of 1951 and for giving me permission to quote; Paul Landis of the University of Illinois, for allowing me to look at the University's collection of Browning manuscripts; the Yale University Library, the Folger Shakespeare Library, and the Pierpont Morgan Library, for permission to examine Browning manuscripts and to quote from them; the Princeton University Library and the Henry E. Huntington Library, for microfilms and photostats; the Boston Athenaeum and the National Library of Scotland, for the use of their collections; and the staff of the Charles Elihu Slocum Library of Ohio Wesleyan University, for copying out marginalia in the books in its possession formerly owned by Mrs. Browning.

In this list of acknowledgments I must also mention Douglas M. Moffat, for sending me a transcript of the marginalia in his copy of a volume once owned by Mrs. Browning; Contessa Maria Datti-Campello, for allowing me to see one of the Brownings' homes in Rome; Signor Amedeo Doberti of Bagni di Lucca, for showing me the rooms and garden of Villa Bastiani (formerly Casa Tolomei), where the Brownings lived in the summer of 1853; the late Stephen Ballard of Colwall, for a photograph of Hope End; and George H. Bird of Port Alberni, B.C., for another photograph of Hope End.

The following persons have kindly answered inquiries: Mrs. Ann Lund and M. C. Duncan, both of Sidmouth; Colonel Ronald Moulton-Barrett, Calbourne, Isle of Wight; Lilla Weed, Wellesley; William O. Raymond, Bishop's University; G. H. Needler, Ontario; Dean Harry Ransom, Fannie Ratchford, and Gertrude Reese Hudson, all of Austin, Texas; Mrs. A. J. Armstrong, Waco, Texas; and Bennett Weaver and R. H. Super, both of Ann Arbor.

The Deans of the Graduate School at Indiana University were interested in this study from its beginning and awarded me several faculty fellowships and generous grants-in-aid.

Barbara McCarthy of Wellesley College read an early version of my manuscript and suggested several improvements. David

Preface

Horne of the Yale University Press has also made many constructive criticisms in preparing my manuscript for the printer. Sir John Murray and John Grey Murray have allowed me to use both unpublished and published Browning materials for which they hold the copyright.

G. B. T.

Wellesley, Massachusetts
August 1956

CONTENTS

Preface		vii
1.	Early Years at Hope End	1
2.	Loss of Hope End	25
3.	Sojourn in Sidmouth	44
4.	First Stay in London: "The Seraphim"	55
5.	Tragedy at Torquay	73
6.	Return to Wimpole Street	88
7.	Friendships and Literary Activities	106
8.	"Poems" of 1844	122
9.	Robert Browning	139
10.	Engagement and Marriage	162
11.	From London to Pisa	181
12.	Italian Affairs and "Casa Guidi Windows"	196
13.	"Poems" of 1850	222
14.	England and Paris, 1851–52	243
15.	Florence, Bagni di Lucca, and Rome	269
16.	England and Paris, 1855–56	290
17.	"Aurora Leigh"	310
18.	War Again in Italy: "Poems before Congress"	348
19.	Last Poems and Final Illness	382
20.	Epilogue: A Century of Criticism	404
Cue Titles		425
Notes		427
Bibliography		455
Index		467

ILLUSTRATIONS

Elizabeth Barrett Browning. From a painting by Michele Gordigiani. By permission of the trustees, National Portrait Gallery, London (*frontispiece*)

	page
Hope End. From an old painting	6
Coxhoe Hall. Photo supplied by the National Coal Board, Darlington	6
The Barretts' house at Fortfield Terrace, Sidmouth. Photo by Hayes	44
Hope End. From an old photograph	44
Collegio Ferdinando, Pisa. Photo by the author	186
Letter from Mrs. Browning to Fanny Dowglass, August 2, 1847. By permission of the Berg Collection, New York Public Library	199
Casa Guidi. Photo by the author	204
Page 215 of *The Seraphim,* with Mrs. Browning's manuscript corrections for her new edition of *Poems* (1850). By permission of Wellesley College	229
Robert Browning. From a painting by Michele Gordigiani. By permission of the trustees, National Portrait Gallery, London	358

1. Early Years at Hope End

SOME TIME during the winter of 1794–95 Mr. and Mrs. Edward Barrett, their ward, their daughter, and their three grandchildren left their comfortable plantation home in the British West Indies to undertake the tedious passage to England.[1] They left behind them both wealth and influence. Ever since Hersey Barrett had landed in Jamaica in 1655 with the British expedition of Admiral Penn and General Venables which wrested control of the island from the Spanish, the Barrett family fortunes had improved. The period of their most rapid expansion was the second half of the eighteenth century, when Edward Barrett and his brothers were buying estates along the western portion of the Northside, in the precincts of St. James and Trelawny, from Montego Bay eastward to Palmetto Point, which later became Falmouth. By the 1790's Barrett prestige was at its peak, the family being ranked among the leading planters of the island.

But in 1794–95 Edward Barrett and his family said goodbye to their relatives and friends at Cinnamon Hill Great House and made their way to the port of Falmouth, ten miles along the shore to the east, to embark for England. The grandparents looked forward to visiting a brother and sisters in London before returning to Jamaica, while the younger members of the party, Miss Trepsack and Elizabeth and her children, were planning to remain in England. Mary Trepsack (Trippy) was an orphan whose father, an impoverished Jamaica planter, had died suddenly and left her without means for her support. She had been accepted as a member of the family by Samuel Barrett, and after he died in 1782 by his brother Edward. The Barretts' daughter Elizabeth, accompanied by her three children, was leaving the only home she had known and the birthplace of herself and of at least two of her children, Edward and Sam, who were then about ten and eight years old respectively. Her twelve-year-old daughter Sarah and, very likely, the tutor of the children, Francis Murphy, completed the group. Elizabeth's reason for transplanting her family in England was that they might receive an English education and an English upbringing. And when the education of these rich children should be completed and they should in turn have established homes for themselves, the family plan was to allow them to remain in England, receiving rents as absentee owners of their vast and profitable Jamaica estates. Elizabeth's husband, Charles Moulton, was not present and in fact had not been within the family circle for several years. The marriage had not been successful, and soon after Sam's birth in 1787 he had wandered off—to New York for the slave sales, and to England, where he fathered several children by various mistresses—never again to return to his wife and legitimate offspring.

It may have been before Edward Barrett's departure from Jamaica that he leased for his daughter Coxhoe Hall in Durham County, through the good offices of a business acquaintance, John Graham-Clarke, a wealthy merchant of Newcastle and the future father-in-law of young Edward Barrett Moulton—though after their arrival in England the Barretts seem to have lived for several months with their London relatives. It was during this interval that Sir Thomas Lawrence painted the now famous portrait of Sarah Goodin Moulton (Pinkie), who died on April 23, 1795, shortly after the canvas was finished. Coxhoe Hall, which became in the spring of 1795 the home of Elizabeth Barrett Moulton, of her life-long companion Mary Trepsack, and of the two remaining Moulton children, is six miles south of Durham. It is a large stone castellated building of three stories set in the middle of a beautiful wooded estate of more than a thousand acres. The hall had been built about 1725 by John Burdon, who is said to have imported Italian workers to make the interior decorations, which were handsome and ornate. The large and elaborate fireplace in the drawing room was of carved wood with figures of floral wreaths and shells. On the ground floor were three reception rooms and a billiard room, and upstairs about twenty bedrooms, many of which had fireplaces decorated with colored marble.[2] As one looks at the estate today, he needs an effort of the imagination to visualize what it must have been like toward the end of the eighteenth century. At that time no village of Coxhoe had yet come into being; about one hundred people lived in scattered cottages in the outlying districts. In all directions from the mansion one would have seen only woodland and pasture and low hills in the distance, with everything rural and unspoiled. Now only the shell of Coxhoe Hall remains, for prisoners of war billeted there during the conflict of 1939–45 completed the ruin of the interior. Since then the building has been allowed by its present owners, the National Coal Board, to fall into even greater disrepair. Huge slagheaps from coal-mining operations disfigure the landscape, and much of the original estate has become an ugly modern town, with rows of cheaply built brick houses all looking much alike.

Mrs. Moulton in her magnificent palace decided that her eldest son should be educated in a style appropriate to a future country gentleman who would inherit much of the Barrett property. Young Edward Barrett Moulton was indeed fortunate. According to the principle of primogeniture he would some day be the chief proprietor of his grandfather's extensive Jamaica plantations. By 1797, when Edward Barrett Moulton entered Harrow, his grandfather Edward Barrett had buried all three of his sons. His eldest, George Goodin, had died a bachelor and had bequeathed £30,000 and other wealth to nephew Edward Barrett Moulton. Another son, Henry, was survived by one daughter, Elizabeth; and the youngest son, Samuel, left four children by an illicit union with a second cousin, Elizabeth Barrett Waite Williams. So shortly before his death in 1798, Edward Barrett made his will in favor of the sons of his daughter Elizabeth, with the provision that the sons adopt the surname of Barrett. Once again John Graham-Clarke acted as intermediary for Edward Barrett and secured in 1798 permission from the King for the change. The full names of Mrs. Moulton's sons were now Edward Barrett Moulton Barrett and Samuel Barrett Moulton Barrett. (In later years the first "Barrett" was usually dropped by both brothers.)

How long the twelve-year-old Edward remained at Harrow is not known. He seems to have entered in October 1797, and may have remained only a few months.[3] Oddly enough, in none of her correspondence did his famous daughter in later years ever refer to her father's education or to his activities during the period he would normally have spent at school and the university. Long after his wife's death, Robert Browning wrote that Edward Moulton Barrett received at Harrow "so savage a punishment for a supposed offence ('burning the toast') by the youth whose 'fag' he had become, that he was withdrawn from the school by his mother, and the delinquent was expelled." [4] Whether or not that old family legend has any basis of truth, it was unfortunate for Edward that his indulgent mother allowed him to remain away from school. Evidence suggests that even as a boy he was permitted to live in a dream world of his own, so that he never had to discipline himself by academic studies or to learn how to get along with other people in the give-and-take of school or college life.

The guardian of the Barrett brothers was James Scarlett, later Lord Abinger, one of the most brilliant lawyers of his time, who had originally come from an estate near Cinnamon Hill, Jamaica. No family records tell whether he took the place of the missing father or whether he was too much occupied with his own practice and his personal affairs to have time to supervise very closely the upbringing of the late Edward Barrett's heirs.

Although in October 1801 Edward Moulton Barrett entered Trinity College, Cambridge, as a fellow-commoner at the early age of sixteen, it would be fruitless to speculate upon the influence his tutor Thomas Jones and other teachers may have had upon him, for there is in fact no proof that he ever resided at Cambridge.[5] From 1798, when he was removed from Harrow at the age of twelve or thirteen, until his early marriage, he apparently had very little formal schooling, except perhaps for some desultory tutoring at home. Free from external pressures and restraints and relieved of the necessity of assuming responsibilities, he no doubt was becoming more and more self-willed, isolated, and insensitive to the feelings of those around him. The large, coarse handwriting and the manner of expression and subject matter of the letters of his mature years reveal him as a man who probably did not often put down his thoughts on paper and one whose mind had a practical bent far removed from the intellectual and artistic interests of his daughter. His younger brother Samuel, who was to become "more than uncle" to Elizabeth Barrett, had a more attractive, more outgoing personality and evidently more facility in self-

Early Years at Hope End 5

expression, since he was for several years a member of Parliament.

On May 14, 1805, Edward Moulton Barrett married Mary Graham-Clarke of Newcastle—he not yet twenty, she some four years older. It would have been very natural for Mrs. Moulton and her sons to visit John Graham-Clarke and his family, for Newcastle is not far from Durham and he had been for many years an adviser and friend of the Barretts in Jamaica. Edward's bride was of a family as wealthy as his own. Her father was one of the first citizens of Newcastle; he took an interest in civic affairs, and had a fleet of ships sailing between England and the West Indies, as well as sugar plantations in Jamaica, and diversified business investments in his home city.

Edward brought his bride to Coxhoe Hall, where they lived with Mrs. Moulton, Trippy, and Sam, and where two of their children were born. While the mansion was large enough to accommodate several families, Edward and Mary, like many young couples who have to live for a while with their parents, must have been hoping they would soon have a house of their own. Their first child was born on March 6, 1806, and was named after Mrs. Moulton; hence the full name was Elizabeth Barrett Moulton Barrett. With her oval face and slightly receding chin, she looked more like her father than her mother. About a year later a son and heir was born whose features had a remarkable resemblance to those of his older sister.[6] The second child was named Edward Barrett Moulton Barrett, after his father and grandfather. The two children were baptized together at nearby Kelloe Church on February 10, 1808.

The owner of Kelloe Manor, which is a mile or two from Coxhoe Hall, was Sir Henry Vane Tempest, whose wife was the proprietor of an estate of about five hundred acres called Hope End (meaning "a closed valley") in the eastern part of Herefordshire. On September 6, 1809, Edward Moulton Barrett wrote his three-year-old daughter, who was staying with Mrs. Moulton at her home in Surrey, that he and several other men were examining Hope End, and he added, "The more I see of the property the more I like it and the more I think I shall have it in my power to make yourself, Brother and Sister and dear Mamma happy."[7] Accordingly, later in the year, several months after the birth of Henrietta, the third child, Edward Barrett bought Hope End and built for himself and his growing family a "Turkish house," as Elizabeth later wrote Robert Browning, "crowded with minarets and domes, and crowned with metal spires and crescents." It is probable that his daughter's words are not literally true; he may have been responsible only for the pseudo-Eastern excrescences of the house Lady Tempest had owned.[8]

Ledbury is approximately in the center of a triangle formed by the three cathedral cities of Hereford, Gloucester, and Worcester. It is an old market town, and many of its buildings, which date from the sixteenth and seventeenth centuries, are in the black and white half-timbered, half-brick style characteristic of the region. In the early nineteenth century the town and its environs must have looked much as they do today. The surrounding countryside is gently rolling and covered with forests, pastures for sheep and cattle grazing, apple orchards, hopyards, and fields of wheat and barley. The Hope End estate, which is three miles from Ledbury, is on the northern edge of a range of hills running north and south immediately to the east of the town. To the south of Hope End is the small village of Wellington Heath; to the east, Barton Court, which was the home of the Peytons, friends of the Barretts; to the northeast, the estate of Old Colwall, where Mr. and Mrs. James Martin lived, also close friends of the Barretts; and to the northwest, the low-lying parishes of Bosbury and Coddington. The highest land in the vicinity, running north and south about two miles to the east of Hope End and Ledbury, is the range of the Malvern Hills, on the sharp eastern slopes of which are Great Malvern and Malvern Wells. It is fortunate that the lovely Hope End estate, with its great forest trees of oak, beech, cedar, and cypress, has been preserved almost as it was when the Barretts lived there. The only important difference is that Mr. Barrett's dwelling was torn down about 1872 and a new house of more conventional design erected on an eminence overlooking the hollow where the older building had stood. Nothing remains of the earlier structure except some of its foundations. The walls which enclosed the courtyard in the rear and the archway and clock turret (though not the clock) have recently been reconstructed, and on the site of the old mansion the present

Coxhoe Hall

Hope End

Early Years at Hope End 7

owner of Hope End has just built a guest house. Neither the suburban areas of Great Malvern nor those of Ledbury have encroached upon Hope End and its neighboring farms and estates, all of which still retain their rural qualities.

However bizarre Edward Barrett's architectural tastes may have been, his mansion was as luxurious as the one he had left in the north. Like Coxhoe Hall, it had twenty bedrooms, many of them with elaborately carved marble fireplaces. Over the main hall, on the ground floor, and the great stone staircase with its mahogany handrail and brass balustrade was a large glass dome. The folding doors between the various drawing rooms were of mahogany, inlaid with pearl and filled with stained glass. From the windows of the reception rooms one could see pheasants parading their plumage on the lawn, beautiful flower gardens and shrubbery, and a small artificial pond.[9] The house was unfortunately situated in a vale, so that the higher land around it obstructed the views of the Malvern Hills and of Eastnor Castle.

WHEN Frederic G. Kenyon edited Mrs. Browning's letters in 1897, he included only three from the Hope End period, because at that time almost no others were available. He was not sure how many had been preserved; more than two hundred letters written during her early years have been saved, however, most of them from Elizabeth to her eccentric and scholarly neighbor Hugh Stuart Boyd but many from members of her own family to her. Furthermore, almost every scrap of paper upon which she placed her childish pen has been piously rescued from oblivion even though most of the material has little biographical significance and no poetical merit. Today one may see in various public and private collections Elizabeth's schoolroom exercises, a succession of birthday epistles in verse to her family, excerpts from plays performed, descriptions of games and entertainments of the Barrett family and their cousins, summaries of her reading, and solemn estimates of her own character and personality, all of them in the open, flowing hand of her teens and even of earlier years. The impression one gains from reading the letters and other documents of the Hope End period is that Elizabeth was a shy, intensely studious, precocious child, yet cheerful, affectionate, and lovable. She was not so much of a recluse as she later believed she had been, for she took delight in planning charades and composing and taking part in plays with her brother Edward and her sisters as fellow actors.

The estate of Hope End and its surrounding hills provided a beautiful and peaceful setting, a "paradise" she always called it in later years. "Beautiful, beautiful hills, they are!" she wrote of the Malvern Hills; and in the same letter to Richard Hengist Horne, viewing in retrospect her life at Hope End and the countryside of Herefordshire, she spoke of "a retirement scarcely broken to me except by books and my own thoughts, and it is a beautiful country, and was a retirement happy in many ways, although the very peace of it troubles the heart as it looks back." [10] And in writing to Boyd in the summer of 1846 at the moment a new happiness was entering her life, she confessed that "looking back to that early time, the hours spent with you, appear to me some of the happiest of my life." [11]

Mr. and Mrs. Barrett had brought with them to Hope End their three children, Elizabeth, Edward, and Henrietta. Between 1810 and 1824 the patient mother bore nine more, and all grew to maturity, except Mary, who died in 1814 at the age of three. Elizabeth's early verse and letters and her mother's letters to her paint a vivid picture of the daily routine of the large household. Mr. Barrett occupied himself with landscape gardening on his estate and with the supervising of his farms. He was elected sheriff of the county in 1812 and again in 1814 [12] and took an active part in the meetings of the Bible and missionary societies at Ledbury and Malvern. Before Elizabeth's long and serious illness at the age of fifteen she often went with him to church services. "I used to go with my father always," she later wrote Browning, "when I was able, to the nearest dissenting chapel of the Congregationalists." Edward (Bro) and Elizabeth (Ba—from the first syllable of "baby" and pronounced as though spelled "bah") studied together their French, Greek, and Latin. The sisters Henrietta (Addles) and Arabella practiced on the piano and played duets with their mother or with their governess Mrs. Orme. The younger brothers Sam and Charles John (Stormie) were often busy copying out French and Latin paradigms. In the afternoons, when school-

Early Years at Hope End 9

work was finished, brothers and sisters, except Elizabeth who was too frail, sometimes went "on some fanciful chase over the hills," [13] in Mrs. Barrett's words, and in the evenings they would often read together. "Books and dreams were what I lived in—and domestic life only seemed to buzz gently around, like bees about the grass," Elizabeth said many years later.

The list of books she read is formidable. At four and a half her "great delight was poring over fairy phenomenons and the actions of necromancers—and The Seven Champions of Christendom in 'Popular Tales' has beguiled many a weary hour." Then she wept over Mrs. Amelia Opie's moral tales *The Father and Daughter, Temper,* and *Valentine's Eve.* Soon afterward she was absorbed in the histories of Greece, Rome, and England and in Pope's Homer, *Paradise Lost,* and Shakespeare.[14]

At the age of twelve the study of metaphysics was her "highest delight." After reading Locke, she "not only felt edified but exalted," and for a time she kept a copy of Hooker's works under her pillow that she might study them at the earliest light of dawn.[15] Her father had told her not to read Gibbon and *Tom Jones* "and none of the books on *this* side, mind!" So she was "very obedient and never touched the books on *that* side, and only read instead Tom Paine's 'Age of Reason,' and Voltaire's 'Philosophical Dictionary,' and Hume's 'Essays,' and Werther, and Rousseau, and Mary Wollstonecraft." When she was thirteen, she "perused all modern authors who have any claim to superior merit and poetic excellence," [16] but she did not particularize. She was overserious in her religious devotion. Her religion at the age of twelve, she wrote four years later in an autobiographical sketch unpublished in her lifetime, was "not the deep persuasion of the mild Christian but the wild visions of an enthusiast." One evening her "whole mind was tortured" after she remembered having accidentally forgotten a prayer. "The next morning I renewed with tenfold ardour my agonising prayers," she wrote. "My God, My God, why hast thou forsaken me I repeated in a tone of anguish." [17]

It is no surprise that such a high-strung and bookish child should have made verses from her infancy. "I used to write of virtue with a large 'V,' and 'Oh Muse' with a harp, and things of that sort," she later told Browning. "At nine years old I wrote what I called 'an epic'—and at ten various tragedies, French and English, which we used to act in the nursery." One which escaped destruction was her drama called "Regulus," in French rhymed verse. Bro took the part of the noble Roman. Elizabeth as his daughter and Henrietta as his wife Marcia both perish from despair at the end when they see the tragic hero leave Rome for his death in Carthage.[18]

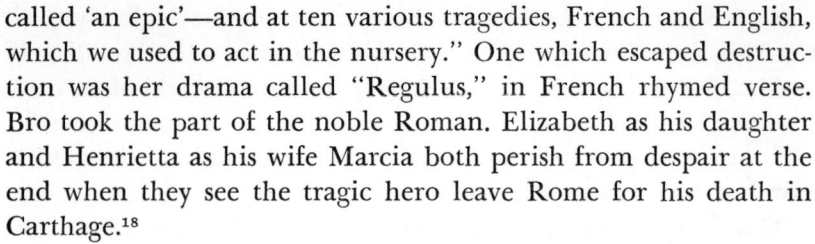

When she was about twelve, a Mr. MacSwiney came to Hope End to tutor Bro in the subjects required for entrance to Charterhouse. Elizabeth eagerly availed herself of the opportunity for instruction, and for two or three years before Bro's departure for the school in 1820 the two of them studied together Greek, Latin, French, and probably some Italian. The type of book which interested her may be seen from her casual remark in a letter to her uncle Sam, written when she was twelve, that she had been reading John Bigland's *An Historical Display of the Effects of Physical and Moral Causes on the Character and Circumstances of Nations,* Frederic S. N. Douglas' *An Essay on Certain Points of Resemblance between the Ancient and Modern Greeks,* Madame de Sévigné's *Letters* (on which Elizabeth commented, "The French is excellent."), and the last canto of *Childe Harold's Pilgrimage.*[19] Her schoolroom translations and paraphrases written during this early period give evidence of an acquaintance with at least Homer, Plato, Bion, Anacreon, Horace, Claudian, and Dante; and she was also familiar with Xenophon, Ovid, the *Aeneid,* and several plays by Racine and Molière. The time when she "read Greek as hard under the trees as some of your Oxonians in the Bodleian" [20] was not to begin until seven or eight years later, after she had been encouraged by H. S. Boyd to renew her Greek studies. "My learning Greek was a child's fancy . . achieved for Homer's sake," [21] she later wrote to Miss Mitford, and she confessed to Boyd that her reading Greek with MacSwiney "was rather guessing and stammering and tottering through parts of Homer and extracts from Xenophon than reading."

Her first volume of verse is the product of her early Hellenic enthusiasm. *The Battle of Marathon,* an "epic" in four books—"Pope's Homer done over again, or rather undone," [22] she later described it—was written in 1817 or 1818 [23] but did not appear until early in 1820, for the inscription in the copy sent to "dearest Grandmama from her affectionate child" was dated March 6 of that year.[24] Just as Elizabeth was beginning her career, several writers of an earlier generation were extending their reputations in 1820. Washington Irving produced his *The Sketch Book,* Scott his *The Monastery* and its sequel *The Abbot,* Shelley his *Prometheus Unbound,* and Byron a portion of *Don Juan.* Elizabeth's book was issued, without any wrappers and with the leaves merely stitched together, under the imprint of W. Lindsell, 87 Wimpole Street, Cavendish Square. On the title page are several verses from Akenside and Byron and the author's name. All of her later publications were to be anonymous until the volume of *The Seraphim* of 1838. No reviews or publishers' notices announced the slight volume, for it was not published but privately printed by her father in an edition of fifty copies. Of more interest than the childish, imitative verse are the dedication and the preface. It is significant that it was not to her mother that she dedicated the book, but "to the father, whose never-failing kindness, whose unwearied affection I never can repay." The tone of the preface is oversolemn and self-conscious, but it shows an appreciation of literature which is extraordinary in a child of eleven or twelve. She first praises Homer and Virgil, "those grand and solitary specimens of ancient poetic excellence." Then she asks, "Who, unsophisticated by prejudice, can peruse those inspired pages emitted from the soul of Byron, or who can be dazzled by the gems sparkling from the rich mine of the imagination of Moore, or captivated by scenes glowing in the descriptive powers of Scott, without a proud consciousness that our day may boast the exuberance of true poetic genius?"

In the following year, 1821, when Elizabeth was only fifteen, she had the satisfaction of making her first public appearance as a poet. Thomas Campbell, who had just undertaken the editorship of the *New Monthly Magazine,* published in that periodical two of her poems, both of them lamenting the present loss of freedom in Greece, in the light of its "glorious" past. Apparently she had no letter of introduction to Campbell but forwarded her verses to him in the hope he might accept them even though they were from an unknown writer. She was so gratified at his response that she sent him a long poem dedicated to him and asked for his opinion of the work. If it had been favorable, she had evidently planned to have it printed as her second volume of verse, for her dedication and preface were ready for publication and have been saved, whereas the poem itself seems to have been destroyed after she received Campbell's adverse comments. Though his reply, dated August 28, 1822, was mainly unfavorable, he assuaged her wounded feelings by telling her that the poem "bespeaks an amiable heart and an elegant mind." In general, he objected to the "lyric intermixtures" which he thought were "the most difficult of all gems to set in a Narrative poem and should always be of the first water." [25] Not long afterward she asked for his opinion of another manuscript, and this time he replied in a much shorter letter that it was impossible for him to "admit of renewed applications for criticisms on the works of young authors however promising they may be." [26] He did not intend to discourage her versifying; nor was she discouraged, since she continued to compose the usual birthday epistles and even attempted several more ambitious pieces, fragments of which were preserved.

On June 30, 1824, one of the leading newspapers in London, the *Globe and Traveller,* printed her "Stanzas on the Death of Lord Byron," with no signature or initials. Mr. and Mrs. Barrett's pride in Elizabeth's accomplishment may be seen in a letter her mother wrote her from Hope End when she was visiting her grandmother, Mrs. Graham-Clarke, and her Aunt Arabella (Bummy) at their home in Cheltenham. "As Papa took up the paper in the Dining Room," Mrs. Barrett wrote,

> a glance satisfied me whence they [the verses] came, but I said nothing till he came into the Drawing Room, when taking the paper with a *becoming carelessness* of air, I asked him what he thought of those lines. He said, "They are very beautiful indeed . . ." "I cannot help thinking," replied I, "that we know something of the Author." "They cannot be Ba's," said he, taking the paper from me to read them again, "tho certainly when I first read them they reminded me greatly of her style. Have you any idea if they are hers?" "I

have a conviction of it," said the conceited Mother, pouring out the tea with an air that threatened to overflow the tea tray."[27]

Two years later, when Elizabeth's next volume was published, she was staying with her other grandmother, Mrs. Moulton, at Hastings. Mrs. Barrett wrote Elizabeth of the arrival of the books and of the eagerness with which she and Mr. Barrett read her poems once again: "The news ran like lightning last night thro' the nursery to me that a brown paper parcel was come for Papa from Worcester 'which *felt* very much like books,' . . . and vain the temptations of our 'rich repast' till I had peeped into those pieces which had not yet delighted our eyes, nor did Papa taste anything, till he had found the paper cutter, so that between every two or three mouthfuls, we had Riga's dying strain." She added with pride: "I wish, my beloved Ba, that I could tell you all Papa said in commendation of this wondrous little book. The preface he says is equal to anything he ever read, and would do honor to any man . . . There never was any circumstance in the existence of your dearest Father or my own that could afford us the same gratified feelings, as this strong evidence that our beloved child, has so well applied and cultivated the talents with which she is gifted." [28] The book which thus pleased Mr. and Mrs. Barrett was *An Essay on Mind, with Other Poems,* a slender duodecimo volume published in London March 25, 1826,[29] by James Duncan, 37 Paternoster-Row. On the title page was a line from Tasso but no indication of authorship. Neither her name nor her initials appeared on the title page or after the preface. Many years afterward in a letter to the American critic Cornelius Mathews Elizabeth wrote that the book was "a girl's exercise . . nothing more nor less!—not at all known to the public," and she called the work "the black-letter offence of my early youth . . . an imitation poem (after Pope and Campbell) as all *young* poems are apt to be . . . *so* pert . . *so* unamiable." [30] Yet if family records are to be trusted, the volume enjoyed a brisk sale in at least one city. About two weeks after its publication Mrs. Barrett wrote Elizabeth that "Granny" (Mrs. Graham-Clarke) had reported that the book had "caused quite a sensation in the North," that nearly fifty copies had been sold in Newcastle, and that more had been ordered.[31] Perhaps the letter which most pleased Elizabeth was one from her future benefactor John Kenyon, who wrote her from Malvern Wells of his approval of the volume. He said that he had heard that she did not spare herself enough, and he asked her to remember that at her age "all need not be done in a day." [32]

The poem for which the book was named bravely attempted in some 88 pages to survey from classical Greece to the present the fields of history, science, metaphysics, and poetry. To the text of the poem were appended eighteen pages of notes in prose on such diverse writers as Plutarch, Condillac, Cicero, Bacon, Herodotus, and Tyrtaeus. The notice of her volume in the *Eclectic Review* [33] was mainly unfavorable. It objected to the obscurity of language, to the "barren and dazzling themes," and to the choice of subject, to succeed in which she should have adopted "a style far more remote from the sparkling, crackling style of Pope, with his sardonic grin and ever-recurring antithesis, or from the tinsel and affectation of Darwin." The reference to Darwin she thought an example of hasty and stupid reviewing, the recollection of which irritated her for many years; she always maintained that she had never read the author of *The Botanic Garden* before she wrote the "Essay." The *Literary Gazette* was more condescending and less sharp in its criticism. Since its editor, William Jerdan, had a year before published her short lyric "The Rose and Zephyr," he may have known who she was. For "the production of a young lady," he wrote, "it certainly displays a much more extraordinary degree of philosophical, we might say, metaphysical acumen, than could be expected either from the youth or sex of the writer." He ended his review with the admonition to "the fair author" that she "address herself more to nature, and undress herself from the deep *blue* in which she is now attired." [34]

The "Stanzas on the Death of Lord Byron" reappeared in *An Essay on Mind, with Other Poems,* and in the same volume was a poem with the cumbersome title, "Stanzas occasioned by a passage in Mr. Emerson's Journal, which states, that on the mention of Lord Byron's name, Captain Demetrius, an old Roumeliot, burst into tears." Throughout her life Elizabeth was again and again to be seized with spasms of uncritical hero worship—"My organ of veneration is as large as a Welsh mountain," she once wrote. "I could kiss the footsteps of a great man." [35]—and Byron was one of her earliest heroes. When she was only a child, she had longed to escape from the nursery, dress up in men's clothes, and become Byron's page. At some time in her teens she read *The Corsair*, which, she reported to her father, was "exquisitely beautiful," [36] and she wrote in imitation of it a poem called "Leila," [37] which told of the tragic fates of Otho the Corsair in his island home, of his beautiful daughter, of a wan and meek minstrel, and of the captive in the dungeon. And it was under the spell of Byron that she had written her early poems on Greece in the *New Monthly Magazine*.

One of the personal poems in the volume of 1826, the "Verses to My Brother," recalls the happy times she spent with Bro, their games and their literary pursuits. Now that her "belov'd and best" is continuing his studies away at school, she wonders whether he has "dreams of me and home"; and as she reads Homer alone, her thoughts "often stray" in search of Bro. In the spring of 1826 (although the poem was probably written several years before) Edward Barrett, who was now within a few months of his nineteenth birthday, was at Charterhouse. His leaving Hope End to go to the school six years earlier had caused Elizabeth great anguish. "My beloved Bro and I have parted on the plain of life," she had written in 1821. "The last farewell is agony, for alas our pursuits will now no longer be the same. . . . I may ascend the delightful hill of classical learning, but he who has added pleasure to every cherished object is no longer with me." Brother and sister had "fagged at the grammar, wept over the torn dictionary." She continued melodramatically, "Let cold reason scoff but let those who have pursued together the Roman and Greek classics, and who have together resisted difficulties of style and language decide whether or not our attachment be founded on folly." [38] After Bro left Hope End, the separation between brother and sister was only partial. He was with her some of the time during the year she was in Gloucester in 1821 and 1822. Her mother had written her from Hope End in August 1821 that someone had been sent "to bring dear Bro to pay us a *visit,* for such it must be, while his dearest Ba is at G." [39] He must have been with Elizabeth at Hope End during his vacations; and when she was visiting Mrs. Moulton at Hastings for a year in 1825 and 1826, Bro was with her for several months, before he returned to school. From 1820, his first year at Charterhouse, to 1826, he had advanced from the ninth to the third form. "How rejoiced we are to hear dearest Sam is in another form!" Mrs. Barrett wrote Elizabeth in April 1826 of her second son, also at Charterhouse. "Would that we had similar good news of Bro. I am every day more anxious about those dear boys, as time advances when they *must* be more actively occupied and *how?* That is the question." [40] Long after Mrs. Barrett's death the question was still being asked, with the answer no less uncertain. At all events Bro was withdrawn from Charterhouse in 1826 before he had completed the last two forms,[41] and there is no evidence that he ever again received any formal education.

IN SENDING to Richard Hengist Horne a few paragraphs about herself for *A New Spirit of the Age,* Elizabeth wrote in 1843, "As to stories, my story amounts to the knife-grinder's, with nothing at all for a catastrophe. A bird in a cage would have as good a story." Perhaps she had in mind the restricted existence which ill health had imposed upon her during the preceding six or seven years. During the Hope End period, however, even though she "had no social opportunities" and had her "heart in books and poetry," she nevertheless took trips around England and to the Continent more than many persons could hope to do in an age when travel was slow and expensive. At one time she seems to have lived for seven months with some of her family at Boulogne "for masters, which are excellent there, and for the acquirement of that habit of talking French, which comes at a call," as she later wrote.[42] More is known about her trip to Paris with her father and mother in October and November 1815, for her "Notes" on the journey have a vividness of phrase and fullness of detail which are remarkable for a child of nine. Her belief in the superiority of English domestic comforts was to be altered many years later after she had acquired a taste for living arrangements on the Continent. "At length Dover Castle rose as from the sea, to our view," she wrote, "and we rejoiced to find ourselves by a good comfortable

Early Years at Hope End 17

English fireside, which, even foreigners must allow, is preferable to all the luxuries in the world." [43] Among her various trips in England, she went with her parents, Bro, and Henrietta in June 1814, to Carlton Hall, between Richmond and Darlington in Yorkshire, the beautiful home of her father's brother, Samuel Moulton Barrett, who was living there with his mother and Mary Trepsack. During the following July, August, and September they stayed with Mrs. Barrett's parents, the Graham-Clarkes, at their dignified and spacious residence, Fenham Hall, in Newcastle.[44] There Elizabeth head Madame Catalani sing at the Grand Musical Festival, of which John Graham-Clarke was one of the patrons.[45] Several times she visited at Cheltenham her Aunt Arabella Graham-Clarke,[46] with whom Mrs. Graham-Clarke lived after the death of her husband in 1818. During the early part of the summer of 1819 she stayed with relatives at Worthing,[47] and she lived with Mrs. Moulton and Miss Trepsack at Hastings from June 1825 until late in May or early in June of the following year.[48] Also she must have visited from time to time her Uncle John Altham Graham-Clarke and his wife in their Elizabethan house called Kinnersley Castle [49] in Hereford.

Another long period away from home was from July 1821 to the spring or summer of 1822. She was suffering from such a serious illness that she had to be taken from Hope End to the Spa Hotel, Gloucester, where more adequate medical treatment may have been available than at Ledbury.[50] Dr. William Coker had written to Dr. G. B. Nuttall on June 24, 1821, about "the case of Miss Barrett, that prodigy in intellectual powers and acquirements!" [51] The symptoms he described, the headaches, the pain and weakness in various parts of the body, the paroxysms and convulsions of the muscles, suggest some kind of nervous disorder, from which she was never to be completely free. She had been treated with many medicines, including opium, Dr. Coker said, and none had proved helpful.

As one might suppose, when she was away from home Elizabeth regularly received letters from her mother rather than from her father. Though only a few of the family letters at this period have been preserved, Mrs. Barrett tried to write or to have her husband or one of her children write Elizabeth almost every day.

Likewise when Elizabeth's parents were visiting friends and relatives, she was asked as the eldest child to send messages from Hope End that all was well. One such letter was saved, written by Elizabeth when she was about eighteen or nineteen, to her mother, who was at Hereford with Mr. Barrett. Her message could hardly have put them at ease, though they may have understood that she was accustomed to exaggerate her illnesses. After commenting on the greatly improved health of her brothers and sisters, she continued, "As for myself the *violent cough* that I had when you were last here has not left me and I fear will accompany me to the end of my life. My constitution and my appetite is as *bad* as ever! But do not be uneasy for you know that *natural ill health* generally continues to *death* so it is nothing *outrée*. And have you really the assurance to suppose that in this short period of separation buried as we are amidst hills rocks and woods that we have any news or even scandal to regale your ear?" [52]

Mrs. Barrett's letters from Hope End to Elizabeth and Henrietta, while chiefly filled with domestic details and neighborhood gossip, are nevertheless of great interest in their revelation of the kind of difficulty she encountered with her husband. Years after her mother's death Elizabeth described her as "very tender . . . of a nature harrowed up into some furrows by the pressure of circumstances . . . A sweet, gentle nature, which the thunder a little turned from its sweetness." Mrs. Barrett, it is clear, was not necessarily consulted when her husband made his household decisions, nor was she always informed of his plans. Therefore she had to resort to indirect means of learning about the arrangements made for her own children. For example, when Elizabeth and Bro were visiting their grandmother in the winter of 1825–26, Mrs. Barrett wrote her daughter on November 25, "I am full of anxiety to hear whether dearest Papa's letter was intended to prevent Bro's going to school, or whether he was gone before it arrived." [53] Bro had not yet departed, and the letter evidently did prevent him from leaving for school at that moment, for Mrs. Barrett wrote Elizabeth again on December 30 that before long the day would come "when Ba must leave dearest Granny . . . and from a hint of Papa's yesterday, I have felt an apprehension that it may come *too* suddenly to admit of your going to Walthamstow

Early Years at Hope End

[the home of Elizabeth's uncle Sam, near London], which I should dread Sam would consider unkind as they took you from hence . . . I know not how to suggest any escape from this danger, as it is only a surmise of my own (tho a *very strong* one) that Papa's cogitations run upon Bro's being your escort home, before he goes to C. House." [54] Mrs. Barrett then suggested that Elizabeth write her father to express her wish of spending at least a week with Uncle Sam on her return from Hastings, and then she appended conspiratorially, "Say nothing of all this when you write, further than any allusion you may think right to Walthamstow." The strong surmise proved incorrect, for Mr. Barrett arranged for Bro's return to school but made no provision for that of Elizabeth and Henrietta. "How little did I think when I saw you drive away in Mary's barouche," Mrs. Barrett wrote Henrietta on April 11, "that I was not to see those dear faces again for ten long months . . . and yet no certain means arranged for your return!" [55] Mrs. Barrett's frustration in the whole episode is clear enough.

Yet it would be an oversimplification to conceive of Mr. Barrett merely as a despot exercising his power upon a defenseless household. In the commonly held view of him which has persisted since the time of Elizabeth's marriage, he was "one of those tyrannical, arbitrary, puritanical rascals who go sleekly about the world, canting Calvinism abroad, and acting despotism at home." [56] This judgment is not altogether fair because it overlooks a more attractive aspect of his personality: "his elastic spirit and merry laugh," [57] in Elizabeth's words—his boyish high spirits, humor, and charm. The evidence in many unpublished letters of Elizabeth and other members of the Barrett family confirms the impression that he was indeed a tyrant; but if he had been no more than that, Elizabeth would never have loved him as she did until the day of his death; nor would his family, at least in the earlier years, have received so much pleasure from his presence. A letter from Mrs. Barrett to Elizabeth which tells of her going out of the house to watch two old apple trees being cut down refers to "Papa's wit" and "the approving laugh of the delighted and busy audience." [58] In a few lines of doggerel which Elizabeth wrote describing a trip she and her family had made early in the summer of 1814 to the caverns of Matlock in Derbyshire, she mentioned "Papa's laugh," which echoed through the caves.[59] And later in the summer, when she was visiting her grandparents Mr. and Mrs. Graham-Clarke at Newcastle-on-Tyne, she wrote in her "Epistle to Dearest Papa in London" that she wished he would return, because in his absence the house seemed "dull." [60]

WHILE Bro was away at Charterhouse, Elizabeth "studied hard" by herself. The titles of many of the books she read and her opinions on them may be found in an unpublished pocket notebook which was recently given to the Wellesley College Library. In this small volume of 230 pages bound in diced Russia calf [61] she commented on about fifty different works to which she had devoted herself for the three years 1823–25. Although she had earlier shown much interest in the classics and was later to become absorbed once again in Greek studies under the influence of her neighbor H. S. Boyd, the only classical work she criticized was the *Ajax* of Sophocles. Most of her comments were in the fields of biography, memoirs, letters, and travel diaries. She read about men and women in many different countries and periods of history. For example, she went through Thomas Roscoe's translation of the *Memoirs of Benvenuto Cellini,* Lord Holland's biographies of Lope de Vega and of Guillen de Castro,[62] a translation of Madame Campan's memoirs of Marie Antoinette, a translation in eight volumes of the memoirs of the Countess de Genlis, a journal of Napoleon at Saint Helena (also in translation) by Las Cases, and another book which also dealt largely with Napoleon: a translation of Madame de Staël's history of the French revolution. In addition to these works on Continental figures, Elizabeth commented on many books of memoirs of her compatriots. She read three volumes of anecdotes and gossip on Garrick, Dr. Johnson, Horace Walpole, and others of the period, compiled by Laetitia Matilda Hawkins; [63] James Boaden's biography of John Philip Kemble, which also told about many other actors of the time; two different books on Charles James Fox; [64] and the memoirs of Richard Edgeworth (the father of Maria), of the younger William Pitt,[65] and of Byron, who was still living in 1824, when Egerton Brydges' volume on him was published.[66]

Among books of travel Elizabeth was chiefly attracted to recent works on Italy and Greece. She found a "sprightliness of style and a freshness of observation" in the anonymous *Diary of an Ennuyée,* in which Anna Murphy (later Mrs. Jameson, who was to accompany the Brownings on their wedding trip to Italy) told of her travels through Italy as a governess. Also Elizabeth was much interested in the three volumes of travel sketches entitled *The English in Italy* [67] and in two newly published books on the Greek Revolution.[68] The only novels which she discussed in her notebook were Lockhart's *Matthew Wald* and Cooper's *The Pilot,* both of which appeared in 1824.[69] Of all the books upon which she commented, none seems to have pleased her more than an "annual" called *The Literary Souvenir; or, Cabinet of Poetry and Romance* for 1826.[70] She wrote that it was "an elegant little book" with "beautiful type" and "pretty graphic illustrations" and was "well worth the 12 good shillings" it cost her. Among the two contributions in this volume which impressed her the most was a sentimental poem by Miss Landon called "The Forsaken," which represented the lament of a country girl whose lover had left her to look for city pleasures. Elizabeth thought the verses were "beautiful and pathetic." She was also much affected by a poem by Mrs. Hemans—it "goes to the heart," she wrote—describing the death of a mother and her baby in a shipwreck.

The longest criticism in the notebook of any one work is the sixteen closely written pages which analyze Locke's *An Essay Concerning Human Understanding.* She also wrote summaries of the philosophical systems of Kant, Berkeley, and Hume and discussed George Campbell's *The Philosophy of Rhetoric,* Southey's *The Book of the Church,* and Jacques Saint-Pierre's *Harmonies of Nature,* which she read in translation. The French writer seemed to her "touchingly amiable"; yet before she dipped into his third volume, she had grown "more than half tired of soli-lunar and luni-solar harmonies." The second longest comment in the notebook is a summary of John Dunlop's *The History of Fiction;* for eleven pages Elizabeth wrote a précis of the author's remarks on Greek and Latin romances, Italian tales, and French and English novels.

Her expressions of approval or of disapproval show her forthright manner of expression. For example, she thought that part of Samuel Parr's *Characters of the Late Charles James Fox* was as "sinewy as Tacitus and graceful as Tully," and she added, "I never read with more admiration, or ceased reading with more regret." She was, however, not impressed with the *Recollections of Foreign Travel* by Egerton Brydges, who, she wrote, "seems to think that by declaring and insinuating on every other page that his genius was first-rate, he might at least make his readers believe so. He certainly has not succeeded with *me*." The dates of the inscriptions in Elizabeth's books indicate that in addition to the works upon which she commented in her notebook, she at this time also came into possession of a copy of the *Works* of Horace, Milton's *Prose Works,* Percy's *Reliques,* Burns' *Works,* and a Spanish grammar [71] (although no evidence exists that she ever became proficient in that language).

Her copies of the two volumes of Milton's prose, which are now in the Turnbull Library in Wellington, New Zealand, have many markings and marginal comments.[72] Elizabeth was particularly interested in "The Reason of Church Government" and "An Apology for Smectymnuus," but she did not accept uncritically everything Milton wrote. For instance, she commented in the margin of the treatise "Of True Religion," that it would have been "more admirable and more amiable, had the great author extended to the Papist the same leniency with which he greeted the Socinian." Milton wrote that popery, "as far as it is idolatrous" could be tolerated neither publicly nor privately. "Nothing can excuse this," Elizabeth protested. "Milton was in my opinion a great bigot. When it suits his purpose he is for liberty, as the sacrifice of a King. If however, any of his preconceived ideas be violated, any of his *'conscientious'* notions called into question, then it is a *'great offence to God,'* an *'insufferable scandal.'* "

Since Elizabeth was apparently never able to visit a bookshop and her father seems to have had little interest in literature, how was she able to buy or have the use of so many volumes? I think that she may have regularly received copies of the *Literary Gazette* or a similar publication, in which she read advertisements and reviews of recent works and thereupon ordered from a London bookseller. Also she probably borrowed books from Mr. Best's

Early Years at Hope End

lending library, to which Henrietta frequently went in Malvern.

Elizabeth's analyses in her notebook and her many references in the text and in the prose footnotes of the "Essay on Mind" to philosophers such as Burke, Leibniz, Condillac, Locke, and Berkeley are not necessarily proof that she read widely in all of these writers. It is likely that some of her knowledge of French and English philosophy was derived from Dugald Stewart's *Philosophical Essays*,[73] which deals with the works of Locke, Berkeley, Burke, and Uvedale Price, and the influence of Locke upon French philosophers in the late eighteenth century. Likewise her information on the ancient and modern drama and on the lives of many English and Continental writers came partly from intermediate sources. For example, in the 1820's, or possibly a little later, she read carefully and made voluminous notes, both in French and in English, on the French translation of A. W. Schlegel's course of lectures on dramatic art and literature.[74] Her comments and summaries were mostly on Greek tragedy and on the English drama, but she paid some attention to the theaters of Rome, Italy, France, Spain, and Germany. In her remarks on the French drama in her "Essay on Mind" she may have been indebted to Schlegel's book.

Elizabeth's footnotes on Bentley, Descartes, and Newton tell several episodes about their lives which were drawn respectively from Isaac Disraeli's *Curiosities of Literature*, his *Literary Character*, and Spence's *Anecdotes*.[75] But I do not wish to give the impression that Elizabeth was not well informed in the subjects she treated, or that she attempted to pass off second-hand information as her own so that she might appear more erudite than she was. Quite the contrary: her command of languages and her wide acquaintance with literature, philosophy, and history were remarkable accomplishments for a girl who was isolated in the country and was without either the resources of a large public library or the stimulus of sympathetic minds engaged in similar pursuits. Like many of us, she derived some of her knowledge from a close study of the original texts and some from a rapid reading of commentaries, histories, compendia, and other books about books.

During the years when Bro was at Charterhouse and before she knew Boyd, Elizabeth had no mentor; she did, however, receive encouragement from Uvedale Price (later Sir Uvedale), who lived on his estate at Foxley, about ten miles northwest of Hereford. He was a cultured country gentleman, who was a warm friend of Charles James Fox, Samuel Rogers, and Wordsworth. Among his many interests were the classics, Italian poetry and art, and landscape gardening. In the Lawrence portrait, now at the Boston Museum of Fine Arts,[76] the features of Sir Uvedale in his later years are those of a studious and sensitive man. By the time Elizabeth knew him he had published a translation from the Greek of Pausanias [77] and had written *An Essay on the Picturesque as Compared with the Sublime and the Beautiful.*[78] Precisely when she first met him is not known, but in 1826, shortly before her return home from Hastings, she received from him a letter of praise for her *Essay on Mind.* Soon afterward she wrote a commentary on the proof sheets of his *Essay on the Modern Pronunciation of the Greek and Latin Languages,*[79] and for the following two years they corresponded on the subjects of classical meters and pronunciation and translations of the classics.[80] A particular reason for Elizabeth's gratitude is that unlike her father he did not discourage her after she had labored for six months on a long poem called "The Development of Genius." According to her autobiographical notes she gave part of her work on February 3, 1827, to her father, who ridiculed it as "a lamentable waste of time" and brusquely told her: "I would not read over again what I have read for fifty pounds . . . I advise you to burn the wretched thing." [81] Elizabeth did not describe the form in which Sir Uvedale's encouragement expressed itself, but apparently his criticism was more constructive than her father's. In her record of the interview in which Mr. Barrett had contemptuously dismissed her verses, she added significantly, "Mr. Price's friendship has given me more continual happiness than any single circumstance ever did—and I pray for *him,* as the grateful pray." Her poem (which remained unpublished in her lifetime) to Price on his eightieth birthday in the following month expresses her thankfulness to him for his sympathy and help.[82] She may have continued to see him occasionally until his death in September 1829, but a year and a half before that event she had found a new guide and ally much closer to her in years and interests than the kind-hearted master of Foxley.

2. Loss of Hope End

HUGH STUART BOYD moved to Great Malvern in 1824 or 1825.[1] His interest in Greek studies made it likely that he and Elizabeth would eventually be attracted to each other, and he evidently wrote to her soon after the publication of her *Essay on Mind*. It is unfortunate that of the hundreds of letters which he must have sent her during the next twenty years, only a handful have survived, for the relationship between them and the resulting tensions within his family and within Elizabeth's must necessarily be viewed only through her eyes. Her letters show that the friendship had a much deeper emotional content for her than for Boyd, that Mr. Barrett was irritated and possibly jealous because of her frequent visits to Malvern, and that Boyd strongly disapproved of Mr. Barrett's possessive and autocratic attitude toward his children. Also it seems that at times there may have been a lack of sympathy between Elizabeth and the two women of Boyd's household, his wife and his daughter. In Elizabeth's letters to him, she wrote not only of Homer and Ossian, of St. Gregory and St. Chrysostom, of neighborhood gossip and the domestic routine, but—more important to her biographer—she revealed her hopes, ambitions, conflicts, and frustrations more intimately than to any other correspondent until she began writing to Miss Mitford in 1836. "Have you ever observed this in me," she wrote Boyd, "that tho' I can restrain myself and mask myself as well as anybody else, in conversation, yet as soon as I begin to *write*,—out everything comes . . . ?"[2]

Since for six or seven years Elizabeth was closer to Boyd than to anyone else outside her immediate family, it is disappointing that the details of his biography are so meager. His father, Hugh Macauley Boyd, had been a handsome, socially brilliant Irishman well known in several London circles and a friend of Goldsmith and Garrick. In 1781 he left a wife, a daughter, and a son only a few months old, and went off to repair his dwindling fortune in India, where he died suddenly in 1794, apparently without accomplishing his aim.[3] His son Hugh was admitted to Pembroke College, Cambridge, in 1799, but he was not serious about his university career and failed to take a degree.[4] All his life he was to remain a dilettante. His first published work was a frigid tragedy in blank verse, *Luceria*,[5] which according to the preface had been submitted to the manager of the Drury Lane Theater and "upon examination it was pronounced to be deficient in interest and effort." In the following twenty-nine years he published several translations of the Greek Fathers—chiefly St. Chrysostom, St. Gregory Nazianzen, and St. Basil—a number of religious tracts, and a dull prose translation of the *Agamemnon* of Aeschylus. Inasmuch as not one of his books could have paid for itself and he never held any salaried post, he must have had independent means. There was never any suggestion of want, and he was free to move himself and his family to a new home every few years.

In May 1826 he was living at Morrison's Hotel, Great Malvern, and the following year he was at Ruby Cottage in Malvern Wells, which was his home when Elizabeth first saw him. Some time in May 1828 he and his family moved to Woodland Lodge in Great Malvern, where they stayed until about May 1831. Then they returned to Ruby Cottage for a year before leaving that part of England forever. At the age of thirty he had become totally blind,[6] after which he had his favorite Greek authors read to him so that he might commit their works to memory. In May 1832, according to a note in Elizabeth's handwriting, he could repeat from memory more than 2,000 lines from Gregory Nazianzen, 1,800 from Aeschylus, and 1,310 from the hymns of Synesius; altogether almost 8,000 lines of Greek verse and prose.[7] Elizabeth later wrote to Browning that Boyd's memory was "merely the mechanical faculty. The *associative*, which makes the other a high power, he wants." She thought Boyd "a very peculiar person . . . in all possible ways," and in the same letter she showed she was not unaware of his defects. "He talks like a man of slow mind, which he is, . . and with a child's way of looking at things . . . He cares for me perhaps more than he cares for any one else . . far more than for his own only daughter; but he is not a man of deep sensibility, and, if he heard of my death, would merely sleep a little sounder the next night." The first letter from Elizabeth to Boyd which has been saved is dated March 11, 1827. In it she referred to a previous note in which she had thanked him for sending her his works, and then she acknowledged his invitation to visit him. Although she had recently celebrated her twenty-first birthday, that event seems not to have conferred upon her any measure of independence. "I very seldom have it in my power to leave home," she said, "and the first time I am able to do so, must visit some friends to whom I am under a long engagement." [8] As for walking across the fields and over the hill from Hope End to Malvern Wells, that would be out of the question: "My health . . . is not bad, but deficiency in strength makes me quite incapable of much exercise." During the spring, summer, and fall letters were sent back and forth, and the possibility of her visiting him was still no less remote. On November 3 she wrote him that he should not feel hurt at her failure to see him because, "My Father has represented to me, that, whatever gratification and improvement I might receive from a personal intercourse with you, yet, as a *female,* and a *young* female, I could not pay such a *first visit* as the one you proposed to me, without overstepping the established observances of society." [9] Elizabeth and Boyd continued to correspond without seeing each other, and she discussed her reading of Greek and Latin, Uvedale Price's recent book on ancient pronunciation, and Boyd's translations.

Perhaps several years might have passed without their meeting each other if a pathetic appeal from Boyd to Elizabeth had not wrung from her father the necessary permission. On Thursday, March 13, 1828, Elizabeth went in the Barretts' phaeton to Great Malvern to visit a cousin of hers, Mrs. Trant. Within a hundred yards of Mrs. Trant's house, she passed Mr. and Mrs. Boyd in the street. "My first impulse was to stop the carriage—but my courage gave way! I COULD *not* introduce myself *then!*" she wrote her grandmother Moulton.[10] The next morning she received from Boyd a long letter dated "Thursday morning," in which he said, "I suppose it was *you* who passed me this morning . . . Whether it was you or not, it awakened within me feelings and reflections which for several months have been *somewhat* repressed! Mrs.

Boyd is tired of this place and wishes to leave it. If I *should* do so, I shall probably write you a letter the *day before,* to tell you more fully what I think and feel! I am now nearly forty seven, but, if I recollect right, this is the longest letter I ever wrote in my life." The letter made her feel so "pained and uncomfortable" that she took it to her father and secured his consent, as she wrote, *"to do as I liked."*

So on Monday Elizabeth undertook the journey with Bro, Henrietta, and Arabel. On the part of the road which descends steeply into Great Malvern the carriage got out of control, and all were thrown upon the bank. Bro then fastened the pony to a tree and after placing Elizabeth in the carriage, dragged it himself into the town. The first people they saw there were Mr. and Mrs. Boyd. Trembling with fright, Elizabeth went toward him, held out her hand, but could not speak. Mrs. Boyd said, "Miss Barrett"; Boyd and Elizabeth, however, shook hands in silence. She thought him "a rather young looking man than otherwise, moderately tall, and slightly formed. His features are good—his face very pale, with an expression of placidity and mildness." He enquired from Elizabeth whether she had been hurt, and Mrs. Boyd asked if "Miss Barrett would allow them to take charge of her." She declined since she wished to rejoin Henrietta, who had been slightly hurt in the accident and had gone ahead to Mrs. Trant's house in the coach. They walked along in silence, broken only by Boyd's saying, "I cannot help thinking that *I* was the cause" and "this is ominous, Miss Barrett." She, however, "was too frightened and nervous for conversation." They finally reached Mrs. Trant's house, where Boyd said to Elizabeth, "God bless you." Thus ended "this extraordinary interview" and began one of the most important friendships of her life.

In a blank page of his copy of Elizabeth's *An Essay on Mind* [11] Boyd wrote that she did him the honor of paying him a first visit on Wednesday, April 16, 1828, and that on Friday, May 16, she came again and read the opening of the *Oedipus Tyrannus.* For the next four years she frequently saw him at his house, occasionally paying visits of a week or more, during which she read widely with him in the Greek classics and the Greek patristic writings. He was not her formal tutor; but if she had never had his encouragement,

Loss of Hope End

his suggestions of different authors and texts to read, and at times his instruction, it is doubtful if she would have been so devoted to Greek studies. As for the Greek Fathers, she later wrote to Boyd that they "would probably have remained in their sepulchres, as far as my reading them was concerned." Only a very rapid reader of that language could have gone through so much material. Although a few years before her death she wrote a friend that she did not consider herself "well-grounded by any manner of means" in her knowledge of Greek, she believed that she had "read over a wider surface than most scholars perhaps." In the same letter she also wrote that in her youth she had read through "nearly every word extant in Greek" and that "for years" she did "nothing else." [12]

Her marginal comments in one of her volumes of Euripides [13] testify to the speed with which she read the language. After each of the ten plays in the book she made a short critical evaluation and entered the date when she finished it. She read all of the *Rhesus* (which seemed to her as a whole "very heavy and uninteresting and cold" in spite of "several beautiful passages"), the first of the dramas in the edition, in January 1832, and by the end of June she had gone through all the plays. She spent a week each in reading the *Bacchae* and the *Heraclidae* and about a fortnight upon the *Hercules furens* (which delighted her more than any other drama in the volume because "few things in real life are so affecting as to see a *man* shed tears"). Boyd's manuscript notes of what Elizabeth read at his house in the summer and fall of 1830 are also evidence of her rapid reading. The usual stint of a morning's visit at that time was somewhat more than one hundred lines from the *Agamemnon,* although occasionally she read two hundred in one day. Boyd mentioned at least twice that she did the translation "extremely well." When she stayed at the Boyds' for some two weeks late in the summer, she read more than one thousand verses from the *Agamemnon* and about twelve hundred lines from Chrysostom, Gregory, and Basil.[14] At times she must have been studying several Greek texts concomitantly. For example, she wrote to Boyd in an undated letter that she had just finished Longinus' work and the *Rhesus* of Euripides and had been reading Chrysostom's commentaries on the Epistles to the Corinthians. If she found a text hard to understand, she did not hesitate to acknowledge her perplexity. For example she wrote to Boyd in 1829 that she was reading a little of Longinus' *De sublimitate* every day and that she hoped he was considered difficult, for she had to look at the Latin every five minutes. On the back of the frontispiece of her copy of Longinus she scribbled a short critical estimate of that author and explained that she had found the Greek hard because of "technicalities in the phraseology" and "the involutions of the style." [15]

All her time was spent in reading and writing, as she said to Boyd quite truthfully. But the writing was mostly of long letters to him and a few other correspondents, for she was not composing much poetry. Between the publication of her volume of 1826 and that of 1833, a few of her *juvenilia,* all of them imitative and without distinction, appeared in the *Literary Gazette,* the *Jewish Expositor and Friend of Israel,* and *The Times.* Her energies were chiefly directed to her reading, which as in earlier years was mainly in the classics and in modern literature. Before she left Hope End at the age of twenty-six, she had read one or two books of the Old Testament in the Hebrew, some of the New Testament in Greek,[16] possibly all of Aeschylus,[17] and most of Euripides.[18] The marginal annotations in her two volumes of Sophocles [19] show that either at this time or a little later she went through all the plays with the possible exception of the *Trachiniae,* the only one upon which she failed to comment. She also studied the *Phaedo* of Plato, the orations and letters of Isocrates,[20] and the *Memorabilia* and *Cyropaedia* of Xenophon;[21] and she no doubt continued with Homer and Pindar. As for the Greek Christian Fathers, she read hundreds of pages in the closely printed folios and quartos of Gregory,[22] Chrysostom,[23] Basil, and Synesius, for all of whom Boyd had published translations.[24] The list of the texts with which she became familiar among the Greek writers of the Roman era includes the *Enchiridion,*[25] a treatise on classical prosody by Hephaestion; the *Manual* [26] of the Stoic philosopher Epictetus; the *Aethiopica,* a romantic novel in Greek by Heliodorus; and Longinus' *De sublimitate.* She also devoted some attention to Latin writers; but since Boyd was not particularly interested in Latin literature, she made only a few references to the subject in her letters to him, which are almost the only source of biographical information during these years. It is certain, however, that she finished the *Pharsalia* of Lucan, whom she described as "an ardent poet," and at this period or possibly somewhat later she read Virgil's *Eclogues,* the *Georgics,* and parts of the *Aeneid;* a number of plays by Terence; some of Lucretius' *De rerum natura;* and selections from Livy, Catullus, Horace, Aulus Gellius, and Erasmus.[27] In addition to the Greek and Latin she read Adam Clarke's commentaries on the Bible and several volumes of sermons and theological treatises, and she continued her study of French literature.

In 1828, when she was writing to Uvedale Price on classical meters and was also reading Sophocles with Boyd, she began what she later called in a letter to Miss Mitford a "lengthy" correspondence with Edmund Henry Barker of Thetford, Norfolk. Because of common interests Barker was an acquaintance of both Price [28] and Boyd, but it was probably the latter who introduced Barker to Elizabeth. At the time of their correspondence Barker was an industrious and productive classical scholar who had edited Lemprière's *Classical Dictionary* and had helped in the production of a Greek thesaurus and a Latin thesaurus. But within a few years he was destined to be financially ruined, placed in the Fleet prison, and die in a shabby London boarding house. It was evidently Barker, not Elizabeth, who initiated and wished to maintain the correspondence. "To tell you the truth," she wrote him on May 12, 1829, "you a little surprised me by proposing to correspond regularly with me; for, having heard a good deal of your extensive correspondences . . . I did not venture to conjecture that you could have any time to throw away. You resemble a Chinese waterman, who, while he conducts the oars with his feet, and regulates the sail with his hands, is able nevertheless to smoke his pipe all the while. I hope I need not say that I am gratified by your promising to *smoke a pipe* now and then for my benefit." [29] Elizabeth thought him a rather silly man. In her letters to Boyd she made fun of Barker's books for children, several of which he had sent her, and she ridiculed his edition of Cicero,[30] with its mixture of English and Latin notes. The volume contained the orations against Catiline, a dialogue by Tacitus, and "several beautiful extracts from English authors, with a suggestion to the conductors of classical schools to devote one day in the week to the study of English literature." Elizabeth might well have hesitated to thank Barker and to have wondered how she could fill a letter about "such a mere compilation" [31] when she saw the titles and authors of some of the passages: for example, a "Description of a Christian Family Spending the Sabbath" from the Rev. Joshua Gilpin's *Monument of Parental Affection to a Dear and Only Son*. A year before the edition of Cicero was published in 1829 Barker issued in two thick volumes his *Parriana: or, Notices of the Rev. Samuel Parr, L.L.D.* (1828-29). The work is a compendium of ill-assorted material, much of which has only a tenuous connection with the life of Parr. Elizabeth struggled through the volumes in the summer of 1828 and presumably at Boyd's request made a list of the passages she thought would interest him.

At about this time Mrs. Barrett, who had been in poor health for a year or two, was encouraged by her physician, Dr. Carden, to go to Cheltenham, where, everyone hoped, she might recover her strength. When she left Hope End late in September with her sister Arabella (Bummy) and possibly Henrietta, no one knew how critically ill she was. From Tewkesbury on the first of October, Mrs. Barrett wrote back to Elizabeth, "My beloved Ba's tearful eyes as I parted with her yesterday have hung somewhat heavily on my heart." [32] On the back of the letter Elizabeth wrote, "The very last I ever received from *her*. One week after it was written, we possessed her no longer. It has been wet with more bitter tears than were those the recollection of which hung heavily on her tender heart, *but may* the Lord's will be done." She died at Cheltenham on the seventh of October, 1828, and was buried beside her daughter Mary in the Parish Church of St. Michael and All Angels in Ledbury. Mr. Barrett, who was neither at his wife's bedside at the time of her death nor at home, wrote Elizabeth on a scrap of paper with no indication of address or date a message which appears to have been scribbled hastily:

> This morning has the afflicting dispensation of our Heavenly Father been made known to me in two hours I shall be on my way to Cheltenham, where I will have this put with the

Post for you. I cannot say what I feel, for I scarcely can define my sensations, the blow is too recent . . . I would say Lord not my will but thine be done, thou knowest best, teach us to submit patiently to all thy excitations . . . She is, I am persuaded . . . now in the presence of him to whom she belongs as a purchased one, and a redeemed one by the pouring out of his precious blood.[33]

Both now and in later years Edward Moulton Barrett was essentially inarticulate, and he bottled up within himself his grief and disappointments, so that no one around him ever knew his feelings. The language of the letter is that of a man who appears never to have had religious doubts and who was, as Elizabeth said of him, "strong in the consolation which is of God." [34]

However much Mrs. Barrett may have been overshadowed by her husband, the ties between Elizabeth and her mother had always been close. In spite of the fact that Mrs. Barrett had been unwell when she left home, her death was for Elizabeth, as she wrote Boyd [35] immediately after the event, an "unforeseen and unexpected" blow, which for a time took away from her the power of thinking. Her agony was the more severe because she had been "denied the consolation" of being with her mother at the end. It seemed to her that she had perhaps had too much natural affection for her mother and that God had thus "reproved" her. In her next letter to Boyd some weeks or possibly months later, she again wrote of her grief: "I never can forget what I have lost. Her voice is still sounding in my ears—her image is in my heart —and *they* are to be loved, however unreal they may be!" [36]

Upon Mr. Barrett now devolved the sole responsibility for bringing up the eleven children, who ranged from the twenty-two-year-old Elizabeth to the four-year-old Octavius. It was an obligation which a greatly reduced income was to render increasingly burdensome. Two or three years before his wife's death he had suffered the first of a series of financial losses which were eventually to alter his way of life and even his personality. The basis of the trouble had been a long-standing dispute over some of the Jamaica properties. After Edward Barrett of Cinnamon Hill, Jamaica, died in 1798, the Moulton-Barretts were the principal inheritors of his Northside estates; they remained absentee owners and entrusted their plantations to resident managers who ran the estates for their own interests rather than for those of the owners. Their cousins, the Goodin-Barretts, instituted a law suit against them in 1801 to recover some property willed them by Edward Barrett, and the case remained in litigation for more than twenty years. In 1824 the court decided in favor of the Goodin-Barretts, and several parcels of the slaves of the Moulton-Barretts were handed over to Richard Barrett as receiver. The Moulton-Barretts then had to hire the slaves back from their cousin Richard and also pay large interest charges which had accrued during the past years when the slaves had been held by them illegally, according to the decision.[37] Richard Barrett was one of the most brilliant lawyers and politicians of Jamaica and was speaker of the House of Assembly in 1830. Elizabeth in a letter to Miss Mitford later described him as "a man of talent and violence and some malice, who did what he could, at one time, to trample poor Papa down . . did trample him at one moment when he felt him under his feet." [38] So in 1825 Edward Moulton Barrett and his brother Sam must have realized that if they were to salvage a portion of their Jamaica investments, they could not both remain in England as *rentiers*. Which of the two would have to pull up stakes and go to Jamaica to run the Northside estates?

Some of the reasons why the choice fell upon Sam are obvious enough. Edward had a large family whose removal to Jamaica would have been very expensive, while Sam had no children. On the other hand Sam must have been very reluctant to live in Jamaica because his wife, whom he had married in 1822, was in such poor health [39] that the harsh climate of the island would hasten her death (as it did four years after her arrival). Furthermore, he had been a member of Parliament since 1820, representing the Borough of Richmond. The brothers seemingly had at one time a serious quarrel which Elizabeth, who was her uncle's favorite niece, may have succeeded in healing. On July 5, 1824, Mrs. Barrett wrote Elizabeth in Cheltenham that she was sending a letter from "Sam offering thro you the olive branch to Papa, and . . . expressing Mary's desire to know Papa and his own

Loss of Hope End

that the past should be buried in oblivion." [40] It seems curious that although Mary Clementina Cay-Adams had been married to Sam for two years, she had never met his brother. Several enigmatic references in Elizabeth's letters suggest that Sam's going to Jamaica, or his remaining there, may have been an act of despair after the failure of everything in England. In all ways he seems to have been in contrast to his inflexible, unimaginative older brother. He was a brilliant conversationalist, "a bright, gifted being," at one time "a man of large fortune." After he had been *"talked into the new South sea bubbles of some years ago,"* failures came, and he "found himself responsible for companies to whom he had simply given his name." Unlike his brother, he had no gift "for battling with adversity"; and leaving "a situation full of perplexity and distress," he "went to the West—and so ended all!" [41] In 1827 he resigned his seat in Parliament and left with his ailing wife for Jamaica; apparently neither saw England again.

Although the change was less drastic than it had been for Sam, Edward Moulton Barrett also had to sacrifice many of his accustomed pleasures in his effort to retain the Hope End estate and prevent any diminution of the capital he hoped to bequeath to his children. From 1827 until the Barretts left Hope End in the summer of 1832, he no longer was able to spend most of his time at home, enjoying the pleasures and performing the duties of a country squire but for business reasons had to live in London during a large part of each year.[42] Because of either poor judgment or bad luck, or a combination of both, he found his financial resources were dwindling so rapidly that it would soon be necessary for him to dispose of his large estate and to live in greatly reduced circumstances. The education of Bro and of Sam at Charterhouse had to be interrupted before either could complete his course. Bro, who had advanced from the ninth form in 1820 to the third in 1826, did not return in 1827. Sam went from the twelfth form in 1822 to the sixth in 1828, which was his last year at that school or any other. None of the other six brothers ever went to a public school. It was evidently in the spring of 1831 that the mortgaged Hope End property, which was then valued at about £50,000, was seized from Mr. Barrett and put up for sale to satisfy the creditors. The great slave insurrection in Jamaica of December 1831–January 1832, with its widespread destruction on the Barrett plantations, increased his difficulties as he tried to find the money to redeem Hope End.

At first Elizabeth had no inkling of her father's changed fortunes. She was absorbed in her friendship with Boyd, riding on her donkey back and forth across the Malvern Hills to read Greek with him. Before long she cared for him far more than she ever had for Uvedale Price. She was attracted to his "unworldliness and enthusiasm" [43] and felt he provided for her the mental companionship and sympathy she could not find at home, except possibly from Bro. In January 1831 when the news reached her of the death of her grandmother Moulton, who had been a second mother to the Barrett children and especially to Elizabeth, she became so ill she could not leave home for several weeks. But she wrote Boyd that even though she could not go to his house, she wished him to know she still cared for him, that "there never were or could be any, out of my own immediate family, towards whom I have felt as I have and must ever feel towards *you*." [44] Her father seems to have been jealous of Boyd for his friendship with Elizabeth. She often wrote to Boyd of her reluctance to ask her father for permission to see him, for fear he might be irritated by her importuning him too often on the subject. Once she said, "He was not pleased on Monday at my having left home on such a day, and told me that I would certainly kill myself—and *then* I might be satisfied." [45] Oddly enough it is likely that Mr. Barrett never visited and hardly ever spoke to the man whose friendship meant so much to his daughter. Although she would have liked her father to call upon Boyd and was distressed at his omission, she never asked him to do so because, as she explained, "from my knowledge of his habits and usual inclinations, there appeared to me no kind of probability of hearing any other than a negative answer." [46]

In the spring of 1831 Elizabeth began to hear rumors that her beloved home might be sold and that the Barrett family would have to move away, though no one knew where, and for the next year she was constantly preoccupied with "THE *subject*," as she called it. Fantastic backstairs gossip and neighborhood talk came to her that her father was so ill he was not expected to live much longer, or that all the servants but one had been discharged because they would not move to the West Indies with the Barretts. She was terrified at the prospect of their going to one of the family's plantations in Jamaica. Since Mr. Barrett never informed his children of the plans he had made for them, it was useless to question him. She had been present when he had received a letter telling him of the loss of his fortune "not down to the point of 'elegant competence' but very far below it!" Several years later she described the scene to Miss Mitford: "He was surrounded by his family—and they, so young—and not educated,—and with not one prospect amongst them. And the letter came—and just one shadow past on his face while he read it (I marked it at the moment) and then he broke away from the melancholy, and threw himself into the jests and laughter of his innocent boys." [47] He bravely faced the misfortune without complaint and was usually able to hide his feelings behind "a thick mask of high spirits." Owing to his "extraordinary power of self-command," [48] she could guess nothing from his expression and manner. One day Elizabeth and Henrietta were discussing in the presence of their father the question whether their aunt Arabella had left her home and was now in London. Mr. Barrett remained "perfectly silent" during the conversation, but the next morning he sent a letter to Arabella Graham-Clarke addressed to her hotel on Albemarle Street. "So you see," Elizabeth wrote Boyd, "he knew all about it, all the time. There is nothing but mysteries!" [49] It was from Mr. Curzon, the minister of the Independent Chapel in Ledbury, that Elizabeth finally learned of the certainty that Hope End would be sold, though he was not sure how much more time the Barretts would be able to remain there.[50]

In April or May of 1831, about the time Elizabeth first heard the rumors concerning Hope End, she also learned that Boyd was planning to move away, possibly to Bath. She was much disturbed at the prospect and immediately suggested in her letters to Boyd many reasons why he should remain: the salubrious climate of Malvern, its social advantages for Mrs. Boyd, and the many temptations and harmful influences at Bath for a young girl like Annie. In the highly emotional language with which she usually expressed her feelings she wrote him that she had lately been suffering such "distress of mind" that her body could scarcely endure any further struggle, and she added, "I would give up all the pleasure and advantage I have derived from your society, for *this*—that you had gone away three years ago instead of now." [51] Boyd's wife and daughter would have preferred to leave immediately, but he persuaded them to remain, took a year's lease on a house in Malvern Wells, and did not move away until May 1832. In her letters to him that year, and probably in their many conversations, she traced the fluctuations of her hope and despair as she learned now good news, now bad, about the fate of Hope End. Once she was so happy she could hardly write and rushed to her room, where she added a few words to a letter she had begun earlier in the morning to Boyd: *"Promise me,"* she wrote in great excitement, "that you will not to *any one person,* say one word of what I am now going to tell you,—and now listen!!" [52] She had been told by her aunt Arabella that Mr. Barrett believed he could retain his home, but Elizabeth, Henrietta, and Bro were warned not to change their expressions before Mr. Barrett, because if he suspected Miss Graham-Clarke had revealed to them any of his communications, "they would cease from that moment."

A "fat gentleman with the rings" came from London and was reported to have said, *"The place is to be sold,"* that he had been appointed to take possession in the meanwhile, and that he had asked a neighboring farmer to plow the Hope End hopyard. According to the rumors from some land surveyors, as Elizabeth told the episode to Boyd, the farmer went to Mr. Barrett for his permission, and since his reply, *"Do as you please,"* was considered too ambiguous, "the fat gentleman's intended ploughing is still unperformed." [53] Another time her father's having a number of his own men work in the Hope End hopyard was interpreted by some as a favorable omen, Elizabeth heard, and by others as without meaning, since he was gathering the crops which already belonged to him.[54]

She was particularly distressed at the loss of privacy in having to put up with visitors at Hope End who came ostensibly to consider the purchase of the property. But some of them, she suspected, were there only to gloat over the misfortunes of her family and to snoop around the grounds and the interior of the house that they might have the perverse pleasure of seeing the Barretts in

Loss of Hope End

the luxurious surroundings they no longer could call their own. One afternoon in August 1831 the vicar of the Priory at Great Malvern, Dr. Henry Card, together with his wife and three friends, all five of whom were acquaintances of Elizabeth, "made a *party of pleasure*" to her home. The ticket of admission which they had secured from a real estate agent in Worcester was invalid, and they were not permitted to go beyond the dining room. Mr. Barrett was not at home. Bro became so angry at the intrusion that he told the butler in a voice loud enough for the unwelcome guests to hear that if he did not show them out of the house immediately, he would do so himself. They left and walked around the grounds, peering into the windows to look at Miss Graham-Clarke in the drawing room. All the time they were laughing and chattering and seemed "satisfied and pleased." And only a short while ago one of the group, a Miss Wall, had written to Eliza Cliffe, a friend of Elizabeth's, of her strong feeling of "compassion" for "those poor girls." [55] Years later, as Elizabeth looked back upon that "miserable time," she told Miss Mitford that they "had to hide, even away from our own private rooms, where we used to be safe from all the world,—and to hear in our hiding-place the trampling and the voices of strangers through the passages everywhere, and in the chambers which had been shut up for years from our own steps, sacred to death and love." [56]

In spite of their unsettled domestic arrangements during their last year at Hope End, Mr. Barrett, Elizabeth, and Bro were very much interested in the debates over the proposed Reform Bill. Late in May 1831 Bro dined at Ledbury in honor of the victory of the reform candidate, a Mr. Hoskins. When Mr. Barrett was not away in London, he used to read to his children in the evenings the reports in the newspapers of the struggles over the bill and to express his own liberal-whig principles. Elizabeth, who always had a propensity for dividing the world into saints and sinners, thought the language of the anti-reform lords was "disgusting" and that Lord Grey's position was "morally sublime." [57] After the bill had passed early in June 1832 she wrote Boyd that the event would be celebrated in Ledbury by a procession, a great dinner, and a giving away of food to the poor. Her father contributed "a very large cow" worth £20.[58]

In the middle of May the Boyds had moved to Somersetshire, eventually to Bathampton. Their alleged reason for going was that the health of their daughter would be endangered by further residence in Malvern, but Elizabeth thought Annie was well enough and that Boyd was yielding to the pressures of his wife and daughter, both of whom considered Malvern a dull town and hoped for a more lively social atmosphere in Bath. His departure was a severe blow which, together with the trouble about Hope End, brought on an emotional upset from which Elizabeth did not recover until several months later, after her arrival in Sidmouth. For the three or four years previous he had been the only person outside her own family whom she had cared to see regularly. A day or two after he left she sent him a letter in which she again expressed her sense of guilt, as she had at the time of her mother's death. She wrote that a recent letter from him had been read by her "with many tears" and that perhaps she deserved the agony of their separation, "because when under the pressure of those heavy afflictions with which God has been pleased to afflict me since the commencement of our intimacy,—I often looked too much for comfort to you—instead of looking higher than you." [59] She begged him to write her frequently and told him that while he might become acquainted with many persons who were in many ways superior to her, "yet you will never never have another friend whose regard for you can be stronger or truer or more incapable of change than mine." [60] She had for this blind, middle-aged, limited, ineffectual, and rather helpless man an extraordinary attachment. But within one or two years the bonds of the relationship were to be loosened at the very moment she was forming a close friendship in Sidmouth with a man who had many similar qualities.

Boyd apparently wrote Elizabeth that he hoped she would visit him at Bath. Her nerves were tense from the conflict in loyalties and from her dread of having to move away from the only home she could remember. She could not go to see Boyd, for her father would neither allow her to remain as a guest in his house nor settle his family near Bath. When he apparently wrote her that she lacked the "spirit and resolution" to secure her father's permission, she replied that she had no desire to give pain to "the person, who loves me better than any person in the world loves me, for the sake of visiting you for a week or two!!"[61] All her energy, she said, was "expended in bearing up against the different deprivations under which I suffer."[62] Such language bears little relationship to the outward circumstances of her life, for she was suffering no physical hardships in the summer of 1832. The Barrett fortune, although greatly diminished, had not disappeared, and her father was still in a position to provide for all of them a comfortable, if less luxurious, home. The threatened loss of Hope End, the absence of Boyd, and his misunderstanding of her position all depressed her spirits. Her letters to him during her last months in Herefordshire are filled with references to her mental suffering and her belief that she was near the breaking point. A passage from her letter to him in July 1832 is typical of many: "I sometimes feel that for the rest of my life, I would barter almost every kind of pleasure for the loss of every kind of pain, and consent to be only tranquil instead of pleased. For a long time my powers of feeling pleasure and pain have been clashing against each other—and neither my body nor mind can bear it any longer."[63]

As a distraction against her anxieties and despondency she absorbed herself in the world of books. With the aid of John Parkhurst's *An Hebrew and English Lexicon* [with] *an Hebrew and a Chaldee Grammar*[64] she read her two quarto volumes of the Hebrew Bible[65] "from Genesis to Malachi, right through, and was never stopped by the Chaldee." After the following winter she gave up Hebrew studies and never resumed them. She also went through the whole of the *Aeneid* except for two books she was already familiar with; two plays of Euripides, the *Alcestis* and the *Troades*, each for the second time; and two novels in Italian. Furthermore she finished for the third time, and admired more than ever,[66] Madame de Staël's *Corinne,* upon which in the maturity of her career she was to draw for some of the characterization and plot of *Aurora Leigh.*

During their last few months at Hope End Elizabeth felt that rather than endure any longer the uncertainty, she would prefer to have the place disposed of and to be far away from her beloved home. Eventually Mr. Barrett heard it had been sold, and he left immediately to spend a week in Devonshire looking for a new home. He went away so suddenly, without telling anyone his plans or his reasons for the trip that Elizabeth did not know five minutes before his departure that he intended to go anywhere,[67] and she could only guess at the nature of his errand from the trembling in his voice as he said goodbye. The friends and neighbors of the Barretts, Lady Margaret Cocks, the Cliffes, the Peytons, the Martins, and the Commelines, were all distressed at their leaving Hope End. In the last letters she wrote to Boyd before going to Sidmouth, Elizabeth described all the details of her family's misfortune and confessed that she gained even "a certain pleasure in saying them." [68] She wrote to him with unconscious understatement, "You will think I dare say, that I am apt to be out of spirits and to look at the gloomy side of everything." [69] One woman was in such an agony of grief that she fell down in what appeared to be a fit after blessing "every hair of Master's head, and all his children from the biggest to the least." [70] Some of the people upon whom Henrietta called in their cottages in Wellington Heath burst into tears and expressed their pity. In contrast to the present, Elizabeth recalled the pleasant time she had spent several years before in France, when she was always joking and in high spirits. Once when smoke from a wood fire had made her weep, an acquaintance was astonished to "have seen the tears in Mademoiselle Barrett's eyes." [71] But recently a number of "desolating changes" had come to her, and now the loss of Hope End was "the last stroke." [72] She hated to think that strangers would soon be living in her home, that they would be laughing and talking in the rooms "too painfully dear" to her, where her mother had lived and where no one of the family had entered since her death.

At the beginning of August workmen came to pack up the furniture to be stored away in Ledbury and the plate to be sent to the bank in London until the Barretts should have another permanent home, and the sound of their hammering and walking about echoed all day long in the empty rooms and halls. Elizabeth was grieved at the sight of "dear Hope End looking so unlike the happy Hope End it used to be," [73] and she would sit at the window and wonder whether it was all a dream. With the assistance of his sons Mr. Barrett dusted the books and wrapped them up in bundles, also to be placed in safe deposit. Of Elizabeth's own library two folios of St. Chrysostom and two quartos of Adam Clarke's commentary on the Bible were put in the warehouse. She sent ahead to Sidmouth her folio of Gregory Nazianzen, Wolf's Homer, the first volume of C. G. Heyne's edition of the *Iliad* and the first volume of his Pindar, possibly her three volumes of the *Odyssey,* two plays of Aeschylus, the complete works of Sophocles and Euripides, a few small Latin books, her Hebrew and Greek Bibles, Boyd's *Select Passages,* and his *Agamemnon of Aeschylus.*[74]

Mr. Barrett's pride was so hurt by having to forfeit his home that he shrank from old friends and many of his customary activities. To his children he never referred to the subject, and "he could play at cricket with the boys on the very last evening." Early in the morning of Thursday, August 23, 1832, two carriages left Hope End for the house Mr. Barrett had rented for his family in Sidmouth, Devonshire, 130 miles away. Fifteen were in the party: nine Barrett children (all but Bro and Septimus, both of whom came later with their father), their aunt Arabella, and several servants. Although most of the Barretts often returned to the neighborhood of Hope End in later years to visit relatives and friends, Elizabeth was never again to set foot in Herefordshire. They spent the night at the York Hotel in Bath, which she thought, "take it altogether, marble and mountains, is the most beautiful town I ever looked upon." She was so tired and out of health from her long drive that she could scarcely stand and had to be content with the view of Bath from her bedroom window. To have visited Boyd at Bathampton was out of the question. Early the next morning they set out toward Sidmouth; and since it was dark when they arrived, they had trouble at first in finding their new home.

3. Sojourn in Sidmouth

IN 1832 SIDMOUTH was rapidly becoming a fashionable "watering place." It is situated in a valley on the southern coast of Devonshire, with high, green hills and moors behind it and with steep, red cliffs above the sea, stretching away both east and west. One of Mr. Barrett's reasons for selecting the town was that its warm climate might help Elizabeth's cough to disappear. He supposed that any place he rented there would be only a *pied à terre* for a few months as he looked for a permanent home. The house at 7 and 8 Fortfield Terrace, where the Barretts first lived in Sidmouth until about June 1833, is in a row of white Georgian buildings which look across the cricket green to the esplanade and the bathing beach. Elizabeth wrote of this new house that it was the "one which the Grand Duchess Helena had, not at all *grand*, but extremely comfortable and cheerful." With its population of about three thousand, the town was larger than Ledbury, and it could have afforded Mr. Barrett's sons and daughters more opportunities to meet people than they had hitherto enjoyed. Elizabeth, however, remained aloof from all its "quadrilling and cricketing." She recovered her strength for the time being and was able to attend Bible meetings and church missionary services; she went on boating expeditions; she rode her donkey along the shore and on the cliffs; and she waded nearly up to her "waist in the wet grass or weeds, with the sun overhead, and the wind darkening or lightening the verdure all round." Yet despite her improved health and the possibility of a more active social life, her instincts were those of a recluse. Immediately upon her arrival she wrote Boyd that although she could not hope to live so secluded as before, she was resolved not to make any new friendships. Her explanation is significant: "Papa might not like my knowing people whom he does not know."[1] Almost a year later she wrote to Mrs. Martin, "Of society we have had little indeed; . . . as for me, you know

44

Hope End

The Barretts' house at Fortfield Terrace, Sidmouth

Sojourn in Sidmouth　　　　　　　　　　　　　　　　　　　　　　45

I don't want any." And so it is not surprising that by the autumn of 1835, when the Barretts left Sidmouth for London, Elizabeth had made only one important new friendship.

Within a few weeks after the Barretts moved to Sidmouth, a misunderstanding arose between Elizabeth and Boyd which could not be settled as long as they remained apart from each other. He had several times reproached her during the summer for not coming to see him in Bathampton, and her replies suggest that she would have been glad to accept his invitations if by so doing she did not have to offend her father. Boyd was very much hurt that she did not visit him when she passed through Bath, which was only three miles from his home, and he apparently blamed Mr. Barrett for the omission. She replied that he had no right to be angry with her father, for he could hardly have been expected to keep fourteen people waiting in Bath an extra day and her father to have spent an additional eight or nine pounds.[2]

Boyd remained unmollified and even hinted that it was a burden to have Elizabeth's long, closely written letters read to him so frequently. When she resolved to give him "negative pleasure" by writing a very short note, he appeared to be even more offended. In a long reply which brought matters to a crisis, she confessed she "could not write the last letter with tearless eyes,"[3] and she told him how greatly she had always valued his friendship. "The charm of my intercourse with you," she wrote, "was the power of communicating with a person who could feel like me and with me, and of saying within myself—*I cannot tire him.*" Although she no longer had that confidence, she still cared for him. "If you could see into my heart," she assured him and underlined the pronouns for emphasis, "you could not suspect *me* of thinking ill of *you!*"

The highly emotional appeal was successful. Boyd was convinced of her sincerity and determined to move immediately to Sidmouth even though the lease on his present house did not expire for six months. Mrs. Boyd accepted the arrangement, possibly with misgivings, but Annie refused to give up the parties of Bath. On December 11, 1832, Elizabeth was astonished to find Boyd and his wife had arrived in Sidmouth. It was their plan to surprise her by not writing that they were coming. Three days later Elizabeth reported to Mrs. Martin that although Boyd was pleased with Sidmouth, "Mrs. Boyd is not satisfied in the *same degree,* but I have no compassion for her." [4] For reasons which can only be surmised, Mrs. Boyd left her husband and returned to Bath, apparently within a few days after their arrival. References in Elizabeth's letters make it clear that Mrs. Boyd was suffering from some kind of nervous disorder, and she may have been irritated at Elizabeth's almost constant presence in her household.

On April 13, 1833, Elizabeth wrote Mrs. Boyd in Bathampton that for the last four months Boyd had been solitary except for the hours that she herself spent with him, and she blamed Mrs. Boyd for not returning. Furthermore she thought that if Annie "was strong enough to attend the Bath parties," she was also strong enough to come to Sidmouth. Annie had evidently tried to hurt her father by some slighting reference to his partiality toward Elizabeth, who said in the same letter to Mrs. Boyd that, "of one thing I am *quite sure*" (underlining each of the words twice), "that Mr. Boyd deserved *no* expressions from Annie which were not *affectionate and grateful ones.*" Elizabeth, it seems, was so weary of the Boyds' family quarrels that she regretted he had ever come, for she continued: "Whatever pleasure I have received from Mr. Boyd's being here, it has not prevented me from wishing more than once, that he had not come here." [5] Again, on May 3, Boyd implored his wife to return, in a letter for which Elizabeth was the amanuensis. Since no further letters from Elizabeth to Mrs. Boyd on the subject have come to light, it may be presumed that she soon arrived at Sidmouth. The Boyds remained there until the spring of 1834.

The three years the Barretts spent in Sidmouth saw many changes in the family pattern. Mr. Barrett had to be in London much of the time to attend to his business interests, usually living in lodging houses and hotels, since he kept no apartment there. The abolition of slavery, decreed by Parliament in September 1833 and taking effect on the first of August 1834, made inevitable a further diminution of income from the Barretts' Jamaica investments, and thus he could not afford to stay long with his children. And when he was at home, he appeared to be restless and to long for the more active rural life he had left. Elizabeth wrote to Mrs. Martin that when her father was in London, he was "more to be missed out of the red arm chair in our drawing room here, than when he used to spend almost all his hours with the cows and sheep," [6] and to another old friend, a Miss Commeline in Herefordshire, she said that she was "afraid Papa misses his farm and his active occupations." [7] At one time three of the Barrett boys were away from home. Bro worked on the family's Jamaica estates for about a year in 1834-35. Since he was Elizabeth's favorite brother and since the two had been inseparable companions, they must have been in frequent correspondence, none of which, however, has been preserved. Thus there is no evidence to indicate whether life on a sugar plantation was congenial to one of Bro's tastes, or why Mr. Barrett recalled him in 1835 and in the following year sent in his place Sam, who was four years younger than Bro. Elizabeth's brothers Charles John (Stormie) and George were students at the University of Glasgow from 1834 to 1835. Charles John did not take a degree; he shrank from the required public examination because of his impediment of speech, a defect which made him very self-conscious in the presence of strangers. George was graduated B.A. in the spring of 1835,[8] and in the following January he entered the Inner Temple as a barrister student.

ALTHOUGH the history of the Barrett family at this time may be traced in its broad outlines, the Sidmouth years are less fully documented than any other period of Elizabeth's adult life. The chief sources of biographical information are her letters to Mrs. James Martin, her life-long friend and former neighbor, and to Boyd before and after his residence in Sidmouth, because they describe her reading, the activities of her family, and her publications.

She wrote to Mrs. Martin on May 27, 1833, that her *Prometheus Bound . . . and Miscellaneous Poems* "came into light" recently. "I dare say," she added, "I shall wish it out of the light before I have done with it." Her later opinion of the work justified her prophecy. "That frigid, rigid exercise," she called it in a letter to Boyd some twelve years later when she told him she had translated the drama. And she once said to Browning that her early translation had been written "in thirteen days—the iambics thrown into blank verse, the lyrics into rhymed octosyllabics and the like, —and the whole together as cold as Caucasus." Her belief that "the little book was unadvertised and unknown" was not quite true, for the duodecimo volume was advertised in the *Athenaeum* May 11, 1833, and briefly reviewed in that journal four weeks later. Like *An Essay on Mind,* the book was issued anonymously. The mottoes in Greek (from Mimnermus and Theognis) on the title page were no doubt intended to impress the reader with the translator's learning. The volume was brought out by A. J. Valpy of London, who published mostly classical texts and translations; it was probably through the good offices of Elizabeth's acquaintance E. H. Barker, one of Valpy's principal editorial assistants, that her manuscript had been directed to his attention. Before they left Hope End, Mr. Barrett had suggested to Elizabeth that she write to Barker to ask whether his friend Valpy would publish her translation in one of the volumes of his Family Classical Library. A brief review in the *Athenaeum* [9] advised "those who adventure in the hazardous lists of poetic translation, to touch any one rather than Aeschylus; and they may take warning by the author before us." The writer of the notice could hardly have looked at the book, for he made no mention of the miscellaneous poems. Her footnotes to the translation were mostly taken, not always with acknowledgment, from C. J. Blomfield's edition of the *Prometheus Bound.*[10] References in the notes indicate that she also received some help from the editions of James Scholefield[11] and Samuel Butler.[12]

Like the translation, the shorter poems were probably all written during her last years at Hope End. Many are of the "vision" or meditation type. "The Picture Gallery at Penshurst" suggests that she may have visited Sydney's home on her return to Herefordshire from Hastings in the spring of 1826, if at that time she stopped at Tunbridge Wells to see her uncle Sam and his wife Mary. "To Victoire, on Her Marriage" was presumably written to a girl she had known when the Barrett family were living at Boulogne:

> And now a change hath come to us,
>   A sea doth rush between!
> I do not know if we can be
>   Again as we have been.
>
> I sit down in mine English land,
>   Mine English hearth beside;
> And thou, to one I never knew,
>   Art plighted for a bride.

The lines "To the Memory of Sir Uvedale Price, Bart." pay tribute to a friendship for which she had been sincerely grateful, but the diction and imagery are trite:

> Upon thy grave my tuneless harp I lay,
> Nor try to sing what only tears can say.
> So warm and fast the ready waters swell—
> So weak the faltering voice thou knewest well!

Several poems which deal with religious subjects, such as "The Appeal," "Idols," and "Hymn," have great evangelical ardor, but like all the writing in the volume they are surprisingly immature in their expression. Elizabeth's only other publication while she was at Sidmouth was a sentimental poem in the *New Monthly Magazine*, September 1835, on the death of Mrs. Hemans.

The five or six short poems she composed from 1832 to 1835 are a meager harvest for such a period. When she left Sidmouth for London she was in her thirtieth year. So far she had published nothing under her own name. She had to her credit only a few poems, scattered about in various journals and newspapers, and three short volumes of imitative verse, the expenses of which had been borne by an indulgent and proud father, none of them with any distinction or promise and all unnoticed by the public. Tennyson, at the age of twenty-three, published "The Lotos-Eaters," "The Lady of Shalott," and "Œnone" in his volume of 1832; Browning his *Paracelsus*, also at twenty-three. Each of the great Romantic poets had spoken with authentic voice long before his thirtieth year. But Elizabeth Barrett, who had amazed her family with the precocious scribbling of her teens, remained immature during her twenties. No one would have supposed that within eight or nine years she was suddenly to emerge from her obscurity to achieve widespread popularity both in her own country and in America.

It was unfortunate that so much of her energy was expended as reader, amanuensis, and research assistant to Boyd. First she helped him in the summer and fall of 1833 as he revised his "Essay on the Greek Article" and his "Postscript to the Essay," both of which had appeared originally in Adam Clarke's commentary on the Bible, and as he wrote a "Supplement to the Postscript." The three essays were embodied in a new edition of Clarke's work and were also published separately, along with a prose tract on the doctrine of the atonement.[13] Early in 1834 Boyd began the preparation of his volume entitled *The Fathers Not Papists*,[14] which was a collection of translations largely from Chrysostom, Basil, and Gregory Nazianzen: a jumble of homilies, orations, discourses, letters, and poems, all of which were supposed to prove that none of the Greek Fathers, indeed, no "first-rate Greek scholar," could ever have been a Roman Catholic. In his preface he maintained that all priests of that church were uneducated and that the most ignorant clergyman of the Church of England was more learned than the Roman Catholic clerics, who read the Bible from a corrupt translation. "If any man should deny this," Boyd wrote, "his denial must be ascribed either to gross ignorance, or to determined knavery, combined with unblushing impudence." Elizabeth frankly expressed to him her disapproval of the narrow, contentious spirit of his preface and said that many readers might consider the language he had applied to himself as "somewhat too *assuming of reputation*." [15] She also told him that the "mere composition" of the passage seemed to her *"rather loose and crude."* [16]

Some time before the end of May 1834 the Boyds moved away from Sidmouth, possibly because of the poor health of Mrs. Boyd, who died during the following autumn. He must have left unexpectedly, for his book was still in the press and Elizabeth inherited the task of reading proof sheets at Sidmouth in the shop of John Harvey, the printer. She attempted, without much success, to persuade Boyd to eliminate or alter the offensive passages of the preface. When a few months later he refused to pay £10 which Harvey believed was due him, she wrote to Boyd that she was

Sojourn in Sidmouth

"very sorry" he had denied the claim of the printer, who, she thought, had done all he could to fulfill his part of the contract and would have fulfilled it if not for the delays and inconveniences caused by Boyd's sudden departure. She concluded that "a remuneration can scarcely be among his prospects, as the book *does not seem to sell here at all.*" [17]

After the Barretts moved to London in the fall of 1835, Elizabeth was within a mile or two of Boyd's house. She continued to write him and saw him occasionally, but new friendships and new interests intervened so that they never resumed the intimacy of the years at Hope End and at Sidmouth. She had worshiped him because he had represented, it seemed to her, the world of literature and philosophy to which she aspired, but after she moved to London she realized she had little in common with any one so limited in his scholarship, so narrow and unenlightened in his literary tastes, and so isolated from all living currents of art and literature. After Annie Boyd married in the summer of 1837, Boyd's sister stayed with him for a short while until her death. He then lived pathetically alone in various houses in Hampstead and St. John's Wood, becoming ever more eccentric and timid, until he finally was afraid to walk out of his house or even to go down stairs. Elizabeth read very little Greek after her middle thirties because it was largely Boyd's special interests which had attracted her to Hellenic studies; after their friendship waned, she directed her attention to other subjects, such as French fiction and current political problems. His influence upon her had not been altogether beneficial, for her time might have been more profitably employed than in reading Gregory, Basil, Chrysostom, Synesius, and the other Greek Fathers.

IN ADDITION to her work in Greek, Elizabeth at this time also went through several volumes of philosophy and religion. She read a discourse on infant baptism by Ralph Wardlaw,[18] who was a Congregational minister and professor of theology at the Glasgow Theological Academy; a biography of an eloquent Baptist preacher at Bristol, Robert Hall; [19] the works of the clergyman Samuel Parr [20] and of the Presbyterian divine James Kidd; [21] the memoirs of Adam Clarke; [22] Lord Brougham's *A Discourse of*

Natural Theology; a treatise by the scientist William Prout entitled *Chemistry, Meteorology, and the Function of Digestion Considered with Reference to Natural Theology;* and selections from the writings of Martin Luther and of the eighteenth-century philosopher Anthony Collins. For diversion she read Edward Bulwer-Lytton's early novels.

While the Barretts were at Sidmouth, Elizabeth became very much attracted to a man who was for a time the minister of the Independent Chapel in that town, George Barrett Hunter. Inasmuch as he remained one of her most intimate friends until her marriage, in many ways superseding Boyd in his influence over her, it is unfortunate that so little is known about him. Of the many letters which must have gone back and forth between Elizabeth and him for more than twelve years, only one seems to have escaped destruction. Although his middle name might suggest the contrary, he had no connection or relationship with the Barrett family. Elizabeth's first reference to him is in a letter to Mrs. Martin, September 7, 1833, in which she mentioned his eloquence in the pulpit, his feeling for literature, his being "so gentle and humble and simple minded." [23] Both she and Mr. Barrett enjoyed Hunter's preaching, and she even wrote extracts from his sermons in one of her notebooks. When the Barretts first became acquainted with Hunter, no doubt shortly after their arrival at Sidmouth, he had living with him only his six-year-old daughter Mary.[24] In May of 1834 Elizabeth wrote of an expedition to Torquay on the steam packet she had made with her sister Arabel, several of her brothers, Mr. Hunter, and Mary; but she did not speak of Mrs. Hunter. Likewise in some manuscript verses, "To G. B. H.," [25] which Elizabeth placed in the presentation copy to Hunter of her *Poems* of 1844, she referred to the walks and conversations she had shared with him in Sidmouth, but she made no suggestion that he was ever accompanied by his wife. Several years later Elizabeth told Miss Mitford that Mary Hunter's mother had been "removed from her by a stroke worse than death . . madness"; [26] apparently the event had occurred before Elizabeth became acquainted with the family. Elizabeth was attached to him because of what appeared to her as idealism, his wide culture, and the sincerity of his religious convictions. And on his side he must have been

Sojourn in Sidmouth 53

gratified at the eager response of such an attractive and intelligent girl. Their close friendship in Sidmouth probably lasted a little more than two years, for on February 4, 1835, she wrote Boyd that Hunter had left the Independent Chapel and that "his absence from its pulpit is not likely to be ever worthily supplied." [27]

For the rest of his life he met with nothing but misfortune as he drifted from church to church and attempted to augment his small income by private tutoring. In the course of time Elizabeth came to see another side of his nature: his abnormal sensitiveness, his violent temper, and his melancholy and bitterness engendered by long years of failure. His delight was to fulminate against the wrongs and abuses of the world until his congregations could bear him no longer. "So unhappy a life! So unhappy a creature!" [28] Elizabeth said of him when she heard of his death in 1857. In describing him to Miss Mitford in 1842, she said that "the power of suffering is not sufficiently balanced by the energy to act,— which produces a despondent character very painful to witness the workings of sometimes, in so dear a friend." [29]

Hunter evidently fell in love with Elizabeth, although it is hard to see how he could have entertained any serious hopes. Her family was financially independent, and she had a modest fortune in her own name; his circumstances were "miserably straitened," [30] his prospects were cloudy, and he was burdened with an insane wife. If he was in love, she certainly never returned it; rather it was for her a warm emotional feeling much like her earlier attachment to Boyd and similar in its sequel of disillusionment. Both men were unworldly, impractical, and idealistic, and both suffered from severe handicaps, mental or physical, which prevented them from earning an adequate living.

The tone and content of the one letter from Hunter to Elizabeth which has been preserved make it clear why she would have become tired of him sooner or later. It was written in September 1838, from Axminster, where he was preaching, to Elizabeth, who had just arrived at Torquay. A large portion of the letter is an apology for a clumsy joke he had made in a previous letter about "aristocracy," a joke which Elizabeth had thought was at her expense. He was "bewildered and astonished" to learn that she was offended and assured her that he had not been angry and had not meant to be unkind. His manner of expression shows that he was very much interested in her. He could not imagine how she could ever have supposed that he had imputed "hard thoughts" to her or " 'silence' called 'ingratitude.' " It seemed to him an unhappy mistake: "Had I ever made such an association . . . I should wear away in the wretchedness of having . . . deservedly and for ever forfeited a regard wh. is dearer to me than that of all the world besides." [31] Until Hunter's death she continued to admire him for the high qualities she believed she saw in him; but for all his assiduous attention toward her, she was increasingly irritated by his awkward, perverse conduct.

Late in the spring of 1833, after the lease on their home at Fortfield Terrace expired,[32] the Barretts seem to have moved into a "ruinous house," [33] which was so unsatisfactory that before long they rented a spacious Georgian mansion called Belle Vue, which was about five minutes' walk from the sea. The building has been somewhat enlarged and is now the Cedar Shade Hotel on All Saints Road. They stayed there until the summer of 1835, when they removed to their "ancient house upon the beach." [34] Soon afterward, either in the summer or in the autumn, they moved to London so that Mr. Barrett might be close to his business and so that those of his sons who were receiving their education in London might live at home.

4. First Stay in London: "The Seraphim"

FOR THEIR FIRST TWO YEARS in London the Barretts rented a house at 74 (now 99 and 101) Gloucester Place, which is between Oxford Street and Regent's Park. The building is on the northwest corner of Gloucester Place and Crawford Street and is a dignified-looking brick structure built about 1805 to accommodate a single family but now divided into several flats. Its outward appearance, however, has not changed since the Barretts lived there.

Elizabeth had not wished to leave Sidmouth. She wondered how she could ever breathe when "walled up like a transgressing nun, and out of hearing of that sea."[1] At first the narrow streets and "want of horizon" severely depressed her, but in a month or two she came to enjoy the parks and felt at home in the city. With her ever-present tendency toward hero worship, she thought of London as "a wonderful place—the living heart and centre of an immense circle of humanity—the fountain of intellect—of Art in all its forms—of the highest memories consecrated by genius: it is your Fletcher's London, our Shakespeare's London, my Chaucer's London," as she wrote Miss Mitford.[2] To remain quietly in her room and contemplate the great movement of life in the city outside was a "miracle" which caused her imagination to "thrill"—a favorite word in Elizabeth's vocabulary.

Whether or not the other members of the Barrett family preferred London to Sidmouth can be only guesswork. Her father, Elizabeth felt, would always miss Hope End. In the summer of 1837 she wrote that he was "not at all a Londoner in his heart and pining I fear sometimes for his old dear rural occupations."[3] Her two sisters were at home: Henrietta, the best-looking of the three, "most caring for the Polka," and Arabel, "for the sermon preached at Paddington Chapel." Sam went to Jamaica and remained there, except for intervals at home, until his sudden death from a West Indian fever at the age of twenty-eight. In the fall of 1836 Henry went to Germany to study with a companion-tutor for about two years. Charles John, who was always painfully shy and inarticulate, stayed at home without any regular occupation until his departure for Jamaica in the spring of 1840. Also at home were the two youngest boys, Septimus (Sette) and Octavius (Occy). Two of the brothers were studying in London: George at the Inner Temple, where he became a barrister-at-law in 1839, and Alfred at the University of London, to read Greek, Latin, and philosophy. What of "dear Bro," Ba's closest companion and idol, who in 1837 had reached his thirtieth birthday? The only evidence is Elizabeth's remark to an old friend in Herefordshire, "My eldest brother . . . is at home. He still draws occasionally." [4] He also studied some German one summer with Elizabeth and Henry before the latter went abroad.

Soon after coming to London, Elizabeth made two significant friendships: those with John Kenyon and with Mary Russell Mitford. The full extent of Kenyon's influence upon her can scarcely be overestimated. Her success as a writer and her happiness as a woman owe more to his sympathetic interest than to any other person in her life, except Browning. He encouraged her in her writing when she was despondent; before her marriage he was her chief link with the world of letters in London, and he introduced her to several persons who became congenial friends; he fostered the romance between her and Robert Browning, aided them financially after their marriage, and bequeathed to them a portion of his fortune. Although he claimed, jokingly perhaps, to have with the Barretts "a cousinship in some degree or other," [5] Elizabeth seemingly considered the "cousin" only a courtesy title. In writing to Browning of "dear Mr. Kenyon's opinion of his 'young relative,' " she pointed out that she was "neither young nor his relative," [6] and in a letter from Pisa to Henrietta, she referred to Kenyon as her "relative scarcely more than by name." [7]

Kenyon, whom Southey described as one of the best and pleasantest of men he had ever known,[8] was a friend of Henry Crabb Robinson, Landor, Southey, and Wordsworth, and he had known

First Stay in London: "The Seraphim"

Lamb and Coleridge. Like Mr. Barrett, he had been born in Jamaica of a wealthy plantation family. He was sent to England to be educated, went first to the Fort Bristol School in Bristol, where one of his schoolfellows was Robert Browning, the future father of the poet, and later he was a student at Charterhouse and at Cambridge, which he left in 1808 without taking a degree. At the time Elizabeth became one of Kenyon's intimate friends in 1835 or 1836 (she had been acquainted with him for many years), he was in his early fifties. Although he had experienced the deaths of two wives, he had remained cheerful and friendly. An American writer and traveler, George Stillman Hillard, spoke of him as a man with "a warm heart, a good digestion, a sunny temper, and an enjoyable nature," and he said that "there was something peculiarly winning in his manner, the tones of his voice, and the expressions of his face."[9] Since he had ample means, he could afford to be a patron of the arts, to help men of letters in many different ways, and to entertain them at his comfortable home at 4 Harley Place, and later at 39 Devonshire Place. Although he was a friend of poets, rather than an original poet himself, he had published in 1833 a short volume entitled *Rhymed Plea for Tolerance* and five years later his *Poems: for the Most Part Occasional.*

It was through his good offices that Elizabeth came to know Miss Mitford. He had urged Elizabeth to come to a large party to meet Wordsworth, but in spite of her veneration of the poet from Rydal Mount, she was too afraid of crowds to accept the offer. Kenyon was somewhat hurt at her refusal, and she was torn between her desires and her fears. Then he invited her to a smaller reception, at which Wordsworth and Miss Mitford would be guests. On the morning of the party, May 27, 1836, Elizabeth received a note from Kenyon, proposing instead a trip with him and Miss Mitford to the Zoological Gardens. "I resolved at once to go," she later wrote, "and set my teeth as for the desperate purpose of it,"[10] thinking all the while how happy she would be when it was over. After several hours of mental anguish, during which she could neither read nor write, she heard the carriage and went down stairs, her knees shaking so that she could hardly walk. Kenyon then took her and Miss Mitford to see the animals in Regent's Park and to the Diorama, which was a building on the east side of Park Square, southeast of Regent's Park, where spectators sat in a darkened room and by means of an optical illusion appeared to see a revolving and changing landscape. The two scenes on view in July of that summer, and possibly also in May, were the falling of an avalanche over the Alpine village of Alagna in the valley of Sesia in northern Italy and the interior of the church of Santa Croce in Florence. According to an article by Lady Morgan in the *Athenaeum*,[11] the visitors could see Monte Rosa and other peaks "reposing in the moonlight," the outline of "a most picturesque cottage," from which the smoke "rises gracefully" and "stains the deep blue atmosphere," the approaching hurricane, and the "heaving sea of snow" which filled the valley while the sun shone the following morning on the obliterated town. They also observed the Florentine church first "in all the lustre and brightness of a sunshiny Italian noon," and then in the "reserved tints of evening," when everything seemed "chill, and grey, and misty," and finally as it was brilliantly lighted for "the august ceremony of high mass," during which they smelled the incense and heard the peal of the organ and the tinkling of the bell when the priest elevated the host.

Miss Mitford wrote to her father that she had met "a delightful young creature; shy and timid and modest." The following evening Elizabeth returned to Kenyon's house, where in addition to seeing Miss Mitford again, she met Wordsworth and Landor. She was "not at all disappointed in Wordsworth," though she confessed that perhaps she would "not have singled him from the multitude as a great man." He seemed reserved, his speech was measured and slow, and his expression did not have Landor's animation. "As to my being quite at my ease when I spoke to him, why how could you ask such a question?" she wrote Mrs. Martin. "I trembled both in my soul and body. But he was very kind, and sate near me and talked to me as long as he was in the room." Landor gave her two Greek epigrams he had recently composed, and he conversed "brilliantly and prominently," until Bro, who was always more loquacious in general company than his sister, "abused him for *ambitious* singularity and affectation." Upon her return home Elizabeth recorded her impressions of Wordsworth and of everything he had said to her. They had discussed the question whether a literary genius must necessarily have moral qualities. He had maintained that the two went together, that no poet had ever lived without developing "the gentle exalted moral humanities," and had cited the examples of Burns and of Byron, in both of whom their "weaknesses of the moral faculty" came from "a want of genius than a redundancy of it." [12] On another occasion Elizabeth went with Miss Mitford and Wordsworth to Chiswick, and all the way she thought she "must certainly be dreaming."

Landor did not forget the young poet he had seen at Kenyon's, for in August he told Lady Blessington the circumstances of his meeting Elizabeth and asked whether she had read Miss Barrett's poems, and he added curiously enough that he had heard Miss Barrett had recently "become quite absorbed in her devotional contemplations." [13] Wordsworth also remembered her; shortly after the publication of *The Seraphim, and Other Poems* in 1838, he wrote from Rydal Mount to Kenyon that he was "so much pleased with the power of knowledge displayed" in the volume that he wished to see also her translations from Aeschylus.[14]

Between Elizabeth and Mary Russell Mitford an intimate friendship came into being. Miss Mitford was the elder by nineteen years, and by 1836 she had long been a well-known writer. Several of her tragedies had been successfully produced at Covent Garden and Drury Lane, with such eminent actors as Macready and Charles Kemble, and her stories of country life called *Our Village* had earned her an international reputation. Elizabeth, however, had not yet begun to write under her own name. Yet despite dissimilarities in literary reputation and in age, each was immediately drawn to the other. Whenever Miss Mitford came to London from her "insufficient and meanly-furnished labourer's cottage" [15] (as H. F. Chorley described it), at Three Mile Cross, near Reading, she called on Elizabeth, who because of her frailty could not return the visits but instead wrote to her long letters in which for the next ten years she reported the minutiae of her life much more fully than to any other correspondent. Elizabeth once wrote Browning that a large drawer in her room in Wimpole Street had been filled with Miss Mitford's "delightful letters, heart-warm and soul-warm, . . driftings of nature," and that if they were all printed they "would assume the folio shape as a matter of course." Elizabeth's replies, which have been preserved but published only in part, would fill several folios. She wrote of the medical details of all her many illnesses, the opinions of her physicians, the books she was reading, gossip about mutual friends and her family, and, sometimes, the different kinds of food she had given Flush to eat.

Although they continued to write to each other as good friends after Elizabeth left for Italy, until Miss Mitford's death in 1855, neither fully understood the other's point of view. Miss Mitford enjoyed her life in the country, was conservative in her social and political views, and was suspicious of "pen and ink folk" because of their eccentricities. For her, writing was a laborious task to be endured only because it provided the money so necessary in a household the resources of which were constantly being depleted by a profligate and selfish father. Elizabeth, on the other hand, naïvely glorified literary life and worshiped writers even because of their unconventional habits. But owing to the circumstances of a comfortable home and of her own independent income she was sheltered, and all her life was to remain so, from the hardships many writers have suffered. And thus knowing only the exhilaration of authorship and nothing of the poverty which often attends it, she could not understand Miss Mitford's longing to be released from the drudgery of writing. Furthermore Elizabeth disliked English country life, "where human creatures ruminate stupidly as the cows do, the 'county families' es-*chewing* all men who are not 'landed proprietors,' and the farmers never looking higher than to the fly on the uppermost turnip-leaf!" It was to her mind "simply and purely abominable." In contrast to Miss Mitford's contentment to remain at home, Elizabeth always had within her an element of repressed bohemianism. Before her marriage she longed to live on the Continent. "If I had strength and liberty,—I would go tomorrow, and divide two or three years between France, Germany, and Italy," [16] she wrote Miss Mitford in 1843. She would "settle in some German town for the summer, and in Rome for the winter, and diverge—and share the intermediate time between various shrines of pilgrimage. What!—you would not like it?" she asked Miss Mitford. *"Can you say so?"* [17]

To Miss Mitford the way of life of the Barrett family appeared "full of quiet respectability," and it seemed to have "all the marks of affluence without the slightest show." [18] She thought that Mr. Barrett was "an exceedingly clever agreeable man with very easy highbred manners." [19] Also she was impressed by Elizabeth's "very simple but graceful and costly dress by which all the family are distinguished." Miss Mitford's description of Elizabeth, before the disaster at Torquay prematurely aged her, emphasizes her youth, health, physical attractiveness, and her bookish qualities: "a slight, girlish figure, very delicate, with exquisite hands and feet, a round face, with a most noble forehead, a large mouth, beautifully formed, and full of expression, lips like parted coral, teeth large, regular, and glittering with healthy whiteness, large dark eyes, . . . a dark complexion, with cheeks literally as bright as the dark China rose, a profusion of silky, dark curls . . . Her talk, delightful as it was, had something too much of the lamp—she spoke too well." [20]

Besides Kenyon and Miss Mitford, Elizabeth occasionally saw Boyd, who was living nearby on Circus Road, Regent's Park, and later in Hampstead; and out of habit she continued to correspond with him. But since he no longer meant much to her, the letters she now wrote him were lacking the intimacy of those she had sent from Hope End.

IT WAS during her early years in London before she left for Torquay that she first gained widespread recognition for her poetry. Charles Wentworth Dilke, editor of the *Athenaeum*, and Samuel Carter Hall of the *New Monthly Magazine* published anonymously between 1835 and 1837 a number of her poems, all of which she revised for inclusion in *The Seraphim, and Other Poems*. In addition to her verses, her prose essay entitled "A Thought on Thoughts" appeared, also anonymously, in the *Athenaeum* of July 23, 1836. It is a schoolgirl exercise which she had written some time before June 1831 [21] and had put away until she found an editor who would accept almost everything she sent him. The *Athenaeum* reviewed briefly two of her poems which were printed in the *New Monthly Magazine* in 1836. Of "The Romaunt of Margret" it said that "We have not read such a ballad for many a day; and if its writer will only remember, that in poetry *manner* is a blemish to be got rid of, and not an ornament to be worn and cherished, he (or she) may rank very high—what if we say, among the highest?" [22] Several months later it noticed the "fine, though too dreamy, ballad, 'The Poet's Vow,'" which it considered to be the work of a writer of "much inspiration and promise." Once again it urged the author to be clearer in his expression and "less quaint" in his diction.[23]

Both poems are humorless, sentimental tales of a type which was to become very popular with Elizabeth's reading public. The "fair ladye" of "The Romaunt of Margret" learns from a phantom that she must die unless she loves someone who loves her "as truly as the sun." Brother, sister, father, none of them, according to the shadow, is wholeheartedly in love with her. What the phantom says does not distress her until she learns that her "more than friend" is no longer living, and then she drowns herself. "The Poet's Vow," although it is a more ambitious effort and has an attached "moral," is similar in content and tone. For some obscure reason a poet vows to live apart from mankind and offers his castle as a dowry to his fiancée Rosalind if she will marry his best friend. She indignantly spurns the offer and soon dies of grief. Her corpse, upon which lies a scroll telling of her frustrated passion, is placed in front of the "hall" of the poet, who forthwith breaks his vow of isolation. After a macabre recognition scene in which "the senseless corpse rocked to and fro," he bewails his broken heart "In a mortal agony." When Rosalind's body is carried away the following morning, "Her bier was holding twain."

Although Landor wrote to Lady Blessington that he doubted whether she would think Miss Barrett's poetry suitable for the *Book of Beauty*,[24] in point of fact some of Elizabeth's most characteristic verses made their first appearance in the "annuals." It was in the 1830's that the annuals, or gift books, achieved their greatest popularity, but their vogue began to die out in the forties and fifties. They had such sentimental names as *Forget Me Not, Friendship's Offering, Flowers of Loveliness, The Book of Beauty, Gems of Beauty, The Amulet, The Diadem*. Their elaborate bindings were of morocco leather, watered silk, or velvet; the paper was smooth and rich-looking; and they were filled with handsome full-page illustrations which were usually more important than the

First Stay in London: "The Seraphim"

texts. The names alone of many of the editors and of the contributors suggest that their "keepsakes" were pervaded with an odor both feminine and aristocratic: the Countess of Blessington, the Hon. Mrs. Caroline Norton, Lady Caroline Lamb, Lady Emmeline Stuart-Wortley, Letitia Elizabeth Landon, Mary Russell Mitford, Felicia Hemans, and Mary Howitt. In June of 1837 Miss Mitford, who had accepted the editorship of one of the annuals, asked Elizabeth Barrett to contribute a poem "in illustration of a very charming group of Hindoo girls floating their lamps upon the Ganges." [25] During the following two months Elizabeth was at work on her "A Romance of the Ganges," which was published anonymously in *Findens' Tableaux: a Series of Picturesque Scenes of National Character, Beauty, and Costume*, for 1838.[26] The album had a series of twelve engravings of insipid-looking "beauties," with each plate representing a different country or part of the world. The drawing which Elizabeth's poem was supposed to "illustrate" depicts five languorous females gazing across a body of water. Upon it are floating two small boats which look like turtle shells, each with a flame spurting upward and each filled with flowers. In the background is a temple vaguely oriental in appearance. To accompany the illustration Elizabeth concocted a melancholy tale, the basis of which was the superstition that after a girl launched a boat, its flame would continue to burn if her lover were faithful. One of the girls finds she has lost her lover to another in the group around her, a discovery which promptly generates an inundation of tears from all five. The *Athenaeum* in its review of the volume said that the poems were better than in most collections of its type, and it mentioned "E.B.B." as one of the "comparatively unhackneyed" writers in the annual.[27] The notice in the *Literary Gazette* said that most of the contributions were "of a very low order." [28] The only work it quoted was that "by an anonymous writer, with the initials E.B.B." In the opinion of the reviewer, it was "incomparably the best poem" in the collection.

Miss Mitford was so pleased with Elizabeth's verses that she asked her to contribute to the volume for 1839,[29] the full title of which was *Findens' Tableaux of the Affections: a Series of Picturesque Illustrations of the Womanly Virtues*. In May and June of 1838 Elizabeth composed "The Romaunt of the Page," to which

Miss Mitford accorded pride of place in her volume. The engraving represents a girl dressed as a squire or page but so obviously feminine in appearance that the identity of her sex could have confused no one but the knight in the poem. She is kneeling at the foot of a tree and looking with a wistful expression toward the back of a fully armed knight on a horse that is pawing the air and is about to charge away. On the ground in front of the page are a casque and a murderous-looking instrument, which seems to be a combination of cross-bow and battle-axe and is called "battle-bow" in Elizabeth's poem. The verses tell of an incredibly faithful bride who masquerades as a page that she might follow her husband to Palestine. She sees in the distance the Saracens rushing toward them, but the extraordinarily imperceptive knight is oblivious of the danger. The page, without revealing her identity and promising to follow him soon after saying a prayer, tells him to ride away by himself. He does so without question, and she is killed by the pagans and dies with a smile because her sacrifice has been successful. The *Athenaeum* in a longer review than it usually granted to annuals, made short, perfunctory remarks about the contributions of Kenyon, Miss Mitford, and the now-forgotten John R. Chorley, but it devoted the rest of its attention to Elizabeth's ballad, which seemed to the writer "one of the most beautiful things from a woman's hand which has appeared for many a day."[30]

THE first work which Elizabeth issued under her own name was *The Seraphim, and Other Poems,* a duodecimo volume published by Saunders and Otley, of Conduit Street, London, who advertised it in *The Times,* Wednesday, June 6, 1838.[31] Her previous books (except for the juvenile *Battle of Marathon*) and her contributions to magazines and newspapers had all been anonymous. The year in which Elizabeth Barrett came before the public was a dead period in English poetry. Keats, Shelley, and Byron had disappeared from the scene in the early twenties, Coleridge had died four years before, and for a long while Wordsworth had added nothing to his reputation. Although Moore, Campbell, Southey, Landor, and Rogers were still living, none was to have any new inspiration. As for the younger generation, both Browning and

Tennyson were known to small groups, but neither had yet achieved general recognition. Among the women who in the thirties were producing verse, all of it flaccid and diffuse, the best known were Felicia Hemans, who died in 1835, Letitia Elizabeth Landon, Caroline Norton, and Caroline Southey.

In writing to Kenyon of her volume of 1838, Elizabeth Barrett said that "with all its feebleness and shortcomings and obscurities," it was yet "the first utterance of my own individuality." More than most poets, she had "found it hard work to *get into expression*," partly because she had always led "so conventual recluse a life." As she later told Browning, her tongue "clove" to the roof of her mouth when she composed the poems of this book. The conclusion of her preface is a sincere expression of her humility and of her hope "to write hereafter better verses." She could never "feel more intensely than at this moment—nor can it be needful that any should—the sublime uses of poetry, and the solemn responsibilities of the poet."

The principal poem in the book is "The Seraphim," a lyrical drama of about the same length as her "Prometheus Bound." When she was writing "The Seraphim" in the fall of 1836, she was "in two panics," first because it seemed to her "a very daring subject —a subject almost beyond our sympathies, and therefore quite beyond the sphere of human poetry"; and secondly, as she said, "because all my tendencies towards mysticism will be called into terrible operation by this dreaming upon angels." The poem is divided into two parts and an epilogue. The first part takes place at the time of the Crucifixion and the scene is "the outer side of the shut heavenly gate." Except for Ador, "the Strong," and Zerah, "the Bright One," all the angels have descended toward the earth at the command of God. The two seraphim speak of the Creation, the Fall, the Birth of Christ, the Incarnation, and the Redemption, all in the tumid diction with which Elizabeth always endowed angel tongues. The place of the second part is "mid-air, above Judaea." Ador and Zerah, both of whom have come down from the heavens and are now "a little apart from the visible Angelic Hosts," describe the scene taking place below them. Their conversation is interrupted from time to time by the Voice from the Cross, Voices of the Angelic Multitude, Voices of Fallen Angels, the Voice of the Earth, and the Voice of All Things. In the epilogue Elizabeth suggests, truthfully enough, that her power of expression is inadequate to deal with such a theme.

In their subject matter and treatment the shorter poems are unreal, sentimental, and some of them fantastic. "Isobel's Child," for example, describes an all-night vigil of a mother and her three-month-old baby, who has been desperately ill. The mother is human enough to pray that he may be spared, but the child has a vision of "celestial places," "high and vista'd palms," and "a little harp" waiting for him. He laments the "dreary earthly love" of his mother, whose "prayers do keep me out of bliss," so that she "changed the cruel prayer" she had made and freed the child's spirit to go "To the place that loving is." Like many other poems in the volume, the concluding passage is one of commonplace moralizing. Among the verses with personal associations "The Deserted Garden" tells of Elizabeth's childhood pleasures at Hope End, of the sanctuary in the woods where she could get away from her family and find for herself a solitude:

> And so, I thought my likeness grew
> (Without the melancholy tale)
> To gentle hermit of the dale,
>   And Angelina too!
>
> For oft I read within my nook
> Such minstrel stories! till the breeze
> Made sounds poetic in the trees,—
>   And then I shut the book.

"The Name" explains the origin of her nickname "Ba":

> My brother gave that name to me
>   When we were children twain;
> When names acquired baptismally
> Were hard to utter, as to see
>   That life had any pain.

Two of the poems which have for their background the years at Sidmouth are "The Sea-Mew" and "The Little Friend," both of which were written for G. B. Hunter's daughter Mary. In "A

First Stay in London: "The Seraphim" 67

Song against Singing," addressed to "my dear little cousin, Elizabeth Jane H———" (Hedley), Elizabeth expresses her reluctance to write a poem for the child:

> How could I think it right,
> Newcomer on our earth, as, Sweet, thou art,
> To bring a verse from out an human heart
> So heavy with accumulated tears;
> And cross with such amount of weary years,
> Thy day-sum of delight?

The doleful self-portrait bears little resemblance to the original; in spite of her physical weakness, Elizabeth's life in London was serene and not unpleasant, and the severer trials of ill-health and grief were still in the future. Two other personal poems are "My Doves" and "To Miss Mitford in Her Garden." "Victoria's Tears," which was republished from the *Athenaeum,* is based on the contrast between the millions who were rejoicing in their new sovereign and the Queen herself, who all alone "wept, to wear a crown!" A month after the accession of Victoria, Elizabeth had written to Miss Mitford, "Those tears, wept not only amidst the multitudes at the proclamation, but in the silence of the dead midnight—(we heard that she cried all night before holding her first privy council . . .) are beautiful and touching to think upon." [32]

Among the shorter poems, the ones on religious topics, like "The Weeping Saviour" and "The Measure," are all of them lachrymose and insipid. In "Cowper's Grave" Elizabeth writes of a place "where happy saints / May weep amid their praying," and she says that all may read "Through dimming tears" of Cowper's tragic life. With all its spurious pathos and religiosity, it became the most popular poem of the volume of 1838.

Although *The Seraphim, and Other Poems* sold slowly and did not even pay for the expenses of publication, it received long and fair reviews in the principal literary journals, so that within two or three months Elizabeth, who had been virtually unknown, was widely acclaimed as one of the most promising of the younger English poets. The most wildly enthusiastic of the reviews appeared in a short-lived magazine called the *Sunbeam,* which expired shortly after its series of articles on Elizabeth Barrett's verse.[33] The editors had announced that "under the head of polite literature" they intended to review "all those works, which, without being abstruse, inculcate religion, morals, and piety"; they evidently considered that Elizabeth's poems were well within their scope. The writer of the article referred to "The Seraphim" as "this divine poem," and he said that the shorter pieces in the volume were "characterised by the distant—the profound and the sublime—by remote analogies, by deep analysis, and by lofty aspirations—all, however, moderated by a spirit of piety and restrained within the scheme of the Christian dispensation." The reviewer declared that Elizabeth Barrett was frequently like Tennyson but that she was "capable of sustaining a more prolonged flight" than he.

Even the more sober notices all hailed the arrival of a poet of "extraordinary" ability—the adjective appears many times—and of still greater promise. John Wilson ("Christopher North"), who reviewed the volume for *Blackwood's Edinburgh Magazine,* said that he had read Elizabeth's book "with love and admiration." Of the shorter poems he wrote, "There is beauty in them all—and some of them, we think, are altogether beautiful." It seemed to him that at least one, "Isobel's Child," was "beyond all dispute" the production of a genius.[34] The *Metropolitan Magazine* referred to Elizabeth as "a truly original and gifted author" of an "extraordinary little book," and it praised its "originality, ideality, earnestness, and masterly power of expression and execution." [35] Likewise, the *Quarterly Review* considered "Miss Barrett to be a woman of undoubted genius, and most unusual learning." [36] Several notices expressed pleasure that such a book had been written by a woman. The *Athenaeum* thought that the volume was "especially welcome as an evidence of female genius and accomplishment," [37] and the *Monthly Review* wrote that the poems "when considered as the compositions of a female, must . . . command admiration and awaken hope." [38] The *Sunbeam* said in the same vein that the themes of Elizabeth's long poem "were wonderful to be spoken of by men—by an Aeschylus and a Shelley; how much more wonderful thus uttered by a woman?"

However much praise and encouragement the reviewers accorded the volume as a whole, almost none of them believed that "The Seraphim" was a success. Even Elizabeth herself later recognized its "complete failure." [39] The *Quarterly Review* objected to the subject of the poem, as one "from which Milton would have shrunk, and which Miss Barrett would not have attempted, if she had more seriously considered its absolute unapproachableness. In the first place, there is not, in the proper critical sense, any human interest in such a subject; and in the next place, the awful narrative of the Evangelist exterminates all parallel or supplement." Although "Christopher North" found both poetry and piety in "The Seraphim," he almost wished that the poem had not been written because "the awful Idea of the Poem—the Crucifixion—is not sustained." The *Examiner* [40] thought that although she was "a genuine poetess, of no common order," she aimed too high and therefore fell "infinitely short . . . of what a proper exercise of her genius would infallibly reach." The *Monthly Review* also believed that in "The Seraphim" Elizabeth was always close to bathos and was constantly "alarming us or making us conscious that we are upon the verge of what will precipitate herself and her readers to an offensive or irrecoverable condition."

In the opinion of most of the reviews the shorter poems were more successful. A brief notice in the *Monthly Chronicle,* after commenting on the "many feeble and affected lines" of the opening poem of the volume, said that, "There are several minor pieces, which, though less ambitious in design, are more perfect in execution. The more simple of these are indeed gems equally pure and lustrous; and in them every lover of poetry must find delight, and every student of poetry a model." [41] Some of the poems most frequently praised in the reviews were "Isobel's Child," "The Deserted Garden," "The Sea-Mew," "My Doves," "The Poet's Vow," "The Sleep," and "Cowper's Grave."

Yet even her shorter poems were marred by frequent lapses in expression. An unsigned review in the *Athenaeum,* probably by Henry Fothergill Chorley, deplored her hazy diction: "A thousand strange and beautiful visions flit across her mind, but she cannot look on them with steady gaze;—her descriptions, therefore, are often shadowy and indistinct, and her language wanting in the simplicity of unaffected earnestness." Likewise the *Atlas* [42] thought that she was "sometimes chargeable with affectation." However much Elizabeth may have considered the *Atlas* "the best newspaper for literary reviews, excepting always the 'Examiner,'" the remark irritated her, for she wrote Miss Mitford that it was "not pleasant to be called 'affected' as in the Atlas . . . I do not understand how anyone who writes from the real natural impulse of feeling and thought . . . can write affectedly, even in the manner of it." [43] The reviewer compared her poetry to an overworked tapestry which "has consequently a cumbrous appearance, here and there, from the excessive weight of the colouring." Although Elizabeth "was much delighted" with the critique in *Blackwood's* and felt that it was "something to be in a cave with . . . dear old Christopher, who is the first *professionally poetical* critic of the day," [44] the reviewer accorded her as much censure as praise. Even the minor poems were "all disfigured by much imperfect and some bad writing—and the fair author is too often seen struggling in vain to give due expression to the feelings that beset her, and entangled in a web of words." The *Literary Gazette*, while admitting that Elizabeth's volume had "a feeling and a flow of true poetry," condemned "the many antiquated and affected phrases with which it abounds." It continued, "Our authoress seems to have modelled herself upon the very worst portion of Keats and Tennyson, in labouring for outlandish compound words, picking up obsolete phrases, and accenting every unnecessary syllable." [45] It objected to such expressions as "the night is in her hair," "a low shadowy laughter," "the silentnesses."

In commenting on the influence upon her poetry of her reading, the *Metropolitan* declared its "great respect for the fair author's uncommon learning." The reviewer believed she must have an intimate acquaintance with Greek and German letters, though by 1838 she had read very little German and was never to be much interested in German literature. It also seemed to him that she was "perfectly imbued" with the spirit of Greek poetry. The critic's opinion notwithstanding, classical repose, clarity, balance, and restraint are precisely the qualities in which she was conspicuously lacking. Why is it that although Elizabeth was an excellent student of Greek and had gone through many of the Latin poets, much of her verse is lawless? The answer may be that for

First Stay in London: "The Seraphim"

her, reading of the classics was largely an escape not a partly creative act; thus she could not assimilate much of what she read or draw upon it in the composition of her own poetry. She later came to feel that she had "lost time . . . and life" from her concentration upon the study of languages.[46] It is significant that in her more active years in Italy she no longer devoted herself to the "dear Greek" but that her reading was mostly of recent French and English novels and of the reports in newspapers and magazines of current events.

Within three years of its publication copies of *The Seraphim, and Other Poems* had found their way to New York and Boston. The first review in the United States appeared in the February 1841 issue of *Arcturus, a Journal of Books and Opinion*,[47] which was edited by two ambitious young New Yorkers, Cornelius Mathews and Evert A. Duyckinck. The critique, which was written by the latter, was generally favorable. It called Elizabeth a "true poet," whose verse could not be read "without a consciousness of love and holy thought." Like the earlier English reviews, he preferred the shorter, simpler poems to "The Seraphim," with its "sense of mysticism and obscurity in a dim philosophizing," which, he believed, had hurt the reputation of "the fair authoress." An unsigned article, possibly by George Stillman Hillard, in the *North American Review* found in her volume "more fertility of invention, more luxuriance of fancy, more boldness and originality of thought, a more expanded poetical horizon, brighter visions of beauty, and tones of more impassioned music" than in *An Essay on Mind*. The reviewer believed, however, that her faults were the same as in her earlier books: "Her great defect is a certain lawless extravagance, which delights in the wild, the mystic, the wonderful; which blends into the same group the most discordant images, and hurries her into a dim cloud-land far remote from human sympathies." [48]

After a year or two in London Mr. Barrett decided that he and his children would settle there permanently. In September 1837 he purchased a house at 50 Wimpole Street, not far from where they were living in Gloucester Place, and they moved there in the following April. Just as Elizabeth had been fearful of leaving her home at Hope End, and later at Sidmouth, she was now reluctant to make the change "on account of the gloominesses of that street . . . whose walls look so much like Newgate's turned inside out." During most of the time she was to live at Wimpole Street, however, she was so confined to her room that she probably saw the street too seldom to be depressed by its unaesthetic appearance. In this building Mr. Barrett lived, with those of his children who remained with him, until his death nineteen years later. The house was destroyed in 1912, but a plaque on the present edifice commemorates the site.

Elizabeth's health, which had improved while she was at Sidmouth, was becoming worse again. In the summer of 1837 she wrote Miss Mitford that she had to spend much of her time on the sofa, and at the end of November she told her that a cough and "bilious fever" had kept her indoors for two months.[49] She was well enough, however, to dine on the evening of March 26, 1838, at Kenyon's home, where she saw the American writer George Ticknor, who recorded in his diary that he had met "a Miss Barrett, who has distinguished herself by a good poetical translation of the 'Prometheus Vinctus' of Aeschylus."[50]

By the summer of 1838 she was suffering from such poor health after the breaking of a blood vessel that her physician, William Frederick Chambers, fearing that one of her lungs might become consumptive, insisted that she live for a while in a warmer and sunnier climate. Torquay, on the southern coast of Devonshire, was suggested. Mr. Barrett did not wish his daughter to leave, and her going away was not "against his desire, but against the bias of his desire," as she later explained to Miss Mitford. "I was persuaded—he was entreated. On his side, it was at last a mere yielding to a majority."[51] About the end of August, Elizabeth, Bro, Henrietta, and George went by ship from London to Plymouth and from there by packet boat to Torquay.

5. Tragedy at Torquay

As ELIZABETH said goodbye at Wimpole Street to those of her family who were not coming along, her feelings must have been deeply stirred. She knew that her condition was so serious that she might never again see her home. "The worst—what people call the worst—was apprehended for me at that time," she later wrote. Furthermore it must have been clear to her that she would be responsible, although through no fault of her own, for keeping her family divided as long as she remained at Torquay. Her nerves were no doubt frayed from her having been the pivot of a family dispute all summer. In such poignant circumstances her chief consolation was the presence of her *alter ego,* "dearest Bro." Her experience of seeing the dawn break on a Sunday morning of her first full day at sea is the background of "A Sabbath on the Sea," which was published that fall in Thomas Kibble Hervey's annual, the *Amaranth.*[1]

Upon their arrival at Torquay the Barretts went to live in the home of Mr. and Mrs. John Hedley on the Braddons, a hill in the northern part of the town. Mrs. Hedley (Aunt Jane) was a sister of Elizabeth's mother. During the following three years almost all of the Barrett family shuttled back and forth between London and Torquay. Bro remained with Elizabeth until his death, but their brother Sam was mostly in Jamaica until he died. Of the others, Henrietta and Arabel were her most constant companions, her father stayed with her for months at a time, and her brothers paid frequent visits. At times more of the family were in Torquay than in London; for example in the winter of 1840-41, Henrietta, Arabel, Stormie, and Octavius (Occy) were all living with Elizabeth. When the time came for Bro to leave, late in the summer of 1838, Elizabeth could not keep back the tears, so that one of her aunts asked Mr. Barrett to allow Bro to remain. "Once *he* held my hand," she later told Browning, "and said that he 'loved me better than them all and that he *would not* leave me . . till I was well.' " Mr. Barrett yielded, but with poor grace, saying "that he considered it to be *very wrong*" in his daughter *"to exact such a thing."* And so for the last two years of Bro's life "there was no separation." The only specific activities of his at Torquay mentioned by Elizabeth are painting in water colors, sailing, and attending occasional parties. Although she believed he had "high talents," he was, she later said of him, "not distinguished among men, because the heart was too tender for energy." [2] Presumably he spent much of his time at the bedside of his invalid sister.

Early in the fall of 1838, after living with the Hedleys for a month or two, Elizabeth, her maid Miss Crow, Bro, and Henrietta moved to 3 Beacon Terrace, which was "considered the warmest situation" in Torquay.[3] It is in the center of the town, looks immediately upon the harbor, and is sheltered behind by the sharp rise of Beacon Hill. It seemed to Elizabeth as if her new home were "in the sea," as she wrote her life-long friend Mary Minto. "From this sofa I cannot see a yard of vulgar earth—except where the undulating hills on the opposite side of this lovely bay bound the clearness of its waters—and whenever the steam packet leaves it or enters it, my bed is shaken with the vibrations." [4] The Barretts' aunt Arabella Graham-Clarke joined them in a few weeks and stayed with Elizabeth until she left Torquay. On about the last day of September 1839 Elizabeth and her entourage moved next door to 1 Beacon Terrace, where they remained for the rest of their sojourn in Torquay. The building in which they lived for two years was originally called Bath House. It is now the Hotel Regina and looks much as it did 120 years ago, but the neighborhood around it has been greatly built up.

Because of Elizabeth's extreme seclusion she scarcely saw anyone besides her family and physicians. Her friend G. B. Hunter, who had a parish nearby at Axminster until the end of 1839, may have come to her occasionally, and his daughter Mary lived with the Barretts for a while. John Kenyon made several visits to Torquay. Elizabeth also received two or three calls from Theodosia Garrow and her half sister, a Miss Fisher, both of whom lived in the town. Miss Garrow, whom Elizabeth was to meet again many years later in Florence as the wife of Thomas Adolphus Trollope, had recently published some verses in one of Lady Blessington's annuals.

At first Elizabeth's health appeared to improve, so that she was able to go boating almost every day. But in January 1839 she suffered a sudden relapse, and for two months she "seemed to hang by a thread between life and death." [5] That attack was followed by a few months of partial recovery in the spring and summer, after which she was besieged with a serious illness for the remainder of her stay at Torquay. The symptoms were general physical weakness, spitting of blood, an apparent "spot" on the left lung (according to stethoscope examination), loss of voice, and a shattered nervous system, which manifested itself in headaches, insomnia, fainting spells, fits of weeping, and palpitations of the heart. During her first year at Torquay she was attended by Dr. Robert Fitzwilliam De Barry, for whose ability and character she soon had the greatest respect. "No one could be more kind and feeling than he was to me in my last illness," she wrote to Arabel in April 1839. "All the professionalisms were cast away from the manner." [6] She told her sister of Dr. De Barry's tedious trips to attend poor patients in districts remote from the center of Torquay, of his refusing to accept fees and even of his paying for the medicines.

To quiet her nerves, Dr. De Barry, and later Dr. Scully, prescribed a mixture of opium and brandy. She mentioned to her sister the "want of calmness in the nervous system" and her belief that "whatever is of a disturbing character to body or mind, must increase the difficulty a little." [7] Thus she came to have a longing for peace and a morbid dread of excitement and change. Early in 1839 she wrote Miss Mitford, "I can't understand the craving for excitement. Mine is for *repose*." [8] And when Dr. De Barry told her in April that she was well enough to leave her sick room, she was fearful of breaking away from her confinement to join in the family life below. "The fact is . . . ," she wrote Arabel, "I did most emphatically abominate and nauseate the going down stairs yesterday. The change from a four-month-long imprisonment to this room, where from habitude I had grown to like the air and the silence, was quite sure to be felt unpleasantly, and pretending to covet the change except at a distance was out of the question." [9]

Dr. De Barry insisted that Elizabeth remain idle and write no letters or poetry. She said that he "groans in the spirit whenever he sees within my reach any book larger and graver looking than 'the last new octavo neatly bound.' " [10] Yet she eluded his vigilance and continued to compose verses and read Greek. By the time she left Torquay, she had "gone through every line of the three tragedians," [11] she had read three or four plays of Aristophanes and selections from three of Aristotle's works: the *Poetics*, the *Nicomachean Ethics*, and the *Rhetoric;* and she had made a careful study of almost all of Plato. Shortly before going to Torquay, she acquired the eleven quarto volumes of Plato edited by Immanuel Bekker.[12] Within three years she "began with the first volume and went through the whole of his writings . . . one after another," so that she had mastered "not only all that is properly attributed to Plato, but even those dialogues and epistles which pass falsely under his name." The reading of the Plato alone was an extraordinary achievement in view of her desperate ill health. The dates in her marginalia show that she had finished the *Parmenides* in the second volume by New Year's Day of 1839, and two sections of the *Laws,* which were in the seventh volume, by February 15, 1840. Her pencil was busiest when she was studying the *Parmenides,* which she found the hardest to understand of all the dialogues. On almost every page she made a comment or ventured a translation. She also underscored many passages and jotted down short critical remarks in the margins of the *Symposium*, the *Republic,* and the *Laws*. Early in 1840 she was also reading the two volumes her father had given her of Shelley's work entitled *Essays, Letters from Abroad, Translations and Fragments,* newly published by Moxon.[13] Her marginalia show that she examined closely several of his translations from Plato and indicated many passages where she thought he had failed to reproduce the sense of the original.

Her reading of Greek did not absorb all her energy, for she continued to compose verses. In 1839 and 1840 she contributed three poems on recent events to the *Athenaeum*. The background of "L. E. L.'s Last Question" was the sudden and mysterious death in Africa of Letitia Elizabeth Landon, who is supposed to have asked as she sailed toward the Cape Coast with her dour bridegroom: "Do you think of me, my friends, as I think of you?"—the refrain of Elizabeth's poem. "The Crowned and Wedded Queen" celebrates the marriage of Queen Victoria and Prince Albert, and "Napoleon's Return" was occasioned by the deposition of the Emperor's ashes in the *Invalides*.

Elizabeth was persuaded by Miss Mitford to write once again for her annual, which was now entitled *Findens' Tableaux: the Iris of Prose, Poetry, and Art for 1840;* so in the summer of 1839 she wrote "The Dream," which served as an introduction to the album, and "The Legend of the Brown Rosarie." As in previous years, Miss Mitford forwarded an engraving to which Elizabeth had to fit her verses. The illustration was as fatuous as the earlier ones for which Elizabeth had supplied poems. In the margins around the central picture of two women and a little boy in a chapel are faint representations of a "brown rosarie," an "old convent ruin," a nun, angels, an "evil spirit," the "bridegroom" and "Leonora" both on horseback, and "the priest at the altar" with his "grave young sacristans." Elizabeth responded to the challenge and devised a wildly improbable ballad of about four hundred lines in which she made use of all the properties and figures. She explained to Arabel, "When you once begin a story you can't bring it to an end all in a moment—and what with nuns and devils and angels and marriages and death and little boys, I couldn't get out of the mud without a great deal of splashing." [14]

Through the help of her friend Richard Hengist Horne, Elizabeth had two poems accepted in 1840 by the *Monthly Chronicle*. "The Lay of the Rose" is a banal representation of the complaint of a rose which blossomed too early and died unknown and of a poet born out of his time. Yet though both are unappreciated, each is "Blessèd still and consecrated." Her other work in the *Monthly Chronicle,* which appeared in the April issue, was "A Night-Watch by the Sea." In its subject matter and imagery it has a remarkable prescience of the deaths which were about to strike at Elizabeth's heart. As she lay awake "every midnight long" and heard the roar of the surf and the "stormy winds" below her window, she must have thought of the many others who were keeping watch: "the fisher's widow'd spouse," "The nurse that came for hire," "the sick man" upon whom "death is winning," "the corpse" which "lies all alone" and never "Sigh or motion can be giving." The diction is trite, but the poem is a more authentic expression of Elizabeth's mood at Torquay than any other she composed while she was living there. It is significant that she never republished the poem in any of her later volumes; the associations of Torquay were to become too painful.

Dr. De Barry died suddenly on October 2, 1839, after a brief illness.[15] He had been a young man of energy and promise, and he left behind him a wife, a daughter, and an unborn child. The tragic event so affected Elizabeth that she became seriously ill for three weeks. Mr. Barrett arrived from London late in October to comfort her and possibly to consult with Dr. Scully, the senior physician of Torquay, who took over the case and remained her physician until she left for London. When she first went to Torquay, she had "felt grief in the air," [16] and now she longed to escape from the place, especially from the chill of its east wind which kept her in bed all winter without any prospect of release until the following spring. It was early in April,[17] just as she was hoping to assume a more active life, that she received news of the unexpected death on February 17, 1840, of her brother Sam in Jamaica. Elizabeth, "being weak . . . was struck down as by a *bodily* blow, in a moment, without having time for tears."

In the middle of May, when she was still in bed, she wrote Miss Mitford in a letter, the handwriting of which is so faint and irregular that it is clear she scarcely had sufficient strength to hold her pen: "I have been very ill with fever—passing from delirium at nights to such extreme exhaustion by day that I never thought to write to you any more. It would have been very melancholy for poor Papa if he had lost two children by one stroke—would it not?" [18] She also said that her father had given her great comfort by his presence for a whole month. At the same time she wrote George of her longing to get back to London and of her strong religious convictions: "What is done is done—and we, knowing that God did it, know in that knowledge the extremity of love and mercy involved in the doing." [19]

Tragedy at Torquay

Sam had died at the age of twenty-eight. Although he was only six years younger than Elizabeth, he had never entered closely into her life, probably because she had given so much of her affection to Bro. Even so, his death had brought her to the verge of a nervous collapse.

ON JULY 8, however, she reported to Boyd that she was "a very great deal better." She was soon to have desperate need of all her strength, for within three days occurred the great tragedy of her life which immediately plunged her into a far more serious illness than any she had hitherto suffered. On Saturday, July 11, 1840, Bro, after parting from his sister "with a pettish word," the recollection of which was to haunt her as long as she lived, went out in a sailboat named *La Belle Sauvage* with two of his friends, Vanneck and (Captain) Clarke, and the boatman William White. A squall arose which caused the boat to capsize in Babbacombe Bay, two or three miles from Teignmouth; according to another account it foundered in the harbor of Torquay within sight of those on shore.[20] The "other boats came back one by one," but not *La Belle Sauvage*. For an "awful agony of three days" Elizabeth and her sisters kept watch. Each day the sun was shining, there was no wind, and the sea was calm. Her sisters "drew the curtains back" that she might observe "how smooth the sea was, and how it could hurt nobody." All the while she thought to herself, "You have done this." Finally their "last hope went." The four men had been drowned, and the bodies of all but Vanneck were washed ashore within the next few weeks. Bro's remains were buried on August 6 in Tor Churchyard, Torquay.

For more than three months Elizabeth suffered from occasional spells of delirium. It was impossible for her to "hold on to one thought for more than a moment," and she could not understand what was being said to her. Visions of "long dark spectral trains" and of "staring infantine faces" seemed to break up her mind into fragments and drove her almost to "madness, absolute hopeless madness."[21] She could not pray; she was "too near to God under the crushing of His hand."[22] Nor could she weep, for "the tears ran scalding hot"[23] into her brain.

When she partially recovered from the shock, she sensed a deep longing to "lie down to sleep among the snows of a weary journey" [24] but was prevented only by "an unnatural tenacity to life." [25] Except for her family and closest friends, she could but "shrink away from the very thought of seeing a human face" so that she did not receive even an old neighbor, a Mrs. Hanford, who had come from Herefordshire to see her. The peculiar quality of her bitterness and anguish stemmed from her belief that she had bestowed "evil, unmitigated evil," [26] that "the crown" of the family had fallen because of her entreaty that Bro stay with her at Torquay. In the first letter she wrote to Boyd after the event, she expressed her strong sense of guilt: "Only I know and recognize God's chastening in it, and my own transgression—my God and my sin . . eminent in the sweeping agony as causes and interpretations." [27] She supposed she had but a short while to live: "Presently, and perhaps very soon, all will be calm and smooth in Christ Jesus. Oh dear friend! what an 'anarithmon gelasma' *that* will be, in the eternal world!"

Elizabeth now felt herself unprotected and bereft of sympathy. All her life she had received only "the tenderest affection" from Bro. "There was no harsh word, no unkind look—never from my babyhood till I stood alone. A leaf never shook till the tree fell. The shade was over me softly till it fell." [28] Part of the anguish may have come from her having subconsciously transferred the symbols; possibly she was the "tree" which had kept Bro in its shade and had drawn too much nutriment from the soil for the other to mature. However much she loved her father, her sisters, and her brothers, she acutely missed the companionship and understanding she had received only from her *"best beloved."* A year after the tragedy she wrote to Miss Mitford, "The nearest sympathy, the natural love which was friendship too, is not close to me now." [29] From her own family she could not hope for consolation, and in her despair she looked "up to that Heaven whence only comes any measure of true comfort and adequate endurance." [30] Bro had been her "first and chiefest affection," whom she had loved "best in the world beyond comparison and rivalship . . far better" than even her father, "as he knew." [31] Mr. Barrett, who was always "so kind, so tender," [32] remained with her throughout her desperate illness, the nearest one to her "on the closed grave

Tragedy at Torquay 81

. . or by the unclosing sea." Not once, at this time or later, did he blame her for what had happened; "he was generous and forbearing in that hour of bitter trial." [33]

Yet notwithstanding his kindness and patience and the solicitude of her brothers and sisters, none of her family could come intimately into her life. Her father, although "full of all sorts of general information" and possessed of "strong and clear natural faculties," was "not poetical, or literary even in the strict sense." [34] None of her sisters and brothers ever had any literary or artistic interests. While neither Henrietta nor Arabel fully understood their eldest sister, both of them were bound to her by ties of affection and loyalty which were dissolved only by death. Except for George, the brothers were mostly indifferent to her in later years. None of them ever went to Italy to see her (though neither did Henrietta or Arabel), and, again with the exception of George, they made little effort to be with her when she returned with Browning on their periodic visits to England.

Soon after she went back to Wimpole Street, Elizabeth wrote to Miss Mitford, "The scars of that anguish I shall take down with me to the grave." [35] For the rest of her life "the thought of *one face*" [36] remained with her every waking moment. Such was her morbid sensitivity that she could never utter Bro's name, not even to her husband. She struck from her vocabulary the word "Torquay" and always substituted the less specific "Devonshire." It was all but impossible ever again to attend chapel services, because whenever she heard the familiar hymns she had sung with Bro, she was immediately overcome with weeping and faintness. Once at Bagni di Lucca, when a friend she had not seen for ten years mentioned Bro's name "in all kindness," she was "literally nearly struck down to the ground," and as the "blue sky reeled" over her, she "caught at something, not to fall." [37] Never again did she return to Herefordshire to see her friends; the thought of looking at the places around Hope End where she had been so happy with Bro made her recoil in terror. "As if any human being could know thoroughly what *he* was to me," she wrote in 1855 in explaining why she could not visit the Martins at Old Colwall.

By November she could again concentrate on her literary activities, and she had regained the will to live. It now seemed to her that her recent illness was the principal dividing line of her life. As she expressed it to Miss Mitford a year or two later, her thoughts of the future were never of joys but only of pains to be suffered and of duties to be performed: "My castle-building is at an end! A great change has passed both upon my inward and outward life within these two years. I scarcely recognize myself sometimes. One stroke ended my youth." [38] She also told Mrs. Martin of her despondency: "My faculties seem to hang heavily now, like flappers when the spring is broken. *My* spring *is* broken, and a separate exertion is necessary for the lifting up of each—and then it falls down again." It was probably during her last winter at Torquay that she composed the verses entitled "De Profundis," which because of their personal associations remained unpublished until the last few months of her life, when she sent them "by an impulse" to the New York *Independent*. The poem "represents a condition from which the writer had already partly emerged, after the greatest suffering," Elizabeth said of her work, and it "exaggerates nothing." [39] The first stanzas are a cry of anguish in which the bereaved sister recalls what her brother had meant to her:

> The face which, duly as the sun,
> Rose up for me with life begun,
> To mark all bright hours of the day
> With hourly love, is dimmed away,—
> And yet my days go on, go on.
>
> The tongue which, like a stream, could run
> Smooth music from the roughest stone,
> And every morning with "Good day"
> Make each day good, is hushed away,—
> And yet my days go on, go on.
>
> The heart which, like a staff, was one
> For mine to lean and rest upon,
> The strongest on the longest day
> With steadfast love, is caught away,—
> And yet my days go on, go on.

Elizabeth's first literary project in the fall of 1840 was her version of "Queen Annelida and False Arcite" for *The Poems of Geoffrey*

Chaucer, Modernized, which was edited by Richard Hengist Horne. She had become acquainted with Horne a year before through Mrs. Orme, who had been her governess for a time at Hope End.[40] Mrs. Orme was now living in London and knew Horne well enough to ask his opinion about some verses written by Elizabeth. He liked her poems, and the two of them began a correspondence which was voluminous until her marriage and infrequent afterward. The man whom Elizabeth considered "one of the very first poets of the day" was a restless, adventurous person; after many escapades in America during the twenties he had entered upon a career of journalism and letters in London in the thirties and forties. In 1852 he was to leave England after "twenty years of public indifference" [41] to become a businessman and a government official in Australia. His three dramas in verse, *Cosmo de' Medici, The Death of Marlowe,* and *Gregory VII,* written between 1837 and 1840, were all very much admired by Elizabeth.

He had suggested to all who were contributing to his volume of Chaucer that they retain as much as possible of the original language and versification. The versions by Wordsworth, Elizabeth Barrett, and Horne himself adhered faithfully to the editor's principle, but those by Leigh Hunt and Robert Bell departed so far from the text that they became almost original poems. Compare the opening lines of Elizabeth's rendition with those of Leigh Hunt's "The Friar's Tale." Elizabeth makes almost no change:

> O thou fierce God of armies, Mars the red,
> Who in thy frosty country callèd Thrace,
> Within thy grisly temples full of dread,
> Art honoured as the patron of that place,
> With the Bellona Pallas, full of grace!

Hunt, on the other hand, eliminates most of the pungent vocabulary of the original and substitutes a more generalized diction so that Chaucer comes alive neither in the spirit nor in the body:

> There liv'd, Sirs, in my country, formerly,
> A wondrous great Archdeacon,—who but he?
> Who boldly did the work of his high station

In punishing improper conversation,
And all the slidings thereunto belonging; . . .

The review in the *Athenaeum* [42] damned the volume as an ill-advised effort to dilute Chaucer's poems "down to the level of cockney comprehensions." It thought that the essential qualities of Chaucer could not be preserved in modern language, which is "vague, characterless, inappropriate," and it said that if the book inspired but one reader to turn to Chaucer himself, he would "despise the copy, in proportion as he prizes the original." Among the best done of the contributions, in the opinion of the reviewer, were those by Wordsworth and Elizabeth Barrett.

In the spring of 1840 Horne had suggested to Elizabeth that the two of them collaborate in the writing of a drama. Before she could consider the project, Bro's death and her own illness intervened. The following winter he brought the matter up again, proposing that they begin at once and that she name the subject. Her "thoughts grew fantastical," and she envisaged a hero who was "neither a Manfred nor a Faust . . . but pretty nearly as mad to vulgar eyes." [43] As she later told Browning, her plan was "of a man, haunted by his own soul, . . (making her a separate personal Psyche, a dreadful, beautiful Psyche)—the man being haunted and terrified through all the turns of life by her." She thought it a "fit subject enough for a wild lyrical drama," while in Horne's opinion it was "a difficult subject but still feasible." They agreed that she would write the plan of the drama and choruses, and he would divide the material into scenes and supply the dialogue. During her last spring and summer at Torquay she prepared several tentative outlines, which he commented upon and revised.

In the opening scene of the projected work, which is called "Psyche Apocalypté," Medon (Cymon in earlier drafts) the hero is speculating upon his own identity as he converses with a child at the foot of an old tomb "in an unknown island of the Greek Archipelago." In the second act the marriage ceremony between Medon and Evanthe (Oenone in several versions) is interrupted "by the wail of Psyche." The guests depart in confusion, and the bride is "paralysed" by what she has heard. By the beginning of the third act she is dead; Medon has found the corpse "half covered with the drifted snow." He realizes that Evanthe "has been the victim of his condition with relation to Psyche." At the end of the drama the hero has a vision of Christ on the cross, is reconciled with his own soul, and promises to pass the rest of his life in a hermitage beside the tomb of Evanthe.[44] Fortunately for Elizabeth's reputation, the work remained in embryo, but its composition had for her a therapeutic value by diverting her mind outward to fresh activity. Within a month after her return to Wimpole Street, Horne urged her to resume the Psyche drama, but by then she had lost interest.

Before she left Torquay, she had written several short poems, at least one of which became widely known in England and in America. "The Cry of the Human," first published in 1842 in the *Boston Miscellany of Literature and Fashion,* is a humanitarian poem written against the background of the "hungry forties," Disraeli's "two nations," the Chartist disturbances, and the agitation for repeal of the corn laws.

> The curse of gold upon the land,
>   The lack of bread enforces—
> The rail-cars snort from strand to strand,
>   Like more of Death's White horses!
> The rich preach "rights" and future days,
>   And hear no angel scoffing:
> The poor die mute—with starving gaze
>   On corn-ships in the offing.
>   Be pitiful, O God! [45]

During all of the spring and the summer of 1841 Elizabeth longed to get away from Torquay, with its terrible associations which lay upon her "like the oppression of a perpetual nightmare." The sound of the dashing waves was fearful to her, and the cold east wind kept her in bed and made her feel as though she were "bound in chains heavier than iron." In May she wrote to Boyd, "You *cannot* know how the only strong earthly wish I have left, relative to myself, is set towards being once more *at home.*"[46] She had been told earlier by "kind, *honest* Dr. Scully" that she might be fit for the journey in June. In the summer, however, her physician seems to have changed his mind, for he thought the trip to London was "an undertaking full of hazard" and that "he was justified by his medical responsibility" in laying before her "all possible consequences." One final agony she had to endure before she was on her way. She was prepared to assume the risk of the journey, but her father's hesitation in deciding on the date and means of her departure tortured her with suspense.

Furthermore she was in despair when she learned that Mr. Barrett was considering the purchase of a house in Black Mountain, an isolated, rural community in the hills of southwestern Shropshire—or possibly he had in mind a place in the Black Mountains on the Welsh border—from which her brothers would have to be mostly away unless they were to "quench the energies of their lives in hunting and fishing." [47] For her, it would be "the knell" of her "perpetual exile." She was equally horrified to find out a few weeks later that he was seriously considering the possibility of moving his family to Michael Church, a small town in Herefordshire. "My wonder is great that he should think of Herefordshire—thickly sown as it is with pain for all of us," she wrote her brother George; "I would rather live in a wilderness than there." [48] She was exhausted by the rise and fall of her hopes and had "little heart or strength left to struggle out towards the light." [49] Soon afterward when Mr. Barrett apparently decided that Elizabeth should stay indefinitely at Torquay, she pleaded with George not to acquiesce tamely in their father's plan but to speak up to him and explain that she could not face the prospect "of remaining another year in this miserable place." [50] Then Mr. Barrett thought of Clifton, a suburb of Bristol. Elizabeth feared that she might be forced to live *there:* "My mind turns round and round in wondering about Papa's fancy for Clifton, that hot, white, dusty, vapory place," [51] she wrote to George in June. Once when she felt she could stand the strain no longer, her father sent her a brief note telling her nothing specific and saying that he was too annoyed to continue the letter because his crops in the West Indies had been poor.[52]

She learned in August that a carriage suspended on "a thousand springs" and with a bed in it was soon to arrive to take her by slow stages to Wimpole Street. On about the first of September 1841 she began the journey to London at the risk of her life in order that "poor Papa's domestic peace" might no longer be jeopardized by a divided household. With her were her maid Crow, Arabel, and an important addition to the family: Flush, a little spaniel Miss Mitford had sent to Elizabeth for company. They traveled slowly, with Elizabeth's "bed being drawn out of the carriage like a drawer out of a table, and deposited (with a shawl over her face) in a bedroom at the different inns," [53] and arrived at their home on Saturday, September 11. The first letter Elizabeth wrote after her return was to Miss Mitford, to whom she confessed that she was "tired of course, with a sense of being thoroughly *beaten*." [54] She looked forward to the quiet life of a recluse, isolated from emotional shock, with "no more partings—nor meetings which were worse." [55]

6. Return to Wimpole Street

FOR FIVE YEARS Elizabeth stayed mostly in her room, up three flights of stairs, at 50 Wimpole Street. The atmosphere of the room was dead, for it was sealed tightly to prevent the entrance of drafts from within the house and fresh air from without. She had "Chaucer's and Homer's busts in guard over these two departments of English and Greek poetry." Later "in right hero worship" she hung on the walls the portraits of Wordsworth, Carlyle, Tennyson, Browning, and Harriet Martineau—"because she was a woman and admirable" and had written several letters to Elizabeth. These five engravings had been given her by R. H. Horne after he had used them in his *A New Spirit of the Age*. To provide herself "with a vain deceit of rural life" and to shut out the sight of chimney pots and grimy brick walls, she had an ivy planted in a box of soil at the foot of her window. All day long she would lie on the sofa in her dark, silent room and look at the vine spread over her windowpane. When she heard the wind rustle the leaves upon the glass, her thoughts were "of forests and groves." Until her emancipation some three years later, her life was confined to "books and thoughts and dreams."

She was no longer so desperately ill as she had been at Torquay. Three years earlier a blood vessel had broken in her lungs, and she had "never quite got over it." As she wrote Boyd, she did not have "tuburcular consumption . . . but an affection of the lungs which leans towards it." At first she could not be carried from her bed to the sofa without fainting; then she was able to walk a few steps with no assistance, although she was "so weak as to stagger like a drunken man"; [1] and during the last year before her marriage she was strong enough to go for short walks away from the house and to take occasional drives. Her nervous system, which had never been strong, was so shattered by the tragedies at Torquay that she was subject to attacks of hysteria during which she became convulsed and lost the power of swallowing. Her physicians made her take a preparation of opium in the form of morphine "to give the right composure and point of balance to the nervous system." She called the drug "my amreeta draught, my elixir,—because the tranquillizing power has been wonderful" and said that sleep did not come readily "except in a red hood of poppies." During the period before her marriage her dependence on opium, it appears, was steadily increasing, for she wrote in the summer of 1846 that her "greatest personal expense lately has been *the morphine.*" Later in Italy, she was to need it less but was never able to dispense with it. In prescribing thus, her physicians no doubt believed that it was a necessary sedative, but her use of morphine may well have increased the severity of the spells of anxiety and depression from which she suffered throughout her life.

Such was her "morbidity"—the word she often used for her moods—that when the moment came for her to see anyone she did not know well, she would "shrink and grow pale in the spirit." Her life was almost as cloistered as the strictest nun's; she wrote B. R. Haydon that she "might as well be in a wilderness—or a hermitage—or a convent—or a prison—as in this dark room," [2] which became for her a symbol of security. She especially liked "the silence" of the room and thought it would be "an effort and a grief to leave it." [3] It seemed to her that her "life was ended" —the phrase occurs many times in the letters she later wrote to Browning—and that she had nothing to live for except her writing. "In other respects, the game is up," she said to Haydon. "If it were not for this poetry which I feel within as a destiny to be worked out, I think I should wish to die to-morrow." [4]

The prospect of any change in the routine of her life—a friend coming to see her or a member of the household going away—so upset her that she was afflicted with headaches and insomnia for days before and after the event. It was "a hard, terrible struggle" to stay calm when she learned that Stormie and George were going away in September 1843 for their holiday trip along the Rhine. The departure a year later of Stormie and Henry for a voyage to Alexandria on their father's ship the *Statira* made her bitter and gave her "many a fearful thought and heavy hour" so that she believed the advantage to her brothers was "disproportionate to the long anxiety of those left at home." [5] When her maid Crow left in May 1844, her going away was "full of pain" to Elizabeth, who was depressed and suffered from headaches for days afterward. During the summer of 1842 Wordsworth asked twice if he might see Elizabeth Barrett, and each time he was politely refused by Kenyon, who knew that his protégée's extreme shyness would make a visit painful to her. In March of 1842 Robert Browning read Elizabeth's articles in the *Athenaeum* on the Greek Christian poets and asked through Kenyon if he might be admitted to her room; but she, while pleased at his interest, declined without a moment's hesitation.[6] Miss Mitford urged her several times to allow her friend H. F. Chorley to call on her. Even though he had often praised her poetry in his reviews in the *Athenaeum*, she bluntly told Miss Mitford that she could not admit him any more than the many others who wished to see her. And Elizabeth wrote to Horne after he had collaborated closely with her on several literary projects: "I sometimes doubt to myself . . . whether if I should ever be face to face with you, the shame and the shyness would not annihilate the pleasure of it to me!" The only four people outside of her family whom she admitted to her room at this time, Kenyon, Miss Mitford, G. B. Hunter, and a Nelly Bordman, all had formed their friendships with her before she went to Torquay. Miss Bordman was an orphan who was now the ward and was later to be the wife of one of Elizabeth's physicians, a Mr. Jago of Hammersmith.

After Elizabeth's return home, her father always spoke to her "kindly and gently," and he talked about her "affectionately and with too much praise." Every evening he came to her room and prayed with her, "not out of a book, but simply and warmly at once," [7] as he held one of her hands in his. She had as much joy as she believed she could ever have again when she heard his approaching footsteps on the stairs. Since she thought that he loved her and did not blame her for the loss of Bro, she returned his apparent affection and "loved him better than the rest of his children." She had "heard the fountain within the rock," and her heart had "struggled in towards him through the stones of the rock." It was her father's essential integrity and the fortitude with which he had faced up to the loss of his fortune which made Elizabeth respect him and love him.

To be sure, he remained as peremptory and obstinate as he had been at Hope End. For example, one evening Elizabeth said that they might hear from George on the following day. Her father replied that nothing could be more unlikely, that if he wrote at all, he would not write then. She received a letter from George the next morning.[8] What is the explanation of "that strange, stern nature," the rule "by divine right," the "incredible system" which isolated Mr. Barrett from his family and made a "cold dead silence all round"? Why did he forbid his children to fall in love and get married? He had, in Elizabeth's words, "an obliquity—an eccentricity, or something beyond—on one class of subjects"; Kenyon called it a "monomania." Bro had been in love shortly before his death; and since he lacked the means to marry, Elizabeth wished to transfer to him part of her fortune, but her "hands were seized and tied." Henrietta also had "offended" and had been "made to suffer." She had been "carried out of the room in strong hysterics" after her knees had been "made to ring upon the floor"; and Elizabeth, horror-stricken by the scene, had fallen down unconscious so that Arabel, who was with her, thought she was dead. Mr. Barrett believed Elizabeth to be "the purest woman he ever knew" because she "had not troubled him with the iniquity of love affairs, or any impropriety of seeming to think about being married."

The reason why his children yielded to such tyranny is clear enough: they were "constrained *bodily* into submission . . apparent submission at least . . by that worst and most dishonouring of necessities, the necessity of *living*"; for all of them except Elizabeth were "dependent in money-matters on the inflexible will." As for Mr. Barrett's make-up, no simple explanation is satisfactory. Elizabeth at first thought that her father had a "deep tender affection" behind his arbitrary nature, but she later changed her mind and realized that he had no conception of love: *"that,* he does not understand, any more than he understands Chaldee, respecting it less of course." She saw that after he used his own children as slaves for a while, "the children drop lower and lower toward the level of the chattels, and the duties of human sympathy to them become difficult in proportion."

His despotic ways and insensitiveness to the feelings of others may have had their origin in his boyhood home, Cinnamon Hill, Jamaica, where he must always have been conscious of the absolute control held by a few white men over the lives and persons of another race. At that time he no doubt had often thought of the power which would be his, as he supposed, when he should inherit from his grandfather the Northside plantations. The prosperous, secure years during his early tenure at Hope End were followed by serious financial reverses which necessitated his living in much more humble circumstances and following a way of life distasteful to him after his earlier freedom. He had enjoyed the active pursuits of a landed proprietor. Now he had to live in a much smaller house in one of the most urban parts of London, and every day he went to the City to attend to his business interests. The loss of financial power and social position hurt his pride and seems to have soured his disposition, so that he became excessively strict with his children and pretended to infallibility in all matters.

"Then the principle of passive filial obedience," Elizabeth wrote, "is held—drawn (and quartered) from Scripture. He *sees* the law and the gospel on his side." Mr. Barrett was a Nonconformist, and the language of several of his letters which have been preserved suggests that he was narrow and fanatical in his religious views. For example, once when he was away from home, he included in a letter to Elizabeth about his activities an irrelevant tirade against the Roman Catholic church: "Popery . . . must succumb to Christianity the revealed and the only pure religion; the Pope of the Vatican . . . must fly and be no more heard of." [9] His outrageously possessive attitude toward his children may have been due partly to an exaggerated notion of the responsibility that was his for the family of which he had been so long the sole parent. A second reason may have been that he wished to make good for his own sons and daughters, and with interest, the loss from which he had always suffered in never having known a father, the philanderer Charles Moulton, as I have said, having disappeared from the Barrett family when Edward was an infant. Yet paradoxically Mr. Barrett took no interest in Elizabeth's literary acquaintances and friends. C. W. Dilke left his card at 50 Wimpole Street, but Mr. Barrett did not return the visit. He did not ask his "cousin" Kenyon, or Horne, to dine, for fear, as Elizabeth said to palliate her father's selfishness, that the Barretts' dinner table and drawing room might seem dull to "pen and ink folk." Also he never called on Browning, when the poet later became one of Elizabeth's regular visitors, or spoke to him at Wimpole Street to thank him for the attention Browning was paying his invalid daughter.

Although at this time neither of the sisters impinged upon Elizabeth's inner life as intimately as her father, both of them were always loyal and affectionate to her. Between Henrietta and William Surtees Cook, her second cousin,[10] an attachment was slowly forming which was to lead to marriage in 1850. Arabel, who was destined to remain unmarried and to minister unselfishly to her father's comforts until his death, was becoming ever more devoted to the Chapel and to "good works." Of the brothers, Charles John, now the eldest, had returned from Jamaica immediately after Bro's death, and until his trip back to the West Indies in 1846 he stayed at home, evidently accomplishing little and always feeling out of place because of his impediment of speech. George, whom Elizabeth described as "good and true, honest and kind, but a little over-grave and reasonable," was away part of the time as a barrister, on his various circuits. Elizabeth thought of him as the most stable and reliable of her brothers, often depended upon his judgment, and occasionally asked him to use his influence with Mr. Barrett in her behalf. It was with George alone among the brothers that Elizabeth maintained a regular correspondence during the last ten years of her life. Alfred had a position as a clerk, and the two youngest brothers were students. Septimus was reading philosophy, history, and literature at the University of London and hoped to become a special pleader,[11] and Octavius was studying architecture. Henry was presumably at home, but he appears seldom in Elizabeth's letters. Mr. Barrett was away from noon until about seven o'clock almost every day (fortunately for Elizabeth when Browning became a regular visitor).

BUT books and the literary gossip she heard from Kenyon, Miss Mitford, and later Browning were much more real to her, one suspects, than the hum of family life in the rooms below. What was she reading during the five or six years before her marriage? She remained the indefatigable reader she had always been, but the reputation she received for being among the most learned of English poets was not fully deserved, as she herself was the first to admit. Now that she was very much less under Boyd's influence, the pattern of her reading had undergone a great change. She rarely went back to her Greek and Latin texts, except for the two or three months when she was preparing her articles on the Greek Christian poets and retranslating the *Prometheus Bound.* Instead, she read much that was merely ephemeral: newspapers, periodicals, travel books, memoirs, and romances, none of which could be considered serious literature. Every week she went through the columns of the *Athenaeum,* which was sent to her without charge, partly in return for her many contributions. C. W. Dilke, its editor, and H. F. Chorley, who wrote many of the reviews, were both much interested in Elizabeth's literary career. Dilke accepted everything she sent him, and Chorley never missed an opportunity to praise her. Although the *Athenaeum* was primarily devoted to reviews of recent books, it also had critical notices of plays, concerts, and operas; reports of the meetings of scientific organizations; and bulletins from foreign countries on travel conditions, local customs, and current artistic and scientific activities. Elizabeth considered that in spite of its niggardly appreciation of contemporary poetry, it was in many respects "liberal and large-hearted." From time to time she also looked at *Tait's Edinburgh Magazine, Blackwood's,* the *Examiner,* and the *New Monthly.*

She read, or at least became slightly acquainted with, almost all the fiction and poetry published in England from about the middle of the thirties to the middle of the forties. Among the minor novelists with whom she was familiar were Frances Trollope, Catherine Gore, Mrs. S. C. Hall, H. F. Chorley, Captain Marryat, and G. P. R. James. She went through all of Chorley's novels and liked especially his *Pomfret,* which seemed to her "a good true and natural book." [12] Furthermore she seems to have read all the novels, as they appeared, of Dickens—whom alone of the English novelists she called "a true genius"—of Thackeray, of Disraeli, and of Bulwer-Lytton. The historical romance *Ernest Maltravers* and its sequel *Alice* delighted her more than any other of Bulwer-Lytton's novels, and she often praised them to Miss Mitford. She knew many of the writings of poetasters now mostly forgotten, such as Mary Howitt, Letitia Elizabeth Landon, Caroline Norton, Philip James Bailey, George Darley, John Edmund Reade, John A. Heraud, Henry Taylor, Robert Montgomery, and Thomas Noon Talfourd. With sympathetic interest she followed the poetical careers of Horne, Milnes, Barry Cornwall, Patmore, and Macaulay. Of the poets of her own generation she reserved the highest praises for Tennyson and Browning, each of whom was, in her characteristic phrase, "a true genius." Ever since her brother George gave her in 1836 a copy of Tennyson's volume of 1830, she had felt that a new star was rising. Her comment in a letter to Thomas Westwood after she had read Tennyson's *Poems* of 1842 is typical of her emotionalism: "I am very fond of Tennyson. He makes me thrill sometimes to the end of my fingers, as only a true great poet can."

Elizabeth had been "a great hero worshipper" of Robert Browning from the time Kenyon gave her a copy of *Paracelsus* a few months after its publication. She immediately admired the poem because of its "height and depth of thought," believed she saw in it "sudden repressed gushings of tenderness," [13] and asked Miss Mitford to read it and agree with her that the author was "a poet in the holy sense." [14] Miss Mitford did not share Elizabeth's enthusiasm and somewhat later irritated her with the remark that it was a pity Browning missed being an engineer or a merchant's clerk. For ten years Elizabeth was to defend her hero against Miss Mitford's charges of obscurity and dreaminess. Elizabeth was annoyed also at the *Athenaeum* because its reviews of Browning's poems were patronizing and ungenerous. Even more than *Paracelsus* she admired *Pippa Passes,* which, she later said to its author, "I could find in my heart to covet the authorship of, more than any of your works." But in all his writings, from *Paracelsus* to the dramas and lyrics of the *Bells and Pomegranates,* she found, as she said in the autumn of 1842, long before she met Browning, "the palpable presence of poetic genius everywhere." [15]

In writing to Chorley in 1845, Elizabeth remarked that two years earlier she "passed through a long dynasty of French memoirs." Of the four principal authors she read, the earliest from the point of view of history was the Duchess of Montpensier, sometimes called *La Grande Mademoiselle,* whose period was that of Louis XIV, her cousin. The memoirs of Louis de Rouvroy, Duke of Saint-Simon, deal with the latter part of the reign of Louis XIV and the regency following his death. The Countess de Genlis spanned the eighteenth and nineteenth centuries, and the Duchess d'Abrantès wrote on French society in the Bonaparte era. Elizabeth must have spent countless hours learning about the French aristocracy of the previous two centuries, for the Paris edition of 1840, if that was the one she used, of Saint-Simon's *Mémoires* was issued in forty tomes, and the other three writers also presented full and detailed pictures of their eras. She read with great eagerness the sensational memoirs of the notorious Madame Marie Pouch Lafarge, who had been arrested, tried in 1840, and found guilty of poisoning her husband with arsenic. For biography and published correspondence Elizabeth always had an insatiable appetite. Besides the memoirs of French writers, she also went through Southey's life of William Cowper (which she confessed to Miss Mitford drew tears from her), Anton Schindler's *The Life of Beethoven,* the autobiography of the German clairvoyant Johann Heinrich Jung-Stilling, Laman Blanchard's *Life and Literary Remains of L. E. L., The Life and Correspondence* of Matthew G. Lewis, William Hayley's *Memoirs,* Fanny Burney's *Diary and Letters,* and the correspondence of Samuel Richardson and of Anna Seward. She was especially attracted to Chorley's *Memorials of Mrs. Hemans*—"Shall I tell you how often I have read those volumes?" she once wrote their author.

No less than memoirs and reminiscences, she enjoyed books of travel. Although in the past she had always dreaded the prospect of being uprooted, she was now developing the romantic and nomadic disposition which was to be characteristic of her mature years and was hoping to travel whenever her health and domestic circumstances might permit. For the moment, however, she made herself content with merely reading about Continental life in Chorley's *Music and Manners in France and Germany,* William

Howitt's *German Experiences,* Talfourd's *Recollections of a First Visit to the Alps* and his *Vacation Rambles and Thoughts,* George Borrow's *The Bible in Spain,* and the writings of two American women: Catharine M. Sedgwick's *Letters Abroad to Kindred at Home* and Lydia Sigourney's *Pleasant Memories of Pleasant Lands.* Of books on the new world she read Mrs. Trollope's *Domestic Manners of the Americans,* Harriet Martineau's *Society in America,* Mrs. Jameson's *Winter Studies and Summer Rambles in Canada,* and Dickens' *American Notes.* She also acquainted herself with Alexander Kinglake's record of his wanderings in the Near East, *Eōthen,* and thought it "a work of genius."

But more than either memoirs or books of travel, Elizabeth's chief literary discovery after her return from Torquay was contemporary French fiction. "I am probably," she wrote Chorley, "not to say certainly, the most complete and unscrupulous romance reader within your knowledge," and most of the romances she looked at were French. Before she left for Italy, she had read widely in Balzac, Hugo, George Sand, Eugène Sue, Frédéric Soulié, Paul de Kock, and the elder Dumas; and she had gone through the early novels of Jules Janin and Stendhal's *Le Rouge et le noir.* In view of the strict Nonconformist background of her family, it is hardly surprising that such writers shocked her by their "perverted moral standards," as she often expressed it in her letters to Miss Mitford. Although she recognized their genius, she deplored their "stench." In writing to Horne of the French novelists she said, "We cannot *wish* them to be popular in England, for obvious reasons," and she told Miss Mitford that she had read all sorts of "corrupting" books which she would not wish her sisters to look at, even though to her they "strengthened the truth . . . through an antagonistical ingenuity."[16] Her father did not know that she was reading such authors, and furthermore he was not acquainted with any of them. If she had told him she admired the novels of George Sand, who was "no better than she should be," he would think she "was mad and required his paternal restraint in all manner of ways."[17]

Balzac's *La Vieille Fille* she characterized as "a prodigy of noisomeness," and she was so disgusted by it that she resolved never to read him again (a resolution she soon broke).[18] Balzac, she said, so "burns and abashes one" that it is impossible to read him without being "acclimated." [19] Even in her hero Victor Hugo she found an "indelicacy and want of elemental morality." Although George Sand was "the greatest female genius the world ever saw," she was sometimes *"shameless."* Elizabeth could not finish *Lélia* on account of its "soul-slime" and "vileness"; but she did read *Indiana, Consuelo* and its sequel *La Comtesse de Rudolstadt, Jeanne,* and *Le Péché de Monsieur Antoine.* As for Paul de Kock, whom she considered a "coarse animal writer," she waded through "most of his forty or fifty volumes" despite their "filth." [20] Her romantic imagination was stimulated by the sensational plots and fantastic characterizations of Sue, Soulié, and the elder Dumas. While she found the material of Sue's *Les Mystères de Paris* "painful and repulsive," [21] she read the novel several times with much interest and was later to draw upon it for several of the characters and situations in *Aurora Leigh*. She also admired Sue's *Mathilde* and his *Le Juif errant. La Guerre des femmes* of the elder Dumas made her weep, and the romantic adventures in *Le Comte de Monte-Cristo* so fascinated her that she re-read the novel twice during her first three years in Florence. For the rest of her life the perusal of George Sand, Dumas, Sue, and their contemporaries remained one of her principal diversions. In eighteenth-century French fiction, however, she had no interest and apparently found much of it too licentious for her taste. She once looked at *Le Sopha* by Crébillon *fils* and after turning the pages a few minutes thought it a "most disgusting sensual book" and "dropped it like a burning iron." [22] If her remarks now seem prudish, it should be remembered that in the moral climate of the Victorian age no "respectable" woman would dare admit having owned or read a French novel of any period.

As for English literature, she browsed widely in all periods from Chaucer's to her own, though she was particularly drawn to the nondramatic verse of the early and middle seventeenth century and to Elizabethan and Jacobean drama. She looked again at Shakespeare and at Ben Jonson, and she read Beaumont and Fletcher in the volumes her brother George presented to her when she was at Torquay, and Massinger in her copy of Robert

Return to Wimpole Street

Dodsley's collection of plays, of which she owned the first nine volumes. The principal Romantic poets, especially Wordsworth, Shelley, and Keats, were among her favorites to the extent that in her own verse she unconsciously absorbed some of their mannerisms of diction and idiom. Finally, as might be expected of one who never lost her simple, orthodox Christian faith, every day she regularly read the Bible.

A surprising hiatus in her reading was in the fields of the natural sciences and of philosophy. Although she did go through the Oxford *Tracts*—and "was disappointed *even* in the degree of intellectual power displayed in them"—and although she was interested in Richard Monckton Milnes' *One Tract More*—her former enthusiasm for metaphysics and theological doctrine had largely disappeared. Instead she was becoming more and more interested in the occult and the spiritualistic. She read Jung-Stilling's *Theory of Pneumatology,* which had a morbid influence upon her, with its reports of trances, apparitions, visions, presentiments, and somnambulistic experiences; also one of Baron Du Potet de Sennevoy's books on animal magnetism and William Newnham's *Human Magnetism,* both of which dealt with a subject much discussed in the middle forties: mesmerism or the treatment of physical disorders by means of hypnotism. From this period, too, stems her lifelong attraction to the writings of the eighteenth-century Swedish mystic Emanuel Swedenborg. The discoveries in geology and biology which contradicted the literal account of the creation in Genesis had no effect upon her imagination. In 1844 Robert Chambers published anonymously a useful compilation of scientific thought entitled *Vestiges of the Natural History of Creation,* in the first part of which he explained the origin of the universe in terms of the nebular hypothesis of Kant and Laplace. In the next section he dealt with the theory established by Sir Charles Lyell a decade earlier that the earth's surface had changed slowly and was still changing, in response to uniform, fixed causes. Then, without denying the existence of the deity or the evidences of "design" in nature, he advanced the evolutionary hypothesis of the development of the individual species from the simple and uniform to the complex and diversified and thus looked forward to Darwin's principle of natural selection. But Elizabeth, who remained untouched all her life by evolutionary thought, dismissed Chambers' important work as "one of the most melancholy books in the world."

WITHIN a few months of her return to London from Torquay, she was very much occupied with her writing and felt that for the first time "the faculty of life" had sprung up in her "again, from under the crushing foot of heavy grief." She submitted to the *Athenaeum* translations of three hymns of Gregory Nazianzen which with an introductory paragraph, were published in the issue of January 8, 1842. Three days earlier she had received a letter from Dilke asking her to contribute some reviews, and she immediately planned a series of articles on the Greek Christian poets, whom years ago she had read with Boyd. Although she had "scarcely sufficient materials for a full and minute survey of them" and could not leave her room to read and collect materials in the British Museum or other large public libraries, she wrote to Boyd, asking for a list of names she might include and for the loan of several texts, and within the next two months prepared very rapidly four connected articles on twenty of the principal Greek Christian poets over a span of sixteen centuries. The papers were published anonymously in the *Athenaeum* in February and March.

Some of the texts she used were her own folios of Gregory Nazianzen and of Chrysostom, a volume containing some of the works of Paul Silentiarius and of George Pisida, which was the thirty-first tome of the *Corpus scriptorum historiae Byzantinae*,[23] and Pisida's *Hexaëmeron,* in a book "as tall as the Irish giants." She borrowed Boyd's copies of Heliodorus, of Synesius, and of John Mauropus; also his volume of Gregory Nazianzen with the *Christus patiens,* which she attributed to Apollinaris, Bishop of Laodicea; and Boyd's two volumes written by Adam Clarke and his son J. B. B. Clarke entitled *A Concise View of the Succession of Sacred Literature,*[24] which was helpful to her in her dating of the poets. Another work she consulted was Henry Alford's *Chapters on the Poets of Ancient Greece,* which irritated her because of its disparagement of Gregory Nazianzen.[25] In her introductory re-

Return to Wimpole Street

marks Elizabeth admitted that in the Christian era the Greek language was "an antique instrument, somewhat worn, somewhat stiff in the playing," that not one of those about whom she was writing was "a true genius." She deplored the fact that the modern Latin poets were now more widely read and better known, for she thought they stood "cold and lifeless, with statue-eyes, near these good, fervid, faulty Greeks," who, while lacking the elegance of the Latin authors, had "that higher distinction inherent in brain and breast, of vivid thought and quick sensibility." Then she explained that her aim was to present the chief characteristics of each writer, with the translation of some of his verses. While several poets, such as Silentiarius and Pisida, were difficult because of their specialized vocabulary, most of them were easy enough to understand with their simple diction and sentence construction. That Elizabeth stayed as close to the original as possible may be seen, for example, in her version of the Ninth Ode of Synesius of Cyrene, which begins:

> Πολυήρατε κύδιμε
> Σὲ μάκαρ γόνε Παρθένου
> Ὑμνῶ Σολυμηΐδος,
> Ὅς τὰν δολίαν πάγαν
> Χθόνιον μεγάλων ὄφιν
> Πατρὸς ἤλασας ὀρχάτων·
> Καταβὰς μέχρι καὶ χθονὸς
> Ἐπίδημος ἐφαμέροις,
> Κατέβας δ' ὑπὸ τάρταρα.[26]

Elizabeth knew Boyd's flowery paraphrase of this ode in his *Select Poems of Synesius and Gregory Nazianzen*.[27] She may have thought that the spirit of the Greek poet was lost in his fanciful rendition, for her own, the opening lines of which follow, is an almost literal translation:

> Well-beloved and glory-laden,
> Born of Solyma's pure maiden!
> I would hymn Thee, blessed Warden,
> Driving from Thy Father's garden
> Blinking serpent's crafty lust,

> With his bruised head in the dust!
> Down Thou camest, low as earth,
> Bound to those of mortal birth;
> Down Thou camest, low as hell, . . .

She was pleased at the favorable reception of her articles from Boyd, Miss Mitford, and Horne. Kenyon, who also liked them but thought they were "labour thrown away, from the unpopularity of the subject," reported the approval of Mrs. Jameson and of Robert Browning. Apparently Dilke was satisfied too, for just as she was completing her final paper, he sent her a recently published anthology of English verse from Chaucer to Beattie, entitled *The Book of the Poets*,[28] for her to review in two articles.

By the time she had finished her critique she had expanded her material to a series of five articles, which were published anonymously in the *Athenaeum* in June and August 1842. In only the first three paragraphs of the initial article did she discuss the anthology, of which she mainly disapproved because she felt that too many insignificant poets were included and that the selections from the better-known writers did not represent their best work. She then undertook a summary of English verse from Langland to such late eighteenth-century Romantic poets as Cowper, Thomas Warton, and Burns. Her most sympathetic remarks were upon Chaucer, Spenser, Shakespeare, the Elizabethan lyrists, and the drama from its medieval origins through Massinger, Ford, and Shirley. Of the Elizabethan era she wrote with unrestrained enthusiasm, "Never since the first nightingale brake voice in Eden arose such a jubilee-concert—never before nor since has such a crowd of true poets uttered true poetic speech in one day!"

Since her poetic sensibility was derived from the generation of Keats and Shelley, she maintained that Dryden, Butler, and Pope were not true poets and that Dr. Johnson was "the ponderous critic of the system." Dryden "had a large soul for a man . . . but it was not a large soul for a poet." Samuel Butler's "business was the business of desecration, the exact reverse of a poet's," and so he was "a natural enemy to poetry under the form of a poet." Likewise Pope "was not a great poet; he meant to be a correct poet, and he was what he meant to be, according to his construction of the thing meant." The only Metaphysical poet she wrote about was Cowley, who was "without the poet's heart" and who was so coarse that "he went to the shambles for his chambers of imagery, and very often through the mud." Her comment on Milton seems perverse; she missed the quality of "spirituality" in his poetry: "His spiritual personages are vast enough, but not rarefied enough." But one might argue that it is precisely because of their intensely human qualities that the characters of Milton's major poems are vivid and authentic, while the personages of Elizabeth's "The Seraphim" and "A Drama of Exile" seem wearisome abstractions. She concluded that in Augustan England "there was no room either for Nature or Art," both of which were "maimed and dejected" until the "revival of poetry" in the time of Burns, Percy, and Beattie, from whose *Minstrel* she had drawn her "childhood's first poetic pleasure."

Two weeks after the publication of her last article on the English poets Elizabeth reviewed anonymously for the *Athenaeum* Wordsworth's volume which had been recently published by Moxon, *Poems, Chiefly of Early and Late Years; Including The Borderers, a Tragedy*. The first part of her notice told of the "noble hearts," Wordsworth and Coleridge among them, who freed English verse from "the 'system' riveted upon the motions of poetry by Dryden and his dynasty." She acknowledged Wordsworth as "poet-hero of a movement essential to the better being of poetry," and she declared with characteristic hyperbole that of all the English poets, living and dead, "not one has swept the purple with more majesty than this poet," when it pleased him to be majestic. His sonnets in particular she thought were the finest in the language: "However the greatest poets of our country—the Shakespeares, Spensers, Miltons—worked upon high sonnet ground, not one opened over it such broad and pouring sluices of various thought, imagery, and emphatic eloquence as he has done." Byron, whom Elizabeth had worshiped as a child, is now placed far below Wordsworth. Poetry, she wrote, should reveal the complete man, and it seemed to her that Byron's life had been incomplete, with its overemphasis upon passion: "His poems discovered not a heart, but the wound of a heart; not humanity, but disease; not life, but a crisis."

While Wordsworth's volume was in her opinion a "true poet's work," it did not present his best writing. For example, she was sorry that he had published the series of sonnets in favor of capital punishment, and she thought that "The Borderers" was uncertain in its dramatic movement and poorly organized as a whole. Yet now and then "there are sweet gushings" (an overused phrase in Elizabeth's critical vocabulary) "of such words as this poet only knows." In the last paragraph she expressed a theme which appears in many of her poems, that "a true poet" must dedicate all of his life to his art and that he must suffer from poverty, from the neglect of the general public, and from the indifference of professional critics. Volumes of verse could not hope to pay for their expenses of publication, and many people feared that English poetry was moribund and would be superseded by prose. Too many poets, she solemnly proclaimed, "hold back their full strength from Art because they do not *reverence* it fully." It would be well for them to keep in mind Wordsworth's example, "to remember *now* what a silent, blameless, heroic life of poetic duty this man has lived." And turning from the elderly, respected bard to the poets of her own generation whom she believed to have the greatest promise, she generously praised two fellow-craftsmen: "In the meantime the hopeful and believing will hope—trust on; and, better still, the Tennysons and the Brownings, and other high-gifted spirits, will work" and wait for their hour to come.

The last prose contribution Elizabeth sent to the *Athenaeum* was her unsigned review in the issue of June 24, 1843, of *Orion: an Epic Poem, in Three Books* by R. H. Horne. The literary world of London thought that Horne had gone mad when he offered his work on May 29 for the price of one farthing at all booksellers, with the stipulation that each customer might buy only one copy and that any person who mispronounced the title should not be allowed to purchase the book at all. It was apparently its nominal price that attracted many buyers, not all of whom perhaps would have cared to spend more than a farthing on an epic poem with a classical background, because two weeks after its publication Horne wrote Elizabeth that his publisher had been almost torn to pieces by requests from would-be purchasers, almost none of whom could he hope to satisfy. Within a year of its appearance the poem reached a fifth edition. In her critique Elizabeth gave a summary of the story and praised the work as "a true poem" even though it seemed to her "scarcely a true epic" because the action was overweighted with philosophical comment. It was, she suggested, possibly "a spiritual epic" telling of the "growth of a poet's mind" and its ultimate triumph over obstacles. What is of greater importance than her analysis of the poem is the fact that she was generous in her praise and gave as much help as she could to her friend and colleague: "To thoughtful minds the poem will be welcome for its original cast and elevated cheerful teaching; and by poetical minds it will be received cordially as a poet's gift." After the publication of her notice on *Orion,* Dilke wrote her that he would send her any book she wished to review for the *Athenaeum.* She thanked him for his offer but declined because she wished to devote more of her time to poetry. Thus she ended her brief career in journalism.

7. Friendships and Literary Activities

IN ADDITION to the reviews and poems Elizabeth published in the *Athenaeum* and in American periodicals in 1842, she also wrote the "Introductory Stanzas" and the verses to accompany the portraits of the Prince of Wales, the Duchess of Orleans, Samuel Rogers, and the King of Prussia in the *English Bijou Almanack* for 1843. This tiny volume—one of the smallest in the British Museum—is less than one half inch in height, and the print can be read only under a strong magnifying glass. According to the *Athenaeum* it came out in December 1842, "under the protecting patronage of Miss Mitford." [1]

But the acquaintances Elizabeth made that year were as important as her publications. Early in January she began a correspondence with Thomas Westwood, a poet eight years younger who had written only one volume of verse. She told him of her own work and related gossip about such people as Miss Martineau, Miss Mitford, Wordsworth, Tennyson, and Browning. Unlike Elizabeth, Westwood was not serious about his poetical career. In 1844 he went to Belgium, where he became the director of a railroad and in his later years devoted his leisure to the bibliography of angling. After 1845 their respective interests had so diverged that they hardly ever wrote to each other again.

A much more important pen acquaintance was the painter Benjamin Robert Haydon, with whom Elizabeth began to correspond in the spring of 1842. A vain, self-assertive, impetuous, quarrelsome, touchy, and embittered man, he was then in his middle fifties and had still to receive the recognition he thought due him. Although she was aware of the obvious weaknesses of his character, she thought he had, as she said to Browning after

Friendships and Literary Activities 107

Haydon's suicide, "a certain fervour and magnanimity of genius." Success had eluded him partly because of his faulty draftsmanship, weak composition, and inability to achieve harmony and unity, and partly because of the change in taste which no longer favored his style of painting: the treatment on a grand scale of a biblical, literary, or historical theme. Subjects such as "Curtius Leaping into the Gulf" or "Christ's Triumphant Entry into Jerusalem" were too remote from the interests of patrons, who mostly preferred portraits of themselves and small, neat canvases in the tradition of the Dutch realists. Miss Mitford introduced him to Elizabeth, and for a little more than a year they not infrequently wrote to each other. "At that time, through caring for nobody and feeling so loose to life," she later told Browning, "I threw away my thoughts without looking where they fell." Early in October 1842 [2] Haydon sent Elizabeth his "Wordsworth Musing upon Helvellyn," which, in spite of the artist's usual distaste for portrait painting, is the one work in which he came closest to the high ideals he fitfully set for himself. "Such a head! such majesty!" Elizabeth said of the picture in her room.[3] She immediately composed a sonnet on the portrait and submitted it to the *Athenaeum*, where it appeared within a few days. In the meantime Haydon had forwarded a copy of the poem to Wordsworth, who wrote to Elizabeth from Rydal Mount of his approval of the sonnet and of the pleasure he had received from her volumes of 1833 and 1838. He thought one sentence in her poem might seem obscure to many readers and proposed a slight revision. When she reprinted the verses in her *Poems* of 1844, she altered the passage to which he had called her attention, though her second version remained different from his suggested lines.[4] Another gift from Haydon which pleased Elizabeth was "two pages, nearly, of Keats' poetry written in the poet's hand," [5] consisting of the last sixty lines of "I Stood Tip-Toe upon a Little Hill." [6]

Both Haydon and Elizabeth had much to offer each other. A friend of Keats, Lamb, Hunt, Hazlitt, Shelley, and Scott, he was the product of a richer culture and had wider sympathies than any other of her acquaintances in 1843. Elizabeth, who had known almost nothing about painters and their works, learned much from him concerning matters of technique and the economic problems of an artist's existence. On her side, in spite of having lived a fantastically restricted life and being twenty years younger, she several times gave him the sane, practical advice of which anyone as impetuous and unbalanced as he was badly in need. For example, in the spring of 1843 she urged him to soften or eliminate the references in the manuscript of the autobiography he was compiling which might be offensive to living persons.[7] In July, after he had failed to win any of the prizes offered for the trial paintings submitted by candidates for the work of decorating the new Houses of Parliament, she counseled him not to accuse the judges of having harbored a feeling of malice against him, or to say publicly that he was the victim of a general "conspiracy."[8]

Two Americans with whom Elizabeth began a correspondence late in 1842 were James Russell Lowell and Cornelius Mathews. The copy of *Arcturus*, edited by Mathews and Evert A. Duyckinck, of February 1841 which contained a review of her volume of 1838 was sent to her from New York the following December with a letter assuring her that her verses would be "heartily received by the lovers of poetry in America."[9] Months later the periodical and the editor's letter arrived, and in July 1842 she acknowledged having received them and enclosed four sonnets and "The Cry of the Human." Meanwhile *Arcturus* had suspended publication. The latter poem was sent by the former editors to Nathan Hale, Jr., who published it in November in his *Boston Miscellany of Literature and Fashion*. Through the good offices of Mathews, the four sonnets appeared in the December issue of *Graham's Magazine* in New York. In introducing Elizabeth to their readers the editors of *Graham's* said that her writings were "unique in this age of lady authors," that they had the " 'touch of nature' . . . sentiment, passion, and fancy in the highest degree." The notice paid extravagant tribute to her learning: "The fine tissue of her flowing style comes to us from the loom of Grecian thought. She is the learned poetess of the day, familiar with Homer and Aeschylus and Sophocles."[10] In October Mathews had written to Elizabeth and had sent her a copy of *Wakondah; the Master of Life*,[11] thus beginning a correspondence which remained active for the next two years. He was an eager New York journalist, poet, playwright, and novelist in his middle twenties. His reason for writing Elizabeth while she was still known only to a few in America may have been a shrewd guess that before long she would become one of England's most popular poets, with a wide following also in his own country, and so would be able to help him secure a reputation in England. He sent her copies of his volumes of poetry of 1841 and 1843, hoping that she would herself write reviews of them or bring them to the attention of the leading English literary journals.[12] Although she was too shy to do either, she quoted a verse from his *Poems on Man* [13] as a motto for one of the poems in her volumes of 1844,[14] and in a footnote she praised his work for being "as remarkable, in thought and manner, for a vital sinewy vigour, as the right arm of Pathfinder." Also she wrote to Horne that Mathews was "full of genial kindness and generosity, upright and warm-hearted" and asked if he could use his influence in behalf of the American writer. In her letters to Mathews she always spoke well of his poetry, which she thought had "more strength, fibre, bone, and muscle" than any other American poetry she had ever read.[15]

It was Mathews more than any other American who helped Elizabeth Barrett to gain a hearing in his own country. He placed eleven of her poems in *Graham's Magazine* during the year and a half before the publication of her volumes of 1844, and he arranged for the firm of Putnam and Wiley, publishers of the magazine, to pay her £10 5s. In the summer of 1844 he had several of her works published in the *United States Magazine and Democratic Review*.[16] Soon afterward he wrote a review of the American edition of her *Poems* which was extravagant in its praise.[17] He signed a contract between H. G. Langley and himself for the republication in America of Elizabeth's volumes of 1844; under the terms of the agreement she was to receive 10 per cent of the net sales.[18] When she later sent him the proof sheets from the English edition, he saw the work through the press. Then he collected many of the American reviews, forwarded them to her, and told her of the enthusiastic reception in America of her *Poems*. Many times in her letters she expressed her gratitude to him for all he had done. She also wrote him of her own work and of the activities of writers in whom he might be interested: Wordsworth, Rogers, Hood, Mrs. Jameson, Mrs. Norton, Horne, Chorley, Tennyson, and Browning. Of the latter she wrote with pride soon after the publication of his *Dramatic Romances and Lyrics* that another number of *Bells and Pomegranates* had appeared, in which its author's "great original faculty throws out new colours and expands in new combinations." She continued, "A great poet he is—a greater poet he will be—for to work and to live are one with him." [19] After 1845 she was too much absorbed in her romance to continue her correspondence with Mathews. One of the last times she wrote to him was early in 1847 from Pisa, when she sent him a long letter telling of her marriage and her change "from the long seclusion in one room, to liberty and Italy's sunshine . . ." [20]

The second American with whom she corresponded before her marriage was James Russell Lowell. In 1842 he was in his early twenties, had recently been graduated from Harvard College and the Harvard Law School, had published a short volume of poems, and was hoping to establish himself in the literary world of Boston. No doubt he had seen Elizabeth's poem in the November issue of the *Boston Miscellany,* edited by his friend Nathan Hale. That month Lowell wrote to her, introducing himself and sending a copy of his *A Year's Life.*[21] After receiving an acknowledgment, he told her in the middle of December that he was going to publish a magazine in Boston in which he hoped to improve the state of literature in his native city, and he asked her for a contribution. Unlike Mathews, he could not offer to pay anything; but he flattered her by saying that unless he had thought highly of her, he would not have requested her verses.[22] She replied graciously early in January, thanked him for his high opinion of her, and enclosed three poems. "From the circumstances of a retired life and ill health," she wrote, "it has happened that I never stood face to face with an American, except in my dreams. But I love the Americans and America for the sake of national brotherhood and a common literature and I honor them for the sake of liberty and noble aspiration, and I am grateful to them,—very grateful,— for their kindness to me personally as a poet." [23] Had she forgotten having met Ticknor at Kenyon's house before she went to Torquay? Lowell printed only one of the three poems he received from her, "The Maiden's Death," which appeared in the *Pioneer* in March 1843. He probably planned to use the other two in later numbers of the magazine, but it ceased publication after the March issue. The other two poems, "That Day" and "Insufficiency,"[24] were included in her volumes of 1844, but "The Maiden's Death," which is in her most humorless and sentimental manner, was not republished during her life.[25] Lowell evidently did not write her again until he sent her a copy of his *Poems* of 1844, which she acknowledged late in July of that year. She mentioned "various beauties and felicities" but frankly criticized the volume as a whole because of its vagueness and "poetical diction."[26] In February 1845 Lowell sent her a copy of his recently published prose work, *Conversations on Some of the Old Poets,* which seemed to both Elizabeth and Browning a naïve and pretentious book. Lowell was "graceful for an American critic," she later wrote her fiancé, "but the truth is, otherwise, that he knows nothing of English poetry or the next thing to nothing." She thought that the publication of such a work was "a curious proof of the state of literature in America." During her first winter in Italy she forwarded to Lowell "The Runaway Slave at Pilgrim's Point," which was printed in the *Liberty Bell* in Boston 1848. It was not until the summer of 1852 that she met Lowell and his first wife. They were in London, breaking their journey between Italy and America, and Elizabeth was particularly impressed by Maria, who, she thought, had a "pure and fragrant" spirit.[27]

In August of 1843 [28] Elizabeth began to correspond with Harriet Martineau, whom she once called "the profoundest woman thinker in England," and another time with even more generosity "the noblest female intelligence between the seas." Although Miss Martineau was only four years older than Elizabeth Barrett, she had been for the previous ten years one of the most successful writers in England. After producing several religious works, such as the *Traditions of Palestine,* she achieved sudden fame in the early thirties with her *Illustrations of Political Economy* in terms of the doctrinaire principles of Ricardo, Malthus, and Bentham. From 1834 to 1836 she was in America and like Mrs. Trollope and Dickens earned her passage money by reporting on her experiences. Later, while traveling in Italy, she was stricken with a uterine tumor. She was brought back to England and lived for a while at Tynemouth, where she received a series of treatments based on mesmerism, from which she seemed to benefit so much that before long, as Elizabeth reported to Cornelius Mathews, she was able to "walk five miles a day with ease." It was Miss Martineau who initiated the correspondence with Elizabeth, possibly because she felt a bond of sympathy between them in that both were invalids. For example, in writing to Elizabeth in the fall of 1843 she said that "we sick people" could have no excuse for delay in their communications to each other.[29]

For about two years they exchanged letters on their respective illnesses and writings. Miss Martineau criticized Elizabeth's poetry for its obscurity and repeatedly advised her to simplify her style. Many of the letters contain references to Miss Martineau's apparent cure as a result of the mesmeristic experiments, a subject which fascinated Elizabeth, who wrote her old friend Mrs. Martin that she "would give a great deal, *not to believe a word of it:* and I believe, in spite of my repulsions."[30] She expressed herself to Westwood on the same subject: "I, who am very credulous, feel my blood running the wrong way as I read. Can it be lawful if it is true? or expedient, if lawful?"[31] What neither Elizabeth nor Miss Martineau knew was that the notorious treatments afforded no cure at all: as a post-mortem examination made clear, at the time the patient was subjecting herself to the experiments, the abdominal cyst happened to shift its position and thus brought relief for many years.[32] After 1845 correspondence between the two women died a natural death. Neither had much to contribute to the other; neither was sympathetic to the other's point of view. For example years later, in 1860, Miss Martineau in a letter to an American paper on European politics greatly offended Elizabeth by commenting with "cool arrogance" on her recent volume of poems on the Italian war. Miss Martineau sharply criticized the poet for her faith in Napoleon III. She said, however, that those who knew Elizabeth realized that in her attitude toward the Emperor she was not guilty of a "vulgar worship of success" but that her position was owing to her *"ideal and unpractical habit of mind which is no secret among her friends."*[33] Although Elizabeth thought the charge was "monstrously unjust and absurd,"[34] she did not reply.

Friendships and Literary Activities

IN 1843 she wrote several of her best-known poems: "The Dead Pan," "The Cry of the Children," "A Vision of Poets," "The Lost Bower," and "To Flush, My Dog." The first of these was inspired by a poem John Kenyon had published in the Countess of Blessington's *Keepsake for 1843*,[35] "The Gods of Greece," paraphrased from Schiller. Kenyon's poem looks with nostalgia to the "sparkling world" where pagan deities "ruled, of old, a happier race." The "generous Creeds" of the South were killed by a "blight-wind from the bitter North" so that the "bright Fictions" of classical myth now "live in Poet's dream alone." Elizabeth's verses, as she herself said, "oppose a doctrine still more dishonouring to poetry than to Christianity." [36] She does not regret the present silence of the "vain false gods of Hellas," for Christian themes are now more appropriate for poetry and "nobler than the Muses." As for the verses to Flush, they were much admired by Cornelius Mathews and his friends in America soon after their publication in the *Athenaeum* in July.

"A Vision of Poets," which is the second longest poem in the volumes of 1844, is an overambitious attempt to summarize, in a few verses for each, the characteristics of the principal European poets from Homer to Keats and Shelley. Several of the descriptions, like that of the author of *De rerum natura,* are happily conceived:

> Lucretius—nobler than his mood!
> Who dropped his plummet down the broad
> Deep universe, and said "No God," . . .

"On calmed brows" is an inappropriate epithet, for Sappho, however; whose poetry is that of a passionate spirit; "infantine" is an unsuitable adjective for Chaucer, who was simple but not childish; nor was Byron "forlorn." Like many of Elizabeth's poems, "A Vision of Poets" suffers from a moralizing passage with which it concludes. As she said in her preface to her volumes, the poem as a whole expressed her view of "the mission of the poet, of the self-abnegation implied in it, of the great work involved in it." [37] This is a theme which appears frequently in her writing.

"The Lost Bower" tells of a childhood incident, her wandering in the woods above her home and entering a glade which she so enjoyed for its "fresh and dewy glitter" that she resolved to return there every day. But never again did she succeed in finding it. She then enumerates all her losses since her early days at Hope End: "Studious health," "sound child-sleeping," "merry leisure" (though she always had unlimited freedom for reading and writing), and "Some respect to social fictions." She had so changed that if any one who had been a friend of hers when she was a girl should now see her lying on her couch, he would "Never know me for the same!" The chief interest in the poem is its description of the scenery at Hope End:

> Green the land is where my daily
> Steps in jocund childhood played—
> Dimpled close with hill and valley,
> Dappled very close with shade;
> Summer-snow of apple blossoms, running up
> from glade to glade. . . .
>
> On your left, the sheep are cropping
> The slant grass and daisies pale;
> And five apple-trees stand, dropping
> Separate shadows toward the vale, . . .

"The Cry of the Children," which was to become one of the best-known of Elizabeth's poems, first appeared in *Blackwood's* in August 1843 and thus anticipated by several months the publication of Hood's "The Song of the Shirt." While both poems are highly effective appeals to the conscience of England to rectify one of the worst abuses of nineteenth-century industrialism, Elizabeth's verses have a greater urgency. Her poem treats the subject with a somewhat wider scope, is slightly longer, but unlike much of her work does not weary the reader with an excessive number of examples to illustrate her theme. It is one of the few times when she knew where to stop. Her imagination had been stirred by the reports from the Commissioners in 1842 and 1843 on children's employment in mines, trades, and manufactures. Her friend Horne, who was one of the investigators for the Commission, reported officially that the rooms in the factories were "crowded

Friendships and Literary Activities 115

with dangerous machinery not boxed off." He described to the Commission the terrible conditions in a typical factory he visited: "It is a frightful place, turn which way you will. There is a constant hammering roar of wheels, so that you could not possibly hear any warning voice. You have but once to stumble on your passage from one place to another, or to be thinking of something else, and you are certain to be punished with the loss of a limb, or of your life if the limb does not come away kindly." Horne then told of the callousness of the employers: "Little boys and girls are here seen at work at the tip-punching machines (all acting by steam power) with their fingers in constant danger of being punched off once in every second, while at the same time they have their heads between two whirling wheels a few inches distant from each ear. . . . 'They seldom lose the hand,' said one of the proprietors to me, in explanation; 'it only takes off a finger at the first or second joint. Sheer carelessness—looking about them —entirely through carelessness!' " [38] The reports on the employment of children in mines said that boys and girls often began to work at the age of five, that they had to draw on their hands and knees a cart of coal through dark, unventilated, foul-smelling passages sometimes no higher than eighteen inches. Since they were compelled to work thirteen, sometimes sixteen, hours a day, they were too tired to do anything but sleep on Sundays. The children were beaten by their masters, they had almost no opportunity for education, the girls were not always decently clothed, both the boys and girls were afflicted with many occupational diseases which often killed them before their time, and almost all had a "crippled gait" and "stunted growth"; these sufferings and shocking conditions they endured to earn about three shillings a week.[39]

Elizabeth based many of the details of her poem on the Parliamentary reports. Her children work in the mines and in factories. They are young, have "pale and sunken faces," and are too tired from overwork to enjoy the open fields:

> "For oh," say the children, "we are weary,
>   And we cannot run or leap—
> If we cared for any meadows, it were merely

To drop down in them and sleep.
Our knees tremble sorely in the stooping—
We fall upon our faces, trying to go; . . ."

In the mines they drag their burdens "Through the coal-dark, underground," and in the factories the "iron wheels" of the machines are close to their faces. They are so poorly educated that they know only two words of prayer: "Our Father." Many die because of the wretched conditions. Elizabeth's verses present a vivid picture of the plight of the children in the early Victorian economy, when labor was abundant, cheap, and unprotected by labor unions or law. With her idealistic and emotional approach to the problem, she saw clearly the abuse but oversimplified the remedy—as she was later to oversimplify the issues of American slavery, of the Italian *Risorgimento,* and of women's rights. The villain in "The Cry of the Children" is the "gold-heaper," the Victorian capitalist; presumably, if he were to repent of his miserly ways, the wrongs would no longer exist.

IN ADDITION to writing poetry, Elizabeth was very busy during the winter of 1843-44, collaborating with R. H. Horne in the preparation of *A New Spirit of the Age,* of which he was the editor. On October 4 he wrote her about the proposed publication and asked for a biographical sketch of herself, a list of her works, and her picture.[40] She complied with the first two requests but did not wish to appear in a portrait. A few days later he asked her to help him in writing some of the critiques, all of which were to be unsigned, and enjoined her to secrecy, since the work was to contain an article on her. His reason for asking Elizabeth to have a part in the project was that he thought she had "a finely suitable intellect" for such writing, that she was "dwelling comparatively out of the world and its conflicting people and opinions, yet taking a deep interest in the best things that are going on," and that she had "magnanimity to admire, as well as moral courage to demur or denounce." He proposed that she should send him her comments on the authors he asked her to discuss, and then he would interpolate throughout her text his own remarks. Thus, as she later wrote to her friend Westwood, she had no *"right to claim any single article"* [41] in the book. Likewise she later explained to Browning that she did not write "one of those papers singly. . . . It was simply a writing of notes . . of slips of paper . . now on one subject, and now on another . . which were thrown into the great cauldron and boiled up with other matter, and re-translated from my idiom where there seemed a need for it." Horne's other collaborator was Robert Bell, who two years earlier had contributed one of the least successful translations to *The Poems of Geoffrey Chaucer, Modernized.* Many of the mottoes at the beginning of each chapter were supplied by Elizabeth Barrett and Robert Browning, although at the time neither knew of the other's part in the work.

Owing to the circumstances of the composition of the essays, the extent to which Elizabeth shared in their authorship is unknown. Since Horne sent her most if not all of the page proofs for her marginal criticisms shortly before the book went to press, she probably offered comments on a majority of the papers. The articles on Landor and Milnes, however, were written mostly by her;[42] those on Wordsworth, Hunt, Tennyson, and Carlyle were produced jointly by Horne and Elizabeth.[43] She contributed to the critiques on Caroline Norton, the Irish novelists (Samuel Lover, Charles J. Lever, William Carleton, and Mrs. S. C. Hall), Henry Taylor, and Philip James Bailey.[44] The notes for her own biography she sent to Horne, who garbled them in his article on her. She may also have supplied a few hints for the chapters on G. P. R. James, Catherine Gore, Captain Marryat, Frances Trollope, Sydney Smith, Fonblanque, Douglas Jerrold, Harriet Martineau, Anna Jameson, Mary Wollstonecraft Shelley, Macaulay, and Talfourd.[45]

When Horne first asked Elizabeth for her help, he told her his aim was not to praise well-known writers but rather to discuss those who were not yet established. In the preface to the work he said that nearly twenty years had passed since the publication of Hazlitt's *The Spirit of the Age* and that now "a new set of men, several of them animated by a new spirit, have obtained eminent positions in the public mind." Hazlitt's compilation dealt with the great Romantic writers who were still living in 1825 (including Byron, who had not yet died when the article on him was written); those in the second rank, such as Southey, Hunt, Campbell, and

Washington Irving; also a clergyman, an economist, and several philosophers, lawyers, statesmen, and critics. In 1838 Chorley had published *The Authors of England,* which Horne referred to scornfully as "Chorley's picture book." The *raison d'être* of the handsome quarto volume was its series of medallion portraits in profile of fourteen writers, engraved by Achille Collas from the works of various British artists. Chorley, who wrote the "illustrative notices," said in the preface that "nothing in the shape of classification in the arrangement or selection of subjects has been attempted." This was true enough, for his work included such diverse figures as Shelley, Wordsworth, Mrs. Hemans, the Countess of Blessington, Bulwer-Lytton, Lady Sydney Morgan, and Mary Russell Mitford. Horne included two writers whom Hazlitt had treated, Leigh Hunt and Sheridan Knowles; and two in Chorley's book, Wordsworth (also in Hazlitt) and Bulwer-Lytton. With these exceptions he made his selection not "from those who are already 'crowned,' and their claims settled, but almost entirely from those who are in progress and midway of fame." More than Hazlitt had, Horne drew almost all his subjects from the field of *belles lettres,* and only five were from somewhat different areas: Macready, Sydney Smith, Pusey, Lord Ashley, and the public-spirited physician Thomas Southwood Smith.

Besides the essays, the *New Spirit* had full-page illustrations of the portraits of Dickens, Smith, T. N. Talfourd, Wordsworth, Tennyson, Miss Martineau, Browning, and Carlyle. One review spoke of Tennyson's "magnificent portrait," which looked like "the head of the wisdom-poet, the master mind, above the littlenesses of humanity"; [46] another wrote of the "striking portrait of Mr. Tennyson . . . the head of a poet, poetically rendered." [47] But the reviews failed to notice the even more arresting picture of the youthful Browning in profile. A lock of dark hair falls over part of the forehead. The face is thin, smooth, and white; the expression is alert; and the features are regular, with full chin, sensuous lips, and prominent, straight nose. It was the engraving upon which this portrait in the book was based that Elizabeth hung in her room.

She was very much dissatisfied with the article on herself, in which she was incongruously paired with the notorious and unhappy Caroline Norton. It dealt too much with her biography, she thought, to the exclusion of her poetry. Furthermore, she felt that Horne overemphasized her invalidism and her erudition, for she wrote him that he had exaggerated in saying that she composed "elegant Latin verse" and that she had been "shut up in one room for six or seven years" and during that time was often "several weeks together in the dark." While she was never vain about her looks, she could scarcely have been pleased when she read that she was "deeply conscious of the loss of external nature's beauty." The reputation for extraordinary learning she was to have among critics and reviewers in future years may be traced to this account of her more than to any other one source. Horne wrote that in spite of her poor health she had been able to "attain and master more knowledge and accomplishments than are usually within the power of those of either sex who possess every adventitious opportunity, as well as health and industry."[48] Then he said without exaggeration that, "Probably no living individual has a more extensive and diffuse acquaintance with literature—that of the present day inclusive—than Miss Barrett." As for her poetry, which Elizabeth thought he disliked, Horne declared that she too often showed "an energetic morbidity on the subject of death, together with a certain predilection for 'terrors.'" He also said that she wrote 'like an inspired priestess . . . whose individuality is cast upward in the divine afflatus, and dissolved and carried off in the recipient breath of angelic ministrants."

Critical response to Horne's work, which was published on March 5, 1844,[49] was almost unanimously unfavorable. Some of the adverse comments were deserved, but reviewers were ignorant of the unusual difficulties Horne faced in preparing his book: the speed with which he had to assemble the material for the publisher, the necessity of having to reconcile with his own the opinions of his two fellow workers, one of whom, Miss Barrett, he never saw, and his lack of the editorial assistance which might have kept several inaccuracies from appearing in the final text. Shortly before publication he was so pressed with work that in passages where Elizabeth had indicated an objection in the margin of the proofs, he simply inserted "not" before a verb to reverse the meaning, or he substituted the name of another author in the same context. In reviewing what it called "The New Gull's Horne-Book," *Ainsworth's Magazine* [50] remarked that Hazlitt had been much wider in his sympathies than Horne and had offered a more comprehensive scheme: "He wrote of Wordsworth, and he wrote also of Bentham. In the number of *his* spirits, he included Moore, and he included Malthus too." The writer thought that the volume could hardly claim to portray the spirit of the age when it omitted almost all distinguished names unassociated with literature. The comment was unfair, for Horne had said in his preface that with two or three exceptions his work considered only names distinguished in literature and that if it were well received it would be followed by other books in the series, dealing with statesmen, scientists, and artists. Yet the review in *Ainsworth's* declared that even as an attempt to picture "a new literary spirit," Horne's effort was a failure, for he had selected the wrong names and had been capricious and offensive in his criticism of several figures who had been chosen to represent the age.

The *Westminster Review,* which was the organ of philosophical and political radicalism, humanitarianism, and social reform, was not always sympathetic to *belles lettres.* Thus it is not surprising that in its long article on Horne's volume, it sharply attacked the assumption that the spirit of the age was to be found in literature.[51] With typical early-Victorian optimism it proclaimed that "the prominent characteristic of the present age is physical progress, *i.e.* progress in all arts tending to diminish human drudgery, and ultimately to extinguish it." It is the inventor of machines, the engineer, the industrialist, and the technician who represent the spirit of the age, rather than the poet, the dramatist, and the novelist. The reviewer then examined Horne's writings, ridiculed most of them, and said that he was incompetent to pass judgment upon his contemporaries, that he was "unfitted even to distinguish them." Like the other notices of the work, it disapproved of the exclusion of many distinguished names in literature, and it thought that not a few of those who were mentioned were undeserving of the honor. Interestingly enough, the one essay which the review considered well done was the paper on Tennyson, which had been written by Elizabeth. An unsigned article in the *Athenaeum,* probably by Chorley, adversely criticized the book because it appeared to be the work only of a "literary *coterie*" and to represent "a peculiar view of a peculiar set of minds." [52] Since Elizabeth had been for a number of years one of Chorley's favorite writers, he complained that Horne's remarks on her did not do her justice: "We have to regret, that some of the peculiar excellencies of the latter lady [E. B. B.] are not so much as touched on. No writer on Miss Barrett's genius should have failed to award high honour to the Romaunt of 'Margret,' or done such scanty justice to the rare lyrical sweetness of some of her measures, as 'The Deserted Garden.' Her deep and quaint learning, her tendency and taste for mystical contemplation, are obvious beyond mistake; but of her merits as an artist, the public has not yet a sufficient relish." In New York, the *United States Magazine and Democratic Review* for July 1844 commented unfavorably on the book for the same reasons expressed in English periodicals.[53] In its review of the work, however, it referred its readers to "A Drama of Exile," the first half of which was printed in the same number, with an introductory paragraph (apparently by Mathews) that heaped lavish praise upon Elizabeth's poetry.[54]

After receiving so much abuse from all quarters, Horne realized that to compile another book in the projected series would prove an equally thankless task. In fact, before long he retreated from the literary world of London and lived for a while in Germany. Before he left, he terrified Elizabeth by asking if he might call upon her. She answered with her "usual 'no,' like a wild Indian," but he persevered and was granted an invitation. He was so busy, however, with preparations for his trip abroad that he failed to appear at the appointed time. "I clapped my hands for joy when I felt my danger to be passed," she later wrote Browning. After Horne left for a sojourn in Germany, his correspondence with Elizabeth became desultory, and they collaborated in no further projects. From Italy she wrote him three or four letters, telling of her experiences in Pisa and Florence. Browning and Elizabeth later saw him several times in England in the summer of 1851. Soon afterwards Horne emigrated to Australia, and Elizabeth heard from him no more.

8. "Poems" of 1844

ON MARCH 20, 1844, only about two weeks after the appearance of *A New Spirit of the Age,* Elizabeth sent to her printer material for the first sheet of her two volumes of verse. For two or three years she had enough new poems in manuscript to fill a volume but had been unable to find anyone who would undertake to publish them. In December of 1842 Edward Moxon had told George Barrett that however much he respected his sister's genius, he could not issue any of her work because of the poor market for poetry. Some two or three months later Moxon asked Kenyon to inform Elizabeth that he would very much like to publish her verses. It was Kenyon who seems to have persuaded Moxon to assume some of the risk, and as she composed further poems for her forthcoming publication, Kenyon was her everpresent confidant and adviser in all matters. Without his help and encouragement the volumes of 1844 would not have appeared in their present form; perhaps they would never have been published. "Dear Mr. Kenyon," she said of him, "has been my friend and helper, and my book's friend and helper! critic and sympathiser, true friend of all hours!"

Late in March Moxon advised her to bring out two volumes instead of the one she had originally planned. As for the title, she suggested they be called "New Poems,"[1] but he preferred simply "Poems"; his choice prevailed. He did not think that such a title would imply to readers the idea that they were being republished. A week before they were due to appear, Moxon noticed that the first volume was about seventy pages shorter than the second, and he proposed to transfer a number of poems from the end of the second volume to the first. Since she did not wish "The Dead Pan," which came at the end of the second volume, removed from that position, she finished a poem which had been lying half completed in her desk, by dashing off nineteen pages in one day. So, when the first volume was printed, the last forty pages comprised the ballad entitled "Lady Geraldine's Courtship."

On August 13 [2] Moxon issued from his establishment at 44 Dover Street Elizabeth's neat octavo volumes in dark green cloth boards. In addition to being a publisher, he was himself a poet and a friend of poets and had produced Monckton Milnes' *Memorials of a Tour in Some Parts of Greece,* Samuel Rogers' handsomely illustrated *Poems,* and the first collected editions of Shelley and of Keats; and he had recently published the verse of Wordsworth, Tennyson, Milnes, Sterling, Patmore, and Browning. The American edition under the title of *A Drama of Exile: and Other Poems* did not appear until October 5.[3] In the first paragraph of the preface of this edition Elizabeth wrote, "My love and admiration have belonged to the great American people, as long as I have felt proud of being an Englishwoman, and almost as long as I have loved poetry itself." She concluded the paragraph by addressing her "thanks to those sons of the soil, who, if strangers and foreigners, are yet kinsmen and friends, and who, if never seen, nor perhaps to be seen by eyes of mine, have already caused them to glisten by words of kindness and courtesy."

In view of all that Kenyon had done for Elizabeth, it would have been appropriate for her to have dedicated her *Poems* to him, but instead she gave that honor to her father, just as she had inscribed to him long ago her earliest printed verses. In the passage "To My Father" Elizabeth wrote, "And my desire is that you, who are a witness how if this art of poetry had been a less earnest object to me, it must have fallen from exhausted hands before this day,—that you, who have shared with me in things bitter and sweet, softening or enhancing them, every day,—that you, who hold with me over all sense of loss and transiency, one hope by one Name,—may accept from me the inscription of these volumes, the exponents of a few years of an existence which has been sustained and comforted by you as well as given." She concluded, "Somewhat more faint-hearted than I used to be, it is my fancy thus to seem to return to a visible personal dependence on you, as if indeed I were a child again; to conjure your beloved image between myself and the public, so as to be sure of one smile,—and to satisfy my heart while I sanctify my ambition, by associating with the great pursuit of my life, its tenderest and holiest affection." In the preface she said that she was offering to the public the poems she had written during the six years since the publication of her volume of *The Seraphim* and that all, "with the exception of a few contributions to English or American periodicals," were now being printed for the first time. But of the sixty-one poems in the volumes, twenty-five had already been published. In the last paragraph of the preface she put on the robes of a high priestess and solemnly explained the mysteries of her calling: "If it must be said of me that I have contributed immemoral verses to the many rejected by the age, it cannot at least be said that I have done so in a light and irresponsible spirit. Poetry has been as serious a thing to me as life itself; and life has been a very serious thing: there has been no playing at skittles for me in either. I never mistook pleasure for the final cause of poetry; nor leisure, for the hour of the poet." Finally, she believed that "the reverence and sincerity with which the work was done, should give it some protection with the reverent and sincere."

By far the longest and most ambitious poem in the volumes was "A Drama of Exile." Late in the previous autumn, as Elizabeth was looking over the manuscripts of her verses, she had come upon a fragment of a masque called "The First Day's Exile from Eden." The twenty lines of the original soon grew to somewhat more than two thousand as she put aside everything else and rapidly finished the work, writing "with continuous flow—from fifty to a hundred lines a day, and quite in a glow of pleasure and impulse all through." But after its completion she doubted whether the poem had any merit and hesitated to offer it for publication. At her request, Kenyon took it home. The next day he praised the poem, which he thought "very superior as a whole" to any of her earlier work. Today, however, much of the blank verse reads like a burlesque of *Paradise Lost,* and the choral passages sound like a parody of the choruses of Shelley's *Prometheus Unbound.* The subject, as she explained in the preface, was "the new and strange experience of the fallen humanity, as it went forth from Paradise into the wilderness; with a peculiar reference to Eve's allotted grief, which . . . appeared to me imperfectly apprehended hitherto, and more expressible by a woman than a man." Elizabeth had "attempted, in respect to Milton, what the Greek dramatists achieved lawfully in respect to Homer." By thus associating herself with some of the greatest writers of the drama and epic she made it clear that she wished to be judged by the highest standards.

The opening scene is "the outer gate of Eden shut fast with clouds." Rows and rows of angels cast from their swords a glare which "extends many miles into the wilderness." Adam and Eve are in the distance, and in the foreground Gabriel is speaking with Lucifer and ordering him to depart. The ruined angel, however, prefers to remain and is unmoved by the rhetoric of the divine emissary. While Adam and Eve "fly across the sword-glare," they hear a chorus of "Eden Spirits" who are "chanting from Paradise," with songs from "Spirits of the Trees," "River-Spirits," a "Bird-Spirit," and "Flower-Spirits." The first parents stop for a moment at "the extremity of the sword glare," where Eve expresses her contrition and the wish that Adam punish her. But he consoles her and thanks God for allowing Eve to stay with him. After a "faint and tender" chant of invisible angels, Lucifer appears again and mocks at the fallen pair. He vanishes as he hears the "Song of the Morning Star to Lucifer," from which the following lines may show why many critics found it incomprehensible:

> Around, around the firmamental ocean,
> I swam expanding with delirious fire!
> Around, around, around, in blind desire
> To be drawn upward to the Infinite—
> Ha, ha!

In the following scene, which takes place in "a wild open country seen vaguely in the approaching night," Eve says that she is terrified at the shapes of the Zodiac. Adam reassures her and explains the signs. Then "Two Spirits, of organic and inorganic nature" rise from the ground and bewail their fate of "undeserved perdition" because of the first sin. Their reproach brings tears to the eyes of Eve, who feels herself "Saddest and most defiled" and asks the spirits to pardon her and Adam. Lucifer returns to curse the two exiles and remind them of the "plagues," the "corruptions," and the "hideous forms of life and fears of death" which will afflict them and their descendants. A choral interlude of "philosophic voices," "love voices," "revel voices," and many other kinds of voices is followed by a "Vision of Christ" rebuking the earth spirits, reconciling them to Adam and Eve, and telling them of the future Incarnation, Crucifixion, and Redemption. The poem concludes with a long choral passage sung by "Invisible Angels," while Adam and Eve "advance into the desert, hand in hand."

Viewed as a whole, "A Drama of Exile" appeared even to Elizabeth's staunch supporters to be a complete failure. As the summary of the plot shows, the work has no central idea, no action, no conflict, no development of character. Elizabeth had only a hazy conception of what she was trying to express. The review in the *Spectator* said that most of the drama was nothing but verbiage, that Lucifer, for example, was "a mere talker, and rather a long-winded one, who is more given to railing and reverie than to practical speech."[4] Likewise *Blackwood's* spoke of the "vague and impalpable conceptions which form the staple of her poem, the dreamy and unpractical character of her style."[5] The reviewer disliked the lyrical passages, which were "frequently so inarticulate, so slovenly, and so defective, both in rhythm and rhyme, that we are really surprised how a person of her powers could have written them." Edgar Allan Poe, who reviewed the *Poems* in the *Broadway Journal*,[6] also disapproved of the choral songs: "We have none of us to be told that a medley of metaphysical recitatives sung out of tune, at Adam and Eve, by all manner of inconceivable abstractions, is not exactly the best material for a poem." Furthermore Poe thought that Elizabeth's Eve was a shadowy character: "She is a mystical something or nothing, enwrapped in a fog of rhapsody about Transfiguration, and the Seed, and the Bruising of the Heel, and other talk of a nature that no man ever pretended to understand in plain prose." As for the appearance of Christ as an interlocutor, an unsigned article in the *New Quarterly Review*, probably by Chorley, expressed the prevailing consensus that it was "a serious defect in poetic taste."[7] Elizabeth herself feared that some of her readers might think that the time of the drama, which was only one sunset, was insufficient for so much traveling and for so many long conversations. To anticipate their objections she wrote in her preface that very little was known about the length of the evenings before the flood and that for her part she could not "believe in an Eden without the longest of purple twilights."

The shorter poems were more admired by Elizabeth's friends and critics than were "A Drama of Exile" and "A Vision of Poets." Among the verses which appeared for the first time in the volumes of 1844, "Lady Geraldine's Courtship: a Romance of the Age" found favor not only with Carlyle and Miss Martineau but with almost all her readers. Lady Geraldine is similar to Tennyson's Lady Clara Vere de Vere in wealth and social status, but Elizabeth's poem has a romantic conclusion. The story is told from the point of view of Bertram, "a poor poet," who was "born of English peasants." He "could not choose but love" Lady Geraldine, "an earl's daughter," with many "halls" and "castles." She has "resonant steam-eagles" (a term which puzzled several reviewers) and retainers who "bow before her, as her chariot sweeps their doorways." Although she has "lovers in the palace," she becomes interested in the poet and invites him to visit her at one of her country houses. Among the other guests are "lovely London ladies" and many high-born suitors. When Geraldine and Bertram are alone together, he reads aloud from Petrarch, Spenser, Wordsworth, Tennyson,

> Or from Browning some "Pomegranate," which, if cut
>   deep down the middle,
> Shows a heart within blood-tinctured, of a veined
>   humanity!—

He later overhears an earl ask for Geraldine's hand and her reply that the man she marries will be "noble" and "wealthy" and that she will "never blush to think how he was born." Bertram supposes that she is scornful of himself and favors her noble suitor. After the earl leaves, he abuses her with so many "mad words" that when she replies by merely uttering his name, he is "struck down before her" and, unconscious, is taken by the servants to his chamber. At the end of the poem Geraldine comes to his room and declares her love, "While the shining tears ran faster down the blushing of her cheeks." Then Bertram falls on his knees in adoration.

The "Rhyme of the Duchess May" is no less ridden with clichés. In its subject matter and treatment it is similar to such earlier poems as "The Romaunt of the Page" and "The Lay of the Brown

Rosary," both of which were reprinted in the volumes of 1844. The Duchess May, "a Duke's fair orphan-girl," is disdainful of "Lord Leigh, the churl," to whom she had been betrothed by her uncle and protector, the elder Lord Leigh, since the age of twelve "for the sake of dowry gold." She escapes from father and son and elopes with Sir Guy of Linteged to his castle, which is soon afterward attacked by the Leighs. After fourteen days of siege Sir Guy resolves to spare further bloodshed by sacrificing himself. He asks that his horse be led up the winding staircase to the top of the turret. His retainers think him "grief-distraught" to make such a strange request, but they obey without question. When he prepares to ride over the edge, his "noble wife" foresees his mad purpose and leaps into the saddle beside him. His knights catch at the rein, but too late, for both horse and riders topple below.

"Bertha in the Lane" is also a sentimental treatment of the subject of death. It represents the last words of a girl who resolved to die as soon as she learned that her supposed fiancé had transferred his affection to her younger sister. The concluding line has the merit of brevity: "I aspire while I expire!" Two other poems in much the same vein are "Catarina to Camoëns" and "The Mournful Mother." In the former, Catarina on her deathbed recalls the verses in which Camoëns, who is now abroad, had "recorded the sweetness of her eyes." The chief interest in the poem is that it "greatly impressed" Robert Browning before he "became personally acquainted with their writer whose condition in certain respects had, at one time or so I fancied," he wrote long after his wife's death, "resembled those of the Portuguese Caterina." [8] The mournful mother in the poem of that title is weeping because of the recent death of her blind child, but the poet tells her to dry her tears, for he now "walks in light," and to wait

>Until ye two give meeting
>   Where the great Heaven-gate is,
>And *he* shall lead thy feet in,
>   As once thou leddest *his!*

In its material and treatment this poem is similar to "Isobel's Child" in the volume of *The Seraphim*. Although "The Mournful

Mother" now seems among the most mawkish of Elizabeth's poems, it had precisely the qualities which appealed to many of her readers. For example, the *Examiner* thought it the "most perfect" of her poems because of the "exquisite pathos in its beauty" and quoted much of it in its review of Elizabeth's volumes.

The verses entitled "A Portrait" describe Mr. Barrett's ten-year-old cousin and ward, Georgina Elizabeth (Lizzie) Barrett, who was a member of the household at 50 Wimpole Street. Her mother was insane, and her father [9] in the West Indies may not have had the right type of home in which to bring up a daughter. She stayed in her foster home until she married Elizabeth's brother Alfred Barrett in 1855. Another poem with personal associations was "Wine of Cyprus," addressed to H. S. Boyd to acknowledge the gift of a vial of Greek wine, the taste of which "reminded one of oranges and orange flower together, to say nothing of the honey of Mount Hymettus." Elizabeth recalls the "golden hours" long ago when she read Greek with him in his cottage at the foot of the Malvern Hills:

> And I think of those long mornings
>   Which my Thought goes far to seek,
> When, betwixt the folio's turnings,
>   Solemn flowed the rhythmic Greek.
> Past the pane, the mountain spreading,
>   Swept the sheep-bell's tinkling noise,
> While a girlish voice was reading,—
>   Somewhat low for $\alpha\iota$'s and $o\iota$'s!

One of the most successful poems was "The Romance of the Swan's Nest." *Blackwood's* praised it particularly for its "graceful playfulness of manner and sentiment, which shows how heartily the amiable authoress can enter into the sympathies and enjoyments of a child." At the beginning "Little Ellie sits alone," dreaming of the noble lover who will come riding on a handsome steed, dismount, and kneel at her feet. Then "soul-tied by one troth," she will take him to her swan's nest. But when on her way home she pays it her daily visit, she sees that "the wild swan had deserted" and "a rat had gnawed the reeds."

> Ellie went home sad and slow!
> If she found the lover ever,
>   With his red-roan steed of steeds,
>   Sooth I know not! but I know
> She could show him never—never,
>   That swan's nest among the reeds!

Among the sonnets, two of the boldest were those addressed to George Sand, whom Elizabeth in a letter to Chorley once called with her usual exaggeration "the first female genius of any country or age." Kenyon told Elizabeth that she was "a daring person" to publish them and that a guest of his had recently said that "no modest woman would or *ought* to confess to an acquaintance with the works of George Sand." [10] The sonnet "Past and Future" affected Browning when he first saw it, as he later wrote, "more than any poem I ever read." It expressed the idea she was to reiterate with many variations in her love letters, that she then thought her "life was ended."

> My wine hath run
> Indeed out of my cup, and there is none
> To gather up the bread of my repast
> Scattered and trampled!

The poems of 1844 represent the fruit of some six years of intermittent poetical activity. Much had happened in her life since the publication of *The Seraphim*. She felt that as she matured, she had gained in constructive ability and had eliminated some of her faults of expression. In comparing "A Drama of Exile" with "The Seraphim," she thought the former was "fuller, freer and stronger, and worth the other three times over," and the two volumes as a whole far superior to all she had written before. She forwarded copies to her close friends and to Wordsworth, Landor, Carlyle, Miss Martineau, and Leigh Hunt, to the latter of whom she was especially grateful for his having written of her as "the most imaginative poetess that has appeared in England, perhaps in Europe." [11] Then she anxiously awaited their replies and the first reviews. "It is awful enough, this looking forward to be reviewed," she wrote to Westwood late in August. She soon heard from everyone who had received the volumes. Carlyle's advice was not helpful: that a person of her " 'insight and veracity' ought to use 'speech' rather than 'song' in these days of crisis." [12] Harriet Martineau wrote of her "immense advance" on her former volume and said that she had greatly improved "in the whole art of utterance." The "predominant impression" of the verse upon Miss Martineau was of its "originality"; it seemed to her as fresh as if no one had ever written poetry before.[13] Elizabeth heard from Thomas Noon Talfourd in the Lake District that he liked her books and that they had been "the companions of his pleasantest walks in that romantic country."[14] Dante Gabriel Rossetti and his brother William Michael "revelled" in her works "with profuse delight." Such poems as "A Drama of Exile," the "Rhyme of the Duchess May," and "Lady Geraldine's Courtship" held the Rossetti brothers "spellbound," so that they read them "more than half-a-hundred times over" and learned to recite them from memory.[15] From America James Russell Lowell and Lydia Sigourney sent messages of congratulation. The latter wrote, as Elizabeth told Boyd with pride, that "the sound of my poetry is stirring the 'deep green forests of the New World.'"

Early in September, Chorley, who had reviewed her sympathetically in two different journals, thanked her for "the pleasant emotions" her *Poems* had excited. He wrote that he had followed her career "step by step" ever since she had begun to print and that her recent volumes "were so much better than any preceding them, and were such *living books,* that they restored to him the impulses of his youth." Chorley was a friend of Miss Mitford, who several times had asked Elizabeth to admit him to her room. But as she had illogically written to Miss Mitford in explaining why she could see Browning, though not Chorley, *"Now a line must be drawn*—or my sepulchre must be prepared—do you not see the necessity?"[16] From that decision Miss Mitford could not appeal. Elizabeth exchanged letters with him from time to time as long as she lived, but she did not see him until the summer of 1852, when she and Browning dined one evening at his London home.

Although the volumes brought her little money at first, they had such a steady sale that a new edition was called for six years later. The *Poems* of 1844 were praised by the leading critical journals and were more widely reviewed than any of her earlier works. Most of the poems now seem diffuse, sentimental, and trite. What qualities did many well-known writers and responsible critics find in her that so delighted them?

Although Elizabeth was "without a single personal friend among these critics," she thought herself "singularly happy" in her reviews and had "full reason for gratitude to the profession." On both sides of the Atlantic the most-respected journals published long and thoughtful reviews; and while they mentioned many deficiencies in her verse, they also found much to praise. The *British Quarterly Review* said that, "She possesses genius, a cultivated mind, a truth-loving heart, quick powers of observation, and luxuriance of fancy and expression." [17] *Tait's Edinburgh Magazine* called her volumes "the out-pourings of a pure and noble spirit, disciplined by study, and by the greater discipline of sorrow, revealed in tones which are musical by the greatness, depth, and music of the thoughts." [18] *Blackwood's* wrote that her "powers appear to us to extend over a wider and profounder range of thought and feeling, than ever before fell within the intellectual compass of any of the softer sex"; and it declared that she was "gifted with very extraordinary powers of mind" and that "her genius is profound, unsullied, and without a flaw." [19] It concluded that, "Were the blemishes of her style tenfold more numerous than they are, we should still revere this poetess as one of the noblest of her sex." H. F. Chorley in the *Athenaeum* added his praise to that of the others by characterizing her volumes as "remarkable manifestations of female power." [20]

Many other journals were even more extravagant in their expressions of approval. The writer in the *Atlas* experienced a "lively pleasure" in reading her poetry, with its "almost endless variety of subject," its "tuneful harmony," its "supreme sense of beauty," and its "happy thought most happily evolved"; he asserted that her volumes showed "extraordinary power, and . . . extraordinary genius." [21] The *Metropolitan Magazine* spoke of her "deep piety," "bold and original thought," "newness of simile," and "suggestive description," and it said that "she seems to us 'one bright particular star,' shining from a firmament of her own." In his concluding sentence the reviewer held "a bright augury" for Elizabeth's poetical reputation—that she would be, "as she deserves to be, esteemed and admired at once and throughout future generations." [22] The *Monthly Review* thought that it "would be difficult to name within the range of the poetry of the last quarter of a century, a publication that presents so much of independent effort, of original power, and of sterling beauties, as do these volumes." [23] And to the *Prospective Review,* Elizabeth's work represented the "Phoenix of true Poetry," which was rising again from its ashes.[24] The *New Monthly,*[25] *Ainsworth's Magazine,*[26] and the London *Globe* [27] were no less favorable. It is no wonder that after reading such glowing estimates of herself, Elizabeth wrote Cornelius Mathews, "Your kindness will be glad to learn of the prosperity of my poems in my own country. I am more than satisfied in my most sanguine hope for them, and a little surprised besides."

While some of the reviews were uncritically laudatory throughout, the notices appearing in the most influential journals were in agreement that the poems had the same lapses in expression which disfigured her former volumes. The *British Quarterly Review,* which Elizabeth later wrote to Browning, "has been abusing me so at large, that I can take it to be the achievement of a very particular friend indeed," objected to her "fantastic images and phrases." Although the reviewer had spoken warmly of her poetry in another part of his article, he felt that much of what she had written was unintelligible because her thoughts did not seem to have been clearly conceived. "And the case is rendered more hopeless by her attributing it, not as one would have expected, to her own feeble grasp of her subject, and defective power of expression, but . . . to her thoughts being too sublime and grand to be spoken out in clear, connected phrase." An article in the *Critic* also condemned her style for its obscurity and affectation; it seemed to the writer that she mistook "vagueness for sublimity, and the chaos of a dream for a creation." [28] Yet reviews often cancel each other, for the *Eclectic Review* named "conciseness as one of Miss Barrett's distinguishing excellencies," and the writer defined "conciseness" as "fulness of meaning, conveyed in few and simple words." [29] The *Prospective Review* said in her defense, "Those who offer . . . objections are not in a position to understand her.

... Our authoress has risen above their horizon, and she must on no account stoop to lift up into it those whom she has left behind."

Almost all the reviewers disliked her false rhymes. In attempting to defend herself against the charge of carelessness, she explained to Boyd that she had used double rhymes with slightly different vowel sounds "after much thoughtful study of the Elizabethan writers," and she added, "If I deal too much in licences, it is not because I am idle, but because I am speculative for freedom's sake. It is possible, you know, to be wrong conscientiously; and I stand up for my conscience only." Nevertheless such rhymes as "shade is" and "Hades," "Hellas" and "tell us," "Niades" and "and breeze," "glories" and "floorwise" can have for most readers only a comic effect.

The *Westminster Review*, which Elizabeth described as "our most influential quarterly (after the 'Edinburgh' and right 'Quarterly')," commented on the absence of humor in her verses. It attributed her style, which was "not unfrequently, wanting the ease of colloquial expression," to her long seclusion during which she had lived too much in the world of books; thus, in the opinion of the reviewer, the development of her poetical powers had been weakened rather than aided.[30] Yet she herself well understood that her ignorance of many aspects of life beyond the confines of her room was a severe handicap to her art. "How willingly," she later wrote Browning, "I would as a poet exchange some of this lumbering, ponderous, helpless knowledge of books, for some experience of life and man." The *Westminster Review* pointed out that the defects of many of her poems were "the result of rapidity of composition." Elizabeth told of the speed with which she wrote "A Drama of Exile" and "Lady Geraldine's Courtship," and no doubt she also finished other poems with equal haste. Yet she always believed that she took great care both in the original composition of her verses and in their revisions. "I have *worked* at poetry—it has not been with me reverie, but art," she said to Horne. In the same spirit she told Kenyon, "Very few writers . . . pay more laborious attention than I do habitually to the forms of thought and expression." The *John Bull*, which Elizabeth learned had cut her up "with sanguinary gashes, for the edification of its

Sabbath readers," poked fun at her prolixity. It gave as an example part of a sentence in her preface, in which she wrote that "A Drama of Exile" was the longest poem which she had ever "trusted into the current of publication," instead of the simpler "published." [31] A review in the *Examiner,* written probably by John Forster, also censured her for verbosity: "She uses *all* her thoughts and feelings for whatever she does. The art of knowing what to keep and what to reject, she has not attained." [32]

IN AMERICA Elizabeth's literary reputation had been steadily increasing for two or three years before the publication in New York of her volumes of 1844. Her poems in *Graham's* and other American magazines were making her known in the literary circles of New York and Boston. The *New York Daily Tribune* for July 15, 1844, printed "Pain in Pleasure" from the August issue of *Graham's* and called the poem "an exquisite thought by Mrs. [sic] E. B. Barrett." In the same newspaper, on November 27, the writer of a review of Rufus W. Griswold's *The Poets and Poetry of England, in the Nineteenth Century,*[33] which contained a critique on Elizabeth Barrett, mentioned having "read, admired, and copied 'The Romaunt of Margret' from a London magazine, years before we heard that it was written by Elizabeth B. Barrett, and even before we knew there was such a woman." Griswold's critical sketch of Elizabeth, which had been written before he saw *A Drama of Exile: and Other Poems,* is remarkably full and generous in its praise. He knew about her because he had been an assistant editor of *Graham's* during the years when it published many of her poems. Although American readers, he said, had not yet seen many of her verses, she had "already made herself a home in the hearts of the people; a proof that the popular taste does not lie altogether in the direction of sing-song echoes, sickly sentiment, or empty blank verse; a proof, too, in her own case, that the most varied acquirements of learning do not impair the subtlest delicacy of thought and feeling." It is of interest that in contrast to these handsome eulogies in *The Poets and Poetry of England, in the Nineteenth Century,* Griswold in the same volume disposed of Robert Browning in only one short paragraph, which dealt mainly with his alleged obscurity.

The many American reviews of Elizabeth's volumes praised and blamed them for much the same reasons which were being expressed in her own country. Cornelius Mathews wrote an article on her poems in the *United States Magazine and Democratic Review*.[34] Since he had been one of her warmest admirers in America and had recently helped her volumes through the press, he spoke with reverence of the "most exquisite utterances of the divine soul of poetry that glows within her, generated of the sweetest union of womanly tenderness of heart and masculine loftiness and power of intellect."[35] He praised "A Drama of Exile" for its "lyrical, descriptive, and dramatic forces all in unison" and for the "complete and harmonious impression" it left in the reader's mind; and he declared that "A Vision of Poets" was "one of the finest pieces of criticism in the language." The *Methodist Quarterly Review* found "no two qualities more manifest in her than *intensity* and *deep religious feeling*" and maintained that among the "spiritual poets" she was "at the very head."[36] The *Christian Examiner* placed her "in the centre of that constellation of our favourites, Keats, Hood, Sterling, Tennyson, Emerson, Lowell," and it declared that in "bold imagination, beautiful fancy, and tender humanity . . . she surpasses all other living writers."[37] The author of the article found it "inspiring to meet such lofty genius blended with such meek simplicity of Christian faith—such purity—such peace." His further assertion that "Elizabeth Barrett is herself, and not another or others" is a characteristic example of the reviewing in the literary journals of that period. The *American Whig Review* in January 1845 said that there were only two English poets of the new generation who were great: Miss Barrett and Tennyson, and the latter was "certainly not as favorable a representative of the manly character as Miss Barrett is of the feminine."[38] And Margaret Fuller, who was to meet Elizabeth in Florence several years later, did not "hesitate to rank her, in vigour and nobleness of conception, depth of spiritual experience, and command of classic allusion, above any female writer the world has yet known."[39]

Some of the American notices, however, strongly disapproved of many aspects of her poetry and were surprised that most critics had treated her with such respect. Edwin Percy Whipple in the

American Whig Review for July 1845 was offended by her many pedantries, her "barbarous jargon compounded of all languages," and her "elaborately infelicitous style"; [40] and the *Knickerbocker* felt "ready to despair of Miss Barrett as an artist." [41] The writer of the critique in *Graham's* was baffled by much of Elizabeth's poetry, the first reading of which, he thought, "produces pain in the eyes." He added that, "The brain staggers beneath the weight of her compound epithets, or falls back exhausted in striving to follow or unriddle her dark subtlety of fancy." [42] The harshest criticism came from the *Southern Literary Messenger,* which expatiated upon all the deficiencies mentioned by other reviews and enumerated many others. The reviewer acknowledged, however, that he was presenting a minority report and concluded that "the more *outré* and unnatural a writer is, the more lavishly and unscrutinizingly is praise heaped over him." [43]

One of the most comprehensive of the American notices was by the poet Poe. Of his review in the *Broadway Journal* Elizabeth later said to Browning, "You would have thought that it had been written by a friend and foe, each stark mad with love and hate, and writing the alternate paragraphs." Rather than her long, ambitious pieces, he preferred the simpler poems like "The House of Clouds" and "The Lost Bower," both of which, he believed, were "superlatively lovely, and show the vast powers of the poet in the field best adapted to their legitimate display." He thought that she was deficient in rhythm, and he disapproved of her inadmissible rhymes, of her overabundant and inappropriate imagery, of her archaic and "quaint" diction (for example, "blé," " 'gins," " 'las," " 'ware," "oftly," "erelong"), of her "excessive reiteration of pet *words*" (such as "chrism," "nympholeptic," "down," "leaning"), and of her fondness for compound epithets (for example, "dew-pallid," "pale-passioned," "silver-solemn"). Poe was evidently puzzled by Elizabeth's character and personality. He wrote that her seclusion from the world gave her "a comparative independence of men and opinions" and "a happy audacity of thought and expression never before known in one of her sex"; yet in the following sentence he contradicted himself by saying that her isolation had perhaps "invalidated her original Will—diverted her from proper individuality of purpose—and seduced her into the sin of imitation." The main theme of his article is that Elizabeth had never shown herself capable of any sustained effort, that "her wild and magnificent genius" seemed to exhaust itself in short passages. Yet in spite of his adverse criticisms he declared that she had "done more, in poetry, than any woman, living or dead," and that she had "surpassed all her poetical contemporaries of either sex (with a single exception)." [44] Only Tennyson, he implied, was a greater poet.

Thus Elizabeth had been welcomed by critics on both sides of the Atlantic as one of England's great poets. But she had been given a friendly warning by most of the reviews to express herself with greater simplicity and compression, to restrict herself to more conventional rhymes, and to deal only with subjects close to her own experience. Unfortunately for her artistic development she was never in her later career (with two or three exceptions) to heed their advice.

9. Robert Browning

"I HAD A LETTER from Browning the poet last night, which threw me into ecstasies [Elizabeth wrote Mrs. Martin]—Browning, the author of 'Paracelsus,' and king of the mystics." Soon after his return from Italy in the middle of December 1844 Robert Browning picked up Elizabeth's *Poems,* which Kenyon had recently sent to Sarianna Browning,[1] the sister of the poet, and found in "Lady Geraldine's Courtship" the lines addressed to himself—the most generous recognition he had yet received from a fellow poet. His friend John Kenyon had often told him about Elizabeth and had encouraged him to make her acquaintance. Once Kenyon had all but introduced him to her, but she had been "too unwell." If Browning could not see her, he would write to tell her how delighted he was with her poems. Kenyon sent him a note to say that Elizabeth would be "pleased" to hear from him. "I love your verses with all my heart," he began his first letter to her on January 10. "Into me has it gone, and part of me has it become," he wrote, "this great living poetry of yours." He was enchanted with "the fresh strange music, the affluent language, the exquisite pathos and true new brave thought." [2]

Into what kind of family had Robert Browning been born, and how had he spent the years before this letter to Elizabeth? Like the Barretts, the Brownings also had a West Indian background, for the first wife of the poet's paternal grandfather, Robert Browning, was Margaret Tittle, who had been brought up in St. Kitts and Jamaica. She and her husband settled in Camberwell, then a quiet village near London, and he was at first a clerk and later a responsible and well-paid official in the Bank of England. Before her sudden death, while her children were still in their infancy, she had given birth to a son Robert, the poet's father; a daughter; and a second son, who died when he was a baby.

Robert Browning the elder married again and before long had

a large family for whom he had to provide. So he made arrangements for his eldest son to work in St. Kitts on the plantation which had formerly been managed by Margaret Tittle's father. But for a boy who was so studious, artistic, and sensitive, a planter's life in the eighteenth century was degrading and inhuman. He "conceived such a hatred to the slave-system in the West Indies," Browning the poet told Elizabeth about his father, "that he relinguished every prospect,—supported himself, while there, in some other capacity, and came back, while yet a boy, to his father's profound astonishment and rage." After his return he "had the intention of devoting himself to art, for which he had many qualifications and abundant love—but the quarrel with his father, —who . . . continued to hate him till a few years before his death,—induced him to go at once and consume his life after a fashion he always detested." Like his father he secured a position in the Bank of England. Just before he retired in 1852, after almost fifty years of faithful service, he was earning about £320 a year,[3] which was very much less than the top salary achieved by his more practical but less complicated father. He merely endured banking to earn a living for his family; his real interests were art, literature, and the collecting of books. Reuben Browning, the half-brother of the poet's father, wrote of "his wonderful store of information" on all subjects, his "love of reading," and his knowledge of old books and of bookstalls in London.[4] In 1811 he married Sarah Anna Wiedemann, of mixed Scottish and German parentage, who had been living recently with an uncle at Camberwell. Mrs. Orr, who was a close friend of Robert Browning the poet in his later years, refers to her "distinctly evangelical Christianity."[5] It was through Sarah's influence, not that of the poet's father, that the Browning family worshiped at the Congregational Chapel at York Street in Walworth.

The Brownings' first child, Robert, was born on May 7, 1812, at their home on Southampton Street, Camberwell; two years later the arrival of Sarianna completed the family circle. Like Elizabeth Barrett, Robert was "precocious" and produced "verses at six years old, and drawings still earlier." His education was like hers also in that he acquired most of it at home, reading at will in his father's library of several thousand volumes in Greek, Latin,

Hebrew, and many modern languages. He did, however, receive some formal schooling, for at the age of eight or nine he was sent to a school in Peckham, run by the Misses Ready and the Reverend Mr. Thomas Ready. For five or six years he boarded there during the week, going home for weekends and vacations. Only once again was he confined to a classroom. In the autumn of 1828 he was enrolled as a student in Greek, German, and Latin at the newly founded University of London on Gower Street, but he suddenly withdrew without completing the following spring term and stayed at home, reading and practicing music. He was no recluse, however, for he took part in "dancing, riding, boxing, and fencing, and excelled in the more active of these pursuits." [6] Another similarity between him and Elizabeth was his unusual dependence upon his family. He had lived in lodgings at Bedford Square, which he had secured to be near the University, only one week before homesickness compelled him to leave. Mrs. Orr says that he never "willingly spent a night away from home" and that "even an agreeable visit had no power to detain him beyond a few days." [7] She also tells of a "tender little bond" between Robert and his mother: as long as he lived at home, "it was his rule never to go to bed without giving her a good-night kiss." [8] Just before he married, he confessed to Elizabeth that if there was one thing he should regret, it was that the close ties between him and his family must be cut. "There was always a great delight to me in this prolonged relation of childhood," he explained.

His first collection of poems, which he wrote when he was twelve or thirteen, was not published at the expense of an indulgent father, like Elizabeth Barrett's *The Battle of Marathon,* but was destroyed by the poet himself. His first published work, *Pauline,* that "altogether foolish" poem, as its author later said of it, appeared anonymously in March 1833. Both in its biographical significance and in the melody of the verse, this "fragment of a confession" has far more interest and merit than Elizabeth's "pedantic" and "pert" *An Essay on Mind,* which was also published when the writer was twenty. In *Pauline* Browning tells of the spell which Shelley had cast over him and his "strange regret" that the "sun-treader" is no longer the sole object of his worship. Elizabeth had also read in her youth Shelley and Tom Paine and

Voltaire, yet she never, like Browning, passed through a phase of atheism and vegetarianism. But for Browning, Shelleyan libertarianism proved too heady a draught, and he soon felt "A need, a trust, a yearning after God." Much shaken by the experience, he returned to his mother's "strict dissent," but the memory of this brief defection colored his thought during the best years of his poetic career. John Stuart Mill wrote in the first sentence of a penciled comment at the end of his copy of *Pauline* that "the writer seems to me possessed with a more intense and morbid self-consciousness than I ever knew in any sane human being." [9] This copy, which had been sent by Browning's friend William Johnson Fox to Mill for him to review, was later returned to Fox, who then gave it back to the poet. It may have been Mill's success in penetrating into the poet's confused mind which made Browning resolve never again to "lay my soul bare"; henceforth he would "only make men and women speak."

Three years before his death Browning said that as far as he knew, "no single copy of the original edition of *Pauline* found a buyer; the book was undoubtedly 'stillborn.'" [10] He exaggerated, for although it had no public sale, it received several favorable reviews. The notice by Fox in the *Monthly Repository* was unstinting in its praise and said that the poem had "truth and life in it, which gave us the thrill, and laid hold of us with the power, the sensation of which has never yet failed us as a test of genius. Whoever the anonymous author may be, he is a poet." [11]

Two years afterward, in 1835, *Paracelsus* was published. Browning later referred to the poem as "a failure" and added that until Forster's notice *"every* journal that thought worth while to allude to the poem at all, treated it with entire contempt." Again, his account of the reception of one of his books is unreliable. Except for a somewhat unfavorable review in the *Athenaeum,* which long rankled within him, almost all the notices were enthusiastic. John Forster's first review, which was in the *Examiner,* called the poem a work of "unequivocal power," predicted for Browning "a brilliant career," and attributed to him "all the elements of a fine poet." [12] Half a year after his first review, Forster praised the volume again, even more warmly, in a long article in the *New Monthly Magazine* of March 1836.[13] He believed that the poem opened "a deeper vein of thought, of feeling, and of passion" than any other work which had appeared in many years. "Without the slightest hesitation," he named Browning "at once with Shelley, Coleridge, Wordsworth" and added, "He has entitled himself to a place among the acknowledged poets of the age." The publication of *Paracelsus* gained Browning an entrée into the literary circles of London. In addition to Fox, who made many of the introductions for him, he soon became acquainted with Forster, W. C. Macready, Bryan Waller Procter, Thomas Noon Talfourd, Landor, Wordsworth, Carlyle, Horne, Kenyon, Miss Martineau, and Mrs. Jameson. Browning at the age of twenty-four might well be satisfied with the rapid growth of his reputation among a small but influential group. He must have been particularly pleased that Wordsworth should have toasted his health at the dinner at Talfourd's home, May 26, 1836, after the opening performance of *Ion*. From the point of view of their importance in their respective literary reputations, Browning's *Paracelsus* may be compared with Elizabeth's *The Seraphim, and Other Poems*. Both volumes were the first works in which their authors' names appeared on the title pages; both writers were reviewed in the leading critical journals, were greeted as poets of unusual ability, and were reproved for incoherence and for mannerisms in diction and grammar. Unlike Browning, Elizabeth made no new friendships from the publication of her volume, for soon after its appearance she had to leave for Torquay.

Since Browning had always been fond of the theater, it is not surprising that he accepted Macready's challenge to him at the *Ion* dinner: "Write a play, Browning, and keep me from going to America." [14] He wrote *Strafford*, which had its first performance at the Covent Garden Theater on May 1, 1837, with Macready and Helen Faucit in the leading parts. The play had a very short run, with steadily decreasing audiences, for *Strafford*, like Browning's other dramas, was not suitable for stage presentation.

How did he appear to one of his friends during these years when he was becoming known in London? Mrs. Bridell-Fox later described him as "slim and dark, and very handsome; and—may I hint it—just a trifle of a dandy, addicted to lemon-coloured kid-gloves and such things . . . But full of ambition, eager for success, eager for fame, and, what's more, determined to conquer fame and to achieve success." [15]

In 1838 he made his second trip abroad; four years earlier he had gone with the Russian consul general to St. Petersburg. He went to Italy, where he remained only a month, visiting Venice, Asolo, Bassano, Vicenza, Padua, and several other nearby cities. Upon his return, with the scenery of northern Italy fresh in mind, he made another attempt to finish *Sordello,* upon which he had been at work a number of years. It was the publication of that poem in 1840 which put his reputation under a cloud for many years and delayed the recognition due him until after his wife's death. Many journals failed to notice the poem, and those which reviewed it were unanimous in their opinion that it was incomprehensible. Elizabeth Barrett, who spoke more kindly of it than anyone else, said it was "like a noble picture with its face to the wall just now —or at least, in the shadow."

After his unhappy experience with *Sordello* he made during the next three years several unsuccessful attempts to become a popular playwright. Macready refused *King Victor and King Charles* and *The Return of the Druses.* Then at Browning's insistence he unwillingly produced at the Drury Lane Theater in February 1843 *A Blot in the 'Scutcheon,* which was an ignominious failure and closed after a run of three nights. At the conclusion of the performances, both the producer and the poet had become so exasperated with each other that their friendship was ruptured, and for many years they did not converse or correspond. The only other stage play from Browning's pen was *Colombe's Birthday,* which had been written for the actor Charles Kean. When Browning showed it to him in March 1844 he was not eager to produce it, and the poet suddenly decided to publish it as one of the pamphlets in his series of *Bells and Pomegranates.* The play remained unacted until Helen Faucit's production at the Haymarket Theater in April 1853. The failures in the early forties of all his stage plays and of *Sordello,* coming as they did so soon after the favorable reception of *Paracelsus,* painfully depressed his spirits. "So glides this foolish life away, week by week," he wrote in 1843 to his old friend Alfred Domett, who was then in New Zealand.[16] When Browning sailed from England in the autumn of 1844, he was in a much less confident mood than he had been when he made his first visit to Italy. This time he stayed longer and visited chiefly Naples and Rome. After his return from abroad, he went back to the home of his parents, with whom he had been living. Mr. and Mrs. Browning had moved late in 1840 from Camberwell and were now in possession of a larger house in New Cross, Hatcham, farther out of the city along "the interminable Kent Road."

It was late in December when Browning first saw Elizabeth Barrett's *Poems*. At that time he "was scheming how to get done with England and go to my heart in Italy," as he later wrote his fiancée, and he was confident that nothing could divert him from his intended way of life. In January 1845 when he wrote his first letter to Elizabeth, he was within four months of his thirty-third birthday. He had never been in love, although he had enjoyed the friendship of three women, all of them interested in literature and the arts and all somewhat older than he: Eliza and Sarah Flower, the wards of W. J. Fox, and Euphrasia Fanny Haworth. Despite his resolve to return to Italy, he was so dependent upon his family that one suspects he would not have gone there later but for the love affair which was so completely to alter the pattern of his life.

WHEN Elizabeth began her correspondence with Browning, she supposed that she had already seen the best years of her life. Her "face was so close against the tombstones, that there seemed no room even for the tears"; many similar expressions appear in her letters and poems. To be sure, she received a lively pleasure from publishing her verse and from reading the many flattering reviews. While she was correcting proof sheets for her volumes of 1844, she wrote to Boyd that, "All the life and strength which are in me, seem to have passed into my poetry." Yet whenever the momentary exhilaration died away, she always felt that her poetry was far outside of herself, that it had a "factitious personality" which was divorced from her own; it was "a mockery and a bitterness when people persisted in confounding one with another." Thus ever since her heart had been "broken by that great stone that fell out of Heaven," she had lived "blindly and darkly" and "completely dead to hope of any kind." It was "a thoroughly morbid and desolate state."

The one living person she loved most was her father. Once his absence for a few days in Cornwall depressed her, she wrote, for "his presence or the sense of his nearness" always had upon her "so much cheering and soothing influence." In the last summer of their courtship she told Browning that her father "might have been king and father over me *to* the end, if he had thought it worth while to love me openly enough." She would have remained so close to him that Browning would never have been permitted the opportunity of proving his affection for her.

Like Browning, Elizabeth had never been in love. When she lived at Hope End, several persons may have asked her to marry them. In writing later to Miss Mitford of her marriage, she said that "years ago, in my best days, as a woman's days are counted," when she had never imagined that a man whom she could love would love her, she had been "gently upbraided for such romantic fancies . . . and for not taking Mr. A or B or C for the 'best possible' whatever might be." [17] And in a letter to Browning she wrote that she had "never thought it probable or possible" that she should ever have occasion for such a choice "except perhaps when the door of life was just about to open . . before it opened." The Barretts lived in such seclusion in Herefordshire, and Elizabeth had so few acquaintances later in Sidmouth, that her remark is puzzling. In her unusually detailed correspondence she mentioned everyone with whom she conversed or exchanged letters from the age of six to the last few weeks of her life, and no one seems to have come close enough to her in her early years to be identified with "Mr. A or B or C."

The four men outside of her own family to whom Elizabeth had been most warmly attached before Browning entered her life were Boyd, Hunter, Kenyon, and Horne. She had always been very fond of Kenyon and was grateful to him for his many kind and generous acts. No one had brought her more cheer and sympathy. He used to come into her room, she told Miss Mitford, "like a flash of lightening, for suddenness and contrast and power, —and like sunshine, for calmness and gentle cheerfulness. He is my epitome of society." [18] Boyd, who now lived at St. John's Wood, had meant much to her during her last years at Hope End and at Sidmouth, but she had long outgrown him. She could not respect the judgment of anyone who preferred Ossian to Homer, who thought Wordsworth a third-rate poet, and who had never heard of Tennyson or of Browning. Except for Elizabeth, almost no one was aware of Boyd's existence. They still wrote to each other, but her letters were no longer so frequent or so intimate as they had been when he was her sole correspondent.

The history of the growth and decay of her friendship with Hunter has many similar elements, but her feelings were more deeply engaged. In the early forties he was the minister of an Independent chapel in Brighton, from which he occasionally came to London with his daughter Mary to see Elizabeth. During the decade since she first knew him, he had grown white-haired and now looked old and worn. His visits could scarcely have been a comfort to her, since he was at odds with the world and was continually complaining about his misfortunes. He was evidently in love with her and jealous of her growing literary reputation. The only unfavorable opinion she received from her articles on the Greek Christian poets was Hunter's: "that the criticisms are not given with either sufficient seriousness or diffidence, and that there is a painful sense of effort through the whole." But these reasons, as Elizabeth reported them to Boyd, were irrelevant. He could not bear to sink into greater indigence and obscurity and at the same time see her become a public figure and grow out of his reach. Early in 1844 his pastorate at Brighton came to an end, and leaving Mary, "by her desire," at school in Brighton, he took lodgings in London to tutor a pupil. A salary of forty guineas a year, out of which he had to pay rent, offered only a precarious living. As he became ever more "incensed with the continual pricks of ill-fortune," his pride was hurt by the contrast between his desperate circumstances and Elizabeth's fame after the publication of her works in the *Athenaeum* and of her volumes of 1844. She wrote to Miss Mitford early in 1845 that ever since the appearance of her *Poems* Hunter had talked to her "gravely and bitterly," and on and on until she was weary, "epigrams about the sin and shame of those divine angels, called women, daring to tread in the dust of a multitude." For "every new review," there was "a burst of indignation." [19] For his image of the ideal woman "who looks languishing in a Book of Beauty," she had only contempt.

To anticipate the story for a moment—in the summer of 1845 he may have asked her to marry him, and she refused "with most absolute calmness," believing "that a moment's enthusiasm had carried him a good way past his discretion." [20] In writing to Robert Browning of the episode a year after the event, she did not name her suitor, but it may well have been Hunter. In their discussions of him, they often called him "poor Chiappino" because of a partial resemblance to that character in *A Soul's Tragedy*. In the context of their remarks he is always seen as a jealous and disappointed lover. When he became aware of her interest in Browning, he repeatedly taunted her with her "New Cross Knight." She respected him for his high qualities, pitied him for his misfortunes, and in deference to their friendship of many years continued to see him. Then he sent her a number of letters which were so "insolent" that she refused to reply; and whenever he came to see her, she asked Arabel to stay in her room because his violence made her fearful. A month before the marriage, he followed Browning upstairs to Elizabeth's room, "white with passion"; after the poet had gone, "there was an explosion . . . among the many." A few days later he wrote that he was going away to live in a village and asked for a "last interview" during which he promised to control himself. "Oh—such stuff!" Elizabeth said to Browning. "Am I to hold a handkerchief to my eyes and sob a little?" Hunter thought she "had shown great want of feeling" in sending him some of Browning's verses and in saying that she was "sincerely sorry for all his real troubles." Toward the end of August, Hunter hurled a final uncomplimentary epithet at Browning as they confronted each other on the steps at 50 Wimpole Street. After Elizabeth's marriage, he sullenly resolved never to communicate with her again and like Mr. Barrett maintained a stubborn silence until his death in 1857. Hunter's name occurs in a letter from Elizabeth at Pisa to Arabel, who had reported that he was still quarreling. "Can anything be in more execrable taste than the whole bearing of him!" Elizabeth wrote.[21]

Of the relationship between Horne and Elizabeth, less need

be said. Although they never saw each other before she went to Italy, they became close friends as they collaborated in their different projects. To Elizabeth he had appeared to be a refined and courteous gentleman. She was naturally disappointed and pained at the reports Miss Mitford sent her in 1843 of his conduct when he had been a guest at her home: his "straining after wit," his taking a bath "three times a day," and his outstaying his welcome.[22] Miss Mitford thought him selfish, inconsiderate, crude, "pushing," and uneducated. In her replies to Miss Mitford, Elizabeth always defended him and suggested that he had been misunderstood. Her faith in him, however, was shattered in the following spring, when she learned from Miss Mitford that Horne had asked one girl to marry him one day and another the next and that each had a fortune. To Elizabeth the "baldheartedness" seemed "ten times over worse than the baldheadedness." (On seeing earlier a portrait of Horne, she had been surprised that he was "absolutely bald.") She admitted to Miss Mitford that her "bubble has broken on its brightest side," for she thought "the pure love of a man of genius is a lofty thing."[23]

AFTER knowing such men as Boyd, Hunter, and Horne, Elizabeth particularly welcomed the friendship of Browning, whose genius she had worshiped for many years. She immediately replied to his first letter that she was delighted that he wished to be her correspondent and assured him she always had "pleasure in letters, and never think them too long, nor too frequent." If he would treat her *"en bon camarade,* without reference to the conventionalities of 'ladies and gentlemen,'" she would be happy "to sign and seal the contract," she wrote, "and to rejoice in being 'articled' as your correspondent." Both had "great sympathies in common," she added, "and I am inclined to look up to you in many things, and to learn as much of everything as you will teach me." Each had the same religious convictions, the same interest in humanitarian and liberal causes, and the same devotion to literature. Owing to his good health, Browning had experienced a greater range of activities and had more acquaintances, and his interests were also wider. He was very much attracted to the opera and the theater, both of which were forbidden to Elizabeth and her brothers and sisters by their father, who sternly disapproved for religious reasons. Also Browning played on the piano and the organ, and he paid frequent visits to the art galleries of London. Elizabeth, on the other hand, had "seen and heard nothing of pictures and music." If she had been well, she might have looked at more paintings; she probably would not have attended concerts, however, since music almost always upset her emotionally. For example, she wrote to Browning in the summer of 1846 that she had just been to Westminster Abbey when the service was about to begin and "was so frightened of the organ" that she had to leave immediately; and "again the other day, in the drawing room, because my cousin sang a song from the 'Puritani,' of no such great melancholy, I had to go away to finish my sobbing by myself."

Both Elizabeth and Browning found an immediate sympathetic response to the other's poetry. "You do not understand," he wrote, "what a new feeling it is for me to have someone who is to like my verses or I shall not ever like them after!" Since Bro's death, no one had been close to Elizabeth to whom she could ask, " 'Is this which I have written good? Is it worth anything?' and be sure of the just answer." [24] In the letters which were passing ever more frequently between Wimpole Street and New Cross, they wrote of their own and of each other's poetry, of the books they were reading, and of their mutual friends. She had just completed a new translation of the *Prometheus Bound,* "except the transcription and the last polishing," and Browning made criticisms "of the greatest value" before she submitted the manuscript to *Blackwood's Magazine.*

In the middle of March he asked, "Do you think I shall see you in two months, three months?" A few days later she wrote at length about her "lonely life" years ago in Herefordshire, of her having "lived only inwardly," while he, it seemed to her, had "drunken of the cup of life full." She implied that one day his request would be granted. "If you think that I shall not *like* to see you, you are wrong, for all your learning. But I shall be afraid of you at first." He had traveled widely and had associated with many men and women in the public eye, while she had "lived with visions" for her company: "You are Paracelsus, and I am a recluse, with nerves that have been all broken on the rack, and now hang loosely—quivering at a step and breath." He made no further request to visit her until almost two months later, when he wrote, "I ask you *not* to see me so long as you are unwell, or mistrustful of—." Then she asked to be forgiven for having "made what is vulgarly called a 'piece of work' about little." Her secluded life had made her "shy," but she was not "mistrustful." Then he read the words for which he had been waiting: "If you care to come to see me you can come." But, she warned him, he must not "talk of having come afterwards." She feared he might not receive "the least straw of pleasure" from knowing her personally: "There is nothing to see in me; nor to hear in me—I never learnt to talk as you do in London." She, who never had any men visitors except her elderly "cousin," suddenly broke the pattern of isolation which had become ever more rigid since Bro's death. It was an extraordinary act of will. She was "vexed" with Browning for asking to come and with herself for yielding, but he had influenced her "in a way in which no one else did." While she was writing that he might see her, she wept for nervousness.

Now that she had finally given her permission, she advised him to stay quiet and "keep away that dreadful musical note in the head" with which he was often afflicted. Later he might come, and her sister would take him to her room, "and we will talk; or *you* will talk; and you will try to be indulgent, and like me as well as you can." He thanked her for the "infinite kindness" of the invitation and asked if he might call at two on Tuesday, May 20. She suggested that he come at three, instead, and in a postscript she said, "If on Tuesday you should not be well, *pray do not come*— Now, that is my request to your kindness." Browning was well, he came at the appointed hour, and he stayed until half past four. A few days afterward she wrote Miss Mitford that she had recently seen Browning "and liked him much. Younger looking than I had expected—looking younger than he *is*, of course —with natural and not ungraceful manners,—and full of his art, which he is destined, I believe, so worthily to sustain." [25] The sense of his presence remained with Elizabeth. On the morning after the visit she said to her father, "It is most extraordinary how the idea of Mr. Browning does beset me—I suppose it is not being used to see strangers, in some degree—but it haunts me . . it is a persecution."

A few hours after he left Elizabeth, Browning wrote her that he was "proud and happy" in her friendship and that he hoped he had not spoken too loud or stayed too long. Elizabeth, who was always very quiet in general company, had probably said less than her visitor. Browning's friend Joseph Arnould described his conversation at this period of his life as "remarkably good . . . anecdotal, vigorous, showing great thought and reading, but in his language most simple, energetic, and accurate. From the habit of good and extensive society he has improved in this respect wonderfully. We remember him as hardly doing justice to himself in society; now it is quite the reverse." [26] Elizabeth assured him that he had not talked too loud or stayed too long, and she insisted on being allowed to say that it had been "kind" of him to come and that she was "grateful."

His next letter so pained and disturbed her because of its "wild speaking" that, as she later explained, "I could not sleep night after night,—could not,—and my fear was at nights, lest the feverishness should make me talk deliriously and tell the secret aloud." Browning, who had come to see her with a "presentiment" that he might fall in love, had in fact immediately lost his heart. "Nothing was *between* the knowing and the loving," as she later said to him in gratitude that his eyes had never at any time been "cold discerners and analyzers" of her. But now his confession of love seemed to her "a mere poet's fancy . . an illusion of a confusion between the woman and the poetry." [27] It was, she supposed, the mere impulse of "a generous man of quick sympathies taking up a sudden interest with both hands!" She replied that he had said "some intemperate things . . fancies,—which you will not say over again, nor unsay, but *forget at once,* and *for ever, having said at all.*" It was only her being "in the most exceptional of positions," she reminded him, which had made it possible for her to receive him alone. If he objected to what she had just written or if he referred to it, she could not see him again, and she hoped he would not cause her "to break through an intercourse just as it is promising pleasure." His answer was ungenerous since it put her in the wrong. "Will you not think me very brutal," he said, "if I tell you I could almost smile at your misapprehension of what I meant to write?" To repair the damage caused by his first "thoughtlessness," he wished her to understand that what he had meant to express was his sense of "real inferiority" to her. She then sent him "the most humble of apologies," said that she was "ashamed" of herself, and added humorously, "I assure you that I never made such a mistake (I mean of overseriousness to indefinite compliments), no, never in my life before." At the end of the letter she said with remarkable prescience, "We shall know each other some day perhaps." After one more awkward reference to the subject, he adhered to the conditions she had imposed and continued to enjoy her friendship.

In her letters to him that summer, and probably in their conversations as they met once a week, she told him about her years at Hope End and about some of the peculiar circumstances of her life. She said that she was "like Mariana in the moated grange," that she had "been ground down to browns and blacks" and had nothing to offer but grief. Weary, discouraged, defeated, she felt her life was without meaning. "Sometimes—it is the real truth," she wrote him, "I have haste to be done with it all." But her feelings were deeply affected by his wishing to see her so often, and he was grateful for the unique privilege she had granted. "The letters and the visits rained down more and more," she later wrote Mrs. Martin, "and in every one there was something which was too slight to analyse and notice, but too decided not to be understood." [28]

In the meantime, after having completed the *Prometheus Bound,* she was writing very little poetry in comparison to her creative activity of 1843–44. During the summer of 1845 she made a few short trips in a brougham for the first time in many years. In July she went up Wimpole Street to the gates of Regent's Park at Devonshire Place, and by September she could go twice around the inner enclosure of the park. "The novelty of living more in the outer life" made her "inclined to be idle." Also she was spending much time in the "pure enjoyment" of reading some of Browning's poems in manuscript and making many detailed suggestions. She commented on at least thirteen of the poems which were published in the *Dramatic Romances and Lyrics* in November 1845. An examination of her proposed emendations shows how greatly they were improved by her advice. In criticizing the poems of others, she always had a very keen sense of rhythm and a feeling for the appropriateness of the imagery. In addition to her remarks on the shorter poems, she recommended a few revisions for *A Soul's Tragedy,* written several years earlier, and she offered many criticisms for *Luria,* which was being composed in the fall and winter of 1845-46.[29] Early in the summer of 1845 she wrote a number of short paraphrases from Apuleius, Nonnus, Homer, Theocritus, Hesiod, Euripides, and Anacreon to be published in a "Classical Album." One of Kenyon's friends, a Miss Thomson (later Madame Emil Braun) had undertaken to edit the work and asked Elizabeth to write the paraphrases "for the sake of the art-illustrations." The book was never published, and Elizabeth's poems remained unprinted until their appearance after her death in *Last Poems.* At about this time she made a translation of Bion's *Lament for Adonis,* which was first published in her volumes of 1850. In the spring of 1846, in response to a request of Mrs. Jameson, she wrote two versions of "The Daughters of Pandarus" based on the *Odyssey,* one in prose and the other in verse which imitated the rhythm of the Greek hexameter. She sent the translations to Mrs. Jameson and asked her to select the one she preferred for her article, "The Xanthian Marbles"; both versions were published. And it was during the months before her marriage that she wrote the first draft of the "Sonnets from the Portuguese."

LATE in August she told Browning in a long "gloomy letter" the details of Bro's death and what his loss had meant to her. He replied that he was "most grateful" for having been permitted to share in her feelings. Now he believed he had gained her confidence and might break the silence she had enjoined upon him. For a second time he declared his love, and in the same letter of August 30 he said in a postscript, "I trust you see your . . dare I say your *duty* in the Pisa affair, as all else *must* see it." Earlier in the summer she had written him that her father and her aunt were considering the possibility of sending her to Alexandria or Malta for the winter, in September or October. She had commented significantly, "in every case, I suppose, *I* should not be much consulted." As the autumn approached, Dr. Chambers gave both his "opinion and injunction" that she spend the winter in Pisa and said that if she had gone to Italy years ago, she would now be well. At the time Browning referred to Pisa, Mr. Barrett had already indicated that he was reluctant to have Elizabeth go, but he had not yet made a final statement. Browning had encouraged her to get away from the dead atmosphere of her room and go out of doors as often as possible. Now that the summer was over, he realized she must exercise her will and go to Italy even if her father selfishly preferred her to remain with him. Boyd and Miss Mitford also thought that Elizabeth should become more independent of her family. For example, Miss Mitford in writing to a friend of hers two years earlier, said that Elizabeth was "so foolish still as to cling to London, and so obstinate as to pretend that there is no difference between the air of Wimpole Street and that of the country." She continued, "I suppose nobody is without faults and hers are those of not choosing to do that which everybody advises for her health." [30] Boyd knew better than Miss Mitford the strength of Mr. Barrett's hold upon Elizabeth; the "affair about Italy made him furious," she later told Browning about Boyd's feeling after he heard of Elizabeth's disappointment in the autumn of 1845. Likewise, in the summer of 1846, when she told Boyd of her approaching marriage, she wrote Browning that she was "sure he triumphs inwardly in the idea of a chain being broken which he has so often denounced in words that pained and vexed me."

When she replied to Browning's renewed avowal of his love, she told him she had nothing but "anxiety" and "sadness" to offer, that in justice to him they must leave the subject "without one word more." So things would have remained indeterminate, had it not been for the outcome of "the Pisa case." Browning was fortunate that within a few weeks after his letter, Mr. Barrett had forfeited Elizabeth's love for him. Early in September she asked Browning and her sisters to inquire about steamer passage to Italy. Dr. Chambers and another physician told her "that to escape the English winter [she wrote Mrs. Martin] will be *everything for me,* and that it involves the comfort and usefulness of the rest of my life." One lung was "very slightly affected, but the nervous system *absolutely shattered.*" It was imperative that she spend the winter in a warm climate, as she explained, for "the cold weather . . . acts on the lungs, and produces the weakness indirectly, whereas the necessary shutting up acts on the *nerves.*" She was convinced there was "a means of escape from these evils, and God has opened the door of escape." Her father, she had supposed, "would catch at any human chance" of helping her to regain her health. One of her brothers would go with her, and she had "good courage" and "sufficient means" of strength. But in her father she found only a "dead silence." Then he wrote her a "hard cold letter" in which he probably gave a grudging permission but made clear his displeasure at the prospect of having his household again divided as it had been when she was at Torquay. He evidently thought Elizabeth would abandon the plan, but after she received "Papa's note of consent," she was advised by George and by her aunt Mrs. Hedley to bring the matter up again and emphasize the unwisdom of acting in defiance of medical opinion. So she "spoke face to face and quite firmly" to her father of the necessity of the trip but said that she "was ready to give up Pisa in a moment" if he wished her to remain because of his affection for her. "Whatever my new impulses towards life were [she later wrote], my love for him (taken so) would have resisted all—I loved him so dearly. But his course was otherwise, quite otherwise, and I was wounded to the bottom of my heart—cast off when I was ready to cling to him." [31]

The chief obstacle to her going was that her father would not permit any of her brothers or sisters to accompany her, and she was too weak to make the trip alone. Even though she knew her health was endangered by staying, she thought it would be unfair to involve them in her father's anger. "I had expected more help than I have found, and am left to myself," she explained. Browning, Kenyon, Boyd, and Mrs. Jameson all encouraged her, but possibly some of her brothers were unsympathetic. When she realized in the middle of September, after two weeks of suspense, that for her there would be "no Pisa," that she could not leave her "prison," she experienced a deeper despair and bitterness than she had known since the death of Bro. "Sometimes it seems to me as if it *could not* end so," she wrote Browning; a few days later she told him, "I feel aggrieved of course and wounded" as she thought of her father's words she would always remember with pain.

The revelation that her father "obviously" did not love her as much as she had believed he did but that he demanded obedience merely because she was his daughter was "the bitterest 'fact' of all." Her feelings had been so hurt that, as she said to Miss Mitford, "nothing could ever induce me to appeal again, on any personal ground whatever, to that quarter." [32] When she asked her father to say he was not "displeased" with her, he answered that for her to take a sister and brother with her "and do such a thing for the sake of going to Italy and securing a personal advantage, were altogether impossible, obviously impossible!" A week later "he complained of the undutifulness and rebellion" of his family and told her, as she wrote Browning, that she might do as she liked but "for his part, he washed his hands of me altogether." When she finally saw the futility of further discussion —"I have no spell for charming the dragons," she told her lover —George "in great indignation, pressed the question fully" and was informed by his father that she might go if she pleased, "but that going it would be under his heaviest displeasure."

Just before the Pisa business came to a crisis, Browning wrote in the middle of September that to join his life to hers would make him *"supremely happy."* He told her of his simple tastes in food and dress and of his potential capacity as a breadwinner. Thus far he had earned no money but had been living, as Miss Mitford expressed it somewhat unfairly, "in contented idleness" upon his father, who had paid for his expenses of travel and also of publishing all but two of his volumes. Each of the pamphlets of the *Bells and Pomegranates* cost £16 to produce, which was as much as the annual salary of Elizabeth's maid Wilson—and she was "an expensive servant." In his letter Browning had said he had no love of money for its own sake, and she answered she was no less indifferent to "the gold and gauds of the world." She explained that she could not be poor even if she wished to be, for she alone among her brothers and sisters was in possession of a fortune of her own. Both her grandmother Mrs. Moulton and her uncle Sam Barrett had willed her money. Now she had some £8,000 invested in government bonds, the interest of which was about £45 each quarter. She also received dividends of almost £200 a year from shares owned in the *David Lyon,* a trading ship between England and the West Indies. Her annual income, tax free, was therefore a little more than £350, and in the early Victorian years the pound had about ten times its present purchasing power. Such an income was more than enough for the average middle-class family in England to live in modest comfort. It was considerably more than Browning's father was then earning. If a couple were at that time to have made their residence in Italy, where English money stretched three or four times as far as at home, they could have hoped with that sum to live in luxurious circumstances. Until her marriage about half her income was regularly reinvested. But the portion available to her was soon spent, she confessed to Browning: "The money flows out of window and door" for medicines, books, gifts to friends, and clothes (although one gown cost only five shillings).

In the same letter in which she told Browning that she could never "be very poor, in the world's sense of poverty," she also said she "would accept the great trust" of his happiness if she could, but that "something worse than even a sense of unworthiness, *God* has put between us!" Browning replied that although she saw at the moment "insurmountable obstacles," he had a "true, honest unfeigned inability to imagine what they are." In order that she might not think herself too old for him, he explained that he was "no longer in the first freshness of life." For many years he had made up his mind to "the impossibility of loving any woman," and when "real love, making itself at once recognized as such, *did* reveal itself to me at last, I *did* open my heart to it with a cry," he wrote. "The *one* poor sacrifice" he could make for her was "this absolute independence," his almost unlimited bachelor's freedom he had "fought so many good battles to preserve." Then he assured her that he would be willing to undertake regular employment to earn a living, "that whenever I make up my mind to that, I can be rich enough and to spare." On September 17, just as he was promising to go to work, if that were necessary, Elizabeth sent him "one word just to say that it is all over with Pisa." A day later she explained that the mysterious barrier or difficulty to which she had alluded was that she had "been a very byword among the talkers, for a confirmed invalid through months and years." As for the "sacrifice" he had promised to make if she would marry him, she thanked him "gratefully" but said she could never accept such an offer, which would involve "an exchange of higher work for lower work."

It was late in September when he realized that the dragon's spell had partially paralyzed her will, that her yielding to her father's decision and staying in London might have a detrimental effect upon her health for the rest of her life and would certainly undo the gains achieved in the summer. He wrote her that she must act, contrary to her father's command if necessary. "You are called upon to do your duty to yourself," he said as forthrightly as he dared, short of giving offense. "I truly wish," he told her, "*you* may never feel what I have to bear in looking on, quite powerless, and silent, while you are subjected to this treatment, which I refuse to characterize—so blind is it *for* blindness." If her father's love had been a necessary protection, he could understand and sympathize, yet "the jewel is not being over guarded, but ruined, cast away." It might be "infinitely harder" to oppose her father's will, but better so "than to blindly adopt his pleasure, and die under it." All the "obstacles" had disappeared: she did not suffer from "an incurable complaint," as he had supposed at first, and she was not financially dependent upon her father. Yet she was in what he "should wonder at as the veriest slavery," he told her, "and I who *could* free you from it, I am here scarcely daring to write."

After three weeks of bitter conflict she knew that Browning loved her as her father never had, and he suddenly took the place her father had held in her affections. She did not openly defy her father and leave, for in the circumstances such an act would have been impossible. Even Kenyon, who well understood Mr. Barrett's "peculiarities," agreed with her that she had no alternative to living at home that winter. But she surrendered to Browning. "Henceforward I am yours for everything but to do you harm," she wrote on September 26. Furthermore she promised that, "None, except God and your will, shall interpose between you and me, . . I mean, that if He should free me within a moderate time from the trailing chain of this weakness, I will then be to you whatever at that hour you shall choose . . whether friend or more than friend . . a friend to the last in any case." She asked him not to consider it a formal engagement or to think he was bound to her in any way. Their decision would depend upon her health after another winter in England. If she were ill again, he would "see plainer the foolishness of this persistence"; if not, she would do as he wished.

"Of all the events of my life, inclusive of its afflictions," she wrote him several months later, "nothing has humbled me so much as your love." She thought he was superior to her in all ways, that he was offering much in return for nothing. Her letters are filled with such expressions: "You see from above and I from below"; "You are too good and too high for me." Much the same thought appears in the "Sonnets from the Portuguese":

> What can I give thee back, O liberal
> And princely giver, who hast brought the gold
> And purple of thine heart, unstained, untold,
> And laid them on the outside of the wall
> For such as I to take or leave withal,
> In unexpected largesse? am I cold,
> Ungrateful, that for these most manifold
> High gifts, I render nothing back at all?
> Not so; not cold,—but very poor instead.
> Ask God who knows. For frequent tears have run
> The colours from my life, and left so dead
> And pale a stuff, it were not fitly done
> To give the same as pillow to thy head.
> Go farther! let it serve to trample on.

Elizabeth told Browning that he might continue to visit her once a week because that was "a thing established," and now and then he might come twice a week. If he were to see her more often and if his visits were noticed by Mr. Barrett, "difficulties and vexations would follow as a matter of course." Between Elizabeth and her father an estrangement slowly grew which was marked at first by his omission of the nightly visits he used to make to her room, where he would sit and talk and then pray with her.

As the chill and fog settled for another season over London, Elizabeth and Browning, each infinitely grateful for the new-found happiness the other had brought, anxiously awaited the winter's outcome.

10. Engagement and Marriage

ALL THAT AUTUMN and winter Elizabeth remained in her room. Although she was anxious about her health, she did not lose more strength than usual. Among her regular visitors, besides Browning, were Miss Mitford, Mrs. Jameson, Kenyon, and his friend Sarah Bailey, the latter of whom repeatedly offered to accompany Elizabeth to Italy whenever she wished. The more Elizabeth saw of Mrs. Jameson, the more she liked her and believed her "the kindest, most affectionate woman in the world," partly, one suspects, because unlike Miss Mitford she had a high opinion of Browning's genius. In October 1844 Elizabeth had received a letter from Mrs. Jameson praising her *Poems*. Just as Kenyon had introduced Miss Mitford to Elizabeth eight years earlier, he now facilitated the acquaintance between Mrs. Jameson and his "cousin." He had known and had unobtrusively aided Mrs. Jameson for a number of years, and it must have been he who encouraged her to write to Elizabeth. In the middle of November another note came from Mrs. Jameson to say that she was living with a friend at 51 Wimpole Street; soon afterward she called upon Elizabeth, who described her visitor as "very light—has the lightest of eyes, the lightest of complexions; no eyebrows, and what looked to me like very pale red hair, and thin lips of no colour at all." Mrs. Jameson, who was already an intimate friend of Lady Byron and of Goethe's daughter-in-law Ottilie, was then fifty years old and had gained a European reputation from having published more than a dozen books. In 1838, after twelve years of a childless, incompatible marriage, she had separated for the last time from her husband in Canada and had returned to Europe to earn her living by her writings. Her first book, the *Diary of an Ennuyée,* published anonymously in 1826, was an immediate success. Since then she had issued her *Characteristics of Women* and her *Winter Studies and Summer Rambles in Canada,* as well as her guidebooks to the art galleries of London. During the remaining fifteen years of her life she was to suffer from increasing loneliness and poor health; yet she courageously struggled to support herself and her parasitic sisters by producing a series of books on early Italian painters and sacred art. Although she was more practical and more realistic than Elizabeth, they were immediately attracted to each other and entered upon a close friendship which was mutually enjoyed until Mrs. Jameson's death in 1860.

Kenyon, who had also helped to introduce Browning to Elizabeth, was no doubt pleased to observe the rapid growth of the friendship of the two poets, but "with his all-scrutinizing spectacles" he made her uncomfortable by constantly asking, "When did you see Browning? When do you see Browning again?" As for the most important of her visitors, Elizabeth was "positively vexed and jealous" of herself for having a "curious double feeling" about him, a sense of discrepancy between the writer of the letters and the man who came to see her. The visitor "confounded" her and left her with the "impression of its being all dream-work on his side." The writer of the letters, on the other hand, was close to her from the beginning; as she later said to him, "the dear letters took me on the side of my own ideal life where I was able to stand a little upright and look around."

At this time Browning completed the *Dramatic Romances and Lyrics,* which he published in November as Number 7 of the *Bells and Pomegranates.* Elizabeth saw in them a "sense of beauty and power everywhere" and asked, "Now if people do not cry out about these poems, what are we to think of the world?" The pamphlet contained some of the finest poems of his career, such as "The Bishop Orders His Tomb at St. Praxed's Church," "Pictor Ignotus," and "The Englishman in Italy." But the world made no outcry. His two dramas *Luria* and *A Soul's Tragedy* were published together as the last of the *Bells and Pomegranates* on April 13, 1846. Elizabeth gave both of them high praise, but they received almost no recognition from the general public or from professional critics.

In October 1845 Elizabeth wrote Browning, "I will never fail to you from any human influence whatever," but she was fearful of jeopardizing his future and of rewarding his generosity with unhappiness. Would she be justified, she asked, in helping him to a step "of wasting, in a sense, your best feelings . . of emptying your water gourds into the sand?" Months later she said in the same vein, "Yet to bring you down into my ashes . . *that* has been so intolerable a possibility to me from the first." She also feared that he only pitied her for her grief and isolation. Although she never doubted the sincerity of his passion, she questioned whether he loved her in the way he believed he did, whether he was not self-deceived. Still another fear was that he might later be disappointed in her from having created during his courtship an ideal which bore no relation to the reality. As late as the following April she wondered whether he were not "deluded, mistaken" in his love. "It seems to me," she wrote, "as if you were in the dark altogether, and held my hand for another's: let the shutter be opened suddenly; and the hand . . is dropped perhaps." Would he continue to love her, she asked, "when the ideal breaks off, when the light is gone"? And only two weeks before her marriage she said that although she did not doubt his affection for her, "Yet you make me uneasy often through this extravagance of over-estimation; forcing me to contract 'obligations to pay' which I look at in speechless despair." But however deep and complex were her uncertainties, she never failed to express her gratitude for his love. She would remember to her "last hour, that *you,* who might well have passed by on the other side if we two had met on the road when I was riding at ease, . . *did not* when I was in the dust."

His unfaltering devotion and understanding of her problems helped her to resolve her doubts and to brace herself for the decisions she must make in the summer. He well knew that although she had assented in principle to the step which would free her from Wimpole Street, she would advance countless reasons for delay when confronted with the necessity of deciding upon a specific date. Soon after the beginning of the year he wrote her, "this living without you is too tormenting now. So begin thinking, —as for Spring, as for a New Year, as for a new life." She replied that it was "advisable to hurry on nothing," for their position was in many ways extremely precarious. If her father were to have suspicions, he would never allow her to see him again, and all letters from him would be destroyed. But she gave him her promise: "Do *you* remember, besides, that there can be no faltering on my 'part,' and that, if I should remain well, which is not proved yet, I will do for you what you please and as you please to have it done. But there is time for considering!" Her sisters *"know,"* she reported, though not her brothers, whom she thought it imprudent to involve in such a responsibility. Henrietta now had an informal attachment to William Surtees Cook (who was admitted to the house only because he was a cousin), and she too had to be cautious. But since Henrietta and Cook would have to delay their marriage for several years because of financial stringency, Elizabeth knew she would be the first in the family to "offend" her father by getting married. Even more than Henrietta, she understood that her father would be implacable in his anger, whether she were merely to ask his permission to become engaged or whether she were to marry without his consent: "For *him* . . he would rather see me dead at his foot than yield the point: and he will say so, and mean it, and persist in the meaning." In his next letter Browning claimed his "promise's fulfilment—say, at the summer's end: it cannot be for your good that this state of things should continue." He suggested that they "go to Italy for a year or two." Her reply was all he could have hoped for: "If in the time of fine weather, I am not ill, . . *then* . . *not now* . . you shall decide, and your decision shall be duty and desire to me." In the next paragraph she repeated herself, "I am yours as *you* see . . and not yours to teaze you. You shall decide everything when the time comes for doing anything."

She was very much aware of the insecurity of their present arrangements and early in March wrote that either they might continue to live as they had been "until an obstacle arises," or, she promised, "I will be yours in the obvious way, to go out of England the next half-hour if possible. As to the steps to be taken (or not taken) before the last step, we must think of those." She reported to him that when her father had come to her room before dinner, "it was plain to see" that he was not pleased at having found him in her room earlier in the day. To Browning it was no less than "SHOCKING" that a father who chose "to give out of his whole day some five minutes" to his invalid daughter should be *"not pleased"* at the kind attention she received from a fellow poet. In the same letter he encouraged her to "go up and down stairs, get strong." He realized that the confinement to her room damaged her nervous system and sapped her will power; so during the spring and summer he urged her to go out as often as she could. Only thus, it was clear to him, could she acquire the physical and moral strength she would need to break the ties between herself and Wimpole Street, when the occasion should arise. By the end of March they agreed to write to each other every day, except when they met, until they should leave England together. About a week afterward he pleaded, "Let us marry soon, very soon, and end all this!"

She now touched with complete frankness upon a somewhat awkward subject she had "often and often mused about saying" to him, but from which she had shrunk "and torn the paper now and then." She informed him that Kenyon had just asked her "what Mr. Browning's objects in life were. Because Mrs. Procter had been saying that it was a pity he had not seven or eight hours a day of occupation." Her "spiteful" reply to Kenyon had been that "if Mr. Procter had looked as simply to his art as an end [as Browning had], he would have done better things." Then she said to Kenyon, as she often had to Miss Mitford, that one does not put "race horses into dray carts." After reporting this conversation to Browning, Elizabeth said that her possession of a private income would enable them "to be free of the world" and to escape the unkind gossip of acquaintances and family. "It is not of the least importance to either of us, as long as we can live," she declared, "whether the sixpence, we live by, came most from you or from me." Browning was offended by Mrs. Procter's comment, which seemed to him "of course purely foolish," and he added, "the world does seem incurably stupid on this, as other points." She pacified him in her next letter by assuring him that nothing had been said of him in disrespect and affirmed that, "if Miss Procter would 'commit suicide' rather than live as you like to live, *I* will not, as long as you are not tired of me." Nothing more was spoken on the subject until two months later, when he asked her to transfer her money to her brothers and sisters. "Does anybody doubt that I can by application in proper quarters obtain quite enough to support us both in return for no extraordinary expenditure of such faculties as I have?" he asked her. She probably did not doubt, but she would not agree to so impractical a suggestion. On the contrary, owing to her frail health and to Browning's need for leisure to develop his art, she could not "cast the burden" of herself upon him, without financial resources of her own. "Supposing that you sought *money*," she wrote him, "you would not be quite so stupid, the world may judge for itself, as to take hundreds instead of thousands, and pence instead of guineas. To do the world justice, it is not likely to make a blunder on such a point as this." But she was to find out, to her disgust, soon after her marriage, that her estimate of the world had been too charitable. He hoped to "write wondrous works," and he commented sarcastically that from them "may easily come some fifty or sixty horrible pounds a year,—on which one lives famously in Ravenna, I dare say."

In July Elizabeth apparently suggested that she will all her property to her sisters and leave him nothing. She also asked whether he would be happier "if a *part* were relinquished *now*" with the provision that the remainder always be his. It would be unwise, he answered, for her to give away any of her funds, "for I have never been so foolish as to think we could live without money, if not of my obtaining, then of your possessing." He would have preferred the former, but he could not be certain of a sufficient income from the sale of his works. He ended further discussion by saying, "I have only to be thankful that you are not dependent on my exertions,—which I could not be *sure* of,—particularly with this uncertain head of mine." His "notion of the perfection of money arrangements" was that "of a fairy purse which every day should hold *so* much, and there an end of trouble." Few would disagree. Just before his marriage he borrowed £100 from his father for traveling and living expenses until the management of Elizabeth's income should be transferred from her father to the trustees of the marriage settlement.

As the summer approached, Elizabeth became stronger and began to emancipate herself from the room which had for so long been her prison. Late in May she walked up the stairs unaided. A few days afterward, accompanied by Arabel and Flush, she went to Upper Montagu Street to pay the first visit in many years upon her grandmother's life-long companion Miss Trepsack, of whom Elizabeth was " 'her child,' *par excellence* . . her acknowledged darling and favourite." She took a walk in Regent's Park and drove in a carriage with her sisters to Hampstead, another time to Harrow, and once as far as Finchley, which in 1846 was "pretty and rural." With Kenyon she saw the train come into the terminus of the recently finished Western railroad, "and Flush was so frightened at the roar of it, that he leapt upon the coach-box."

On the twentieth of June she visited Boyd's house at 24A Grove End Road, St. John's Wood, "not to see him, but as a preliminary step to seeing him." Arabel went inside to tell him that Elizabeth was in the carriage, and then they drove away. Elizabeth had been too overcome with emotion to see him, because of his associations with her life at Hope End and Sidmouth. "We are both perhaps rather afraid of meeting," she wrote Browning, "after all these years of separation." Soon afterward she overcame her reluctance and returned to see him. Her "heart was too full to speak at first," but she "stooped and kissed his poor bent-down forehead, which he never lifts up, his chin being quite buried in his breast." They talked not about their former homes and acquaintances in Herefordshire and Devon, but about "Ossian and Cyprus wine," and he may have asked her how she could believe "the stupid story" that Macpherson had forged the poetry of Ossian. As if with a premonition that she would never see Boyd again after her marriage, she went to him five or six times that summer. In August he was the one person outside the immediate families who was informed of Elizabeth's plans before the celebration of the marriage in September. He "approved highly," she told Browning, and "exhorted me, with ever such exhortation, to keep to my purpose, and to allow no consideration in the world or out of the world, to make any difference."

She also took several drives with her sisters in Hyde Park, went to Westminster Abbey, to Paddington Chapel, and to the Scotch Church in her neighborhood, and visited with Mrs. Jameson the private art gallery of Samuel Rogers at his mansion on St. James' Street. Over a period of fifty years Rogers had brought together, in Mrs. Jameson's words, a "small but most beautiful collection," in the formation of which could be traced the "union of exquisite taste with good sense." [1] In it were represented many of the best-known painters of the various European schools: Fra Angelico, Tintoretto, Titian, Velazquez, Claude de Lorraine, Poussin, Salvator Rosa, Holbein the younger, Gainsborough, Reynolds, and Elizabeth's friend Haydon. The paintings which most impressed Elizabeth were Rubens' version of Andrea Mantegna's "Triumph of Julius Caesar," "a divine Virgin and child, worn and faded to a shadow of Raphael's genius," and a self-portrait by Rembrandt: "Such a rugged, dark, deep subterraneous face, . . yet inspired—! seeming to realize that God took clay and breathed into the nostrils of it." She was also deeply affected by the sight of the agreement between Milton and his publisher for the sale of *Paradise Lost.* "How was it possible not to feel giddy with such sights!" she exclaimed.

Among all her short excursions from home that summer, she paid no visit to New Cross. Since Browning had told both his parents and Sarianna of his plans, he hoped that they might see Elizabeth before she left with him for Italy. For Mr. and Mrs. Browning to have come to Elizabeth's room would, in the circumstances, have been impossible. And "the usual worldly form," she explained to her fiancé, "would be *against* my paying such a visit." But for her a more important reason why they should not meet was that Browning's parents might be kept "quite safe and away from all splashing of the mud." When Browning asked her to receive Sarianna, she recoiled from the suggestion and offered an incoherent excuse. The principal reason for her reluctance was probably her "blind dislike to seeing strangers." "I was afraid of not being liked enough," she explained to him. "There would be the need in me of being affectionate to your sister! how could I not? and yet, *how could I?* Everything is at once too near and too far—it is enough to make me tremble to think of it."

On June 2 Elizabeth asked whether it might not be "wiser, more prudent" for them to remain "quietly as we are, you at New Cross, and I here, until next year's summer or autumn?" Browning, who had been gratified at Elizabeth's steady increase in strength, answered immediately that they must not waste another year: "Every day that passes before *that day* is one the more of hardly endurable anxiety and irritation, to say the least; and the thought of another year's intervention of hope deferred—altogether intolerable!" She agreed they had nothing to gain by delay and possibly everything to lose: "We are standing on hot scythes, and because we do not burn in the feet, by a miracle, we have no right to count on the miracle's prolongation."

Soon afterwards Mrs. Jameson said to Browning at a party, "How I should like to introduce *you* to Miss Barrett . . did you ever see her?"—"To which I answered in the old way," he told Elizabeth, "that nobody, as she knew, saw you." He could no longer endure "the sense of mask-wearing," as Elizabeth had called it, and asked her whether the time of waiting might end soon: "May I count by months, by weeks?" Any form of secrecy or of equivocation was repellent to both Browning and Elizabeth. He would have preferred to inform everyone of his intentions and to make a straightforward application to Mr. Barrett. But, as Elizabeth warned him many times, such a course would prove fatal to their hopes. She still had great fear of her father and knew that to tell him of her plans would be, as she expressed it, to place a dagger in his hand. "I would rather be kicked with a foot," she wrote Browning, "than be overcome by a loud voice speaking cruel words." Her spirit would not yield, but she "could not help *dropping,* dying before them." To save her fiancé from another embarrassing encounter with Mrs. Jameson, Elizabeth told her "what might be told," that the poet was one of her regular visitors. Browning and Elizabeth after much discussion decided that it would be unwise to let Kenyon know of their intentions. Since he was a friend of both families, he might, if he were told, consider it his duty to inform them. Furthermore, in "his irresolution, his apprehensiveness," he might endeavor to separate them by saying to Browning and to Elizabeth individually that each would be hurting the other. "Let him, on the contrary, see the thing done, before he sees it at all," she correctly prophesied, "and *then* he will see the best of it."

A tragic event interrupted them as they were making plans for Italy. On the afternoon of June 22, when Elizabeth was looking at Rogers' art collection, she noticed Haydon's "Napoleon Musing at St. Helena," but she did not know that the artist had that very

Engagement and Marriage 171

morning taken his life. Although her brief correspondence with him had lapsed two years earlier, she had received from him during the week before his death three notes, on one of which he had written "that he *couldn't and wouldn't die.*" In April he had shown his paintings at his own expense in Egyptian Hall, but the public had ignored his exhibition. Thousands streamed past the room where his paintings were on view, without looking in, as they went to see Barnum's "General Tom Thumb" in the same building. Haydon never recovered from that humiliating experience. The news of his death shocked and depressed Elizabeth: "Oh, that a man so high hearted and highly endowed," she said to Browning, "a bold man, who has thrown down gauntlet after gauntlet in the face of the world—that such a man should go mad for a few paltry pounds!" She unreasonably blamed herself for not having sent money, but he had made no request. John Forster asked Kenyon to inform her that in a paper in which he gave his reasons for his self-destruction, he left directions that Elizabeth Barrett should arrange for the publication of the twenty-six manuscript volumes of his journals. Before his death he had committed to her care "all his private papers in a great trunk . . one of three" which he sent to her house. Since she was acquainted with almost none of the persons and events he wrote about in his memoirs, she realized that she was not qualified to edit them. "Some competent and sturdy hand" was needed. Talfourd recommended to her, through Browning, that she leave the material untouched, since it was the property of Haydon's creditors. And that was the course she followed. The autobiography and journals were ably edited by Tom Taylor, a well-known journalist, dramatist, and professor of English for a short time at University College, London. The publication of the three volumes in 1853 was one of the literary sensations of the year.

TOWARD the end of June Browning again reminded Elizabeth of the uncertainties of their situation, of the necessity of her making an immediate decision. Because of her delicate health, their flight from England would be impossible after September. The reason she could not make up her mind was that she had, in her words, "lived so in a dream for very long!—and everything, all undertakings, all movements, seem easy in dream-life." In asking her again and again to decide upon their final step, he was trying to reinforce her will power, which was still partly dormant. Many expressions in his letters seem to indicate a disinclination on his part to assume responsibility: "I hate being *master*"; "My own will has all along been annihilated before you"; "Think for me,—that is my command"; "It is pleasanter to lie back on the cushions inside the carriage and let another drive,"—to cite only a few of many similar passages. But in writing thus, he was not allowing himself to be dominated by Elizabeth. On the contrary, he was encouraging her to assert herself against the tyranny at home, to make up her mind to leave while the weather and her health were still in their favor. It was Browning who finally insisted that they should be married immediately and go abroad as soon as possible after the wedding. In the middle of August he wrote her, "I hope if you want to please me especially, Ba, you will always remember I have been accustomed, by pure choice, to have another will lead mine in the little daily matters of life." But in the larger decisions during their marriage each had an equal share.

Elizabeth's immediate reply to Browning's earnest entreaty of June 26,—"*do* decide, Ba . . . do *think,* to decide"—must have profoundly discouraged him. For she still had no sense of urgency: "Seriously . . there is time for deciding, is there not? . . even if I grant to you, which I do at once, that the road does not grow smoother for us by prolonged delays." When they were conversing on Tuesday, July 28, she "vexed" and "teazed" him by saying, "You had better give me up!" In her letter the next day she explained that her remark had been "only the reflection, in the still water, of what *had been* a proposition. 'Better' perhaps!—'Better' for you, that you should desire to give me up and do it—my 'Idée fixe' you know." But he "ought certainly to know," she assured him, "that I am your own, and ready to go through with the matter we are upon, and willing to leave the times and the seasons in your hand!" Yet even though August was near, she thought that "there was no need yet of specifying the exact time." Although he knew it was perilous to delay the decision another day, he wrote with his customary patience that "if no new obstacles arise," he would agree to their remaining as they were through September and October, "if your convenience is attained thereby in the least degree."

Their situation was more difficult in July and early in August, when Arabella Graham-Clarke and the Hedley family came to London on the occasion of the marriage of Elizabeth's cousin Arabella Hedley to James Johnstone Bevan. They spent much of their time at 50 Wimpole Street. Neither Miss Graham-Clarke nor the Hedleys (Aunt Jane and Uncle Hedley) had heard of Browning the poet, nor did it occur to them that Elizabeth might ever wish to live away from her home. Soon after her arrival, Miss Graham-Clarke said to Mr. Barrett: "I have not seen Ba all day —and when I went to her room, to my astonishment a gentleman was sitting there." Arabella Barrett explained who it had been. Her aunt continued, "And Ba bowed her head as if she meant to signify to me that I was not to come in."—"Oh, *that* must have been a mistake of yours," Henrietta said; "perhaps she meant just the contrary." Mr. Barrett ended the discussion by saying: "You should have gone in and seen the *poet*." Later, when Bevan came to her room, she was "nervous . . oh, so nervous!" Mrs. Hedley introduced him to Elizabeth and told him it was an honor to be so received, "for she never lets anybody come here except Mr. Kenyon, . . and a few other gentlemen." Mr. Barrett corrected her: "Only *one* other gentleman, indeed. Only Mr. Browning, the poet—the man of the pomegranates."

An episode in Elizabeth's home on Saturday, August 1, made her ever more uncomfortable and apprehensive. A severe thunderstorm detained Browning in her room longer than he was accustomed to stay. It was possibly because the Hedleys had not yet left London that Mr. Barrett spent most of that afternoon not at his office but in one of the reception rooms at his home. All the while Browning sat with her, she "was looking at Papa's face," as she "saw it through the floor," terrified lest he appear and touch off an explosion which would put an end to all their hopes. By seven o'clock her guest was no longer there, and Elizabeth "was lying on the sofa and had on a white dressing gown." Her father, who had already shown anger that afternoon when he had been told that during the storm "only Mr. Browning" was with her, came into her room, looking "a little as if the thunder had passed into him." He asked, "Has this been your costume since the morning, pray?"—"Oh, no," she answered, "only just now, because of the heat."—"Well," he said, "it appears, Ba, that *that man* has spent the whole day with you." While he was making that "appalling commentary," he had "a still graver aspect" and appeared "so displeased." The conversation was "brief enough—but it took my breath away," she wrote Browning the next day, "or what was left by the previous fear." He answered promptly on Monday morning, "See! *Now* talk of 'three or four months'! And is not the wonder, that this should wait for the eighty-second visit to happen?"

Mrs. Jameson was planning to leave for France and Italy early in September, with her niece Gerardine Bate, to collect material for her forthcoming *Sacred and Legendary Art*. Not long before her departure she more than once asked Elizabeth to travel with them and was somewhat puzzled by her cryptic refusals. On the Wednesday after the thunderstorm she called on Elizabeth and again brought up the matter. Elizabeth thanked her but said "it was in vain . . impossible." Mrs. Jameson said, "Mr. Kenyon threw cold water on the whole scheme. But *you!* Have *you* given up going to Italy?" Elizabeth answered that she was grateful for her interest but that she "could not be frank—there were reasons which prevented it." Mrs. Jameson looked at her "a little curiously, but asked no more questions until she rose to go away." Then she asked, "But you will go?"—"Perhaps—if something unforeseen does not happen."—"And you will let me know, and when you can,—when everything is settled?"—"Yes."—"And you think you shall go?"—"Yes."—"And with efficient companionship?"—"Yes."—"And happily and quietly?" But Elizabeth "could not say the full 'Yes,' to *that*."

In the meantime Browning and his fiancée were reading guidebooks on Italy and comparing the advantages and disadvantages of Palermo, Salerno, Sorrento, and La Cava. They finally rejected southern Italy because of the extra distance and decided upon Pisa, which was recommended for its mild winter climate.

Among the members of her own family, almost everyone suspected that Elizabeth and Browning had a romantic attachment for each other; everyone, that is, except Mr. Barrett, who was

Engagement and Marriage 175

always the last to learn of any event in his family. In the middle of August Miss Trepsack told Arabel she would not be surprised if Elizabeth married and went to Italy. A fortnight later, Stormie asked Arabel, "Is it true that there is an engagement between Mr. Browning and Ba?" She answered, "You had better ask them, if you want to know." George, who had overheard the conversation, looked "as grave as if antedating his judgeship."

As August drew to a close, Browning had still failed to make Elizabeth understand the importance of making an immediate decision. In his letter of August 28 he referred to "the shortness of the remaining travelling season serving to compel a speedy development" of some definite plan. An episode on the same day gave evidence of her father's increasing displeasure in her, though for reasons he probably failed to analyze. She was talking in her room with Mr. and Mrs. Hedley, when her father came in. To Mrs. Hedley's comment that Elizabeth was looking very well, that she saw a "surprising difference in her," Mr. Barrett answered, "Oh, I don't know. She is mumpish, I think. Mumpish! She does not talk."—"Perhaps she is nervous," her aunt suggested. During the conversation, Elizabeth herself "said not one word." She later explained to Browning, "When birds have their eyes out, they are apt to be mumpish." It is clear from an expression in her letter on Sunday, August 30, that at that moment she had no intention of fixing a date and was willing to allow at least two more months to slip away. Her visit with Browning the day before had been cut short by the appearance of Kenyon, who was planning to leave London soon and to be away for a month or two. She wrote Browning that it was "delightful to have heard of those intended absences one after another till far into October: which will secure us from future embarrassments." On that same Sunday he wrote of "the hatefulness of this state of things which is prolonged so uselessly." If she could show how they might "gain anything by deferring our departure till next week instead of to-morrow," he would "bear to perform yesterday's part for the amusement of Mr. Kenyon a dozen times over without complaint," he continued. "But if the cold plunge *must* be taken, all this shivering delay on the bank is hurtful as well as fruitless." Close to despair, he asked her to inform him at once if she were "unable, or unwilling to make this effort"; he would "not offer a word in objection" but continue his life as at present and "wait till next autumn, and the next and the next, till providence end our waiting." On the following morning he again counseled her not to delay her departure and used the "homely illustration" of the apple his mother had failed to pick, until it was too late. Elizabeth then reminded him that while his present position was indeed awkward for him, their marriage would be "the occasion of new affronts, sarcasms, every form of injustice." As for her promise, she said, "I will keep it freely at any time you choose." Each was placing the burden of choice upon the other.

Her attention was suddenly distracted by the disappearance of Flush. On Tuesday, the first of September, as she and Arabel left a shop on Vere Street to return to their carriage, they "looked round for Flush—there was no Flush!" Once again, after suffering the same fate twice in earlier years, he had imprudently strayed from his mistress and had allowed himself to be stolen and held for ransom by a gang of dog thieves. "It was such a shock to me —think of it! losing him in a moment, *so!*" she told Browning.

In each of his letters on Sunday, Monday, and Tuesday he had reported that his mother was not feeling well, and Elizabeth thus found another excuse for procrastination: "We may talk of September, but you cannot leave her, you know, dearest, if she should be *so* ill!" When he wrote on Wednesday, his mother was "very much better," and he urged Elizabeth once again to make a decision. "Do not let our happiness be caught up from us, after poor Flush's fashion—there may be no redemption from *that* peril." At the moment, the abduction of Flush overshadowed all other matters: "You may think it absurd," she wrote Browning, "but when my dinner is brought to me, I feel as if I could not (scarcely) touch it —the thought of poor Flush's golden eyes is too strong in me."

Just as Elizabeth was bemoaning the absence of her pet, Browning became ill on Thursday and had to go to bed. Although he felt better on Friday and Saturday, he got up on Sunday, September 6, "with the old *vertiginousness,* or a little worse," and was told by his physician to stay in bed and eat nothing until Wednesday morning. "The root of the evil" was not what the doctor thought he had found, but the long strain from which Browning had been

Engagement and Marriage

suffering, his anxiety that another year would pass with still no decision from Elizabeth. In the meantime she had paid the ransom of six guineas and again had Flush beside her. On Wednesday evening, September 2, Taylor, the leader of the thieves, had come to the Barretts' house to receive the money. Mr. Barrett told Henry not to pay and to say nothing to Elizabeth. She found out, however, what had happened, and the next morning asked Henry to go and pay the ransom. But he would not help her because of his fear of "Papa." After other unsuccessful appeals she herself finally went on Saturday in a cab with Wilson to Taylor's house. That evening Flush was returned—but not until after one further imbroglio. When Taylor arrived at Wimpole Street, Elizabeth sent down the money; but just as the affair was being settled, Alfred came in and called him "a swindler and a liar and a thief." Since "no gentleman could bear" such language, he left immediately, with the threat they would never see Flush again. Elizabeth was "very angry" with her brother, "who had no business to risk Flush's life for the sake of the satisfaction of trying on names which fitted," and she was on the point of going again to Shoreditch in the hope of "saving the victim at any price." Her brothers pacified her, Septimus went out to conclude the business with Taylor, and soon afterward Flush arrived, looking frightened and bedraggled.

BY WEDNESDAY, September 9, Browning was well enough to visit Elizabeth. Again he warned her of "the extreme perilousness of delay," but nothing was decided. In his letter Thursday morning he explained why he had all along been reluctant to decide on their last step. "You *give* me yourself," he wrote. "Hitherto, from the very first till this moment, the giving hand has been advancing steadily—it is not for me to grasp it lest it stop within an inch or two of my forehead with its crown." Two or three hours after he wrote those words, he returned home from London and found waiting for him a note from Elizabeth, dated "Wednesday Night," saying that the house at Wimpole Street would soon be vacated for a month, possibly for longer, while it was being cleaned and repaired. "Now!—what *can* be done?" she asked. He must "decide, after thinking," she told him. Again in her short letter she emphasized that he must now make the final decision: "Therefore decide! It seems quite too soon and too sudden for us to set out on our Italian adventure now." And in her last paragraph she said, "Well—but you must think for both of us." He made up his mind that moment, broke open the letter to her he had not yet posted, and added: "We must be *married directly* and go to Italy. I will go for a licence to-day and we can be married on Saturday. I will call to-morrow at 3 and arrange everything with you." In a note Elizabeth wrote that same Thursday she repeated, now for the last time, the burden of her earlier letters: "I shall not fail to you—I do not, I will not. I will act by your decision, and I wish you to decide." On Friday afternoon, when the Barrett family were having a picnic at Richmond, Browning paid his last, the ninetieth, visit upon Elizabeth, during which they made their final arrangements.

When he left, Elizabeth told her plans to Wilson, who was "very kind, very affectionate, and never shrank for a moment." After a sleepless night she went out with Wilson on Saturday morning, September 12, 1846, to the cab stand at Marylebone Road. Elizabeth "staggered" so that they "both were afraid for the fear's sake." But they "called at a chemist's for sal volatile and were thus enabled to go on" to Saint Marylebone Parish Church, where Browning and his cousin James Silverthorne were waiting. Browning thought that Elizabeth looked "more dead than alive." This was the only time before they left for Italy that they ever met each other away from the house at Wimpole Street. "There was no elopement in the case, but simply a private marriage,"[2] she later wrote her sisters; as she explained to Mrs. Martin, they were "*constrained* to act clandestinely, and did not *choose* to do so." Of all the women who had been married in that church, none had such strong reasons, Elizabeth thought to herself, as hers "for an absolute trust and devotion towards the man she married,—not one!" To carry out their plans, few women had sacrificed so much or had suffered so bitterly. "We parted, as we met, at the door of Marylebone Church," she wrote; "he helped me at the communion table, and not a word passed after."[3] By mutual agreement they did not meet again until their departure from England a week later. After the ceremony Elizabeth sent Wilson home and went directly to Boyd's house, where she "was able to lie quietly on the sofa in his sitting-room down-stairs" before he was free to see her. Her sisters had planned to meet her there at noon, and before they came she had "some bread and butter for dinner" that she might not appear "too pale in their eyes." She went away with them and "to complete the bravery" drove to Hampstead Heath before returning to Wimpole Street. "How I suffered that day . . . when I had to *act a part to you*—how I suffered!" she later wrote her sisters. "And how I had to think to myself that if I betrayed one pang of all, I should involve you deeply in the grief which otherwise remained my own." Even so, Arabel appeared "to see through it," for she looked at Elizabeth "so intently, and was so grave." [4] Browning woke the following morning "*quite well*—quite free from the sensation in the head." He wrote his bride, "I have not woke *so*, for two years perhaps—what have you been doing to me?"

In the last letters they ever wrote to each other (because after their marriage they were never separated for more than a day or two), they discussed the wording of the marriage announcement for the newspapers and the arrangements for their journey. She suggested, "You might put in the newspaper . . of Wimpole Street and Jamaica, or . . and Cinnamon Hill, Jamaica"; but Browning wisely replied, "Jamaica sounds in the wrong direction, does it not?" And so the announcement on page 7 of *The Times* on Monday, September 21, read as follows: "On Saturday, at St. Marylebone Church, by the Rev. Thomas Woods Goldhawk, M. A., Robert Browning, jun., Esq., of New-cross, Hatcham, to Elizabeth Barrett, eldest daughter of Edward Moulton Barrett, Esq., of Wimpole-street."

Elizabeth wrote on the Thursday after the marriage that the Barrett family were to move to a house in Little Bookham on Monday: "I would rather have waited—indeed rather—only it may be difficult to leave Bookham . . yet *possible*—so tell me what you would have me do." In the same letter she said she would have to send ahead her box and carpet bag on "Friday evening, if we went on Saturday." He interpreted the conditional clause as an affirmative statement: "But now,—you propose *Saturday*." They could not go to Italy by a direct passage on a steamer from the Thames because all such ships left in the morning. Since Arabel slept on a sofa in Elizabeth's room, it would be impossible to leave early in the day without implicating her. They planned therefore to take the five o'clock train from Nine Elms, Vauxhall, for Southampton, where they would embark on the night packet for Le Havre. In his last letter to Elizabeth on Friday, he said he would be at Hodgson's, the bookseller's shop near the Barretts' house, *"from* half-past three to *four precisely."*

"It is dreadful . . dreadful . . to have to give pain here by a voluntary act—for the first time in my life," she wrote her husband on her last evening at Wimpole Street. Her last hours in her home, she later wrote, were filled with "agitation and deep anguish—for it was the deepest of its kind, to leave Wimpole Street and those whom I tenderly loved." The inner conflict which so tortured her, the rival claims of her family and of her new love, would never be wholly resolved. She had been so close to her father, her sisters, and some of her brothers that she would suffer if they should no longer respond to her affection. Her father, she was certain, would explode with fury when he learned she had gone with Browning, but she hoped that "at last, perhaps" he would forgive them. She prophesied that her brothers would be "displeased" and "vexed at the occasion given to conversation" but that it would be "a passing feeling, and their hearts and their knowledge of circumstances may be trusted to justify me thoroughly." As for her sisters, with whom she had lived in great intimacy for many years, she dreaded to say goodbye to them. She knew they wholeheartedly approved of her step, and she hoped that all three would continue to share in one another's lives.

Elizabeth, Flush, Wilson, and Browning went to Southampton, according to plan, and then they suffered from a "miserable" passage all night. Browning had courageously assumed the responsibility for Elizabeth's health, but she was no less courageous in undertaking a trip which was to cost her much weariness and suffering before she finally reached Pisa.

11. From London to Pisa

ON SUNDAY MORNING, September 20, 1846, Elizabeth felt "sad at heart," and all three travelers were so "exhausted either by the sea or the sorrow" that they rested all day at Le Havre before setting out in the diligence for Rouen in the evening. As she sat in the coupé of the stagecoach that night, she noticed in front of her "now five horses, now seven . . all looking wild and loosely harnessed . . some of them white, some brown, some black, with the manes leaping as they galloped and the white reins dripping down over their heads . . such a fantastic scene it was in the moonlight! [she wrote Arabel]—and I who was a little feverish with the fatigue and the violence done to myself, in the self-control of the last few days, began to see it all as in a vision and to doubt whether I was in or out of the body." [1] Upon arriving at Rouen at one in the morning, they were told that their baggage must go on immediately to Paris by railroad. They had hoped to spend the rest of the night at Rouen, but instead Browning carried Elizabeth into the travelers' room of the Rouen hotel, where they had light refreshments before proceeding with their journey. After two successive nights without sleep, they were received at their hotel in Paris at ten o'clock Monday morning.

Robert then went directly to the Hotel de la Ville de Paris to call on Mrs. Jameson, who was out but later received his message and came that evening to see the Brownings. Elizabeth was so tired she could hardly speak, and she looked, as Mrs. Jameson later told her, "frightfully ill." On coming into their suite, Mrs. Jameson was "out of breath with wonder," and her "eyes opened as wide as Flush's." Although she had been told that Browning was the only man except Kenyon who was admitted to Elizabeth's room at Wimpole Street, she had never suspected a romance. But she left no doubt in their minds how she felt about the marriage: "He is a wise man in doing so . . and you are a wise woman, let the world say as it pleases! I shall dance for joy both in earth and in heaven, my dear friends." ² To her friend Lady Byron Mrs. Jameson wrote that Elizabeth was "nervous, frightened, ashamed, agitated, happy, miserable." ³ Then she added: "I have sympathized, scolded, rallied, cried and helped, and now they want me to join them on the road to the South." It had been the Brownings' intention to remain in Paris for two days only in order to await the arrival of their passports which had been taken from them at Le Havre by mistake. Also Elizabeth had, in Mrs. Jameson's words, "a feverish desire to go *on on*—as if there was to be neither peace nor health till she was beyond the Alps." But when the Brownings called upon Mrs. Jameson at her hotel the next morning, she persuaded them to remain with her in Paris for a few days before all of them should leave for Italy. Then they engaged a comfortable suite at her hotel. On Wednesday, September 23, Mrs. Jameson wrote that Elizabeth was "now better, more quiet, and willing to rest here a few days. Rest is indeed most necessary for her."

A day later she was still "in a most feeble state," according to Mrs. Jameson, who believed that she had "saved her life by persuading her to rest." She wrote Lady Byron that she found the Brownings "a great interest and a great care" and feared the marriage might not end well, for she did not have "faith in the poetical temperament as a means of permanent happiness." In the evenings Mrs. Jameson and the Brownings dined together at nearby restaurants, with Robert "pouring out rivers of wit and wisdom" and with Mrs. Jameson proving herself to be even more pleasant and congenial than she had been with Elizabeth in London. In the first letter Elizabeth wrote to Arabel after leaving her home, when the Brownings were still in Paris, and in many of her later letters from Pisa and Florence, she spoke of her never-ending wonder at the "miracle" that a man so gifted and brilliant, as she expressed it many times, would have fallen in love with her. His constant high spirits, tact, sense of humor, and tender care fully compensated her, she told Arabel, for her earlier sorrows and for the unjust attitude toward her of most of her family. Owing to her infirm health the Brownings had to stay in their apartment most of the time and to be "satisfied with the *idea* of Paris," which seemed to

From London to Pisa 183

Elizabeth a city "infinitely" beyond London in its magnificence. Yet they went once to the Louvre, with Mrs. Jameson on one side of her and Browning on the other, and Elizabeth had a brief glimpse of "the divine Raphaels . . unspeakable, those are." [4] Curiously enough, Mrs. Jameson had hesitated at first to accept the Brownings' invitation to go to Italy with them for fear her niece Gerardine—"a quiet earnest-looking little girl," in Browning's words—might be infected with the virus of romance. The Brownings could hardly have been blamed, however, when Gerardine, though still in her teens, surprised and dismayed her aunt in the spring of 1847 by becoming engaged to an impecunious painter in Rome, Robert Macpherson, whom in spite of Mrs. Jameson's dissuasion she later married.

All six (including Flush) left Paris on the evening of September 28, and the next day were at Orleans, from which Mrs. Jameson again wrote Lady Byron of the couple who had entreated her help and confidence. She no longer feared for Gerardine, since "the deportment of both is in the best taste." Browning seemed to her "altogether a most charming companion" with his gay and witty conversation and "his poetical fancies and antics, with every now and then the profoundest seriousness and tenderness interrupting the brilliant current of his imagination." In Elizabeth she saw "not a trace of animal spirits, tho evidently a sense of deep happiness, gratitude and love."

Elizabeth could not have been light-hearted after reading her letters from Wimpole Street. For the last few days she had been looking with increasing dread to the time when she would receive at Orleans her first mail since she had left. Finally the hour came— "my 'death warrant' I called it at the time, I was so anxious and terrified," she wrote her sisters—and Browning brought in "a great packet of letters." She sat holding them in her hands, "not able to open one, and growing paler and colder every moment." That she might "meet the agony alone," she asked Browning to go away for ten minutes, and then she read the "very hard letters, those from dearest Papa and dearest George." [5] The letter from her father was no less terrible than she had feared. He accused her of having sold her soul "for *genius* . . mere genius," as she reported to her sisters, and he informed her that he had disinherited her, cast her off forever, and for the rest of his life would consider her as dead. He was true to his word, for he never saw her again and left her nothing in his will. It did not seem to her that she had "deserved that full cup," but she did not feel called upon to judge her father, who had "peculiar tendencies," for which she could only pity him. But "more than all papa's dreadful words," George's letter particularly irritated her and, as she said, almost broke her heart. He told her bluntly that she had "sacrificed all delicacy and honour." [6] She explained to Henrietta that George had written "in only treating the whole case, I must say, precisely as if I had run away without being married at all in 'leaving the weight of sorrow and shame to be borne by my family' (the quotation is genuine.)." [7] What "vexed" Elizabeth most in George's letter "was something about 'Mr. Browning.'" She did not mention to Robert the slur her brother had cast upon him. It was hard for her to believe that George could have written thus, for only a year ago it was he who had taken her part, as far as he dared, in the Pisa dispute. Her other brothers simply ignored her, and she was not to hear from any of them until several months later. After she had read the harsh letters from home, Browning sat by her "for hours, pouring out floods of tenderness and goodness." As if to compensate her for the affection she had lost from her family, he loved her "more and more." A few days later he said (as Elizabeth wrote to her sisters), "I kissed your feet, my Ba, before I married you—but now I would kiss the ground under your feet, I love you with a so much greater love."

After the news from Wimpole Street, Kenyon's message of wholehearted approval was a great comfort to both Elizabeth and Robert. "Nothing but what is generous in thought and action could come from you and Browning," he wrote. "And the very peculiar circumstances of your case have transmuted what might have been otherwise called 'Imprudence' into 'Prudence,' and apparent wilfulness into real necessity." [8] The Brownings also received letters of best wishes from Chorley, Miss Mitford, Milnes, Barry Cornwall, Carlyle, and Elizabeth's physician Mr. Jago.

From Orleans the party went to Bourges, where Elizabeth entered the cathedral; it seemed to her "as if all the sunsets of time had stained the wonderful painted windows." [9] Thence they

From London to Pisa 185

traveled to Roanne and Lyons, from which, on October 6, they went down the Rhone to Avignon "in a dirty confined steamboat, the rain pouring in torrents," Mrs. Jameson wrote. Elizabeth peeped through the windows of the "miserable" cabin at the misty landscape and looked at the trellised vineyards and here and there a ruined castle. She was disappointed that the poor weather prevented her from catching a glimpse of the Alps. Her own letters to her sisters gave no hint of the physical suffering she had to endure but spoke only of her great happiness in her marriage and of her pleasure in seeing the monuments and scenery of the Continent. But Mrs. Jameson, in writing from Avignon of "our poor invalid," said that they not only "had to carry her fainting from the carriage but from her extreme thinness and weakness, every few hours journey has bruised her all over, till movement became almost unbearable." Through all her trials she had been patient, Mrs. Jameson wrote Lady Byron, and had shown an "unselfish sweetness of the temper" and an "unfailing consideration for others." Browning, according to Mrs. Jameson, was "most devoted." The day after their arrival at Avignon Elizabeth remained in bed, while the others went through the Palace of the Popes. The most celebrated episode of the wedding trip took place on Thursday, October 8, when they visited at Vaucluse the fountain which, as Elizabeth said, "in its dark prison of rocks flashes and roars and testifies to the memory of Petrarch." While all of them were standing beside the pool—"a most tumultuous torrent," wrote Mrs. Jameson—Elizabeth without a word suddenly began to walk across the slippery rocks, with the spray flying upon her from all sides. Browning asked in amazement, "Ba, are you losing your senses?" He followed and helped her, and they sat amidst the spray; while they watched the water boiling and churning around, Mrs. Jameson on the shore sketched them.[10]

They went from Vaucluse to Aix and Marseilles, where on the "burning, glaring afternoon" of October 11 they embarked as the only first-class passengers on the French steamer *L'Océan* for Genoa and Leghorn. (Except for their passage on the Rhone, the entire trip from Paris to Marseilles had been accomplished by diligence and by *vettura*. In the middle forties railroads were more of a novelty than a reality of public transportation.) After a miserable night, during which the ship rolled and pitched in the heavy sea, Elizabeth and Browning early the next morning left their cabins and, wrapped in heavy cloaks, stood on the deck to watch the "magnificent coast along which a thousand mountains and their rocks leapt up against the morning-sun." [11] Although the vessel did not stay so close to the shore as in calm weather, Elizabeth could see clearly the green blinds to the windows of the houses of one small Italian town after another. "It was all glorious, and past speaking of," she wrote Arabel. They arrived at Genoa on the evening of the twelfth and spent the night "under the frescoed roof" of an old palace, while their ship tied up for twenty-four hours. When Mrs. Jameson and Gerardine went off the next day by themselves to see the monuments of Genoa, Elizabeth in spite of her weakness took a short walk with Browning. The scenes she remembered from her first view of an Italian city were the narrow alleys and streets, the "palaces looking all strange and noble," and the inside of a church where the mass was being celebrated.[12] The church was more gorgeously decorated than any she had hitherto seen, with its altars of "a shining marble encrusted with gold," its "great columns of twisted porphyry," and its "frescoed angels glancing from the ceiling." On the marble pavement were kneeling monks dressed in brown serge and girded with ropes, nuns of various orders, and Genoese ladies whose heads were covered with the national veil. "Beautiful Genoa—what a vision it is!" she wrote ecstatically. Elizabeth, when she traveled, was always enthusiastic; she liked to go to new places, remembered all the things and people she saw, and described them fully in long letters to her sisters (much longer than the ones she received from them) in which every quarter inch of the almost transparent paper was covered on both sides with her microscopic but very legible handwriting. On the night of the thirteenth they suffered from an even more stormy passage to Leghorn, where they arrived at eight the next morning. Soon afterward they all went by railroad to Pisa.

When Mrs. Jameson had first seen the Brownings in Paris, she had thought them "a pretty pair to go thro this prosaic world together!" In Pisa, after observing them closely for almost a month, she wrote to Lady Byron that although Browning was "the very prince of travelling companions" because of his charm and intel-

Collegio Ferdinando, Pisa

From London to Pisa

ligence, he was, however, "in all the common things of this life the most impractical of men, the most uncalculating, rash, in short the worst *manager* I ever met with." And Elizabeth, she said, was "in her present state, and from her long seclusion almost helpless." She continued pessimistically: "Now only conceive the ménage that is likely to ensue and without FAULT on either side!" Before long, however, Elizabeth wrote that Mrs. Jameson was praising them for their "miraculous prudence and economy."

After a few days in a hotel, the Brownings rented an apartment in a handsome sixteenth-century palace designed by Vasari and called the Collegio di Ferdinando, which is within a few minutes' walk of the cathedral and the leaning tower. Their weekly rent, which included the use of linen and eating utensils, was £1 6s. 9d. In her first letter to Arabel from Pisa, Elizabeth boasted of the cheapness, in comparison with rents in England, but later the Brownings realized the sum was exorbitant and that their "padrone" had taken them for "millionaires" because they had failed to bargain. Mrs. Jameson (Mona Nina or Aunt Nina, as the Brownings came to call her) and Gerardine remained near by in a hotel until about November 4, when after "a painful parting to everybody," that "affectionate, generous woman" and her niece went to Florence.

MEANWHILE Mr. Barrett at Wimpole Street gave no outward appearance of having been affected by Elizabeth's action, and the sisters reported to her that he was in fine spirits and often entertained at dinner. He sent one of Elizabeth's letters back to her unopened, complained to his family that she had "deceived" him by marrying without his consent, and refused to be any longer a trustee of her funds.[13] Toward Arabel he was for several months cold and peremptory, because he suspected her of complicity; in his anger he turned her out of her old room where she had been with Elizabeth. Furthermore he had all of Elizabeth's books removed from that room and placed in storage and instructed that the bills be sent to her. She had to pay £5 a year until she sent for them in the summer of 1848.[14] Her father's unrelenting anger greatly depressed Elizabeth. "If I had committed a murder and forgery," she wrote Henrietta, "I don't see how Papa could have shown his sense of it otherwise than he has done. . . . Oh, how unkind it all is. Set my fault at the largest, call it fault or crime if you choose and the unkindness covers and overpasses the whole. I could not have had the heart to act so to anyone I had ever loved had that person wronged me more than I ever wronged an enemy —it is hard and cruel I think." [15] And after she had her first miscarriage in March, she thought "somewhat bitterly" that if she had died that day, her husband would not have been able to communicate with any of her male relatives. She then resolved never again to live in England, for beside the climate "there would be bitterness on all sides . . bad enough as it is, but intolerable under nearer circumstances." As she wrote Henrietta on March 31, "I cannot *help* considering myself *wronged.*" [16]

The attitude of the brothers astonished and embittered her even more, and she regretted that she had ever taken them into her confidence, as she partially had. Did they secretly admire her for having asserted her independence but fear to express themselves because of their father? The answer is probably that although they were not angry at her for leaving home, they shared in his disapproval of Browning because he was living on Elizabeth's fortune. Many years later, at the time of the publication of the love letters, Charles John took it upon himself as the eldest surviving brother to protest the decision of the Brownings' son and "to relate the facts." From the tone of the letter, which he wrote from Jamaica in 1899, it is clear that he had always sided with his father. He implied that Browning the poet had behaved surreptitiously during his courtship, and he asserted that Mr. Barrett had "lost" his daughter and had "never recovered" from the episode. "I venture to say," he wrote, "few fathers would take the hand of a man who had so acted." [17]

Early in 1847 Septimus hinted in a letter to Elizabeth that she had been "foolish" in allowing herself to be "overpersuaded" by Browning, "who was the real criminal." George sent a second "unkind" note, in which he seems to have intimated that he would "forgive" her but would not accept Browning.[18] She quite properly refused to reply to such a letter. "Those insinuations about money [she wrote Henrietta] and 'Mr. Browning' being reiterated are really 'de trop' altogether," and they angered both her and Robert.

"Money, money, money, nothing but money," she continued. "My brothers are all of them considerably younger than my husband and have seen less of the world; but that he is infinitely less worldly than any of them, taking no thought of this filthy money, money . . is as true . . as that he would be no husband of mine if it were otherwise. I wish with all my heart that my sense of duty (with this uncertain future as concerns my health and other things) would allow me to go to him and say, 'Now let us do as you have wished; let us throw this money back to my family and trust to ourselves for the rest. Accept such a situation and let us be clean of the imputation of which now for the first time I will tell you.' Good Heavens!—how little they know *him* . . and how ungenerous men can be in their guesses at the unknown. Would George himself act so, for instance, if he married a woman under informal circumstances so that her money became his? . . . I wonder they do not say in Wimpole Street that he married me in order to murder me at leisure." [19] It seemed to Elizabeth that Browning, with barely enough money to live by and the possibility of her future sickness had made a "fair exchange for freedom and a brilliant life in London."

Her aunt Arabella Graham-Clarke, who had been with her at Hope End and during the terrible years at Torquay, wrote that Elizabeth had been very "wicked" not to ask her father's permission first, that "the world" blamed her "dreadfully," and that her conduct would be a "drawback" to her happiness for the rest of her life.[20] Mrs. Hedley (Aunt Jane) was more sympathetic but was sorry that Elizabeth had not made known her plans in advance. Elizabeth's old friends the Martins, who knew Mr. Barrett better than anyone else outside the family (except Kenyon) sent their unqualified approval. Kenyon "thrust his hand into the fire" by managing Elizabeth's financial affairs after her father had given them up and by speaking to him in favor of the Brownings "with the whole weight of his personal influence." Later he became a trustee of her funds, along with Browning's old friends Joseph Arnould and H. F. Chorley. Elizabeth and Robert never forgot their gratitude toward Kenyon for his many kind acts in their behalf.

From her cottage at Three Mile Cross Miss Mitford continued

to send benevolent letters. Elizabeth had written to her, "Nothing is changed between us, nothing can ever interfere with sacred confidences, remember." But everything was changed between them. Miss Mitford, for whom the future was to be one of increasing loneliness and poor health, lost more by their physical separation than Elizabeth. It seemed to Miss Mitford that Elizabeth had forgotten their "tender friendship of twelve years." She felt that Elizabeth, like many women who marry "after the usual time" doted upon her husband and cared "for none but his admirers," and Miss Mitford was "none of those." Browning she had always considered indolent and effeminate; she could not forgive him "for not working" and for living on his wife's money, as before he had lived on his father's. "I fear that marriage much," she wrote to a friend.[21]

HOWEVER much some of her relatives censured Elizabeth for improper conduct, the culprit herself was not *"improved,* but *transformed* rather," in the opinion of Mrs. Jameson. Likewise Browning said that if her sisters could see her as he had the "happiness to see her, so changed as to be hardly recognisable, and with a fair prospect of life and enjoyment for many years to come . . they could *not* be very angry I am sure!" [22] To the satisfaction of both her sisters and of Browning, Elizabeth found that she was able to reduce gradually the amount of morphine she needed, although for the rest of her life she was always somewhat dependent on the drug.

With her health thus improved, she was enjoying her liberty and was happier than ever before. A few days before Christmas she wrote to Miss Mitford of herself and Browning that there had "not been a shadow between us, nor a *word,*" that the only difference in her husband was "simply and clearly an increase of affection." Pisa she thought was a beautiful little city, with its great palaces and with "the rolling, turbid Arno, striking its golden path between them underneath the marble bridges." In spite of her delight in Pisa, during all the time she lived there she was unable because of her frailty to visit most of the churches or to climb the leaning tower, but every day before the cold weather set in she went for a short walk with Browning. Week after week they were flooded with "a divine sunshine" and enjoyed such a stretch of "cloudless, exquisite weather" that they wondered whether it were June instead of November. Now and then they visited the Campo Santo to look at the fourteenth and fifteenth-century frescoes, which were to retain their clarity and freshness until they were mostly destroyed in the war of 1939–44. They lived very quietly, seeing almost no one at Pisa, and for amusement they read together Vasari's *Lives,* Stendhal's *Le Rouge et le noir* (for Elizabeth a second time), and Soulié's *Saturnin Fichet,* the latter of which finally became so tedious to Browning that he allowed Elizabeth to finish it by herself. Both of them were impressed with Stendhal's power. "What a book it is really [Elizabeth wrote Miss Mitford], and so full of pain and bitterness, and the gall of iniquity!"

Their way of life, "free from domestic cares and the ordering and cooking of dinners," was in Elizabeth's words, "a continental fashion which we never cease commending" and one which she never tired of praising to her sisters (neither of whom ever had the slightest desire to live outside of England) for its inexpensiveness and simplicity. They dined "on thrushes and chianti with a miraculous cheapness," having their meals sent to their apartment at two o'clock from a *trattoria* at the cost of 8*d.* each, with "no trouble, no cook, no kitchen; the prophet Elijah or the lilies of the field took as little thought for their dining." At six they had their "coffee, and rolls of milk, made of milk, I mean," and at nine their "supper (call it supper, if you please) of roast chestnuts and grapes." Prices were so cheap that contrary to the experience of most travelers, they were able to stretch their money even further than they had hoped. Their first six months of spending for the three adults, inclusive of the journey from London and the two weeks in Paris, was only £150. Elizabeth heard that in Pisa they could live for £250 a year in an excellent apartment and could have their own carriage and two horses "and a man servant to boot." And at Florence, she was told, all prices were astonishingly low. Another freedom they enjoyed was the freedom from Grundyism; Elizabeth believed that it was much easier for them to live their own lives on the Continent without interference from relatives and friends than it would have been in England.

"The worst of Pisa is, or would be to some persons," she wrote Mrs. Martin, "that, socially speaking, it has its dullnesses." But to her sisters she later conveyed a different impression. In a letter to Henrietta she said that she had heard to her surprise that Pisa was "very 'gay' just now . . a weekly 'reception' at the Governor's, besides the Baroness," [23] and to Arabel she complained that "this place is too English for us, in the social party-giving sense." [24] She learned that two English women who had recently called on her, a Mrs. Young and her daughter, gave "great soirées" to which "everybody" was invited: the "Religious" on one night "to tea and serious conversation" and the "Irreligious" on another to enjoy "music and dancing," [25] It is interesting that it was Robert more than Elizabeth who objected to intrusions upon their privacy, but neither of them wished to take part in the trivial social affairs of the English colony. Elizabeth wrote Henrietta that in Florence, "We mean to cut everybody we ever knew, so that nobody need be offended. Robert works himself up into a fine frenzy in talking of the horrors of mixed society, and sometimes exhorts me just as if I wanted exhortation—'Those people will spoil all our happiness, if we once let them in,—you will see— If you speak of your health and save yourself on that plea, they will seize upon *me*— oh, don't I know them?' He walks up and down the room, thoroughly worked up." [26] He urged her particularly not to receive Mrs. Trollope, who was living permanently in Florence: "I do hope, Ba, if you don't wish to give me the greatest pain, that you won't receive that vulgar, pushing, woman who is not fit to speak to you." But in both Florence and Rome the Brownings were always gracious to all their visitors.

While Elizabeth soon became very fond of Italy because of its simple domestic and social arrangements, its cheapness, its warm climate, and its beautiful scenery and monuments, she was disillusioned about the state of its literature and of the Church. "There seem to be no *men* here," she complained to Arabel, and she commented on "the intellectual and moral degradation" in Italy, comparing the country unfavorably with France and England, both of which she thought were "centuries before these Italians —to judge from the *writings*." [27] Elizabeth had arrived in Italy with the expectation, apparently, of coming upon a literary and artistic renaissance. Yet what she found were "translations, translations, translations from third and fourth and fifth rate French and English writers, chiefly French; the roots of thought, here in Italy, seem dead in the ground." In her opinion Italian writing was "purely dull and conventional"; she could find "no breath nor pulse in the Italian genius." The comparison with France and England was not altogether fair, because Italy was then under the domination of Austria. The atmosphere prevailing throughout the peninsula was indifferent and even hostile to creative activity in the arts, and for the first two-thirds of the nineteenth century the energies of most Italian writers and artists were absorbed in the political and military phases of the *Risorgimento*. As for the Church, nothing struck Elizabeth so much as "the want of all reverence and decency" in the congregations. On Christmas eve she had wrapped herself up in shawls, furs, and a great cloak and had gone with Browning to the midnight service in the cathedral. Accustomed as she was to the quiet and serenity of Paddington Chapel, she was surprised to see that the Italians, who have always been an intensely individualistic and communicative people, retained both those characteristics even when they were in church. Elizabeth had been looking forward to a thoughtful sermon, but none was preached because "the giving of religious instruction in that form, seems shrunk from." While the mass was being said, the people walked about and conversed loudly enough for Elizabeth "to hear three yards off," and two signoras on their knees beside her were laughing and talking to each other "with all their might." The gestures of the priests as they chanted hoarsely at the altar she thought "insignificant and feeble." Both the services and the response of the congregation seemed to her "most melancholy,—melancholy beyond all my expectations." The Italians, she wrote Arabel, "have the sun, and no light." [28]

During her first winter in Italy, Elizabeth did little to advance her career as a poet. She and Robert hoped to publish jointly a volume of poems on Italian subjects, but they later abandoned the project; with one minor exception (*Two Poems* of 1854) they continued to issue their volumes separately. She sent to *Blackwood's* some sonnets, for which she received £25, and they were published in the issues of May and June 1847. Of the eight sonnets which appeared, all had been written several years earlier. Two had personal associations: the "Two Sketches" of her sisters, although neither of them is named in the title or in the text. Henrietta had a cheerful smile and regular features:

> The shadow of her face upon the wall
> May take your memory to the perfect Greek, . . .

and Arabel had "high-hearted fortitude" and gave Elizabeth "sympathy" and "comfort." *Blackwood's* made no mention of the fact that any of the poems had been published elsewhere, but the sonnet describing Arabel, which was entitled "Sketch II," had already been printed in the *Christian Mother's Magazine.* Elizabeth's volumes of 1844 were enjoying a steady sale; in March 1847 she wrote to one of her sisters that only 180 copies of her *Poems* remained and that Moxon had sent them £75 that year,[29] an amount which was largely Elizabeth's earnings, rather than Robert's, whose last three numbers of the *Bells and Pomegranates* had barely earned expenses of publication. But with great pride Elizabeth told Arabel that Moxon had not rendered her husband a bill for several years. "I assure you," she wrote, "we shall make our way by poetry yet." Late in December 1846 she sent a poem across the Atlantic in aid of the abolitionist cause, "too ferocious, perhaps, for the Americans to publish," called "The Runaway Slave at Pilgrim's Point," to the *Liberty Bell* of Boston, where it appeared in the edition of 1848. The subject had been given her by a cousin Richard Barrett, Speaker of the House of Assembly in Jamaica, whom she had seen in England when she was a child. It is a horrifying story told from the point of view of a dying negro slave, who is standing at the place where the first band of Pilgrims landed in search of liberty. She had fallen in love with another slave, who had been killed by the overseers. Then she had been tied up and flogged, was forced into concubinage with a white man, gave birth to a child who resembled the father in color, and strangled her baby out of hatred toward the white man. Like "The Cry of the Children," the poem was written to redress a great social wrong. It is, however, too blunt and shocking to have any enduring artistic worth and lacks the compelling rhythm of the earlier work.

From London to Pisa

After the Brownings had been in Pisa for two months, they regretted having taken their apartment for half a year, since they would have preferred to spend the early part of the spring in Florence. There was less to see in Pisa than in Florence, and Browning found the countryside monotonous in his daily walks. Elizabeth had a miscarriage late in March, which made it impossible for them to move until she had recovered some of her strength. On April 20, however, she was well enough to go to Florence with Browning in the diligence. The Tuscan countryside "with vine-festooned plains and breaks of valley and hill— ridges of mountain and sweeps of river" was much more beautiful than she had expected to see between Pisa and Florence. She had only a glimpse of Florence as she crossed one of the bridges of the "old dear yellow Arno" to the Hotel du Nord, into which Browning carried her and placed her on the sofa, where she "could only wait for coffee and dream of being in the city of the Medici." After staying at the hotel for two days, they took a lease of two months, which they later extended to three, on an apartment at 4222 Via delle Belle Donne, just off the Piazza Santa Maria Novella.[30] Elizabeth thought the rooms "infinitely superior" to their accommodations in Pisa, and the rent was only £4 monthly. Within three or four days after their arrival she was looking forward to enjoying the artistic treasures of "divine" Florence. And so the Brownings began their lives in the city which more than any other is associated with their names.

12. Italian Affairs and "Casa Guidi Windows"

FLORENCE, with its Arno river, which "rushes through the midst of its palaces like a crystal arrow," seemed to Elizabeth, as it has to countless other visitors, "the most beautiful of the cities devised by man." If Browning and she could now stand, for example, near the Church of San Miniato and look down once again upon their favorite city, they would see that its fabric had suffered only slight damage in the course of a century. The principal landmarks would all be familiar: the dome designed by Brunelleschi for the cathedral, Giotto's *campanile,* the great, massive tower of the Palazzo Vecchio, the lesser tower of the Bargello, and the slender, delicate spire of the Badia. The white houses among the vineyards and silver-gray olive orchards on the opposite hill stretching up toward Fiesole, with its convent, cathedral, and bell tower, also present much the same appearance. They would notice three temporary bridges replacing the Carraia, the Santa Trinità, and the Grazie, but from their vantage point they would not be aware of the destruction of the buildings around each end of the Ponte Vecchio in the war of 1939–44. The population of the city has increased fivefold in the last hundred years, and it has been built up far beyond its earlier boundaries. The Brownings must have considered the medieval walls one of the most characteristic sights in Florence; all of them on the north side of the Arno were demolished three or four years after Elizabeth's death to make room for broad boulevards around that portion of the city. Another change they would observe in the outline of Florence is that made by the large postwar skyscraper, which is fortunately not in the older section.

The Brownings would no doubt be surprised to see many thousands of tourists in Florence, most of whom spend only two or three days of frenzied sight-seeing before rushing away for an equally short stay at Rome or at Venice. One hundred years ago almost no foreigners came to Florence or remained there during the summer. At other seasons it had fewer visitors than now, but those who came were apt to be more leisurely travelers. Painters, sculptors, writers, and many persons who had no intellectual or artistic abilities but ample funds visited the city with the intention of sojourning several months or a year, but often, like the Brownings, they became so enchanted with Florence that they never again called any other place their home. The English colony tended to become a closely knit community who lived their lives insulated from those of the Italians around them. English society was "kept up much after the old English models," Elizabeth wrote, "with a proper disdain for continental simplicities of expense." Almost every woman had her "day" when she "received," and some, like Mrs. Trollope, who was, Elizabeth said, "in the full flood and flow of Florentine society," had their public days for the many and their private days for close friends. The Irish novelist Charles Lever had a series of "grand English private-theatricals" at his house, and a James Montgomery Stuart gave a course of lectures on Shakespeare. According to Murray's *Hand-Book* (1847), there were grocers and "fancy shops" well supplied with all English articles, a *farmacia* "where every English patent medicine may be obtained," "an English chemist and druggist," "two excellent English physicians," "a good English tailor," "an English lady" who was the proprietor of a school "for all branches of general female education," and an English chaplain to provide the girls with religious instruction. In 1844 a building was erected in Florence for the Church of England to hold its services; much to Elizabeth's disgust everyone had to pay at the door the price of admission, which was about 1s. 6d. Elizabeth was not usually well enough to attend any church in Florence, while Robert often went to the services of the Church of Scotland, of which a Reverend Mr. Hannah was the preacher.

The fantastically low prices of everything in Florence surprised and delighted the Brownings. A large roast turkey cost them only 1s. 10d.—"just such an one, Wilson thinks, as at this time of year would cost twenty shillings in London." It seemed to Elizabeth that "the wheels of life slide on upon the grass (according to continental ways) with little trouble and less expense." Their *donna di servizio* came to them for a few hours every day to make beds, clean the rooms, and brush Robert's clothes, all for six shillings a month. Just as in Pisa, the Brownings arranged to have their dinners delivered regularly to them from a *trattoria*. Elizabeth did not even have to order the meals. "They send us what they like [she wrote Henrietta], and everything cooked excellently and well served and hot." A typical meal for three, which consisted of vermicelli soup, sturgeon, turkey, stewed beef, mashed potatoes, and cheese cakes, cost two shillings and eightpence. Wine, which Browning bought separately, was about three pennies a bottle.

What especially charmed Elizabeth was "the innocent gaiety of the people, who, forever at feast day and holiday celebrations, come and go along the streets, the women in elegant dresses and with glittering fans, shining away every thought of Northern cares and taxes, such as make people grave in England." She felt that at such times no class distinctions were maintained among the crowds on the streets, that rich and poor alike, from grand duchess to charwoman, were "listening to the same music and walking in the same gardens, and looking at the same Raphaels even!" Everyone "appears dressed for a drawing room," she wrote Miss Mitford, and among all the people she found only "the most gracious and graceful courtesy and gentleness." The one drawback to the city was the noise of people walking, talking, and singing under her windows all night long. "The worst of Florence is the noise," she wrote Arabel. "I do believe that the people never sleep at night except by the merest accident." [1]

During their first two or three years in Florence the Brownings lived very quietly, as they had at Pisa, with Robert never going "anywhere except to take a walk with Flush"; their days passed happily "with music and books and writing and talking." They continued to read together Vasari, and Elizabeth devoured as many as she could find of the latest novels of Sue, Soulié, George Sand, and Dumas. On some evenings they strolled to the Trinità bridge: "Oh, that Arno in the sunset," she wrote, "with the moon and evening star standing by, how divine it is!" In her enthusiasm

August 2. Palazzo Guidi, near
 but direct Poste Restante .. it is safer.

I hasten to thank you my dearest kindest friend, with all my heart, for your goodness to me & mine. This must be the first word,—but the next purpose is to set myself a little right with you & the matter of what must have struck you probably as most unfriendly & unaffectionate reserve & silence — Do pardon me for all things which have seemed unkind. Your name has again & again been present to my thoughts, though I could come & stay so long in your Italy without a word or sign .. yes, and leave England nearly at the same time with you & not say distinctly that I was going & how. Oh .. among many painful feelings this was one .. that you must be displeased with me — and then I had no courage to write, & preferred to wait & see you face to face in Rome & show you my heart at the same time. Was it not pricked, do you imagine, when Mr! Going found me out at Pisa & told me that you had bade a friend of yours enquire about me? yes indeed. — Still I did not write .. I would wait I thought — And I waited till on the only evening I have spent in society since my marriage (or for how many years before?) I met your friend Mr! Collyer & heard of your being at the Baths of Lucca, & was promised your address which she sent to me a few half hours before we proceeded to scale the heights of Vallombrosa & persuade the monks to take us in

Letter from Mrs. Browning to Fanny Dowglass, August 2, 1847

Elizabeth used that adjective indiscriminately for works of art, scenery, and cities. On other evenings they crossed the Ponte Vecchio to look at "Cellini's god-like Perseus" in the *Loggia dei Lanzi*.

Often they went for a drive late in the afternoon in an open carriage, with Elizabeth holding a parasol over her head. They would usually begin by looking at Masaccio's frescoes in the Brancacci Chapel of the Church of the Carmine, or they would go into the Church of Santa Croce for a view of Michelangelo's tomb and Giotto's frescoes. Afterward they would take a long drive in the park of the Cascine before returning home. Now and then they went for a walk in the Boboli gardens and saw "the great fountain, surrounded with the famous nudities which overwhelmed Wilson at her first arrival at Florence." [2] In this beautiful park behind the Pitti Palace, they strolled "into the arbor-walks, with lattices cut out of the deep green, showing glimpses of the Apennines, of Fiesole, of olive grounds grey against the hills," and when Elizabeth was tired they sat down on the marble benches and talked.

In June the Brownings made one of their rare appearances at an evening reception, in order to meet R. B. Hoppner, the former English consul at Venice, and his wife. Mrs. Hoppner amused Elizabeth by telling her of the visit which "poor Shelley and his wife" made to the Hoppners' home in Venice. Upon their arrival they ate nothing but some thin gruel, boiled cabbages, and cherries, but Mrs. Hoppner before long "seduced" Shelley from vegetarianism by tempting him with thick slices of roast beef.[3] When the grand festa of San Giovanni, the patron saint of Florence, was held during the Brownings' first June in their new home, they saw the chariot races in the Piazza Santa Maria Novella. "On all sides up against the houses, up against the great church, up against the convent walls [she wrote Arabel] seats were raised, one over one, and the people crowded everywhere close as bees, only shining like butterflies, with their pretty dresses and glittering fans. Every seat, every window looked alive. The monks stood at the monastery windows, and we laughed to observe that there was room for just two at each." [4]

After the Brownings had been in Florence about five weeks,

Elizabeth wrote Arabel that she had been once each to the Uffizi gallery, the Pitti Palace, and the studio of Hiram Powers.[5] She implied that if the galleries, which were open in the morning and until three in the afternoon, were not closed so early, she would have gone more frequently. "You may conceive the impossibility of going out in the morning," [6] she wrote her sister; but it is not clear why she would not have preferred to visit the museums early in the day and thus avoid the heat of an Italian afternoon. Her comments on the art she saw in Florence and later in Rome, Siena, and other Italian cities are almost always disappointing. Two of her favorite paintings, as for many other nineteenth-century travelers to Florence, were the "Madonna della Seggiola" and the "Madonna del Granduca." Of these and the other Raphaels she wrote to Arabel, "Divine, divine, they are," and to Henrietta, "I am giddy . . . with the Raphaels." The "Venus" of the Tribune had no effect upon her, whereas the "Eve" of Powers, which she saw in the original clay, before the Italian marble cutters had polished away its originality, she thought "very serenely beautifully sad" as she stood "in divine unconsciousness of naked beauty." She much preferred it to the ringleted "Venus" of Canova, which for her had "such suggestion of indecency" from the way she was "huddling her drapery round her waist." [7]

Hiram Powers was one of a group of romantic expatriate artists, most of them American or English, who lived in Italy in the middle of the nineteenth century. Many had gone there for the training in sculpture or painting they could not find in their own countries. While a few, like William Page, eventually returned to their native lands, the majority found the atmosphere of Rome or Florence so congenial that they preferred to remain in Italy. For most of them, the drive and originality they may have possessed in the beginning died away gradually in the pleasant circumstances of their exile. Although Powers took himself seriously as a sculptor and although his studio was one of the chief tourist attractions of Florence, he was essentially a mechanic and a shrewd Yankee businessman rather than an artist. He came originally from a small town in Vermont and like the other American carvers in Italy at that time had no training in his craft, little knowledge of human anatomy, and only slight ability in modeling. Hawthorne was one of the few observers of his studio who recognized his limitations. While he was attracted to Powers because of his frankness, good humor, and unaffected ways, he thought that he saw "too clearly what is within his range to be aware of any region of mystery beyond." After talking with him for a while, Hawthorne wrote, "you feel inclined to think and see a little further for yourself." [8] Within the Brownings' first month in Florence, Powers called on them; Elizabeth declared the following day that he was a "true genius." She wrote Henrietta, "I took one of my fancies to the man, and might well do so as he was very kind to me . . ." Early in the autumn she said that Powers was their "chief friend and favorite," and in the same letter she referred to this "most charming, simple, straightforward, genial American" as a "man of genius." Rather more than Robert, she became a very close friend of Powers because of their common interest in Swedenborgianism and spiritualism. She wrote a sonnet on his statue the "Greek Slave," finished in the middle forties, which achieved a sensational success when it was shown at the International Exhibition in London in 1851. The work looks in some ways like an uninspired imitation of the "Venus de' Medici." The face is without expression, the modeling is lean and monotonous, much of the anatomy is incorrect, and the sculptor devoted too much attention to the accessories of the chains and shackles and the embroidery of the cloth on the post upon which the right hand is resting. The influence of art "against man's wrong" is the theme of Elizabeth's sonnet on the "fair stone," with its "passionless perfection" and its "divine face."

The Brownings' first guest was not Powers but Mrs. Jameson, who came to their new apartment on Friday evening, April 23. Just as Robert was playing to Elizabeth "prostrate on the sofa, Shakespeare's favourite air (as discovered by poetical antiquaries) a voice said 'upon my word here's domestic harmony!' and lo! Mrs. Jameson stood in the room!" She had arrived with Gerardine a day earlier than expected, so that all of them might celebrate Shakespeare's birthday together, and she brought "a bottle of wine from Arezzo in order to do it the due honors in company with 'two poets.'" Elizabeth she thought was "looking very well considering everything," and Robert seemed the same "inexhaustible man." Upon that last remark Elizabeth commented to Mrs. Jameson, "and think of the stream running just the same for these six months past, ever since we parted!" For a week the Brownings entertained her and her niece before they began their trip back to England. A fortnight later Elizabeth wrote Mrs. Jameson to tell her how much Robert and she missed her; in the same letter she spoke again of her new happiness in life which was, however, tempered by "some griefs, which are and must be griefs."

She was thinking of the birthday which would soon be celebrated in Wimpole Street, the first May twenty-eighth since the estrangement between her father and herself. The day after her father's anniversary she wrote to Arabel that her heart had been full, for "to be so cast off" was "a lasting grief" to her, "notwithstanding all other sources of happiness." [9] Unfortunately for her peace of mind, she kept brooding over the wrongs she had received from her old home and expended her energy in fruitless regrets. She wrote that she could never forget what she had left behind, since her love for her father had "always been a peculiar thing" and that he could have held her "by a thread" [10] if he had so wished. About a month later she let Henrietta know how bitterly she resented the attitude of her brothers. She hoped that they might wish to visit her in Florence: "If Papa knows that they are on the Rhine or at Milan, that will be enough: there need be no scrape with him. I long to see some of them; and such a proof of their still caring for me would go to my heart." [11] Their point of view, she thought, was indefensible: "I have no pride for my own part, only let me say: for having grieved and displeased any of them, I am sorry . . and not least sorry when I enter least into their views. But whether I *have been right or wrong, they are wrong now,* or there is no right and love. . . . They are wrong who stand aloof from me thus and thus."

By the middle of July Elizabeth's health had so improved that she and Robert were able to make their first trip away from Florence. One morning at four o'clock they set off for Vallombrosa in the foothills of the Apennines, about twenty miles east of Florence. As their carriage stopped in front of a small hotel in the village of Pelago, Elizabeth started at hearing someone say in a hearty American accent, "Why Mrs. Browning!" It was a young writer from Boston, George William Curtis, who had recently visited the Brownings. Several other Americans and Curtis were also going to Vallombrosa, but they were too polite to intrude on the Brownings and went ahead of them on horseback. From Pelago Elizabeth and Wilson "travelled in basket sledges drawn by four white oxen," with Robert riding beside them. "Such pine woods, supernaturally silent, with the ground black as ink, such chestnut and beech forest hanging from the mountains, such rocks and torrents, such chasms and ravines!" Elizabeth wrote with her characteristic verve. To their great disappointment their hoped-for visit of two months at the ancient monastery was cut short after five days, when they were "expelled ignominiously" by the new abbot, "a St. Sejanus of a holy man, and a petticoat stank in his nostrils."

Upon their return, the heat in their old apartment was so intense that Browning found a spacious and much cooler suite of seven rooms on the *primo piano* of the Palazzo Guidi, where as "successors to a Russian prince," they enjoyed the use of "marble consoles, carved and gilt," armchairs of crimson and white satin, and "noble mirrors," for about a guinea a week and an additional nine shillings a month to the porter.[12] Casa Guidi is a great dark, grim-looking palace dating from the fifteenth century, with two features characteristic of Florentine architecture: the overhanging eaves and the rough stonework on some of the lower portions of the building. It is situated between Via Maggio and Via Mazzetta, where the two streets converge at an angle, and from the front of the palace, which faces a *piazzetta* at the end of Via Romana, may be seen a part of the Piazza Pitti and one wing of the great palace behind. On one side of a central passage in the apartment were Robert's room, Wilson's bedroom, and her sitting room, with all three looking toward the Pitti. The principal chambers of the suite were on the other side of the passage: the dining room, the drawing room, Elizabeth's own room—all three of which were of magnificent proportions, with high coffered ceilings, and the somewhat smaller sitting room.[13] Eight windows of the main sitting rooms opened on a small stone balcony, supported by arches, which projected slightly from the first story over the sidewalk below. Across the street was the blank gray wall of an ancient

Casa Guidi

convent church "called San Felice for good omen." On the evenings when Elizabeth and Robert did not stroll to the Arno, they paced up and down their small terrace, "where there is just room for two to walk," listened to the organ and choir, and waited for the moon to rise above the church building.

Early in October 1847 when the propietor of Casa Guidi demanded a higher rent for the winter season, the Brownings moved to an apartment in the same neighborhood, at 1881 Via Maggio.[14] Although their new lodgings were quieter at night, since Elizabeth's bedroom looked into a courtyard, they were much smaller and more expensive, costing £5 7s. a month. But after ten days there they found the rooms too cold to stay in them any longer, and they "had to pay heaps of guineas away" to break the lease. They moved to furnished rooms "yellow with sunshine from morning to evening" in the Piazza Pitti just opposite the palace where Leopold II, the Grand Duke of Tuscancy, lived. The Brownings remained in this apartment until early in the following May. From her windows Elizabeth could see the civic guard on *festa* days show the Florentines their "new helmets and epaulettes and the glory thereof." Crowds came to view the spectacle in the Piazza Pitti "like children to see rows of dolls, only the children would tire sooner than the Tuscans."

The most frequent visitor to the Brownings' new apartment that fall was the niece of Lord Corke, Mary Boyle, who brought a letter of introduction from one of Elizabeth's English friends, Miss Fanny Dowglass, whom Miss Boyle had met at Bagni di Lucca. Every so often at nine in the evening Miss Boyle caught the Brownings at their "hot chestnuts and mulled wine" and sat with them at their fireside. She seemed to Browning "a little lively aristocrat," and Elizabeth wrote that "a kinder, more cordial little creature, full of talent and accomplishment, never had the world's polish on it." Miss Boyle in her memoirs spoke of Elizabeth's "pale, thin hand," her "small delicate face," her "clusters of long curls," and her figure, which was "so fragile as to appear but an ethereal covering."[15] Another visitor was George S. Hillard, a graduate of Harvard College and a Boston lawyer, politician, and writer on literary subjects, who had reviewed Elizabeth's poetry in 1842; she thought him "a very intelligent man, of a good, noble spirit."

He too remembered her slight figure and her face "expressive of genius and sensibility, shaded by a veil of long brown locks." Like many others who recorded their impressions of her, he noticed that her voice was "tremulous" as it "flutters over her words." Also he was impressed by her extreme fragility; he had "never seen a human frame which seemed so nearly a transparent veil for a celestial and immortal spirit." [16]

DURING the autumn and winter of 1847-48 Elizabeth wrote "A Meditation in Tuscany" on Italian affairs and sent the poem in the spring to *Blackwood's,* the editor of which did not publish it, however, because he felt the military and political situation had changed so greatly that everything in the poem was out of date, and also that the struggle for freedom in Tuscany would be a subject too remote from the interests of most of the readers of the magazine.[17] The "Meditation" later became the first part of *Casa Guidi Windows,* which was published in 1851. Soon after the death of the reactionary Gregory XVI on June 1, 1846, Cardinal Giovanni Maria Mastai-Ferretti was elected Pope Pius IX. Within a month of his elevation to the Papacy he delighted all of liberal Europe and irritated Austria by proclaiming a somewhat more generous amnesty than was customary for a new Pope, freeing thousands of political prisoners. With the Pope's approval, plans were made to modernize both in the Papal State and in the States of the Church the courts, prisons, and education; also to take the first steps toward a parliamentary form of government for the Commune of Rome and its provinces. In the following March the Vatican conceded to the press a limited freedom; in April arrangements were made for a *Consulta* of the State, which was to be nominated by the provincial councils; in June a ministerial cabinet was appointed which, though composed mostly of churchmen, was a step in the direction of freer institutions; and in July permission was granted for a civic guard. The sincere though cautious liberalism of Pius so angered Vienna, especially when he allowed some of his own Romans to arm themselves, that the Austrians occupied Ferrara, where they had garrison rights, in the States of the Church. This act of aggression provoked a protest from the Pope which made him appear more anti-Austrian and

Italian Affairs and "Casa Guidi Windows"

nationalistic than he was. As a result of his qualified approval of reform and progress, a wave of unrest rolled across the peninsula, and reactionary régimes everywhere were swept out of power or placed on the defensive. There were disturbances in Genoa, Milan, Palermo, Naples, Lucca, Pisa, Leghorn, and Florence. In May 1847 the Florentines were granted a free press; in September they were allowed their civic guard; and in the following February a constitution was proclaimed in Tuscany. In the first half of *Casa Guidi Windows* Elizabeth gave expression to her generous but naïve faith in the liberalism of the Hapsburg Grand Duke of Tuscany and voiced her hope that the Pope would continue to aid the cause of reform and of Italian unity and independence.

On the day of the Brownings' first wedding anniversary they saw from the windows of their apartment in Casa Guidi a great demonstration of the people to celebrate the establishment of a civic guard and the prospect of independence and unity. Elizabeth's account of the event to Henrietta was breathless with excitement. A comparison of the prose passage with the description of the same scene in her poem will illustrate why her letters (in contrast to Robert's) have all the charm, ease of manner, and vividness which are lacking in much of her verse. "Ah, you should have seen our day!" she wrote.

> For above three hours the infinite procession filed under our windows—with all their various flags and symbols, into the Piazza Pitti where the Duke and his family stood in tears at the window to receive the thanks of his people. Never in the world was a more affecting sight—nor a grander if you took it in its full significance. The magistracy came first, with their flag, and then the priesthood—and then and then—class after class—troops of peasants and nobles, and of soldiers fraternizing with the people. Then, too, came the foreigners, there was a place for them; . . . French, English, Swiss, Greeks (such a noble band of Greeks!) all with their national flags. Meanwhile there was no lack of spectators. The windows dropping down their glittering draperies, seemed to grow larger with the multitude of pretty heads, and of hands which threw out flowers and waved white handkerchiefs. There was

not an inch of wall, not alive, if the eye might judge. Clouds of flowers and of laurel leaves came fluttering down on the advancing procession; and the clapping of hands, and the frenetic shouting, and the music which came in gushes, and then seemed to go out with too much joy, and the exulting faces, and the kisses given for very exultation between man and man, and the mixing of elegantly dressed women in all that crowd and turbulence, with the sort of smile which proved how little cause there was for fear—all these features of the scene made it peculiar, and memorable and most beautiful to look back upon." [18]

The verses in *Casa Guidi Windows* telling of the Grand Duke standing in a window of his palace may serve as one example among many of Elizabeth's emotionalism:

> Nor was it ill, when Leopoldo drew
> His little children to the window-place
>   He stood in at the Pitti, to suggest
> *They* too should govern as the people willed.
>   What a cry rose then! some, who saw the best,
> Declared his eyes filled up and overfilled
>   With good warm human tears which unrepressed
> Ran down. I like his face; . . .

A fortnight after the amiable but weak Leopold, fearful of offending either his own Florentines or Vienna, halfheartedly granted Tuscany a constitution, Elizabeth described the rejoicing of the people when they recognized "our good, excellent Grand Duke" one evening at the opera and took him back in triumph to the Pitti Palace: "The *'Evvivas'* were deafening. So glad I was. *I, too,* stood at the window and clapped my hands. If ever Grand Duke deserved benediction this Duke does. We hear that he was quite moved, overpowered, and wept like a child." And in another letter Elizabeth wrote of the "excellent constitution" Leopold had given to Tuscany, "and this by his free will and after long reflection. Nights after nights he has spent, they say, without sleep, in painful thought—and his face expresses it. I like him, **and I like his face.**"

Italian Affairs and "Casa Guidi Windows"

She also had great confidence in the new Pope. In September 1847 she wrote of the "new animation and energy given to Italy by this new wonderful Pope, who is a great man and doing greatly." Her optimistic point of view in *Casa Guidi Windows* was qualified by her suspicion of the Papacy as an institution with vested interests:

> He is good and great
> According to the deeds a pope can do;
> Most liberal, save those bonds; affectionate,
> As princes may be, and, as priests are, true;
> But only the ninth Pius after eight,
> When all's praised most. At best and hopefullest,
> He's pope—we want a man!

Elizabeth was looking for "a perfect man," "some high soul, crowned capable to lead" the Italian people against their Austrian oppressors. "Where is the teacher?" she asked in *Casa Guidi Windows*,

> What now may he do,
> Who shall do greatly? Doth he gird his waist
> With a monk's rope, like Luther? or pursue
> The goat, like Tell? or dry his nets in haste,
> Like Masaniello when the sky was blue?
> Keep house, like other peasants, with inlaced,
> Bare, brawny arms about a favourite child, . . . ?

The man who was to be the principal architect and builder of Italian independence and unity under a constitutional monarchy —and one of the great heroes in Elizabeth's life—was at this moment not a monk, a goatherd, or a peasant fisherman. In the fall of 1847 Count Camillo Benso di Cavour was still comparatively young and unknown in Italy. He had traveled widely throughout his country and the rest of Europe, had acquired a thorough knowledge of practical agriculture and an understanding of the political and social problems of his own country, and had managed for a while his father's estate at Leri. When late in October the Piedmontese government allowed greater freedom of the press, Cavour then gave up his work in behalf of the Piedmontese agricultural society he had founded and taking advantage of the new law made plans for the publication of a daily newspaper with liberal principles. The first number of *Il Risorgimento* was printed in Turin, December 15.

DURING that winter and the following spring Elizabeth looked from her apartment upon the popular demonstrations in the Piazza Pitti to celebrate the government's liberal concessions and the first steps toward independence. But she was not confined to her rooms and was well enough to walk for half an hour in the piazza when it was sunny or now and then "to go over to the gallery and adore the Raphaels." Early in May 1848 the Brownings moved back to their old apartment, this time unfurnished, in Casa Guidi, which was to become for them a kind of permanent *pied à terre,* their home to which they would always return from their many trips. Their annual rent for their "noble suite" was about twenty-five guineas,[19] which was only half of what it would have been if the rooms were furnished. The Brownings filled them slowly with "rococo chairs, spring sofas, carved bookcases, satin from cardinals' beds" as they spent the proceeds from Elizabeth's books during the previous two years. Thus their furniture was "antique and worthy of the place" and was bought at prices which were "something quite fabulous." In view of their absurdly low rent, they planned to augment their income by subletting the apartment when they were away for about £10 monthly, which could be used to defray traveling expenses. After they had lived at Casa Guidi for several years, their guests would have seen hung on the dining room walls medallions of Tennyson, Carlyle, and even of Robert Browning. The large drawing room where they entertained their friends was dimly lighted because the windows were partly covered by plants. According to Kate Field, it had "a dreamy look, which was enhanced by the tapestry-covered walls and the old pictures of saints that looked out sadly from their carved frames of black wood."[20] Their guests in the drawing room would also have noticed Dante's profile, a plaster cast of Keats's face taken after his death, and pen-and-ink sketches of Tennyson and of John Kenyon.

Among the Brownings' most intimate friends were Count Cottrell and his wife Sophia, with whom they became acquainted soon after arriving in Florence, probably because of a family connection between the Countess and Ann Eliza Gordon, the second wife of Elizabeth's uncle Sam Barrett. Cottrell, who made no effort to earn a living because of a regular allowance from his father-in-law, spent some of his time as an amateur painter. When their fifteen-month-old daughter Alice died in November 1849, the Count was so "unmanned by grief" that Browning had to attend to the details of the funeral. Within a week or two after the baby's death Elizabeth wrote "A Child's Grave at Florence," which appeared late in December in the *Athenaeum*. One of the Brownings' visitors who came to have coffee with them once or twice a week in the summer of 1848 was William Ware. He was a Harvard graduate who after fifteen years as a Unitarian clergyman in New York City had resigned his pulpit to write several historical novels and to edit the *Christian Examiner*. Elizabeth thought him "a delightful, earnest, simple person."

Some months earlier the Brownings had met two other Americans, the sculptor William Wetmore Story and his wife, who were passing through Florence on their way to Rome. When the Storys returned to spend the autumn in Florence, they became close friends of the Brownings. Story wrote to James Russell Lowell that Browning had a nervous, rapid manner and "a great vivacity, but not the least humour, some sarcasm, considerable critical faculty, and very great frankness and friendliness of manner and mind." He described Elizabeth as "very unaffected and pleasant and simple-hearted," and like many other persons who recorded their impressions of her was surprised to find her "listening and talking very quietly and pleasantly, with nothing of that peculiarity which one would expect from reading her poems." [21] At Rome later and at Bagni di Lucca and at Siena, the Storys were to become the most intimate friends the Brownings had in Italy; for the American couple their association with the two English poets was, in the opinion of Story's biographer Henry James, "the most interesting friendship of their lives."

Another visitor at Casa Guidi that autumn was Francis Sylvester Mahony (Father Prout), who was then the Roman correspondent of the *Daily News,* which was being edited by Dickens.

Browning had been ill for nearly a month with a fever and an ulcerated throat, and Mahony, "knowing everything as those Jesuits are apt to do," prepared a soothing drink of eggs and port wine which effected a prompt cure. Elizabeth was most grateful to him, for during Robert's illness she had become lonely and frightened and had fallen "into a paroxysm of most unChristian humour." [22] Her whole being had been filled with the old bitterness at the unbroken silence of her brothers and of her father, so that she had resolved never to "set foot on English ground again . . never." Now that Robert was well, her feeling of desolation had passed away. Mahony "came to doctor and remained to talk," visiting the Brownings every evening for several weeks. Each time he would "plant" himself close to Elizabeth's sofa, smoke two or three cigars, call for wine, and take one of the Brownings' "Raffael-basins for a spitting convenience" so that after three hours both Robert and Elizabeth "were fairly *sick*." Although he always behaved with "the utmost kindness and warmheartedness" toward the Brownings, he was far too worldly and outwardly cynical for Elizabeth's taste. It seemed strange to her "to see the priestly vesture . . . heave with such laughters and jests as seem characteristic of the laity." [23]

In the spring of 1848 Elizabeth suffered from her second miscarriage,[24] but in the summer she was well enough to make with Browning *"un bel giro"* along the Adriatic coast. Early in the evening of July 17 they left in the diligence for Arezzo, from which they crossed the mountains to Fano by way of Borgo Sansepolcro. Fano proved to be impossibly hot and dull, although Elizabeth enjoyed looking at the churches and the paintings. She was especially impressed with "a divine picture of Guercino's . . . worth going all that way to see," namely "The Guardian Angel" in the Church of San Agostino, and with "a very expressive picture of Domenichino's," the "David with the Head of Goliath" in the Collegio Folfi. After three days at Fano they went down the coast to Ancona, which was also too hot and sunny for comfort. They stayed there, however, for a week, "living upon fish and cold water," and then went to Loreto for a day, retraced their steps to Fano, and journeyed northward through Pesaro and Rimini to Ravenna. There Elizabeth was again disillusioned, for with the

Italian Affairs and "Casa Guidi Windows"

exception of Dante's tomb and the churches with their marvelous Byzantine mosaics, she found the city unattractive and the stench from the marshes unendurable. On the return by the route through Forli, Elizabeth was once more delighted with "the exquisite, almost visionary scenery of the Apennines." It was during the brief sojourn at Ancona that Browning wrote one of his few poems without a dramatic mask, "The Guardian-Angel: a Picture at Fano." Its personal quality and its sincere religious tone owe much to Elizabeth's influence.

> We were at Fano, and three times we went
>   To sit and see him in his chapel there,
> And drink his beauty to our soul's content
>   —My angel with me too: and since I care
> For dear Guercino's fame, (to which in power
> And glory comes this picture for a dower,
>   Fraught with a pathos so magnificent)
>
> And since he did not work so earnestly
>   At all times, and has else endured some wrong,—
> I took one thought his picture struck from me,
>   And spread it out, translating it to song.

During the last half of July and the first week in August, while the Brownings were on their tour, Charles Albert, King of Piedmont, had been defeated at Custoza, a few days later had attempted with the remnant of his army to defend Milan, and, believing that his cause was hopeless, had capitulated to the Austrian Radetzky. To go back to the origins of the Italian war—in the spring of 1848 much of Europe had been in revolt. The Orleanist Louis Philippe was driven from his throne in Paris, Baden was granted a constitution, and Metternich fled from Vienna. As the revolution spread to Italy, an almost unarmed populace forced 20,000 Austrian troops to withdraw from Milan after the "Five Days" of hand-to-hand fighting; Daniele Manin with the help of a few citizen guards proclaimed the Republic of St. Mark after compelling the Austrians to evacuate Venice; Austrian dukes with their garrisons fled from Parma and Modena; and hundreds of volunteers in Bologna and Florence joined the national uprising.

Earlier in the year Naples and Sicily had risen in revolt and had obtained a constitution from their Bourbon King Ferdinand. Charles Albert, after much indecision, fearing on the one hand a subversive republican movement within his kingdom if he were to remain inactive, and on the other hand, the wrath of official Europe if he opposed Austria with military force, finally declared war on March 24 and two days later sent his troops across the frontier at Pavia. In the early battles of the ensuing campaign the Sardinians made an effort to drive the enemy from several of their fortresses in the "Quadrilateral," where they were strongly entrenched. On April 30 the King successfully attacked the Austrian General D'Aspre at Pastrengo, near Verona, but recalled his army when it might have overtaken the demoralized Austrian troops. A week later he showed the same timidity when he withdrew from his position after cutting the Austrian line in two at Santa Lucia and thus lost his last chance of capturing Verona before the arrival of Radetzky's large reinforcements. Charles Albert's reverses at the battle of Custoza late in July and his surrender some ten days afterward at Milan were by no means all his fault. Although his own generalship and that of his subordinates had many faults, he was beset by political uncertainties, and he also failed to receive the number of troops promised him, because almost everyone was too busy planning for peace after the expected victory. The Austrians were far superior in discipline and in the organization of their army, and Vienna had given Radetzky a free hand in the conduct of the war.

The Papal Allocution of April 29, in which Pius declared that he could not sanction a war against a Catholic nation, was a shock to many of his liberal supporters. As the head of the Church, he could have taken no other position, but his action gave proof that he was first a Pope and secondly an Italian nationalist. All that spring and summer progressive and patriotic groups in the Papal State clamored for further democratic concessions and for military action against Austria. In the autumn the Pope appointed as his chief minister a well-known economist and statesman of liberal principles, Count Pellegrino Rossi, who aimed at administrative reform, stable constitutional government, and the development of an Italian league. Although he was disliked by extreme democratic and reactionary factions alike, he, more than any other political leader, might have saved the Papal State from anarchy, but on November 15, as he was on the point of presiding at the first sitting of the Chamber of Deputies, he was assassinated. Pius then yielded to the demands of the radical groups who wanted a constituent assembly, a republican government, and war against Austria. On November 24, 1848, disguised as a simple priest, he left Rome for the protection of the King of Naples at Gaeta, on the coast south of the Papal State.

Meanwhile in Tuscany the ministry of the liberal, scholarly, yet rather ineffectual Montanelli and of the shrewd, quarrelsome, energetic, opportunist Guerrazzi was encountering difficulties similar to those faced by Rossi. Almost no one had any understanding of the nature of a constitutional form of government, riots broke out everywhere, local authorities were indifferent to the central government and made no effort to restore order, and both the radical and conservative factions sabotaged all measures of reform and the efforts toward stability and peace.

Amid the turmoil Elizabeth suddenly abandoned her optimism of the preceding summer and fall and went to the other extreme in losing all confidence in the ability of the Italians to win their independence. "Dante's soul has died out of the land," she wrote in disillusionment to Miss Mitford. Her "faith in every species of Italian" was "nearly tired out," and she did not believe they were "men at all, much less heroes and patriots." She was disappointed that she had not seen great deeds enacted before her eyes. A year or two earlier she had fallen in love with the Italians because they had appeared to her a civilized, courteous, and refined people; now she complained to Henrietta that they lacked martial prowess and had little integrity or stamina: "There must be honesty, there must be union, there must be zeal and strength of some kind, intellectual *or* moral—and here, there are men only fit for the Goldoni theatre, the coffee houses and the sunny side of the Arno when the wind's in the north."

Early in January 1849 both chambers of the Tuscan Assembly in Florence voted to send representatives to the parliament at

Rome, which had recently been proclaimed the Constituent Assembly of all Italy. Guerrazzi obtained the Grand Duke's approval, but rather than offend the Pope by signing the bill Leopold left Florence for Siena, telling his ministers, however, that he would soon return. When he learned a few days later of Radetzky's promise of eventual military aid in restoring him to his dukedom, he decided that instead of going back to his subjects during the interregnum he would accept the hospitality of Pius at Gaeta. After the Grand Duke's intention became known in Florence, the two legislative houses elected Guerrazzi, Montanelli, and Mazzoni to form a provisional government. The most able member of the triumvirate was Guerrazzi, whose firmness saved Tuscany from civil war and whose liberal program of union with Rome won him for a short while the support of several moderate groups.

In the proud, independent kingdom of Piedmont, Charles Albert and his subjects were angry at the Austrians for their outrageous treatment of the aristocrats of Milan, and the Piedmontese government was finding it impossible to reach agreement with Austria on just and honorable peace terms. The King finally surrendered to the pressure of the war party, declared on March 20 that the truce with Austria was no longer in force, was decisively beaten by Radetzky at Novara on March 26, and abdicated his throne the same evening in favor of his son Victor Emmanuel II, the Duke of Savoy. After the disaster at Novara the Tuscan Assembly made Guerrazzi dictator. He had the impossible task of attempting to reconcile many opposing groups, republicans, legitimists, constitutionalists, and factions within those factions; also of trying to organize a defense of volunteers against an expected Austrian invasion. But he failed to secure the support of the moderate parties, several of which were secretly hoping for the Grand Duke's return; and after a riot in Florence against some arrogant and unruly troops from Leghorn, the Municipal Council on April 12 seized power from the Assembly, declared itself a provisional government, put Guerrazzi in jail, and invited Leopold back to the Pitti Palace. In May the Austrians occupied Florence, and on July 28 the cowardly Grand Duke came home again, under the shadow of Austrian bayonets.

Italian Affairs and "Casa Guidi Windows" 217

By the middle of May 1849 Elizabeth was thoroughly disillusioned with the Florentines. "O heavens! how ignoble it all has been and is! A revolution made by boys and *vivas*, and unmade by boys and *vivas*—no, there was blood shed in the unmaking—some horror and terror, but not as much patriotism and truth as could lift up the blood from the kennel. The counter-revolution was strictly *counter*, observe. I mean, that if the Leghornese troops here had paid their debts at the Florentine coffee houses, the Florentines would have let their beloved Grand Duke stay on at Gaeta to the end of the world." Leopold, whose part Elizabeth had been taking because he had seemed to her "a good man, more sinned against than sinning," she now gave up "from henceforth, seeing that he has done this base thing of taking again his Austrian titles in his proclamations coincidentally with the approach of the Austrians."

The second part of *Casa Guidi Windows*, which was finished in 1851, tells of the events in Tuscany in 1848 and 1849. Elizabeth repented that she had been gullible enough to believe the oath of the Grand Duke. The Pope, to whom she had at first been attracted because of his early professions of liberalism, has disgraced both himself and the Church:

> Peter's chair is shamed
> Like any vulgar throne, the nations lop
> To pieces for their firewood unreclaimed,—
> And, when it burns too, we shall see as well
> In Italy as elsewhere. Let it burn.

Partly because of their own faults, she feels, the Italians failed in their uprising, but the people cannot be held down forever and will some day crush their overlords. "Life throbs in noble Piedmont!" and "New springs of life are gushing everywhere . . ." In the meanwhile Elizabeth has faith in the future:

> We will trust God. The blank interstices
> Men take for ruins, He will build into
> With pillared marbles rare, or knit across
> With generous arches, till the fane's complete.
> This world has no perdition, if some loss.

Elizabeth's approach to the political problems of the *Risorgimento,* as she expressed herself in *Casa Guidi Windows* and in her letters, was based on emotion rather than logic. She had little understanding of the complexity of the issues and merely condemned all people and nations if they appeared to be cautious in their support of the Italian effort or hostile to the cause. Her heroes at this time were Garibaldi, Charles Albert, Louis Napoleon, and Mazzini. Among her notable villains were the Tuscan Grand Duke and the Pope, and she had nothing to say in favor of Guerrazzi. Although many liberal-minded Florentines questioned Guerrazzi's integrity, Elizabeth's condemnation of him in her letters seems much too harsh. She thought him a traitor who was "false as falsehood." Although she admitted that he had more energy than any one else in Tuscany, she failed to give him credit for his patriotic efforts to hold the state together. Her partisan attitude toward personalities and political programs led her into a number of inconsistencies. For example, she wrote in May 1849 of the new régime in Rome that, "If a republic *in earnest* is established there, Louis Napoleon should not try to set his foot on it." The republic had been in existence since February and was being heroically defended against General Oudinot by Mazzini and Garibaldi. On the last day of August Elizabeth spoke about the intervention in Rome: "I, for my own part (my husband is not so minded), do consider that the French motive has been good, the intention pure." The new president of the French republic, Louis Napoleon, had unfortunately persuaded himself that it was in the best interests of France and of the Catholic Church to destroy the Roman republic and restore to the Pope his former temporal power, with the hope that Pius, under the protection of the French government rather than of the Austrian oligarchy, would institute a mild and progressive rule. At the beginning of July Oudinot's superior forces overcame the resistance of the defenders, who were fewer and less well trained than the French troops, and at the end of the month Oudinot handed Rome over to a harsh and reactionary Papal Commission.

In her attitude toward English diplomacy Elizabeth was also inconsistent. She declared in the first part of *Casa Guidi Windows* that England should give up its militarism:

> O my England, crease
> Thy purple with no alien agonies!
> No struggles toward encroachment, no vile war!
> Disband thy captains, change thy victories,
> Be henceforth prosperous as the angels are,
> Helping, not humbling.

Yet in the second part she accused England of staying out of war for selfish, commercial reasons:

> A cry is up in England, which doth ring
> The hollow world through, that for ends of trade
> And virtue, and God's better worshipping,
> We henceforth should exalt the name of Peace,
> And leave those rusty wars that eat the soul,—
> Besides their clippings at our golden fleece.

A more noble policy, she believed, would be to rescue by military force all subjected peoples. The British government's course of action in her opinion was not one of true peace; on the contrary,

> 'Tis treason, stiff with doom,—
> 'Tis gagged despair, and inarticulate wrong,
> Annihilated Poland, stifled Rome,
> Dazed Naples, Hungary fainting 'neath the thong,
> And Austria wearing a smooth olive-leaf
> On her brute forehead, while her hoofs outpress
> The life from these Italian souls, in brief.

Both now and later when the Italians renewed the war in 1859, Elizabeth greatly underestimated England's help to Italy. She did not understand that Palmerston, who became secretary of state for foreign affairs in 1846, tried to advance everywhere the cause of constitutional government and of ordered liberty and that he was out of sympathy with the Austrians because of their autocratic ways and urged them to make democratic concessions in Italy. In the spring of 1848 he put pressure on the Papal government to admit a few laymen to the council of state and to take the first steps toward a constitution. He was friendly toward the Sicilians when they were revolting against the Bourbon Ferdinand, and after

Charles Albert's defeat at Custoza Palmerston tried to persuade the Austrians to grant generous terms: the surrender of Lombardy to Sardinia and a constitution to Venetia under the hegemony of Austria. It seemed likely to him that Austria would soon lose Italy, but he felt that Hungary, which was in revolt in 1849, was necessary to the Austrian empire as a check against possible Russian aggression.

By the summer of 1849 all Italy except Piedmont was again under the domination of Austria and of the Papacy. Garibaldi had gone to America, Mazzini was in London, and Charles Albert had died that summer at Oporto. In the following decade the Piedmont of King Victor Emmanuel under the leadership of Cavour was, alone among Italian states, to retain its constitutional government and to modernize and strengthen itself so that it gained the confidence of Europe and was strong enough in 1859 to lead most of Italy to unity and independence. However much Elizabeth oversimplified the problems of European diplomacy, she was well aware, from what she had observed in Florence, of the chief reasons for the failure of 1848–49. The people enjoyed marching in processions on feast days, wearing velvet costumes with feathers in their hats, and crying *vivas,* but many were loath to make the necessary sacrifices:

> And yet, to leave our piazzas, shops, and farms,
>   For the simple sake of fighting, was not good— . . .

Popular enthusiasm was a poor substitute for organization and discipline. A general ignorance of the issues deprived the movement of the support of the masses and split the patriotic few into factions who fought more among themselves than against their oppressors. The peasants had failed to join the revolution because of their essential conservatism and more specifically because their priests were opposed to the war against Austria. What strength there was for this early and abortive phase of the *Risorgimento* came chiefly from the better-informed artisans and middle-class groups in the cities. Owing to jealousy and distrust among the states, the war had never been a crusade for Italian unity; at the most, Piedmont had hoped to be the nucleus of a northern Italian kingdom. Mazzini alone had preached independence, unity, and republicanism, and few throughout the peninsula had his idealism and foresight. Elizabeth realized that another attempt of the Italians to win their independence and to unify their country could not be successful until all classes of the people had become better educated and politically mature and had learned the necessity for cooperation, patient planning, self-control, and sacrifice. She did not again become absorbed in Italian affairs until the renewal of the conflict in 1859.

13. "Poems" of 1850

AT FOUR O'CLOCK in the morning of March 9, 1849, Browning wrote Elizabeth's sisters that "thro' God's infinite goodness our blessed Ba gave birth to a fine, strong boy at a quarter past two: and is doing admirably." [1] After her baby was born, Elizabeth did not sink with exhaustion but "rose up into a state of ecstasy" so that she "could scarcely be kept quiet." She was relieved to see that the child was rosy, fat, healthy, and normal-looking, for she had feared a malformation or "some evil" on account of the morphine she regularly took and also because of a serious fall upon the floor of her apartment in the autumn. The child, who was named Robert Wiedeman Barrett Browning,[2] inherited his mother's oval features; in the long years ahead he was to become in his personality and way of life much more like a Barrett than a Browning.

Soon after the birth of his child, Robert's joy was cut short when he heard from New Cross of his mother's sudden death. He had "loved his mother as such passionate natures only can love"; Elizabeth "never saw a man so bowed down in an extremity of sorrow —never." The Brownings had hoped to go to England in the summer to show their baby to friends and relatives, but Robert told Elizabeth that "it would break his heart to see his mother's roses over the wall, and the place where she used to lay her scissors and gloves." By the middle of May Robert was still "looking very unwell—thinner and paler than usual" and remained depressed in spirits.

Early in the summer his loss of appetite and of sleep and his worn, dejected appearance so alarmed Elizabeth that she insisted on his traveling with her to find some place where they, Wilson, the manservant Alessandro, the baby, and his Italian nursemaid might spend the summer away from the heat of Florence. They went along the coast past Carrara to La Spezia, near which, at

Lerici, a glance at Shelley's house made her "melancholy . . . of course." Then they retraced their steps southward to a mountain village named Seravezza, soon abandoned it because of high prices, proceeded to Bagni di Lucca, rented a house there until the end of October for £12, and returned for the other four members of the household. The road from Lucca to the Baths winds upward along the embankment of the Serchio past great white houses surrounded by vineyards and olive orchards, with steep hills on both sides covered with chestnut forests. About fourteen miles from Lucca the road leaves the Serchio, turns east, and runs for a mile beside the Lima, a rushing mountain stream, to Ponte a Serraglio, the first of the three villages. From there a road winds up the side of a mountain to the second of the villages, Bagni Caldi, where the Brownings spent the rest of that summer in "a sort of eagle's nest" perched high above the valley. The road from Ponte a Serraglio upward along the Lima comes at the end of a mile to the third of the villages, the Villa, which is mostly a long street of private residences, boarding houses, and shops.

In the nineteenth century the Baths of Lucca were a fashionable summer resort for the Anglo-American colony in Italy, who took part in the same social activities which they enjoyed for the rest of the year at Florence and Rome. Now, however, few foreigners spend their holidays there. One of the principal monuments of a vanished era is the simple wooden building of the English Protestant Chapel, which is falling into disrepair and appears to have been empty for several years. Elizabeth wrote from Bagni di Lucca in the summer of 1849 that Stuart was "enlightening the English barbarians at the lower village" with his lectures on Shakespeare and that Lever "presides over the weekly balls at the casino where the English 'do congregate' (all except Robert and me)." Nor did the Brownings ever attend, either at Lucca or Florence, lectures, amateur theatrical performances, or anyone's "days." Their friends and acquaintances were mostly American and English writers, painters, and sculptors, and visitors who were admirers of their poetry. Even though the Brownings lived for many years in Italy, none of their intimate friends and few of their acquaintances were Italians.

The Brownings were attracted to their home high in the Bagni

Caldi because of "the coolness, the charm of the mountains, whose very heart you seem to hear beating in the rush of the little river, the green silence of the chestnut forests, and the seclusion which any one may make for himself by keeping clear of the valley-villages." Almost every day they would go out and lose themselves "in the woods and mountains, and sit by the waterfalls on the starry and moonlit nights," and in their wanderings they "never met anybody except a monk girt with a rope, now and then, or a barefooted peasant." One day in the middle of September the entire household, including the baby, made an all-day excursion along the dried-up beds of mountain streams to the top of Prato Fiorito, five miles from the Baths. Elizabeth, Wilson, and the *balia* rode on donkeys, and Browning and Alessandro on mountain ponies. The scenery was "magnificent," Elizabeth wrote one of her sisters. "At the top you look round on a great world of innumerable mountains, the faint sea beyond them, and not a sign of cultivation—not a cottage—not a hut." There they sat down with their guides to a picnic lunch, during which the baby lay "rolling and laughing" on the shawl Elizabeth had spread on the grass. By the middle of October it had become so cool that they had to cut short their idyllic, carefree way of life in the mountains and return for another season at Casa Guidi, where they arrived on the seventeenth.

During the following autumn and the winter, the Marchesa d'Ossoli, formerly Miss Margaret Fuller, often called on the Brownings. Elizabeth wrote Henrietta that she was "one of the very plainest women I ever saw in my life, and talking fluent Italian with a pure *Boston* accent. Still she is a woman of a good deal of generous and womanly goodness." [3] Miss Fuller had first achieved recognition in Boston with her series of very successful "conversations" on serious subjects conducted for the young women of that city. Along with Emerson and George Ripley, she was later an editor of the *Dial,* the organ of the Concord transcendentalists, and then she became a protégée of Horace Greeley and for almost two years wrote reviews and articles for his newspaper, the *New York Daily Tribune.* In the summer of 1846 she sailed for England, where she hoped to meet, among others, Elizabeth Barrett, to whom she was carrying a letter of introduction from Cornelius Mathews.[4] Elizabeth's marriage and removal to Italy had prevented their meeting in London. Miss Fuller traveled around the British Isles, France, and Italy, and then settled in Rome for the winter of 1847–48 and astonished her acquaintances by marrying an Italian military officer about a decade younger than she, penniless, and with no pretension to her degree of intellectual culture. Both she and her husband aided the cause of the Roman republic, and when it fell in July 1849 they went with their child to Florence, where she undertook the writing of a history of the Roman revolution. "Over a great gulf of differing opinion" both of the Brownings "felt drawn strongly to her." Elizabeth was liberal in her political views and much more progressive and broad-minded than many of her acquaintances and relatives, but she was shocked at Madame Ossoli's radical socialism; she later described her guest as a woman "of noble instincts, but a very hampered intellect, and of opinions quite the wildest."[5] When Madame Ossoli paid a farewell call upon the Brownings during her last evening in Italy, she was filled with "gloom" and "sad presentiment" and gave as a parting gift from her child to the Brownings' baby a Bible, with the inscription *"In memory of Angelo Eugene Ossoli,"* which seemed to Elizabeth "a strange, prophetical expression." On the voyage back to America, the ship (the *Elizabeth*) carrying Madame Ossoli, her husband, and their child sank, and all three were drowned. Elizabeth was very much depressed when she heard of the tragedy, "affecting in itself," she wrote Miss Mitford, "and also through association with that past, when the arrowhead of anguish was broken too deeply into my life ever to be quite drawn out."

Both of the Brownings were busy with their own poetry in the winter of 1849–50. Robert was writing his *Christmas-Eve and Easter-Day,* and Elizabeth was revising her volumes of 1838 and of 1844 in preparation for a new edition. Browning's poem was not brought out by Moxon, possibly because the poet considered him too slow and too conservative, but by Chapman and Hall. Elizabeth thought that the new work, which was issued on the first of April, was "full of power," but it received few acceptable reviews and the sales were poor.

Indeed, during Elizabeth's lifetime all of Browning's poetry failed to win general recognition, and his reputation was very much overshadowed by that of his wife. For example, when the post of poet laureate became vacant after Wordsworth's death in April 1850 it was Elizabeth, not Robert, whom the *Athenaeum* recommended to the position. On June first the first paragraph of "Our Weekly Gossip," a column probably written by H. F. Chorley, said that to grant the laureateship "to a female would be at once an honourable testimonial to the individual, a fitting recognition of the remarkable place which the women of England have taken in the literature of the day, and a graceful compliment to the Sovereign herself." [6] The writer added, "There is no living poet of either sex who can prefer a higher claim than Mrs. Elizabeth Barrett Browning." Three weeks later the *Athenaeum* reported that Leigh Hunt was being considered for the post. Although the author of the article believed that Hunt had a claim, he thought that it was "not of the kind which can be properly recognized by the laureateship," [7] and again suggested Elizabeth's name. After the position was granted to Tennyson, the writer in the *Athenaeum* regretted the decision because the award had not gone to a woman and because Tennyson already had a pension.[8] Elizabeth had at first favored Leigh Hunt, who was "a great man and a good man in spite of all," but she later said that Tennyson was "in a sense" worthier of the laureateship than Hunt; "only Tennyson can wait, that is the single difference."

Although Elizabeth had not published much poetry since her volumes of 1844, she had not been altogether forgotten either in America or England before the discussion about the laureateship. An American critic and traveler, Henry Theodore Tuckerman, who had been for a while editor of the *Boston Miscellany of Literature and Fashion,* in which Elizabeth had published in 1842, wrote an appreciative review of her work in his *Thoughts on the Poets,* which appeared in New York in 1846. He emphasized her classical scholarship and declared that her poems were "imbued with the spirit of antique models." [9] A Scottish preacher and journalist, George Gilfillan published an article on her poetry in *Tait's Edinburgh Magazine* in 1847.[10] He praised several of her shorter poems but counseled her to simplify her style, "to sift her diction of whatever is harsh and barbarous," and to write "in the clear articulate language of men." Clarity of expression, he implied, was primarily a masculine characteristic. An American clergyman, musician, and minor poet, George W. Bethune, wrote in 1848 in his *The British Female Poets* of Elizabeth's "high religious faith, her love of children, her delight in the graceful and beautiful, her revelations of feminine feeling, her sorrow over the suffering, and her indignation against the oppressor." [11] Thomas Powell, an Englishman who had collaborated with R. H. Horne in *The Poems of Geoffrey Chaucer, Modernized* and who later became a journalist in New York, published there in 1849 *The Living Authors of England,* in which he described Elizabeth as *"the greatest poetical intellect ever vouchsafed to an English woman."* [12] That same year an English editor and author, Frederick Rowton, paid tribute to her genius in his *The Female Poets of Great Britain.*[13] He found in her precisely the qualities she seems now to lack: "She is chief amongst the learned poetesses of our land: at least, I know of no British female writer who exhibits so intimate an acquaintance with the *spirit* of both antique and modern philosophy, or so refined a perception of intellectual purity and beauty. Her poetry is the poetry of pure reason."

Elizabeth herself probably did not know of all these flattering articles which had appeared on both sides of the Atlantic, but she was much pleased to have been suggested for the laureateship. While she was awaiting the critical reception of her new volumes, she suffered in the summer of 1850 from her fourth, her last, and by far her worst miscarriage and her most serious setback since she had left England. For six weeks afterward she could not walk and was thin and white and greatly depressed. Her physician Dr. Harding realized that no amount of medicine could effect a cure and that she would have to move to a cooler place in the country as soon as she was well enough to travel. At seven in the morning of August 31 the Brownings left Florence by railroad for Siena, with Elizabeth "in a miserably helpless state, having to be lifted about like a baby, looking ghostly rather than ghastly, and feeling as if it were a most uncongenial effort." They spent the month of September about two miles from the city in a small villa which cost only eleven shillings a week. It was in the midst of its own vineyard, olive orchard, and flower garden and was on a hill called *poggio dei venti*. The villa was cool and had splendid views in all directions. Elizabeth wrote, "From one window you have a view of Siena, with its Duomo and its campanile, and its Italian colouring over all! . . . From another, the whole country leaps under the sun, alive with verdure and vineyards." Her health soon improved enough so that during the first week of October, which the Brownings spent inside the city of Siena, she was able to walk through the cathedral and the Academy, where she admired "the divine Eve of Sodoma." Although she was to live in Siena parts of the summers of 1859 and 1860 and to pass through the city many times on her journeys between Florence and Rome, she was never again strong enough to climb the steps into the cathedral.

ABOUT the first of November Elizabeth's "new edition" was brought out by Chapman and Hall, who had published Browning's *Christmas-Eve and Easter-Day*.[14] The *Poems* were issued in two octavo volumes bound in dark gray-blue cloth boards. Elizabeth included all of the poems in the volumes of 1844 and all but nine of the poems in the volume of *The Seraphim* (omitting the weakest, such as "The Little Friend," "Victoria's Tears," and "The Weeping Saviour") and all the verses which had appeared in periodicals since 1844, most of them in *Blackwood's*, two in the *Christian Mother's Magazine,* and one each in the *Liberty Bell* of Boston and the *Athenaeum;* also "A Sabbath Morning at Sea" from an annual in 1839 and "The Claim," which had been published in the *Athenaeum* in 1842. She had not been writing for magazines so frequently as before her marriage. Browning strongly disapproved of the publication of poetry in a periodical before it should appear in a book, because he felt the practice was a deception of the future buyers of the book. The most important of her works being published for the first time were the new translation of the *Prometheus Bound,* a translation of Bion's *Lament for Adonis,* and the "Sonnets from the Portuguese,"[15] as well as three short poems which also were inspired by her love for Browning: "Life and Love," "Inclusions," and "Insufficiency."

In the preparation of her new edition she made many revisions among the poems of 1844 and had to rewrite many pages of the sent to William Blackwood in Edinburgh. In 1848 he also had the manuscript of "A Meditation in Tuscany" but later returned both works because of their unsuitability for publication in his magazine. Elizabeth included them in the *Poems* of 1850. Her translation of the *Prometheus Bound,* which received Browning's careful attention in the spring of 1845, is a great improvement upon her earlier attempt. It is a spirited and readable, rather than a pedantically literal, version; although in many passages she does not pretend to convey every idiosyncrasy of the Greek, she nowhere misleads the reader. She did not make Browning's mistake years later in his translation of the *Agamemnon,* which remained so close to the original that it was generally considered incomprehensible. One example out of many may serve to illustrate her skill in preserving the meaning of the Greek despite the demands of rhyme. Prometheus, hearing the approach of the Chorus of the daughters of Oceanus, says to himself:

> φεῦ φεῦ, τί ποτ' αὖ κινάθισμα κλύω
> πέλας οἰωνῶν; αἰθὴρ δ' ἐλαφραῖς
> πτερύγων ῥιπαῖς ὑποσυρίζει. [124–126] [17]

> Alas, alas, what rustling motion of birds of prey do I again hear near by? The air is whirring under the light flutterings of wings.

In Elizabeth's translation, Prometheus says:

> Alas me! what a murmur and motion I hear,
> As of birds flying near!
> And the air undersings
> The light stroke of their wings—

Indeed throughout her version Elizabeth happily reproduces many of the original figures of speech. For instance, in the following passage she makes clear the meaning of the verb ῥυθμίζω, "to bring into harmony," as one forces words into their appropriate rhythms in verse. Prometheus says to the Chorus that he alone had the courage to make a stand against the tyrant Zeus. Therefore he is suffering fearful tortures; and although he gave mortals first place in his pity, he himself is thought unworthy of pity,

ἀλλὰ νηλεῶς
ὧδ' ἐρρύθμισμαι, [242–243]

But without mercy I have
been thus disciplined.

Elizabeth makes Prometheus say:

... while I render out
Deep rhythms of anguish 'neath the harping hand
That strikes me thus!—

At times for the sake of clarity she expands a metaphor which is merely suggested in the Greek. As an example I quote once again from the two versions. When the members of the Chorus arrive at the scene, they express their compassion for the hero. They well understand the reason for his punishment:

νέοι γὰρ οἰακονόμοι
κρατοῦσ' Ὀλύμπου· νεοχμοῖς
δὲ δὴ νόμοις Ζεὺς ἀθέτως κρατύνει.
τὰ πρὶν δὲ πελώρια νῦν ἀιστοῖ. [148–151]

For new helm-directors hold sway in
Olympus; and with new laws Zeus is
lawlessly ruling, and the mighty things
of old he is now annihilating.

The following paraphrase is much more effective than if it had been an exact translation:

For new is the Hand and the rudder that steers
The ship of Olympus through surge and wind—
And of old things passed, no track is behind.

Among the poems in the volumes of 1850 with personal associations are three sonnets to H. S. Boyd: "His Blindness," "His Death," and "Legacies," the latter of which is filled with lachrymose recollections. The copies of Aeschylus and of Gregory Nazianzen which came to her after his death were

those I used to read from, thus
Assisting my dear teacher's soul to unlock

> The darkness of his eyes: now, mine they mock,
> Blinded in turn, by tears: now, murmurous
> Sad echoes of my young voice, years agone,
> Entoning, from these leaves, the Græcian phrase,
> Return and choke my utterance.

Another poem with the background of Herefordshire was "Hector in the Garden," which had been written before she left Italy and published in *Blackwood's* in October 1846. Elizabeth recalls the pleasure she experienced at the age of nine from tending in the Hope End garden a "huge giant" of many different kinds of flowers—daffodils, violets, lilies, daisies, and others. In spite of its descriptive charm, the poem is spoiled by the "moral" of the concluding stanzas. The poet will not allow herself "this dreaming" about the past, but she thirsts for action, "Life's heroic ends pursuing."

It was in the new edition of her *Poems* that Elizabeth first published the sonnet sequence she had composed before her marriage. On July 22 of her last summer in London she had said to Browning, "You shall see some day at Pisa what I will not show you now. Does not Solomon say that 'there is a time to read what is written.'" Except for that cryptic remark she told him nothing of the sonnets she had been writing on the miracle of her life: her former isolation, ill-health, and sense of deep grief followed by the triumph of love over doubts and fears. Just before the last, the forty-fourth of the sonnets which Elizabeth copied into her small white notebook, she wrote, "50 Wimpole Street 1846, Sept."[18] In this poem she spoke of the many flowers Browning had brought her from his garden, and in return she presented him with her sheaf of sonnets:

> So, in the like name of that love of ours,
> Take back these thoughts, which here, unfolded too,
> And which on warm and cold days I withdrew
> From my heart's ground.

But neither at Pisa nor for the next two years at Florence did she show her husband the sonnets written for him. It was not until the Brownings were at Bagni di Lucca in the summer of 1849[19] that Elizabeth first placed "that wreath of Sonnets" on Robert "one morning unawares, three years after it had been twined." [20] Her reluctance to let him see them all this time may have been due to her shyness or to a chance remark Browning had once made "against putting one's loves into verse." At Lucca he had suddenly spoken "something else on the other side," and the following morning Elizabeth "said hesitatingly 'Do you know I once wrote some poems about *you?*'—and then—'There they are, if you care to see them,'—and there was the little Book"—the same one which Browning had beside him when he later wrote these words to Julia Wedgwood three years after Elizabeth's death. When Robert saw the manuscript, he was "much touched and pleased" and thought so highly of the poetry that he "could not consent," Elizabeth wrote Arabel, "that they should be lost" to her volumes.[21] Browning and she decided "to slip them in under some sort of veil" and chose the title "Sonnets from the Portuguese," which might seem to mean *"from the Portuguese language,"* but which really referred to "Catarina to Camoens," the poem immediately preceding the "Sonnets." Browning had read this poem before he made Elizabeth's acquaintance, and it "had affected him to tears, . . . again and again." Ever since then he had "in a loving fancy" associated her with the Portuguese Catarina. According to legend she was the girl with whom the Portuguese poet Camoëns fell in love, and she is supposed to have died during his absence abroad and to have left him "the riband from her hair," as Browning said.[22] And so Elizabeth and Robert gave the "Sonnets" their ambiguous name and allowed the public, "who are very little versed in Portuguese literature," as Elizabeth wrote, to interpret the title as they pleased.

Forty-three of the "Sonnets" came at the end of the second volume of the new edition. "Future and Past," which was the last poem of the first volume, later became the forty-second of the sonnet sequence in the fourth edition of 1856. Elizabeth did not place the sonnet with the others in 1850 because of its association with "Past and Future" published in the *Poems* of 1844, and she thus hoped to preserve the anonymity of the new sequence. In the earliest of the three manuscripts of the "Sonnets" which have been preserved,[23] she gave titles to eight of the poems: "Death

"Poems" of 1850

and Love" (No. 1), "Love's Obstacles" (2), "Love's New Creation" (7), "Love's Expression" (13), "Love's Causes" (14), "Love's Repetitions" (21), "Love's Refuge" (22), and "Love's Sacrifice" (23). But she wisely decided that forty-three titles all somewhat similar to one another would have a monotonous effect and crossed out the eight she had tentatively chosen so that in the published form the individual poems were designated only by numerals. Elizabeth took more pains in the composition of the "Sonnets" than in any of her former poems. For once the expression was concise and coherent, the rhymes almost all conventional, the imagery in better taste, the syntax clear, and the diction simple and unaffected.

A study of the significant revisions of one of the sonnets will illustrate the great care with which she wrote and later emended them. The "Sonnets" may be seen in five different stages of development: the manuscript in the Pierpont Morgan Library, the George Murray Smith Memorial Manuscript in the British Museum,[24] the new edition of the *Poems*,[25] the third edition of 1853 (in which she made only three or four slight revisions of the "Sonnets"), and the fourth edition of the *Poems* in 1856. The earliest manuscript reading of "Sonnet 16," for example, is as follows:

> And yet because thou art above me so,
> Because thou art more strong, and like a king,
> Thou canst prevail against my fears and fling
> Thy purple round me till my heart shall grow
> 5 Too close against thy heart to henceforth know
> Its separate trembling pulse. Oh, conquering
> May prove as noble and complete a thing
> In lifting upward as in beating low!
> And as a soldier, struck down by a sword,
> 10 Cries "Here my strife ends", and sinks dead to earth,—
> Even so, beloved, I, at last, record . .
> "My doubt ends here—" If *thou* invite me forth,
> I rise above abasement at the word!—
> 14 Make thy love larger to enlarge my worth.

The words "art above me" were given a stronger meaning by the substitution of "overcomest." "Strong" in line 2 was changed to "princely" and later to "noble." The awkward and needless splitting of the infinitive in line 5 was corrected so that the phrase became "henceforth to know." Perhaps since the movement of the first four words in line 6 was hindered by the excessive number of *s* and *t* sounds, she eliminated the expression and substituted "How it shook when alone." The word "noble" had been used in the revision of line 2 and was therefore removed from line 7 in favor of "lordly." In line 8 "beating" was replaced by the more vivid "crushing." In the change of the next two lines, the figure became much happier: the wounded soldier raised by his gallant enemy is compared to the poet herself, whose hesitations were conquered by a generous lover.

    9 And as a vanquished soldier yields his sword
  10 To one who lifts him from the bloody earth,—

The first four words of line 12 became in 1850 the more emphatic sentence, "Here ends my doubt!" and in 1856 the meaning was enlarged by the change: "Here ends my strife."

Yet despite Elizabeth's conscientious craftsmanship the freshness of the "Sonnets" has faded, and they no longer evoke the eager response of earlier generations; with all their singing angels, floods of tears, chrisms, lutes, and golden thrones, they are very much in the idiom of the period. But no poems were ever called into being by a love more true and sincere.

SHE received fewer reviews of her new edition than she had in either 1838 or in 1844. The *Poems* of 1850 were almost unnoticed in the United States, because no separate American edition was issued. A Boston publisher had agreed to reprint her two volumes and to pay for the rights, but he was anticipated by C. S. Francis of New York, who pirated the two volumes of her *Poems* without any of the alterations or new material. "I don't know when I have been so provoked," Elizabeth wrote to Arabel [26] of the failure of the Boston publisher to honor his agreement because the volumes had already appeared in New York. "So I lose everything—both money and reputation." A brief, perfunctory notice of one paragraph in the *Christian Examiner* of Boston referred to Elizabeth's "possession of the richest poetical gifts." [27] An equally short paragraph in *Harper's Magazine* spoke of her "peculiar boldness, originality, and beauty" and said that the new edition would be "thankfully accepted by the wide circle which has learned to venerate Mrs. Browning's genius." [28]

In England the most favorable review was in the *Athenaeum* [29] and was probably written by Elizabeth's friend H. F. Chorley. He quoted from many of her best-known poems, such as "The Cry of the Children" and "Catarina to Camoens" and concluded with handsome praise: "Mrs. Browning is probably, of her sex, the first imaginative writer England has produced in any age:—she is, beyond comparison, the first poetess of her own." The *Eclectic Review,* which was also extravagant in its commendation of the *Poems,* spoke of her "splendid poetry," her "profound thought," and her "pervading spirit so pure and so womanly." The writer thought that the romantic ballad "Bertha in the Lane" was "unrivalled in its pathetic beauty" and that the carelessly written "Lady Geraldine's Courtship" was "one of the most charming and finely-elaborated poems in the language" and had an effect which was "indescribably delightful." No other woman writer, in the reviewer's opinion, had such a combination of "solemn purpose with large intellect and the same intensity of imagination." [30] But the *Guardian,* the *Examiner, Fraser's Magazine,* and the *English Review* were all more temperate in their praise and believed that even her most recent poetry had the same faults of style mentioned in the reviews of earlier volumes: diffuseness, obscure and affected diction, ungrammatical syntax, inappropriate and absurd images, confusion of the parts of speech, slovenly versification, and faulty rhymes.[31] Each of the four reviews, however, found something to commend. The *Guardian,* for example, said that "in melody of verse, in tenderness, in true pathos, in abundant language, command of rhyme, and affluence of imagery, she is quite in the first ranks of living writers. In all her works she evinces marks of a truly poetical mind." The *English Review* asserted that Elizabeth took "high rank among the bards of England" and that there was perhaps none who surpassed her "in her especial beauties—in the combination of romantic wildness with deep, true tenderness and most singular power." Yet unlike many critics at that time the reviewer considered Browning a greater poet than his wife: "Upon the whole, we think Browning's the higher and the master spirit; hers the more tender, and the more musical also." A remark in the *Examiner* on "Lady Geraldine's Courtship" and "The Romaunt of the Page" was expressed with the characteristic glibness of reviewers: that both poems "show how delicate, pure, and intense a spirit of womanly love is connected with this masculine and far-reaching intellect."

On the whole the reviewers had curiously little to say about either the new translation of the *Prometheus Bound* or about the "Sonnets from the Portuguese." It is doubtful whether the writer of the notice in the *English Review* understood Elizabeth's responsibility as a translator, for he wrote of her *Prometheus Bound* that the hero's "complaints are rather too rhetorically rendered, without sufficient dramatic earnestness." The *Eclectic Review* called her version of the drama "a noble achievement" and said that it was one of the many evidences in the volumes of the poet's "solid classical scholarship." None of the reviewers made a close examination of the *Prometheus Bound* by comparing it with the original, nor did any of them appear to know that the new translation was her second of the same drama.

The reviewers were equally imperceptive in their comments on the "Sonnets from the Portuguese." They mostly ignored these new poems, and the two or three which mentioned them failed to grasp their significance. The writer in *Fraser's Magazine* did not understand that the sonnets were a revelation of the poet's own love, but he suggested that they were more than translations: "From the Portuguese they may be: but their life and earnestness must prove Mrs. Browning either to be the most perfect of all known translators, or to have quickened with her own spirit the framework of another's thoughts, and then modestly declined the honour which was really her own." The *Examiner* described the themes of the "Sonnets," which it thought a "remarkable series," but it gave no hint that they might have been based upon Elizabeth's personal experiences.

The *Spectator* [32] was the only important journal which found almost nothing of merit in the new edition. The reviewer believed that although Elizabeth had shown great promise in her earlier volumes, she had made almost no progress in her art: "Mrs. Browning has given no single instance of her ability to compose finished works. Diffuseness, obscurity, and exaggeration, mar even the happiest efforts of her genius." It seemed to the writer that most of her poems were only "rough sketches, thrown off, it is to be supposed, in one or two sittings."

Elizabeth was not exhilarated by the notices of her volumes of 1850, as she had been in 1844, probably because copies of the reviews did not arrive in Italy until months after they had been published. Since many of the reviews had been kind to her, she could not have been disappointed (for example, the article in the *Guardian,* which she read early in May 1851, just as she was beginning her journey to England, gave her great pleasure). But the authors of the articles had mostly read her poems with the same carelessness and haste they had imputed to her writing, and they had expressed themselves superficially and in clichés.

In November and December a young American paid a number of calls at Casa Guidi. Charles Eliot Norton, who was later to be the first professor of fine arts at Harvard, was on a leisurely tour of the East and of Europe. At their apartment in Florence he found the Brownings "sitting in a pleasant home-like room, surrounded with pictures and books, with an open fire shedding a genial light through it." Browning, as Norton described him, had "a pleasant open expression and manner" and seemed in his looks and conversation quite unlike the idea of him he had received from his poems. Elizabeth's appearance was also altogether different from what he had expected after reading her works. He noticed her slight and delicate figure, her "reserved and timid" manner, her quiet plaintive voice. At first she had little to say, and Norton felt "as if she were so distrustful of herself that she kept back the expression of her sentiments and thoughts from all but those with whom she was familiar." Her face, like her voice, was "melancholy" and "full of sensibility" so that she looked like "the most delicate and sensitive of poets," rather than the author of poems of "very great intellectual strength and power of expression." The more he saw of the Brownings, the more he liked them. Browning's conversation he thought extraordinary, with its quick flow of ideas and its inexhaustible fund of anecdotes told "with such entire straightforward earnestness that one cannot but like him." Norton continued, "He is quite unconscious and never even in the slightest way claims any regard for himself as a poet, or shows that he expects you to remember that he is one. Indeed one of the most charming characteristics of both him and his wife is their self-forgetfulness." [33]

IT WAS during the winter of 1850–51 that Elizabeth wrote the second half of *Casa Guidi Windows* on the events which had taken place two years before. Early in the spring she sent the manuscript to London, and the work was published as a slender octavo volume by Chapman and Hall on the last day of May.[34] Later in the year C. S. Francis in New York pirated the poem in a volume which included the revised *Prometheus Bound* and the other new poems of Elizabeth's edition of 1850.[35] The *American Whig Review*,[36] which was one of the few journals in the United States to notice it, was unsympathetic and made fun of almost all the poems because of their unconventional diction, syntax, and rhyme. The writer of the article, which was a joint review with Browning's *Sordello* and the series of *Bells and Pomegranates,* believed, however, that the Brownings had "two of the greatest poetical minds of the day" and were "possibly the most interesting married couple on record." Elizabeth knew that her sharp criticism of British foreign policy in *Casa Guidi Windows* would offend many English critics. Nor was she mistaken; a number of journals ignored the poem, and those which reviewed it were mostly unfriendly. To many English people the Italian situation seemed remote, and the war of 1848–49 was all but forgotten. None of the reviewers was interested enough in the work to discuss in detail Elizabeth's attitude toward Pius IX, Duke Leopold, Guerrazzi, and Garibaldi, and her reasons for the failure of the liberal movement. The *Athenaeum,* the *Guardian,* and the *Prospective Review* condemned the poem for its diffuseness, its excessively colloquial style, and its poor choice of subject matter.[37] According to the *Prospective Review,* one of the chief defects of the work was "its limitation in scope and topic"; it was "too truly and too literally described by its title." But Elizabeth had already explained in the introductory "Advertisement" in her volume that she was attempting "no continous narrative, nor exposition of political philosophy" and was presenting only "a simple story of personal impressions." The *Guardian* called the poem "an unmistakeable and complete failure," filled with "a great deal of diffuse and rather commonplace reflection and regret." Miss Mitford, who had always preferred Elizabeth's romantic ballads to her other types of poems, described her recent work as "a dull tirade on Italian politics" and added that the treatment of the material was "so unreal that it excites no sympathy." [38]

The *Eclectic Review,* on the other hand, considered that the poem was "perhaps, the finest which she has produced, and is certainly one of the noblest productions of female genius. The language is singularly eloquent and strong; the feeling which pervades it is in the highest tone of humanity." [39] The writer was surprised, however, at her "crying so coldly and cruelly for war" after advocating in the first part of the same volume that England should remain at peace. The *Literary Gazette,* which found in the poem "all the charm which might be expected from Mrs. Browning's fine and original perceptions and ardent style," praised her for having "systematically adopted a chaster and severer style." [40] The reviewer thought that many passages were "dashed off with a fiery energy and a picturesque brevity which are almost Dantesque." Although the *Spectator* had spoken harshly of her new edition of the *Poems,* it said that *Casa Guidi Windows* was a great improvement and admired Elizabeth for her "womanly faith and trust" which had remained firm in the face of many disappointments. Unlike almost all the other journals, it approved of her writing on the politics of the hour and strongly recommended the book "as a proof of the feminine warmth of heart that may coexist with a vivid sympathy with the public affairs of nations." [41] But whether the notices were laudatory or censorious, Elizabeth paid less attention to them than she had to the reviews of some of her earlier books, for she was making her first trip back to England. Except for a few remarks in the letters which she received at Lucerne and at Paris from Arabel, she heard little about the reception of the volume.

The Brownings had not been able to return to England in the summer of 1849 because of the death of Robert's mother, or in 1850 because of Elizabeth's pregnancy and severe illness. By the winter and spring of the following year she had fully regained her health and was stronger than she had been at any time since her childhood. Once she even walked up the long steep hill to the ancient Basilica of San Miniato al Monte. Several years after Elizabeth's death, Browning referred to this period as the time when she "was at the very height of her health, so far as she ever recovered it: but we returned for the first time to England, and there was fatigue, and afterward, other troubles began, and she never touched that height again." [42]

It was probably on May 3, 1851,[43] that Elizabeth, Browning, the baby, and Wilson left Casa Guidi for a tour of northern Italy and Switzerland on their journey to England. They planned to settle in Paris for the winter and to visit Rome in the following spring, but they were not to see Italy again until the autumn of 1852.

14. England and Paris, 1851-52

ON THE TRIP TO VENICE with the Brownings were Mr. and Mrs. David Ogilvy, "upright, excellent people," who had been living in an apartment above them at Casa Guidi. Mrs. Ogilvy, Elizabeth wrote, "aspires strenuously towards poetry," and two books which were the product of that aspiration were *A Book of Highland Minstrelsy* and *Traditions of Tuscany, in Verse*. The party spent the first night at a village in the Apennines, two days at Bologna, a few hours at Modena, and a day at Parma; at Mantua they took the railroad and went past Verona, Vicenza, and Padua and then "shot into the heart of Venice."[1] As they visited churches and art galleries on their trip from Florence, Elizabeth had become tired and confused because of too much conversation, even though the Ogilvys were congenial and intelligent. She always liked "to receive impressions quietly and deeply, without so much talk of this and that."[2]

After Elizabeth had been at Venice a few days, she wrote that although her "fancy had of course been brim-full of floating sea-pavements, marble palaces with seaweed on their marble steps, and black gondolas sweeping through sunlit and moonlit silence . . . the real *sight* exceeded the imagination."[3] She was in "a sort of rapture" every moment after she arrived and would have been content, if circumstances permitted, to live out her life there. Venice held her spellbound: "Never had I touched the skirts of so celestial a place [she wrote Miss Mitford]. The beauty of the architecture, the silver trails of water up between all that gorgeous colour and carving, the enchanting silence, the moonlight, the music, the gondolas—I mix it all up together, and maintain that nothing is like it, nothing equal to it, not a second Venice in the world."

The Brownings rented for thirty shillings a week a spacious apartment in "a noble palazzo" with private balconies looking upon the Grand Canal in "the best situation in Venice." [4] Because of her frail health, Elizabeth left unseen most of the churches, except for the basilica of San Marco, nor was she able to go to the Academy to see the paintings of the Venetian masters. But she led what she considered "a true Venetian life"; Browning and she went to a festa at Chioggia in a steamer and frightened Wilson by staying out until two in the morning; they attended two operas by Verdi (for which Elizabeth apologized to her unworldly sister Arabel) and a play, all for less than a shilling each; and once they visited the Armenian convent where Byron had studied. As they went through "the pretty, bowery garden," they saw an old man "with a white beard long below his waist," who was sitting under a rose tree in bloom. To their surprise he spoke to them in English and asked, "You are English?" He told them he was the superior of the convent and had taught Armenian to Byron.[5] In the evenings Robert and Elizabeth sat under the gas lamps in the piazza of San Marco, reading newspapers, drinking coffee, and watching the people around them, who were a typical Italian crowd, Elizabeth wrote Arabel, "of a good breathing living humanity." With their parents were "such heaps of rosy children, not asleep yet," and all classes of people were mingling freely as they walked about or sat side by side, enjoying the same music and "eating the same ices (ices are so cheap)." [6]

Their two-year-old baby, who was now beginning to talk, called himself Wiedeman, which he gradually "turned into Peninny, by an extraordinary violation of syllables," [7] and later the name was shortened to Pen. Elizabeth had been making him wear a lace cap under his hat and would have continued to do so had not Robert objected. She wrote from Venice to Arabel:

> Robert wants to make the child like *a boy*, he says—(because he is a man)—and I because I am a woman perhaps, like him to be a baby as long as possible. . . . The truth is that the child is not "like a boy," and that if you put him into a coat and waistcoat forthwith, he only would look like a small angel travestied. For he isn't exactly like a girl either—no, not a bit. He's a sort of neutral creature, so far. But it vexes Robert when people ask if he is a boy or a girl—(oh, man's

pride!) and he will have it, that the lace caps and ribbons help to throw the point into doubt.[8]

The Brownings were in no hurry to leave Venice, for they were waiting to hear whether they would have enough "ship money" (from Elizabeth's shares in the *David Lyon*) to make a long tour of Switzerland. But while she and Pen were thriving and growing fatter in the relaxing, humid climate of Venice, Robert became "uncomfortable, and nervous, and unable to eat or sleep," and Wilson felt even worse. So after a month Elizabeth was forced "out of pure humanity and sympathy" to cut short their sojourn in the city where she felt so much at home, and they left in the middle of June for Padua, Brescia, and Milan. When they were at Padua, they hired a *calèche* and made a pilgrimage to Arquà because of its association with Petrarch. "The sight of that little room where the great soul exhaled itself" moved her profoundly, and "even Robert's man's eyes had tears in them," she observed. During their two days at Milan Elizabeth was well enough to climb the 350 steps of the "glorious" cathedral. She also visited Da Vinci's "Last Supper" and thought it "divine." Guido and Guercino and "those soulless Caracci" at Bologna she no longer admired after knowing more about them. But Correggio was "sublime" and "wonderful" and besides had "the sense to make his little Christs and angels after the very likeness" of her child. From Milan they went to Como, took a steamer along the lake to Menaggio, thence by carriage to Porlezza at the tip of Lake Lugano, and by boat to Lugano, from which they traveled by carriage to Bellinzona in the foothills of the Alps. Then after a day of steaming down Lake Maggiore and back again, they journeyed north to Faido and by means of a carriage crossed the St. Gotthard pass to Flüelen, where they took a boat to Lucerne, arriving on June 24 "with just *ten francs*." Everywhere the scenery had been "most exquisite." Elizabeth wrote that during the "sublime" passage across the Alps "the tears overflowed my eyes."

At Lucerne they received "desperately bad news" about their finances: that they were to get only £50 that year from the *David Lyon*. It was impossible for them to visit the Swiss lakes and mountains and to make the trip by steamboat down the Rhine to

Cologne, all of which they had hoped to do; they would have to go to Paris the most inexpensive way. Browning upbraided himself for having attempted the long journey with such slender resources and was "in a high fever of anxiety," but Elizabeth begged him not to worry. She felt that she had "twice the share of artistic temperament" that he had. As she wrote Arabel, "It's impossible to fret me about money-matters. If we can't live on bread and cheese, we must live on bread alone . . and that's better than cheese alone, isn't it?" [9] But it was easier for her than for Robert to appear unconcerned about money, since she had enjoyed an independent income for many years. She always told him that he "ought to have five thousand a year," all of which he needed "to meet the exigencies of his nature." [10] But their income, which at this time was far below that sum, consisted of about £200 a year from Elizabeth's government bonds, £100 annually which Kenyon gave them after the birth of Pen, and varying amounts from her ship shares and from her books. They went immediately to Basel by diligence and from that city to Paris via Strasbourg by a combination of railroad and diligence. The whole journey of seven weeks, including the month at Venice, had cost exactly £77, Elizabeth wrote to Arabel, who had apparently implied that the Brownings were spending too much money in travel.[11] In a number of her letters to Arabel she could hardly conceal her irritation at her sister's belief that money should be put aside and not spent.

Although Elizabeth did not love Paris the way she did Florence and Venice, she admired it once again and thought it a beautiful and brilliant city. She liked "the bright green trees and gardens everywhere in the heart of the town" and enjoyed the carefree dining at restaurants. They secured a comfortable apartment of seven rooms for six francs (five shillings) a day at the Hotel Aux Armes de la Ville de Paris on the Boulevard de la Madeleine. There Elizabeth rested and gathered her courage for the inevitable trip to London— "Ah, if you knew how abhorrent the thought of England is to *me!*" she had written from Venice. She was distressed that she would soon be so near yet so far from her father and the other members of the Barrett family who had rejected her.

One evening Tennyson called on the Brownings and asked them

to his hotel to meet his wife. Elizabeth, "(though tired half to death with the Louvre) rose up from the sofa in a decided state of resurrection, and acceded at once." They became good friends, and Tennyson offered them the use of his house and servants at Twickenham as long as they were in England. Elizabeth liked them both very much. Of Mrs. Tennyson she wrote with her usual superlatives to Arabel, "She has the sweetest manner, the gentlest smile, the softest tone of voice, that a woman can have." [12]

The Brownings might not have gone to London that summer but for the entreaty of Arabel, who could not come to Paris to see her sister. They left on July 22 and arrived the following morning at the small apartment they had rented at 26 Devonshire Street. It was, as Elizabeth said, a "miserable accommodation," having only two rooms on the ground floor and a dressing room in the garret; yet it cost £2 a week.

Elizabeth missed the amenities of the Continent and felt strange and uncomfortable and almost like a foreigner. Arabel was the only member of the Barrett family with whom she could be intimate. All her brothers had remained obdurate in their disapproval of her marriage. Charles John (Stormie), for example, had written her a short note in 1850 in which he sent "not a single word of remembrance to Robert" and said that as soon as she *"was reconciled to Papa, he would write often."* [13] Elizabeth had expressed to Henrietta her amazement at her brothers' conduct: "If the universe had attested to me that they would have acted so, I, with my former impression of and trust in their generous, affectionate dispositions, would never have believed it." [14] Henrietta had married William Surtees Cook on April 6, 1850. She had asked her father for permission to marry and had received a harsh note upbraiding her for the "insult" and threatening to cast her off forever if she married. The letter made her realize the futility of further discussion, and they were married immediately. The brothers, however, were very cordial toward her husband because he was their cousin. Several members of the Graham-Clarke family had been "insolent" toward Henrietta, just as they had been cool to Elizabeth. "How different with both of us," she wrote Henrietta, "had we married rich men under ever such offensive circumstances. It is that conviction which makes me angry." [15] In the summer of 1851 Henrietta and Cook were living in Taunton, Somersetshire, but Henrietta was able to come to London for a week to see Elizabeth.

The Brownings stayed two days at New Cross with Robert's father and Sarianna, both of whom were "most affectionate" to Elizabeth, and Sarianna in return was "constantly" at the Brownings' apartment. Of all her brothers and sisters only Arabel still needed and missed Elizabeth. The eldest of the brothers, Charles John, was a planter in Jamaica, but the others were all at home and saw her from time to time. George became reconciled to both her and Robert before they left for Paris in the autumn; he was the only one of the brothers with whom she regularly corresponded for the rest of her life. Elizabeth's aunt Arabella Graham-Clarke, who had been close to her at Hope End and later at Torquay, paid her a call out of curiosity but was "most offensive" in her manner; on her return to the country she wrote "an extraordinary letter" to Elizabeth asking her to become reconciled to her father. Both she and Robert did write to Mr. Barrett before they left England, and Elizabeth asked him at least to see her child. In reply Browning received "a very violent and unsparing letter" and two packets enclosing all of Elizabeth's letters, none of which had been read.

> I could never tell you [Elizabeth said to Henrietta], if I tried, what I felt when those letters came back to me, nine or ten of them, all with their unbroken seals testifying to the sealed up heart which refused to be opened by me. Oh, if my child were cast out of society for the most hideous of possible crimes, could I keep my heart so sealed up towards *him*? Not while a pulse of life stirred in it. If God and man cried aloud to me not to open, I should yet open—I could not help it. Think of the black unbroken seals, Henrietta, and the black-edged paper! How did he know that I might not have been widowed and childless and calling out to him in my desolation? . . . He fulfilled what he considered (he said, writing to Robert) "his duty to himself, his family, and society." May God pardon what we call our virtues! For my part I look upon

it all with profound pity and sorrow, and now with little hope.[16]

Yet notwithstanding the coolness of Elizabeth's aunt Arabella and the unrelenting anger of her father, she and Browning were "both giddy with the kind attentions" they received from many friends. They dined at Kenyon's house, where they saw Bryan Waller Procter, Carlyle, John Forster, H. F. Chorley, and Mrs. Jameson. Once they met at Kenyon's the American traveler, journalist, and poet Bayard Taylor, who later wrote of Elizabeth's "thin, pale face, half hidden by heavy brown ringlets." [17] It was at the same house, though possibly on another occasion, that they saw Samuel Taylor Coleridge's daughter. In a letter written in August to a friend, Sara Coleridge described Elizabeth. She mentioned the thin face and long ringlets Taylor had noticed and also said that Elizabeth was small and hard-featured and had a weak, plaintive voice but that there was "something very impressive in her dark eyes and her brow." [18] Fanny Kemble called on the Brownings, John Forster gave them "a magnificent dinner," and they received visits from Procter, R. H. Horne and his wife, and Mrs. Jameson. They also went to see Miss Mitford, Browning's old friend William Johnson Fox, the aged Samuel Rogers, and Carlyle, who was, Elizabeth said, "one of the great sights in England."

As autumn drew near, Elizabeth was fearful of remaining longer in London because of the damp fogs; so they made plans to leave on September 25. Two or three days before that, Carlyle, who was also about to set out for Paris, heard of the Brownings' intentions and delayed his departure that he might travel with them. On that Thursday morning he went to the London Bridge Railway Station and found the Brownings, their child, Wilson, and Flush. They all got into their compartment in the train for Newhaven. Off they went, with Robert "talking very loud and with vivacity," Carlyle wrote, and himself "silent rather, tending towards many thoughts." [19] Elizabeth, on the contrary, found Carlyle's conversation vigorous and picturesque and thought she had hardly ever heard a literary man speak so well. He "left a deep impression" upon Elizabeth, who found it "difficult to conceive of a more interesting human soul." Both Carlyle's journal and Elizabeth's letters describe the rough passage on the Channel. As soon as they were on the open sea, the decks were swept by the water, and everyone was startled to hear crockery falling to the floor and tables and chairs tumbling about the saloon. Elizabeth was relieved when they arrived that evening safely at Dieppe at twenty minutes past nine and she could throw herself upon the sofa in her hotel. The next morning, while Carlyle and Browning strolled around the old city, Elizabeth was characteristically engaged in writing to one of her sisters a letter in which she related in minute detail every event of the trip.[20] In the afternoon they took the train to Paris, where the Brownings returned to the hotel from which they had departed two months earlier. About October 10 they moved into a cheerful, sunny apartment of six rooms and kitchen at 138 avenue des Champs-Elysées, which they rented for two hundred francs (£8) a month. It had a large private terrace which overlooked the avenue and was almost surrounded by trees. Since Elizabeth was not strong enough for housework, they had a *femme de service,* whom they paid twenty-two francs (about eighteen shillings) a month, and she prepared the meals and kept the apartment clean.

Now that Elizabeth was on the Continent again, she felt more at home and happier. For Browning it had been "pure joy" to be with his friends and family in England, and Elizabeth believed "he would have been capable of never leaving England again" if it had been possible for her to live there. She, however, had left for France with mixed feelings, grateful for the love and many acts of kindness shown her, but at the same time bearing a wound which would never heal: "Where love of country ought to be in the heart," she wrote, "there is the mark of the burning iron in mine." The Brownings' apartment was warmer, more conveniently arranged, and less dear than any she had known in England. "Talk of English comforts!" she wrote Miss Mitford. "It's a national delusion. The comfort of the continental way of life has only to be tested to be recognised." In contrast to England, the climate of which Elizabeth believed had "a supremacy in badness," Paris was warm and sunny. Her cough disappeared, and once in a while she was strong enough to walk with Robert along the Champs-

Elysées early in the evening and stand on the Pont de la Concorde and look down the Seine at "the fantastic city drawn out in gas light." [21] She always thought it "an enchanted scene."

That autumn Browning was busy writing the introduction to his volume of Shelley's letters, to be published by Moxon, letters which were later proved to be forgeries. Elizabeth wrote Henrietta that she was about to prepare a third edition of her poems, but she lost interest and did not make the necessary revisions until the spring of 1853. The contest between President Louis Napoleon and the legislative assembly caught her imagination, and she seems to have spent much of her time reading about the subject in newspapers and magazines. For relaxation she was absorbed in Eugène Sue's long, involved *Mystères de Paris,* which she had first read not long after it had appeared in 1842.

James T. Fields, the Boston publisher, called on the Brownings in November on his way to Italy. He explained to Elizabeth that he had wished to bring out a new edition of her works on the model of her *Poems* of 1850 and to pay for them as though she were an American author. C. S. Francis, however, had protested against the "injustice and cruelty" of issuing the volumes to compete with his piracies but had promised that whatever Fields would give her he too was ready to pay. "Very generous intentions on both sides," Elizabeth commented, "and between the two I get nothing!" [22] She was annoyed that Fields appeared to condone Francis' most recent piracy, the volume containing the "Sonnets from the Portuguese" and "Casa Guidi Windows." Fields had published late in 1849 the first American edition of Browning's poems,[23] which Elizabeth believed had almost sold out, but he had sent the author no money. In view of the apparent success of the *Poems,* she did not understand why "the profits of it go exclusively to Mr. Fields' pocket." It seemed to her a "curious" arrangement.

Although the Brownings did not have so many friends in Paris as in London, they did not lack for society. "People are inclined here to be over-kind to us, I see, rather than the contrary," Elizabeth wrote. One evening they went to a reception at the home of Lady Elgin, the widow of the English statesman who, when he was ambassador to Turkey, had arranged for the removal of the sculpture from the Parthenon. Elizabeth thought her a "highly cultivated" and "generous and noble" woman, with wide sympathies and a kindness to everyone "which nobody can well exaggerate." [24] She became one of the Brownings' most intimate friends. At her home they met the English-born wife of the professor of Persian at the Collège de France, Madame Julius Mohl, who was "very clever and agreeable," Elizabeth wrote, "knowing everybody worth knowing, in French society." [25] She too was soon to be a favorite with the Brownings, who frequently went to her *salon* and in turn entertained both her and Lady Elgin in their own apartment.

Another close friend was the French critic Joseph Milsand, of whom Elizabeth wrote with her usual fervor that he was "altogether admirable. A more noble and conscientious intellect it would be impossible to find." [26] He had published an "excellent and most pleasant" article on Browning's poetry in the issue of August 15 of the *Revue des Deux Mondes*, "elaborately written and so highly appreciatory as well nigh to satisfy *me*," as Elizabeth described it to Miss Mitford. For the next in this series of articles, which had the general heading "La Poésie anglaise depuis Byron," Milsand wrote for the issue of January 15, 1852, a critique on Elizabeth's work. He had nothing but praise for her romantic ballads and for the "meditations on life," such as "A Drama of Exile," but her most recent publication *Casa Guidi Windows* was in his opinion a strange confusion. He objected to its choice of subject; great poetry, he maintained, should not deal with the political issues of the moment. But he concluded gallantly, "Mistress Browning me semble être un honneur pour son sexe et son pays." [27]

While Elizabeth very much enjoyed her friendships with Lady Elgin, Madame Mohl, and Milsand, there was no one in Paris whose acquaintance she would rather make than that of Madame Dudevant (George Sand), whom for many years she had worshiped as one of the great geniuses of the age. The Brownings sent her a letter of introduction from Mazzini and received from her an invitation to call at her home on Sunday afternoon, February 15. After the interview Elizabeth's faith in George Sand was still unshaken. She had the impression that Madame Dudevant was "a noble woman" and that she had "great moral as well as intellectual capacities." What chiefly surprised Elizabeth, however, was that the woman who had been the mistress of Sandeau, Mérimée, Musset, and Chopin could never have been beautiful. To Elizabeth's mind, her face had several poor features and was lacking in sweetness. During the three quarters of an hour the Brownings stayed, George Sand talked in a low, rapid voice to two or three men about politics; as she listened, Elizabeth "felt the burning soul through all that quietness." A few days later they paid a second call, and this time they remained for half an hour, during which Madame Dudevant sat by the fire with eight or nine men about her and was silent except to answer with "calm disdain" a few questions addressed to her. Browning was offended by the untidy, bohemian atmosphere, the "crowds of ill-bred men who adore her *à genoux bas* [Elizabeth wrote], betwixt a puff of smoke and an ejection of saliva," and he said to Elizabeth that "if any other mistress of a house had behaved so, he would have walked out of the room." He later met George Sand five or six times and once, seeing her near the Tuileries, walked the length of the gardens with her. He could not get on with her, however, and complained to Elizabeth that as soon as the ice was broken, then a new frost came between them. "I would break it and break it again," Elizabeth wrote to Arabel,[28] who had not concealed her disapproval of Madame Dudevant or of Elizabeth for calling on her. George Sand must have thought she had little in common with the Brownings, for she left Paris without returning their calls, to Elizabeth's keen disappointment. "We both tried hard to please her," she said; "only we always felt that we couldn't penetrate—couldn't really *touch* her—it was all vain."

Robert had objected to Elizabeth's exposing herself to the winter winds to visit George Sand; but she had "smothered" herself with furs and had gone "in a close carriage" so that she did not catch cold. Thereafter she took no further risk with her health and mostly remained indoors until April, when she attended with Browning a performance of *La Dame aux camélias* by Dumas *fils*. Both of them were so affected by "the exquisite acting, the too literal truth to nature everywhere," that the tears rolled down their cheeks, Elizabeth wrote, and she herself had a headache for a day afterward. Early in May she went with Mrs. Jameson, who had recently rented an apartment in the building where the Brownings lived, to the Champ-de-Mars to see the military *fête* of Louis Napoleon, the giving of the eagles. A week or two later Browning and she attended a *matinée musicale* at the home of Ary Scheffer, a painter of dreamy, sentimental pictures mostly on biblical and literary subjects. Although he was then much in fashion, his works soon became outmoded. After Elizabeth met him, she wrote that she had not believed "so sublime an artist" still existed, nor had she been "prepared for anything so divine as those pictures."[29] As she heard Beethoven being played at the home of the French artist, she was so deeply moved she could hardly keep from fainting. Late in May she went with Mrs. Jameson and Madame Mohl to the Institute to see the reception of the poet Alfred de Musset. Although she had to sit for four hours in the heat with the fear every moment of "dropping down under an avalanche of Parisian bonnets,"[30] her endurance was rewarded by a view of Musset, who "looked like a poet," and of Guizot, to whose "noble, pale, melancholy face" she was drawn again and again.

Besides writing to her sisters about her friends and her engagements in Paris, Elizabeth also described at length her child, who was three in March. Pen must have been an unusual sight in his red velvet frock, chattering in Italian to Wilson as she took him to the Punch and Judy shows along the Champs-Elysées. To anyone inquiring about his nationality he would always reply that he was a *"iano"* (*Italiano*). Once he saw the wine knocked out of a marionette's hand in a farcical scene, and for days afterward he was seized with spasms of uncontrollable laughter at the memory of Punch's surprise and discomfiture. "No dinner, Punch —no vino, Punch," he would cry out.[31] Elizabeth realized that her child was delicate and high-strung and was much worried about his attacks of hysteria. A friend of the Brownings invited Pen to a New Year's Eve party where about thirty children were to enjoy games around a Christmas tree.[32] Since the affair was scheduled for seven o'clock and the child usually went to bed at six, Browning said that it would not be good for Pen to stay up late and that it would be "very foolish" of Elizabeth to send him.

But she wanted "to show him off" and bought a black velvet frock, broad blue satin ribbons for the sleeves, and shoes with blue rosettes.[33] With his "fair skin and bright golden ringlets," Pen in his new frock "will look like a picture," Elizabeth wrote Arabel with parental pride. "So I shall have my way," she said, and a few days after the new year she informed Henrietta that Pen went to the party and "looked perfectly lovely." Not long afterward a visitor at the Brownings' said to Elizabeth, "Take care of making an idol of that child."[34] She was impressed by this warning, for she quoted the words in a letter to one of her sisters and said that she had often thought of them since they had been spoken.

It was from Paris that Elizabeth first mentioned the subject of spiritualism, about which she and Arabel were to disagree for the rest of their correspondence. At this time Elizabeth discussed the "rapping spirits" chiefly with Lady Elgin, but she had first learned about them from Hiram Powers in Florence. In the early fifties a craze for table turning, séances, and other spiritualistic experiments swept through America and Europe. Under the influence of the spirits, tables spun around or shot upward, pencils wrote messages from the other world, rappings were heard upon wood, people who knew no Greek suddenly wrote the language, watches were wound up without keys, and accordions sailed through the air, playing tunes while in flight. According to a popular book Elizabeth read on the growth of the "manifestations" in America, Henry Spicer's *Sights and Sounds,* published in 1853, the "rappings," which had first been heard four years earlier in Rochester, New York, had spread all over the Union. Messages were supposedly conveyed to the living from the souls of the dead through a clairvoyant, who because of his role as the connecting link between the two worlds was called a "medium." Spicer said that there were at that time "not less than *thirty thousand* recognised *media* practising in various parts of the United States," and that in Philadelphia alone there were at least three hundred "magnetic circles" holding regular meetings.[35] In England and on the Continent interest in the subject was no less prevalent.

From the beginning Elizabeth was convinced of the authenticity of almost all spiritualistic phenomena, read the chief articles and books on the topic as they appeared, and in conversation with friends eagerly exchanged gossip about the latest "incidents." She was "in a state of high expectation just now" and was certain that "wonderful things will soon be learnt." [36] Although Robert always remained skeptical, most of the Brownings' acquaintances in Italy—for example, Story, Page, Jarves, and Powers—became as credulous as Elizabeth. In view of her ardent, generous, if somewhat naïve disposition, she could hardly have been indifferent to such a mass of apparently well-founded evidence, with its promise of hope to mankind. She wrote to Arabel in the spring of 1852 that she was greedy for all the facts of spiritualism. "I want a knowledge of real life," she said, the lack of which she felt a severe handicap in her profession as a writer. She had read too many books, she believed, and now was "most greedy of actual sights, sounds, facts, faces." The "rapping spirits" she longed to hear were to her mind an aspect of life she had been missing, and she was convinced that she would "think and write better and stronger" for having known them.[37]

ANOTHER subject about which Robert and she disagreed was Louis Napoleon, for whom three-fourths of the electors had voted in the presidential election of December 10, 1848. Soon afterward the elected head of the nation was engaged in a struggle with the legislative assembly in which he had the backing of the majority of the people, while many of the deputies represented vested interests and some were hoping to restore the monarchy. According to the constitution he could not have a second term as president. The vote to amend that law passed in the assembly by a wide margin but failed to secure the required three-fourths of the ballots. After that he no longer felt obliged to observe the letter of the law; and when he appealed to the people and to the army for their support in the autumn of 1851, almost everyone supposed he would eventually depose the assembly and declare himself the ruler of France. Elizabeth wrote on November 12 that she believed he was "honest" and that he meant to be Napoleon the Second. Since she always longed for great events to take place around her, she was not disappointed in the *coup d'état;* she "would not have missed the grand spectacle of the second of December for anything in the world." The entrance of the troops into Paris on that morning, she wrote Henrietta, "was very grand —the military music and the shouting of the people, as the president rode under our windows, the manoeuvring of the splendid cavalry, the white horses, glittering helmets, all that 'pomp and circumstance,' might well move older children than our babe." [38]

Elizabeth approved of what the president had done, and for the rest of her life she gave unqualified support to all of his policies. Since she was "by temperament perhaps over hopeful and sanguine," as she wrote Kenyon, she felt that the president's régime would be mild, beneficent, and democratic. It was her belief that he had broken only "the husk of an oath" and that he was justified "in throwing back the sovereignty from a 'representative assembly' which had virtually ceased to represent, into the hands of the people." The English, she thought, took such a "pedantic view" of the matter that in their minds "constitutional forms and essential principles of liberty . . . are apt to be confounded." In all her letters at this time she maintained that in the circumstances Louis Napoleon had the moral right to disregard the law of the land: the lion must come to the rescue. On Thursday night, December 4, Elizabeth sat up until after midnight, "listening to the distant firing from the boulevards." Louis Napoleon had allowed his troops to break down the barricades built on the streets and to kill some 1,200—possibly more—of the citizens of Paris who resisted him. It was an unpardonable act and also a stupid blunder, for the brutality with which he came into power made it less easy for him to restore to the people their former liberties. Elizabeth's comment to Henrietta is a good example of her special pleading: "To talk about 'carnage' is quite absurd. The people never rose—it was nothing but a little popular scum, cleared off at once by the troops." Louis Napoleon took away the freedom of the press, and his government treated with great harshness many republican and socialist opponents, banishing them to Algeria and French Guinea. Elizabeth had to admit that the French under their new ruler did not enjoy "the liberty and ease of a regular government"; yet she prophesied optimistically that the dictatorship would soon be less severe.

In the plebiscite of December 20, 1851, the French people voted 7,400,000 to 640,000 in favor of Louis Napoleon. Elizabeth's sisters and her brother George, like most of the British press, were suspicious of the French leader and felt that he had not yet made evident the good intentions he professed. In writing to her family in England, Elizabeth often referred to "the falsifications of *The Times*" and to the "insular fog" which she thought characteristic of British foreign policy. "You are all wrong in England," she railed at Arabel, "frightfully wrong, immorally wrong, some of you." [39] She maintained that the election had not been "managed," but that, on the contrary, it expressed "the most extraordinary unity of national will almost ever manifested." [40] What she neglected to say was that the people had been presented with a *fait accompli* and had been given no one else for whom they might cast their ballots. In such circumstances the more than half a million votes of protest were significant. Also she asserted that Louis Napoleon had the support of the Parisians: "The result of my own impressions is a conviction that *from the beginning* he had the sympathy of the whole population here with him," and she reported that all their tradesmen were "in a glow of sympathy and admiration." She did not understand that many of the artisans of Paris held radical political views and were hostile to Louis Napoleon, whose strength came mostly from the Parisian middle classes and from the provinces, which were in general more conservative than the capital. Browning was more "English," as Elizabeth said, in his point of view, for he had little confidence in the president. He saw that Louis Napoleon was not keeping his promises now that he had power, and he believed that in England the public was better informed than in France, where almost every voice against the government had been stifled.

Soon after the *coup d'état* Elizabeth heard of a reference to herself in an English publication which upset her more than any other episode in many years. Miss Mitford in her *Recollections of a Literary Life,* published late in 1851,[41] told the story of Bro's death, with embellishments drawn from gossip and from her own imagination. "I have so often been asked [Miss Mitford wrote] what could be the shadow that had passed over that young heart, that now that time has softened the first agony it seems to me right that the world should hear the story of an accident in which there was much sorrow, but no blame." The *Athenaeum* in its review of the volumes quoted by an unhappy chance the entire passage describing the tragedy at Torquay. The reviewer seemed to consider Miss Mitford's disclosure the most sensational information in the book. In his opinion, however, she had treated the subject "with the delicacy of true sympathy." [42]

A lecturer on English poetry at the Collège de France, Philarète Chasles, announced a talk on Mrs. Browning, "from whose private life the veil had been raised in so interesting a manner lately by Miss Mitford," but Milsand, who was preparing his article on Elizabeth for the *Revue des Deux Mondes,* tactfully asked Browning whether in deference to her feelings he ought not to disregard the recent biographical information. Elizabeth, as she often admitted, had always been "morbid" on the subject of Bro's death, and never in her poetry or in conversation with friends and relatives—not even to Browning—had she been able to make "one direct reference" to that subject. "Good Heavens—how obtuse of feeling . . . some people are," she wrote hysterically to Arabel. "She has pulled out the very heart from me, to hold it up to the world, with its roots still bleeding!" [43]

A month later she was still brooding over the matter and wrote in the same vein to Arabel that people had "grown peculiarly disagreeable just now," that she was being "pricked at every turn" when she wished to live quietly, and that if she were bothered much longer she would have to "take lodgings in the desert." [44] Browning had always been aware of Miss Mitford's disapproval of him and did not hesitate to write to Kenyon of the difference between the sensitivity of the French critic and the "stupidity" of Miss Mitford, who was "always abusing literary men." Elizabeth immediately wrote Miss Mitford a letter in which she began by assuring her that she had always been "the most generous and affectionate of friends." She then frankly told Miss Mitford of the great pain she had received from her action, and Miss Mitford sent back a note of apology and explanation, in which she said that before her marriage Elizabeth had "scandalized horribly" a portion of the reading public; many persons in the world of letters had attributed to her "a most desperate state of love-affairs, and an habitual wearing of 'widow's weeds' which was anything but respectable."[45] Miss Mitford's reasons were fantastic, but fortunately the friendship between the two women remained unimpaired. An aftermath of the episode was that Chasles in his lectures on her poetry embroidered so greatly upon Miss Mitford's narrative that Elizabeth was again much offended. He said that she was the daughter of a Calvinist minister, that she had been faithful to a fiancé for some six years before she met Browning, that she used to hire a large room in London, and that she and her husband had been living in a palace of the Medici in Florence.[46] Some writers would be merely amused to learn that such myths were being circulated, but Elizabeth was profoundly disturbed.

Another incident which took place soon afterward was almost equally distressing. Sarianna wrote to Robert to ask him out of respect for the family to attend the funeral in London of their cousin James Silverthorne, who had accompanied Browning at his wedding. Elizabeth pleaded with him not to leave her and said she doubted that his presence at the rites was necessary, since many other members of the family would be there. When Browning received a second message from his sister, again urging him to come, Elizabeth was deeply shaken and told him he had better go. Just as he was about to leave, she looked so pale and wretched that Browning changed his plan and stayed with her. "Sarianna understands nothing about Robert's susceptibilities," she wrote Arabel. However "good and true, affectionate and generous" Sarianna had always been, she "*is* not made of the same stuff as Robert," Elizabeth said, and did not seem to have "a notion of what he would suffer in going."[47]

ON JULY 5, 1852,[48] the Brownings left Paris to spend three or four months in London, chiefly for Browning's sake, that he might enjoy his relatives and friends. Elizabeth dreaded both the English climate and the prospect of being hurt once again by her father's refusal to see her. Early in the morning of July 6 they arrived in London and went to "very respectable rooms" Arabel had rented for them at 58 Welbeck Street, which was not far from the Barretts' home.

England and Paris, 1851–52

Meanwhile a situation had been developing in England which was soon to prove much more upsetting to the Brownings than either Miss Mitford's book or the request to attend a cousin's funeral. Four days before the Brownings left Paris, Robert's father appeared in the Court of Queen's Bench at Guildhall before Lord Campbell and a special jury as the defendant of an action brought against him by a forty-five-year-old widow, a Mrs. Von Müller, to recover compensation for breach of promise and defamation of character. In December 1850, according to the plaintiff's counsel, Sir A. Cockburn, Robert Browning the elder wrote an anonymous letter to Mrs. Von Müller, who lived near him in New Cross, and afterward "he used to pass the house waving his hand, and looking with great earnestness." [49] Cockburn read more than fifty letters which were "couched in terms of the greatest warmth, and professed the most intense love of the writer for the lady whom he was addressing."

In the autumn of 1851 Browning's father and Sarianna had lived with him and Elizabeth in Paris for about three weeks, and at that time he first learned from his father of his attachment to the widow. He seems to have been so shocked by what his father told him that the elder Browning attempted to mollify his feelings by misrepresenting the situation to convince his son and possibly himself too that he was being persecuted by Mrs. Von Müller. The younger Browning immediately wrote her a letter, saying that she had been annoying his father. Furthermore the elder Browning informed her that he had changed his mind about marrying her, accused her of misconduct from the time she was a girl, and charged her with marrying her second husband when she knew her first was still alive. At the trial, counsel for the widow said that the elder Browning was "guilty of the most cruel cold-blooded cowardice" and produced documents to prove the falsity of the defendant's accusations, and even his counsel could say in his favor only that he was "a poor old dotard in love." The jury gave a verdict for the plaintiff and assessed the defendant £800 for damages.

The younger Browning was crushed by the news of the result of the trial, since he had not known that his father had written so many letters or had expressed himself so warmly. He could have appealed the case, but he did not wish any more unfavorable publicity. The alternate course was for his father to leave England immediately so that the amount awarded by the court could not be collected. And so Browning took his father and sister from their new home in London to Paris, where he found them an apartment. From there the elder Browning received the pension which the Bank of England eventually granted him. He was soon contented with Paris and went for walks in the Bois de Boulogne or made sketches in the Louvre. Sarianna, however, would have preferred to remain in London; her pride was hurt, and, as Elizabeth said, Paris could scarcely have seemed "much better to her than a penal settlement." [50] Elizabeth was loyal to Browning and his father, as she explained the proceedings in letters to old friends and to her sisters. Browning's father, she declared, was a pure, simple, innocent man, who had been ensnared by a villainous and scheming woman. She deplored the fact that so much "mud" had been "thrown about" for her friends and family to see in the newspapers (*The Times* carried a long, detailed report the day after the trial). She was, however, chiefly anxious about Robert, who was much troubled. On July 24 she wrote Henrietta that Robert had recently returned from Paris: "He had safely deposited the poor victim, and left him tolerably composed and comfortable. I do hope it may all end well. In any case the end can't be worse than the beginning. Robert's spirits are better, I think, but the vexation of it all is immense." [51]

A week or two earlier Henrietta had made a trip to London to be with Elizabeth. George came to see her often, but her "chief joy" in London was her intimacy with Arabel, whom she saw as frequently as she had during the previous summer. From time to time she took Pen to 50 Wimpole Street, where they dined with Arabel in her room. Every evening they were there, Elizabeth became very much frightened at six o'clock, fearful that her father might come in and see her. Once she noticed her father in front of her as the two of them were approaching each other on Wimpole Street, and Elizabeth "only had time to turn abruptly round Hodgson's corner." [52] Again this summer she wrote him, though with a feeling of "utter hopelessness," that she was in London and asked for an interview. He replied with a brutal note telling her not to annoy him with further communications. She was severely shaken by this letter as she acknowledged to Henrietta:

> Nothing could be worse than the manner of the written answer, of that, you may be sure. I have looked tenderly, and even pityingly at all these things, always trying to conjecture the best; but it was, I confess to you, with a revulsion of feeling that I read that letter . . written after six years, with the plain intention of giving me as much pain as possible. It was an unnatural letter, and the evidence of hardness of heart (towards *me,* at least) is unmistakable. May God alter these facts—men cannot deny them. I have a child myself. I know something of the parental feeling. There can be no such feeling . . There never can have been any such . . where that letter was produced. Certainly the effect of it is anything but to lead me to *repentance.* Am I to repent that I did not sacrifice my life, and its affections to the writer of that letter? Indeed no.[53]

Though Elizabeth was filled with bitterness, she nevertheless had much pleasure visiting with old friends and making new acquaintances. The Brownings once again saw W. J. Fox, H. F. Chorley, and Mrs. Jameson. Elizabeth received a call from Florence Nightingale, whom she later described as "a pretty and highly accomplished woman—even *learned.*" The young novelist Dinah Mulock also came. She had recently published an anonymous poem in the *Athenaeum* [54] expressing her gratitude for the comfort and inspiration she had derived from Elizabeth's poetry, and she had just dedicated her novel *The Head of the Family* to Mrs. Browning, "one who has for years been the good influence of my life. . . . the mere naming of whom includes and transcends all praise." Another visitor was Mrs. Newton Crosland, who was later to write a book on her spiritualistic experiences.[55]

The Brownings had luncheon at the home of John Ruskin and his wife at Denmark Hill, where Elizabeth looked at his collection of Turners, "which, by the way, are divine," she wrote Miss Mitford. Elizabeth was greatly attracted to Ruskin, whom she thought "very gentle, yet earnest—refined and truthful," but was less impressed with his wife because she seemed merely pretty and vivacious but without intellectual capacity. It is interesting that when Elizabeth heard two years later of the failure of the marriage, she refused to believe in the truth of the imputations against Ruskin which have since been authenticated.

The Brownings also met the Christian Socialist Charles Kingsley, who in spite of his "wild and theoretical" ideas appeared to Elizabeth "original and earnest, and full of a genial and almost tender kindliness." Richard Monckton Milnes and his "quiet and kind" wife entertained the Brownings at dinner and later had them to "a brilliant christening luncheon." At Kenyon's house Elizabeth met Henry Crabb Robinson, who recorded in his diary that she had "a handsome oval face, a fine eye, and altogether a pleasing person." [56] According to him she had no opportunity of taking a prominent part in the conversation and apparently no desire. They also saw James Russell Lowell and his wife Maria, who were in London for a brief stay before their return to America.

Soon after the Brownings' arrival in London, Mrs. Tennyson had sent Elizabeth a letter of welcome to England. Upon the birth of their son Hallam, Tennyson wrote her "such three happy notes" that Elizabeth "really never liked him so well before." Her letter of congratulation on August 12 was the first he received. Late in September she sent a note of thanks to Mrs. Tennyson for asking Robert and her to the baby's christening and promised they would come, but she was too unwell to attend.[57]

Jane Welsh Carlyle came with Mazzini to call upon the Brownings. "Oh, such a fuss the Brownings made over Mazzini this day!" Mrs. Carlyle wrote on July 27. "My private opinion of Browning is, in spite of Mr. C's favour for him, that he is 'nothing,' or very little more, 'but a fluff of feathers!' *She* is *true* and *good*, and the most *womanly* creature." But after she saw the Brownings again at a tea given by John Forster, she confessed, "I like Browning less and less; and even *she* does not grow on me." [58] Mrs. Carlyle, however, was "a great favorite" with Elizabeth and seemed to her "full of thought, and feeling, and character." Mazzini, "with that pale spiritual face of his, and those intense eyes full of melancholy illusions" was at that time one of Elizabeth's heroes,

England and Paris, 1851-52

although she was later to consider him an unscrupulous person who deserved a fate she would "be sorry to inflict."

A few days before this visit, Mrs. Carlyle and her American-born friend Mrs. Edward Twisleton called on Elizabeth. Like almost all others who recorded their impressions of Elizabeth, Mrs. Twisleton mentioned her small size, her thick brown hair which fell in curls, her face of great refinement and sensibility, her low, gentle voice, her "quiet, well-bred manner," and her fine-looking forehead and "soft grey eyes." Elizabeth, she thought, looked "like an invalid, but a self-controlled one, one who made no fuss." She was "dressed in black and not with any particular care or nicety, but not at all sluttish either, only as if she did not spend money or thought upon the matter." [59] Some months later Mrs. Twisleton, after calling with her husband upon the Brownings in Florence, wrote that Elizabeth told her "she was of an anxious disposition and always building 'dungeons in the air,'" which Mrs. Twisleton though a "forcible" phrase.[60] She also noticed that Elizabeth avoided all gossip and small talk.

Kate Field, who was one of the Brownings' close friends in Florence during the last few years before Elizabeth's death, also spoke of the serious tone of her conversation, which was usually about "books and humanity, great deeds, and, above all, politics, which include all the grand questions of the day." As Kate expressed it, "One never dreamed of frivolities in Mrs. Browning's presence." [61] According to her, Elizabeth's talk had no sallies of wit or brilliant repartee, but it was often "intermingled with trenchant, quaint remarks, leavened with a quiet, graceful humor of her own." Mrs. Andrew Crosse in her somewhat unsympathetic portrait of Elizabeth said that in her conversation she "seemed reserved, with a certain proud aloofness of manner; at the same time there was a listening reticence in her attitude that did not help the playful tossing to and fro of talk." [62] Her remarks appeared to Mrs. Crosse too carefully meditated for general company, and Elizabeth spoke as though she had spent all her life in a library. Thackeray's daughter, who became Lady Anne Ritchie, remembered Elizabeth as she saw her in Rome, "in soft falling flounces of black silk, and with her heavy curls drooping, and a thin gold chain hanging round her neck." The atmosphere Elizabeth carried about her, Lady Ritchie said, was "serious, motherly, absolutely artless, and yet impassioned, noble and sincere." [63] She observed that Elizabeth rarely laughed but was always kind, cheerful, and smiling.

THE lengthening shadows and foggy weather of October made it imperative for the Brownings once again to leave their many friends in England and cross to the Continent. They went by way of Folkestone and Boulogne about the twelfth of the month and found rooms in Paris at the Hotel de la Ville l'Évêque. Elizabeth wrote to Arabel on the morning of her arrival that she felt as though her soul had been dragged through a hedge and had "left some torn shreds of itself on the thorns." [64] But Paris so charmed her that she soon forgot the pain of recent farewells. Among their friends who welcomed them were Mr. and Mrs. John Frazer Corkran. He was the Paris correspondent of several English newspapers, and she conducted a *salon* much frequented by literary and artistic groups. Elizabeth wrote enthusiastically that he was "the kindest, widest-hearted of men" and his wife an "intellectual woman . . . good and noble in *all* her impulses." [65] Many years later their daughter Henriette described the Brownings' visit to the Corkrans' apartment. She recalled that Elizabeth was exhausted and out of breath after climbing to the fifth floor and was placed gently in an arm chair by her mother.[66] Browning was cheerful and pleasant, but it was Elizabeth and Pen whom she remembered. The Brownings' child had "long golden ringlets" and wore "white drawers edged with embroidery," so that Henriette thought he was a girl. After a few minutes Elizabeth said to her in a low, gentle voice, "You and Penini must be friends, dear. He is my Florentine boy," stroking his head as she spoke. "Has he not got beautiful hair? so golden—that is because he was born in Italy, where the sun is always golden." During her visit Elizabeth kept her arms around Pen's neck, "running her long, thin fingers through his golden curls."

It was from the balcony of the Corkrans' apartment near the Boulevard des Italiens that the Brownings saw on October 16, 1852, "the great spectacle" of Louis Napoleon's triumphant entrance into Paris. "Nothing so magnificent was ever seen before," Elizabeth wrote. Amidst "all the military and civil pomp of France," crowds swarmed along the broad boulevard, as far as she could see, under a cloudless, sunny sky. "It was wonderful!" Elizabeth exclaimed. She wrote that Louis Napoleon "showed his usual tact and courage by riding on horseback quite alone, at least ten paces between himself and his nearest escort," and as the people cheered, he bowed to right and left. Pen, no less than Elizabeth, was "in a state of ecstasy." The American actress Charlotte Cushman, who was sitting beside Elizabeth, was no admirer of Louis Napoleon; but when she saw him, she pleased Elizabeth by crying out, "That's fine, I must say." [67] Thus Elizabeth had a view of the man who to her mind represented the will of the people. She was more hopeful and more excited than she had been since the demonstrations of 1847 in the Piazza Pitti, and at the moment she forgot her beloved Italy: "For the drama of history we must look to France, for startling situations, for the 'points' which thrill you to the bone."

Despite the possibility that even greater events might soon take place in Paris, the Brownings went back to Florence for the sake of Elizabeth's health. On the morning of October 23,[68] they left by railroad for Chalon, whence they went down the Saône through rain and mist on a steamboat to Lyons. From there they traveled for two nights and two days by diligence to Chambéry and then proceeded to Lanslebourg, at the foot of the Alps. For the ascent over the Mont Cenis pass they had to rent a private carriage. All day long as they climbed high on the mountain and descended in the evening toward Susa, Elizabeth suffered painfully from pressure on the chest, more so than on any of her previous trips. After spending the night at Susa, they went to Turin, where she had two days of rest and gathered her strength for the trip to Genoa. When they arrived there, she was "extremely unwell," she wrote Sarianna, "to the extent of almost losing heart and hope." They had to stop for ten days at a hotel in Genoa, where Elizabeth slowly recuperated. Before they left, she was able to visit one or two churches and the Andrea Doria Palace. From Genoa they went by diligence all night and the following day to Pisa, where they slept. The next morning at eleven they took the train and after three hours entered Florence, to Elizabeth's great joy. When they saw their home, they found that though the apartment had been occupied during their absence of a year and a half, the carpets and furniture looked even better for the wear. Furthermore the Brownings had gained six months' free rent because of the money they had received from subletting their furnished apartment while they had been away. There they remained until the following summer.

15. Florence, Bagni di Lucca, and Rome

"FOR MY PART, I love Florence. I love casa Guidi," Elizabeth wrote a few weeks after her arrival. Besides its "lovely climate, and the lovely associations," it was the "sense of repose" which attracted her, the promise of health and uninterrupted quiet for writing poetry. Browning, on the other hand, who had been demoralized by the excitement of Paris, found Florence a dull place, but to him nothing was more important than Elizabeth's health. Tuscany, like all of the peninsula except for Piedmont, was quiet and subdued, under the rule of Austria. Elizabeth sympathized with the Italians and looked hopefully to the time when they would attempt another revolt.

Among the most frequent visitors to the Brownings' apartment that year was Sir Edward Bulwer-Lytton's son, Robert Lytton (Owen Meredith), who had just come to Florence as an attaché at the British legation. He was a frail, slender youth in his early twenties who was shy and inarticulate in large gatherings but a brilliant talker among intimate friends. While he was a great favorite with both of the Brownings because of his interest in literature, his refinement, and his courteous manners, Elizabeth was particularly attracted to him through their common interest in spiritualism. The following summer, when he was staying several weeks with the Brownings at Bagni di Lucca, she wrote of the future ambassador at Paris and viceroy of India that he was "full of all sorts of good and nobleness . . . and gifted with high faculties and given to the highest aspirations—not vulgar ambitions, understand—he will never be a great diplomatist." Of his ability in poetry she spoke more hopefully and said that his "Clytemnestra," the classical drama he had recently written, was full of promise, and she expected "great things from him."

Another member of the Anglo-American colony whose friendship the Brownings enjoyed was Alfred Tennyson's brother Frederick, an eccentric, shy, dreamy man, "good and pure minded," Elizabeth said of him, and "an earnest Christian too." A year after he had graduated from Cambridge, he inherited enough property to insure him a modest, secure income for the rest of his life and immediately left England for Corfu and later for Italy, where he stayed and was now living with his Italian wife and four children. The poetry he wrote was melodious and graceful, but unoriginal, vague, and too filled with personification. He occasionally came to Casa Guidi to engage in table-turning experiments with Elizabeth, of whom he wrote that she was "never so happy as when she can get into the thick of mysterious Clairvoyants, Rappists, Ecstatics, and Swedenborgians." [1] But more than poetry or "the spirits," his great interest was music. The chief advantage for him in living at Florence was that he could hear all the music he wished at little cost. Elizabeth reported that he once hired a full opera orchestra to come to his villa and play to him while he sat alone in his arm chair.

In the spring of 1853 two American diplomats and their wives became friends of the Brownings. The minister to Turkey under President Taylor's administration and later the first minister to the new kingdom of Italy, George Perkins Marsh and his wife spent some evenings at Casa Guidi and invited the poets to visit them in the summer at Constantinople, but they had to refuse because of lack of funds. William Burnet Kinney and his wife were the other American couple whom the Brownings met late in the spring. Kinney had been the United States minister at Turin from 1850 to 1853, and afterward they lived in Florence for twelve years, where Mrs. Kinney (mother of the poet and critic E. C. Stedman) wrote a now-forgotten metrical romance called *Felicità* and Kinney collected materials for a book on the Medicis which never appeared. He was an "admirable, thoughtful, benevolent person," Elizabeth said, and as liberal as an American diplomat could hope to be; and she, though "rather over-lively

Florence, Bagni di Lucca, and Rome

and not over-refined" for a diplomat's wife, was "clever, literary, critical, poetical," and a favorite with Elizabeth "through her truth and frankness, besides her warmheartedness." [2]

Both the Brownings were hard at work upon their poems. Elizabeth informed Arabel in April that Robert had nearly enough lyrics for a new volume and that she was writing a long poem and was only a quarter of the way toward her goal. A fortnight earlier she had told Mrs. Jameson that her poem would fill a volume when it was finished, that it was the romance she had been "hankering after so long, written in blank verse, in the autobiographical form," and that it was "intensely modern, crammed from the times . . ." For the next three years she was to be absorbed in the work she knew would be by far the longest and most important of her career. Now that the Italian situation was quiescent, she had more peace of mind and was able to gather her energy for this long creative effort. In the spring she interrupted her work upon the new poem long enough to make revisions for the third edition of her *Poems*, because the second had been exhausted. Although she promptly sent the manuscript to Chapman and Hall, she was vexed that the volumes did not appear until October 15.[3] The arrangement of the individual poems was the same as in the edition of 1850, but she made many revisions in "The Seraphim" and "Prometheus Bound," added a preliminary speech by Lucifer in "A Drama of Exile" and altered it slightly in other ways, made a few unimportant changes, mostly in punctuation, in the "Sonnets from the Portuguese," and revised the punctuation and the text of a number of poems throughout the two volumes.

Robert and Elizabeth had been looking forward to a trip to Rome in the winter or spring, but they had to abandon the idea because the expenses would have been too great. Browning's drama *Colombe's Birthday* was revived by Helen Faucit at the Haymarket Theater in April, but as Elizabeth said, "there could be no 'run' for a play of that kind; it was a *succès d'estime* and something more"; but it was not commercially profitable. Furthermore, Elizabeth was receiving no money from her publishers because they had delayed the production of her third edition.

The Brownings consoled themselves with trips around Florence and with a short excursion to Prato. Once they went in an open carriage to a high point in Fiesole, and Elizabeth sat on an old wall and saw the sunset as she "looked across that wonderful valley where Florence lies enchanted." Almost every evening some of their friends came to see them, but once in July they went to a reception at Lytton's villa on Bellosguardo hill south of the Arno. Powers, Frederick Tennyson, and Pasquale Villari, who was a professor of history at Florence, were also present. "We were all bachelors together there," Elizabeth wrote, "and I made tea, and we ate strawberries and cream and talked spiritualism through one of the pleasantest two hours that I remember. Such a view! Florence dissolving in the purple of the hills; and the stars looking on." All were "believers" except for Robert, who persisted in "wearing a coat of respectable scepticism."

Two days afterward, on July 15, 1853, the Brownings escaped from the heat of Florence and went to Bagni di Lucca for the rest of the summer. For less than £11 they rented during the season a large house with a private garden, a row of plane trees, and a fine view of the steep, green hills. Casa Tolomei, which is on the main street of the village called the Villa, still looks much as it did when the Brownings lived there. But the town itself, which to Elizabeth had a "fresh, unworn, uncivilised, world-before-the-flood look," would now seem less isolated and much larger and more lively.

Not long after their arrival they were astonished to have William Wetmore Story and his wife Emelyn call upon them and invite them to their summer home high in the Bagni Caldi. The only people the Storys cared to meet at the Baths were the Brownings, with whom they had, Story wrote, "constant and delightful intercourse, interchanging long evenings together two or three times a-week." [4] Elizabeth said that Robert and she and the Storys went "backward and forward on donkeyback to tea-drinking and gossiping" at each other's houses. The Storys' children, Edith and Joe, and Pen Browning, who was now four, also entertained each other at tea parties and receptions in their parents' homes.

Mrs. Story impressed Elizabeth as being "kind and pretty, fresh and innocent, and intelligent enough besides," and her husband, she wrote, was "a sculptor, poet, lawyer, mover of tables." He had been born into a distinguished and wealthy New England family. His father Joseph Story was an associate justice of the Supreme Court in Washington and later a professor at the Harvard Law School. William was graduated from Harvard College and the law school, was an intimate friend in Cambridge of James Russell Lowell, Charles Eliot Norton, and Charles Sumner, and in his early twenties presented an astonishing versatility. He became an unusually successful lawyer, was appointed a commissioner in bankruptcy, and wrote *A Treatise on the Law of Contracts* and *A Treatise on the Law of Sales of Personal Property*, both of which proved to be standard works. He also published literary criticism, issued a volume of poems, and dabbled in painting and modeling. When his father died, he was asked to make a statue of him and went to Italy at about the age of twenty-eight to draw a sketch, which was accepted upon his return. But Rome had so charmed him that he had abandoned his legal career, gone with his family to Italy, and determined to become a sculptor. He eventually gained an international reputation, especially after the spectacular reception of his "Cleopatra" and his "Libyan Sibyl" at the Exposition in London in 1862, but notwithstanding his aspirations he remained essentially an amateur. With no early systematic training in his craft, he had little understanding of the problems of sculpture. He succeeded in making his sculpture popular with the unsophisticated by emphasizing the accessories and drapery, in the fashion of the day, and by treating familiar subjects drawn from literature and myth, such as Cleopatra, Medea, and Salome. Hawthorne, seeing him in Rome and Siena in 1858, thought him the most brilliant conversationalist he had ever met but hinted that his failure as an artist was due to his "perplexing variety of talents and accomplishments." The circumstances of his life in Rome were so delightful and his creative energies so diffused that he expended himself, as Henry James said, "for results of which, when time had sifted them, little remained but the appearance of his having been happy."[5] Such was the man, now in his early thirties, who was to become one of the Brownings' most intimate friends.

At times with the Storys, and at times by themselves, the Brownings went on expeditions into the chestnut forests, with Elizabeth riding on a donkey and Robert holding the reins and walking slowly beside her. She was well enough for them to stroll along the Lima mountain stream and to venture on makeshift bridges thrown across the river. In spite of their many excursions, they succeeded in writing some poetry almost every day; Robert a number of the lyrics he was to publish in *Men and Women* and Elizabeth part of her novel in verse. Once in September they went with the Storys and Lytton on an all-day trip to Prato Fiorito. For six miles they ascended the mountains on the backs of donkeys and horses, along dried-out river beds. The weather was beautiful, and after climbing for an hour, they "arrived at a little old church," in Story's words, "near by which the view was magnificent." [6] As they rested for a while under the trees, they saw the limestone mountains and grayish-white hill towns in the distance. After another hour and a half of passing through "wild and grand scenery, with mountain-streams dripping and tumbling," they reached the height and saw before them "the soft green velvety dome of Prato Fiorito, adorable name, covered with its short golden grass." There they lay for a time and talked and "gazed at the tumbling waves of mountains below." The trip so tired Elizabeth that she "could not stir for days after," but she wrote in great happiness, "Who wouldn't see heaven and die? Such a vision of divine scenery . . . !"

The church mentioned by Story was the scene of part of Browning's "By the Fire-Side," one of his few personal poems, in which he expresses his gratitude to his wife for allowing him to love her, as they sit together in their Italian home,

> And to watch you sink by the fire-side now
>   Back again, as you mutely sit
> Musing by fire-light, that great brow
>   And the spirit-small hand propping it
> Yonder, my heart knows how!

He imagines that in old age he will be reading Greek by the fire, and his recollection will be of his youth in Italy and his excursion into the mountain and "the ruined chapel," where, in his poet's fancy, he and the woman who became his "perfect wife" first declared their mutual love:

> Hither we walked, then, side by side,
> > Arm in arm and cheek to cheek,
> And still I questioned or replied,
> > While my heart, convulsed to really speak,
> Lay choking in its pride.
>
> Silent the crumbling bridge we cross,
> > And pity and praise the chapel sweet,
> And care about the fresco's loss,
> > And wish for our souls a like retreat,
> And wonder at the moss.

Early in October the weather became so cool that the Brownings returned on the tenth of the month to Florence, where they remained only a few weeks, preparing for the trip to Rome to which they had long been looking forward. They left on November 15, 1853, had "a most exquisite journey of eight days," stopping to see Perugia, the convent and churches of San Francesco at Assisi, and the waterfalls at Terni. All of them were "in the highest spirits" as they entered Rome, with both Robert and Pen singing for joy, and they went immediately to their rooms, which the Storys had secured for them on the third floor at 43 Via Bocca di Leone. Lamps had been lighted and fires were burning, because of the kindness of the Storys, who came to see them that evening from their rooms near by, in the Piazza di Spagna.

The Brownings' apartment was in the heart of the foreign quarter of Rome. In the middle of the nineteenth century this occupied the triangular area of which the northern point was the Piazza del Populo, with one of its sides along the Corso and another extending southward along Via del Babuino at the foot of the Pincian hill to the Piazza di Spagna and Via Sistina on the hill above. The base of the triangle was one of the streets between the Corso and the Piazza di Spagna, such as Via Frattina. The last hundred years have seen little change in the appearance of the building where the Brownings lived that winter or of the neighborhood, although the quiet which was necessary for Elizabeth's nerves is now broken by the cries of vendors in their stalls at the open-air food market which every morning fills the street in front of the apartment house. Since the city then had a population of only about 175,000, it was more intimate and friendly, and most of the English and American travelers there knew about one another.

But the picturesque, leisurely Rome of the nineteenth century was to have little appeal to Elizabeth. On the morning after the arrival of the Brownings, Edith Story was brought to their house by a servant with a message that little Joe was seriously ill. The Brownings went immediately to the Storys and spent the day with them at the bedside of the child until his death that evening. Edith, who had been left in the Brownings' rooms, had meanwhile been attacked by the same disease, "gastric fever, with a tendency to the brain"; and since the Brownings had no separate bedroom for her, she was removed to the apartment below, that of Mr. and Mrs. William Page. Then as both the Storys' English nurse and the Pages' youngest daughter were stricken by the malady, Elizabeth fell "into a selfish human panic" about Pen and wished to fly from Rome with her child. But she stayed, no one else died, and Pen did not suffer from the illness. Her first drive in Rome was with the Storys to the Protestant Cemetery, where Joe's remains were buried near the heart of Shelley. The tragedy had spoiled Rome for Elizabeth, and henceforth she associated it with plague and terror. She wrote to an American friend Mrs. Francis George Shaw, "I cannot fancy that I shall escape having the taste of these aloes always on my lips in this Rome. The impression has been profoundly saddening. I do not make out that it can be Rome at all." [7]

Partly because of the recent shock to her nervous system and partly because of her physical frailty, Elizabeth did little sightseeing in Rome. She visited only the most obvious places: St. Peter's, part of the Vatican Museum, the Sistine Chapel, the Forum, and the Colosseum. Of the great collections of painting and sculpture in the Borghese casino, the museums on the Capitoline, and the many palaces and churches, she was to have little first-hand acquaintance. On Christmas morning, to be sure, she went to St. Peter's "and saw pope and cardinals and all." The music, she wrote Henrietta, was "sublime," and she "was very much impressed and affected." And like many other tourists of that age, she made pilgrimages to the studios of the best-known English and American artists: Gibson, Crawford, Story, Harriet Hosmer, and William Page. John Gibson was an elderly, much-respected English sculptor, whose marbles were in the severely classical tradition of his instructor Canova. One of his worst mistakes was the notorious "Tinted Venus," which had warm flesh tints, blue eyes, blond hair, and a golden net over the hair. Elizabeth did not like the "Venus," which seemed "rather a grisette than a goddess," for the statue had "come out of her cloud of the ideal," and to her mind was "not too decent." She also went to the studio of the commonplace, much over-praised American sculptor Thomas Crawford and thought it "far more interesting" than Gibson's. Harriet Hosmer was "a great pet" of Elizabeth's. She was "a perfectly 'emancipated female,'" who, Elizabeth wrote, worked all day long "as a great artist must." When Hawthorne saw her a few years later, he said that she had "a small, brisk, wide-awake figure" and that she was "frank, simple, straightforward, and downright." She had arrived in Rome in 1852, soon became Gibson's protégée, and worked in his studio. Like the other well-known American sculptors in Italy, Miss Hosmer did not have the instincts of an artist, her modeling was poor, and the accessories were too prominent. Her work was commercially successful, however, especially her "Puck," copies of which she sold for a thousand dollars each, as fast as the Italian marble workers could manufacture copies in her shop.

Another of Elizabeth's close friends in Rome was the American painter William Page, to whom she was attracted because of his interest in spiritualism and Swedenborgianism. "We are warm appreciators both of his paintings and of himself," she wrote their mutual friend Mrs. Shaw. "We reverence and quite love the man, he lives habitually in a high sphere of thought and art, and is a Christian it seems to me, to the end of his paintbrush. A noble man, of whom America may be proud."[8] But she had little interest in his second wife, with whom he was then living, and spoke of her as young and naïve. Elizabeth was a warm admirer of his portraits, especially those of Charlotte Cushman, who was spending the winter in Rome, and of Browning. "His portraits are like Titian's—flesh, blood, and soul," Elizabeth wrote enthusiastically. "I never saw such portraits from a living hand." The portrait of Miss Cushman was "a miracle" and that of Browning "a wonderful picture, the colouring so absolutely *Venetian* that artists can't (for the most part) keep their temper when they look at it." But owing to his method of painting, which caused some of his work to darken rapidly, the surface of Browning's portrait has now so blackened with age that the features can scarcely be recognized. Besides his portraits, Page produced several "Holy Families" and some large narrative paintings in the romantic tradition, such as his "Flight into Egypt" and his "Moses, Aaron, and Hur on Mt. Horeb." It was not only Elizabeth who was spellbound by Page's work and personality; in his lifetime he was regarded by most of his contemporaries as one of the greatest painters of the age. But although he had high ideals, he veered in direction according as he was inspired by one master after another and frittered away his energies in experimenting with various techniques and media, leaving behind a mass of paintings most of which were uneven in execution and have long since been forgotten.

Two English women whom Elizabeth mentioned frequently in her letters that winter were the Kemble sisters. Adelaide (Mrs. Edward John Sartoris) had given up her operatic career after her marriage and lived mostly in Rome, and Fanny (Mrs. Pierce Butler) had recently left an uncongenial American husband in Philadelphia and was spending the winter with her sister. Elizabeth wrote that the only redeeming feature of Rome was her friendship with the Kembles, both of whom she described to Sarianna as "noble and upright women, whose social brilliancy is their least distinction!" Mrs. Sartoris often had the Brownings at her home for musicales, where one met, Elizabeth said, "the best society at Rome." There they saw the aged Lockhart, whose remark about Browning—"he isn't at all like a damned literary man"—so pleased Elizabeth that she quoted it in letters to several correspondents. Also the Kemble sisters had the Brownings with

Florence, Bagni di Lucca, and Rome

them at their picnic excursions at Vallerano and other places on the Campagna and at Hadrian's Villa in Tivoli; Elizabeth went on five such trips, all of which she enjoyed, and Browning on no less than fourteen.

"As for the society, it rains lords and ladies for the especial benefit of Thackeray perhaps," Elizabeth wrote Arabel.[9] The Brownings met Thackeray and his daughters; although Elizabeth found him courteous and amusing, he was too worldly for her taste. "I never should get on with him much, I think," she wrote Henrietta; "he is not sympathetical to me." Although Elizabeth did not often leave her fireside in the evening, she and Robert once went to a musical reception, which she thought "dull according to the most excellent English provincial pattern,"[10] at the home of the English novelist and poet Mrs. Archer Clive. "Relays of young ladies at the piano" were playing and singing in "that sixth rate amateur-manner" which Elizabeth found "altogether intolerable." Another concert which proved to be more enjoyable was held one noon at the home of Madame Emil Braun, the wife of a German archeologist and a close friend of John Kenyon. Beethoven was played for the Prince of Prussia, and Elizabeth reported to Arabel with pride that except for the Brownings no visitors were admitted.[11]

Besides her work on the long novel in verse, which was still less than half finished, Elizabeth wrote two or three short poems that winter. Arabel had asked the Brownings to contribute a poem each, to be printed and sold, including the holographs, in April 1854, for the benefit of the Ragged Schools, in which she was interested. Though they doubted the wisdom of the plan, the Brownings generously wrote the poems and paid for the paper and printing. The pamphlet entitled *Two Poems* was an octavo volume of sixteen pages issued by Chapman and Hall in pale buff-colored paper wrappers, with the price of sixpence printed on the cover. Elizabeth's work, "A Plea for the Ragged Schools of London," was a straightforward request in verse that the citizens of London give help to "Little outcasts from life's fold." On April 3 she wrote Arabel that she had done as well as she could and that what came from her heart "must have some sort of good in it after all."[12] Browning wrote "The Twins" with the motto, " 'Give' and

'It-Shall-Be-Given-Unto-You,' " a poem which was, Elizabeth said, "a simple versification of a fable of Martin Luther's."

Bryan Waller Procter had asked the Brownings to contribute to an annual called the *Keepsake,* the editor of which, Marguerite A. Power, he was trying to help. Both of them responded to his request. Of the two short poems Elizabeth sent, "My Kate" was printed in the *Keepsake* of 1855 and "Amy's Cruelty" in the same publication of 1857.

Although they had enjoyed seeing old friends again and making many new acquaintances, the winter in Rome had not been an entire success for either of the Brownings. "Rome is enough to ruin us with its dearness!" Elizabeth complained to Henrietta. Their weekly living expenses were £3 instead of the two it cost them at Florence, and they were "reduced" to living upon "woodcocks, snipes, hares, and turkeys" because of the high prices of beef and mutton. Pen had lost his appetite and looked pale after a slight attack of "Roman fever." Elizabeth herself had liked the climate of Rome, which is much milder in winter than Florence, with its treacherous, cold winds. Also she received much pleasure from occasional drives and short walks with Browning, when the weather was fine. As she admitted to Arabel, it was wrong to say she did not like Rome: "If I might have leave to stand alone with Robert and look at the campagna, the far opal mountains, the forum, the blue sky flowing in full tide through the rifts of the Colosseum, I can enjoy it intensely." [13] Early in May, however, Elizabeth was anxious to leave the city about which she did not "pretend to have a rag of sentiment." She wrote her American friend Mrs. Shaw that she would avoid the fountain of Trevi: "The climate would suit my chest, but I would not live here with anyone dear to me, for fifty chests—though you filled them for me with Californian gold." [14] Furthermore, as a result of the death of the Story child, "the sense of physical and moral miasma" had weighed upon her more and more heavily ever since she had been at Rome. For Browning too the city was "ill-starred, under a curse seemingly," as he wrote John Forster, and he "would not live there for the Vatican with the Pope out of it." [15]

Yet he had been well and had gone to many dinners and receptions by himself, since Elizabeth was not strong enough to accompany him. Early in February she wrote Arabel, "We have invitations heaped upon us . . for every day of the present week, one a night at least—but I can go nowhere. I make Robert represent me." [16] For the first time since their marriage Elizabeth and Robert were often separated in the evening; she stayed at home to talk about spiritualism with Page or to read a novel or a volume of memoirs.

Before the Brownings left Rome that spring, Elizabeth received another severe shock. Since Edith Story had suffered several relapses during the winter, her parents decided to move to Naples early in the spring. At Velletri, the first stopping place of their journey, the child was stricken with "congestion on the brain and heart" and was "in a state of almost insensibility." [17] Story sent Browning a message that "all hope was over" and asked that he come immediately "and be with them at the end." [18] Elizabeth dreaded to see Robert go, and Pen, in sympathy with his mother, did not help matters by "uttering the most piteous screams and sobs" when he saw the carriage move away. All night she scarcely closed her eyes; she did not know when she had experienced "such a concussion of nerves." At four o'clock the following afternoon Robert returned, laughing, with the news that the child was much better. Elizabeth had been so agitated by the episode that in a letter to Arabel [19] she blamed Story for not facing up to the situation "in all manliness and fortitude," especially since he had with him at Velletri a wife, two servants, three physicians, and "full pecuniary resources."

THE Brownings left Rome by *vettura* about May 28 [20] and arrived at Florence four or five days later. Once again Elizabeth was conscious of her love for her adopted city, which looked "exquisitely beautiful in its garden-ground of vineyards and olive trees, sung round by the nightingales day and night." It had been their intention to travel in June to London or Paris, where they might live for a year or longer so that both of them could see their volumes through the press. Browning planned to be ready to publish in the autumn and Elizabeth in the following spring. But she thought that after their stay in the north they would return to live permanently in Florence. "Cheap, tranquil, cheerful, beautiful, within the limit of civilisation yet out of the crush of it," Florence, she was persuaded, was the one place in the world where she would always feel at home. They suddenly postponed their trip for a year, because Elizabeth realized that she was still far from the completion of her verse-novel [21] and because they did not have enough money.

Their funds were so low in fact that they could not leave that summer—not even for a week or two at Siena or Bagni di Lucca. She wrote Arabel in the middle of June that they had only £100 to spend during the next six and a half months.[22] There had been no ship money that year, and Kenyon had forgotten to pay the £50 due every six months by his generous arrangement. At least twice that summer Robert asked Chapman and Hall to send the financial statement of himself and his wife to the end of June. Late in August Elizabeth informed Arabel that the account had just arrived, and she added, "There's not much for us." Her third edition, which was published in October, had come within £9 of paying its expenses after six months and by now was presumably earning royalties; *Casa Guidi Windows* was selling very slowly and was "not out yet by about a hundred copies"; [23] and Robert's books were keeping "much the same proportion." They had complained of Moxon, but now they thought their present publishers were even slower and more unsatisfactory. Although Elizabeth was usually not worried by money matters, she was for once depressed and wondered why no one ever thought of them for government pensions, but she added generously that as long as Carlyle was forgotten, it was "a distinction not to be remembered." In September they were relieved to hear that the *David Lyon* had finally come in and would eventually pay them the "immense" dividend of £175, the largest since their marriage. Their trip to England the following summer was now assured.

Yet even though their purse was low, the summer of 1854 passed agreeably. The only unhappy event was the death of Flush, Elizabeth's inseparable companion for thirteen years. Although he no longer had a hair on his back and his infirmities had made life only a burden, his death was "quite a shock" and "a sadness" to her.[24] Among their friends, Mrs. Sartoris at Bagni di Lucca came over to see them now and then; Harriet Hosmer, who was

Florence, Bagni di Lucca, and Rome

spending the summer at Florence, was a frequent guest at Casa Guidi; and the Kinneys used to take them out to drive. Also Miss Isabella (Isa) Blagden often drove them in her carriage along the Arno to the Cascine and then to her villa almost a mile from the center of the city, and after tea Elizabeth was usually well enough to walk home with Robert "by moonlight or starlight at worst, through that exquisite avenue of grand cypresses half a mile long." Miss Blagden, with whom the Brownings had been acquainted for the past four years, was to become their most intimate friend in Florence. She was, Elizabeth said, a woman with a "warm heart and active mind," [25] who had come to Florence to live in 1849 and made it her home more than any other city, until her death in 1873. During the years when Elizabeth knew her, she appears to have had no regular occupation and was looking for a way to augment her income. In the sixties she succeeded, through the influence of Browning and T. A. Trollope, in publishing at least five novels, none of which, however, brought her much fame. And yet, though she had neither wealth nor unusual literary talent, her home became the center of social life for the Anglo-American community in Florence; there at different times might have been seen the Brownings, Landor, Robert Lytton, T. A. Trollope and his mother, Harriet Hosmer, Charlotte Cushman, Kate Field, Seymour Kirkup, and the Hawthornes.

Another well-known expatriate in Florence was James Jackson Jarves, with whom Elizabeth always liked to converse. Although he was one of the few mid nineteenth-century writers who perceived the essential hollowness of many of the Anglo-American painters and sculptors in Italy, it was not his shrewdness as an art critic but his interest in spiritualism which served as a bond between him and Elizabeth. He had been born into a family of a wealthy glass manufacturer of Boston, Massachusetts, had tried to run a newspaper in the Sandwich Islands, and had come with his wife and children in 1852 to Florence, where he began to write a series of books on fashions in art and on manners and customs in Paris and Italy. His most enduring accomplishment is his large collection of early Italian masters, which is now at Yale University, the first important collection of its type to come to America. Elizabeth read with astonishment his description in a letter to her of a séance conducted in London by the notorious American medium Daniel Dunglas Home. With no visible intervention, a table turned upon its edge with the lamp on it remaining upright all the while; many kinds of raps spelled out messages; spiritual hands "softer and more thrilling than any woman's"[26] knotted his tie, played an accordion, or untied a woman's apron strings and "in an undulating gliding movement" carried the apron across the room. Once at Casa Guidi Jarves showed her some "perfectly legible" writing made by the spirits themselves "without the mediation of any mortal fingers,"[27] but whenever Browning entered the room the conversation was changed to another topic.

Elizabeth also heard fantastic stories about "the spirits" from an English antiquarian, Seymour Kirkup, described by Frances Power Cobbe as "an old man with long white beard and glittering eye, the nearest approach to an ancient wizard that well might be conceived."[28] He had studied art in London, where he was an acquaintance of Blake and B. R. Haydon, and owing to delicate health settled in Italy about 1820. When the Brownings knew him, he had given up painting and was absorbed in the study of demonology, witchcraft, and alchemy, having collected a remarkable library in those occult subjects. His dusty, dark apartment cluttered with books, medieval manuscripts, and old paintings was in a house overhanging the Arno, near the Ponte Vecchio. Although T. A. Trollope called him "a besotted old man,"[29] Hawthorne, who visited him in 1858, was much impressed with his refinement and courtesy. In a letter filled with gossip about spiritualism Elizabeth mentioned Kirkup's "pet medium" Regina. Living as a servant with this eccentric, untidy, deaf old man was an Italian girl, Regina Ronti, of whose portrait Hawthorne said that he had never seen "a more beautiful and striking face claiming to be a real one." She pretended to be a medium and to have communications with the spirit of Dante. A year or two before her death in 1856, at the age of nineteen, she bore Kirkup a child, Imogene, who stayed with him and duped him as her mother had done by means of alleged messages from the souls of Dante and some of the poet's companions in the spirit world. Trollope, who was outraged at Imogene's constant deception of Kirkup and of her mocking him in the presence of others for his credulity, thought her "a clever, worthless hussy." Years after the Brownings left Italy, Kirkup at the age of eighty-seven was to marry an Italian girl of twenty-two. The most amazing of the tales Kirkup told the Brownings was of some rings and crosses he placed on the inside sill of an open window, high over the Arno, in an uninhabited room, carefully locking the door and putting a straw inside the lock so that he could later tell whether any one had tampered with it. When he returned the next day, the lock was untouched; yet the deposit had disappeared. Three days later he went to the room again, found the lock intact and the materials mysteriously restored. Browning and Trollope went to the apartment, saw that the locks had been properly sealed, and could suggest no explanation except for a fastened door behind a bookcase which could not be moved. Browning was not sure in which direction the door opened; but if inwards, Elizabeth concluded it was indeed "the work of spirits." [30] Robert, however, believed Kirkup was a "humbug."

THE autumn, winter, and spring of 1854–55 were serene and happy for the Brownings, both of whom were trying to finish their respective volumes. By the middle of January, Elizabeth had written some 4,500 lines of her novel in verse, and four months later more than seven thousand.

Almost every morning she heard Pen read from his story books for an hour before she began her own work, and then Robert gave him a music lesson for an equal length of time. It seemed to Elizabeth that the boy was remarkably quick, that "by a little *pushing*" they might "make him do anything," but she did not want her child to be a prodigy and was fearful that if he were made to apply himself for more than an hour, he would be liable to fever of the brain. In her letters to Henrietta she asked if her son ever had "naughty tempers," and said with pride that Pen never fell into a tantrum because "his nature is made of silk." [31] With his "infantine way of speaking," which she refused to correct, his "melodious voice," and his "sweet manner," he was the light of his mother's eyes. She admitted, however, that he was "by no means fond of his lessons and has no general passion even for story books" but was convinced that "if he would but set his mind to a thing steadily, there's nothing he can't do." [32] And in a letter to Arabel she confessed that Pen "was never much trained to obedience," that he believed he "ought to do what he likes himself generally, and generally does it." [33] But Robert was "strictly obeyed for the most part," for Pen detected in his father "a potentiality of wrath." Although the child's penmanship was good, he spelled so badly that he had to ask his mother about almost every word. Once she insisted that he go to the table and write by himself. He was "very unwilling" and came back in a minute with three words carefully written: "POOR LITTLE PENINI!" Elizabeth was "quite touched," she wrote Henrietta. "It sounded so like the bleating of a lamb left alone." One of the reasons why she so worshiped and spoiled the child may have been that she subconsciously identified Pen, whose features were much like Bro's, with her favorite brother who had been suddenly taken from her. Also Pen was her only child and had come to her when she was no longer young.

But if he was not sure of the spelling of the simplest words, his pronunciation of Tuscan was flawless, and he gave himself "immense airs" in correcting Wilson's Italian and even at times his mother's, always telling them, "I *must* know, because I was born in Florence." [34] He always wished to be considered Italian rather than English and used to say, "Sono Italiano, voglio essere Italiano." Once when he was with Wilson and the Brownings' servant Ferdinando at a day-time theater where monkeys and dogs were acting in the open, he began to scream in Italian "till the audience accepted him as a part of the performance." A jeweler from the Ponte Vecchio asked Ferdinando whose child he was. He replied, "His master's."—"Then you live with an Italian," said the jeweler.—"No, with an Englishman,"—"And the child speaks Italian so? *ma pare impossible,*" was the reply.

Late in the afternoon and in the evening, after Pen had been given his lessons, and after the Brownings had completed for the day their stints of composition, they received visitors or went to see their friends. Frederick Tennyson asked them to several *soirées musicales* at his large, handsome Villa Torrigiani, and once or twice the Brownings made excursions into the country

Florence, Bagni di Lucca, and Rome 287

with the Tennysons and with the Nortons, who had an apartment in Tennyson's house. Brinsley Norton, the son of the writer Caroline Norton, had married in 1853 a Capri peasant girl, "who knows nothing about anything—shoes and brushes included." [35] Elizabeth was shocked at the idea of such a marriage—"The inconsistencies of men are stupendous," she wrote—but she accepted both him and his wife until he tired the Brownings with constant self-admiration.

While the members of the Anglo-American colonies in Florence and in Rome were writing poetry, dabbling in music and the fine arts, and receiving messages from "the spirits," the peace of Europe was being disturbed more seriously than it had been since the Napoleonic era. England and France as allies had gone to war in March 1854 to preserve the Ottoman Empire, which was being threatened by the dynastic ambitions of Nicholas I of Russia. Sardinia later entered the conflict on the side of the Allies when Cavour sent a contingent of troops to the Crimea. Since the Brownings had no close relatives or friends fighting in the Crimean War and since it had only a remote connection with Italian politics, Elizabeth spoke less about it in her letters than she had about the war in Italy in 1848-49. When Arabel wrote to ask whether she ever thought about the war, Elizabeth said in November to Henrietta that the subject interested her very much. With characteristic hopefulness and oversimplification, she called it "a most righteous and necessary war" and said that there were "great interests involved besides the specific Turkish interests— the liberty and civilization of all Europe, and the good of the world for centuries." Although she was horrified at the thought of the agonies endured by thousands, she was somewhat comforted by the idea of the alliance. "Nothing so good ever happened either to England or France as their union," she wrote, much pleased that English soldiers were fighting beside those of Napoleon III. In February 1855, long before the Allies captured the fort of Sevastopol, winning that victory largely because of French efforts, Elizabeth declared, "How well and magnanimously the French have behaved!" In June she shrewdly observed that the fault of the English was not their lack of experience, as the government alleged in order to excuse its failures, but the system of favoritism and patronage: "We have soldiers, and soldiers should have military education as well as red coats, and be led by properly qualified officers, instead of Lord Nincompoop's youngest sons." She thought that Florence Nightingale, whom she remembered seeing in London, was "acting greatly on this occasion," and Elizabeth honored her for having "fulfilled her woman's duty where many men have failed." Yet she considered Miss Nightingale's step not a solution of the "woman's question," but on the contrary a movement backward to older values. Elizabeth did not believe "the best use to which we can put a gifted and accomplished woman is to *make her a hospital nurse*. If it is, why then woe to us all who are artists!"

That winter Elizabeth had "the worst attack on the chest" from which she had ever suffered in Italy. Owing to a long period of unusually cold weather and bitter winds, she became so ill with a constant cough and fever that for a time she could not eat, and when she finally convalesced late in the spring she was thinner and weaker than she had been for many years. Browning had been up, night after night, "keeping up the fire, boiling the coffee, and listening to the horrible cough which made sleep out of the question for either of us," Elizabeth said in gratitude. "Nothing could exceed his tender patience." In June she was well enough to travel, they had the means they lacked a year earlier, and Browning had completed eight thousand lines, according to Elizabeth, and was "at his mark." As usual, Elizabeth was reluctant to leave Italy, for she dreaded to expose herself to the English climate, but she eagerly looked forward to her reunion with Arabel, Henrietta, George, and some of the Brownings' close friends.

A few days before their departure rumors came to Elizabeth that the section of the city where they lived was being attacked by cholera. She heard that fourteen people had died in the street behind Casa Guidi and that the bodies had been carried under her windows and placed for a time in San Felice Church across from her balcony. Fearful of Pen's safety, she "fell into a sort of panic" [36] and insisted that Robert take them away within twenty-four hours to wait at Leghorn for their ship. He begged her "to be quiet and wait till the next day," when, if the rumors were worse, he would do whatever seemed best. On the following day, however, physicians assured everyone that "there was no epidemic, nor would be an epidemic." It was merely that a number of people had been ill from "imprudences in diet" because of the "excessive abundance and cheapness of fruit and vegetables." [37] A day or two after the scare they embarked in the middle of June at Leghorn on a ship bound for Corsica and Marseilles.

16. England and Paris, 1855-56

AFTER the Brownings were deposited at their hotel in Marseilles, where they planned to break their journey for two or three days before proceeding to Paris, they were surprised and delighted to learn that Alfred Barrett was staying in a room next to theirs. He had come to France to marry his pretty, young cousin Lizzie Barrett, who had for a number of years been living at 50 Wimpole Street as Edward Moulton Barrett's ward. Alfred showed "great affection" toward the Brownings, treated them to champagne, and won Pen's favor by heaping him with gifts. Although Elizabeth well knew from her sisters' letters about the step her brother was planning, "not a word did he tell" her of his intentions. His reticence seems extraordinary, but perhaps he suspected that she disapproved. If so, he did not wish to embarrass her by placing her in the position of having to congratulate him for a marriage about which she had grave misgivings. She had written to Arabel that she was "very very sorry" about the engagement, partly because Alfred was heavily in debt and his prospects seemed uncertain. Later in the summer he wrote his father of his plans, and upon receiving no reply, married his cousin on the first of August at the British Embassy in Paris. As soon as Mr. Barrett heard of the event, he disinherited his son, just as he had Elizabeth and Henrietta.

At seven o'clock in the evening, June 24, 1855, the Brownings reached Paris and immediately secured a suite of rooms below the apartment of the elder Browning and Sarianna. In the middle of May, Elizabeth had written to Arabel that Wilson was engaged to their Italian manservant Ferdinando Romagnoli. Although Elizabeth felt that marriages between Roman Catholics and Protestants should not, as a general rule, be encouraged, she thought that Wilson had made a good match. About Ferdinando, Elizabeth wrote that it would be hard to find "a better man, more upright, and of a more tender nature."[1] In Paris the Brownings had trouble in securing a priest who would be liberal enough when he married them to waive the usual requirement that the children be brought up as Catholics. They had expected to remain for only a week but had to extend their sojourn for another ten days before they could conclude the business. Elizabeth was "horribly vexed" at the delay and irritated at having to spend extra money for expenses at hotels and restaurants. After Wilson finally agreed to submit to her husband's wishes in regard to the religious training of the children, they were married on Tuesday, July 10.[2] Elizabeth, who had been reminded by Browning that "you can't separate a man and his wife,"[3] was very much upset to think that Wilson presumably would no longer sleep beside Pen. She wondered what would happen to her child, who needed someone with him always, as she explained to Arabel, for whenever he woke at night he cried instantly for attention. Her attitude toward the marriage changed early in September, when Wilson, whom she had always supposed to be a model of propriety, had to confess that she was expecting a baby in October. "Oh so shocked and pained I have been through Wilson," Elizabeth wrote Henrietta. "But after the first, I turn and try to think chiefly of her many excellent qualities and of what she has done for me in affectionate attention and service. Human nature is so full of failures, at its best."[4] In December, two or three months after the birth of Wilson's son Orestes, Elizabeth was convinced that the marriage was unfortunate in all ways. Wilson, who was with her family in England, wished to return with her child and live with the Brownings in Paris and later go with them to Italy. As for Ferdinando, Elizabeth wrote Henrietta that Robert and she were "enraged" at him for grumbling about the work he had to do, for complaining that his wife and child were not with him, and for having "shown a great want of moderation and conduct under the late circumstances."[5] Since she could not turn her present maid into the street, Ferdinando's attitude seemed to her unreasonable. Her nerves were jarred by the discussions; "the discomfort is terrible to one's arrangements and thoughts," she wrote Henrietta.[6]

The Brownings during their last few days in Paris before they left for London saw such old friends as Thackeray and his daughters, Milsand, Mrs. Jameson, and the Corkrans. Once they went to Madame Mohl's to meet "heaps of celebrities," especially the French writers François Auguste Mignet, Victor Cousin, Prosper Mérimée, and Adelaide Ristori, one of the most celebrated actresses of her time.[7] They also visited Rosa Bonheur, "the greatest woman-painter, it is considered, who ever lived," as Elizabeth wrote to Arabel.[8] She thought the pictures "wonderful" and the artist herself "charming." On Wednesday, July 11, the day after the wedding of their servants, the Brownings left Paris and at three o'clock the following morning arrived at their new apartment at 13 Dorset Street, in the section of London where they always stayed.

Elizabeth looked forward to talking with her friends once again, although this time she would not be able to see Miss Mitford, who had died early in the year. Before long the Brownings had seen Carlyle, Forster, Mr. and Mrs. Bryan Waller Procter and their daughter Adelaide, Mrs. Sartoris, W. J. Fox, Philip James Bailey, and Alexander W. Kinglake, who wrote *Eōthen,* a travel book about the Near East. It was during this summer that Frederick Locker (later changed to Locker-Lampson) first made the acquaintance of the Brownings, whom he met at their apartment. "At her own fireside she struck me as very pleasing and exceedingly sympathetic," he later wrote. "Her physique was peculiar: curls like the pendent ears of a water-spaniel, and poor little hands—so thin that when she welcomed you she gave you something like the foot of a young bird."[9] But it was Tennyson who paid the most memorable visits to the Brownings' apartment, when he came on September 26 and 27. "The Laureate took us by surprise last week while Arabel was here," Elizabeth wrote in great excitement to Henrietta; "dined with us two successive days, and spent the mornings, and threw us in the nights. He read us the whole of Maud, and exquisitely—the voice hangs in my ear still. We dined and smoked together and were so happy and affectionate as possible; and I didn't get to bed on the second day till three o'clock in the morning. So that altogether I nearly died of the joy of it. But I seriously love Tennyson." In her report of the event to Mrs. Martin she said in the same tone of rapture that Tennyson had dined with them, smoked with them, and opened his second bottle of port, and she added: "If I had had a heart to spare, certainly he would have won mine. He is captivating with his frankness, confidingness and unexampled *naïveté!* Think of his stopping in 'Maud' every now and then—'There's a wonderful touch! That's very tender. How beautiful that is!' Yes, and it *was* wonderful, tender, beautiful, and he read exquisitely in a voice like an organ, rather music than speech." On the second evening, when Tennyson recited "Maud," Browning, not to be outdone, read aloud his "Fra Lippo Lippi." William Michael Rossetti was present on the 27th, and his brother Dante Gabriel, who came both evenings, secretly sketched Tennyson as he was reading his poem.[10]

Another important social occasion, but one which was to leave a bitter aftertaste, was the visit the Brownings paid on July 23 in Ealing at the home of Mr. and Mrs. Rymer, who were friends of Mrs. Jameson, to attend a séance conducted by Daniel Dunglas Home (or Hume). Thomas A. Trollope, who entertained Home at his house in Florence, described him as "about nineteen or twenty years of age . . . rather tall, with a loosely put together figure, red hair, large and clear but not bright blue eyes, a sensual mouth, lanky cheeks, and that sort of complexion which is often found in individuals of a phthisical diathesis."[11] The impression left on Trollope after seeing Home for a month was one of doubt and perplexity; he was not able to convince himself that the medium was trustworthy and sincere. The accounts of what happened that evening, as told by Home, by Browning, and by Elizabeth, are in agreement about most details. When the Brownings arrived at the Rymers', Home showed Robert and Elizabeth a wreath of flowers which he and one of the Rymer girls had just made, and he told Elizabeth that he would afterwards ask "the spirits" to place the garland on her head. The wreath was then put on the table. When they were later sitting around this table, it was so dark that it was hard for Browning to distinguish anything. It seemed to him, however, that a hand pushed the wreath off the table, picked it up from the floor, and took it to Elizabeth, who had left his side and at Home's request had taken a chair beside the medium. Then in accordance with Elizabeth's wishes, so Browning said, the garland was carried under the table and given to him. Both Elizabeth and Home tell the story somewhat differently from Browning's version. She wrote Henrietta: "At the request of the medium, the spiritual hands took from the table a garland which lay there, and placed it upon my head. The particular hand which did this was of the largest human size, as white as snow, and very beautiful. It was as near to me as this hand I write with, and I saw it as distinctly." In none of her accounts of the episode did Elizabeth say that the wreath was then sent to Browning. Home wrote that the wreath was raised from the table "by supernatural power," that Browning, who had been seated at the opposite side of the table, left his place and stood behind Elizabeth, upon whose head the wreath was placed. Home then made the unfair comment, "It was the remark of all the Rymer family, that Mr. Browning seemed much disappointed that the wreath was not put upon his own head instead of his wife's, and that his placing himself in the way of where it was being carried, was for the purpose of giving it an opportunity of being placed upon his own brow." [12]

After the garland was on Elizabeth's head, as Browning reported the episode, "the spirits" supposedly played tunes on an accordion under the table, which was lifted from the ground a foot or two and tilted, and Home fell into a trance and pretended to speak for the spirit of the Rymers' child who had died three years earlier. Elizabeth also mentioned to Henrietta the nonsense uttered by Home: "I think that what chiefly went against the exhibition, in Robert's mind, was the trance at the conclusion during which the medium talked a great deal of much such twaddle as may be heard in any fifth rate conventicle." Browning wished to hold the spirit hand and to make investigations, but the Rymers gave him no opportunity; and since it was an informal family party, he could not press the matter. Both Elizabeth and he had diametrically opposing views on the authenticity of the manifestations. "For my own part [she wrote Henrietta] I am confirmed in all my opinions. To me it was wonderful and conclusive; and I believe that the medium present was no more *responsible* for the things said and done, than I myself was." She also expressed her convictions to Mrs. Jameson: "The least doubt does not remain to me of the verity of a certain class of most wonderful facts, and that in the absence of any physical solution, I stand firm before the spiritual hypothesis. Not only the Ealing phenomena constrain me to this— On all sides of us testimonies would crowd, if there were but a general tolerance." [13] Browning, on the other hand, believed that the table-turning, the spirit hands, and spirit voices were all "a cheat and imposture." It seemed to him that the entire performance was very clumsy and that a competent magician could have made his "tricks" appear more natural. He thought that it would have been possible for Home to have had a tube and some strings under his loose clothes to manipulate the fantoccini hands. Although there was no proof that Home possessed such skills, he was often said to have been a conjurer, ventriloquist, hypnotist, and prestidigitator. Elizabeth, however, was certain that the hand which passed slowly between her lap and her eyes was not made of gutta-percha, but was a living, human hand.

Several days after the Brownings' visit to Ealing, Robert was so much dissatisfied with what he had seen that he asked Mrs. Rymer if he might witness another séance conducted by Home but was refused because of other engagements of hers. Soon afterward Home, together with Mrs. Rymer and her son, called at the Brownings' apartment. The only account of the ensuing fracas is that told by Home, who may have exaggerated, but at all events the scene must have been painful, especially to Elizabeth, who was always upset by the slightest disturbance. Browning greeted Mrs. Rymer and her son. He would not shake hands with the medium, however, but "with a tragic air, he threw his hand on his left shoulder, and stalked away." Elizabeth, who was standing in the center of the room, looked "very pale and agitated," turned to the medium, and, placing both her hands in his, said with great distress, "Oh, dear Mr. Home, do not, do not blame me. I am so sorry, but I am not to blame." Amidst the confusion Browning returned to the group and began "in an excited manner" to tell Mrs. Rymer of his disapproval of the proceedings at her home and to ask why she had not arranged for another séance as he had requested. When Home attempted to reply for Mrs. Rymer, Browning told him to be quiet. Home maintained that he had a right to speak in his defense, and the Rymers supported him.

Browning's face then became "pallid with rage, and his movements, as he swayed backwards and forwards on his chair, were like those of a maniac." Home decided to leave the room immediately and as he was going out shook hands with Elizabeth, "who was nearly ready to faint." She said to him, as she had at first, "Dear Mr. Home, I am not to blame. Oh, dear! oh, dear!" In a letter, written in the formal third person, which Browning sent to a Miss de Gaudrion about the Ealing manifestations, he referred to his contemptuous treatment of Home: "Mr. Browning had some difficulty in keeping from an offensive expression of his feelings at the ———'s; he has since seen Mr. Hume and relieved himself." [14]

After the séance at the Rymers', Elizabeth took the wreath home and hung it on her dressing glass. When it had almost withered, Robert seized it and thew it out of the window into the street, with an expression of scorn for her having kept it.[15] It is not true, however, that the Brownings quarreled between themselves about spiritualism and the notorious Home. Each realized that the other held an altogether different opinion and that any discussion would be fruitless. Since Browning was "a good deal irritated" by any reference to the Ealing affair and its aftermath, Elizabeth begged her correspondents not to mention the matter in their letters. " 'Spirits' are *tabooed* in this house," [16] she explained to Mrs. Jameson. Browning's violent language to Home in Elizabeth's presence had made her suffer. In the letter to Henrietta in which she described the séance, she said significantly, "It has been a most uncomfortable and unprofitable visit to England." She wrote in a similar vein to Mrs. Jameson, "I will say briefly now that a good deal has happened which gave me at the time much pain and still fills me with regret." In this letter to Mrs. Jameson she referred sadly to the opposing views held by Robert and herself: "I never could understand why, considering different idiosyncrasies, and unequal perceptions of truth, we should not all consent to tolerate the differing opinions of one another: but this is difficult, difficult, in practice. Thinking Robert wrong in his view, I could certainly do that for him, which (thinking me very wrong), he can't do for me, or at least will not." [17] It was easy enough for Elizabeth to talk about tolerance, but she always insisted that her view of spiritualism was the only correct one and that if "unbelievers" would only open their minds to the new evidence, they would all agree with her.[18]

In addition to being agitated over Wilson's enforced marriage and Browning's dispute with Home, Elizabeth was much depressed, as she had been during previous summers in London, because of her father's attitude toward her. Early in the year Henrietta had written to Mr. Barrett to ask if she might appear at Wimpole Street, and he gave directions that she should not be admitted. In the middle of February, Elizabeth had written from Florence to Henrietta that she would not venture the risk of forcing an interview because of the inevitable bitterness. "For my part I begin to despair," she continued. "I begin to hate to write about it. I never could have thought such obduracy possible, such and so long, no! not even in *him*."[19] That summer Elizabeth went to her old house at Wimpole Street three or four times to see the housekeeper "Minny," whom she had known and liked for many years, and also to be with Arabel. Once when Pen was visiting Arabel and George, he was seen by Mr. Barrett: "George was playing in the hall with him [Elizabeth wrote Henrietta] and he was in fits of laughter. Papa came out of the dining-room and stood *looking* for two or three minutes. Then he called George and went back, 'Whose child is that, George?'—'Ba's child,' said George.—'And what is he doing here, pray?' Then, without waiting for an answer he changed the subject."[20] Thus Mr. Barrett showed, as Elizabeth expressed it, "an absolute state of indifference" toward her and her family. Late in August, Mr. Barrett announced that he would soon rent a house at the shore for the rest of the season and issued a decree that all the family would have to live there. "Arabel *swears* that if he take a house where *I* cannot follow, she will not leave London, but live *incognita* in a room at Trippy's," Elizabeth wrote Henrietta. But Mr. Barrett treated his forty-two-year-old daughter as though she were a child and insisted that she go with the rest of the family to Eastbourne. Elizabeth was greatly disappointed that Arabel went away, just as her father had demanded. On the day before the departure of Mr. Barrett's children, Elizabeth wrote Henrietta, "Wimpole St. refused us everything except knead cakes and grapes and melon, which George gave us in his kindness. None of them would come because of its being the last hours with Papa." [21] The Brownings hoped to go to Eastbourne about ten days later so that Elizabeth might be near Arabel, but they had to abandon the plan because they lacked the extra money and they were both very busy seeing Robert's volumes through the press. Elizabeth was also disappointed that she did not have a reunion with Henrietta, whose poor health prevented her from coming to London.

DURING that summer Elizabeth was so much occupied helping Robert with the proof sheets of *Men and Women,* seeing relatives and friends, and giving Pen his lessons, that she did not add a line to her long verse-novel. As usual the climate and the associations of London depressed her: "For my part [she wrote Mrs. Jameson], I am ready at melancholy with anybody. The air, mentally or physically considered, is very heavy for me here, and I long for the quiet of my Florence, where somehow it always has gone best with my life. As to England, it affects me so, in body, soul, and circumstances, that if I could not get away soon, I should be provoked, I think, into turning monster and *hating* the whole island." But they could not leave for Paris until the volumes had been sent to the press.

On August 17, Elizabeth informed Henrietta that the books were partly printed. It may have been in September that Browning wrote "One Word More. To E.B.B.," which he placed at the end of the second volume as a dedicatory poem to his wife. Together with "The Guardian-Angel" and "By the Fire-Side," it is one of his most personal utterances and perhaps the finest expression of his love for Elizabeth. Every artist, he said in the poem, wishes to please the woman he loves by attempting just once in his career to devote his talents to a medium different from the one in which he excels. "Rafael made a century of sonnets" in honor of his lady, and Dante began to paint an angel for the sake of Beatrice. But he, Browning, will never be able to express his love by creating pictures, statues, or music, since he must stand on his attainment of verse alone. Instead he will write a poem with a unique meter, used for the first and last time in these verses to his wife, just as an artist who usually paints in fresco might take a hair-brush and illuminate the margin of a missal with minute figures or as a worker in bronze might transfer his efforts to silver. He says that his wife has seen him gather his men and women, whose joys and sorrows, hopes and fears are described in the verses of the two volumes, but in this one poem he wishes to speak in his true person, "Not as Lippo, Roland or Andrea." Thus he presents her with his fifty poems and asks her to keep them: "Where my heart lies, let my brain lie also!" The moon always shows only one face to the earth, but if the moon could fall in love with a mortal and desired to charm him with her magic, she would turn to him a new side which would fill him with awe:

> What were seen? None knows, none ever shall know.
> Only this is sure—the sight were other,
> Not the moon's same side, born late in Florence,
> Dying now impoverished here in London.
> God be thanked, the meanest of his creatures
> Boasts two soul-sides, one to face the world with,
> One to show a woman when he loves her.
>
> This I say of me, but think of you, Love!
> This to you—yourself my moon of poets!
> Ah, but that's the world's side—there's the wonder—
> Thus they see you, praise you, think they know you.
> There, in turn I stand with them and praise you,
> Out of my own self, I dare to phrase it.
> But the best is when I glide from out them,
> Cross a step or two of dubious twilight,
> Come out on the other side, the novel
> Silent silver lights and darks undreamed of,
> Where I hush and bless myself with silence.

By the middle of October 1855, after the Brownings had finished with the proofs of *Men and Women,* they went to Paris for the winter and waited for the critical reception of the volumes, which appeared on the tenth of the following month.[22] They were the fruit of the creative activity of the previous ten years, for Browning had published no collection of shorter poems since his *Dramatic Romances and Lyrics* of November 1845. "Robert will stand higher than ever through these poems," Elizabeth wrote; "I am ready to die for them, at the stake, that they are his ablest works." She thought that for "variety, vitality, and intensity" they were indeed worthy of their author. The volumes which so aroused Elizabeth's enthusiasm contained many poems which have since become favorites with Browning's admirers: "Fra Lippo Lippi," "Andrea del Sarto," "Old Pictures in Florence," "The Statue and the Bust," "Cleon," and "A Grammarian's Funeral"—to name only a few. The two books showed the full maturity of Browning's art and were the product of some of the best years of his life. Yet except for a thoughtful and sensitive study of the poems by the Brownings' friend Milsand in the *Revue des Deux Mondes* and a warm-hearted but naïve notice written by an Oxford student—the future artist and poet William Morris in the *Oxford and Cambridge Magazine*—the volumes failed to gain for their writer a sympathetic hearing from either the general public or the professional critics.

The poems were too original to be appreciated. As Browning himself said in explaining the failure of his recent work, the public is always demanding something new and different; yet it is repelled by true originality. It prefers the old and the familiar, seasoned with the spice of novelty. The depreciatory article in the *Athenaeum* is typical of the many notices which irritated and discouraged Browning because of their unfairness and their failure to make any effort to understand him. The reviewer began: "These volumes contain some fifty poems, which will make the least imaginative man think, and the least thoughtful man grieve. Who will not grieve over energy wasted and power misspent,—over fancies chaste and noble, so overhung by the 'seven veils' of obscurity, that we can oftentimes be only sure that fancies exist? What they are meant to typify or illustrate cannot always be detected by the eyes of even kindred dreamers." [23] Likewise many other critiques were, as Browning wrote to his publisher, "mostly stupid and spiteful, self-contradicting and contradictory of each other." [24] Some of his close friends, like Ruskin, Carlyle, and Dante Gabriel Rossetti, were well aware of the greatness of his verse, but their praise was not publicly expressed and thus did not come to the attention of the professional critics and of the small number of people who occasionally bought volumes of poetry.

MEANWHILE the Brownings were living in an unsatisfactory apartment at 102 rue de Grenelle in the Faubourg St. Germain. Through some misunderstanding their friends Mr. and Mrs. Corkran had signed a lease on their behalf for six months. The Corkrans had evidently been attracted to the suite because of its yellow satin sofas, which they thought worthy of the two poets. Elizabeth wrote to Arabel a few days after arriving in Paris a long letter "full of groans from end to end." [25] The landlady would not cancel the agreement even though they were most discontented. They had to pay £2 a week for their apartment, which they were not allowed to sublet except for £2 10s. It had one room less than they needed; Robert had to dress in the *salon*. "There's only a roof above us," Elizabeth complained to Arabel, "and under us nothing at all,"—referring perhaps to the fact that the rooms were not carpeted. "Altogether we are utterly wretched," she added. Besides her domestic irritations, she was vexed at Arabel for not coming to Paris, as Mr. Barrett had suggested that she or some of her brothers might do after the holiday at Eastbourne, but Arabel was so sure the invitation had been given with the expectation it would be politely refused by all that she dared not bring the matter up.

Elizabeth, however, had to admit that she liked the section of the city where they were living because the English were scarcely ever seen there and it was much more characteristic in appearance than the right bank. Also the markets were less expensive since they were not inflated by English and American influences. A fine goose, for example, cost them 3s. 4d., and a fowl large enough for their whole dinner 2s. 1d. In contrast to London, the French capital seemed "beyond description beautiful," all the streets were clean, and the new buildings being erected as part of the public works program of Napoleon III harmonized "wonderfully with the old." Before the cold weather came she liked to wander through the streets with Robert to look into shop windows or to stroll in the garden of the Tuileries. Besides Ferdinando, who purchased the food and did the cooking, they had an English girl,

Harriet, to keep the apartment clean, so that Elizabeth enjoyed her usual freedom from domestic chores.

The first visitors to their "detestable" apartment were Sir Edward Bulwer-Lytton (later First Lord Lytton) and his son Robert (later First Earl of Lytton). Elizabeth described Sir Edward as young looking, with fair, curly hair. In her opinion he spoke as with authority and rather too emphatically, but his conversation was informative, fluent, and brilliant. His manner was too worldly and his clothing too ornate to please Elizabeth, who thought him "less deep, less sweet, less pure" than his son. She was much more in sympathy with Robert Lytton than with Sir Edward. According to her letters to Arabel and Henrietta, the conversation was mainly on the subject of spiritualism. James Jackson Jarves, who was also present during part of the evening, spoke to Elizabeth of the spirit voices he had recently heard. Both Sir Edward and his son had attended a séance led by Home at the Rymers' in Ealing two days before the performance witnessed by the Brownings. Sir Edward said that at first he had doubted the authenticity of the manifestations and had accused Home of deceit and had told him that he believed that the "spiritual" hands he saw actually belonged to the medium. Home then went to the window and wept hysterically. When he regained control of himself, he returned to the table and placed both his hands into one of Sir Edward's. With his disengaged hand, the elder Bulwer-Lytton then distinctly felt three different spirit hands: one large and rough as a sailor's; one small, smooth, and delicate woman's hand, with polished nails; and the third a child's hand. Sir Edward felt for the arm beyond the wrist and discovered to his horror that "there was *nothing . . nothing.*" Then he was certain that there had been no imposture. He also said that water-color drawings had been produced by the spirits and that letters had not only been written but folded and put into his hand, "and this not once, but by hundreds." Robert Lytton then told the Brownings of having heard from the Cottrells in Florence that Home, who was staying in that city with the Trollopes, was the cause of great excitement. Mrs. Trollope swore that she had seen the medium lifted high into the air and whirled about the room.[26] As Sir Edward was leaving the apartment, he asked Browning and Elizabeth to go with him and his son the next morning to see a French girl conduct a séance. Much to Elizabeth's surprise, Browning accepted and encouraged her to go. So all four went to hear the raps and to see the spirit-writing. Bulwer-Lytton's testimony made Elizabeth feel triumphant over Robert. "The manifestations seem deepening and strengthening on all sides [she wrote Henrietta], and soon will be too strong for the sceptics and the intolerant."

On October 31 Elizabeth informed Arabel that her landlady had agreed to cancel the lease if they would pay rent for two months at the rate of £2 10s. a week and that she had magnanimously refused an offer of three hundred francs (£12) Robert had made her if she would release them. Though they were now free, they did not move until the middle of December, when Elizabeth, "swathed past possible breathing, over face and respirator in woollen shawls," was carried by Robert down the steps of the apartment into a fiacre, which took them to their new suite at 3 rue du Colisée, off the avenue des Champs-Elysées. Here they stayed until their trip to England the following summer. Elizabeth found this apartment more to her liking, but late in the winter she wrote that her health had been impaired because she was confined in her small rooms. She missed the palatial chambers of her Florentine home.

The Brownings saw many of their friends that winter, especially Madame Mohl, Adelaide Kemble, Isa Blagden, Monckton Milnes, and Dante Gabriel Rossetti. W. C. Macready, who was in Paris for a few days, called several times at the Brownings' apartment, and the two men were happy to bury the quarrel which had kept them apart for thirteen years. Whenever visitors came, Elizabeth would thrust under a cushion the manuscript of the long poem she was writing. Yet in spite of the distractions caused by her child and by the people who came to call, she was able to write thirty or forty lines almost every day. By the end of February she had made a fair copy of the first five books, containing more than six thousand lines, and had put together and was ready to transcribe another book. "Oh, I am so anxious to make it good," she wrote Mrs. Jameson. "I have put much of myself in it—I mean to say, of my soul, my thoughts, emotions, opinions." In March Browning saw the first six books and greatly admired them. Early in May she said that she had finished the seventh and was writing the eighth and hoped to finish the transcription of the two books by the middle of June. After she had composed eight books, she decided to add one more, which she may have begun before she left Paris.

In addition to the work on her verse-novel, she prepared a fourth edition of her *Poems,* because the third had been exhausted, sent the material to Chapman and Hall in May, and made corrections on the proof sheets in June. The three octavo volumes were issued on the first of November [27] in dark green cloth boards. The sonnet "Future and Past," which had been at the end of the first volume in the editions of 1850 and 1853, was inserted after the forty-first of the "Sonnets from the Portuguese" and became "Sonnet 42" of the sequence. Elizabeth revised the "Sonnets from the Portuguese," and added *Casa Guidi Windows* and three short poems, "A Denial," "Proof and Disproof," and "Question and Answer," all of which had been written before her marriage and dealt with the new love in her life. Otherwise the three volumes were the same as the *Poems* of 1853.

In contrast to the continuous demand for Elizabeth's works, the sales of *Men and Women* had been slow. Elizabeth had written to Henrietta about a week after its publication that the bookstores had placed large orders and the expenses had been covered within three days. But soon afterward the demand for the volumes slackened, and Browning realized that except for a small group of young Pre-Raphaelites, of whom Dante Gabriel Rossetti was one of the leaders, most of the British reading public still failed to understand his unusual gifts. For a while he undertook to revise *Sordello* but soon became discouraged and occupied himself with drawing. Early in May Elizabeth wrote to Mrs. Jameson that after thirteen days of work Browning had "produced some quite startling copies of heads." She explained that he could not rest from serious work by absorbing himself in light literature as she could: "It wearies him, and there are hours which are on his hands, which is bad both for them and for him. . . . So while I lie on the sofa and rest in a novel, Robert has a resource in his drawing."

IT WAS apparently late in June 1856 that the Brownings felt that although the transcription of Elizabeth's long poem had not yet been finished, they should no longer delay their trip to London.

They came, and at the invitation of Kenyon, who was then in the Isle of Wight, they lived most of the summer in his home at 39 Devonshire Place. During July, even though she was almost incapacitated from the cold, she worked steadily upon her novel in verse. On August 3 she wrote Henrietta that she had eleven thousand lines ready to print and that both Robert and she had to stay in London to attend to the proof sheets. Her American publisher C. S. Francis promised her £100 for the right of printing simultaneously with the English edition, and so she had to prepare a fair copy for him in addition to the one she was about to send to Chapman and Hall.

Mary Howitt, translator, editor, and one of the most prolific writers of the age, came to see Elizabeth not long after the Brownings arrived. One evening Charles Eliot Norton called on them and found that William Morris and Edward Burne-Jones were also present. Norton later wrote that Burne-Jones, who seemed very shy and quiet, appeared almost overpowered by Browning's warm praise of one of his drawings. He remembered Elizabeth's expression of her pleasure in the drawing and the success with which she set the young artist at his ease.[28] The Brownings dined at the Procters on Sunday, July 6. A week afterward they went to a late breakfast party at the home of Monckton Milnes, where Elizabeth sat next to Nathaniel Hawthorne, who had been since 1853 the American consul at Liverpool. He recorded in his notebook that Elizabeth and he had a lively conversation during the meal, for she seemed to him "of that quickly appreciative and responsive order of women" with whom he could talk more freely than with any man. Furthermore she had her own originality to facilitate the flow of ideas, though he supposed she was not usually loquacious. She introduced the subject of spiritualism, and Hawthorne could not but wonder why "so fine a spirit as hers should not reject the matter, till, at least, it is forced upon her." He concluded that he liked her very much, "a great deal better than her poetry, which I could hardly suppose to have been written by such a quiet little person as she." [29]

As soon as Mr. Barrett heard that the Brownings were living in London, he gave orders that his family should spend the rest of the summer at Ventnor, on the southern coast of the Isle of Wight.

In order to see more of Arabel and George, the Brownings at great inconvenience to themselves went on August 23 to Ventnor, where they continued work on the proofs and also saw as much as they could of the Barretts. Two weeks later they traveled to the north of the island to live for a fortnight with Kenyon in his home at West Cowes. Elizabeth thought that he looked thin, pale, and very ill, and she was pained to see how hard it was for him both to breathe and to walk. It was clear that his strength was ebbing away and that he had only a few months to live. In his large, silent house overlooking the Parade and the sea the Brownings talked with him when he was well enough to receive them and spent most of their time working on the proof sheets, which they kept sending to the publishers with the dispatch of almost every post.

Elizabeth wrote Mrs. Martin that Robert and she had spent "a happy sorrowful two weeks together" with Arabel, who was in low spirits and very much aggrieved at having been sent away from London. She had sworn that she would join the Brownings at Taunton when they made their visit to Henrietta and her family. But she did not go because she knew that if her father should come and find her absent he would never forgive her.

> The fact is, she wants companionship [Elizabeth wrote from West Cowes] and never have I been so near to repent my marriage, as in seeing how dull she is, dear thing, all alone. Nobody else misses me, and as to Papa . . really, I don't believe he cares one straw (or ever could have done, much!) whether I am alive or dead. It was *hard*, Henrietta, his resolving to send his family away, the very day on which he knew I was near—hard, almost inhuman. But I won't talk of it here. Let Arabel offend him, and he would turn her out at a moment's notice, which she is so prepared for, that she was considering in London, whether, in that case, she would go out as a companion, or apply herself among the wood-engravers.[30]

After many years of self-sacrifice and of devotion to her father, Arabel had received from him no evidence of gratitude, no intimation that he understood her. She had less security than one of the Barretts' servants.

Before Elizabeth left Kenyon's house at West Cowes, she showed

England and Paris, 1855-56 307

him the dedication in his honor of the poem which was the fruit of some four years of intermittent labor. He was much pleased when he read in the inscription his protégée's handsome acknowledgment of her indebtedness to him for his never-failing encouragement and generosity, "far beyond the common uses of mere relationship or sympathy of mind." Elizabeth took particular pleasure in dedicating the poem to Kenyon because she believed it to be, as she wrote in the inscription, "the most mature of my works, and the one into which my highest convictions upon Life and Art have entered."

From West Cowes the Brownings went to Taunton to be with Henrietta and her family during the week of September 22. She was happy, well, and prosperous, and had a large, comfortable home, with four servants. While Elizabeth and Robert conversed with Henrietta and Surtees, Pen enjoyed the companionship of his three first cousins Altham, Edward, and Mary. The shortness of the Brownings' visit was no measure of the affection the two families had for each other, or of the hospitality of Henrietta and Surtees, but it was necessary for Elizabeth to return to London promptly in order to finish the proof sheets before the cold weather would drive her from England. When she left on Tuesday, September 30, she grieved to say goodbye and hoped that before long they might be with each other again. But that was the last time she saw her sister; four years later Henrietta died of cancer after a short, painful illness.

During the following three weeks after the Brownings' return to London, Elizabeth suffered from a severe cough which kept her awake night after night. The east wind and heavy fogs robbed her of her strength; and both the news that her father had been less well than usual and the recollection of Kenyon's pitiful appearance filled her with foreboding. "I have been very anxious—and shall be sadder than usual in leaving England this year. May God help us all," she wrote Henrietta. Yet in spite of her depression of spirits and her physical weakness, she made corrections with Robert's help on the proofs and struggled desperately to complete the work before her departure. On October 11 she informed Henrietta that they were still within eighty pages of completion of the book. Although they hoped to begin their trip to Florence within a week, it was not until October 21 [31] that Elizabeth wrote that they had made definite plans to leave on the following day but would return the next summer if it should please God. As she looked, however, from her channel steamer that Wednesday afternoon upon the steep, gray cliffs fading away behind her, she had no premonition that she would never see them again. The Brownings stopped in Paris only a day or two and went immediately to Marseilles, from which they hoped to go by land to Genoa that they might enjoy the scenery of the Riviera. But she wrote her brother George from Marseilles on October 27 that the land journey would be too expensive and that instead they were sailing the next day.

Upon their return they were happy to find their carpets and furniture in excellent order. Casa Guidi seemed pleasant, even after living in Kenyon's well-appointed house, and Elizabeth enjoyed being in Florence again, though it was duller and quieter than Paris and London and they seemed to themselves "to have dropped suddenly down a wall out of the world." The novel in verse was to be published on November 15.[32] While Elizabeth waited for critical notices and opinions of friends, she was immured in her apartment because of a bitter *tramontana* wind and eagerly listened to gossip about "the spirits." One of her most intimate friends, Sophia Cottrell, told her that she had held her dead baby in her lap for a quarter of an hour and had asked the spirit of the child, "Darling, won't you give your hand to papa?" The ghost responded, and Count Cottrell swore to Elizabeth that he had held the baby's hand in his own. He also claimed that he had seen an arm veiled in white, with a woman's hand visible, come out of the ground, take a sheet of paper, and write on it. Home, who had been living in Florence, had amazed a large group of spectators at a séance by causing spirit hands to untie a mass of ropes which had bound his arms and legs, and on another occasion he caused the room to shake as violently as if there had been an earthquake. Mrs. Kinney told Elizabeth of a table which had been raised and tilted so that the pencil on it began to roll off. "She put out her hand to prevent its falling—when lo, there it remained—and she could not *with all her force*, separate it from the table," Elizabeth wrote Henrietta on November 18.

It must have been one or two weeks afterward that Elizabeth first heard the anxiously awaited news about the reception of her long poem, the work upon which she was staking her final reputation as a poet.

17. "Aurora Leigh"

THE POPULARITY of *Aurora Leigh* far exceeded Elizabeth's most sanguine hopes; never before had a book of hers sold so well. Some London booksellers, in letting it out, limited the time to two days, and the Florentine bookshops had no copies available within a few hours after they were placed on sale. "I am surprised, I own, at the amount of success [she wrote Sarianna]; and that golden-hearted Robert is in ecstasies about it—far more than if it all related to a book of his own. The form of the story, and also something in the philosophy, seem to have caught the crowd." Although Elizabeth was never boastful or conceited, she was human enough to enjoy the sudden acclaim and to believe that it was not altogether undeserved, for in her opinion the poem was "nearer the mark . . . fuller, stronger, more sustained" than any of her former efforts.

Browning had finished "this divine Book"[1] in London on July 9, 1856, and had been enchanted with its beauty and power. Upon its publication many of the Brownings' friends sent Elizabeth messages of approval and described its sensational reception both in England and in America. "The advent of 'Aurora Leigh' can never be forgotten by any lover of poetry who was old enough at the time to read it," Swinburne later wrote. "Of one thing they may all be sure—they were right in the impression that they never had read, and never would read anything in any way comparable with that unique work of audaciously feminine and ambitiously impulsive genius. It is one of the longest poems in the world, and there is not a dead line in it."[2] A few weeks after the publication of Elizabeth's novel in verse, Leigh Hunt wrote Browning of his admiration for this "unique, wonderful and immortal poem; astonishing for its combination of masculine power with feminine tenderness; for its novelty, its facility, its incessant abundance of thought, and expression; its being an exponent of its age, and a prophetic teacher of it, its easy yet lofty triumph over every species of common place." Even Wordsworth, he maintained, "veritable poet as he is, is barren and prosaic by the side of the ever exuberant poetry of this book." In short, it was a production worthy of "the greatest poetess the world ever saw." [3] Bryan Waller Procter said to James T. Fields that *Aurora Leigh* was "the most successful book of the season . . . by far (a hundred times over) the finest poem ever written by a woman." [4] Within a few weeks after the publication of Elizabeth's poem, Ruskin wrote from Denmark Hill a wildly enthusiastic letter to Browning, in which he called *Aurora Leigh* the greatest poem in the English language, the finest poem which the nineteenth century had produced in any language, and "the first perfect poetical expression of the Age." Walter Savage Landor asserted in a letter to John Forster soon after the appearance of the volume that it had "the wild imagination of Shakespeare" and that he had no idea that any living writer could produce such poetry. "I am half drunk with it," he exclaimed. "Never did I think I should have a good hearty draught of poetry again." [5]

Among the Brownings' younger friends Robert Lytton was equally unstinting in his praise. He wrote in December from the Hague that the poem was "the perfectly successful expression of a whole civilization—that it is not only the solitary epic of this age, but also a noble epic—I almost think not inferior to those of Milton and Dante. . . . In some respects you are here, to my thinking, superior even to those greatest singers by just so much as this age is superior to theirs; for like them you have taken the whole age on your shoulders, this age of complicated sorrows, and scattered knowledge." [6] The members of the Pre-Raphaelite group were also generous in their estimates of the book. The sculptor Thomas Woolner wrote Browning that everyone in the literary circles of London was talking about the poem and that the first question of the day was, "Have you read *Aurora Leigh?*" Many people thought it a "very clever, oh, very clever, very clever book," and others found it "such a marvellous book" that it left them too dumbfounded to reply when they were asked for their opinions. "The truth is," Woolner added, "that such a flood of originality and inspiration as that book must take a long time before it can at all be fully appreciated . . ."[7] He felt "envious and malignant" to think that Elizabeth did not live in England. The Rossetti brothers were no less enthusiastic. William Michael declared that the volume was "stuffed and loaded with poetic beauty and passionate sympathy and insight."[8] Dante Gabriel called it "an astounding work, surely" and acknowledged that he had been in a rapture ever since reading it and could only say, "Oh, the wonder of it! and oh, the bore of writing about it."[9] Across the Atlantic Lydia Maria Child, novelist and author of many antislavery and religious tracts, wrote from her home in Wayland, Massachusetts, early in December 1856 to an American friend that she was delighted with Elizabeth's book, which seemed to her "full of strong things, and brilliant things, and beautiful things."[10]

To some readers and critics *Aurora Leigh* appeared to be shamefully immoral and to be couched in language too coarse for respectable women to read. The *Dublin University Magazine,* for example, asserted, "There is nothing that detracts so much from the pleasure which the perusal of this poem has given us, as this conviction, that the authoress has written a book which is almost a closed volume for her own sex."[11] Elizabeth could hardly conceal her delight in writing to Arabel[12] that she had been told of a woman sixty years old who believed that her morals had been injured by reading *Aurora Leigh* and that her character was in danger if it were known that she had looked at the book. George Barrett "swore" to Arabel that Elizabeth's poem was "worse than Don Juan" and "unfit for the reading of any *girl!*"[13] A number of elderly women complained that they had never felt pure after reading the volume. Stories reached Elizabeth "of women in England, who read it in secret, and sweep it from their drawing-room tables, lest a man should see it."[14] And she was assured by a friend (who may have exaggerated) that the "mamas of England" in a body refused to allow their daughters to look at the volume for fear of contamination. Many years earlier Elizabeth had said to Kenyon that she hoped to write a long poem some day like "Lady Geraldine's Courtship"—"a poem comprehending the aspect and manners of modern life, and flinching at nothing of the conventional." It was her treatment in *Aurora Leigh* of tabooed subjects, especially her references to prostitution in England and her consideration of the problem of the unmarried mother, which offended some of her more conservative readers.

The main theme of the poem, however, was not seduction but "the woman's question"—the difficulties which a gifted and cultured English woman inevitably encountered in the nineteenth century when she attempted to express herself beyond the narrow limits established by a society which both idolized and enslaved its women. Aurora Leigh, who is the heroine and chief companion of the reader of this long novel in verse, is in many respects Elizabeth Browning herself, even though Elizabeth assured Mrs. Jameson that "there is not a personal line, of course." She may have thought that she was presenting her material objectively, but both she and her heroine had much in common. Aurora spent many of her early years in a small English town, was precocious, had literary and intellectual interests with which her family was not in sympathy, published verse when she was a child, continued her career in London, spent some time in Paris, and went to live in Florence, where she found happiness in marriage. Throughout the poem Aurora thinks, talks, and acts much like Elizabeth herself at their corresponding ages; both the character and the poet who created her had many of the same interests and problems.

AURORA tells the story of her life in the first person. Her father was an Englishman who belonged to an old and distinguished Shropshire county family. In his later years he went to Florence, where he fell in love with and married a Florentine girl. Their only child, who was born in Florence, was called Aurora. (In choosing this name for her heroine, Elizabeth may have been unconsciously influenced by the example of the French writer she had worshiped for many years, Madame Dudevant, whose first name was Aurore.) When the child was only four years old, her mother died. Aurora and her father then moved from Florence to Pelago, a small village to the east of the city. There in the foothills of the Apennines they lived a quiet, idyllic life, with her father teaching her Greek and Latin and sharing with her his library, until he died when she was thirteen. Soon afterward she went to England to live with her father's sister in Shropshire. The sharply etched portrait of the aunt is one of the most successful descriptions in the poem. As she waited on the steps of her beautiful country house to greet Aurora,

> She stood straight and calm,
> Her somewhat narrow forehead braided tight
> As if for taming accidental thoughts
> From possible pulses; brown hair pricked with grey
> By frigid use of life (she was not old
> Although my father's elder by a year),
> A nose drawn sharply, yet in delicate lines;
> A close mild mouth, a little soured about
> The ends, through speaking unrequited loves
> Or peradventure niggardly half-truths;
> Eyes of no colour,—once they might have smiled,
> But never, never have forgot themselves
> In smiling; cheeks, in which was yet a rose
> Of perished summers, like a rose in a book,
> Kept more for ruth than pleasure,—if past bloom,
> Past fading also.
>   She had lived, we'll say,
> A harmless life, she called a virtuous life,
> A quiet life, which was not life at all
> (But that, she had not lived enough to know) . . .
> The poor-club exercised her Christian gifts
> Of knitting stockings, stitching petticoats,
> Because we are of one flesh after all
> And need one flannel (with a proper sense
> Of difference in the quality) . . .

Aurora felt as though she were a wild bird confined in a cage with her narrow-minded, conventional aunt. Outwardly the child was docile and quiet, and to please her aunt she learned the collects, the catechism, the creeds, and a smattering of French, German, mathematics, history, and geography. Because the aunt "liked accomplishments in girls," her niece took music and drawing lessons, danced the polka, became proficient in sewing, "Spun glass, stuffed birds, and modelled flowers in wax." Aurora suffered tortures during these years of her education and would have died, she said, if she had not been sustained by inner resources. She used to rise early to look at the dawn or (following the example of Elizabeth herself) to read a book she had been keeping under her pillow all night. The house in which she and her aunt lived was similar to the Hope End mansion in its natural setting. It was hidden away from the world in the midst of a beautiful private park. The countryside through which Aurora walked was much like the part of Herefordshire that Elizabeth knew as a girl:

> Hills, vales, woods, netted in a silver mist,
> Farms, granges, doubled up among the hills;
> And cattle grazing in the watered vales,
> And cottage-chimneys smoking from the woods,
> And cottage-gardens smelling everywhere,
> Confused with smell of orchards.

Aurora's private retreat was her small chamber with carpets, walls, and curtains all in green. Here she often sat and (like Elizabeth) read from her father's large library:

> Books, books, books!
> I had found the secret of a garret-room
> Piled high with cases in my father's name,
> Piled high, packed large,—where, creeping in and out
> Among the giant fossils of my past,
> Like some small nimble mouse between the ribs
> Of a mastodon, I nibbled here and there
> At this or that box . . .

She read all types of books but was especially drawn to the poets, and she published volumes of her own poetry, which she later realized, however, were "Mere lifeless imitations of live verse." Her aunt disapproved of her devotion to impractical subjects and kept reminding her of her household tasks, so that Aurora felt she was trying to grind her down and crush her into a conventional mold. Not far from the aunt's house, on the other side of a hill, was Leigh Hall, the home of Aurora's cousin Romney Leigh, who during his vacations from the university often used to visit Aurora and her aunt. To Aurora he seemed cold, shy, absent-minded, but tender when he wished to be. Whenever he came to her house, he had in one hand the gift of a basket of fruit and in the other a book of "mere statistics" on economics and social problems.

Early in the morning of Aurora's twentieth birthday, in June, she went for a walk in her aunt's garden, where Romney suddenly came upon her. He spoke with condescension about her poetry, which he thought was as well written as the works of most women authors. In spite of progress in many fields, he told her, serious economic and social problems remained unsolved; the gulf widened between the rich and the poor; the workers were exploited by employers; living conditions for many people were becoming worse; and so Romney's soul was "grey / With poring over the long sum of ill." He believed that the times were not propitious for making idle verses and that women, since they could never hope to write as well as men, should help mankind in more practical ways. Then he suddenly asked her to marry him, but he broached the matter so obscurely that Aurora could hardly have been blamed for failing at first to understand. He asked for her love and a life "in fellowship / Through bitter duties" and said that although women had little ability in art, they were "strong / For life and duty." It might well have appeared to Aurora that he was offering her a kind of alliance between them for the purpose of alleviating the social abuses of their age. He promised her they would go "hand in hand" and touch "These victims, one by one" and thus spend their lives among those who needed their help. Aurora replied that what Romney loved was not a woman but a cause, and what he desired was a helpmate rather than a wife. She too had her own work in life and maintained that art was nobler and higher than Romney's philanthropical endeavors, his plans "Of barley-feeding and material ease."

Aurora's rejection of Romney is reminiscent of Jane Eyre's refusal of St. John Rivers in Charlotte Brontë's novel, which Elizabeth had read and admired a few years before she began the composition of her epic poem. Rivers had asked Jane to marry him, to travel with him to India, and to be his fellow laborer in their missionary activities. But he said nothing about love, and

Jane realized that with his inflexible, despotic nature he would crush her individuality. Romney and St. John were alike in their idealistic aims, but Elizabeth's hero was in love with the girl to whom he proposed marriage, and he shyly told her of his love, though he placed more emphasis upon the idea of their service to mankind. Aurora's refusal was less plausible than Jane's. Although the heroine in the poem gave as her pretext for dismissing Romney that if she were to marry him she would not dare to call her soul her own, she was nevertheless subconsciously in love with him throughout the story. The decision proved to be the right one for Jane, but wrong for Aurora, who remained unhappy until she was finally aware of her mistake.

The aunt was very much displeased to hear that her niece had refused Romney and supposed that she was waiting for a more glamorous lover. She then explained to the girl the financial circumstances of the family. The house and lands now in the possession of the aunt and formerly the property of Aurora's father were to revert to Romney at the aunt's death because of a clause in the entail which excluded all children by foreign wives. Thus Aurora would inherit none of the estate. She also said that she had noticed how much Aurora had loved Romney, and the girl seemed to acknowledge the truth of her aunt's observation by blushing deeply.

A few hours after Romney's conversation with Aurora, he sent her a note in which he declared his love and promised that if she would marry him she would always have freedom for her literary pursuits. Aurora did not change her mind, and for six weeks she endured her aunt's cold, silent hostility. Then the aunt died suddenly and left to her niece all her invested funds, which had an annual income of £300. (Elizabeth too had inherited a modest fortune.) At the moment of her death the aunt had held in her hand a letter, of which the seal was still unbroken, from Romney giving her £30,000 from his own property. On the day of the funeral he told Aurora that in his opinion the sum he had mentioned in the letter rightfully belonged to her, since she had been willed all the aunt's money. Aurora, however, wished to accept nothing from Romney and in his sight impulsively tore up the document he had sent the aunt so that all proof of his generosity might be destroyed. Soon afterward she went to live in London, "the gathering-place of souls," while Romney, who was "elbow-deep / In social problems," devoted himself to his hospitals, his almshouses, and his infant schools.

The description of Aurora in her early years until her departure for London was based partly on Elizabeth's own life, but it also owes much to Madame de Staël's *Corinne,* one of Elizabeth's favorite novels, which she had read three times when she was living in Herefordshire. Like Aurora, the heroine in the novel was born in Italy. Her father was an English nobleman and her mother an Italian woman. When Corinne was still a child, her mother died, and after staying for a few years with her aunt in Florence, she was sent by her father to live in England with his second wife, Lady Edgermond, who was a cold, dignified, taciturn woman. Corinne's stepmother resented the child's Italian ways and advised her to adopt English manners. The girl was much attracted to the theater, music, literature, and art, but neither her stepmother nor her father—nor anyone else in the small town in Northumberland where they lived throughout the year—shared her interests, and so Corinne had to cultivate her talents alone in her chamber. Like Aurora's aunt, Lady Edgermond believed that it was wrong for Corinne to be so attached to the arts; women, she maintained, were supposed to be concerned only with their households. Because of the narrow, utilitarian point of view prevailing in her home and in the town, Corinne was most unhappy and always longed to return to Italy. Her stepmother had a favorite nephew, a country squire about thirty years old, who was rich, handsome, well born, and blameless in his morals. When he asked Corinne to marry him, she refused because of his conviction that a wife should confine herself to her domestic duties. She realized that her suitor was well meaning but unimaginative and that he had no understanding of her complicated nature and no sympathy with her intellectual and artistic pursuits. Lady Edgermond was angry with Corinne for rejecting the squire, and everyone in town blamed her for having declined such an apparently desirable offer. When Corinne was twenty, her father died, and a year later she entered into possession of her mother's fortune and also the money her father had left her. After six years she was as unhappy as when she had first arrived. Since she was financially independent, she did not have to remain in England with her foster family, and when a convenient opportunity came, she left suddenly for her native Italy with her maid, Thérésine, who all along had been as despondent as her mistress.

Unlike Madame de Staël's heroine, Aurora did not immediately escape to Italy but rented an apartment in Kensington. Despite her youth and innocence, within a year or two she had acquired in some unexplained way a national reputation as a writer and was receiving many flattering letters from her readers, from professional critics, from other authors, and now and then from men who offered to marry her. All day long, as she sat in her room and worked, she looked from her windows upon the chimney pots and slanting roofs upon which the sun struggled to shine through the fog. Or she saw

> Fog only, the great tawny weltering fog,
> Involve the passive city, strangle it
> Alive, and draw it off into the void,
> Spires, bridges, streets, and squares, as if a sponge
> Had wiped out London . . .

Although her health began to fail from overwork, she did not deviate from her high aims. "I ripped my verses up," she said (though many critics of *Aurora Leigh* felt that Elizabeth had never made much effort to revise her work), but she found no vitality in her writing. It seemed to her that her heart had never developed. "Being but poor," Aurora was constrained to write for a living with one hand while with the other she produced the poetry to which she had dedicated her life. She realized that "In England, no one lives by verse that lives" and therefore spent some of her time compiling articles for encyclopedias, magazines, and the weekly journals (somewhat like Elizabeth, who wrote a few book reviews and prose essays for the *Athenaeum*). Then when she had earned enough money to pay household bills, she returned to her "veritable work." (Elizabeth made her heroine worry too much about financial matters. In the middle of the nineteenth century a single person was able to live in pleasant circumstances, and with money to spare, on an annual income of £300 tax free.) Before long Aurora felt that her verse had improved so that it had life in it; "even its very tumours, warts, and wens" implied vitality.

It was after three years of this solitary existence in London that Aurora received an unannounced visit from a stranger who introduced herself as Lady Waldemar. She informed Aurora that she had news about Romney and would frankly tell her all she knew. Lady Waldemar said that she felt that she need have no modesty in speaking to Aurora, who was an artist and hence, in her ladyship's opinion, different from ordinary women, just as many a papist would never admit to her maid she wore a ribbon to attract a man's attention yet counted adulteries on her beads and felt no shame because the saints were far away. The image is an example of the coarseness of Lady Waldemar's language which pained some of Elizabeth's readers. Aurora's visitor confessed that she was in love with Romney and said that he was on the point of marrying a young girl of no family, wealth, or education, who lived in one of the most wretched slums of London. To please Romney, Lady Waldemar had taken an interest in "reports / Of wicked women and penitentiaries," had gone through the works of such socialistic writers as Fourier, Proudhon, Considérant, and Blanc, and had learned by heart Romney's speeches in the House of Commons on social problems. Yet despite her obvious efforts to attract his attention, he had taken no notice of her, except to commend her for her social conscience. Lady Waldemar's reason for having come to Aurora was to ask her to go to Romney and plead with him not to make such an unsuitable marriage. (It is incredible that an adventuress like Lady Waldemar would have thus confided her schemes and hopes to a stranger and a potential rival.) Aurora replied that even if she had the power she would not endeavor to break the match. Soon afterward she went to a dark, dilapidated tenement building in St. Margaret's Court to see Marian Erle, the girl who was to be Romney's wife. Marian was at home, greeted Aurora cordially, and told the story of her life.

In her narrative, which is a long interruption of the main plot, Marian said that she was born on the ledge of Malvern Hill (within sight of Elizabeth's childhood home) in a rude hut of mud and turf. Her father was a migrant worker who kept swine or picked hops, and when he had no employment he used to drink himself into insensibility. After he had spent all his money on gin, he ill-treated his wife, who thereupon revenged herself by beating their child. The girl grew up without any formal education except what she learned in Sunday school. There she became a friend of Rose Bell, a pretty and cheerful girl whose mother died when she was a baby. It was just last night, Marian told Aurora, that she saw Rose walking along Oxford Street as a prostitute.

Elizabeth knew that her frankness in calling attention to this social evil would cause great offense. Soon after the publication of her poem she explained that she had referred to the subject because her conscience would not allow her to ignore it even though convention forbade women from talking about such matters: "If a woman ignores these wrongs, then may women as a sex continue to suffer them; there is no help for any of us—let us be dumb and die."

To continue Marian's story—her father and mother took her on their trips when they tramped like gypsies around the west of England looking for seasonal jobs. She seemed to her parents a strange and sickly child, incapable either of working outside the home or of performing household duties. When her mother tried to force her to accept the advances of a lecherous landowner, she was so shocked and frightened that she ran away, never to see her parents again. She fled along the road until she fainted from exhaustion and was carried to a nearby hospital. When the time came for her to leave, she dreaded to go because she had no work in prospect and she knew of no one to whom she could turn for help. On the day before her scheduled departure, Romney happened to visit the wards and after speaking to all the patients asked her where she was going. On learning of her plight, he himself took her to London, where he found her a position as a seamstress. Marian told Aurora how she felt when Romney spoke to her in the hospital:

> And when he said "poor child," I shut my eyes
> To feel how tenderly his voice broke through,
> As the ointment-box broke on the Holy feet
> To let out the rich medicative nard.

(It is inconceivable that such language, which is a fair sample of Marian's speech, could be natural for an illiterate child who had been raised by brutal, intoxicated parents in the country, far from all civilizing influences.)

Marian worked faithfully for a year until she forfeited her position by going away to nurse a dying girl who had been a fellow worker. Just as the girl was in her final agony, Romney appeared as though by magic to comfort and help the family and was surprised to find Marian. After the funeral he astonished her by suddenly proposing marriage. He said nothing about love but asked her to work with him as his wife and suggested that since they came from the two extremes of the social classes, their marriage would thus be a protest against the wrongs inflicted upon the poor. Marian accepted his offer and promised that she would "Serve tenderly, and love obediently."

For the character of Marian Erle, Elizabeth may have been indebted to Eugène Sue's *Mystères de Paris,* which she had read for a second time in the winter of 1851–52. Perhaps the most attractive, if least credible, figure in Sue's novel is la Goualeuse, who is called Fleur-de-Marie (slang for "the virgin"). When only a baby, she had been abandoned by her mother, was later savagely beaten and tortured by her stepmother, and was raised in a home which was a cabaret or drinking shop of ill repute in one of the most degraded sections of Paris. All her associates were freed felons, thieves, assassins, and other members of the underworld. Yet in spite of her debased surroundings and depraved acquaintances she was of a sweet, innocent, angelic type. When she enters the story at the age of seventeen, she speaks like a highly educated woman, has elegant manners, refined literary and artistic tastes, and the morals of the purest nun. An equally fantastic character, le grand-duc de Gerolstein, who has adopted the pseudonym of M. Rodolphe, is often dressed in the garb of a French workman. Throughout the story he hastens from one part of Paris to another, engaged in a rapid succession of charitable acts for many people. At the beginning of the novel he rescues Fleur just as she is about to be roughly treated by a hideous-looking criminal who has escaped from the galleys. The eccentric and gallant nobleman soon afterward pays Fleur's stepmother an enormous sum of money, takes the girl away from the cabaret, and places her with a respectable family in a charming country estate far from the base influences which would have contaminated anyone but her.

Just as Marian Erle may have been modeled upon Sue's incredibly virtuous heroine, some of the characteristics of Romney Leigh may be traced to the energetic and noble M. Rodolphe. Both men give evidence of extraordinary good will and apparent omniscience as they effect a succession of miraculous rescues of persons who but for their timely interventions would have shortly been overwhelmed with misfortunes. Furthermore, neither expects nor receives any material reward for his many unselfish actions. Romney, who is a characteristically English counterpart of the very continental M. Rodolphe, is more bookish, austere, and shy. M. Rodolphe's forte is saving pretty, young women from being ruined by avaricious and lecherous men. He devotes less time to civic affairs than Romney, is more elegant in his costume and manners, more flexible in his personality, more gallant toward women, more ingenious in his schemes for the punishment of hypocrites and bullies, and much less intellectual and less concerned with social theories.

Nothing in the *Mystères de Paris* is so bizarre as the ensuing episode at the church in *Aurora Leigh*. "Half Saint Giles in frieze" was invited to meet "Saint James in cloth of gold," and after the ceremony everyone was to participate in a marriage feast on Hampstead Heath. From their shabby, noisome tenement houses in Pimlico the poor people swarmed into the church. Many were lame, blind, and ill, and most were clothed in soiled, patched garments. Their faces were so degenerate in appearance that they could not have had "A finger-touch of God left whole on them."

> 'twas as if you had stirred up hell
> To heave its lowest dreg-fiends uppermost
> In fiery swirls of slime . . .

Elizabeth had almost no first-hand knowledge of the working classes of England, but however desperate their condition in the middle of the nineteenth century, only a person with the wildest imagination would have used this image to describe them. When the ladies from Mayfair became aware of the ill-dressed, foul-smelling rabble on the other side of the main aisle, some stood up in the pews, some were pale with fear, and others flushed with anger. They exchanged gossip while they were waiting for the bride; a few lines from their conversation will show the unfitness of blank verse for such trivial talk:

> —"Yes, really, if we need to wait in church
> We need to talk there."—"She? 'tis Lady Ayr,
> In blue—not purple! that's the dowager."
> —"She looks as young"—"She flirts as young, you mean.
> Why if you had seen her upon Thursday night,
> You'd call Miss Norris modest."—"*You* again!
> I waltzed with you three hours back. Up at six,
> Up still at ten; scarce time to change one's shoes:
> I feel as white and sulky as a ghost,
> So pray don't speak to me, Lord Belcher."—"No,
> I'll look at you instead, and it's enough
> While you have that face."—"In church, my lord! fie, fie!"

After everyone had been kept waiting for several hours, Romney stood on the altar stairs clutching a letter in one hand and announced that there would be no marriage ceremony, for he had just learned that Marian had left him. Then a man from the Saint Giles part of the congregation broke the silence by shouting to his friends to be on their guard lest they be cheated of their promised food and drink. The crowd shouted, "We'll have our rights. / We'll have the girl, the girl!" Men cried for the police, and women swooned or tried to escape from the building, but many fell and were trodden under foot. When some of the disgruntled crowd from Pimlico rushed toward Romney, Aurora struggled to save him but was overcome. The last words she heard before she fainted were, "Pull him down! / Strike—kill him!" She was carried from the melee by a friend of hers, Lord Howe, who afterward showed her Marian's letter to Romney. Even though the intended bride was supposed to have great difficulty with penmanship and spelling, she wrote a letter of ninety-five lines in the euphuistic style she had acquired from Romney, conveying little specific information about herself except that she still loved him but had gone far away, never to return, since she could not be happy as his wife. Romney searched everywhere but could discover no clue. Aurora unaccountably failed to tell her cousin about Lady Waldemar's efforts to prevent the marriage from taking place; had Aurora revealed what she knew, she would have helped Romney to find the girl and would have saved him from being duped in the future by the hypocritical Lady Waldemar.

After an interval of two years, during which Aurora had continued her literary career in London, she expressed in a long passage her views on many of the problems which had been troubling her. As she recalled her published verse, she felt that much of her early poetry was merely a series of surface pictures which were pretty but without significance. With the hope of coming closer to life, she was now writing a long poem dealing with her own times (like *Aurora Leigh* itself), for she was convinced that the present age was worthy of an epic. Most poets and thinkers believed, mistakenly, in Aurora's opinion that the middle of the nineteenth century was

> A pewter age,—mixed metal, silver-washed;
> An age of scum, spooned off the richer past,
> An age of patches for old gaberdines,
> An age of mere transition, meaning nought
> Except that what succeeds must shame it quite
> If God please.

On the contrary, it seemed to Aurora that every age appeared unheroic to those who lived in it. She distrusted the writer who, finding no inspiration in his own times, took his material from romantic legends of the Middle Ages. Thus her own poem did not deal with the period of Charlemagne, but with

> this live, throbbing age,
> That brawls, cheats, maddens, calculates, aspires,
> And spends more passion, more heroic heat,

> Betwixt the mirrors of its drawing-rooms,
> Than Roland with his knights at Roncesvalles.

Aurora then said that she had dedicated herself to her art with the utmost seriousness (as Elizabeth often maintained, in prefaces and letters, about her own poetry) and would not allow herself to be influenced either by the critics or by the public. As for her medium of expression, she had determined to write no stage plays because in her opinion (which was also Elizabeth's) the drama of the present age pandered to the lowest tastes of the public.

Aurora's ever-present solitude depressed her. She reflected sadly that while her books were being enjoyed in family circles and by lovers, her own life was a blank. Other artists had sympathetic, affectionate husbands, wives, or parents, but she herself had no close human ties. Of all the people with whom she had been intimate, she felt that only her father had understood her, and they had long been separated by death. But she knew a number of people, "veracious, nowise mad," who had testified that the souls of the dead communicated with the living, and so Aurora resented the attitude of some whose skepticism prevented communion with the unseen world. (Thus Elizabeth introduced the topic of spiritualism, which had obsessed her during the years when she was composing her long poem.)

One evening Aurora went to a reception at the home of her friend Lord Howe, where she heard about the most recent undertaking of Romney Leigh, who was called by one of the guests "a Christian socialist." He had turned Leigh Hall into a phalanstery inspired partly by the *phalanges* suggested by Fourier and partly by the ideas of the Christian Socialists of England. Aurora also learned that Lady Waldemar would soon marry Romney and that she had spent several days at Leigh Hall,

> And milked the cows, and churned, and pressed the curd,
> And said "my sister" to the lowest drab
> Of all the assembled castaways; such girls!
> Aye, sided with them at the washing-tub— . . .

The picture of a horde of undisciplined, uneducated female waifs swarming about the valuable furniture, books, and art galleries of Leigh Hall was a burlesque of both French and English socialism. At about the time Elizabeth was planning her modern epic, she wrote to a friend that although many socialists were pure, noble, disinterested, and benevolent, they still held in their hands "ideas that kill, ideas which defile, ideas which, if carried out, would be the worst and most crushing kind of despotism." If she might choose her *pis aller,* she would rather live "under the feet of the Czar than in those states of perfectibility imagined by Fourier and Cabet." Her chief objection to the French socialists was that they wished to eliminate "antagonism," as she described it, which seemed to her necessary to all progress.

But it was precisely because of laissez-faire principles of economics that the majority of the workers had failed to benefit from the industrial revolution, the success of which had been due partly to their own efforts. Fourier believed that most of the people were swindled by a few powerful, wealthy, and monopolistic corporations and that the workers by competing with one another for jobs received a steadily diminishing proportion of the products of society. In place of competition he proposed to substitute cooperation and advocated a new system which, he thought, would allow a fuller expression of human impulses. According to his plan, society was to be divided into self-sufficient economic units called *phalanges,* each having about sixteen hundred persons, who were to be allowed to devote themselves to any occupations they found congenial.

Among the leading Christian Socialists in England, both Charles Kingsley and Frederick Denison Maurice were broad churchmen who had a desire not to destroy the present social system and build anew but rather to eliminate some of its inequalities and harsh features which they considered inconsistent with Christian principles. They were successful in extending education to women and to laboring men and used their influence to improve living conditions of the workers and to establish cooperative societies and working men's associations. Why was the author of *Aurora Leigh* indifferent, even hostile, to the progressive social thought of her age when she was so largehearted and idealistic in many other respects? The answer may be that she was fearful that a socialistic state would crush the human spirit, that literature and the arts would shrivel away to make room for a world of soulless technicians.

AFTER Aurora returned from Lord Howe's reception to her apartment, she thought about Lady Waldemar's engagement to Romney and was pained that her cousin should have been trapped by such a coarse, unprincipled woman. Aurora now decided to make her home in Italy and to leave as soon as possible. The reasons why she had not gone there years earlier when she received her inheritance, or why she chose to go at this time are not made clear. She merely said, "And now, my Italy."

Her first stop was the French capital, which seemed to her (as it had to Elizabeth when she first saw it) a beautiful city in comparison with the one she had left. Lost in thought, she went up and down

> the terraced streets,
> The glittering boulevards, the white colonnades
> Of fair fantastic Paris who wears trees
> Like plumes, as if man made them, spire and tower
> As if they had grown by nature, tossing up
> Her fountains in the sunshine of the squares . . .

Aurora (like Elizabeth herself) glorified the new French emperor and was irritated at anyone who maintained that he was an undemocratic ruler:

> —this Caesar represents, not reigns,
> And is no despot, though twice absolute:
> This Head has all the people for a heart;
> This purple's lined with the democracy . . .

Once when Aurora was walking along the boulevards, absorbed in her reflections upon art and life, she caught sight of Marian Erle, but by the time Aurora had emerged from her trance, the girl had disappeared. Later, when Aurora was about to write Romney that she had seen Marian, she suddenly recalled that the girl had been carrying a baby. What right, Aurora asked herself, had such a "castaway" to take a child in her arms? She feared that Marian was defiled and had "damned" herself. For several weeks Aurora searched everywhere in Paris but discovered no trace of her. By chance she recognized Marian one morning and immediately spoke to her. Although at first the girl seemed timid and suspicious, she was soon convinced of Aurora's good will and offered to take her home. They then walked to a dreary suburb and into Marian's tiny, bare room. Just as Aurora had suspected, in front of her was the tangible evidence of Marian's guilt:

> There he lay upon his back,
> The yearling creature, warm and moist with life
> To the bottom of his dimples,—to the ends
> Of the lovely tumbled curls about his face . . .

Aurora wondered how such an innocent-looking baby could be the symbol of Marian's degradation. She was shocked at the way Marian fondled the child with no display of shame and sternly reproved her for touching the baby with unclean palms. Aurora, who had often been out of sympathy with many people because of their "conventional" attitudes, was now horrified that Marian had apparently been unconventional in her love. She harshly called her a thief for having given birth to a child in defiance of Christian principles and of the laws of the state and reminded her that in the years to come her son would consider himself an orphan and would keenly feel the lack of an honorable home and of "a pure good mother's name." Marian was so agitated at hearing herself described as a thief that she picked up the baby, burst into tears, and was seized with uncontrollable spasms of sobbing. In spite of having thus upset both Marian and the baby, Aurora believed that the girl had not yet shown sufficient penitence. She continued to lecture Marian, declaring that it was very wrong for her to have left the pure and noble Romney in order to accept the hand of a seducer. Marian, who by now had reached the limit of her endurance, told Aurora that her accusations were unfounded. She explained that she had not been seduced but "murdered" and then related the story of her life from the time of her engagement to Romney.

At first she had been very happy, but Lady Waldemar called on her and persuaded her that the gulf between Romney and her was so great that they could never be a compatible couple and that Romney's marriage to her would draw upon him the jibes of his friends, all of which would make him suffer. Almost every day Lady Waldemar came to Marian's room with the intention of destroying the girl's faith in herself. Then the lady confessed that she was in love with Romney and said that he returned her affection and that Marian stood between them. Since Romney was an honorable man, Lady Waldemar told the girl, he would make Marian his wife without ever hinting of his preference. Finally she asked Marian to say nothing about her visits. For the girl to have believed everything she was told, to have remained silent to Romney about the conspiracy, and then to have consented tamely to be spirited out of England in the company of a woman about whom she knew nothing are all as implausible as any of the episodes in Sue or Dumas. The woman who was to conduct Marian to Australia, one of Lady Waldemar's former waiting-maids, is a stock figure in novels of seduction. She took the money Lady Waldemar had sent her for Marian's expenses and made the girl disembark in France, where she was placed in a brothel, given a "damnable drugged cup," and then raped. The seasickness from which Marian suffered does not fully explain why she left the ship without raising an alarm; she surely could not have supposed she had come to the end of the voyage. The episode of giving the victim a drug before sexually abusing her may have been taken from Sue's *Mystères de Paris*. Louise Morel was put under the influence of a drug and raped by the notary Jacques Ferrand. Like Marian, she conceived a child, but the baby died of exposure to cold soon after birth. Marian, on the day following the terrible event, was "Half gibbering and half raving on the floor," and for weeks afterward she was utterly mad and wandered through the countryside, receiving food and shelter from charitable peasants. Later her son was born, she found a job as a seamstress, and since then she had been eking out a meager life by working all day long and half the night.

When Aurora returned to her apartment that morning, she had Marian and her baby come with her to spend the rest of the day, and she generously made arrangements to take mother and child to Italy. The next day the three of them were on the train for Marseilles, where they went on board a ship bound for Genoa.

(This was the route Elizabeth had taken when she first went to Italy.) All that night, while Marian slept, Aurora sat on deck, too excited to stay below, and looked at the mountains along the shore of France and of her beloved Italy:

> Peak pushing peak
> They stood: I watched, beyond that Tyrian belt
> Of intense sea betwixt them and the ship,
> Down all their sides the misty olive-woods
> Dissolving in the weak congenial moon
> And still disclosing some brown convent-tower
> That seems as if it grew from some brown rock,
> Or many a little lighted village, dropt
> Like a fallen star upon so high a point,
> You wonder what can keep it in its place
> From sliding headlong with the waterfalls
> Which powder all the myrtle and orange groves
> With spray of silver.

At dawn the ship entered the harbor of Genoa; as Aurora saw the long, gray Andrea Doria Palace ahead of her, she was thankful to have returned to her Italy. They went immediately to Florence and settled in a large, beautiful villa, which was similar in its setting to the homes of the Brownings' friends Robert Lytton and Isa Blagden:

> I found a house at Florence on the hill
> Of Bellosguardo. 'Tis a tower which keeps
> A post of double-observation o'er
> That valley of Arno (holding as a hand
> The outspread city) straight toward Fiesole
> And Mount Morello and the setting sun,
> The Vallombrosan mountains opposite,
> Which sunrise fills as full as crystal cups
> Turned red to the brim because their wine is red.

Beyond the outer walls of her garden an olive orchard covered the hill sloping sharply downward to a line of cypresses which shaded the road toward the center of Florence:

> Beautiful
> The city lies along the ample vale,
> Cathedral, tower and palace, piazza and street,
> The river trailing like a silver cord
> Through all, and curling loosely, both before
> And after, over the whole stretch of land
> Sown whitely up and down its opposite slopes
> With farms and villas.

For many weeks Aurora received no news from England, and then she had a letter from her friend Vincent Carrington, the painter, who congratulated her on the success of her recent book and expressed his own approval, even though it had been written by a woman. Romney Leigh, he reported, had been ill with fever, and he added that as an old friend of both of them he had always supposed that one day Aurora and her cousin would marry each other, though Carrington was disappointed that her removal to Italy made that event less probable. In thinking about this letter, Aurora felt ever more dissatisfied with herself. It seemed to her that her books had succeeded, but not her life. She realized that she was in love with Romney and that years ago she had been very foolish to have rejected him.

Like Tennyson's Lady of Shalott, Aurora had a sense of futility from her solitary existence and her excessive devotion to art. The merely spiritual, she had come to feel, was insufficient; she longed to share her life with another's and to participate in the affairs of the community. Meanwhile she was absorbed in her contemplation and her writing and stayed aloof from everyone in Florence except for the members of her household. In the evenings she wandered by herself to the Ponte Vecchio to see the sunset along the Arno, to have an ice at Doney's café, where she listened to the animated conversation about her, and afterward to enter some church. In the Santissima Annunziata she once saw an English friend of hers, Sir Blaise Delorme, who half bowed to acknowledge her smile, but they did not speak. Somehow the encounter so disturbed her that afterward she mostly remained at home, wrapped in her thoughts and unable either to read or to write.

ONE EVENING as she thus sat alone on the terrace of her villa, she was half aware that the cathedral bell had struck ten and that the gas lamps were flooding the Piazza Pitti with light and outlining the quays along both sides of the river. Then she sensed that Romney was standing in front of her. In great surprise she said to him, "You, Romney!—Lady Waldemar is here?" Within the past few months Romney's phalanstery had burned down, he had become stone blind, and Lady Waldemar had left him. He had written of these events in a letter which he sent to Aurora by Sir Blaise Delorme, but since she had never received it, she was ignorant of her cousin's misfortunes. When he began to speak to Aurora, he said nothing of what had happened to him, supposing that she had already learned from his communication. Elizabeth makes great demands upon the reader's patience as she prolongs the conversation between Romney and Aurora, during much of which the heroine of the poem assumes that Lady Waldemar is Romney's wife. A straightforward explanation from Romney when he first appeared would have eliminated the need for the long, wearisome passage of ambiguous talk which follows, but it would probably not have shortened the discourse of two such articulate persons who here even more than elsewhere in the poem are not living characters but mouthpieces for the expression of many of the author's ideas. All the while the reader is confident that in such a romantic story Romney will reveal everything before he leaves and that they will then declare their passion for each other.

Although Aurora had asked about Lady Waldemar, Romney did not speak of her except to say that he would later show his cousin the note her ladyship had written her. When she asked him to sit down beside her on the terrace, he placed himself in the chair "a little slowly" as though he were in doubt; but Aurora could not have guessed the nature of his infirmity from this hesitation. Instead of saying that he was blind, he spoke mysteriously of the "night" and the stars shining on his "dark." He then acknowledged that he had been wrong in ministering too exclusively to the material needs of man. The world had seemed to him one great mouth which needed to be fed. He had not stopped to ask himself why rich men who wished only for creature comforts to satisfy their bodily needs gave money to eighty thousand prostitutes in England—the second reference in the poem to this subject.

Aurora replied that she too had failed and that on her birthday when she and Romney had been together in Shropshire she should have been less arrogant. Yet she believed that she had always been right in maintaining that it was impossible "To get at men excepting through their souls" and that poets came closer to the souls of men and women than economists. But they had both been wrong, she added, for they had left too small a part for God; Romney had been too much absorbed in his philanthropic activities and she in her literary career.

After a number of long platitudinous speeches, with confessions of failure from each of the interlocutors, Romney told of the destruction of Leigh Hall. His socialistic experiment, he admitted, had been a failure from the beginning. The inmates of the phalanstery, who had led disordered lives before they came to him, cursed him for imposing moral restraints. His neighbors threw stones at his windows, shot at him, and finally set fire to his mansion. The spacious and magnificent art galleries burnt down with the loss of all but one of the Van Dyck portraits. When Romney was carrying that painting from the blazing house, he was struck on the forehead by a beam which had been hurled at him. By a malicious turn of fate the blow came from the father of the girl he had befriended, William Erle, whom he had rescued from a shiftless, brutal existence and had taken into his phalanstery. In his account of the catastrophe Romney made no mention of his becoming blind, but soon after the loss of his house the optic nerve had wasted away because of some mysterious nervous disorder, although outwardly the eyes appeared undamaged.

Aurora felt that he was appealing for sympathy, but that she had no right to respond with too much warmth. She said to herself in her overemphatic idiom, "A woman stood between his soul and mine." In the course of the conversation Aurora believed that Romney was mocking her by using expressions too affectionate to come with propriety from the husband of Lady Waldemar, and she politely requested him to leave. She wished him happiness in his marriage and bade him farewell, saying that they would probably not see each other again, for it would not be right for her to greet Lady Waldemar, the new mistress of Romney's household, with outstretched hands "still warm and thrilling" from Marian's clasp. The mention of her ladyship's name so startled Romney that he exclaimed that no one had wronged his soul so much as Aurora by thus calling Lady Waldemar his wife. He then gave Aurora Lady Waldemar's letter, in which she attempted to explain that in all her actions she had meant well. Lady Waldemar wrote that when she finally realized that she could never hope to gain Romney's affection, she had left him, vowing henceforth to admit "No socialist within three crinolines."

At first Aurora was so dazed by what she had learned that she could not speak. Then Romney said that in the eyes of God Marian Erle was his wife. At the mention of her name the girl herself conveniently appeared on the terrace and cried out, "My great good angel, Romney." He had come to Florence to see Aurora, not Marian, but he loyally promised that he would forthwith marry the girl who had deserted him at the wedding ceremony. Marian knew that he would suffer for this quixotic gesture, that his acquaintances would "ever twit him with his bastard child / And married harlot." Then Marian made an incredible request; she asked Aurora to give her opinion whether she should accept Romney's generous proposal and said that she would be bound by Aurora's decision. But although Aurora without hesitation advised her to marry him, Marian surprised them both by telling them that she could not think of Romney as a husband. She felt that she was emotionally dead, that she no longer loved him—if indeed she ever had—and that there was no room in her life for another lover. All her affection was concentrated upon her child, and she did not wish to have another baby, whose position would be more secure than that of her first child. After her boy had grown up, she planned to devote herself to good works and to help everyone who needed her aid.

In Marian's rejection of marriage and her hope that some day she would be a comfort to widows and orphans, Elizabeth was perhaps indebted to Eugène Sue for a similar episode in his *Mystères de Paris*. The heroine, Fleur-de-Marie, was discovered by her father, le grand-duc de Gerolstein, many years after he had lost her as a baby. At the end of the novel she is no longer a poor and homeless waif, but with her name changed to la princesse Amélie she is living at her father's home in luxurious circumstances. She uses her influence to found an establishment for orphans and abandoned girls and spends much of her time there. With the recollection of the degrading background of her youth, she rejects an offer of marriage from a respectable and accomplished prince because she will not, in her words, profane the sacred name of mother. In addition to Sue's novel, Elizabeth may also have drawn upon Mrs. Gaskell's *Ruth,* which she had read in 1853. She had found it a powerful and penetrating book and had approved Mrs. Gaskell's courageous treatment of a subject which shocked many readers: the problem of the unmarried mother. Elizabeth, however, was sorry that Mrs. Gaskell had her heroine die at the end of the novel but acknowledged that if she had not, the English reading public would have been outraged. Ruth is a girl with the almost saintly characteristics of unusual purity, innocence, innate refinement, forbearance, and every other imaginable virtue. She is callously tricked into a brief liaison with a wealthy young man who has none of her fine qualities and soon afterward abandons her. Then she gives birth to a son and is taken into the home of a kindly clergyman and his sister, both of whom risk the disapproval of the community for their generous act. Ruth never again falls in love, devotes her life to her child, and despite her equivocal position in her small town is respected by almost everyone for her courtesy, her simple way of life, her industriousness, and her high Christian principles. Marian Erle's character and situation are somewhat similar to those of Ruth, except that at the end of the story Marian does not die of the plague while nursing her seducer. Thus Elizabeth was more daring than Mrs. Gaskell in her portrait of the woman who had been led astray and oppressed. But Aurora's reprimands to Marian when she saw she had a baby with no visible father make it clear that Elizabeth would have little patience with a woman who enjoyed an illicit love affair. Indeed one recalls her displeasure after learning of Wilson's first pregnancy.

After Marian left, Romney said to Aurora that the girl's instincts were holy, that she had no further need of him, and that for the rest of her life the angels of heaven would be sufficient for her "To fight the rats of our society." Just as he was preparing to go, he told her that he lost his eyesight. Although Aurora's pride as a woman would have prevented her from expressing her love to Romney if he had not been blind, she could not restrain herself from blurting out, "I love,— / I love you, Romney." (For the details of the burning of the house, the beam falling on the hero's forehead, and his subsequent blindness, Elizabeth may have been indebted to *Jane Eyre,* although soon after the publication of *Aurora Leigh* she wrote Mrs. Martin that in spite of the apparent similarities between her poem and Miss Brontë's work, the circumstances of Romney's loss of eyesight were different from those in the novel.) Romney then assured Aurora that he had always loved her from the time when he had first seen her as a girl fresh from Italy and that after she had refused to be his wife, he had immersed himself in his career of public service and private philanthropy in a desperate effort to fill the emptiness of his life —though earlier in the story he had been portrayed as a rather cold and priggish youth.

Near the end of the poem he expressed his doctrine of work and love and his faith in the new order of things which Aurora and he would help bring into being. "It is the hour for souls," he declared to Aurora and suggested that in some mysterious way their two souls should climb upward, taking with them the souls of everyone on earth, until they all reached "some purer eminence" than anything mankind had hitherto seen. With unclouded optimism he prophesied the coming of a new age in which the human race would have purged itself of its lower desires, a new society from which all falsehoods had been excluded, new churches, new and more equitable economic systems, and laws granting new freedoms. And so Elizabeth concluded her long poem in this apocalyptic strain, far above the unruly passions of living men and women. Had she written a sequel, its theme would have been the founding of the new Jerusalem.

IN COMPARISON with the letters of praise and congratulations the Brownings received from many of their friends, the reviews of Elizabeth's most popular work were generally unfavorable.

They said that a poem which had such a broad scope and was longer than *Paradise Lost* or the *Aeneid* and almost as long as the *Odyssey* would rank as the greatest literary production of the century if it did not have serious shortcomings. To be sure, they were mostly agreed that in writing the book Elizabeth had been very much in earnest, that she had an abundance of ideas and a certain masculine vigor of intellect, that her sympathies were broad and generous, and that many of her descriptions of the countryside and of cities and the portraits of her characters were well done. Yet the notices in the more influential periodicals were unanimous in their opinion that the defects in the poem far outweighed its merits. They asserted that it was too hastily and carelessly written, that it was far too long, that it was lacking in dramatic appeal, that the characters were poorly conceived, that the incidents in the story were hackneyed, implausible, and many of them unnecessarily coarse and revolting to good taste, that the flow of the narrative was interrupted and the reader's attention distracted by an overemphasis of trivial and secondary material and by a profusion of glittering and discordant imagery, that in expressing her "highest convictions upon Life and Art" she was inconsistent and obscure, and that for most of the material of the book verse was an inappropriate medium.

A typical notice in the *Saturday Review* harshly condemned the poem for many reasons: "The characters are few and unreal—the incidents, though scanty, are almost inconceivable—and the heroine and autobiographer, as a professed poetess, has tastes and occupations which are, beyond all others, incapable of poetic treatment." The writer thought that the practical details of authorship were not a suitable subject for an epic poem. He also objected to the sex of the author and maintained with masculine pride that women had never known how to write poetry, thus nicely illustrating one of the main themes of the poem: "The negative experience of centuries seems to prove that a woman cannot be a great poet. Those who are curious in intellectual physiology may find, in *Aurora Leigh,* some materials for the explanation of feminine misadventures in art." [15]

The article in the *Athenaeum* was characteristic of most reviews in their bewilderment at the strange mixture of refinement and coarseness, of the poetical and the prosaic. "The huge mistake of its plan," the review concluded, "the disdain of selectness in its details, could not be exhausted were we to write for column and column,—nor would page on page suffice to contain the high thoughts, the deep feelings, the fantastic images showered over the tale with the authority of a prophetess, the grace of a muse, the prodigality of a queen." [16]

It was the consensus of the critical notices that the poem was not a finished epic but an amorphous, chaotic mass of material which needed a master's touch to compress it to one-half or one-fourth of its present length and shape it into an artistic form. For example, the *Spectator* wrote that to organize all the elements of the work "into a poem of which each part should grow from the expanding life of the central idea, and be necessary to the completeness of the whole . . . would require a more patient endurance of intellectual toil, a more resolute hand upon the reins, more thought, more pains, less self-indulgence in composition, less wilfulness." The critic added that the poet's honest treatment of social and intellectual problems and her sensitive descriptions of persons and places made her book interesting and showed that she had unusual talents, but that in spite of her many fine qualities she had not written a great poem. A work of art, he thought, was quite different from "the finest discursive talk." [17]

Many reviews said that the discussions on art and life and some of the narrative and descriptive elements should have been presented in the form of a novel in prose. *Blackwood's*, for instance, disagreed with Elizabeth's doctrine that poets should deal with the great issues of their own age. The reviewer maintained that art should ennoble and purify the materials which it treated rather than present an unselective, photographic reproduction of the trivial and sordid aspects of life. To illustrate the unfitness of the verse as a vehicle for conveying everyday conversation in Mayfair circles, it quoted a passage from the description of the party at Lord Howe's, as though it were prose. The poet had dislocated the joints of the following lines to make them sound like blank verse: "We are sad to-night, I saw (—Good night, Sir Blaise! ah, Smith—he has slipped away), I saw you across the room, and stayed, Miss Leigh, to keep a crowd of lion-hunters off, with faces toward your jungle. There were three; a spacious lady, five feet ten and fat, who has the devil in her (and there's room), for walking to and fro upon the earth, from Chipewa to China; she requires your autograph upon a tinted leaf 'twixt Queen Pomare's and Emperor Soulouque's." The reviewer thought that these lines were neither prose nor poetry and "would not pass muster even in a third-rate novel." [18]

As for the characters in the poem, the critical notices mostly said that they were no more than puppets which represented different sets of ideas. The characters did not act upon one another, and none of them developed as an individual in the course of the story. In the words of the *Spectator,* "the writer never conceived them from beginning to end of their careers in one coherent effort of imagination." Aurora at thirty was no different from what she had been at twenty, and Marian Erle was "a statue of heroic goodness, out of whom circumstances bring the varying expressions of that goodness, but who can scarcely be said to change, to learn anything, to develop powers or virtues though she manifests them." Elizabeth made all her personages speak alike and often in a euphuistic manner. The literary and somewhat aloof spinster, the aristocratic philanthropist, the fashionable lady of the world, the girl of the streets—all talked as though they had an equally high degree of intellectual culture.

Even though Aurora told her own story, the author of the notice in the *National Review* felt that he did not know her personally and was unable to pierce beyond one or two of her characteristics. She existed only to give voice to the author's convictions and doubts. The critic believed that Elizabeth's total lack of dramatic power, her inability to speak from a point of view not her own, stemmed from her long isolation: "It is from the strength of her own soul, the resources of her own intellect, and the riches of her own heart, that she writes. She gives no voice to the world around her." [19]

Almost none of the reviews considered Aurora an attractive character. For example, the *Blackwood's* reviewer wrote, "After making the most liberal allowance for pride, and fanaticism for art, and inflexible independence, she is incongruous and contradictory both in her sentiments and in her actions. She is not a genuine woman; one half of her heart seems bounding with the beat of humanity, while the other half is ossified." The reviewer for the Dublin *Tablet* was repelled by the heroine of the poem, thought her ridiculous and unbearably tedious, and indeed could find no redeeming qualities: "The *femme incomprise,* the artist-workwoman, the high-souled female with 'a mission,' is a terrible companion in a journey of twelve thousand lines. [The reviewer overestimated the length by about one thousand lines.] . . . Miss Aurora Leigh is a bad specimen even of her very unattractive class." [20] The *Dublin University Magazine* observed that throughout the thoughts and feelings to which she gave expression there ran "a jealous and morbid sense of the misappreciation of woman by man." [21]

The character of Romney also filled the majority of reviewers with repugnance. The writer of the notice in the *Dublin University Magazine* disliked him even more than the heroine and believed that he was "exaggerated and unnatural; weak and almost silly at times; impractical in his schemes of social regeneration, and absurd in his theories; a modern Quixote, more mad than the errant knight who assailed windmills and slaughtered sheep; and with all this is mixed a nobility of nature and a grandeur of sentiment that make him as a whole, a moral monster." The *Blackwood's* critic was also out of patience with him: "Though honourable and generous, he is such a very decided noodle that we grudge him his prominence in the poem, do not feel much sympathy for his misfortunes, and cannot help wondering that Aurora should have entertained one spark of affection for so deplorable a milksop. Excess of enthusiasm we can allow; and folly, affecting to talk the words of wisdom, meets us at every turning: but Romney is a walking hyperbole."

Of the two other principal characters the reviews considered Lady Waldemar revolting in her conduct and unnecessarily coarse in her language; Marian Erle, on the other hand, they thought the most attractive figure in the poem. In contrast to the self-centered, inflexible Aurora, she seemed unselfish, spontaneous, and feminine, and her pathetic story appealed to all of Elizabeth's readers. In the opinion of the reviewers, however, Marian's thoughts and language were hardly characteristic of a girl reared in poverty and ignorance.

Elizabeth's style both in the dialogue of the characters and in the narrative and reflective passages was spoiled by excessive imagery, much of which was in deplorable taste. She was strangely insensitive to the demands of her material and treated a passionate love scene no differently from passages of ordinary conversation or narrative. Everything was made to glitter with blazing metaphors and similes, which both puzzled and distracted the reader. Like almost all the other journals, the *Westminster Review* commented on her want of taste: "By a single ugly phrase, a single hideous word, dragged in, one would think, from the furthest ends of the earth, she every now and then mars the harmony of a whole page of beauty. She sadly wants simplicity, and the calm strength that flows from it. She writes in a high fever. She is constantly introducing geographical, geological, and antiquarian references, almost always out of place, and often incorrect." [22] In the opinion of many reviews her overwrought style was due to her intense intellectual activity; her mind jumped from one idea to another in short, nervous movements so that she often lost sight of her unifying theme. As an example of her jarring metaphors, the *National Review* cited the following lines, which expressed the poet's responsibility to write about his own times:

>   Never flinch,
>   But still, unscrupulously epic, catch
>   Upon the burning lava of a song
>   The full-veined, heaving, double-breasted Age:
>   That, when the next shall come, the men of that
>   May touch the impress with reverent hand, and say
>   "Behold,—behold the paps we all have sucked!"

The almost savage comparison of burning lava to a woman's breasts gave the reviewer exquisite pain to read. As an illustration of the poet's distracting the reader by carrying the image one step too far, the article quoted the verses in which Aurora speaks of her father's Elzevirs with their faded notes:

>   *conferenda haec cum his—*
>   *Corruptè citat—lege potiùs,*
>   And so on, in the scholar's regal way

> Of giving judgement on the parts of speech,
> As if he sate on all twelve thrones up-piled,
> Arraigning Israel.

The simple word "regal" would have sufficed.

According to most of the reviews the plot was as absurd as the language employed by the characters. Although Aurora's life was devoid of outward action, the poem as a whole had many incidents, most of them so startling, as the *Spectator* wrote, "that they might serve for the plot of a Victorian melodrama." *Blackwood's* also commented that in constructing her plot the author had made no effort to give it an air of probability: "It is fantastic, unnatural, exaggerated; and all the worse, because it professes to be a tale of our own times. . . . Mrs. Browning has been perpetrating, in essentials, an extravaganza or caricature, instead of giving to the public a real lifelike picture; for who can accept, as truthful representation, Romney's proposal of marriage to an ignorant uneducated girl whom he does not love . . . ?"

I might add that the episodes, characters, and paraphernalia of the poem are typically mid-Victorian. With its strong-minded, intellectual heroine, its meek, saintly, female character "seduced" and having to bring up a child who had never seen his father, its utopian community led by an indefatigable zealot, it is a characteristic document of the period which produced *The Blithedale Romance, Ruth,* and *Jane Eyre.*

The meaning the poet was attempting to convey seemed to most reviewers as obscure as her manner of expression and as unreal as her characters and plot. The London *Press* observed that although the author had announced in the preface her intention of communicating her convictions on life and art, it was not easy to tell what her ideas were. Throughout the poem she had inveighed against conventional habits of thought, but the *Press* remarked that nothing could have been more conventional than the conclusion of the story with its promise of a happy marriage and an abundance of the world's goods. The hero's final speech to Aurora was, in the words of the newspaper, "in the loftiest style of incomprehensibility." Romney asked his cousin to put her lips to the trumpet and blow down the walls dividing one class from another, even though his own attempts to surmount class distinctions had ended in failure. Did Elizabeth wish to imply that Romney had learned nothing? [23] The Dublin *Tablet* also expressed bewilderment at the conclusion: "It is announced to us (not clearly, for anything so crazily obscure was never penned,) that, in some perfectly insane manner, the great scheme of working for humanity is still to be carried out as a partnership concern. . . . It seems difficult to carry nonsense further."

The *Westminster Review* sharply disagreed with the doctrine expressed many times throughout the poem that art had more power to elevate the condition of the masses than the material agencies of civilization. The review maintained that first of all men and women had to be fed, clothed, washed, and given the rudiments of knowledge, that poetry about poetry would be of no benefit to the rank and file. What was needed, the writer believed, was an adequate system of public education, and in the wilder districts of England and Ireland it was of more importance for the waste lands to be drained, for windows to be placed in the mud cabins, and for their ragged inmates to be taught ways of earning their living than for an epic poem to be published on "the woman's question." The large sales of *Aurora Leigh,* he suspected, had not improved conditions in the slums of London. The objection of the *Westminster Review* to Elizabeth's poem because of her apparent indifference to the efforts of practical reformers and social workers was irrelevant. She would have had no disagreement with the point of view of the journal, but in *Aurora Leigh* she was addressing herself to a different problem, the growing secularization and materialism of the age.

One of her most obvious deficiencies upon which the reviews generally failed to comment was her lack of humor. Yet at times she had a sarcastic wit, as in her description of Aurora's aunt:

> she owned
> She liked a woman to be womanly,
> And English women, she thanked God and sighed
> (Some people always sigh in thanking God),
> Were models to the universe.

If Elizabeth's poetry had been quickened by the droll humor often found in her letters and in her conversation, she would never have written *Aurora Leigh* in anything like its present form.

The reviews, then, mostly censured the poem for its excessive length, high-flown style, absurd characterization and plot, and ambiguous theme. Yet even though the trend of the notices was unfavorable,[24] almost every article found much to praise. For example, *Blackwood's* wrote: "Still, with all its faults, this is a remarkable poem; strong in energy, rich in thought, abundant in beauty; and it more than sustains that high reputation which, by her previous efforts, Mrs. Browning has so honourably won." The *Dublin University Magazine,* which had also disparaged the poem, said at the conclusion of the review: "Be the faults what they may in conception or in execution, we almost forget them in the charm of the language, and the thoughts which surprise and delight us everywhere; and we respect the high purposes of the writer and the enthusiastic earnestness with which she has penned them." Although the *National Review* disapproved of almost every aspect of the poem, it nevertheless acknowledged that its author had extraordinary gifts which placed her among the greatest of the English poets. It said that she surpassed all her contemporaries in abundance of ideas and in vigor of intellect and that a noble spirit could be seen in all her work: "Her muse has a sort of proud virgin carriage. No eyes dare gaze on her disrespectfully. Clear air hangs about her. She writes as from the unsullied ideal of a girl of fifteen, and with the same sort of freshness and intellectual eagerness. She puts aside the shortcomings of the world, half in ignorance, half in disdain."

In contrast to the judicious articles in the leading journals, several of the less influential magazines and a number of daily newspapers reviewed the poem as enthusiastically as if they were greeting the work of a new Homer or Dante. The London *Globe* called it "a gem for this age to wear with other imperishable jewels on its forehead, as it marches onward to join the past ages in the Judgement Hall of Eternity." [25] The London *Daily News* believed that the chief merits of the volume were "in the astonishing power of subtle mental analysis, in the art which fuses incidents almost abruptly startling into a faultless unity." The writer added, "We scarcely ever lose perception of the large throbbings of passion, except when we follow with absorbed attention the eloquent exposition of a great truth." [26] In a review that was equally enthusiastic the *Literary Gazette* said that the genius seen in her former works was "displayed in the present poem in perfection." The writer found variety and power throughout the work and thought that "the pure white flame of inspiration" was no less surely present than in the Hebrew prophets or "in the grandest periods of Milton or Jeremy Taylor." As the reviewer expressed it, the ground was everywhere "strewn with gems which drop from the singer's garment as she passes on her way." [27] The *National Quarterly Review* of New York was also awe-struck by the magnitude of Elizabeth's accomplishment: "This *Aurora Leigh* is a great poem. It is a wonder of art. It will live. No large audience will it have, but it will have audience; and that is more than most poems have. To those who know what poetry is . . . this work will be looked upon as one of the wonders of the age." [28]

"The extravagances written to me about that book would make you laugh, if you were in a laughing mood," Elizabeth wrote to Mrs. Martin late in December 1856, "and the strange thing is that the press, the daily and weekly press, upon which I calculated for furious abuse, has been, for the most part, furious the other way. . . . I don't know upon what principle the public likes and dislikes poems. Any way, it is very satisfactory at the end of a laborious work (for much hard working and hard thinking have gone to it) to hear it thus recognised." In a letter to Arabel she reported that Charlotte Cushman was about to give "readings" of *Aurora Leigh* in Rome and that the poem had found great favor in Florence, where the people said that it "magnetized" them.[29] She also informed her sister that the American reviews were "ecstatical" and that they praised her for having eliminated all her earlier deficiencies and going far beyond herself in all ways. Yet two of the most influential American journals, the *North American Review* [30] and *Putnam's Monthly Magazine*, [31] disapproved of almost all aspects of the poem. To be sure, she received praise out of all proportion to her merits from several magazines on both sides of the Atlantic; but although she acknowledged that she had read unfriendly notices in such journals and newspapers as the *Press,* the *Tablet, Blackwood's,* the *Athenaeum,* the *Westminster Review,* and the *North British Review,* she was not discouraged. She had special reasons for dismissing several of the more disparaging articles as captious or prejudiced. For example, the analysis in the *Athenaeum* was "so very unfair and partial"; the critique in *Blackwood's* was written by the poet W. E. Aytoun and came "from the camp of the enemy (artistically and socially)"; another poet, Coventry Patmore, was "somewhat depreciatory" in his article in the *North British Review;* [32] and she was vexed at the attitude of the *Dublin University Magazine,* which scolded her "all because certain rampant vices are not ignored."

Elizabeth seems to have been oblivious of the fact that the most authoritative critical opinion was largely unsympathetic. Since she was so far from London, she no doubt failed to see many of the reviews, but of more importance to her than the opinions of professional critics was the immediate popular success of *Aurora Leigh*. It continued to sell in large numbers; in June 1860 she wrote both her sister Arabel and Fanny Haworth that it was passing through a fifth edition.

18. War Again in Italy: "Poems before Congress"

Aurora Leigh was Elizabeth's last major poetical work. The effort of composition had exhausted her; afterward she had almost nothing new to say, and for the remaining four and one-half years of her life she produced only a few short poems, most of which were written to express her sympathy with the Italian cause after the outbreak of fighting in 1859. Her loss of creative energy was due partly to a series of bereavements which depressed her spirits and sapped her strength. First of all, Kenyon, who had been a kind and generous friend of the Brownings and more than a father to Elizabeth, died at his home on the Isle of Wight on December 3, 1856, only a few weeks after the publication of the poem which had been dedicated to him. "It has been a sad, sad Christmas to me," wrote Elizabeth, who could scarcely imagine England "without that bright face and sympathetic hand, that princely nature." The Brownings heard that they had received a legacy from Kenyon of £11,000, of which the sum of £6,500 was left to Robert, "marking delicately a sense of trust" for which Elizabeth acknowledged that she was especially grateful. They invested most of the amount in Tuscan bonds, which brought them an annual income of about £550, and they also continued to receive small royalties from the sale of Elizabeth's books and about £175 a year from her investments in British government bonds. Henceforth their total income was to be more than enough for their needs; "altogether, we want nothing," Elizabeth wrote Henrietta.[1] The next death which saddened Elizabeth was that of her old friend G. B. Hunter, who had never resumed his correspondence with her after she had left her home on Wimpole Street. "So our dear friend, dear Mr. Hunter, with all his morbid sensitiveness and many high qualities, is at rest from the turbulence of this world at last,"[2] she wrote Arabel in February 1857. In the same letter she said that for two or three days before she heard the news, her thoughts had strangely gone back to her days at Sidmouth and to her friendship there with "poor dearest Mr. Hunter." When she first learned of his death, she was deeply shocked and spent a sleepless night thinking "of all that past at Sidmouth." Although she realized that life would have continued to separate them more completely than death, the certainty that Hunter and she would never see or write to each other again was "painful, painful."

She sustained a much severer blow soon afterwards when she received word from England of her father's death on April 17, within a month of his seventy-second birthday. He was buried beside his wife in the Parish Church of St. Michael and All Angels in Ledbury. On May 3 Browning informed Mrs. Martin that Elizabeth had been sadly affected and that she was still weak and prostrated. "So it is all over now," he wrote, "all hope of better things, or a kind answer to entreaties such as I have seen Ba write in the bitterness of her heart. There must have been something in the organisation, or education, at least, that would account for and extenuate all this; but it has caused grief enough, I know; and now here is a new grief not likely to subside very soon." A few days later he wrote that he thought that the death had been "very strange and sudden and mournful." Early in the summer Elizabeth described in a letter to Mrs. Martin the great bitterness she had felt within her and the recoil against herself. Long ago she had lost hope of reconciliation; yet strangely enough, what she had for many years called "unkindness" had left within her, now that it was gone, "such a sudden desolation!"

During the previous summer both Mrs. Martin and Mrs. Hedley (Aunt Jane) had made a last attempt to persuade Mr. Barret to "forgive" the three of his children who had married and to treat them no differently from the other members of his family. That Mrs. Hedley failed in her effort may be seen from three sentences in Elizabeth's letter to Henrietta postmarked at Florence January 11, 1857: "I am glad that dear Aunt Jane is to be received in W. St. after all. It would have been too painful if her solicitude and kind feeling toward *us* had been visited on her unpleasantly. Now it is all over (hopelessly for us, Henrietta) she will be held in higher esteem for it even by the person whom she irritated for the moment." [3] Just before Mr. Barrett's death, Elizabeth heard from Mrs. Martin that in reply to her letter of intercession, he had written her that he "had forgiven" and that he even prayed for the "well being and well doing" of the three families he had never recognized. "Those were his words," Elizabeth wrote a few weeks after her father's death. "Let us hold them fast beloved Henrietta. He prayed for us. Our poor little children had so much from him. And *we* when we pray, may thank God for so much comfort." [4] What Mr. Barrett wished to signify by the word "forgive" is not clear, for he refused to tell Kenyon's executor the address of Henrietta, who had been willed £100. He never communicated with Elizabeth, Henrietta, or Alfred after their marriages, nor did he leave them anything in his will.

In spite of Elizabeth's distance from England she had never abdicated her right as the eldest of the children to advise her brothers and sisters from time to time how they should arrange their lives. As she acknowledged half in jest, "I am moved in the spirit always to get up and meddle, and put everybody in the place I want them to stand in—which is foolish, and very provoking, I dare say." [5] After her father's death she pleaded with Arabel to visit Robert and her in Italy, thinking that her sister would prefer something more cheerful and less sectarian than her way of life in London, with her devotion to the Chapel and to the Ragged Schools for destitute girls. She seems to have hurt Arabel to the point of tears by assuming that she would leave London immediately. Even though Arabel had the means and the leisure, she had no desire for a trip to Italy or anywhere else and firmly told Elizabeth that the life she had been living seemed worth while and congenial in all ways and that she had no plans ever to change the pattern. To calm Elizabeth she vaguely promised that some day she would come to Florence, but she never went to see the Brownings in Italy. Then Elizabeth hoped that the Barrett family would remain under one roof and not scatter themselves throughout England. Now that they were financially independent, however, they preferred to live in separate establishments. Elizabeth was distressed to learn that the house at Wimpole

Street was soon disposed of and that Arabel, instead of spending some of her money to see Italy, was buying furniture for a home of her own, facing the Paddington Canal at 7 Delamere Terrace. As soon as the eldest living son, Charles John, heard in the West Indies of his father's death, he sailed immediately to England, where he secured for a time possession of a country estate in Shropshire, near the Welsh border. Some months later Elizabeth wrote both to Henrietta and to Arabel that she thought it was absurd for Charles John, Septimus, and Octavius to go to Jamaica, since she could see no valid reason for their wishing to live on the family plantations far from friends and relatives in England.[6] She disapproved of Alfred's going to a distant country—possibly China—on a government mission and leaving his young and attractive wife in Cheltenham, with all its temptations, and she expressed to Arabel the wish that he return from "that unhealthy climate where he professes to find no overwhelming advantages."[7] Not long after George Barrett received his share of his father's estate, he bought a house in Devon and gave up his law practice. Elizabeth wrote to him that she was vexed to learn that he was planning to settle in the country, with no specific occupation in view. She reproved him for failing to gain a wider view of the world before burying himself in a place remote from any center of intellectual activity.[8] In spite of all advice from their eldest sister, the brothers and sisters continued to manage their affairs just as they pleased.

After the publication of *Aurora Leigh,* Elizabeth's literary reputation far exceeded Robert's. An Irish traveler and writer on many different religious and philanthropical subjects, Frances Power Cobbe, who knew the Brownings at this time, wrote that she thought that no one of the group which surrounded them in Florence considered Robert as a great poet or in any way equal to his wife, whose long novel in verse had recently appeared. She added that Browning's unselfishness in constantly speaking of Elizabeth's fame, in showing to his friends favorable reviews of the poem, and in referring to the many editions through which the work had run perhaps obscured his own claims. He himself always maintained "the simple truth" that Elizabeth was "the poet" and he "the clever person by comparison."[9] Miss Cobbe remembered Robert as a kindly man with a pleasant face and cordial manners who had a fund of droll stories to tell.[10] Elizabeth also observed that, "As a sort of lion, Robert has his range in society, and, for the rest, you should see Chapman's returns," which indeed must have been negligible. Although she could scarcely complain on her own account of an unappreciative public, she felt that "the blindness, deafness, and stupidity of the English public to Robert are amazing." It seemed to her that no one in England pretended to do him justice except a small group of Pre-Raphaelite writers and artists.

The most interesting visitor to the Brownings' apartment in the spring of 1857 was Harriet Beecher Stowe, whose *Uncle Tom's Cabin*—"the most successful book printed by man or woman," Elizabeth called it—had made her one of the best-known women novelists in the English-speaking world. Elizabeth was happy to discover "no rampant Americanisms" and found Mrs. Stowe pleasant appearing, with a mass of dark, wavy hair, and more refined than she had imagined her to be. She wrote to Mrs. Jameson, however, that Mrs. Stowe's "brow has not very large capacity; and the mouth wants something both in frankness and sensitiveness." Three years later Mrs. Stowe called again on Elizabeth when Browning and she were in Rome, and the two women talked about spiritualism and the French emperor. Since Mrs. Stowe also believed in "the spirits" and was becoming more of a Napoleonist, their conversation must have been harmonious. After this visit Elizabeth wrote Isa Blagden that she liked Mrs. Stowe very much and thought her "surprisingly large and open, considering her antecedents and early associations." [11]

During the winter of 1856–57 and the following spring Elizabeth mostly led a very quiet life at home because of her frail health. One evening, however, she went with Robert to a masked ball at the opera house, which was the last time in her life she ever thus "dissipated." Browning had engaged for £2 5s. a box for the ball at the close of the carnival season, intending to repay a number of people who had entertained him, and had made for himself "a beautiful black silk domino." On the evening of the ball it was so warm that he urged Elizabeth to accompany him. Although she had scarcely left her fireside for three months, she immediately sent out to hire a domino and buy a mask. The Brownings arrived at the theater at half past ten. Elizabeth felt too adventurous to remain all evening in her box, and so Robert and she went down into the masked dancers below and made their way through the crowd to every corner of the theater. When someone hit her playfully on the shoulder and cried, "Bella mascherina," she replied in the spirit of the occasion, knowing that no one could recognize her under a mask. In all her years in Italy she had never failed to be delighted with the courtesy of the crowds, and this evening not a coarse word or rough gesture came from anyone, with all the social classes enjoying one another's company in a way which would have been impossible in England. At one o'clock in the morning Ferdinando served for the Brownings and two or three of their friends their supper of *gallantina*, rolls, cakes, ices, and champagne. Elizabeth was enjoying the party and would have stayed if she were well enough. "The brilliancy and variety of the sight," she later wrote, "were well worth coming for." At two o'clock, however, she felt so much oppression in her chest that she went home by herself in a carriage, leaving the others to come later, "as Robert did at four in the morning."

ON JULY 30, 1857, the Brownings went to Bagni di Lucca, where they remained until October 7. They rented a pretty house in the Villa, with a great terrace overlooking a private garden surrounded by oleanders and peach trees, only a few doors away from the place where they had spent the summer of 1853. Two or three days after they moved to the Baths, Isa Blagden, her friend Annette Bracken, and Robert Lytton arrived and stayed at a nearby inn. Elizabeth was physically weaker than usual and very much depressed in spirits, having made but slight recovery from the shock of her father's death, and looked forward to the repose of their summer retreat. Lytton, however, soon became ill with a kind of "gastric fever" and had to be nursed day and night by Isa Blagden and Browning. Pen later caught the same infection and was in bed for two weeks. In the midst of the Brownings' troubles Wilson had to go away because of her pregnancy, and their Italian maid Annunziata was also seized with gastric symptoms. Elizabeth had been "peculiarly brittle" when she left Florence, and Pen's illness, as she later wrote Arabel, "ended by breaking me to pieces." [12]

The following winter, therefore, which the Brownings spent in Florence, was no better for Elizabeth. She informed Arabel that the weather, which was colder than usual, had undermined her health, that her nervous apprehensions also kept her unwell, and that her poor physical condition made her ever more uneasy in her mind. Her past griefs hung heavily on her, and she spent much of her time "brooding, brooding, brooding, and reading German, German, German." [13] She resolved to take an interest in life once again, to do some writing before the year was over, and to "get out of the cloud if God lets me." In the daytime Robert left the apartment to take drawing lessons, and three or four evenings a week he was at Isa Blagden's villa or at the homes of other friends, while Elizabeth went to bed with a book. With his "enormous superfluity of vital energy," as Elizabeth put it, he felt the need of much more activity than did his invalid wife, and so they were necessarily apart more than during the early years of their marriage.

Elizabeth was not too unwell, however, to receive calls now and then from her friends in Florence and from writers and artists who were passing through the city. The Brownings' most memorable visitors in the spring of 1858 were Nathaniel Hawthorne and his wife, both of whom came to Casa Guidi in the evening of June 8. William Cullen Bryant and his daughter and the Brownings' friends Fanny Haworth and Mr. and Mrs. David Eckley were also present. Hawthorne immediately noticed Pen's strange likeness to his mother. Both seemed to him tiny, fragile, elflike creatures almost without substance, who might fly off some day when Browning least suspected it. The nine-year-old child with his long curls and velvet frock was in Hawthorne's eyes "as un-English a production as if he were native of another planet." During the evening Pen helped to serve the cake and strawberries, conversed with the guests, and meditated by himself on a couch. Hawthorne wondered what would ever become of such a fairy-like being and thought he would look queer if he were to wear boys' trousers.

Browning, who was agreeable and vivacious, appeared to carry on an animated conversation with all groups at the same moment. Hawthorne was more impressed with Elizabeth than when he had seen her at a breakfast party at Monckton Milnes' home in London two years earlier. He thought it wonderful to see how small she was, how bright and dark her eyes, how pale her face, which was framed with her black ringlets. It was marvelous to him how "so extraordinary, so acute, so sensitive" a person could make him feel assured of her benevolence. "There is not such another figure in the world," he wrote in his notebook. Although there were four well-known writers in the room, the conversation in Hawthorne's opinion was dull. It was largely on "that disagreeable and now wearisome" subject of spiritualism, and in particular the Brownings discussed the notorious affair at Ealing. While Robert in his hearty manner exposed Home as a charlatan, Hawthorne felt that he had dispelled the mystery of the subject, but Elizabeth "ever and anon, put in a gentle word of expostulation." [14] According to Julian Hawthorne, both his father and Browning "abominated" the whole business from the beginning. Late in June, Hawthorne met Browning at Isa Blagden's villa on Bellosguardo. Although both T. A. Trollope and the American composer Francis Boott were in the room, Hawthorne felt that Browning had the most powerful personality of the group. The English poet seemed amiable and filled with energy, as always, and spoke "most rapturously" of Gordigiani's portrait of Elizabeth, which had been commissioned by Mrs. Eckley. Hawthorne recorded that when Browning talked, even his nonsense was "of very genuine and excellent quality, the true babble and effervescence of a bright and powerful mind." [15]

The Eckleys, whom Hawthorne had seen at Casa Guidi, were for two or three years close friends of the Brownings, and the two couples used to see each other almost every day at Florence and at Rome. The Eckleys were wealthy Americans whom the Brownings had first met at Bagni di Lucca in 1857.[16] The British Museum has copies of five books published by Mrs. Eckley, possibly at her own expense; four are slender volumes of verse and of short sermons and meditations for the Lenten season, and the fifth describes a trip to Egypt, Palestine, and Syria.[17] Elizabeth wrote Arabel that Mrs. Eckley (Sophie) had "fallen in love" with her and worshiped her "with a blind passion in all sorts of ways." [18] At this time Elizabeth was convinced that Mrs. Eckley had "a pure, sweet, and noble nature." [19] Almost every day she came to see Elizabeth, who thought her "so delicate and refined" that her visits were never boring or upsetting.[20] It was a "peculiar and a most *delicate* affectionateness—more delicacy is impossible." [21] Their common interest was spiritualism, and Mrs. Eckley used to tell Elizabeth such stories as having heard at church sounds which followed her to the communion table and were so loud that she feared the rest of the congregation might have been disturbed. Elizabeth was astonished at the simplicity, enthusiasm, and generosity of both the Eckleys, who were in her opinion characteristically American (though she realized that not all her transatlantic friends were either so naïve or so generous) and could scarcely have been English. It seemed to her that everything and everyone Mrs. Eckley loved her husband also loved "with a sort of child's devotion" and a desire to give away everything in his pockets to show the sincerity of his feelings, "with tears in his eyes and a trembling in his voice." He would lay his head under the Brownings' feet, Elizabeth added, and beg them to walk over him, not because his wife told him to do it, but "because she feels so herself." [22] When the Eckleys heard that the Brownings had plans to spend the summer of 1858 on the French coast in order that a change of air might help Elizabeth regain her strength, Mrs. Eckley at once hoped that her husband and she might go with them, but she evidently realized the idea would be impracticable because both Robert and Elizabeth would necessarily be with their respective families almost every minute of the day. She then resigned herself to an absence of two or three months from Elizabeth and heaped up parting gifts: a ring, a brooch, a traveler's bag, Damascus slippers, and a rosary from the Holy Sepulchre. "Such floods of tears there have been—floods," [23] Elizabeth wrote of Mrs. Eckley's farewell as the American woman went with her husband to Bagni di Lucca for the summer.

The Brownings traveled by steamer from Leghorn to Marseilles and from thence to Paris by express trains, arriving in the French capital on Tuesday evening, July 6. They stopped there for about a fortnight before going to Le Havre, where they stayed until

War Again in Italy: "Poems before Congress"

September 20. In a letter from Paris, Elizabeth told Mrs. Eckley that Charles Sumner visited Robert and her and greatly pleased them by his "frank, generous, simple bearing."[24] Sumner was traveling in Europe for medical treatment to recover from the brutal physical attack he had received on the floor of the United States Senate.

Although Elizabeth became somewhat stronger because of the sea air at Le Havre, she wrote Mrs. Eckley that she detested the section of the city where they were living because it was ugly, dull, and foul smelling. Sarianna and Browning's father were in adjoining apartments, and they all came together for their meals. Also Milsand was with them for a time, as well as Arabel, George, and Henry, who came with his recent bride. Much to Elizabeth's distress, her other brothers did not make the trip to see her, although at the moment the three who had gone to Jamaica were living in England. The longer she stayed at their house on the shore, the more she disliked it. There was no sandy beach, their view of the sea was obliterated by a succession of bathing houses, and the great, flat stretch of sand around them seemed "as dismal as possible."[25] Also Elizabeth had become tired from having too many visitors and from hearing too much conversation, so that she was counting the days until she could return to the silence of Italy. She wrote to Mrs. Jameson that after the seclusion of her life in Florence she realized that she was no longer "fit for the common everyday life of sensible people here,"[26] although she begged Mrs. Jameson not to refer to the subject in any letters to her since she did not wish Robert to think she was not enjoying her holiday. And to Mrs. Eckley she wrote in the same vein that it seemed to her now as if she "must needs go out of the world to get rest."[27] After their sojourn at Le Havre, Elizabeth took Arabel back to Paris with her to "dissipate" for a few weeks by looking at the shops. Arabel then returned to London, and the Brownings left Paris on October 13 for Genoa by way of Chambéry and the Mont Cenis pass, the crossing of which caused Elizabeth much suffering, just as it had six years earlier. From Genoa they went by steamer to Leghorn, where they stayed for a day to recuperate after their rough passage, before returning to their apartment in Florence.

Elizabeth was still in such poor health that she realized another winter in Florence would be impossible. Robert and she leaned toward Rome because of its milder climate. While they were debating whether or not to go, Mrs. Eckley "kept her family for weeks" [28] in a hotel in Florence, waiting to see whether or not the Brownings would travel to Rome or remain at Casa Guidi, because if they did not move away, Mrs. Eckley also wished to stay. As soon as the Eckleys learned of the Brownings' decision to go to Rome, they told them they were also making the trip to that city and had two carriages ready, one of which they asked the Brownings and their servants to use, as a special favor to them. The offer was accepted with thanks, and Mrs. Eckley to show her pleasure later gave Elizabeth a "most expensive pair of fur cuffs." The party left Florence on Thursday, November 18, 1858,[29] and journeyed about thirty miles a day by way of the scenic route of Arezzo, Perugia, Spoleto, and Terni, arriving at Rome on the afternoon of the twenty-fourth. In the course of the trip "the spirits" several times "made signs" both to Elizabeth and to Mrs. Eckley.[30] But more startling than the supernatural visitations were two events which almost cost several lives. Once during the descent of a mountain, with one side of the road overlooking a precipitous cliff, the horses rebelled and nearly dragged the Brownings' carriage over the edge. Another time, two drivers of the oxen teams who came to pull the carriages up a mountain began to fight each other. When one drew out a knife and was on the point of stabbing the other, Browning rushed forth from the barouche and although successful in disarming the man was thrown on the ground. Pen shrieked "in an agony of fear," as Elizabeth wrote to Arabel, "Oh, that naughty man is killing papa," and then she all but fainted.

The Brownings reached their destination with no further disturbances and once again rented for about £11 a month their former apartment at 43 Via Bocca di Leone. Within a few weeks they had seen many of their old friends, such as the Storys, Charlotte Cushman, Harriet Hosmer, W. C. Cartwright, who was later a member of Parliament in London, the young English artist Frederick Leighton, and the English diplomat Odo Russell. They also met two distinguished Americans from Boston: the historian

Robert Browning

John Lothrop Motley and Charles Callahan Perkins, who was a wealthy art critic. Even though Elizabeth had many congenial friends in Rome, her increasing frailty made it impossible for her to go out except for short drives in the daytime. On Christmas morning, however, she was strong enough to attend with Robert and the Eckleys the grand mass at St. Peter's, where the blast of the silver trumpets—as she put it—"thrilled" through her bones.[31]

Robert, who appeared more robust than ever before in his life, was "plunged into gaieties of all sorts," Elizabeth wrote Isa Blagden, "caught from one hand to another like a ball, has gone out every night for a fortnight together, and sometimes two or three times deep in a one night's engagements. So plenty of distraction, and no Men and Women. Men and Women from without instead!" If they had an evening together once in several weeks, they called it a holiday. Since Elizabeth was not well enough to receive guests when she was alone, she retired early to conserve her strength. She wrote Henrietta that she was pleased to see Robert thus amused, but it is clear that she did not like Rome as much as he. The climate, she was convinced, was unhealthy for most people, and the members of the foreign colony were filled with "reckless dissipation." The city seemed to her "like a great roaring watering place . . Cheltenham or Baden Baden—nothing thought of but dancing and dining, and crowding in some way or another." [32] She wondered how the Caesars were able to sleep amidst such confusion and confessed to Isa Blagden that the atmosphere was not conducive to work.

In February, Field Talfourd made a drawing of Elizabeth which had been commissioned by her English friend now living in Rome, Ellen Heaton, who wished to "have the only portrait in the world of Mrs. Browning." [33] Although it would have been impossible for Miss Heaton to have achieved such an ambition because Gordigiani had already painted Elizabeth in Florence, "dear Sophie Eckley"—as Mrs. Browning wrote her sister Arabel—said that she was wounded by the "slight." A curious aspect of the last years of Elizabeth's life was the series of petty jealousies to which her women friends gave expression as they vied with one another for first place in her favor. Ellen Heaton *"never could bear* Mrs. Eckley"; [34] Fanny Haworth thought that Isa Blagden was "cold" to her; Elizabeth reproached Isa for being "as cold as ice" to Mrs. Eckley at Casa Guidi; Isa used to speak to Elizabeth of "those horrid Kinneys," and she never cared for Mrs. Story; and Mrs. Jameson was rather cool toward Elizabeth after a visit in Florence during the summer of 1857, possibly, as Elizabeth explained to Henrietta, because Isa was such a frequent visitor at Casa Guidi.[35]

It was also in February that Elizabeth first spoke of the subject with which she was to be obsessed from now until the last hours of her life—the last phase of the Italian *Risorgimento*. Early in the month she wrote Sarianna of the "ignoble way" in which the English were treating Italy, in contrast to the "generous and magnanimous" action of Napoleon III, the "only great-hearted politician in Europe." In a letter to Arabel in March she told of the pleasure she had received from a visit by one of the greatest of Italian statesmen and patriots, Massimo d'Azeglio, who was then the Piedmontese ambassador in Rome. Elizabeth's attention was drawn to his "chivalrous, noble head," and she felt the "moral grandeur of the man, in a moment." [36] Elizabeth's comment that he was "one of the very noblest men in Italy" was scarcely an exaggeration; without doubt he was the most important figure in Italian politics whom she met in Italy. In the same letter to Arabel she again spoke in disparagement of English policy, which she believed too narrow and based on unfounded jealousies.

AFTER Orsini's attempt in Paris on the life of the emperor and the empress in January 1858, Napoleon had resolved to do something for Italy, and in his obscure, tortuous fashion he had been working steadily toward war with Austria. In the following July he had secretly met Cavour at Plombières, where the two men conspired to bring about the freedom of Italy. Napoleon promised to liberate Italy from the Alps to the Adriatic and to make war at the right moment against Austria with 200,000 troops, if the Italians would also provide 100,000 men. He envisioned a kingdom of upper Italy in which Lombardy, Venetia, Parma, Modena, Bologna, and possibly the Marches were to be fused with Piedmont; and a kingdom of central Italy, uniting Tuscany and Umbria under the Duchess of Parma. The Pope was to retain

Rome and King Ferdinand Naples. The four states thus constituted were to form a loose confederation under the presidency of the Pope. The price Italy would have to pay for its freedom was the cession to France of Savoy and possibly of Nice. Napoleon fixed the late spring of 1859 for the outbreak of the war and left it to Cavour to find a plausible *casus belli* in which Austria was the aggressor. By the end of the year the treaty informally discussed at Plombières was officially signed. In January 1859, when Victor Emmanuel in his address to the Sardinian Parliament in Turin said that he could not remain insensible to the "cry of grief" which had reached him from many parts of Italy, a phrase which had been approved by Napoleon, all Europe realized that France and Italy were intending to make war within a few months.

The British government, with Derby as Prime Minister and Malmesbury in the Foreign Office, was against any change in the Vienna Settlement of 1815 and in particular did not want to see the balance of power in the Mediterranean upset; nor did it wish to weaken Austria, which was England's traditional ally. Malmesbury, hoping that the matter might be settled by Austria's reforms in Italy, had no understanding of the desire for independence throughout the length and breadth of the peninsula. The Derby government was not prepared, however, to intervene on the reactionary side to maintain the *status quo,* because the English people as a whole were friendly to Italian aspirations. Malmesbury determined to keep the peace if he could and hoped that the Italian question might be solved not by war but by a congress of the five powers, which was proposed in March by the Russians. Although Napoleon had promised to come to Piedmont's aid if it were attacked by Austria, he was in a difficult position because most of his ministers and the business interests were opposed to the idea of a war against Austria, and Roman Catholic Frenchmen had no enthusiasm for military action which would diminish the Pope's temporal power. The emperor secretly instructed Cavour to continue his preparations for war, hoping, however, for delay in the outbreak of hostilities to give him time to win the approval of official Europe to the French-Italian point of view.

When Napoleon finally yielded to Malmesbury's proposal of

simultaneous disarmament by France, Piedmont, and Austria as a preliminary step to the congress, a joint English-French demand was sent to Turin. Cavour was on the verge of suicide after receiving this note on April 18. He supposed that the war would not take place, and he knew that a congress would never sanction Italian independence and an enlarged kingdom of northern Italy. Since the emperor had apparently deserted him by succumbing to English pressure, he had no choice but to telegraph his acceptance of the note from Paris and agree to disarm along with France and Austria. But the intransigence of Vienna in scorning the French-English offers of conciliation saved the day for Cavour. On the twenty-third an ultimatum from Vienna that Piedmont disarm within three days was presented at Turin. If the Italians failed to comply, they would be immediately attacked. Cavour's policy had triumphed; he had provoked Austria into the war he had long desired. Napoleon, faithful to his word, entered the struggle late in April and began to transport to Italy the troops he had promised. On May 12 he arrived at Genoa and prepared for the advance.

The first of the two principal battles of the campaign was fought on June 4 on the plain of Lombardy a few miles to the west of Milan, at Magenta, from which the Allies expelled the enemy after two hours of severest fighting. The Austrians then evacuated Milan and retreated eastward across Lombardy to the Mincio, along which the final battle took place at Solferino, south of Lake Garda. Again the Allies under the leadership of Napoleon, Victor Emmanuel, and the French general MacMahon gained a decisive victory. A few days later Napoleon's forces crossed the Mincio and established their headquarters at Villafranca and Sommacampagna and were about to undertake the siege of the Austrian fortress at Peschiera. An Allied fleet was stationed in the Adriatic and was ready to attack the coastal forts of Venice. Just when everyone supposed Napoleon was on the point of taking the last step toward the fulfillment of his promise to free northern Italy, the Italians suddenly had their hopes dashed. On July 6 Napoleon asked for an armistice, which was signed on the eighth, and on the eleventh he met Franz Joseph at Villafranca, where the emperors agreed upon the following terms: Austria was to cede Lombardy—except for the fortresses at Mantua and Peschiera—to Napoleon, who in turn would hand it over to Piedmont; Venice was to remain in the possession of Austria; and the Grand Duke of Tuscany and the Duke of Modena were to be restored to their states, though apparently without the use of force.

Why did the French emperor disappoint the Italian people by bringing the war to an inconclusive end when ultimate victory against Austria seemed within his grasp? First of all, Prussia had 400,000 armed men along the Rhine, and Napoleon had to protect his country against this threat. He had suffered casualties of 17,000 troops at Solferino, about 10 per cent of his army, and was horrified at the prospect of further bloodshed. In spite of the popular enthusiasm of the Italians for their cause, the response to the appeal for recruits had been disappointing; not many more than 12,000 men out of Italy's millions had joined the colors. The Austrians could draw upon vast reinforcements and might well win another battle. Besides the military situation, Napoleon realized that Cavour had seized the political initiative and was using his influence to make northern and central Italy one great kingdom under Victor Emmanuel. Cavour's policy was directly opposed to Napoleon's, for the emperor did not wish Italy to become united, strong, and independent of France. Napoleon had hoped the Italians would gain their freedom, but his plan was for them to become a confederation of small, autonomous states, looking to France for their protection. Another reason for making peace was his reluctance to offend the clerical party in France by giving too much help to the Italians in their struggle against the Pope.

IN THE meantime Robert Browning was following the situation with friendly interest, and Elizabeth had become a violent partisan of the movement. She wrote Arabel from Rome in April 1859 that there was "one unity of burning enthusiasm" from the north to the south of Italy, that if war had not come, there would have been a revolution, and that Piedmont would have been crushed by Austria but for Napoleon's noble act.[37] In May she expressed her conviction that the emperor was acting sublimely; his generosity, she said, touched her to the heart. The faith and constancy of the Italians and the prospect that their land would soon be free and united seemed to her "like a beautiful dream,—too beautiful to be other than a dream!" She thought it "a holy cause" and a war on which she might "lawfully ask God's blessing." The "lies" in *The Times,* which Elizabeth believed had for two years been "a tool of Austria," and the cautious, neutral policy of the Derby régime filled her with rage, so that she wrote again and again to relatives and friends in England that the British government, press, and people had all covered themselves with dishonor.

The Brownings left Rome late in May, making the trip by carriage with the Eckleys, and arrived at Florence in the midst of the excitement over the war. The Grand Duke had fled from the Pitti Palace in April, and the government of Florence was now in the hands of three men, of whom Ricasoli was fast becoming the dictator as he led Tuscany toward a fusion with Piedmont, which was a step toward the creation of a strong constitutional kingdom. The Tuscan cabinet voted for Victor Emmanuel's sovereignty, and the communes declared themselves in favor of annexation by an overwhelming majority. In August a representative assembly met in the Palazzo Vecchio and passed a resolution that it was the firm intention of Tuscany to become a part of an Italian kingdom under Victor Emmanuel.

Elizabeth was delighted that her hopes were being realized much faster than she had thought possible, but she became so tense that she could not write, eat, or sleep and spent much of her time talking with friends about Italian politics. As she read in the newspapers of Napoleon's military victories and of the success of the cause which mattered more to her than almost anything else in her life, she lived "in a glow of triumph and gratitude"; it seemed to her as if she "walked among the angels of a new-created world." After the peace of Villafranca she wrote to Mrs. Martin about this period of ecstasy before her disillusionment: "All faces at Florence shone with one thought and one love. You can scarcely realise to yourself what it was at that time. Friends were more than friends, and strangers were friends." Almost never before had she been so happy, she wrote, and she

War Again in Italy: "Poems before Congress"

was happy not only for Italy but also for the world because she thought "that this great deed would beat under its feet all enmities, and lift up England itself (at last) above its selfish and base policy." She was emotionally involved with the issues of the moment and owing to her physical weakness had less control over herself than during her first period of excitement when the Italians fought in 1848–49. She wrote Arabel that she had "literal *physical* palpitations" [38] after reading the newspapers, that tears came into her eyes and sobs to her throat. She was especially upset when she heard of such events as the attack on Perugia, where the Papal Swiss Guard put down a revolt with the greatest brutality, killing women and children in the streets. Also she wept with vexation when she read Tennyson's verses "Riflemen Form!" which had appeared in *The Times,* May 9:

> True we have got—*such* a faithful ally
> That only the Devil can tell what he means.
> Form, Form, Riflemen Form!
> Ready, be ready to meet the storm!

She was offended at Tennyson's scornful reference to the French emperor and wrote her relatives that the British fear of Napoleon was hysterical, for the French were not going to attack the English.

Besides the excitement of a war and a new government in Tuscany, Elizabeth had upon her return to Florence another cause for anxiety. Her former maid Wilson, who through the years had been on the whole reliable and possessed of common sense, had become partially insane and appeared to have wasted away as though by an inner fire. She told Elizabeth that from much reading of the Bible she was convinced that the world was soon coming to an end and that she could not live with her husband Ferdinando any longer, for they were "too near in blood" and their two children Orestes and Pilades were the "first fruit of the first resurrection." A few weeks later she said to Elizabeth that she had seen an angel carrying Orestes past her house in Florence. As Elizabeth looked at Wilson's mad expression and heard her uttering such nonsense with a strange intensity, it was all she could do, she wrote her sister Arabel, to keep from screaming and fainting away.[39] Wilson had a rooming house in Florence, and Elizabeth realized that if it were known that the proprietor was mad, the business would be doomed and Wilson would have to be sent back to her relatives in England.

While Elizabeth was thus worrying about her maid and about the Italian cause, she heard without any warning the news of the cessation of hostilities and of the terms to which the emperors had agreed at Villafranca. At first she could not believe the re port was true:

> Peace, peace, peace, do you say?
>   What!—with the enemy's guns in our ears?
>   With the country's wrong not rendered back?
> What!—while Austria stands at bay
>   In Mantua, and our Venice bears
>   The cursed flag of the yellow and black? . . .
>
> No, not Napoleon!—he who mused
>   At Paris, and at Milan spake,
>   And at Solferino led the fight:
> Not he we trusted, honoured, used
>   Our hopes and hearts for . . till they break—
>   Even so, you tell us . . in his sight.[40]

The Italian people were sullen and felt aggrieved with the emperor for not having won Venetia for them. Elizabeth, however, after her momentary reaction of incredulity and despair, was convinced that Napoleon had behaved magnificently and had been true to the cause from first to last. In a letter to Henrietta she blamed England for frustrating Napoleon's generous impulses: "I *never will forgive* England for her part in these things—*never*—in helping Prussia and confederated Germany, by a league of most inhuman selfishness, to prevent the perfecting of the greatest Deed given to men to do in these latter days." But she was misinformed, because the new British government which had come into power in June had three members of the cabinet who were friendly to the Italian cause and helped it in countless ways: Palmerston, who was the Prime Minister, Lord John Russell, the Secretary for Foreign Affairs, and Gladstone the Chancellor of the Exchequer. Russell understood that the agreement at Villa-

War Again in Italy: "Poems before Congress"

franca left Austria the virtual ruler of Italy, and he brought pressure upon Napoleon to revise the treaty in favor of the Italians. Also he warned that his country would protest the restoration of the Dukes by force. Elizabeth, however, had no faith in England's good intentions toward Italy and did not realize that it was Palmerston's régime, not Napoleon's, which was sympathetic to the idea of a strong Italian kingdom independent of France. She wrote Fanny Haworth that she still believed in the emperor: "He did at Villafranca what he could not help but do. Since then, he has simply changed the arena of the struggle; he is walking under the earth instead of on the earth, but *straight* and to unchanged ends."

After living among the stars for months, Elizabeth was struck down by the sudden announcement from Villafranca. "It was as if a thunderbolt fell," she wrote. She was filled with grief and "impotent rage against all the nations of the earth," which had, as she believed, forced Napoleon's hand. Her nerves were so agitated that she suffered from a severe cough, "the worst attack on the chest" she had ever experienced in Italy. For two days it seemed as though she had been stricken with *angina pectoris*, so that Browning must have feared the worst, and for somewhat more than two weeks afterward her health was scarcely better. When her physician prescribed an immediate change of air and warned that failure to leave Florence might have fatal consequences, she decided to risk the journey to Siena, where Browning and she planned to remain until the arrival of cooler weather. On July 30, looking like "a dark shadow," she was taken downstairs into a carriage, from which she was lifted into a train compartment, and at Siena was carried to her bed in the hotel where the Brownings stopped for two days before they moved into the Villa Alberti. Her physician E. G. F. Grisanowsky was so much concerned over her health that he followed them to Siena by the next train and stayed at their hotel to be near his patient. It was he who selected for the Brownings' summer residence the Villa Alberti, a large, cool house in the low hills about two miles from the center of the city. After they had been there a week, Robert wrote Mrs. Eckley that Elizabeth had not yet been able to walk three steps without help and that she had been too unwell to write anything or to see anyone except her family. Every day, however, she was dressed and seated in a large, airy room and was slowly recovering strength.

In the Villa Belvedere nearby lived the Storys, who had been "most kind in every way," and their guest Walter Savage Landor. Early in August, Story had written Charles Eliot Norton of the recent arrival of the Brownings and of Landor's having come to stay with him three weeks earlier. Landor, who had been living for almost a year with his wife and children in a most unhappy and stormy relationship at the family villa in Fiesole, was turned out of the house one noon early in the summer of 1859 "with some fifteen pauls in his pocket" and was told "to be off and never to come back." [41] Tired and ill, the eighty-four-year-old man walked along the burning streets to Florence, where after wandering around aimlessly he saw Browning, who took him back to Casa Guidi. In Story's words, "It was the case of old Lear over again."

Browning and Kirkup went to Fiesole to try to persuade the family to take him back, but their trip accomplished nothing. Then Mrs. Landor came to Casa Guili, and the aged poet, hearing that his wife was at the door, cried, "Let her come in, and I throw myself out of the window." The wife replied to Browning, "The best thing he could do." In writing of the episode to Henrietta, Elizabeth said that Landor's daughter had told Robert that "to save her father's life, she wouldn't give him a glass of water." [42] Browning, who had "always said that he owed more as a writer to Landor than to any contemporary," showed his gratitude by becoming his guardian and the trustee of his funds. He placed Landor in a hotel for a short time, since Elizabeth's poor health would not permit his living at Casa Guidi, and in the middle of July he accompanied him to the Storys' villa in Siena. One sultry morning Landor arrived with his benefactor, "looking very old, and almost as shabby and dusty and miserable as a beggar." Three weeks later, when the Brownings came, Robert arranged for Landor to move from the Storys' house to a cottage near the Brownings' villa. It was probably not until her last few weeks at Siena that Elizabeth was well enough to sit on the lawn in the evening under the ilexes and cypresses and talk with Landor and the Storys. In view of his strong antipathy against Napoleon III, he must at times have seemed to her a most unsympathetic conversationalist. Story's daughter Edith remembered how "Mrs. Browning, with her face hidden under her large hat and curls, would be stirred past endurance by these assaults on her hero who was her 'Emperor evermore,' and would raise her treble voice even to a shrill pitch in protest, until Mr. Browning would come into the fray as mediator." [43] Emelyn Story, however, recalled that the many anecdotes narrated by Landor were amusing and full of charm and that "Mrs. Browning was often convulsed with laughter at his scorching invective and his extraordinary quick ejaculations, perpetual God-bless-my-souls, &c.!" [44]

In the middle of September, Elizabeth wrote Henrietta that she was well enough to go for a drive every day but that she would not be strong enough to stay for more than a few weeks in Florence after their return early in October. Robert and she were thinking of Palermo because of its warm climate, but since she did not look with pleasure upon the prospect of passing "a winter without civilization," she supposed they would once again go to Rome. Meanwhile she was taking great pleasure in her quiet, comfortable house: "Our villa is really enjoyable—great rooms, with beautiful views. Sunsets red as blood, seen every evening over deep purple hills, with intermediate tracts of green vineyards. And the silence, the repose. I drink them from this full 'beaker of the warm south.'"

After the Brownings went back to their apartment in Florence, they planned to stay only a few weeks before proceeding toward Rome. They were delayed in their departure, however, by a cold wind which kept Elizabeth confined to two or three rooms and also by the arrangements which Robert was making to settle Landor in his apartment at Wilson's lodging house on Via Nunziatina, not far from Casa Guidi. Wilson was to receive £30 a year for taking care of him, "which sounds a good deal," Elizabeth wrote; "but it *is* a difficult position." She added that he had "excellent, generous, affectionate impulses, but the impulses of the tiger every now and then." When the Brownings went away, they left Landor "in great comfort." Elizabeth visited his suite of a sitting room, bedroom, and dining room and found that though they were small, they were quiet and cheerful and looked into a pretty garden.

Now that Landor had been settled for the winter and the weather had become milder, the Brownings were able to leave. As they set forth in their carriage on November 28, 1859, toward Perugia, Foligno, Terni, and Rome, they had with them, in addition to Ferdinando and the maidservant Annunziata, a second manservant who had recently been hired to take care of the pony which Robert had bought for Pen. The pony was fastened by a rein to the other horses, and although the Brownings feared they might have to leave him on the road with his groom, the animal surprised them by coming in fresh at every stage, and Elizabeth was convinced that it "would have travelled to the end of the world on the same terms." [45] After a pleasant excursion of six days, during which Elizabeth suffered no more fatigue than was usual on such trips, they arrived at Rome on Saturday, December 3, and were met at the outskirts of the city by the carriage of the Storys, who for several days had been driving out to greet them. The Storys escorted them to a hotel and then found them an apartment at 28 Via del Tritone in a building which has long since been destroyed when a wide, modern thoroughfare was built from the Piazza Barberini to the Corso. Owing to the war scare which kept all but a few English and Americans from visiting Rome, the Brownings were able to rent for only £11 a month a large and elegant suite, beautifully furnished and carpeted, with two *salons* besides the dining room, all with full exposure to the sun.

Although Elizabeth was careful of herself, she was less well that winter than ever before in Rome. One evening at about five o'clock Robert and she went in a carriage from their apartment to the shop of Castellani the jeweler to see the display of swords presented by the grateful Romans to Napoleon III and Victor Emmanuel. The Brownings were received "most flatteringly as poets and lovers of Italy; were asked for autographs; and returned in a blaze of glory and satisfaction, to collapse [as far as Elizabeth was concerned] in a near approach to mortality." As she wrote to Fanny Haworth, she could not catch just a simple cold: "All my bad symptoms came back. Suffocations, singular heart-action, cough tearing one to atoms." Although she partially recovered from the attack, she felt herself "brittle" afterward and said that she had become "aware of increased susceptibility" and had to live for a while on a diet of ass's milk.

IN THE same letter to Fanny Haworth she also said that she was "going into the fire" for Louis Napoleon by issuing "a little 'brochure' of political poems." Her book, which was called *Poems before Congress,* was a slender octavo volume published in London by Chapman and Hall on March 12, 1860,[46] and in New York by C. S. Francis under the title of *Napoleon III in Italy, and Other Poems.* The Brownings had Chapman sent complimentary copies to their close relatives and to many of their friends, such as Forster, Chorley, W. J. Fox, Monckton Milnes, Ruskin, the Rossetti brothers, Thomas Woolner, William Allingham, and Francis Sylvester Mahony. The congress to which Elizabeth referred in the title of her English edition was supposed to have taken place in January at Paris. When the peace treaty had been signed at Zurich on November 10, invitations for a congress of the leading powers had been issued and accepted. On December 22 an anonymous pamphlet was published in Paris entitled *Le Pape et le congrès,* which, though not written by the emperor, was inspired by his ideas. The aim of the work was to urge that the congress reduce the Pope's territory and leave him only Rome. Napoleon had decided that the Romagna, which had already secured a *de facto* separation from the Papal State, must not again return to the domain of the Church. Austria asked if the French emperor intended to advocate at the congress the principles enunciated in the pamphlet, and on being given an affirmative answer withdrew early in January. Thereafter the congress was indefinitely postponed. Thus when Elizabeth's volume appeared in March, the title of the Engish edition was somewhat misleading.

In the preface of her book she expressed with her characteristic idealism the doctrine that truth and justice must transcend national boundaries and that even at the risk of being called unpatriotic she could not approve England's policy of nonintervention. Patriotism, she felt, did not mean "an exclusive devotion to one's country's interests," which would be a narrow and selfish attitude. "Let us put away the little Pedlingtonism unworthy of a great nation," she continued, "and too prevalent among us. If the man who does not look beyond this natural life is of a somewhat narrow order, what must be the man who does not look beyond his own frontier or his own sea?" She hoped that some day an English statesman would have the courage to propose a policy which would be of more benefit to the peoples of the world than to British trade.

Of the eight poems in the volume, one had no connection with the Italian cause: "A Curse for a Nation," which had been published in the *Liberty Bell* in Boston, 1856. It was unfortunate that Elizabeth included these verses against Negro slavery in the United States because a number of critics thought, after a superficial reading of the lines, that she was cursing her own country for its failure to enter the war on the side of Italy. The other seven poems all dealt with the Italian situation in 1859. "A Court Lady" tells of a beautiful and aristocratic woman in Milan who, after putting on a robe of silk and còvering herself with diamonds, goes in an open carriage to a hospital where she comforts the wounded Italian and French soldiers. Elizabeth does not explain in the poem why the heroine thought it appropriate to display all her jewelry while she was on this errand of mercy, but she informed a number of correspondents that the idea of the verses was based "on the general fact that the ladies of Milan went in full dress through the streets to the hospitals." [47] "The Dance," which is somewhat similar, relates the story of a titled Florentine woman asking the French soldiers stationed in the Cascine park to dance with her and the other Italian women who are present. When the dancing is finished, the Frenchmen take their partners back to their Italian husbands, who thereupon "kissed the martial strangers mouth to mouth." Then a great cry of gratitude for "the gallant sons of France" went up from all the Italians who participated in the episode. "Christmas Gifts" describes the fear of the Pope and Cardinals at the growing power of the Kingdom of Northern Italy; the joyful people, however, have been given the present they have long desired: the prospect that within a year or two their land would be free and united. One of the poems on Italian affairs, "A Tale of Villafranca," was

War Again in Italy: "Poems before Congress"

already familiar to many English readers because it had appeared in the *Athenaeum* several weeks after the announcement of the armistice. In these verses the poet tells her Florentine son why his native city is in mourning:

> A great man (who was crowned one day)
>   Imagined a great Deed:
> He shaped it out of cloud and clay,
>   He touched it finely till the seed
> Possessed the flower: from heart and brain
> He fed it with large thoughts humane,
>   To help a people's need.

But sovereigns and statesmen were angry and fearful that the doer of the deed threatened the right of the great powers to bully the weaker nations and destroy all which aimed at independence. Thus Napoleon's noble aims were "truncated and traduced" by men who were too narrow and mean to understand him. "An August Voice" also deals with Napoleon's action and represents him in August 1859 ironically urging the Florentines to take back their worthless Grand Duke.

The longest poem in the volume is "Napoleon III in Italy," which is a glorification of the "Sublime Deliverer," the man "who has done it all." The emperor is greater than "All common king-born kings" because he represents the will of the people. All his policies are unselfish and straightforward; he would never "barter and cheat" or act from base motives, as "vulgar diplomates" do. Thanks to him, Italy lives anew, and patriots are swarming from every province to enlist. The poet is sure that historians will always say of him,

> That he might have had the world with him,
> But chose to side with suffering men,
> And had the world against him when
> He came to deliver Italy.
>   Emperor
>   Evermore.

This portrait indeed flatters its subject almost beyond recognition. Yet in spite of all the faults which liberal historians have seen in the main figure of the Second Empire, it is none the less true that he was genuinely interested in the cause of Italian freedom, though not of its political unity, and that as a result of the contribution of the French army in the spring of 1859, the country achieved independence years earlier than it would have without that help. Elizabeth was grateful to the emperor for his deed of knight-errantry in behalf of her adopted country, in the struggles of which she had taken an almost personal interest. She saw a great, liberal movement taking place around her, and she assumed that the chief actors on the scene, the French emperor and the brilliant, wily first minister of Piedmont, were honest and without blemish in both motive and deed. In thus oversimplifying issues and recognizing only the best qualities in people, she remained true to character.

The most idealistic poem in the volume is "Italy and the World," in which Elizabeth rejoices that, thanks to France, the provinces of central Italy—"Florence, Bologna, Parma, Modena" —have risen from their graves to become the nucleus of a free and united kingdom. As for England, the poet is angry because of its refusal to go to war alongside the Italians, and she wonders at the hysterical efforts of her native country to defend itself against a nonexistent aggressor:

> I cry aloud in my poet-passion,
> Viewing my England o'er Alp and sea.
> I loved her more in her ancient fashion:
> She carries her rifles too thick for me,
> Who spares them so in the cause of a brother.

She urges the central Italian provinces to extinguish their separate lives and to merge themselves in the newly created kingdom, which, in its turn, she hopes, will some day become an integral part of a world community based on Christian ideals, a brotherhood far above "earth's municipal, insular schisms." With the coming of this era of universal benevolence, there will be

> No more Jew nor Greek then,—taunting
> Nor taunted;—no more England nor France!

> But one confederate brotherhood planting
> One flag only, to mark the advance,
> Onward and upward, of all humanity.

Elizabeth wrote Fanny Haworth that she expected "to be torn to pieces by English critics"; her prophecy was fulfilled. Almost all the reviews objected to her point of view and felt that contemporary political events were not fitting material for poetry. The two critical notices which were strongest in their condemnation appeared in *Blackwood's* [48] and the *Saturday Review*,[49] both of which irritated Elizabeth because of their virulent and unfair attacks. In a letter to Mrs. Jameson she referred to "that mob of 'Saturday Reviewers,' who take their mud and their morals from the same place, and use voices hoarse with hooting down un-English poetesses, to cheer on the English champion, Tom Sayers," —a popular prize-fighter. The tone of the article in the *Saturday Review* was so ill-tempered that it seemed as though the writer had a personal grudge against the poet because of her disapproval of British neutrality. The notice was probably written by G. S. Venables, who was a wealthy lawyer and a well-known writer for the *Saturday Review* and *The Times*.[50] Since the *Saturday Review* was insular in its point of view, hostile toward Napoleon III and indifferent to the Italian cause, the reviewer's unfriendly treatment of the volume is not surprising. In order that he might not appear to be condemning Elizabeth herself, he pretended that the opinions in the book were expressed not by its author but by a fictitious character conceived to be a "bearded exile" from England who was also a poet and a long-time resident of Florence. The main theme of the article was that this "illogical renegade" had lived away from England so long that he had forgotten the meaning of liberty and of constitutional government. The reviewer scoffed at the "cosmopolitan English exile" who frittered away his time between "dilettante Liberalism and dilettante art." He spoke of the "delirium of imbecile one-sidedness" with which this "denationalized fanatic" protested against the Volunteer movement in England, and he referred to the "servile and seditious platitudes" uttered by the "poor prattler" who praised the emperor in "Napoleon III in Italy." According to the review, the speaker of the poems had no ideas of his own except for the ones heard in "Liberal Italian casinos," all of which were influenced by French thought, and thus the English convert "echoes their ignorant calumnies in the shape of unauthorized apologies." Throughout the article the author ridiculed ideas which were "democratic," "liberal," "cosmopolitan," and "Continental."

He particularly objected to the abolitionist poem: "When an angel enjoins her [the speaker of the poem] to indite her superfluous execration, she endeavours, with more than the perversity of Balaam, to express by preference that hysterical antipathy to England which Mrs. Browning attributes in turn to almost all her characters." He then quoted some twelve lines from the "Curse" in which the poet spoke of the "sins" she believed were still characteristic features of English life: "little feet / Of children bleeding along the street," the House of Parliament representing the few rather than the many, and the wide-spread system of bribery. The reviewer replied contemptuously to her allegations of British injustice: "This is the kind of stuff which ignorant foreigners delight to repeat; and their pleasure is multiplied tenfold when English renegades can be found to vent calumnies against a land which they have forgotten. There are more barefooted children and rough pavements, and a greater amount of neglected poverty in any Italian village than in an English town of thrice the population." This article was perhaps the most harshly expressed and unjust review of Elizabeth's poems which came from any critical journal during her lifetime.

In a notice entitled "Poetic Aberrations," *Blackwood's* was almost as unfriendly as the *Saturday Review*. The writer was pained that "one of England's most gifted daughters" had published a volume which was "so ineffably bad" in its poetical composition, "so strangely blind" in its political principles, and "so utterly unfair to England and English feeling." In the eyes of the reviewer, the principal fault of the poems was that they were composed by a woman. He believed that women ought not to write about controversial issues of the day but should confine themselves to their household duties and that if they had to go out of their homes, they should become nurses, like Florence Nightingale: "We are strongly of opinion [the article began] that, for the peace and welfare of society, it is a good and wholesome rule that women should not interfere with politics. We love the fair sex too well, to desire that they should be withdrawn from their own sphere, which is that of adorning the domestic circle, and tempering by their gentleness the asperities of our ruder nature, to figure in the public arena, or involve themselves in party contests." The reviewer continued that women were like angels when they visited the sick, provided food for the hungry, and prayed at lonely deathbeds; when they discussed politics, however, they "overstepped the pale of propriety" and no longer resembled angels but "so many *tricoteuses* in the gallery of the National Convention." He implied that a sensible person would not have written on Italian nationalism but that the poet might be forgiven her choice of subject because of her long residence in Italy. It also seemed to him that the Treaty of Vienna, which in 1815 placed Italy under Austrian rule, was in many respects a satisfactory arrangement, since it procured for Europe a long period of peace; he thought that the Italians were now somewhat unreasonable in asking for the control of their country. The writer had a strong aversion to the French emperor, rebuked Palmerston and Russell for having been sympathetic to the French expedition in Italy, and maintained that Elizabeth in writing her "Napoleon III in Italy" had been "seized with a . . . fit of insanity." The review concluded with a meaningless and unfair comparison between two greathearted Englishwomen: "To bless and not to curse is woman's function; and if Mrs. Browning, in her calmer moments, will but contrast the spirit which has prompted her to such melancholy aberrations with that which animated Florence Nightingale, she can hardly fail to derive a profitable lesson for the future."

Fraser's Magazine [51] was also unfavorable, but it was more temperate in its language than *Blackwood's* and the *Saturday Review*. It disagreed with her high estimate of the French emperor and thought that her portrait of him was "a monstrous caricature of history." The writer of the notice believed that Napoleon's reign was based on fraud and force, and he maintained that the sense of insecurity which then paralyzed the commerce and arts of Europe "might convince the most incredulous, might convince Mrs.

Browning herself, how mischievous to steady progress this disturbing element invariably proves." To the reviewer the most painful feature of the volume was the bitterness with which the poet had spoken of her own country. In his opinion, she had completely misjudged English policy, which seemed to him "upon the whole wise and honourable, prudent and resolute." As far as the poetry was concerned, the reviewer wrote that it was "the weakest, most inchoate, most unmusical, and most ineffective" that he had seen for a long time. The London *Globe* [52] reminded Elizabeth that rulers had to work hopefully with mixed evil and good and that instead of impatiently scolding and vilifying people, she should try to convert them.

More than all the other vituperative notices, H. F. Chorley's remarks in the *Athenaeum* [53] gave Elizabeth the greatest pain. He wrote that her art suffered from the violence of her temper and that in this political pamphlet of sixty pages he found "not so much of lute as of marrow-bone and cleaver." Elizabeth was especially irritated that Chorley, who had followed her career with sympathetic interest longer than any other Engish critic and who was a close friend of both Robert and herself, should have supposed that the last poem of the volume was a curse against England. Yet he was not greatly to blame, for it is not immediately clear against whom or what country the poet vented her curse. She herself admitted to Isa Blagden that "certain of those quoted stanzas do 'fit' England 'as if they were made for her.'" Furthermore no critic would have supposed that a volume apparently devoted to the Italian movement would contain a poem written for the American abolitionist cause. Elizabeth should not have expected to receive a friendly review from Chorley because in his *Roccabella,* published in 1859, he had already shown himself to be hostile to the Italian effort. This novel, which was ironically dedicated to Elizabeth, had an Italian patriot for its chief villain. In acknowledging the dedication, she had written Chorley that she was in complete disagreement with his views, especially with his apparent assumption that "God made only the English." After a copy of the *Athenaeum* containing the review of *Poems before Congress* reached Casa Guidi, both of the Brownings were much upset at the treatment of the volume by the anonymous reviewer whom they supposed to be Chorley. Robert, who was more angry than Elizabeth, expressed in letters both to Edward Chapman the publisher and to Isa Blagden his belief that Chorley had not made a thoughtless error but had intentionally maligned Elizabeth.[54] It was evidently at Browning's insistence that Elizabeth wrote Chorley a letter of protest and explained her "Curse," which she said a more careful reading would have made clear to him. Through no fault of Chorley's, as he later claimed, the *Athenaeum* did not print this letter but merely said in its weekly gossip column that Mrs. Browning wished the editors to state that her "Curse" was aimed not against England, "as is generally thought," but against the United States, not on account, "she now tells us," of the Italian cause but of the Negro question. The writer of the paragraph then asked, in extenuation of the reviewer's "hasty and incorrect" reading of the "Curse," why a poem on the issue of Negro slavery should have appeared among *Poems before Congress*.[55] When Elizabeth saw these words of apology instead of the text of her letter, she was more vexed than she had been at first and wrote Chorley that the wording of the paragraph implied that she had been ungenerous and cowardly, "as if, in haste to escape from the dogs in England," she had thrown them the good name of another country. She emphasized to him that in publishing her volume she had not written to please anyone, not even her husband, and that she had not expected to advance her reputation in England, "but simply to deliver my soul, to get the relief to my conscience and heart, which comes from a pent-up word spoken or a tear shed." She added, "Whatever I may have ever written of the least worth, has represented a conviction in me, something in me felt as a truth." Her attitude throughout the exchange of these letters with Chorley shows the extent to which her obsession with Italian affairs had destroyed her sense of proportion.

A London weekly, the *John Bull*,[56] found much to praise in the volume, although it did not agree with all her views. It said in her favor that her enthusiasm and sympathy had "lent fire and energy to her verse" and that in many passages she still possessed "her old power in wielding the English language and her wonderful gift of rhythmic melody." The critic believed, however, that she had "some impatience of strict justice and some blindness to historic truth." The writer quoted her remark in her preface—"Non-intervention in the affairs of neighbouring states is a high political virtue; but non-intervention does not mean, passing by on the other side when your neighbour falls among thieves"—and then he asked, "But which is the neighbour and which is the thief?" The reviewer thought that an ambassador sent from the Court of Turin to Florence who made use of his position in Tuscany to stir up a conspiracy against his own Prince in Piedmont was a thief rather than a neighbor. Likewise he believed that the threats of assassination made publicly by the secret societies at Parma against all who would give any help to the cause of the exiled Duchess were also the devices of thieves. "In this diversity of opinion and sympathy," the reviewer maintained, "no English Ministry would be likely to interfere on either side. Nor would they, notwithstanding Mrs. Browning's indignation, have been justified in so doing." He also did not share her hope that the steps which were being taken to amalgamate the provinces of northern and central Italy might foreshadow an eventual world community of Christian nations. In his opinion the spirit of 1848 and more recently of 1859 was one of nationalism and should not be confounded with any notion of universal brotherhood. Her idealistic dreams were "flatly contradicted by the instincts of our age." He reminded his readers that "these cants" about international fellowship had been tried and had failed years ago: "One would suppose that Mrs. Browning had gone to sleep in the days of Marat and Danton, and had just now awoke with these specious chimeras fresh in her recollection."

Although almost all newspapers and literary journals were outraged by the book,[57] she received at least two generous and friendly reviews, both of which gave her much pleasure to read after the other hostile criticisms. The London *Daily News* thought that the volume was "a work of considerable power—rough, wild, savage even in parts, yet all a-glow with enthusiasm, from the first page to the last." [58] It was also welcomed by the *Atlas,* which said that it had been much interested in the Italian movement and the greatness of the French emperor.[59] Although in the opinion of the journal the poems were not without some eccentricity and obscurity of expression, they nevertheless were "luminous with noble thought and nobler feeling—harmonious with a harmony beyond mere sweetness." Elizabeth's relatives and most of the Brownings' English friends apparently did not share her political views. William Michael Rossetti, however, wrote Elizabeth from London within a week or two after receiving his copy of *Poems before Congress* that he too believed that Louis Napoleon was a great and noble leader and that he honored her for courageously asserting her ideas in the face of a "blatant and intolerant" public opinion in England.[60]

This was Elizabeth's last volume published in her lifetime. Twenty-two years earlier she had issued her first book under her own name. The *Seraphim* volume was filled with angels, wandering souls, lovelorn maidens, ancient halls, and proud knights; everything was weak, imitative, and sentimental. The reviewers had liked her romantic idiom and had greeted her as a poet of unusual promise but had warned her to come down from the clouds and to write about the world she knew. In her poems of 1860 she dealt earnestly with what she considered the greatest issues of her time and vigorously defended her right to do so, but the change in subject matter from romantic ballads and pseudoreligious dramas to journalism in verse about the politics of the hour was not altogether a gain.

19. Last Poems and Final Illness

DURING the winter of 1859-60 and the following spring Elizabeth was weaker than usual; she had never completely recovered from her desperate illness after the peace of Villafranca. Not only was she ill and tired—she was agitated and distressed by the Italian situation and by the loss of two of her closest friends, one from death and the other as a result of many acts of unforgivable treachery to her. In view of her lowness of spirits and physical frailty, she was not able to do much more than receive a few guests now and then in the daytime, write a number of short poems mostly on Italian politics, and help Pen with his lessons.

Mrs. Jameson died at her home in Ealing on March 17, 1860. "Mona Nina," as Elizabeth called her, had been a favorite with both of the Brownings ever since their marriage trip, had often visited them during her travels on the Continent, and had always maintained an intimate correspondence with Elizabeth. Only a week or two before her death she had received from Elizabeth a long letter on her recent volume of Italian poems and their reception in England and America. Elizabeth could scarcely refer to the loss of Mrs. Jameson in a letter to Sarianna; "it's a blot more on the world to me," she wrote.

The greatest shock she received that winter was the sudden break with Mrs. Eckley, who had been almost a daily companion for more than two years. Besides often driving the Brownings around Rome in their carriage, the Eckleys had also tried to show their affection by giving elaborate Christmas gifts: an expensive brooch to Elizabeth, a bronze inkstand to Robert, and books and toys to Pen. In spite of Mrs. Eckley's overwhelming generosity and friendliness Elizabeth discovered that she had been deceiving her from the time the two first met by pretending to have participated in many different spiritualistic experiences. The reason for this long-continued imposture may have been that Mrs. Eckley knew of Elizabeth's interest in spiritualism and determined to gain and to keep her friendship by constantly talking about her supposed communications from the other world and about the news she heard from persons who also pretended to be mediums. She was not malignant, in Elizabeth's opinion; her fault was vanity, which was, however, "monstrous enough to present a large foundation for an extraordinary falseness of character." [1]

That the basis of Mrs. Eckley's offense was her simulation of spiritualistic powers is clear from Elizabeth's letter to Isa Blagden. Mrs. Browning wrote that she had received from Mrs. Eckley a letter begging forgiveness. The American woman, Elizabeth said, had also written that she was no longer practicing as a medium.[2] Long before Elizabeth knew that Mrs. Eckley could not be trusted, Robert had suspected that she had been telling lies. He warned Elizabeth that she was taking advantage of her innocence like two other American spiritualists, Jarves and Home, both of whom he detested. But she would not listen to Robert, continued to see Mrs. Eckley every day, and had full confidence in her until her impostures were evident. Years after Elizabeth's death Browning wrote Julia Wedgwood that in this episode his wife had "suffered miserably through her ignorance," [3] and in a letter to Isa Blagden in 1869 he also referred to the event which still festered in his memory: Mrs. Eckley had "cheated Ba from the beginning—and I say, in the bitterness of the truth, that Ba deserved it for shutting her eyes and stopping her ears as she determinedly did." [4] Elizabeth, who appears to have been severely shaken by the experience, was angry, hurt, and disillusioned. In a letter to Sarianna, February 18, 1860, she asked why she always had to be the one who was "taken in." She confessed that she was "nearly sick" of the Americans and English in Italy—especially the women—who pretended to be noble and sincere: "They come to me, lay themselves under my feet—and end by tripping me up. Oh, the want of truth, the want of moral cleanliness! it is dreadful." [5]

Her changed attitude toward Mrs. Eckley is the basis of a poem she wrote at this time entitled "Where's Agnes?" In these verses she told of her astonishment that the woman in whose presence she had "dared not name a sin" and who had always been chaste in her appearance and language had "turned mere dirt." Mrs. Eckley's name is not mentioned, or the specific nature of her fault, except that she had been "false." The poem was not published while Elizabeth was alive and presumably was not seen by "Agnes" until its appearance in *Last Poems* almost a year after Elizabeth's death. She was surprised that Mrs. Eckley had no sense of shame after she had been unmasked—"Not a throb of real feeling, nor symptom of wounded honesty anywhere," she wrote Isa Blagden in April.[6] When Mrs. Eckley kept sending her letters in which she asked for a renewal of their friendship, Elizabeth could hardly refrain from grinding her teeth and stamping the floor in anger. Once she had praised the American woman for her sweetness; now she felt "very sick at the adhesiveness." In spite of the entreaties she refused to have any further intercourse with Mrs. Eckley, who complained to Elizabeth late in the spring that her coolness toward her had brought on an ailment for which her physician prescribed a change of air. The Eckleys spent the summer of 1860 at Bagni di Lucca and after the preceding winter in Rome seem never to have had any further contact with the Brownings in Italy.

But more than the treachery of a close friend, it was the growth of Italy which chiefly absorbed Elizabeth's attention that winter and spring. After the agreement at Villafranca both Tuscany and Emilia had remained firm in their resolves to become fused with Piedmont and thus frustrate the French emperor's plans for a kingdom of central Italy. Cavour, who had been out of office for six months, became the Prime Minister of Piedmont again in January 1860. His first concern was the unification of northern and central Italy, and to gain this he was prepared to sacrifice Savoy and, if necessary, Nice. At this point his position was strengthened while he was bargaining with Napoleon by Russell's promise of British recognition of the central kingdom as soon as constitutional forms had been established. Russell also helped Cavour by inducing Napoleon to agree to an Italian plebiscite and to the withdrawal of French troops from parts of Italy. The

Last Poems and Final Illness

French emperor, however, soon became suspicious of Cavour, who now felt assured of acquiring central Italy, and caused several articles to be written in the press on the French claims to Savoy and Nice. In spite of Napoleon's antagonism Cavour planned for the immediate fusion of all central Italy with Piedmont and Lombardy. On the first of March therefore he arranged for plebiscites to take place within a few days in central Italy and for the states to be amalgamated with the North if they so voted.

When Napoleon heard of the announced elections, he was alarmed lest Cavour present him with a *fait accompli* so that he might still lose his coveted provinces. He had so little trust in the Piedmontese government that he demanded that Cavour sign a secret agreement to give up Savoy and Nice if they declared themselves in favor of joining France. Although the Italian statesman abhorred the meanness, the trickery, and the unconstitutionality of Napoleon's methods, he dared not refuse to sign but still hoped, however, that a local movement against France might save the loyal Italian province of Nice. Tuscany and Emilia voted for fusion and were incorporated within the enlarged state, and the first Italian parliament met at Turin early in April 1860 to celebrate the creation of a new kingdom. In the meantime Napoleon had incurred the anger of England by sending his army into Savoy and Nice just as though the provinces were already his. He was accustomed to solving problems by force and had no sympathy with Cavour's notions of civil liberties and constitutional sanction. In the plebiscites which were held in April under the shadow of French guns, the people in both provinces voted almost unanimously for annexation to France. If the elections had been free, it is probable that not more than half the Savoyards would have wholeheartedly favored the arrangement. The inhabitants of Nice, however, who were Italian both in language and in feeling, had almost no sentiment for the French. But they could not escape their fate.

As Elizabeth read the newspapers and conversed with friends who came to her apartment, she followed closely all these events. In spite of the emperor's tortuous policies and his shabby treatment of Cavour and of the young Italian kingdom, she still wrote in countless letters to relatives and acquaintances that Louis Napoleon was the greatest democratic leader in Europe and that from first to last he had been loyal to the cause which had become so much a part of her. Now that central and northern Italy were united under Cavour and Victor Emmanuel, she confidently expected that the rest of the peninsula would soon be added to the new state, which at present was only the nucleus of the Italy to come. "We mean to annex the Neapolitan states, and then the Papal will fall in," she wrote Arabel in June 1860; "that can scarcely be done without strokes. Afterwards comes the Venetia affair." [7] She was greatly irritated at the English for their "wailing" because of Napoleon's premature seizure of Savoy and Nice and his manipulation of the plebiscites. Although she admitted that the emperor had been indelicate and hasty, she felt that the exchange of territory was "pure justice." To her mind, the Savoyards were not "victims," nor was Italy being "robbed," as many of the English had maintained. She wrote Henrietta late in March, after Savoy had been occupied by the French, that "The question of Savoy is little understood among you," and explained that the province was essentially French, had long desired to be united to France, and was now being given that opportunity by a popular vote, just as the people of central Italy had recently expressed themselves in favor of a union with Piedmont.[8] But in this letter to her sister she made no mention of the fact that in the one instance the elections represented the will of the people but that in the other they had been managed and were no valid indication of the general sentiment.

She frankly defended Napoleon's *Realpolitik* in a letter to John Forster, who had disagreed with her in regard to the motives of the French emperor: "If I differ from you, I seem to have access to another class of facts than you see. If Italy, for instance, expands itself to a nation of twenty-six millions, would you blame the Emperor . . . for providing an answer to his own people in some small foresight about the frontier . . . ?" In her discussions of contemporary politics in her letters she did not attempt to defend the rape of Nice but said only that she felt "tenderly for poor heroic Garibaldi, who has suffered, he and his minority." She added, "He is not a man of much brain; which makes the subject

Last Poems and Final Illness

the more cruel to him." But it was natural enough for him to be angry when he heard that his boyhood home had been bartered away.

Among all the new visitors to the Brownings' apartment that winter and spring, none impressed Elizabeth so much as Theodore Parker. He was a learned and courageous Unitarian clergyman from Boston, liberal in his theology and political opinions and a champion of unpopular, progressive causes. After a long and successful ministry he had come to Italy in a vain effort to regain his health. Just after his removal from Rome to Florence and his death there in May, Elizabeth wrote, "There was something high and noble about the man—though he was not deep in proportion." The tone of the second half of the comment may have been caused by Parker's having told her (as she reported, perhaps with exaggeration) that *"all learned persons of the present day* who prefer to believe in the divine aspiration of John's Gospel, are false and lie." [9] Unitarianism seemed to her a "negative" creed. But what may have irritated her much more than his advanced theology was his acknowledgment to her that he placed no credence in the recent "spiritualistic" phenomena, although the subject "had taken strong and extensive hold upon his congregation." In writing to Isa Blagden of Parker's visits, Elizabeth said that he appeared to her too intolerant in his denials. She added that teachers were apt to be scornful of all who held views opposed to their own: "Clergymen and schoolmasters are nearly always narrow men, and in the grades far above them intellectually there is something of the same straitness." Her indictment of these two professions was in itself too dogmatic. Such a sweeping generalization could not have been based upon a wide personal experience, for few of her intimate friends had been teachers or clergymen.

Besides receiving friends now and then in the daytime, she read German with Pen and helped him prepare his lessons for the priest who was giving him instruction in Latin. Unfortunately the child had never learned to apply himself to his studies unless his mother sat beside him and offered encouragement. Elizabeth explained to Henrietta that although she did not criticize her for the educational arrangements of her children, she felt that Pen was "not fit for a school—he would be broken to pieces in it." [10]

Another reason for keeping Pen at home was that Robert and she had "only one, and couldn't lose his presence *so*." She admitted that her child "wants more independence and self-reliance than he was attained to by our process," but she trusted to the future for that. In addition to her theories of education, Elizabeth had equally strong beliefs on how Pen should be clothed. Although he was now ten years old, he still wore a velvet blouse and looked "perfectly lovely,—the burnished curls hanging over it!" She believed that coarse clothing upon children developed rough manners: "Pen tugs at me in vain for very thick shoes—which he thinks manly—because he has seen great boys wear them. I won't let him wear a shoe except of the soft polished leather," she wrote Henrietta. She assured her sister that he was admired everywhere for his "graceful manners" and that people said, "Not a child like him in Rome."

After completing the manuscript of *Poems before Congress,* Elizabeth did not produce much verse during the winter months. In the spring she wrote "A Musical Instrument" and sent it to Thackeray, the new editor of the *Cornhill,* who had asked her for a contribution. It was published in the July issue of the magazine, was reprinted in *Last Poems,* and has become one of her best-known shorter pieces. The main theme of the poem, which is based on the myth of Pan and Syrinx, is an idea frequently seen in Elizabeth's poems and letters: the true poet dedicated to his art must endure many sufferings and sacrifices and cannot hope for the ordinary satisfactions of life.

> Yet half a beast is the great god Pan,
>   To laugh as he sits by the river,
> Making a poet out of a man:
> The true gods sigh for the cost and pain,—
> For the reed which grows nevermore again
>   As a reed with the reeds in the river.

This spring she also wrote on her favorite subject of Italian affairs a number of poems, most of which were published in the New York *Independent.* Theodore Tilton, the editor, had liked her *Poems before Congress* so much that he offered her one hun-

Last Poems and Final Illness

dred dollars for every poem she would send him. She was pleased that her volume had found favor in America, if not in England, and in the course of the following year contributed to the *Independent* some eleven poems, the last two of which appeared a few weeks after her death. "The Forced Recruit, Solferino, 1859" tells of a Venetian youth who, placed against his will by the Austrians in their army, was killed in battle and given a hero's burial by the Italians. In the verses entitled "King Victor Emmanuel Entering Florence, April, 1860" Elizabeth describes the event as she imagines it to have taken place. Since she was in Rome when she wrote the poem, she must have depended upon the Florentine newspapers and the letters of friends. The occasion is "our beautiful Italy's birthday," to celebrate which people from all of Tuscany have brought gifts. To show their gratitude for his help in their liberation, the people "in wild exultation" are throwing flowers in his path and inviting him to live in the Pitti Palace and "evermore reign in this Florence of ours." The King, who is the "first soldier of Italy," is so moved by the demonstrations that he can hardly restrain himself from showing his emotion. Outwardly he appears calm and grave, but if he were to relax for a moment, he "would break out into passionate tears." His joy, however, is tempered by the thought that the deed is only half finished, that Venice and southern Italy must be redeemed.

Another poem on contemporary events written at this time was the "Summing up in Italy." The tone is bitter and sarcastic, as often in both her poems and letters when she referred to the attitude of official Europe toward the aspirations of Italy. In these verses she says that the great powers will eventually approve of the liberation of the peninsula and will "honour the deed and its scope." They will, however, vilify the chief figures—Louis Napoleon, Cavour, Victor Emmanuel, d'Azeglio, Garibaldi, Ricasoli, and the others—and will end by hanging them all:

> True, you've praise for the fireman who sets his
>   Brave face to the axe of the flame,
> Disappears in the smoke, and then fetches
>   A babe down, or idiot that's lame,—

> For the boor even, who rescues through pity
>   A sheep from the brute who would kick it:
> But saviours of nations!—'tis pretty,
>   And doubtful: they *may* be so wicked.

After Rome became too hot for Elizabeth to remain any longer, the Brownings left on June 4, 1860, for Florence, where they arrived a few days later after traveling "through some exquisite scenery" by way of Orvieto and Chiusi. They stayed at their apartment in Casa Guidi for only a month, during which they made preparations to return to the same large, cool villa in Siena where they had lived the preceding summer. Once again they planned to take Landor from Florence and place him in a cottage near their house. During the winter Wilson's querulous lodger had been writing to Robert of the poor quality of the food offered him, of the uncomfortable living arrangements, and of the city itself, which he thought a "very ugly town" with fogs worse than any he had seen in London. As soon as the Brownings reached Florence, Landor came to Casa Guidi to complain that Wilson had thrown a dish in his face and to say that he intended to go to Leghorn and never come back to his present rooms. According to Elizabeth, who described the episode in a letter to Arabel, Landor's charge was baseless.[11] He had been so irritated when his dinner from the *trattoria* arrived eight minutes later than usual that he at first threw the soup out of the window and then the vegetables. Just as he was disposing of the mutton in the same fashion, Wilson seized the dish. "Her eyes flashed fire" as she did so, Landor told the Brownings, and Wilson admitted that she "felt in a passion." Since Wilson had been for more than a year "in a most excitable condition of nerves," Elizabeth feared that there might be further trouble between her and this "poor headstrong old man." Although she had at first pitied him because of the outrageous way in which he had been treated by his wife and children, she now lost all patience and was convinced that he was "without truth and incapable of any steadfast feeling, whether of simple affection or common gratitude."[12]

Early in July the Brownings went to Siena, where they remained until their return to Florence on October 11. The Storys

Last Poems and Final Illness

were a mile away, Isa Blagden was living in a rough cabin within a few minutes' walk from the Brownings' house, and Landor had been deposited in a cottage nearby with Wilson for a housekeeper. The loneliness and the quiet would have helped Elizabeth had it not been for her anxiety and unhappiness which preyed upon her thoughts and were like a "black veil" between her and whatever she tried to do. First of all, she suffered bitterly after having heard in June that Henrietta, who had always been the strongest of the three sisters, had an internal growth and was in great pain. Her first impulse had been to go immediately to her bedside, but Browning had dissuaded her from so rash a step. Now she could only wait helplessly for letters telling of her sister's increasing illness. Also she was worried about the fighting in Sicily and dreaded the possibility that Austria might soon make war against the new Kingdom of Northern Italy.

Like millions of others throughout Europe, she had been stirred by the astonishing achievements in Sicily of Garibaldi, who had sailed with his "Thousand" in two old ships from Genoa early in May. "We are all talking and dreaming Garibaldi just now in great anxiety," she had written to Sarianna in June. "Scarcely since the world was a world has there been such a feat of arms. All modern heroes grow pale before him." In August she was much depressed at the thought that Italians were fighting Italians in Sicily, in contrast to the war a year ago when the enemy was the hated Austrian. Furthermore, she was indignant, as always, that no military help had come from England and hoped that the Palmerston-Russell ministry would soon fall. She wrote Mrs. Martin, "The statesmanship of England pines for new blood, for ideas of the epoch, and the Russell old-fogyism will not do any more at all." And so she passed her last summer at Siena and returned to Florence stronger than when she had left but in the greatest anxiety over Henrietta.

The Brownings planned to spend the winter in Rome as usual. While they were preparing in November for the trip, Elizabeth received such a gloomy letter from George Barrett about Henrietta's condition that she was almost prostrated. Browning was aware of her acute distress and prevailed upon her to set forth toward Rome the next morning [13] so that she might have a few days' respite from the ever more depressing bulletins. She was in agony every moment of the journey; as she expressed it in a letter to Arabel soon after reaching Rome, "It seems as if the blood of my heart *must* be left in stains on the stones of the road." [14] For Browning too, who suffered for Elizabeth's sake, the trip was "a wretched business." She felt bitter because her weakness had prevented her from being with her sister during her last moments.

Henrietta died on November 23, 1860, the day the Brownings arrived in Rome. Elizabeth expected to find letters fom England waiting for her, but there was nothing. For ten days she remained in suspense while she waited for the messages which by a mistake of the post office had not been forwarded from Florence. Although she had long steeled herself to receive the blow, the final announcement, which arrived on December 3, was a severe shock. A few hours after the communication arrived, Browning wrote Isa Blagden that Elizabeth had not been out of her rooms since they came to Rome and that she had seen no one. In a letter he sent at the same time to George Barrett to thank him for his many messages about Henrietta, he said that Elizabeth was bearing up "on the whole, as well as I should have thought possible, but the wounds in that heart never heal altogether, tho' they may film over." [15]

DURING that winter, their last in Rome, the Brownings lived at 126 Via Felice (now Via Sistina) in a quiet and respectable district not far from the top of the Spanish Steps. All winter and the following spring until their return to Florence early in June, Elizabeth was so depressed and weak that she never walked more than two steps outside her rooms, which she left only to take three or four short drives. In about the middle of December she wrote Fanny Haworth that she felt tired and beaten and was struggling hard to live on, and a month or so later she sent her another report of her poor health: "If you laid your hand on this heart, you would feel how it stops, and staggers, and fails. I have not been out yet, and am languid in spirits, I gather myself up by fits and starts, and then fall back."

Her chief consolation was a letter she received from Mrs. Stowe,

Last Poems and Final Illness 393

who wrote from America of some recent communications from the spirit of her dead son Henry. Elizabeth replied that the letter had brought her great comfort and that she did not understand how people could retain their prejudices against spiritualism.[16] Early in January she wrote Arabel that Mrs. Stowe's letter had done her more good than anything else which had happened to her since Henrietta's death, and she copied out extracts from it and sent them to her sister in an attempt to convince her of "the truth." [17] If people could not communicate with the souls of the dead, Elizabeth thought that the fault was theirs. She assured Arabel that there was "a growing cloud of witnesses in England" and in many other countries who believed in these mystical phenomena. Both Mrs. Stowe's letter and the one she had recently received from Jarves, who was also in America, convinced her that humanity was then "in a strange phase" and that everywhere there was "a silent opening of mystic doors and a rolling away of stones before sepulchres." [18] In spite of her bitterness toward Mrs. Eckley for having tricked her, Elizabeth's faith in spiritualism was never shaken. Pen Browning many years after the death of his parents wrote from Florence that his mother's views concerning spiritualism "were much modified" toward the end of her life, after she had been duped by a friend in whom she had great trust: "her eyes were opened and she saw clearly." [19] But at the time of the Eckley episode Pen was much too young to understand his mother's feelings on the subject. The reason for the statement by Pen to *The Times* in 1902 was that he had been irritated and embarrassed by the recent publication of two letters by his parents giving their respective impressions of the séance at Ealing, and he naturally wished to place his mother's memory in as favorable a light as possible.

In contrast to Elizabeth, who was worn and thin, Browning was "looking remarkably well and young" and seemed very gay. He spent part of every day with Story, modeling in clay, and in the evening, as Elizabeth wrote Fanny Haworth, he generally went out "as a bachelor—free from responsibility of crinoline." Once he came home between three and four in the morning from a great ball at which were present "all the princes in Rome (and even cardinals)." Elizabeth on the other hand usually went "early to bed, too happy to have him a little amused." Although Browning did not deny himself the pleasures of society either in Rome or Florence, there is no suggestion that he selfishly pursued his own amusements to the neglect of his invalid wife. Elizabeth wrote in many letters in the last year or two of her life, just as she had from their earliest days together, that she was grateful to Robert for his constant love and tenderness.

She was not so absorbed in her grief that she failed to keep herself informed of Italian politics. On the contrary, her nervous energies were further depleted on the one hand by her excitement in reading and hearing about the final success of Cavour's policies as the country moved toward unification and independence and on the other by the anxiety she felt with the Papal States and Venetia still in bondage, much of southern Italy in a condition of anarchy, and Austria ever threatening another war. During the previous summer Napoleon had looked with dismay at Garibaldi's successes in Sicily and the prospect that Italy would soon be one nation. Since the French emperor's original plan for the peninsula to be divided into four confederate states (northern Italy, central Italy, the Papal States, and the Two Sicilies) had been thwarted by Cavour, he now wished Italy to be composed of a northern and a southern kingdom with the Papal areas between them. He suggested that the English and the French fleets should jointly patrol the Straits of Messina and prevent Garibaldi's army from crossing to the mainland. But the English, except for the Court, were friendly to the Italians and turned down Napoleon's proposal. (Although Elizabeth always believed that her country was in league with the reactionary powers against Italy, this refusal of the British government to act against Garibaldi and the protection he had received from British warships at Marsala in May 1860 are examples of the encouragement and substantial aid from the English, who thus helped Cavour to gain southern Italy.)

Early in September Garibaldi had reached Naples, where he announced his intention of marching to Rome. Cavour then sent the Piedmontese army southward across the border into the States of the Church and encouraged Victor Emmanuel to lead the troops from Ancona to Teano, where they met Garibaldi. This invasion of the Royal army of the Papal territories had been a critical

Last Poems and Final Illness 395

moment for Italy. France, Austria, and Russia withdrew their ministers from Turin, and Cavour feared that the Continental powers would send their forces to Italy to restore the *status quo*. Once again England came to the rescue with the dispatch sent on October 27, 1860, by Lord John Russell (with whom Elizabeth was always irritated because she felt that his liberalism toward Italy was based on words rather than upon deeds). More than anything else, it was Russell's note which discouraged the reactionary powers from intervention against Cavour's new state. In the memorandum to the British Minister at Turin the Secretary had expressed his wholehearted approval of the Italian movement toward constitutional liberties and independence. After Garibaldi's campaign King Francis of Naples took refuge in his fortress at Gaeta, where he was aided by the French emperor, who would not allow the Italians to blockade the stronghold by sea. To cite another example of English friendship toward Italy at this time, the British government insisted early in January that Napoleon withdraw his fleet and give a free hand to the Italians, who soon afterward subdued the fortress. In the plebiscites which had taken place in October, the peoples of Sicily, Naples, Umbria, and the Marches voted overwhelmingly for annexation, and soon afterward Italy was united, with the first national parliament meeting at Turin in February 1861 under the leadership of Cavour.

Elizabeth had been alternately buoyed up and depressed as she followed the ebb and flow of the fortunes of the new country. Many aspects of the situation filled her with anxiety; yet in spite of some temporary setbacks she was convinced in the spring of 1861 that victory had been virtually achieved. The one Italian figure in whom she always had complete confidence was Cavour. As for Garibaldi, she had great respect for his military genius but felt that in political matters he was a child and allowed himself to be influenced by men whose programs were opposed to Cavour's. Mazzini, who was radical in his theories and out of sympathy with Cavourian constitutional methods, she thought "a man without conscience." She was distressed that the Neapolitans and Sicilians were making poor use of the freedom they had recently gained, that the area was being administered by inefficient and corrupt officials, and that brigandage was rife. In a letter to Mrs. Martin she admitted that the Neapolitans were not equal to the other Italians, but she believed that "a little time will give smoothness to the affairs of Italy."

Meanwhile she had lost none of her old hopes and refused to be convinced that conditions were as bad as some observers maintained. For example, she mentioned in a letter to Arabel that an English traveler who had recently come from Naples told her that there had been "some confusion and dissatisfaction" in the South but that the reports of trouble had been greatly exaggerated in the newspapers.[20] Since the Pope obstinately refused to give up any temporal power or to look with favor upon the secular reforms suggested by the French, the Roman question remained a continual embarrassment to Napoleon, who had no choice but to protect the Holy Father. She believed that the aim of the Italian government was apparently "to let the rotten fruit fall at last as much by its own fault as possible, and by the gentlest shake of the tree." Reports came to her that some who had "doubted most in the Emperor's designs" were beginning to say that "he can't mean ill by Italy." As events were to prove, however, she was too optimistic about Rome. In the spring the political situation seemed encouraging to Elizabeth in all ways except for Venetia, to gain which she feared the Italians would have to fight Austria. As usual, she thought that the British government was responsible for most of the troubles in Italy and maintained that the anticipated war "might have been unnecessary if England had frankly accepted co-action with France, instead of doing a little liberalism and a great deal of suspicion on her own account." In reality there was but slight danger of immediate war, for Cavour was trying to avoid armed conflict with Austria for at least two years, and in the meanwhile he hoped that he might reach a peaceful solution with a new and more liberal régime in Vienna. In a letter to Arabel in May [21] Elizabeth referred to the painful scene several weeks earlier in the Chamber of Deputies in which Garibaldi had impugned Cavour's honesty and patriotism. She wrote that although the attack was too much to bear, the Prime Minister had shown remarkable self-command in not replying. Her admiration for Cavour was greater than ever. "There's a great man!" she wrote her sister; "complete in the head and the heart!" At this time she also made known to Sarianna Browning that Robert and she had lost none of their strong faith in Italy and its leaders: "there are great men here, and there will be a great nation presently."

Among the few poems she composed that winter, most dealt with Italian politics. They were published in the New York *Independent,* and she hoped later to place them, along with others which had already appeared in that journal, in a second and greatly enlarged edition of *Poems before Congress.* Two of the poems describe individual human tragedies caused by the recent wars. In "Parting Lovers," a girl declares her love for the man she is sending away to fight, and if necessary to die, for their "noble Italy." "Mother and Poet, Turin, after News from Gaeta, 1861" represents the cry of despair from a woman who has learned that both her patriot sons were killed, one at the battle of Ancona in September 1860 and the other at the siege of Gaeta:

> Dead! One of them shot by the sea in the east,
> And one of them shot in the west by the sea.
> Dead! both my boys! When you sit at the feast
> And are wanting a great song for Italy free,
> Let none look at *me!*

The poem was based upon the personal tragedy of the poet Laura Savio of Turin. Elizabeth's other verse efforts of this period are similar in subject matter and treatment and equally devoid of inspiration.

At least three of the visitors to the Brownings' apartment discussed Italian problems with Elizabeth and shared her liberal sympathies. The world traveler and plenipotentiary Sir John Bowring, who had been a friend of Jeremy Bentham and one of the first editors of the *Westminster Review,* pleased her by saying that nothing could have been more "ludicrous and fanatical" than the English Volunteer movement to prepare for the anticipated invasion from France and that Napoleon, whose intentions had been greatly misunderstood in England, was thoroughly democratic in his domestic policies and Italy's loyal friend. No wonder that she called Bowring a "true liberal of distinguished intelligence." Another visitor was Diomede Pantaleoni, a physician and patriot who as an agent for Cavour was treating with some of the less reactionary cardinals on the Roman question. In March, Cardinal Antonelli had him expelled from the Papal States. Edward J. S. Dicey, "an Englishman of intelligence and impartiality," as Elizabeth called him, also came to her apartment and told of conditions in southern Italy. He was a traveler and journalist who had just written and dedicated to the Brownings a volume entitled *Rome in 1860,* which condemned the Papal government for its inefficient, corrupt, and repressive administration. Besides Bowring, Pantaleoni, and Dicey, all of whom were chiefly interested in politics, Elizabeth spoke with the recently appointed British consul in Rome, Joseph Severn, who gave her fresh details about the death of Keats. One of the last visitors Elizabeth received before returning to Florence was Hans Christian Andersen, who kissed her hand "and seemed in a general *verve* for embracing." She was much attracted to him and thought that he was "very earnest, very simple, very childlike." In his honor she wrote "The North and the South," the last poem of her career.

When Rome was becoming intolerably hot with the approach of summer, the Brownings looked forward to a holiday in Paris and the French coast that they might once again be with Robert's father and sister and with Arabel, who had agreed to make the trip from London. Owing to the wars in Italy they had not seen their families for almost three years. Late in May, however, Browning realized that Elizabeth was far too weak to travel so far and therefore canceled all plans for the journey to France. Although she protested the decision for Robert's sake, knowing his disappointment that he could not see his father and sister for at least another year, she was much relieved at not having to undertake the long, tiresome trip. Five months had passed since she had received the news of Henrietta's death, but she had still not recovered from the shock. A day or two before Browning called off the holiday across the Alps, Elizabeth wrote Arabel [22] that she had been in nobody's house since she arrived in Rome, that even a short drive made her tired, and that she loathed the idea of leaving Italy. She acknowledged that she was "in a morbid sort of state, hating the idea of an old friend, an old association, the face of anyone who ever looked at me in my 'previous state of being.'" It seemed to her that she was made of paper and tore if anyone so much as touched her.

IN VIEW of her weakness and depressed spirits, she hoped to spend the summer in some quiet, airy place not too far from Florence. On Wednesday evening, June 5, 1861, after a carriage trip which had tired her more than usual, she arrived with her family at Casa Guidi, where they planned to stay only a few weeks. On the following day the unexpected news of the death of Cavour, who was but fifty years old, was a severe blow, which actually hastened her own death. She suffered as though from a personal bereavement and was struck down at a time when she had lost her powers of recuperation. Owing to her weak lungs and almost continuous cough, her health had always been precarious even in the most favorable circumstances. During her first ten years in Italy she had been stronger than at any time of her life; then a series of shocks gradually undermined her health: the death of her father, the peace of Villafranca, the death of Henrietta, and finally the death of Cavour. "I can scarcely command voice or hand to name *Cavour*," she wrote Sarianna on the day after she heard the news. "That great soul, which meditated and made Italy, has gone to the Diviner country. If tears or blood could have saved him to us, he should have had mine. I feel yet as if I could scarcely comprehend the greatness of the vacancy. . . . May God save Italy."

On June 13 Browning wrote the Storys that Elizabeth had not left the apartment since her return. In the three or four sentences which Elizabeth added to this letter, she again referred to the loss which had so deeply affected her: "Ba can only write a word— She has not the heart—in the face of this great calamity—what a return to Florence!—I have felt beaten and bruised ever since —though the banners are all out this morning for the as-good-as-official 'recognition of Italy'—but there's a crepe on the flag, and the joy is as flowers on graves." [23] One of the last pieces of writing from her pen was a half-finished letter to Jessie White Mario, which Story found in Elizabeth's portfolio; it was, he said, "full of noble words, about Italy."

After her return to Casa Guidi, Elizabeth took no drives, made no visits, and saw no one at her home except two or three intimate friends, who thought that she was beginning to look well again. According to Kate Field, people who knew Elizabeth in her later years believed that she never looked better than immediately after her return to Florence. But whatever appearance of good health she may have had was deceptive. After she had been at home for a few days, Browning said to her, pointing to the balcony which looked toward San Felice Church, "We used, you know, to walk on this verandah so often—come and walk up and down once. Just once." [24] She went to the window, took two steps, but was so fatigued that she went back into the room and lay down on the sofa. Thus she passed a fortnight, during which she stayed mostly in seclusion and tried to recapture enough strength to escape from the stifling heat of Florence and go away possibly to Siena that they might be near the Storys for another summer.

Late in the afternoon of Thursday, June 20, when Browning was away at a newsroom, Elizabeth opened the windows to feel the cool evening air and placed herself in the midst of several cross-drafts. Isa Blagden, who was paying her daily visit, warned her of the imprudence of thus exposing herself. She replied that there was no danger, for she was protected from the breeze by the cushion at the back of her chair. When Browning returned and had tea, Elizabeth said, "I think I have a sore throat." The next day she had a heavy cold and coughed during much of Friday night. She was so distressed Saturday night that Browning went out and brought back Dr. Wilson,[25] an English physician practicing in Florence, who treated her in various ways until he left at five o'clock in the morning. From Sunday until Friday her condition was much the same, although the symptoms were always said to be "a little better." Dr. Wilson reported that the right lung was congested and that he suspected it had an abscess. She had no anxiety about herself and believed that her illness was less severe than the one from which she suffered two summers ago. "It is the old story," she said to Browning; "they don't know my case— I have been tapped and sounded so, and condemned so, repeatedly . . . This is only one of my old attacks. I know all about it and I shall get better." Every day Browning carried her into the drawing room, where she read the newspapers, took no nourishment other than a little clear soup, and was too weak to talk to anyone outside her family.

On Thursday evening, June 27, she said to Isa Blagden, who had been allowed to make a short call, that she was "decidedly better," and Isa returned to her villa convinced that Elizabeth was gaining strength. The following day Elizabeth and Browning discussed the possibility of renting a villa in Florence. For several months he had been negotiating for an apartment in the Palazzo Barberini in the opposite wing of the building from the Storys' suite. Suddenly it seemed to the Brownings that Casa Guidi, which had been their pleasant home for thirteen years, was hot, noisy, and uncomfortable. Robert agreed that it would be best to take a villa, since they had decided upon Rome as their permanent winter residence, and asked what benefit they derived from returning each spring to a town house where they could not live for more than a few weeks. Elizabeth replied that she could not leave Florence, which she liked as much as ever. He mentioned the Villa Niccolini, which was available, and she asked him to make enquiry right away.

That evening Signora Romagnoli (Wilson) thought that Elizabeth was much improved and more cheerful. Elizabeth told of her desire to get away to Siena as soon as possible, and when Wilson left, she supposed that all was well with her mistress. Pen came in, said good night to his mother, and asked twice, "Are you really better?" Each time she replied, *"Much* better." Dr. Wilson also encouraged Browning when he gave his cautious opinion that she was "perhaps a little better." Isa Blagden came at eight o'clock and spoke about the new Italian Prime Minister, Baron Bettino Ricasoli, whose career Elizabeth had followed with approval when he was an able and patriotic President of the Council of Tuscany after the treaty of Villafranca. Elizabeth showed so much excitement as she talked about the Italian situation that Browning asked Isa to leave. While he was preparing some medicine, with his back turned for a moment, Elizabeth whispered, "Did you say Ricasoli said his politics were identical with those of Cavour, only they took different views of the best way of carrying them out?" When Isa replied "Yes," Elizabeth said, "Ah, so I thought." [26] And so in the last conversation Elizabeth had with her closest friend in Florence, she expressed her concern for the future of the country for whose cause she had used up much of her strength. Isa left the room with the feeling that Elizabeth was much better.

As Browning sat beside her that night, he was worried at her uneven sleep. Whenever he spoke to her, she knew him, smiled, and assured him she was better. At three o'clock he noticed that her feet were cold. He was alarmed, sent the porter immediately for Dr. Wilson, bathed her hands and feet in warm water, and fed her some jellied chicken broth. When Elizabeth heard Browning ask Annunziata to fetch some hot water, she said in amusement, "Well, you *are* making an exaggerated case of it!" Then followed "the most perfect expression of her love" to Browning he had ever known from her. Afterward he sponged her hands a second time, and she fell asleep again almost immediately. In her last moment of consciousness she had no inkling that death was about to come, felt no pain, and supposed only that she was much better and before long would go to the villa where she had earlier lived in Siena. At half past four, Saturday morning, June 29, 1861, she died in Browning's arms. When her head fell down on him, after a moment of suspense while she was struggling to cough, he thought at first she had fainted. Then the brows contracted slightly, and Annunziata cried out that she had passed away. After her death she looked, as Browning later told Story, "like a young girl; all the outlines rounded and filled up, all traces of disease effaced, and a smile on her face so living that they could not for hours persuade themselves she was really dead." As day was breaking, Dr. Wilson arrived and said that her death was probably caused by the breaking of the abscess in the lung. He had realized that her condition was serious but had not thought the end so near.

Isa Blagden, who had been summoned at dawn, came down immediately from her villa, spent the day with Browning, and in the evening took Pen back to her home, where he stayed until his father and he left Florence. The Storys, who were in Leghorn waiting to learn whether the Brownings would join them for another summer in Siena, came immediately to Florence. As Story

Last Poems and Final Illness

looked at Elizabeth's table with her letters and books and her small chair beside it, Browning said to him, "The cycle is complete; here we came fifteen years ago; here Pen was born; here Ba wrote her poems for Italy. She used to walk up and down this verandah in the summer evenings, when, revived by the southern air, she first again began to enjoy her out-doors life." Little by little she had lost strength, and her walks had become shorter and shorter. Only a few hours before her death she had talked of leaving Casa Guidi for a villa outside the gates of Florence. And so it was that in their home they had rounded the circle, and in a sense Browning had come again to the point he had left long ago. Looking back upon the years since his marriage, he could see that Elizabeth and he had "been all the time walking over a torrent on a straw."

On Monday, July 1, the shops in the section of the city around Casa Guidi were closed, while Elizabeth was mourned with unusual demonstrations, for the Italians, as Browning said, "seem to have understood her by an instinct." The Florentine newspapers announced with sorrow the death of the greatest living woman poet, one of the city's most distinguished residents, and a true friend of the Italian cause.[27]

That evening at seven o'clock in a service conducted by a Church of England clergyman [28] the remains of Elizabeth Barrett Browning were interred in the old Protestant Cemetery, near the heart of the city she had come to love and call her home.

20. Epilogue: A Century of Criticism

ALTHOUGH after his mother's death Pen had been staying with Isa Blagden, Browning remained alone at Casa Guidi until the day after the funeral, when he suddenly became so ill with grief that he left the empty apartment and walked up to Miss Blagden's villa. Until his departure from Florence a month later, he went to the villa every night, returning to his own rooms in the daytime. He realized that in spite of his love for Florence, he could not remain in that city because the associations would have been too painful. So he immediately decided to go to London and there to devote himself to his poetry and to the education of Pen. "Life must now be begun anew," he said to Story; "all the old cast off and the new one put on. I shall go away, break up everything, go to England and live and work and write." Likewise he wrote to his sister Sarianna, "I shall never again 'keep house,' nor live but in the simplest manner, but always with reference to Pen."

The boy who in Browning's opinion had become too Italian in his costume and manners was to receive an English education and upbringing. "Of course Pen is and will be English as I am English and as his Mother was pure English . . . ," Browning maintained to John Forster. Only four days after the funeral Browning wrote his sister that, "Pen, the golden curls and fantastic dress, is gone just as Ba is gone: he has short hair, worn boy-wise, long trousers, is a common boy all at once." After having sold some of his possessions and placed the rest in storage, Browning left for Paris, together with Pen and Isa Blagden, on August 1. He was never again to see the city where he had spent the happiest years of his life. At Paris, Isa left Browning and Pen and went to England, where she lived for a year, part of the time near the

Epilogue: A Century of Criticism

bereaved poet, before returning to her Florentine home. After spending most of August and September at St. Enogat on the coast of France with his father, his sister, and his son, Browning went with Pen to London in the autumn. He eventually settled at 19 Warwick Crescent in order to be near Arabel Barrett, who was living in the same neighborhood at Delamere Terrace.

In the long, busy years ahead Browning's "heart was buried in Florence," as he himself said; he never remarried. After the death of his father in 1866, his sister came to live with him in London and thereafter was his constant companion. The child upon whom so much care had been lavished by a devoted mother was equally spoiled by the father. Pen was not sent away from home to a private or to a public school and was educated in such a haphazard manner that he failed in several examinations for entrance to Baliol. For a year or two he was enrolled at Christ Church, Oxford, but was interested primarily in rowing and in billiards. Later he became a sculptor and a painter, without achieving much success in either field, and eventually made his home in Italy.

Robert Browning gained belated recognition as one of England's greatest poets after the publication in 1868–69 of *The Ring and the Book* and received honorary degrees from Oxford, Cambridge, and Edinburgh. In later years volume after volume came from his prolific pen, but much of his poetry was less creative, less dramatic, and more analytical and reflective. He not only continued to publish with unflagging energy, but also was a prominent figure in London society, attending countless dinner parties, concerts, art exhibitions, and receptions. It was not until 1878, after an absence of seventeen years, that Browning again saw the country where he had lived during his marriage. For all but three years afterward he returned late in the summer to northern Italy. It was during one of these annual visits that he died at Venice in his son's home, the magnificent Palazzo Rezzonico, at the age of seventy-seven—twenty-eight years after his wife's death.

ALTHOUGH Mrs. Browning's poetical reputation in England had suffered during the last two or three years of her life because of her political poems, the writers of obituary notices in the leading critical journals rescued her from the disfavor into which she had fallen. They were shocked to learn of her untimely death, which in their opinion prevented her genius from reaching its fullest development. For example, the *Saturday Review,* which had ridiculed *Aurora Leigh* and attacked *Poems before Congress* because of her "un-English" point of view, said, "In English literature, as well as in Italian society, her premature death will leave a visible and melancholy blank." [1] Most of the announcements of her death reviewed her career almost from the beginning. The unanimous opinion was that in spite of her many offenses against poetic taste and her isolation, which hindered her from observing life in its fullness and complexity, she was the greatest woman poet in English literature—in the judgment of several writers, the greatest in the history of the world. The *Spectator* said that she had been "one of the very few truly creative minds of whom England could still boast—one who in poetic gifts ranked far above all her countrywomen" and that she was the only English woman who deserved a place among "our genuine poets." [2] Although the *Edinburgh Review* found a sense of unreality in much of her verse because of her confinement to a sick chamber, it nevertheless asserted that her equal could not be found in the literary history of any country: "Such a combination of the finest genius and the choicest results of cultivation and wide-ranging studies has never been seen before in any woman, nor is the world likely soon to see the same again." [3] It was probably her old friend Chorley who wrote the article in the *Athenaeum,* which announced with regret the death of "the greatest of English poetesses of any time." [4] He traced her career from the time when he first saw her anonymous "The Romaunt of Margret" in the *New Monthly Magazine* in 1836 and had been struck by its "daring and deep originality." Chorley had stabbed her in the back when he harshly criticized her *Poems before Congress,* but he tried to make amends by writing of her literary skill, her intellectual ability, her absence of pretension, her fearlessness in treating unpopular subjects, and the affection and loyalty she had always shown to relatives and friends.

Among the American notices, Kate Field in the *Atlantic Monthly* [5] and George William Curtis in *Harper's Magazine* [6] both described Mrs. Browning as they had remembered her and told of

Epilogue: A Century of Criticism 407

her appearance, personality, and surroundings. Curtis, who had seen the Brownings in Florence early in their years together and had joined them in a trip to Vallombrosa, ranked her "among the chief English poets of this century" and believed that she was unusual among poets in that she was "not only a singer but a hearty, active worker in her way, understanding her time, and trying, as she could, to help it." He thought that since the *Vita nuova* and the sonnets of Shakespeare and Petrarch, almost no one had written poems on the subject of love "so true and sweet and subtle" as the author of the "Sonnets from the Portuguese." Perhaps the highest praise in any American periodical came from the *Southern Literary Messenger*,[7] which called her "the Shakespeare among her sex" and was convinced that among all the poems written by women of all eras and nations, there was "absolutely nothing which deserves to be compared for a moment with the marvellous effusions of this poetess." The writer placed her among the four or five greatest authors since the beginning of civilization: "Mrs. Browning has planted her feet on the mountains of Immortality, and stands glorified with Homer, Dante, Shakespeare, Milton, Goethe, and Shelley,—that august circle of laurelled bards, whose names will go down in music through the echoing aisles of the future." It is clear that immediately after her death she was at the pinnacle of her poetic reputation both in England and in America.

On March 20, 1862,[8] Chapman and Hall brought out her *Last Poems*, which had been collected by Browning. It was a slender octavo volume composed mostly of translations she had made before her marriage for a classical album which had never appeared and of the Italian pieces written after *Poems before Congress*. The reviews mostly commented on and quoted from such poems as "De Profundis" and "A Musical Instrument," which they preferred to the Italian lyrics. Besides discussing the recent volume, most of the notices considered her entire poetic career, of which they spoke no less warmly than when they had announced her death in the preceding summer. The *Dublin University Magazine* expressed the prevailing judgment when it said that she was "one whom many will doubtless rank as the greatest poetess the world has ever known." [9] Once again Chorley in the *Athenaeum* recalled the delight he had experienced when he came upon her first published poems, reaffirmed his belief that her name would live among the first rank of English poets, and declared that "in sweep of thought, in richness of culture, in pertinence of language" she was the greatest of all English woman poets.[10] The volume of *Last Poems* which was published in New York simultaneously with the English edition contained a preface, or "Memorial" as it was called, of more than seventy pages written by Theodore Tilton, editor of the *Independent*. In his opinion Mrs. Browning had both a wider range of subjects and more readers than her husband. Much of her work, he believed, was the finest since Shakespeare and Milton. He thought that her greatness lay in her eloquent expressions of human hopes, fears, joys, and sorrows and in the profound religious quality of her verses, which brought comfort and inspiration to her readers. As a religious poet she was "more devout than George Herbert, more fervid than Charles Wesley."

The fifth edition of her *Poems*, which was a reprint of the fourth edition of 1856, was also issued in 1862 and received even more critical attention than the *Last Poems*. Except for the unfavorable notice in the *Saturday Review*,[11] the other influential journals were extravagant in their praise. The *Christian Examiner*[12] wrote that Mrs. Browning's career was unique in the history of distinguished women, for "the lives of women of genius have been so frequently sullied by sin, as well as darkened by sorrow, that it has been accepted almost as an axiom, that their intellectual gifts are a curse rather than a blessing." Mrs. Browning, however, had been "pure and lovely" in her private life and "noble and dignified" in her authorship. The writer thought that "In Memoriam" and "Aurora Leigh" were the two greatest poems of the age, just as "A Blot in the 'Scutcheon" was its greatest drama. Furthermore, he believed that Tennyson was the most finished artist of the trio, that Browning had the greatest dramatic power, and that Elizabeth excelled in nobility and in strength of thought. It seemed to him that there were no finer love poems in English than the "Sonnets from the Portuguese." "Such purity, sweet humility, lofty self-abnegation, and impassioned tenderness have never before found utterance in verse," he continued. "Shakespeare's son-

Epilogue: A Century of Criticism

nets, beautiful as they are, cannot be compared with them, and Petrarch's seem commonplace beside them."

Similar expressions appear in almost all the notices. The *North American Review* called her "the queen of song" and said that although she was not another Shakespeare, "she came nearest to being Shakespeare's counterpart." [13] The *North British Review* believed that if a "poetess" like Sappho could see the wealth of poetry produced by Mrs. Browning, she "would shrink from her own fame." It seemed to the reviewer that "in passionate tenderness, capaciousness of imagination, freshness of feeling, vigour of thought, wealth of ideas, and loftiness of soul," her poetry stood alone among all that had been written by women.[14] The *Eclectic Review* was also convinced that she was "universally now crowned chief woman-poet of any age or time" and that among the greatest writers of world literature including Homer, Shakespeare, and Milton, "with the exception of Dante, not one had, as she had, entered into the scenery, the mystery, the majesty, the sorrow and glory of the higher life." [15] *Blackwood's* was certain that her place among the immortals was secure and that however much she might be criticized in the future for her faults of style, "the final result will still leave her immovable on her high pedestal." [16] According to the writer, she was almost unique in that she had both exquisite sensibility and unusual intellectual activity, with each intensifying and aiding the other. In general, the reviews of the fifth edition of the *Poems* preferred the "Sonnets from the Portuguese" and such poems as "The Cry of the Children" and "Cowper's Grave" and considered that her political poems were a misdirected effort and that *Aurora Leigh* contained a mixture of both her best and her worst qualities.

In 1863 Browning issued under the imprint of Chapman and Hall *The Greek Christian Poets and the English Poets,* the text of which was based on his wife's essays as they had appeared originally in the *Athenaeum* in 1842. He said in the preface that his reason for publishing the book was that his wife had always had it in mind eventually to make additions and corrections to the essays, which had been all but forgotten by the public, and to bring them together in a new volume. The enthusiastic response from almost all professional critics must have gratified Browning.

The *Athenaeum* asserted that the work was "one of remarkable and abiding interest" and that Mrs. Browning's prose was "from first to last always the richer for her poetry."[17] A new periodical in London entitled the *Reader* thought that the book contained "a wonderful amount of sound criticism and valuable thought."[18] Among the American reviews the *Knickerbocker Monthly*[19] welcomed the volume for the "elasticity and exuberance" of its prose and for the "exquisite" translations. The review in the *Christian Examiner* was probably by Kate Field, who called Mrs. Browning a true scholar (for she had seen the poet's Hebrew Bible with her marginal notes in Greek), a consummate artist, and a perfect woman.[20]

IT WAS not until 1877 that the public had an opportunity to see some of Mrs. Browning's correspondence. Her letters to R. H. Horne, who had received permission to publish from Browning, were edited by S. R. Townshend Mayer and issued in London in two volumes by Richard Bentley and Son. The correspondence, which was most active between 1840 and 1846, dealt largely with such literary projects as *The Poems of Geoffrey Chaucer, Modernized, A New Spirit of the Age,* and the projected drama "Psyche Apocalypté." In the memoir which served as an introduction to the New York edition of the letters, the American critic and poet Richard Henry Stoddard told of Mrs. Browning's life and writings. He said that although sixteen years had passed since her death, no biography had yet been written, that less was known of her than of any other English woman of genius, and that the sum of the present knowledge about her consisted of the dates of the publications of her writings and a few facts about her life found in the published reminiscences of travelers and in the recently issued correspondence of Miss Mitford.

The letters to Horne were well received both in England and in the United States. The critical notices were in agreement that the tone of her correspondence was natural and spontaneous and that it had more gayety than a reader of her poetry would have expected. The New York *Nation*,[21] for example, said that the letters were charming and that they offered "a peculiarly pleasing mixture of the ladylike and the highly-intelligent." The impres-

Epilogue: A Century of Criticism 411

sion they left upon the reviewer was "somewhat akin to that of an agreeable woman's voice—soft, substantial, and expressive." The *Literary World* of Boston referred to her as "true woman and true poet" and believed that many people had "not yet unlearned their reverence for her womanhood nor their love for her pure and noble verse." [22] It was apparently the fresh interest in Mrs. Browning's life and works which stimulated the writing of an article in *Lippincott's Magazine* in 1878.[23] The author coupled Mrs. Browning with Shakespeare, both of whom had "a lavish spontaneity, a swift, uncontrollable impulse of emotional force, a daring freedom of utterance." He added that the greater were her faults of style, "the more her transcendent genius shines in them and through them and over them."

Late Victorian criticism of Mrs. Browning placed great emphasis upon the ethical and religious values of her poetry. It was especially in America that writers dwelt on this aspect of her work. For example, an article published in 1887 in the *Andover Review,* which was edited by the professors of the Andover Theological Seminary in Massachusetts, said that such "pure and sympathetic" poems of her early career as "Isobel's Child," "Bertha in the Lane," or "Lady Geraldine's Courtship" could not fail to stir the depths of the reader's conscience or to arouse his spiritual energies. The writer was convinced that her triumph both in her writings and in her life was "of a distinctively Christian order." In the following grandiloquent passage he was apparently referring to her humanitarian poems: "She descended from the Mount of Transfiguration, where the glory of the Christ had been revealed; but, unlike the useless disciples, she brought with her the mountain splendor and the mountain power to confront and drive away the sin and suffering in the plains of humanity." [24]

A few years later Theodore W. Hunt published in the *Presbyterian and Reformed Review* of Philadelphia an article with a similar theme. Hunt, who was a professor of English literature at Princeton University and an ordained Presbyterian clergyman, believed that through her teaching, English womanhood had become "a more sacred thing than ever." In his opinion everything she wrote "was suffused and surcharged with the very essence of piety; clean and chaste and white as the snow of heaven." He felt that although Mrs. Browning's verse was not widely popular, it was best appreciated by the few readers in every country who look for "character" in literature, and he added, "So intensely transforming is this illuminating presence, that at times it assumes a kind of beatific charm and makes it impossible for any mind within the area of its influence to think of anything but God and goodness and truth and virtue." [25] It was not only in America that critics wrote thus. In 1896, the year of Hunt's publication, an article entitled "The Ethical Impulse of Mrs. Browning's Poetry" appeared in the *Westminster Review*.[26] The writer had nothing but praise for her work because it had a deeper spiritual content than any other poetry of the century. In his vague expression, her verses were "largely charged with the sensitive vibration of the spiritual transports of our inmost consciousness."

A notice of her *Poetical Works* in the Boston *Literary World* in 1885 was somewhat more realistic in its estimate of her reputation, which the reviewer believed had lessened since her death.[27] He suggested that the reason for this apathy was that the present age had little interest in poetry, and he complained that the spirit of the times was scientific, materialistic, and utilitarian. It seemed to him that no one in America wrote or discussed poetry except a small literary class and that the general reading public was devoted to mechanical contrivances and to superficial amusements. He thought, however, that Mrs. Browning was a true poet, that her faults were trivial, since she often gained in spontaneity whatever she might have lost in carelessness of expression. In his opinion, the "Sonnets from the Portuguese" were both the finest sonnets and the greatest love poems in English literature. It was his prediction that one hundred years hence her fame would be much greater.

After the appearance of the letters to Horne in 1877, the next important date when the literary world focused its attention upon Mrs. Browning's life and work was 1888, the year in which John H. Ingram issued the first full-length biography of her for his "Eminent Women Series." Ingram had applied to Browning for permission to draw upon some of her unpublished correspondence, but Browning, who was out of sympathy with the project, did not grant the request. Therefore Ingram had no new material to pre-

Epilogue: A Century of Criticism 413

sent and had to fall back on published reminiscences which had long been familiar. Furthermore he was inaccurate in several of his statements. For example, he asserted that his researches had proved without doubt that Mrs. Browning was born in London in 1809,[28] and he rejected as impossible Browning's recent statement that the date was 1806. The book had an unhappy reception from almost all critics, who deplored the dispute and felt that if the poet had not wished a full-dress biography of his wife to appear during his lifetime, his feelings should have been respected. In addition to its dearth of new biographical information, the volume was also censured for its long quotations of hackneyed poems and for its stale and meaningless criticism. On the other hand, most of the notices of the biography spoke respectfully of Mrs. Browning's verse. The *London Quarterly Review* believed that her poems furnished "the most astonishing and beautiful contrast to the heart-chilling and melancholy pessimism" which was becoming fashionable. In protest against the agnostic spirit of the age, the reviewer asked God to have mercy "on these erring poet-souls" but gave thanks for the work of Elizabeth Browning.[29] Arthur Christopher Benson in his review of Ingram's book entered a minority report with his acknowledgment that he could no longer read with pleasure much of Mrs. Browning's verse.[30] Yet he liked her romantic ballads and thought she would be remembered for these, for her simpler lyrics, and most of all for the "Sonnets from the Portuguese."

As long as Browning was alive there was no possibility of the publication either of an adequate biography of his wife or of a comprehensive selection of her correspondence. Eight years after the poet's death in 1889, Frederic G. Kenyon helped to supply one of these two needs by editing a large collection of Mrs. Browning's letters. The publication of the two volumes by Smith, Elder, and Company in October 1897 was one of the most important literary events of the season. The letters were mostly addressed to her life-long friends Mrs. Martin, Miss Mitford, Boyd, Mrs. Jameson, Kenyon, Sarianna Browning, Isa Blagden, and Fanny Haworth. A comparison of Kenyon's text with the holographs, most of which are in the Wellesley College Library, shows that he omitted remarks about her pregnancies, her use of morphine, other medical details about herself and her friends, family gossip, and uncomplimentary or equivocal references to persons who were still alive in 1897.

Her correspondence is unusually repetitious because she often wrote almost identical letters to four or five different persons. By skillful selection Kenyon eliminated much of this overlapping material. His most serious omissions were the hundreds of letters both to Boyd and to Miss Mitford before Mrs. Browning's marriage and the many intimate letters to Henrietta and to Arabel, but all these portions of the correspondence were not yet available. The reviews were almost unanimous in their feeling that Kenyon had edited the letters with good taste, and they approved of his supplementing the correspondence with biographical information. Many critics wondered how a person whose health was so fragile could have had the strength to produce such a mass of letters, little realizing that the two volumes contained only a small proportion of her total correspondence. In general, the writers of the notices in the newspapers and journals were especially interested in the first 300 pages which came from the pen of Miss Barrett, since the story of her married life had been somewhat familiar after the publication of Mrs. Orr's biography in 1891. Several of the reviews regretted the iteration of her faith in spiritualism and in Napoleon III, and they were surprised that she made so few references to serious intellectual pursuits after her marriage.

The consensus of the reviews was that her poetical reputation was lower than it had been and that in another generation much of her writing would be forgotten, or else, in the words of the *Spectator,* "her best work will have shaken itself free of the dross and superfluity, and stand or fall with the language." [31] All of the notices spoke well of Mrs. Browning's prose style, which they thought sincere, natural, human, and often lightened with humor. There was nothing in Kenyon's volumes which detracted from her reputation; her letters indeed added to her stature, so that to almost everyone she appeared to have the "most wonderful spirit," the "greatest soul," the "most truly passionate nature"—these and many similar expressions appear in the reviews—of anyone who wrote English verse in the nineteenth century. The poet was being

Epilogue: A Century of Criticism 415

replaced by the personality, the woman, the wife, the friend. The New York *Nation,* which was typical of the other journals and newspapers in its approval of the letters, wrote, "We are enabled as never before to conceive of her character in its entirety; and there is nothing in the conception which does not enhance our sympathy with her aspirations as a poet and our admiration for her conduct of her life in every personal way." [32] The most respected newspaper in Boston, the *Transcript,* which was enthralled by this "pair of wonderful volumes," declared in the flowery language of the age that in the letters "there is a true life poem, an expression of a personality sound and sweet and wholesome, rounded and healthful, out-giving in loving kindness and in all the graces of beneficence, of unpretentious economy and of hospitality, with a firm unwavering hold of all the simplest, sweetest sources of happiness in life." [33] If similar passages from other reviews were cited, they would be in agreement that the letters showed Mrs. Browning to have been a woman with ardent impulses, wide and generous sympathies, independence of judgment, a rare faculty for seeing the best in people and institutions, a loving disposition, and a hatred of any kind of tyranny and injustice.

Early in 1899 and somewhat more than a year after the appearance of the Kenyon volumes, the love letters written by Elizabeth Barrett and Robert Browning were published at a time when there was a great public interest in the two poets. Pen Browning explained in a prefatory note that ever since his mother's death the letters had been kept by his father in an inlaid box, with each in its consecutive order and numbered by him. The poet destroyed the rest of his correspondence and not long before his death handed the love letters to Pen, saying, "There they are, do with them as you please when I am dead and gone!" Many of the reviews expressed astonishment that the son would have published the letters, particularly in view of the pain his mother experienced whenever she felt that anyone had infringed upon her privacy. Although they questioned the propriety of Pen's decision, they agreed that his choice was lucrative for him and agreeable for the readers of the two volumes. The *Athenaeum,* for example, said, "We should like to think that Browning never conceived the possibility of his son's publishing them; but, even if he had such an unexpressed idea, more honour would have been done to a great poet's memory by destroying them than by allowing it for a moment to be thought that he sanctioned their publication." [34] Leslie Stephen felt that in reading the letters, which had been printed without omissions or alterations, he was overhearing confidences which neither of the correspondents had ever intended should one day be broadcast to the common ear.[35] It seemed to him, as it did to several other critics, that it might have been wiser to present a selection than the complete text. Everyone was agreed that there was nothing in the closely packed 1,100 pages which did not redound to the credit of both correspondents. To cite from a typical review, the Boston *Literary World* asserted, "Such a high-minded, delicate, unselfish pair of lovers as Robert Browning and Elizabeth Barrett it would be hard to parallel in fact or fiction." [36] The critics were charmed by the correspondence and thought that it was one of the most precious contributions to nineteenth-century literary history. As the *Spectator* expressed it, "We venture to think that no such remarkable and unbroken series of intimate letters between two remarkable people has ever been given to the world." [37]

On the whole the reviews were more interested in Elizabeth's than in Robert's letters. It was through her eyes that the readers of the volumes saw for the first time the extent of Mr. Barrett's tyranny and the shock she received from the Pisa business in the fall of 1845. With two or three exceptions everyone believed that her letters justified the private marriage and the removal to Italy. The critics also maintained that Elizabeth, with her courage, her absence of pretension and self-pity, and her breadth of outlook was indeed worthy of the noble passion she had inspired. In the words of the *Edinburgh Review,* the woman seen in these letters was "a poet in every fibre of her, but adorably feminine, weak with more than a woman's weakness and strong with more than a woman's strength." [38] In comparing her prose style with Browning's, many of the journals commented upon the ease with which she expressed herself, in contrast to her fiancé's stiff, awkward manner and his long, contorted sentences in which he often failed to make his meaning clear. Furthermore, a number of critics observed that she had more humor in her letters than he. As the

Edinburgh Review wrote, "she could be relied upon never to see the droll side of a thing at the wrong moment, either for herself or for another."

It may have been the publication of part of Mrs. Browning's correspondence and of the love letters which awakened a fresh interest in her poetry. In commenting on the various editions of her *Poetical Works* which were issued during the later Victorian years, critical journals repeatedly placed her far above Emily Brontë and Christina Rossetti and declared that she stood alone in the expression of the womanhood in her. Her poetry, they said, appealed chiefly to women because of her understanding of the depth, tenderness, and humility of the love which is given by women.[39] Her works were also being read and discussed in French periodicals, and it was a French woman, curiously enough, who produced the first full-length biography based on the recently published letters. Germaine-Marie Merlette issued in 1905 *La Vie et l'œuvre d'Elizabeth Barrett Browning,* which was her thesis for the doctorate at the University of Paris. Although Mlle. Merlette did not have access to Mrs. Browning's manuscripts and presented no biographical information which had not appeared in print, she succeeded in compiling a sound, well-balanced study which was well received in England [40] and long remained the standard work in its field.

THE YEAR 1906 was marked by many publications in observance of the centenary of Mrs. Browning's birth. The March issue of *Book News,* which was published in Philadelphia, was devoted to a series of articles on her life and writings. In one of these essays Thomas Wentworth Higginson [41] recalled the day more than sixty years ago when a cousin brought him a manuscript copy of "The Lay of the Brown Rosary," which had not yet been published in America. Along with many of his young friends in Boston, he had soon learned it by heart, and a few months later they also memorized "Lady Geraldine's Courtship," a copy of which they saw before its publication. Afterward he had shown great interest in her career and now and then heard James and Maria Lowell in Cambridge read from the letters they had received from her in Italy. In this commemorative issue of *Book*

News another American critic Henry S. Pancoast wrote on her present reputation. He maintained that although her vogue had passed, her place among the great English poets was secure because she "gave something to English poetry that with all its riches it had never before possessed. It is the woman that speaks in her descriptions of babies; in her love of children, in her heartbreak over pain." [42] The editors of the New York *Bookman* announced that they were not planning to issue a special number to commemorate the anniversary.[43] They added, however, that if they had done so, they would certainly have made "more of a to-do over Mrs. Browning than over her husband, for she was undoubtedly in pure poetry a greater genius than he." That Browning had the greater intellect was in their opinion indisputable, but they thought that "for sheer beauty of diction and for perfect music" her best work was finer than anything he achieved. Few critics at this period were so generous in their judgments of her poetry. Percy Lubbock, who published in 1906 a volume of Mrs. Browning's selected letters interspersed with his own comments on her life and writings, expressed the prevailing opinion that much of her work which had been enthusiastically received two generations earlier was unfamiliar to many readers. Now that poets were paying more attention to form, he believed that her careless craftsmanship could not be condoned. Yet he was convinced that she had possessed a great soul and was one of the most fiery geniuses of the nineteenth century and that however much her poetic reputation had declined, her point of view had become all the more interesting since the publication of her letters.

It was not many years after the centenary of his mother's birth that Pen Browning died at his home in Asolo, Italy, after an uneventful and fruitless life. Since he had no children, the books, manuscripts, art objects, furnishings, and other relics which he had inherited from his parents were bequeathed to a number of relatives, who had the collections sold at auction in May 1913. The decision of the Moulton Barrett cousins to dispose thus of the property may have been justified economically, but Browning scholarship would have been better served if the materials had been kept together and made available for future students. After the Sotheby sale the holographs of Mrs. Browning's poems and

Epilogue: A Century of Criticism 419

letters went into the hands of dealers and collectors on both sides of the Atlantic and remained in hiding for more than a generation until they found their way into permanent collections. Thus no one during this long period attempted any serious study of her life or writings. Many critics and poets during the late Victorian and the Edwardian eras had been discussing her poetry, but they did so only on the basis of her published letters and poems. In America E. C. Stedman, Richard Watson Gilder, Lewis Edwards Gates, and William James Dawson were drawn to her, and among British critics Edmund Gosse, Theodore Watts-Dunton, Edward Dowden, George Saintsbury, Henry Jones, and many others dealt sympathetically with her poetry. While all of these writers admitted her shortcomings, they were in agreement that in a few poems she rose to the highest levels and was unsurpassed by any other woman poet. Furthermore they all realized that no one had taken her place since her death.

Although her poetry was read and discussed during the first World War and the following decade, it was not until the late 1920's that the story of the Brownings seemed once again to captivate the public, even more so than it had a generation earlier at the time of the publication of the love letters. In response to this great interest at least eight volumes were issued between 1928 and 1931 on Elizabeth or on the Brownings as a couple, with most of the books dwelling on the romance.[44] One of the most important contributions to Browning studies during this period was the volume of Elizabeth's letters to her sister Henrietta, edited by Leonard Huxley and published by John Murray in 1929. Huxley left out about one third of the text: medical details, repetitious comments on Pen, discussions of family matters, and remarks about obscure friends, all of which he thought would be of little general interest. In the passages he published, however, some of the names of the men and women to whom Mrs. Browning refers are indicated by blanks, even though in 1929 the persons whose names were thus erased had long been dead and, furthermore, had not been treated with disrespect in the letters. The correspondence, which was written between 1846 and 1859, presented a new aspect of Mrs. Browning's life; as more than one reviewer noticed, the most important figure to emerge from the letters was Pen, with his burnished curls and velvet frocks. As for the mother herself, the critical notices agreed that she seemed more attractive in her personality and richer in human sympathies than they had supposed her to be. In the opinion of the *London Mercury,* she portrayed herself as a woman who was "eager, warm-hearted, emotional, a little inclined to gush, full of the typical prejudices of her time, yet very human and likeable after all." [45] Likewise Bonamy Dobrée wrote in the *National Review* that in spite of the bric-a-brac of her surroundings, she was still an appealing figure not only because of the poetic quality in her but also because of the emotional richness of her life.[46] Although the letters to Henrietta explained the mother, the wife, and the sister rather than the poet, several reviews, after describing the new material, considered her present position among English women poets. In their judgment she was in her artistic achievement below Christina Rossetti, though they felt that without doubt Mrs. Browning's letters were by far the more interesting.[47]

But even more than the correspondence to Henrietta and the romantic biographies, it was Rudolf Besier's play *The Barretts of Wimpole Street* which made the story familiar to hundreds of thousands in London and New York. After the appearance of the Hollywood screen version of the play, the romance of the Brownings was known to millions, many of whom had never before even heard of the two poets. Although Besier took many of his lines from the published letters, he manipulated his material freely for dramatic purposes. The scene is Elizabeth's room, and the action is concentrated in the few months before her wedding, to which the Barretts refer at the end of the play after the heroine has fled to France. With the exception of Elizabeth and Henrietta, the family is dominated by the tyrannical and almost insane father, who is tormented by sexual repressions and has an affection for Elizabeth which she herself perceives is incestuous in its impulses. At first Elizabeth appears to be sick, apathetic, and resigned to her prison, but in the course of the action she is drawn to Browning because of his high spirits, his courage, and his faith. The play is true to the spirit of the romance since it presents the noble qualities of both Browning and Elizabeth. There is, however, no historical basis for the final scene in which Mr. Barrett expresses

Epilogue: A Century of Criticism 421

his rage and frustration after he has heard of Elizabeth's marriage. In point of fact, no one knows precisely what he did or said on that occasion. Nor is there any evidence that Elizabeth's father had the abnormal desires with which Besier endowed the character. (Three of Mrs. Browning's nephews vigorously protested in a letter to *The Times* the "disgusting" charge which had been brought against their grandfather, whose memory, they asserted, had been sullied by this "gross violation of the canons of literary decency.") [48]

Besier's play, which was first produced at the Malvern Festival in England in the summer of 1930 and enjoyed a long run in London during the following season, apparently stimulated Virginia Woolf to write about Mrs. Browning's poetry and life. In an article which appeared simultaneously in the *Yale Review* and *The Times Literary Supplement*,[49] Mrs. Woolf introduced her discussion of *Aurora Leigh* by suggesting that as a result of an irony which might have amused the Brownings themselves they were now better known in the flesh than they had ever been in the spirit: "Like so many other Victorian worthies they have been transformed in the past few years into figures of romance, passionate lovers with curls and side whiskers, peg-top trousers and sweeping skirts. In this guise thousands of people must know and love the Brownings who have never read a line of their poetry." However much *Aurora Leigh* had been applauded during the decade or two after its publication, Mrs. Woolf believed that no one looked at it any more. Yet in spite of its many absurdities the poem held her enthralled with its speed, energy, and self-confidence. It seemed to Mrs. Woolf that *Aurora Leigh* gave the reader a feeling of life, that the characters were struggling bravely with the great problems of the Victorian age. She thought the poem still inspired respect and deserved a better fate than the oblivion into which it had fallen. Two years later, in 1933, Mrs. Woolf added her contribution to the many popular treatments of the lives of the Brownings with her charming and original study entitled *Flush, a Biography*.

IN HER essay on *Aurora Leigh* Mrs. Woolf wrote with humorous exaggeration that no one now read Mrs. Browning's poetry, which was considered by all primers of literature to be second-rate and hopelessly old-fashioned. To be sure, few cultivated people on either side of the Atlantic probably had a first-hand acquaintance with her novel in verse, her angel poems, or her romantic ballads. The "Sonnets from the Portuguese," however, have not been forgotten. After Mrs. Browning's death late Victorian critics ranked them with Shakespeare's sonnets and without hesitation asserted that they were of their type among the greatest poems in the language. E. C. Stedman thought it "no sacrilege to say that their music is showered from a higher and purer atmosphere than that of the Swan of Avon." [50] Likewise Edmund Gosse believed that although Shakespeare's sonnets had a more admirable style, "those addressed by Elizabeth Barrett to her lover are hardly less exquisite to any of us, and to many of us are more wholesome and more intelligible." [51] James Ashcroft Noble was "thrilled and melted" by the "Sonnets," and it seemed to him that it could "hardly be presumptuous to predict that for generations to come the *Sonnets from the Portuguese* will remain, what they undoubtedly now are, the noblest anthology for noble lovers which our language has to show." [52] Quotations from almost all the other late-Victorian critics would show opinions no less enthusiastic.

Serious literary historians are now less impressed by the "Sonnets"—which nevertheless have continued to fascinate a portion of the general reading public. In 1886 Ticknor and Company issued in Boston the first separate edition of the "Sonnets," in the form of a large, heavy folio with elaborate border designs. Since that date scarcely a year has passed in which an edition has not been published in some country. The catalogue of the Harvard College Library records forty different editions (including translations), which have appeared in America, England, France, Germany, Italy, and Spain; and both the Library of Congress and the British Museum have copies of editions which are not in the Harvard collection. Although many readers may have purchased the "Sonnets" with a firm belief in their high literary qualities, the arrangements of publication of the various separate editions are evidence of an attitude which has some of the characteristics of a cult. Most of the editions have been produced in a limited number of copies and by private, noncommercial presses rather

Epilogue: A Century of Criticism 423

than by large publishing houses. In some editions each copy is numbered and signed by the illustrator and was originally offered for sale in an attractive-appearing publisher's box. Various editions were bound in white pigskin, calf, morocco, and gay-colored cloth. Some were printed on English handmade paper; others on Japanese vellum. Many have rubricated initials, decorated borders, and different kinds of ornamental designs. One edition is a series of photographs of the poems, with each elaborately illuminated in the manner of a medieval manuscript.[53] In one of the most striking editions, each poem was sketched on a separate plate, with different drawings above the poems.[54] One hundred years after the first publication of the "Sonnets," the firm of Philip C. Duschnes of New York issued in 1950 the "Centennial Variorum Edition" in a printing limited to five hundred copies.[55] The volume, which was daintily bound in flowered cloth, served a useful purpose by giving variant readings from the three original manuscripts, but it unfortunately failed to indicate the differences among the published texts of 1850, 1853, and 1856. New editions have been published since 1950, and it seems likely that the "Sonnets" will be available at bookshops for many years to come because of their appeal to readers with romantic tastes. One of the most interesting of the recent editions is the Spanish verse translation by an Argentine poet which was published as a modest-looking paperbound pamphlet in Madrid in 1954.[56] It is scarcely surprising that the editors of a number of handsome, limited editions were more than generous in their estimates of the poems. For example, William Andrews Clark, Jr., in the introduction to his volume which he issued in San Francisco in 1927, for private distribution only, wrote that the "Sonnets" had secured Mrs. Browning's fame for all time and entitled her "to a high seat on Mount Parnassus beside Shelley, Keats, Byron, Browning, and other great gods of poesy." On the sound foundation of these sonnets "rests her renown as a poet—a foundation as eternal as the hills of Rome." [57]

In addition to the "Sonnets," the story of her life, especially the romance is still of interest to the public. Within the last few years a full-length biography of her and two separate volumes on the Brownings have been published.[58] As a literary craftsman she is now ranked by many critics below Emily Brontë and Christina Rossetti, both of whom in their day received much less acclaim. Yet most of Mrs. Browning's verse, in spite of its fire and energy, gives only a feeble representation of the exalted ideas which she was struggling to express. Except for a handful of her short poems, her ability to create failed to keep pace with her abundant thoughts and turbulent feelings. And so it is not altogether as a poet (although she did have many poetical qualities) that she is attractive, but as one of the greatest personalities of an age which included among other English women of unusual abilities Charlotte and Emily Brontë, George Eliot, Mrs. Gaskell, Christina Rossetti, and Florence Nightingale. With all of Mrs. Browning's foibles, her erratic poetical taste, her naïve acceptance of ready-made formulas to solve political problems, and her violent enthusiasms and antipathies, it is probable that she will be remembered as long as any woman of her time. It is the quality of her life even more than her artistic achievements which will live. Countless men and women will continue to find inspiration in the romance and the flight to Italy—where she found fulfillment as wife and mother—in her devotion to scholarship and letters, in her courageous and impassioned protests against injustice to individuals and subject peoples, and in her broad, generous, idealistic, Christian point of view.

CUE TITLES

Berg	The Henry W. and Albert A. Berg Collection in the New York Public Library
BM	The British Museum
BMType	Kenyon's transcriptions in the British Museum of EBB's letters
Dearest Isa	*Dearest Isa,* ed. McAleer, 1951
DeVane	*New Letters of Robert Browning,* ed. DeVane and Knickerbocker, 1950
Folger	The Folger Shakespeare Library
Harvard	The Harvard College Library
Hood	*Letters of Robert Browning* . . . , ed. Hood, 1933
Horne	*Letters of Elizabeth Barrett Browning Addressed to Richard Hengist Horne,* ed. S. R. Townshend Mayer, 1877
Houghton	The Browning Collection of Arthur A. Houghton, Jr., New York
	The Henry E. Huntington Library
HUP	*Hitherto Unpublished Poems and Stories,* 1914
Huxley	*Elizabeth Barrett Browning: Letters to Her Sister, 1846–1859,* ed. Huxley, 1929
Illinois	The Library of the University of Illinois
Kenyon	*The Letters of Elizabeth Barrett Browning,* ed. Kenyon, 1897
Letters	*The Letters of Robert Browning and Elizabeth Barrett Barrett,* 2 vols. in one, London, John Murray, 1946
Maggs	*Elizabeth Barrett Browning. Unpublished Correspondence,* London, Maggs Bros., 1937
Marks	*The Family of the Barrett,* 1938
McAleer	"New Letters from Mrs. Browning to Isa Blagden," ed. McAleer, 1951
McCarthy	*Elizabeth Barrett to Mr. Boyd,* ed. McCarthy, 1955
Miller	*Elizabeth Barrett to Miss Mitford* . . . , ed. Miller, 1954
MLN	*Modern Language Notes*

NYPL	The New York Public Library
PMLA	*Publications of the Modern Language Association of America*
Shackford	*Letters from Elizabeth Barrett to B. R. Haydon,* ed. Shackford, 1939
Sotheby	*The Browning Collections. Catalogue of Oil Paintings, Drawings and Prints; Autograph Letters and Manuscripts . . . Which Will Be Sold by Auction, by Messrs. Sotheby, Wilkinson, and Hodge,* London, May 1, 2, 5–8, 1913
TLS	*Times Literary Supplement*
Weaver	"Twenty Unpublished Letters of Elizabeth Barrett to Hugh Stuart Boyd," ed. Weaver, 1950
Wellesley	The Wellesley College Library
Yale	The Yale University Library

NOTES

CHAPTER 1. Early Years at Hope End

1. For all references to the history of the Barrett family and their Jamaica background, I am indebted to Jeannette Marks' indispensable study, *The Family of the Barrett*, New York, 1938.

2. For a description of Coxhoe Hall see Robert Surtees, *The History and Antiquities of the County Palatine of Durham* (London, 1816), *1*, 70; Charles Geeson, *A Short History of Kelloe Church and District* (Kelloe Church, n.d.); "Mrs. Browning's Birthplace," *Monthly Chronicle of North-Country Lore and Legend* (July 1889), pp. 303–6.

3. In *The Harrow School Register, 1571–1800*, ed. W. T. J. Gun (London, 1934), there is no entry for Moulton. The following entry for "Barrett" apparently refers to Edward Barrett Moulton Barrett: "Barrett (2) Ent. Oct. 1797, aged 12. Left 1797-8." Edward Barrett Moulton added the name of Barrett in 1798.

4. From RB's prefatory note (dated Dec. 10, 1887) in the first volume of EBB's *Poetical Works*, London, 1889.

5. See *Admissions to Trinity College, Cambridge* (London, 1911), *4*, 5: "Barrett, Edward Barrett Moulton, son of Charles Barrett of Jamaica. School, Harrow (Dr. Drury). Age 18. Fellow-Commoner, October 15, 1801. Tutor, Mr. Jones. (Doubtful if resided. Did not matriculate or graduate.)" There are two errors here: he was 16 years old, and his father's surname was Moulton.

6. See the portrait of EBB, Edward, and Henrietta as children, reproduced opposite the title page in Huxley.

7. Houghton.

8. J. Barrett in *A Description of Malvern and Its Environs* (Worcester, 1796), p. 81, refers to the Hope End estate as "partly a modern structure."

9. From details supplied by the late Stephen Ballard, owner of Hope End, in a conversation with me at Colwall, 1948. For descriptions of the old Hope End mansion and estate see Charles John Robinson, *A History of the Mansions and Manors of Herefordshire* (London and Hereford, 1873), pp. 71–2; "The Particulars and Conditions of Sale of . . . Hope End . . . which will be sold by auction . . . on Wednesday, the 24th day of July, 1867" (British Museum, Maps, 137 a.1 [8]).

10. Horne, *1*, 160–1.

11. McCarthy, p. 279.

12. See the *Hereford Journal*, Nov. 18, 1812; Feb. 9, 1814.

13. Mrs. Barrett to EBB, Jan. 2, 1822 (Houghton).

14. See "Glimpses into my Own Life and Literary Character," *HUP, 1*, 3–28.

15. See EBB's poem written in childhood, "On Laying Hooker under my Pillow at Night" (Houghton).

16. *HUP, 1*, 15.

17. *Ibid.*, pp. 13–14.

18. *Ibid.*, pp. 110–21.

19. See EBB, *The Poets' Enchiridion* (Boston, 1914), p. 27.

20. *Horne, 1,* 161.
21. EBB to Miss Mitford, n.d. (Folger).
22. *Horne, 1,* 159.
23. EBB refers to her " 'epic' of eleven or twelve years old" in a letter to Horne (*1,* 159); in an unpublished letter to Miss Mitford, Nov. 21, 1843 (Wellesley), she says that she wrote an epic at the age of twelve.
24. This copy, with EBB's inscription to her grandmother, is in the Pierpont Morgan Library.
25. National Library of Scotland, MS 1808, fol. 79.
26. *Ibid.* (Dec. 1, 1822), fol. 81.
27. Mrs. Barrett to EBB, July 5, 1824 (Houghton).
28. *Ibid.,* Feb. 28, 1826 (Houghton).
29. "This day is published . . . price 5s 6ds., An Essay on Mind, with Other Poems" (*The Times,* March 25, 1826).
30. EBB to Cornelius Mathews, July 17, 1844 (Berg); quoted in *The Collector,* 5 (1892), 89.
31. Mrs. Barrett to EBB, April 11, 1826 (Houghton).
32. Kenyon to EBB, n.d. (Wellesley).
33. New ser. 26 (1826), 78-82.
34. *Literary Gazette* (July 15, 1826), p. 436.
35. Miller, p. 50.
36. EBB to EMB, n.d. (Houghton).
37. "Leila," which was not published in EBB's lifetime, was "printed for private circulation only" for Thomas J. Wise, London, 1913. It is included in *New Poems,* ed. F. G. Kenyon, London, 1914.
38. "My Character and Bro's Compared," Hope End, Feb. 1821 (Houghton).
39. Mrs. Barrett to EBB, Aug. 13, 1821 (Houghton).
40. Houghton.
41. For information about the dates at Charterhouse of Edward and Sam I have consulted the "Charterhouse School Lists, 1816-1832" in the British Museum.
42. EBB to Miss Mitford, Friday, March 1844 (Wellesley).
43. *HUP, 1,* 172-3.
44. See EBB's verses describing her trips in the summer of 1814, in *ibid.,* pp. 45-60.
45. For an advertisement of the musical festival see the *Newcastle Chronicle,* Aug. 13, 1814.
46. EBB was at Cheltenham in Jan. 1819; see "Lines extempore on taking my last farewell of the statue of Nigeia at Cheltenham," dated Jan. 17, 1819 (Houghton). She was there also in 1824; see Mrs. Barrett's letter to EBB, Cambray Street, Cheltenham, July 5 [1824] (Houghton).
47. See *HUP, 1,* 125.
48. Mrs. Barrett's letter of April 11, 1826, to Henrietta (Houghton) refers to the absence of EBB and Henrietta from home for "ten long months." EBB wrote to Uvedale Price in June 1826 that she had recently returned from Hastings after an absence of eleven months; see *Letters to Robert Browning and Other Correspondents, by Elizabeth Barrett Browning,* ed. T. J. Wise (London, 1916), p. 11.
49. For a description of Kinnersley Castle see Charles John Robinson, *A History of the Castles of Herefordshire and Their Lords* (London and Hereford, 1869), pp. 88-92.

50. The first reference to her being in Gloucester is an inscription in her copy of Horace, "E. B. Barrett, July 20, 1821, Gloucester" (Sotheby).
51. The letter is partly reproduced in Maggs, pp. 10–11.
52. Houghton.
53. *Ibid.*
54. *Ibid.*
55. *Ibid.*
56. J. Arnould to A. Domett, Nov. 30, 1846, in *Robert Browning and Alfred Domett*, ed. F. G. Kenyon (London, 1906), p. 133.
57. Miller, p. 138.
58. Houghton, n.d.
59. *HUP, 1,* 46.
60. *Ibid.,* p. 54.
61. This is Lot 110 of Sotheby: EBB's pocket diary for 1823 and notebook for 1824–25.
62. Henry Richard, Lord Holland, *Some Account of the Lives and Writings of Lope Felix de Vega Carpio and Guillen de Castro,* 2 vols. London, 1817.
63. *Anecdotes, Biographical Sketches, and Memoirs,* London, 1822; *Memoirs, Anecdotes, Facts, and Opinions . . . ,* 2 vols. London, 1824.
64. Ralph Fell, *Memoirs of the Public Life of the Late Right Honourable Charles James Fox,* 2 vols. London, 1808; Samuel Parr, *Characters of the Late Charles James Fox,* 2 vols. London, 1809.
65. By George Pretyman Tomline, 3 vols. London, 1821.
66. *Letters on the Character and Poetical Genius of Lord Byron.*
67. Anon., London, 1825.
68. Leicester Stanhope, *Greece in 1823 and 1824* (London, 1824), which EBB thought "a fine, spirited generous book which lets us look on the face of Greece unmasked"; Edward Blaquière, *The Greek Revolution* (London, 1824), which EBB praised for "the comprehensive and masterly manner in which general views are given, and particular facts stated." EBB also gained some geographical instruction from Frédéric Guillaume de Vaudoncourt's *Memoirs of the Ionian Islands,* London, 1816.
69. The date of the American edition of *The Pilot* is 1823.
70. Ed. Alaric A. Watts, London, 1825. The "annuals" were usually published late in the autumn preceding the year given on the title page.
71. According to Sotheby the inscriptions in EBB's copies are dated as follows: Milton (1824), Percy (June 1826), Burns (July 1824), and *A New Practical Grammar of the Spanish Language* by F. Fernandez (April 11, 1824). For the inscription in her copy of Horace see above, n. 50.
72. For EBB's marginalia in *The Prose Works of John Milton; Containing his Principal Political and Ecclesiastical Pieces,* ed. George Burnett (2 vols., London, 1809), see the *Turnbull Library Record,* Wellington, New Zealand, No. 2 (July 1940), pp. 5–7.
73. EBB received the *Philosophical Essays* (Edinburgh 1816) in Dec. 1824. On May 12, 1829 (NYPL) she wrote E. H. Barker that she had read Dugald Stewart's *Essays* somewhat earlier.
74. *Cours de littérature dramatique,* 3 vols. Paris and Geneva, 1814. EBB's notes on this translation are in her Commonplace Book in the Huntington Library (H.M.

4934). In eighteen closely packed pages she summarized or copied out passages from all three volumes.

75. See *Essay on Mind:* Note *a*, p. 89; Note *i*, p. 93; Note *q*, p. 97. The inscription in EBB's copy of *The Literary Character Illustrated by the History of Men of Genius* (1818) is dated 1822. She also owned a copy of Spence's *Anecdotes* (1820).

76. Reproduced in Marks, facing p. 331.

77. *An Account of the Statues, Pictures, and Temples in Greece; Translated from the Greek of Pausanias,* London, 1780.

78. Two vols. London and Hereford, 1794–98.

79. Oxford, 1827.

80. See a description of the correspondence in Maggs Bros., Catalogue No. 773 (1948), Lot 26.

81. *HUP,* 2, 77.

82. *Ibid.,* pp. 83–6.

Chapter 2. Loss of Hope End

1. The preface to *The Agamemnon of Aeschylus* was finished at Margate, Oct. 29, 1823. In his next published volume, *The Catholic Faith: a Sermon by St. Basil* (London, 1825), Boyd refers in his preface to a sermon he had recently heard in Great Malvern.

2. McCarthy, p. 132.

3. See Lawrence Dundas Campbell, *The Miscellaneous Works of Hugh Boyd . . . with an Account of His Life and Writings,* 2 vols. London, 1800.

4. See J. A. Venn, *Alumni cantabrigienses, Part II, from 1752 to 1900* (Cambridge, 1940), *1,* 348.

5. London, 1806.

6. In his preface to *Select Poems of Synesius and Gregory Nazianzen* (London, 1814) Boyd refers to a severe ophthalmia from which he has been suffering for the past three years.

7. *HUP,* 2, 134–5. Forman supposes that the "Number of lines which I can repeat" is a record of EBB's own accomplishments. That it clearly refers to Boyd may be seen from her remarks upon the subject in her letters to him. See Weaver, p. 405.

8. McCarthy, p. 4.

9. *Ibid.,* p. 11.

10. The episode is related in her letter printed in *HUP,* 2, 87–93.

11. At Wellesley.

12. McAleer, p. 601.

13. *Tragoedeorum pars altera* (Heidelberg, 1597), in the possession of Douglas M. Moffat, New York. EBB finished the *Troades* Feb. 3, the *Bacchae* Feb. 12, the *Cyclops* "early in April," the *Heraclidae* April 15, the *Ion* June 12, and the *Hercules furens* June 28.

14. See "Some Unpublished Papers of Robert Browning and Elizabeth Barrett Browning," ed. George S. Hellman, *Harper's Monthly Magazine, 132* (1916), 530–9.

15. EBB's copy of the *De sublimitate,* ed. Zachary Pearce (London, 1724) is in the Slocum Library of Ohio Wesleyan University.

16. She owned a copy of the *Vetus et Novum Testamentum Graece* (1828).

17. EBB had copies of F. H. Bothe's edition of Aeschylus (Leipzig, 1805) and

Notes. Pages 30-35   431

C. J. Blomfield's editions of *Prometheus vinctus* (Cambridge, 1810), *Septem contra Thebas* (1824), and the *Agamemnon* (1826).

18. EBB owned Euripides' *Tragoediae XX*, ed. J. Barnes, 6 vols. Oxford, 1812; *Tragoediae IV*, ed. Richard Porson, 1824; and *Tragoediae priores quatuor*, ed. Porson, Cambridge, 1829.

19. *Tragoediae septem*, ed. Thomas Johnson, Eton, 1799. The two volumes are in the Slocum Library of Ohio Wesleyan University.

20. EBB's copy of the *Orationes et epistolae*, ed. H. Wolfius (Basel, 1613), is inscribed "Hope End, 1831."

21. Boyd gave EBB a copy of the *Memorabilia* in April 1829. She owned a copy of the *Cyropaedia*, but the inscription does not record the date she received it.

22. EBB's copy of Vol. *1* of Gregory Nazianzen, *Opera Græc. Lat.* (Cologne, 1690), with marginalia indicating the dates when she read various passages with Boyd, is at Wellesley. Boyd gave her the book in 1829, according to the inscription in EBB's handwriting.

23. EBB owned Chrysostom's *Opera Graece*, Vols. *3* and *8* (Eton, 1612) and his *De sacerdotio libri VI*, ed. J. Hughes, Cambridge, 1710.

24. *Select Passages of the Writings of St. Chrysostom, St. Gregory Nazianzen, and St. Basil*, 2d ed. London, 1810; *Tributes to the Dead; in a Series of Ancient Epitaphs, Translated from the Greek* [of St. Gregory], London, 1826; *The Fathers Not Papists* [translations from the Greek Fathers, especially Gregory, Chrysostom, and Basil], London and Sidmouth, 1834; see also above, p. 430, nn. 1, 6.

25. Her copy (Oxford, 1810), which is at Wellesley, is inscribed "EBBarrett, 1828."

26. Her copy (ed. Joseph Simpson, 1758) is inscribed "Hope End, July, 1831."

27. The inscriptions in her copies of Livy and of the *Attic Nights* give no indication when she received them. The dates of her inscriptions in her copies of Erasmus, *Colloquia* (1727) and *Dialogus, cui Titulus Ciceronianus* (Oxford, 1693) are 1827 and 1829 respectively.

28. See Barker, *Literary Anecdotes* (London, 1852), *2*, 36-7, for part of a letter from Price to Barker, March 24, 1827.

29. NYPL.

30. *Cicero's Catilinarian Orations*, London, 1829.

31. EBB to Boyd, Feb. 2, 1829 (Wellesley).

32. Houghton.

33. *Ibid.*

34. McCarthy, p. 62.

35. *Ibid.*

36. *Ibid.*, p. 63.

37. See Marks, pp. 347-8.

38. Miller, p. 100.

39. Mr. Barrett wrote EBB, Aug. 16, 1825 (Houghton): "I am rejoiced to find our beloved Sam has quite recovered but am concerned to hear his Mary is complaining." On April 11, 1826, Mrs. Barrett wrote EBB (Houghton): "How anxiously do I hope dear Mary may find health and strength at Tunbridge."

40. Houghton.

41. Miller, p. 101.

42. Miss Marks suggests that Mr. Barrett may have gone to Jamaica in 1825, and in support she prints (p. 349) two poems addressed to EMB on his birthday,

May 28, 1826, one of them from EBB and the other from Bro. The reason the two children had not seen their father during the preceding year, as they say in the poems, was that they, not he, had been away from home. Bro had been at Charterhouse, and during the vacations he had been visiting his grandmother Mrs. Moulton at Hastings; EBB had spent about a year at Hastings.

43. Weaver, p. 408.
44. McCarthy, p. 114.
45. *Ibid.*, p. 164.
46. EBB to Boyd, n.d. (BMType).
47. Miller, p. 150.
48. McCarthy, p. 124.
49. *Ibid.*, p. 127.
50. *Ibid.*, p. 134.
51. *Ibid.*, pp. 131–2.
52. *Ibid.*, p. 137.
53. *Ibid.*, p. 124.
54. *Ibid.*, p. 129.
55. The episode is related in McCarthy, pp. 143–4.
56. Miller, p. 151.
57. McCarthy, p. 173.
58. *Ibid.*, p. 177.
59. *Ibid.*, p. 169.
60. *Ibid.*, p. 170.
61. *Ibid.*, p. 181.
62. *Ibid.*
63. *Ibid.*, p. 185.
64. Second ed. London, 1778.
65. Ed. Nathaniel Forster, Oxford, 1750; according to Sotheby, EBB's copies contained many of her marginal notes.
66. See McCarthy, p. 176.
67. *Ibid.*, p. 188.
68. *Ibid.*, p. 190.
69. *Ibid.*, p. 174.
70. *Ibid.*, p. 190.
71. *Ibid.*, p. 174.
72. *Ibid.*, p. 192.
73. *Ibid.*, p. 191.
74. *Ibid.*

CHAPTER 3. Sojourn in Sidmouth

1. McCarthy, p. 195.
2. *Ibid.*, p. 197.
3. Weaver, p. 408.
4. EBB to Mrs. Martin, Dec. 14, 1832 (BMType).
5. BMType.
6. Dec. 14, 1832 (BMType).
7. Sept. 22, 1834 (BMType).
8. See *A Roll of the Graduates of the University of Glasgow, from 31st December, 1727, to 31st December, 1897*, compiled by W. Innes Addison (Glasgow, 1898), p. 36.

Notes. Pages 48-57

9. June 8, 1833, p. 362.
10. Cambridge, 1810; EBB owned a copy.
11. *Aeschylus,* Cambridge, 1828.
12. *Aeschyli tragoediae, 1,* Cambridge, 1809.
13. *An Essay on the Greek Article; to Which Is Added, an Essay on the Atonement,* 2d ed. London, 1835. The added essay had originally been published at Margate, 1817, with the title *Reflections on the Atoning Sacrifice of Jesus Christ.*
14. London and Sidmouth, 1834.
15. Weaver, p. 410.
16. McCarthy, p. 203.
17. *Ibid.,* p. 205.
18. *A Dissertation on the Scriptural Authority, Nature, and Uses of Infant Baptism,* Boston and New York, 1832.
19. John Williams Morris, *Biographical Recollections of the Rev. Robert Hall,* London, 1833.
20. Eight vols. London, 1828.
21. Possibly EBB read *A Course of Sermons* (Aberdeen, 1808) or *A Short Treatise on Infant Baptism,* Aberdeen, 1822.
22. *An Account of the Infancy, Religious and Literary Life of Adam Clarke,* ed. J. B. B. Clarke, 3 vols. London, 1833.
23. BMType.
24. EBB in a letter to Miss Mitford, Nov. 8, 1842 (Wellesley), mentioned that Mary Hunter was then sixteen years old.
25. Printed in *HUP, 2,* 234-6.
26. EBB to Miss Mitford, n.d. (Folger).
27. Weaver, p. 413.
28. EBB to Arabel, postmarked Feb. 19, 1857 (Berg).
29. Miller, p. 141.
30. EBB to Miss Mitford, n.d. (Folger).
31. Maggs, p. 37.
32. See Kenyon, *1,* 20-1.
33. *Ibid.,* p. 22. It is possible that this may be 8 Fortfield Terrace and that the Barretts had only two different homes in Sidmouth.
34. Weaver, p. 414.

CHAPTER 4. First Stay in London: "The Seraphim"

1. EBB to Boyd, n.d. (BMType).
2. Miller, pp. 123-4.
3. EBB to Miss Commeline, Aug. 19, 1837 (BMType).
4. *Ibid.*
5. Kenyon to EBB, n.d. (Wellesley).
6. *Letters, 1,* 448.
7. March 31, 1847 (Houghton). There was, however, a distant connection between Kenyon and a branch of the Barrett family. See Marks, pp. 198-9, 234.
8. See Mrs. Andrew Crosse, "John Kenyon and his Friends," *Temple Bar, 88* (1890), 477-96.
9. See *Diary, Reminiscences, and Correspondence of Henry Crabb Robinson,* ed. Thomas Sadler (London, 1869), *3,* 452.
10. Miller, pp. 114-15.

11. Aug. 13, 1836, pp. 570–2.
12. The unpublished MS of EBB's account of her first meeting with Wordsworth is at the Berg.
13. *The Collection of Autograph Letters and Historical Documents Formed by Alfred Morrison*, Ser. 2, 1882–93. *The Blessington Papers* (privately printed, 1895), p. 120.
14. Wordsworth to Kenyon, Aug. 17, 1838 (Berg).
15. Henry Fothergill Chorley, *Autobiography, Memoir, and Letters,* compiled by Henry G. Hewlett (London, 1873), *1*, 201.
16. Miller, p. 205.
17. *Ibid.*, p. 204.
18. Miss Mitford to Miss Anderdon, Dec. 5, 1841 (Yale).
19. *Ibid.*
20. *Letters of Mary Russell Mitford*, ser. 2, ed. Henry F. Chorley (London, 1872), *1*, 180–1.
21. "A Thought on Thoughts" is in EBB's letter to Boyd, June 24, 1831 (Wellesley).
22. July 9, 1836, p. 491.
23. Oct. 8, 1836, p. 723.
24. See *The Blessington Papers*, p. 120.
25. *The Life of Mary Russell Mitford*, ed. A. G. L'Estrange (London, 1870), *3*, 76–7.
26. Published in the autumn of 1837.
27. Oct. 21, 1837, p. 783.
28. Oct. 21, 1837, pp. 668–9.
29. Published in the autumn of 1838.
30. Oct. 20, 1838, pp. 757–8.
31. Page 6.
32. Miller, p. 16.
33. Sept. 1, 1838, p. 243; Sept. 8, p. 254; Sept. 22, pp. 269–70; Oct. 6, p. 287; Oct. 13, p. 293.
34. See "Christopher in His Cave," *Blackwood's Edinburgh Magazine, 44* (1838), 279–84.
35. *Metropolitan Magazine* [London], 22 (Aug. 1838), 97–101. Here, as elsewhere in similar references, the pages cited are of the entire reviews.
36. Vol. *66* (1840), 382–9.
37. July 7, 1838, pp. 466–8.
38. New ser., *3* (1838), 125–30.
39. Kenyon, *1*, 193.
40. June 24, 1838, pp. 387–8.
41. [London] 2 (1838), 195.
42. June 23, 1838, p. 395.
43. Miller, p. 32.
44. EBB to Boyd, Weaver, p. 417.
45. Dec. 1, 1838, pp. 759–60.
46. EBB to Isa Blagden [1855], McAleer, p. 601.
47. Vol. *1* (Feb. 1841), 171–6.
48. Vol. *55* (1842), 201–18. By George S. Hillard, according to the marked copy at Harvard.
49. Miller, p. 22.

Notes. Pages 72–81 435

50. George Ticknor, *Life, Letters, and Journals* (Boston and New York, 1909), 2, 146.
51. Miller, p. 73.

CHAPTER 5. Tragedy at Torquay

1. The date of the imprint is 1839, but the book appeared in 1838.
2. Miller, p. 96.
3. *Ibid.*, p. 40.
4. EBB to Mary E. Minto, Jan. 15 [1839], Add. MS 41,323 (BM).
5. McCarthy, p. 232.
6. EBB to Arabel, April 1 (Berg).
7. EBB to Arabel, postmarked July 15, 1839 (Berg).
8. *The Friendships of Mary Russell Mitford*, ed. A. G. L'Estrange (New York, 1882), p. 264.
9. EBB to Arabel, April 29 (Berg).
10. Miller, p. 44.
11. Kenyon, *1*, 101.
12. *Scripta Graece omnia*, London, 1826. The volumes, with EBB's marginalia, are in the Slocum Library of Ohio Wesleyan University.
13. London, 1840. The volumes, with EBB's marginalia, are in the Princeton University Library. See James Thorpe, "Elizabeth Barrett's Commentary on Shelley: Some Marginalia," *MLN, 66* (1951), 455–8.
14. EBB to Arabel, postmarked July 15, 1839 (Berg).
15. According to the Register of Deaths at Torquay, in the office of E. Laws, Esq., Supt. Registrar, Newton Abbott.
16. EBB to Miss Mitford, Nov. 14, 1842 (Miller, p. 142).
17. EBB wrote to Miss Mitford, May 14, 1840 (Miller, p. 65), that she heard the news "five weeks ago."
18. EBB to Miss Mitford, May 14, 1840 (Miller, p. 65). It seems to me that the date should be "14," rather than Miss Miller's conjectural "17."
19. Maggs, p. 18.
20. Besides the accounts given by Miss Mitford see Arthur Charles Ellis, *An Historical Survey of Torquay* (Torquay, 1930), p. 364; J. T. White, *The History of Torquay* (Torquay, 1878), pp. 166–7.
21. EBB to Miss Mitford, n.d. (Wellesley).
22. *Letters, 1*, 177.
23. EBB to Miss Mitford, n.d. (Wellesley).
24. Kenyon, *1*, 87.
25. Miller, p. 73.
26. EBB to Miss Mitford, Nov. 9, 1841 (Wellesley).
27. EBB to Boyd, May 10, 1841 (Harvard).
28. Miller, p. 73.
29. Miller, p. 74.
30. EBB to Miss Mitford, Nov. 9, 1841 (Wellesley).
31. *Letters, 1*, 175.
32. Miller, p. 74.
33. *Letters, 1*, 175.
34. Miller, p. 74.
35. EBB to Miss Mitford, Nov. 9, 1841 (Wellesley).

36. Kenyon, 2, 206.
37. *Ibid.*, p. 49.
38. EBB to Miss Mitford, n.d. (Folger).
39. Kenyon, 2, 415.
40. *Horne, 1,* 7-8. Horne says that EBB's poem sent by Mrs. Orme was forwarded by him to *Colburn's New Monthly* and that the next MS sent to him was "The Dead Pan." Both statements are wrong. Horne knew the editors of the *Monthly Chronicle*, which accepted two of her poems in 1840 (see below, Bibliography), but did not print the two poems EBB had sent to Horne through Mrs. Orme, namely "The Madrigal of Flowers" (later "A Flower in a Letter") and "The Cry of the Human." EBB wrote to RB (May 6, 1845) that she and Horne "approached each other on the point of one of Miss Mitford's annual editorships." On Aug. 3, 1839 (Wellesley), EBB sent Miss Mitford extracts from Horne's letter to her (EBB) making fun of the annuals, but EBB promised nevertheless to write for Miss Mitford's *Findens' Tableaux*.
41. Quoted by Eric Partridge in his introduction to Horne's *Orion* (London, 1928), p. xiii.
42. Feb. 6, 1841, pp. 107-8.
43. EBB to Miss Mitford, May 30, 1841 (Wellesley).
44. For various plans of the drama submitted by EBB, and for Horne's interpolations as well as his account of the genesis of the project, see *Horne*, 2, 61-110; *HUP*, 2, 201-21; and *Psyche Apocalypté*, London, privately printed, 1876.
45. This stanza was not included in the poem as it first appeared in the *Boston Miscellany* but was added to the version in *Poems* (1844).
46. EBB to Boyd, May 10, 1841 (Harvard).
47. Maggs, p. 19.
48. *Ibid.*, p. 20.
49. *Ibid.*
50. *Ibid.*
51. *Ibid.*, p. 21.
52. See EBB to George Barrett, July 25, 1841 (Illinois).
53. Miss Mitford to Miss Anderdon, Oct. 4, 1841 (Yale).
54. Miller, p. 84.
55. *Ibid.*

Chapter 6. Return to Wimpole Street

1. Shackford, p. 9.
2. Shackford, p. 20.
3. EBB to Miss Mitford, June 13, 1842 (Folger).
4. Shackford, p. 32.
5. Miller, p. 219.
6. See EBB to George Barrett, March 30, 1842 (Illinois).
7. Miller, p. 138.
8. The episode is related in EBB's letter to George Barrett, March 2, 1842 (Illinois).
9. Mr. Barrett to EBB, n.d. (Houghton).
10. Surtees Cook and Henrietta had the same great-grandfather, Roger Altham, whose daughter married John Graham-Clarke, Mrs. Edward Moulton Barrett's father.
11. See EBB to George Barrett, Oct. 21, 1841 (Illinois).
12. Miller, p. 261.

13. *Ibid.*, p. 10.
14. *Ibid.*
15. *Ibid.*, p. 134.
16. EBB to Miss Mitford, n.d. (Folger).
17. Miller, pp. 226–7.
18. EBB to Miss Mitford, n.d. (Folger).
19. *Ibid.*
20. EBB to Miss Mitford, March 1844 (Wellesley).
21. Another unpublished letter from EBB to Miss Mitford, n.d. (Wellesley).
22. EBB to Miss Mitford, Dec. 19, 1842 (Wellesley).
23. Bonn, 1837. In the two sets at Harvard one copy of this volume is numbered "31" and the other "32." No volume number appears on the title page. EBB owned a copy of the volume.
24. London, 1830–32. EBB twice asked Boyd for his copies of "Mr. Clarke's book." See Kenyon, *1*, 96 f.
25. See Chapter 5, "Fragments of the Lost Poets of Greece," London, 1841.
26. J. P. Migne, *Patrologiae cursus completus*, Series Graeca, 66 (Paris, 1859), p. 1614.
27. Pages 1–3.
28. No editor is mentioned on the title page; published by Scott, Webster, and Geary, London, 1841.

Chapter 7. Friendships and Literary Activities

1. Dec. 17, 1842, p. 1085.
2. See Miller, p. 135.
3. The painting, which is in the National Portrait Gallery, London, is reproduced in Eric George, *The Life and Death of Benjamin Robert Haydon 1786–1846*, London, 1948.
4. For all three versions, and Wordsworth's letter, see Kenyon, *1*, 113–14.
5. Miller, p. 160.
6. See *The Papers of Lt.-Col. Harry Peyton Moulton Barrett*, Sotheby Sale Catalogue, June 7, 1937, Lot 40. According to the marked copy in the BM, the manuscript was sold to Rosenbach for £950.
7. Shackford, Letter 14.
8. *Ibid.*, Letter 16.
9. EBB quoted these words in a letter to the editors of *Arcturus*, July 18, 1842 (Princeton University Library).
10. Vol. *21* (1842), 343.
11. New York, 1841.
12. In many of his letters to EBB Mathews asked for her help in making his poetry better known in England. See the collection of unpublished letters at Illinois from Mathews to EBB written from 1842 to 1844.
13. New York, 1843.
14. "A Rhapsody of Life's Progress," *Poems*, 2, 209.
15. EBB to Mathews, March 1844; quoted from *The Collector*, 5 (1892), 76.
16. In addition to the publication listed in the Bibliography, below, there appeared "A Drama of Exile," new ser. *15* (July 1844), 74–88, and (Aug. 1844), 142–52; "Work" (Sept. 1844), 249. These publications do not appear in the Bibliography because they were not original contributions to periodicals. "A Drama of Exile"

and "Work" were in the sheets EBB sent to Mathews for the American edition of her *Poems.*

17. *United States Magazine and Democratic Review,* new ser. *15* (1844), 370–7. On Mathews' having written the review, see Kenyon, *1,* 214.

18. See Mathews to EBB, June 27, 1844 (Illinois).

19. EBB to Mathews, Dec. 3, 1845; quoted from *The Collector,* 5 (1892), 107.

20. Quoted from Thomas Powell, *The Living Authors of England* (New York, 1849), p. 150.

21. Boston, 1841.

22. See Lowell to EBB, Dec. 13, 1842 (Illinois).

23. EBB to Lowell, Jan. 4, 1843 (Harvard).

24. Entitled "Imperfect Manifestations" in the letter to Lowell.

25. It was published in *New Poems,* pp. 132–3.

26. EBB to Lowell, Aug. 1, 1844 (Harvard).

27. EBB to Mrs. Francis George Shaw, April 1, 1858 (Harvard). Mrs. Shaw, whom the Brownings met in Europe, was a close friend of Emelyn Story and Maria Lowell.

28. The holographs of the earliest letters from Miss Martineau to EBB, which are at Wellesley, date from August 1843. Marks (p. 477) says that the correspondence began in 1838 and cites as proof a remark in EBB's letter to John Kenyon in *Letters, 1,* 58–9. But the date of the letter is probably 1843, not 1838, as given by the editor.

29. Miss Martineau to EBB, Oct. 16, 1843 (Wellesley).

30. EBB to Mrs. Martin, Tuesday, Dec. 1844 (BMType).

31. EBB to Westwood, Nov. 4, 1844, Add. MS. 40, 689 (BM).

32. See Theodora Bosanquet, *Harriet Martineau* (London, 1927), p. 202.

33. EBB to Arabel Barrett [June? 1860?] (Berg).

34. *Ibid.*

35. Pages 77–80.

36. *Poems* (1844), *2,* 262.

37. *Poems* (1844), *1,* xii.

38. *Reports from Commissioners: Children's Employment (Trades and Manufactures),* "Great Britain, House of Commons Papers," *13–15,* Feb. 2–Aug. 24, 1843. The quotation is from "Reports by R. H. Horne, Esq., on the Employment of Children and Young Persons in the Iron Trades and Other Manufactures of South Staffordshire, and the Neighboring Parts of Worcestershire and Shropshire; and on the Actual State, Condition, and Treatment of Such Children and Young Persons" (Wolverhampton, May 25, 1841), *15,* Q9.

39. *Reports from Commissioners: Children's Employment (Mines),* "Great Britain, House of Commons Papers," *15–17,* Feb. 3–Aug. 12, 1842.

40. See letter of that date from Horne to EBB (Illinois).

41. EBB to Westwood, April 16, 1844 (BM).

42. For the review of Landor see *Horne, 1,* 137–8. For Milnes see *ibid.,* pp. 204–5.

43. For the notices of Wordsworth and Hunt see *ibid.,* pp. 135, 176–7. For Tennyson see *ibid.,* pp. 179, 191, 199; also "An Opinion on Tennyson, by Elizabeth Barrett Browning," *Literary Anecdotes of the Nineteenth Century: Contributions towards a Literary History of the Period,* ed. W. Robertson Nicoll and Thomas J. Wise (London, 1895), *1,* 35–41. For Carlyle see *Horne, 2,* 29; also "Carlyle: a Disentangled Essay, by Elizabeth Barrett Browning," *Literary Anecdotes of the Nineteenth Century* (1896), *2,* 105–19.

Notes. Pages 117–133

44. For the notice of Norton see *Horne, 1*, 227–30. For Lover, Lever, and Hall see *ibid.*, pp. 266–71. For Taylor see *ibid., 2*, 5–12. For Bailey see *ibid.*, pp. 12–15.

45. For James, Gore, Marryat, and Trollope see *ibid., 1*, 213–16. For Smith, Fonblanque, and Jerrold see *ibid., 2*, 152–3. Horne asked about Carleton, Martineau, Jameson, Mary Wollstonecraft Shelley, Macaulay, and Talfourd in his unpublished letters to EBB, written from Oct. 1843 to Feb. 1844 (all at Illinois). EBB may have sent opinions about some, possibly all.

46. *Westminster Review, 41* (1844), 383.

47. *Athenaeum* (March 30, 1844), p. 291.

48. "Miss E. B. Barrett and Mrs. Norton," *2*, 131–40.

49. According to an advertisement in the *Athenaeum* (March 2, 1844), *A New Spirit of the Age* was to be published on the following Tuesday, March 5.

50. Vol. *5* (1844), 317–25.

51. Vol. *41* (1844), 357–87.

52. March 23, 1844, pp. 263–5; March 30, pp. 291–2.

53. New ser. *15* (1844), 49–62.

54. *Ibid.*, p. 72.

Chapter 8. "Poems" of 1844

1. See an unpublished letter from EBB to Moxon, n.d. (Berg).

2. EBB wrote Miss Mitford August 9, 1844 (Wellesley) that her volumes would not be out until the following Tuesday, which was the thirteenth. They were advertised as "just published" in *The Times*, August 14, and in the *Athenaeum* and the *Spectator*, both on August 17.

3. New York, Henry G. Langley, 8 Astor House.

4. August 24, 1844, pp. 809–10.

5. Vol. *56* (1844), 621–39.

6. Vol. *1* (1845), 4–8, 17–20.

7. Vol. *5* (1845), 84–97. For the authorship of the article see *Kenyon, 1*, 229.

8. RB to Mrs. Mary Talbot, Dec. 12, 1887; quoted by Rowland Grey, "Browning's Answer," *Cornhill Magazine*, new ser. *68* (1930), 430.

9. George Goodin Barrett. He was the natural son of Samuel Barrett, who was the brother of Elizabeth Barrett Moulton, EMB's mother.

10. Miller, p. 225.

11. *Men, Women, and Books* (London, 1847), *2*, 111.

12. Miller, p. 221.

13. Harriet Martineau to EBB, Sept. 16, 1844 (Yale). EBB proudly quoted several sentences from this in her letter to Boyd, Sept. 22, 1844 (Huntington).

14. EBB to Boyd, Sept. 22, 1844 (Huntington).

15. William Michael Rossetti, *Some Reminiscences* (London, 1906), *1*, 232.

16. Miller, p. 248.

17. Vol. *2* (1845), 337–52.

18. Vol. *11* (1844), 720–5.

19. Above, n. 5.

20. August 24, 1844, pp. 763–4. For the authorship of the review see *Kenyon, 1*, 229.

21. August 31, 1844, pp. 593–4.

22. Vol. *42* (1845), 322–34.

23. New ser. *3* (1844), 300–6.

24. Vol. *1* (1845), 445–64.

25. Vol. 72 (1844), 282–4.
26. Vol. 6 (1844), 282.
27. August 22, 1844.
28. New ser. 1 (Nov. 1, 1844), 148–52.
29. New ser. 20 (1846), 573–85.
30. Vol. 42 (1844), 381–92.
31. August 31, 1844, pp. 551–2.
32. Oct. 5, 1844, pp. 627–9. For the authorship of the review see Kenyon, 1, 204.
33. Philadelphia, 1845 (entered 1844). See pp. 422–37 for the article on EBB.
34. For the authorship of the review see Kenyon, 1, 214. See Mathews' preliminary notice, new ser. 15 (1844), 72–3, and his full-length review, pp. 370–7.
35. Quoted from the preliminary notice, p. 72.
36. Ser. 3, 6 (1846), 54–68.
37. Vol. 38 (1845), 206–7.
38. Vol. 1 (1845), 38–48.
39. See Margaret Fuller [Ossoli], *Papers on Literature and Art* (New York, 1846), Pt. II, pp. 22–30. The essay is a reprint of her review in the *New York Daily Tribune*, Jan. 4, 1845. See also Margaret Fuller's references to EBB in her *Woman in the Nineteenth Century* (New York, 1845), pp. 63–4, 150.
40. See Edwin Percy Whipple, *Essays and Reviews* (New York, 1848), 1, 345–7. The remarks on EBB were originally published in the *American Whig Review*, 2 (July 1845), 53–55, as part of a review of Rufus W. Griswold's *The Poets and Poetry of England, in the Nineteenth Century*.
41. Vol. 25 (1845), 541–2.
42. Vol. 26 (Jan. 1845), 46–7.
43. Vol. 11 (1845), 235–43.
44. Above, n. 6.

CHAPTER 9. Robert Browning

1. These two volumes are at Harvard. Each is inscribed as follows: "John Kenyon to Miss Browning, Decr. 1844."
2. *Letters*. These two volumes are the chief source for the material quoted in this and the following chapter.
3. So stated in the account of the case of Von Müller vs. Browning, *The Times*, July 2, 1852.
4. See W. Hall Griffin and Harry C. Minchin, *The Life of Robert Browning* (London, 1910), pp. 8 ff.
5. Mrs. Sutherland Orr, *Life and Letters of Robert Browning*, new ed. revised by Frederic G. Kenyon (Boston and New York, 1908), p. 18.
6. *Ibid.*, p. 41.
7. *Ibid.*, p. 44.
8. *Ibid.*, p. 43.
9. The volume is in the Dyce and Forster Collection, Victoria and Albert Museum, London. Mill's comment is quoted by Griffin and Minchin, pp. 59–60.
10. RB to Thomas J. Wise, July 6, 1886 (Hood, p. 251).
11. New ser. 76 (April 1833), 252–62.
12. Sept. 6, 1835, pp. 563–5.
13. "Evidences of a New Genius for Dramatic Poetry—No. 1," 46 (1836), 289–308.
14. Orr, p. 82.

Notes. Pages 144-184 441

15. *Ibid.*, p. 86.
16. *Robert Browning and Alfred Domett,* ed. Kenyon, p. 55.
17. Miller, p. 275.
18. *Ibid.*, p. 137.
19. *Ibid.*, p. 235.
20. *Letters,* 2, 164.
21. EBB to Arabel, postmarked March 11, 1847 (Berg). For a full discussion of the relationship between Hunter and EBB see Betty Miller, "Miss Barrett and Mr. Hunter," *Cornhill Magazine, 165* (Spring 1951), 83-96.
22. Miller, pp. 191, 194.
23. EBB to Miss Mitford, May 3, 1844 (Wellesley).
24. Miller, pp. 73-4.
25. *Ibid.*, p. 244.
26. *Robert Browning and Alfred Domett,* ed. Kenyon, p. 86.
27. Miller, p. 273.
28. Kenyon, *1,* 289.
29. For the text of EBB's criticisms of the poems in the *Dramatic Romances and Lyrics* and of *Luria* and *A Soul's Tragedy* see *New Poems,* pp. 139-73. Edward Snyder and Frederic Palmer, Jr., give a detailed discussion of EBB's comments on "The Flight of the Duchess" in "New Light on the Brownings," *Quarterly Review, 269* (1937), 48-63.
30. Miss Mitford to Mrs. Partridge, June 22, 1843 (Yale). Chorley in his edition of the *Letters of Mary Russell Mitford* (second series, London, 1872), *1,* 216-17, prints the letter but omits the words quoted.
31. Kenyon, *1,* 291.
32. Miller, p. 259.

Chapter 10. Engagement and Marriage

1. Anna Jameson, *Companion to the Most Celebrated Private Galleries of Art in London* (London, 1844), p. 385.
2. *Twenty-two Unpublished Letters* (New York, 1935), p. 4.
3. *Ibid.*, p. 3.
4. *Ibid.*

Chapter 11. From London to Pisa

1. EBB to Arabel, Paris, Saturday [1846] (Berg).
2. *Ibid.*
3. See George K. Boyce, "From Paris to Pisa with the Brownings," *New Colophon, 3* (1950), 110-19, for five letters written by Mrs. Jameson to Lady Noel Byron. For other details of the trip to Pisa see Anna Jameson, *Letters and Friendships (1812-1860),* ed. Mrs. Steuart Erskine (London, 1915), pp. 233-5; Gerardine Bate Macpherson, *Memoirs of the Life of Anna Jameson* (London, 1878), pp. 228-32.
4. EBB to Arabel, Paris, Saturday [1846] (Berg).
5. The episode is told in *Twenty-two Unpublished Letters,* pp. 1-2.
6. EBB to Mrs. Martin, Feb. 1, 1847 (Wellesley).
7. EBB to Henrietta, Nov. 24, 1846, No. 1 (Houghton). Here, as elsewhere in similar references, the numbers correspond to those in Leonard Huxley's edition.
8. *Twenty-two Unpublished Letters,* pp. 4-5.
9. EBB to Arabel, Pisa [Oct.-Nov. 1846] (Berg).

10. The episode is told in EBB's first letter from Pisa to Arabel [Oct.–Nov. 1846] (Berg). Mrs. Macpherson (p. 231) tells much the same story but differs in detail.
11. EBB to Arabel, Pisa [Oct.–Nov. 1846] (Berg).
12. *Ibid.*
13. See EBB to Arabel, Dec. 14 [1846] (Berg).
14. See EBB to Henrietta, June 24 [1848], No. 15 (Houghton).
15. EBB to Henrietta, Dec. 19 [1846], No. 2 (Houghton).
16. No. 3 (Houghton).
17. *Literary Digest, 18* (May 20, 1899), 578.
18. See EBB to Arabel, Feb. 24, 1847 (Berg).
19. EBB to Henrietta, No. 2 (Houghton).
20. See EBB to Arabel, Dec. 14 [1846] (Berg).
21. See Miss Mitford to Mrs. Partridge, Oct. 27, 1847; Dec. 18, 1847; Jan. 2, 1849 (Yale).
22. *Twenty-two Unpublished Letters,* p. 14.
23. *Ibid.,* p. 38.
24. EBB to Arabel, April 12 [1847] (Berg).
25. *Ibid.*
26. *Twenty-two Unpublished Letters,* p. 19.
27. EBB to Arabel, Feb. 8 [1847] (Berg).
28. The description of the service is in EBB's letter to Arabel, Dec. 24, 25 [1846] (Berg).
29. See EBB to Arabel, postmarked March 11, 1847 (Berg).
30. See an unpublished letter from this address written by EBB to George L. Duyckinck [1847] (NYPL).

CHAPTER 12. Italian Affairs and "Casa Guidi Windows"

1. EBB to Arabel, Aug. 29 and 31 [1847] (Berg).
2. *Ibid.*
3. EBB to Arabel, June 22–25 [1847] (Berg).
4. *Ibid.*
5. For an illustration of Powers' studio between 1850–60 see Albert Ten Eyck Gardner, *Yankee Stonecutters* (New York, 1945), Plate I, Fig. 2.
6. EBB to Arabel, May 29, 30 [1847] (Berg).
7. EBB's description of the trip one morning to the Pitti and to Powers' studio and another morning to the Uffizi is in her letter to Arabel, May 29, 30 [1847] (Berg).
8. *Passages from the French and Italian Note-Books* (London, 1871), 2, 66; entry for June 27, 1858.
9. EBB to Arabel, May 29, 30 [1847] (Berg).
10. *Ibid.*
11. EBB to Henrietta, July 9 [1847], No. 6 (Houghton).
12. EBB to Arabel, July 26 [1847] (Berg).
13. EBB drew a floor plan of the apartment in her letter to Arabel, May 10, 11 [1848] (Berg).
14. See EBB to Henrietta, 1881 Via Maggio, Florence, n.d. [1847], No. 9 (Houghton).
15. See *Mary Boyle, Her Book,* ed. Sir Courtenay Boyle, 2d impression (London, 1902), pp. 219–20.

16. See George S. Hillard, *Six Months in Italy* (Boston, 1853), *1*, 177–8.
17. See EBB's letter to William Blackwood, Dec. 1 [1848], Acc. 1424A (National Library of Scotland). She writes of returning a proof of the "Meditation," which had been in his hands since the previous spring and suggests that Blackwood may question its acceptability to his readers. In the same letter she refers to her unpublished MS of "Prometheus" also in Blackwood's possession. On Oct. 7–11 [1848] (Berg) EBB wrote Arabel that she had just received a letter from Blackwood saying that the "Prometheus" was to appear. In the same letter EBB said that Blackwood had sent a full proof of the "Meditation," which he thought a " 'grand poem' but past all human understanding" and asked EBB to attach notes to make the work comprehensible.
18. Huxley, pp. 43–4.
19. See EBB to Arabel, May 10, 11 [1848] (Berg).
20. See "Elizabeth Barrett Browning," *Atlantic Monthly, 8* (1861), 368–76.
21. Henry James, *William Wetmore Story and His Friends* (Edinburgh and London, 1903), *1*, 172.
22. EBB to Arabel, Oct. 7–11 [1848] (Berg).
23. *Ibid.*
24. For details of this illness see EBB to Henrietta, March 7–April 1 [1848], No. 13 (Houghton); EBB to Henrietta, April 22 [1848], No. 14 (Houghton).

CHAPTER 13. "Poems" of 1850

1. *Twenty-two Unpublished Letters*, p. 63.
2. In referring to her son, EBB always spells "Wiedeman" thus.
3. Dec. 22 [1849], No. 24 (Houghton).
4. See EBB to Margaret Fuller, March 3, 1848 (Harvard). The letter was published by Leona Rostenberg in *Notes and Queries, 184* (1943), 252–3.
5. EBB to Arabel, Feb. 11, 12 [1852] (Berg).
6. Page 585.
7. June 22, 1850, p. 662.
8. Nov. 23, 1850, p. 1218. See Leslie A. Marchand, *The Athenaeum, a Mirror of Victorian Culture* (Chapel Hill, 1941), pp. 79, 274.
9. For his remarks on EBB see pp. 281–9.
10. "Female Authors.—No. II: Mrs. Elizabeth Barrett Browning," *Tait's Edinburgh Magazine, 14* (1847), 620–5. The article was reprinted in Gilfillan's *A Second Gallery of Literary Portraits* (2d ed. Edinburgh, 1852), pp. 185–94.
11. Philadelphia, 1848; for his critique of EBB see pp. 452–87.
12. Page 137.
13. Philadelphia, 1849; see his notice on EBB, pp. 500–21.
14. EBB's *Poems* were advertised by Chapman and Hall under their "New Publications" in the *Athenaeum* (Nov. 2, 1850), p. 1130, and in the *John Bull* (Nov. 2, 1850), p. 690. The *Poems* were announced for "Early in November" in the *John Bull* (Oct. 26, 1850), p. 674. For a discussion of the two different title pages and three different bindings of the *Poems* see John Carter, "Mrs. Browning's Poems, 1850," *TLS* (May 30, 1936), p. 464.
15. The edition of the "Sonnets from the Portuguese," supposedly printed in Reading, 1847, is a forgery. See John Carter and Graham Pollard, *An Enquiry into the Nature of Certain Nineteenth Century Pamphlets* (London and New York, 1934), pp. 8–41, 167–8.

16. EBB's copy for preparing the two volumes of *Poems* (1850), with thousands of corrections in her hand, is at Wellesley.

17. The text is from the Loeb Classical Library, ed. Herbert Weir Smyth, London and New York, 1922. The translations are mine.

18. George Murray Smith Memorial Manuscript, Add. MS. 43,487 (BM). See note 24 below.

19. RB wrote in three letters that EBB first showed him the "Sonnets" at Bagni di Lucca in the summer of 1849: to Leigh Hunt, Oct. 6, 1857 (Hood, pp. 47–9); to Julia Wedgwood, Nov. 1864 (*Robert Browning and Julia Wedgwood. A Broken Friendship as Revealed in Their Letters*, ed. Richard Curle, London, 1937, pp. 114–15); to Mary Talbot, Dec. 12, 1887 (published by Rowland Grey, "Browning's Answer," *Cornhill Magazine*, new ser. *68*, 1930, 423–30). EBB wrote Arabel, Jan. 12 [1851] (Berg) that she "never showed them to Robert till last spring," but she was confused, for she had sent her MS of the new edition to England some time before Feb. 18, 1850, as she explained to Miss Mitford; see Kenyon, *1*, 436. Edmund Gosse wrote that EBB gave RB the "Sonnets" at Pisa early in 1847 and with the help of Miss Mitford had them printed later in the year at Reading. See Gosse, "The Sonnets from the Portuguese," *Critical Kit-Kats* (London, 1896), pp. 1–17. See also W. O. Raymond, "Thomas Wise and Edmund Gosse," *TLS* (Dec. 14, 1946), p. 620.

20. Quoted from RB's letter to Julia Wedgwood, Nov. 1864.

21. EBB to Arabel, Jan. 12 [1851] (Berg).

22. Quoted from RB's letter to Julia Wedgwood, Nov. 1864.

23. This MS, which contains Sonnets 1–28, except for Sonnet 17, is at the Pierpont Morgan Library. It was Sotheby's Lot 153.

24. The MS was presented by the Brownings' son to Mrs. George Murray Smith in 1898 and by her to the British Museum in 1933. It contains the 44 "Sonnets" and seven other poems: "A Denial," "Life and Love," "Verses" ("Inclusions," 1850), "Only" ("Insufficiency," 1850), "Proof and Disproof," "Question and Answer," and "A Ring" (the latter unpublished in EBB's lifetime). See "Sonnets from the Portuguese," *TLS* (June 21, 1947), p. 316.

25. The text of the third MS of the "Sonnets from the Portuguese" is the same as that of the *Poems* of 1850. It is owned by Arthur A. Houghton, Jr.

26. Jan. 12 [1851] (Berg).

27. Vol. *49* (1850), 495.

28. Vol. *1* (1850), 714.

29. Nov. 30, 1850, pp. 1242–4.

30. Vol. *93* (1851), 295–303.

31. See the *Guardian* (Jan. 22, 1851), pp. 55–6; *Examiner* (Jan. 25, 1851), pp. 52–3; *Fraser's Magazine*, *43* (1851), 178–82. I have consulted the review of EBB's *Poems* in the *English Review*, as it was reprinted in the New York *Eclectic Magazine*, *22* (1851), 337–44.

32. Jan. 25, 1851, pp. 85–6.

33. For Norton's description of the Brownings see *Letters of Charles Eliot Norton*, ed. Sara Norton and M. A. DeWolfe Howe (Boston and New York, 1913), *1*, 72–9.

34. The volume was advertised in the *Athenaeum* (May 31, 1851), p. 589, under the heading "This day is published," though it was advertised under the same heading in the *Guardian* (May 28), p. 388.

35. *Prometheus Bound, and Other Poems; Including Sonnets from the Portuguese, Casa Guidi Windows*, etc., New York, C. S. Francis and Co., 1851.

Notes. Pages 240–254 445

36. Vol. *14* (1851), 462–6.
37. See the *Athenaeum* (June 7, 1851), pp. 597–8; *Guardian* (June 11, 1851), p. 424; *Prospective Review,* 7 (1851), 313–25.
38. Mary Russell Mitford, *Correspondence with Charles Boner and John Ruskin,* ed. Elizabeth Lee (London, 1914), p. 188.
39. Vol. *94* (1851), 306–17.
40. May 31, 1851, p. 372.
41. June 28, 1851, pp. 616–17.
42. RB to Isa Blagden, March 19, 1866 (*Dearest Isa,* p. 232).
43. See EBB to Arabel, May 1, 2 [1851] (Berg).

CHAPTER 14. England and Paris, 1851–52

1. EBB to Arabel, May 16 [1851] (Berg).
2. *Ibid.*
3. *Ibid.*
4. *Ibid.*
5. The episode is told in *ibid.,* June 5 [1851] (Berg).
6. *Ibid.*
7. *Ibid.,* postmarked Oct. 14, 1851 (Berg).
8. *Ibid.,* June 5 [1851] (Berg).
9. June 26 [1851] (Berg).
10. *Ibid.,* postmarked July 10, 1851 (Berg).
11. Postmarked July 6, 1851 (Berg).
12. Postmarked July 22, 1851 (Berg).
13. EBB to Henrietta, Feb. 20 [1850], No. 25 (Houghton).
14. *Ibid.*
15. *Ibid.,* Nov. 15 [1850], No. 30 (Houghton).
16. *Ibid.* [1851], No. 35 (Houghton).
17. *At Home and Abroad* (New York, 1860), p. 444.
18. *Memoir and Letters* (London, 1873), 2, 389.
19. See "Excursion to Paris," *The Last Words of Thomas Carlyle* (New York, 1892), pp. 207–66.
20. EBB to Arabel, Sept. 26 [1851] (Berg).
21. EBB to Arabel, postmarked Oct. 14, 1851 (Berg).
22. *Ibid.,* Nov. 18 [1851] (Berg).
23. Boston, Ticknor, Reed, and Fields. The publication date on the title page is 1850.
24. EBB to Arabel, April 28 [1852] (Berg).
25. *Ibid.,* Nov. 18 [1851] (Berg).
26. *Ibid.,* postmarked Oct. 23, 1852 (Berg).
27. "La Poésie anglaise depuis Byron," *Revue des Deux Mondes, 13* (1852), 339–61. The article was reprinted in *Littérature anglaise et philosophie* (Dijon, 1893), pp. 147–72. Although the article dealt principally with EBB, it also contained critiques on Henry Taylor and John Edmund Reade.
28. March 23 [1852] (Berg).
29. EBB to Arabel, May 25 [1852] (Berg).
30. *Ibid.,* May 29, 30 [1852] (Berg).
31. *Ibid.,* postmarked March 5, 1852 (Berg).
32. The episode is related in EBB's letter to Arabel, Dec. 25, 26 [1851] (Berg).

33. See EBB to Henrietta, Jan. 5, 6 [1852], No. 40 (Houghton).
34. EBB to Arabel, postmarked March 5, 1852 (Berg).
35. *Sights and Sounds* (London, 1853), p. 4.
36. EBB to Arabel, April 30 [1853] (Berg).
37. *Ibid.*, April 28 [1852] (Berg).
38. Huxley, p. 150.
39. EBB to Arabel, postmarked Feb. 18, 1852 (Berg).
40. *Ibid.*, Dec. 25, 26 [1851] (Berg).
41. Three vols. London, 1852. The account of EBB's life is in *1*, 268–72.
42. See the *Athenaeum* (Jan. 3, 1852), p. 10.
43. EBB to Arabel, Jan. 13 [1852] (Berg).
44. *Ibid.*, Feb. 11, 12 [1852] (Berg).
45. EBB to Mrs. Martin, Feb. 27 [1852] (Wellesley).
46. So EBB wrote Arabel, March 23 [1852] (Berg).
47. *Ibid.*, May 25 [1852] (Berg).
48. See EBB to Mrs. Jameson, postmarked July 8, 1852 (Wellesley).
49. From the account of the trial, Von Müller v. Browning, in *The Times* (July 2, 1852), p. 7.
50. EBB to Arabel, Dec. 21, 1852 (Berg).
51. EBB to Henrietta, postmarked July 24, 1852, No. 44 (Houghton).
52. EBB to Henrietta, postmarked Sept. 25, 1852, No. 47 (Houghton).
53. EBB to Henrietta, postmarked Sept. 16, 1852, No. 46 (Houghton).
54. "To Elizabeth Barrett Browning on Her Later Sonnets," *Athenaeum* (Feb. 15, 1851), p. 191.
55. *Light in the Valley: My Experiences of Spiritualism*, London and New York, 1857.
56. *Diary, Reminiscences, and Correspondence of Henry Crabb Robinson*, ed. Thomas Sadler (London, 1869), *3*, 402.
57. The holograph, with the postmark Sept. 29, 1852, is at Yale; also at Yale are her note to Mrs. Tennyson, July 21, 1852, and to Tennyson, Aug. 12, 1852. The notes of Aug. and Sept. were printed with minor alterations in Hallam Tennyson, *Alfred Lord Tennyson: a Memoir* (London, 1897), *1*, 357–8, 360.
58. *New Letters and Memorials of Jane Welsh Carlyle* (London and New York, 1903), 2, 39, 45.
59. *Letters of the Hon. Mrs. Edward Twisleton* (London, 1928), p. 35.
60. *Ibid.*, p. 64.
61. See "Elizabeth Barrett Browning," *Atlantic Monthly, 8* (1861), 368–76.
62. See "The Brownings," *Littell's Living Age, 192* (1892), 719–28.
63. See her description of EBB in *Records of Tennyson, Ruskin, and Browning* (2d ed. London, 1893), pp. 204, 240–3.
64. EBB to Arabel, postmarked Oct. 13, 1852 (Berg).
65. *Ibid.*, postmarked Oct. 23, 1852 (Berg).
66. See Henriette Corkran, *Celebrities and I* (London, 1902), pp. 31–4.
67. EBB to Arabel, postmarked Oct. 17, 1852 (Berg).
68. *Ibid.*, postmarked Oct. 23, 1852 (Berg).

CHAPTER 15. Florence, Bagni di Lucca, and Rome

1. *Letters to Frederick Tennyson*, ed. Hugh J. Schonfield (London, 1930), p. 99.
2. EBB to Arabel, Aug. 22 [1854] (Berg).

3. Chapman and Hall advertised the *Poems* in the *Athenaeum* (Oct. 15, 1853), p. 1212, as published on that day.
4. James, *William Wetmore Story and His Friends*, *1*, 267.
5. *Ibid.*, 2, 222.
6. For a description of the expedition see *ibid.*, *1*, 273–4.
7. [1853 or 1854] (Harvard).
8. May 4, 1854 (Harvard).
9. EBB to Arabel, Feb. 2 [1854] (Berg).
10. *Ibid.*
11. *Ibid.*, Feb. 28 [1854] (Berg).
12. April 3 [1854] (Berg).
13. EBB to Arabel, Feb. 2 [1854] (Berg).
14. May 4, 1854 (Harvard).
15. DeVane, p. 77.
16. See EBB to Arabel, Feb. 2 [1854] (Berg).
17. *Ibid.*, April 3 [1854] (Berg).
18. DeVane, p. 73.
19. April 3 [1854] (Berg).
20. See EBB to Arabel, postmarked May 27, 1854 (Berg).
21. See "A Visitor to the Brownings," ed. Leonard Huxley, *Yale Review,* new ser. *13* (1924), 228–46, esp. p. 243.
22. EBB to Arabel, June 17, 18 [1854] (Berg).
23. *Ibid.*, Aug. 22 [1854] (Berg).
24. *Ibid.*, June 17, 18 [1854] (Berg).
25. *Ibid.*, Sept. 12, 13 [1854] (Berg).
26. *Ibid.*, May 15 [1855] (Berg).
27. *Ibid.*, Oct. 21 [1854] (Berg).
28. *Italics* (London and Edinburgh, 1864), p. 395.
29. See Thomas Adolphus Trollope, *What I Remember* (London, 1887), *1*, 386 ff.
30. The episode is told in EBB's letter to Arabel, Jan. 25 [1857] (Berg).
31. EBB to Henrietta, March 4 [1856], No. 75 (Houghton).
32. *Ibid.*, Jan. 1 [1856], No. 74 (Houghton).
33. EBB to Arabel [summer of 1853] (Berg).
34. *Ibid.*, Jan. 10, 11 [1855] (Berg).
35. Huxley, p. 204.
36. EBB to Arabel, June 25 [1855] (Berg).
37. *Ibid.*

CHAPTER 16. England and Paris, 1855–56

1. EBB to Arabel, May 15 [1855] (Berg).
2. Lot 175 of Sotheby (p. 39) includes an autograph note by RB stating that the marriage took place on July 11. But he seems to have made an error, for EBB's letter to Arabel, dated "Tuesday morning" (i.e. July 10) and postmarked July 10 (Berg) refers to the marriage having just taken place.
3. EBB to Arabel, June 25 [1855] (Berg).
4. EBB to Henrietta, Sept. 6 [1855], No. 67 (Houghton).
5. *Ibid.*, Jan. 1 [1856], No. 74 (Houghton).
6. *Ibid.*, postmarked Dec. 8, 1855, No. 73 (Houghton).
7. EBB to Arabel, postmarked July 9, 1855 (Berg).

8. *Ibid.,* June 30 [1855] (Berg).

9. See Locker-Lampson's description of EBB in *My Confidences* (London, 1896), pp. 157–8.

10. See William Michael Rossetti, *Some Reminiscences* (London, 1906), *1*, 235–6; Sotheby, Lot 11, p. 6.

11. *What I Remember, 1,* 374 ff.

12. See Daniel Dunglas Home, *Incidents in My Life* (second series, New York, 1872), pp. 105–8.

13. EBB to Mrs. Jameson [Oct.? 1855?] (Berg).

14. See RB's and EBB's letters to Miss de Gaudrion in *TLS* (Nov. 28, 1902), p. 356.

15. See EBB to Mrs. Jameson, Jan. 9 [1857] (Berg).

16. [Oct.? 1855?] (Berg).

17. *Ibid.*

18. For further references to the Ealing affair see EBB to Mrs. Kinney, Dec. 19, 1855 (Yale); *William Allingham: a Diary,* ed. H. Allingham and D. Radford (London, 1907), pp. 101–2; William Lyon Phelps, "Robert Browning on Spiritualism," *Yale Review,* new ser. *23* (1933), 129–35.

19. EBB to Henrietta, postmarked Feb. 12, 1855, No. 59 (Houghton).

20. *Ibid.,* postmarked Aug. 18, 1855, No. 62 (Houghton).

21. *Ibid.,* postmarked Aug. 30, 1855, No. 66 (Houghton).

22. They were advertised for "this day" in the *Athenaeum* (Nov. 10), p. 1315.

23. *Athenaeum* (Nov. 17, 1855), pp. 1327–8.

24. DeVane, p. 87.

25. Postmarked Oct. 23, 1855 (Berg).

26. The conversation of Bulwer-Lytton and his son is told by EBB in her letter to Arabel, Oct. 31 [1855] (Berg).

27. They were advertised for "this day" in the *Athenaeum* (Nov. 1, 1856), p. 1328.

28. See *Letters of Charles Eliot Norton, 1,* 341–2.

29. See *The English Notebooks,* ed. Randall Stewart (New York, 1941), pp. 381–2.

30. EBB to Henrietta, postmarked Sept. 19, 1856, No. 82 (Houghton).

31. *Ibid.,* Oct. 21 (postmarked Oct. 22, 1856), No. 86 (Houghton).

32. It was advertised for "this day" in the *Athenaeum* (Nov. 15, 1856), p. 1411.

CHAPTER 17. "Aurora Leigh"

1. At the foot of page 347 of the MS of *Aurora Leigh* at Harvard, RB wrote: "Read this Book, this divine Book, Wednesday Night, July 9th '56. R. B. 39 Devonshire Place."

2. From his introduction to *Aurora Leigh* (London, 1898), p. ix.

3. See "Aurora Leigh. An Unpublished Letter from Leigh Hunt," *Cornhill Magazine,* new ser. *3* (1897), 738–49.

4. James T. Fields, *Yesterdays with Authors* (Boston, 1885), p. 414.

5. John Forster, *Walter Savage Landor* (Boston, 1869), p. 64.

6. *Letters from Owen Meredith to Robert and Elizabeth Barrett Browning,* ed. Aurelia Brooks Harlan and J. Lee Harlan, Jr. (Waco, Texas, 1937), pp. 129–30.

7. A. N. L. Munby, "Letters of British Artists of the XVIIIth and XIXth Centuries—Part VI," *Connoisseur, 122* (1948), 102.

8. *Autobiographical Notes of the Life of William Bell Scott,* ed. W. Minto (London, 1892), *2,* 34.

Notes. Pages 312-351

9. *Letters of Dante Gabriel Rossetti to William Allingham, 1854-1870*, ed. G. B. Hill (New York, 1897), p. 189.
10. *Letters of Lydia Maria Child* (Boston, 1883), p. 87.
11. Vol. *49* (1857), 460-70.
12. Postmarked Feb. 19, 1857 (Berg).
13. S. Musgrove, "Unpublished Letters of Thomas De Quincey and Elizabeth Barrett Browning," pp. 26-7. See the Bibliography, below.
14. EBB to Mrs. Shaw, April 1, 1858 (Harvard).
15. Vol. *2* (Dec. 27, 1856), 776-8. Merle M. Bevington, *The Saturday Review, 1855-1868* (New York, 1941), p. 215, says that the review was written by G. S. Venables.
16. Nov. 22, 1856, pp. 1425-7.
17. Vol. *29* (Nov. 22, 1856), 1239-40.
18. Vol. *81* (1857), 23-41.
19. Vol. *4* (1857), 239-67. The review, which was written by William Caldwell Roscoe, later appeared in his *Poems and Essays* (London, 1860), 2, 80-106.
20. Nov. 29, 1856, pp. 762-3.
21. See above, n. 11.
22. Vol. *68* (1857), 399-415.
23. Nov. 22, 1856, pp. 1120-2.
24. For other unfavorable reviews of *Aurora Leigh*, almost all with similar remarks on the deficiencies of the poem, see *John Bull and Britannia* (Dec. 27, 1856), p. 827; London *Atlas* (Dec. 13, 1856), pp. 794-5; London *Monthly Review of Literature, Science, and Art, 1* (1856), 743-54; *Guardian* (Dec. 31, 1856), pp. 999-1000; New York *Eclectic Magazine, 56* (1862), 74-8; London *National Magazine, 1* (1857), 314-15; London *Morning Post*, Dec. 15, 1856.
25. Nov. 20, 1856.
26. Nov. 26, 1856.
27. Nov. 22, 1856, 917-18.
28. Vol. *5* (1862), 134-48.
29. Jan. 25 [1857] (Berg).
30. Vol. *85* (1857), 415-41.
31. Vol. *9* (1857), 28-38.
32. Vol. *26* (1857), 443-62. For the authorship of the review see Kenyon, 2, 255.

CHAPTER 18. War Again in Italy: "Poems before Congress"

1. Postmarked June 4, 1857, No. 91 (Houghton).
2. Postmarked Feb. 19, 1857 (Berg).
3. No. 88 (Houghton).
4. EBB to Henrietta, May 13 [1857], No. 90 (Houghton). The letter is partly printed in Huxley. Huxley reproduced the entire letter in "Mrs. Browning and Her Father's Forgiveness," *Cornhill Magazine*, new ser. *74* (1933), 331-6.
5. Huxley, p. 277.
6. See Huxley, p. 289; EBB to Arabel, Nov. 22 [1857] (Berg); *ibid.*, postmarked Feb. 25, 1858 (Berg).
7. *Ibid.*, Nov. 22 [1857] (Berg).
8. See EBB to George Barrett, postmarked April 30, 1861 (Illinois); **EBB** to Arabel, postmarked May 15, 1861 (Berg).

9. *Dearest Isa*, p. 365.
10. See *Life of Frances Power Cobbe by Herself* (London, 1894), 2, 14–18.
11. McAleer, p. 607.
12. April 12 [1858] (Berg).
13. Postmarked March 24, 1858 (Berg).
14. *Passages from the French and Italian Notebooks*, entry for June 9, 1858, 2, 1–16.
15. *Ibid.*, entry for June 21, 1858, 2, 68.
16. Mrs. Eckley is mentioned in EBB's letter to Fanny Haworth (Kenyon, 2, 149–51), dated 1853 by Kenyon, but the subjects discussed in the letter show that it was probably written in 1858.
17. She may also have written a novel with an Italian background: according to the catalogue of the Boston Public Library the anonymous novel *Orsilia: or, the Ordeal* (London, 1867) is by Sophia May Eckley.
18. Postmarked Nov. 26, 1858 (Berg).
19. *Dearest Isa*, p. 35.
20. EBB to Arabel, postmarked March 6, 1859 (Berg).
21. *Ibid.*, postmarked Nov. 13, 1858 (Berg).
22. *Ibid.*, postmarked Nov. 26, 1858 (Berg).
23. *Ibid.*, London postmark of June 18, 1858 (Berg).
24. EBB to Mrs. Eckley, July 12 [1858] (Berg).
25. EBB to Arabel, July 30 [1858] (Berg).
26. See EBB to Mrs. Jameson, Aug. 25 [1858], reproduction in NYPL.
27. EBB to Mrs. Eckley, Aug. 28 [1858] (Berg).
28. EBB to Arabel, postmarked Nov. 26, 1858 (Berg).
29. EBB wrote Sarianna Browning (Kenyon, 2, 295) that they left Florence on the "next day" after her letter of "Wednesday, 18th." But in 1858 Wednesday was the 17th.
30. The trip is described in EBB's letter to Arabel, postmarked Nov. 26, 1858 (Berg).
31. EBB to Arabel, Dec. 24, 25 [1858] (Berg).
32. *Dearest Isa*, p. 32.
33. EBB to Arabel, postmarked March 6, 1859 (Berg).
34. EBB to Fanny Haworth, BMType; the letter is partly in Kenyon, 2, 420–3.
35. Postmarked Aug. 5, 1857, No. 92 (Houghton).
36. EBB to Arabel, March 29 [1859] (Berg).
37. Postmarked April 30, 1859 (Berg).
38. EBB to Arabel, June 3 [1859] (Berg).
39. *Ibid.*
40. *Last Poems*, pp. 57–8.
41. From Story's *Conversations in a Studio*, quoted by James, 2, 18.
42. EBB to Henrietta, Sept. 13 [1859], No. 107 (Houghton).
43. The Marchesa Peruzzi de' Medici [formerly Edith Story], "Walter Savage Landor," *Cornhill Magazine*, new ser. *38* (1915), 494.
44. James, 2, 20.
45. EBB to Arabel, postmarked Dec. 8, 1859 (Berg).
46. Advertised in the *Athenaeum*, Saturday, March 10, 1860 (p. 325) for the following Monday.
47. *Twenty-two Unpublished Letters*, p. 89.

Notes. Pages 375–393   451

48. Vol. 87 (1860), 490–4.
49. Vol. 9 (March 31, 1860), 402–4.
50. See Merle M. Bevington, *The Saturday Review, 1855–1868* (New York, 1941), p. 215.
51. Vol. 61 (1860), 818–23.
52. April 16, 1860.
53. March 17, 1860, pp. 371–2.
54. See also RB's sarcastic remarks on this subject in an unpublished letter to Kate Field, March 29, 1860 (Boston Public Library).
55. April 7, 1860, p. 477.
56. Vol. 40 (April 7, 1860), pp. 218–19.
57. For other unfavorable reviews of *Poems before Congress*, see *Chambers's Journal*, 13 (1860), 251–3; *Examiner* (March 24, 1860), p. 181; London *Observer*, April 23, 1860. William Howitt in an article entitled "The Earth-Plane and the Spirit-Plane of Literature" in the *Spiritual Magazine, 1* (July 1860), 293–5, reviewed EBB's career and deplored the change from the "spirit-plane" of her early verse to the "earth-plane" of her present poetry. Also he was horrified that she had "become fascinated with the second modern Moloch, Louis Napoleon."
58. March 29, 1860.
59. March 24, 1860, pp. 231–2.
60. See W. M. Rossetti to EBB, March 27 [1860] (Wellesley).

CHAPTER 19. Last Poems and Final Illness

1. EBB to Fanny Haworth, Aug. 25, 1860, BMType; part of the letter is in Kenyon, 2, 405–8.
2. See EBB to Isa Blagden [Nov.–Dec. 1860], BMType. Kenyon omitted the passage dealing with Mrs. Eckley; for the rest of the letter see 2, 411–14.
3. *Robert Browning and Julia Wedgwood*, ed. Curle, p. 168.
4. *Dearest Isa*, p. 314.
5. *Letters to Robert Browning and Other Correspondents, by Elizabeth Barrett Browning*, ed. Wise, pp. 52–3.
6. April 2 [1860], BMType; part of the letter is in Kenyon, 2, 373–5.
7. [June? 1860?] (Berg).
8. *Twenty-two Unpublished Letters*, pp. 87–8; conjecturally dated 1857 by the editor. The correct date is 1860, when the Brownings were living at 28 Via del Tritone.
9. McAleer, p. 608.
10. *Twenty-two Unpublished Letters*, p. 85.
11. [June? 1860?] (Berg).
12. EBB to Sarianna Browning [possibly June 1860], BMType; part of the letter is in Kenyon, 2, 396–400.
13. See Maggs, p. 56. EBB wrote George Barrett (Illinois) in a letter postmarked at Florence Nov. 19, 1860, that they were going to Rome the following day.
14. [Dec. 8?] London postmark of Dec. 17, 1860 (Berg).
15. Maggs, p. 56.
16. See Hazel Harrod, "Correspondence of Harriet Beecher Stowe and Elizabeth Barrett Browning," *University of Texas Studies in English*, 27 (1948), 28–34; Charles Edward Stowe, *Life of Harriet Beecher Stowe* (Boston and New York, 1889), pp. 356–9.

17. London postmark of Jan. 14, 1861 (Berg).
18. *Ibid.*
19. *TLS* (Dec. 5, 1902), p. 365.
20. [Feb.–April 1861] (Berg).
21. Postmarked May 15, 1861 (Berg).
22. London postmark of May 29, 1861 (Berg).
23. Hood, p. 58.
24. James, 2, 65.
25. Mentioned in various editions of Murray's guides of Florence as licentiate of the Royal College of Physicians, London, and of the College of Physicians, Göttingen, formerly physician to a London hospital, physician to the British Legation at Florence—"the Watson of Florence."
26. Hood, p. 61. For details of EBB's death see RB's letters to Sarianna Browning (Hood, pp. 58–63; DeVane, pp. 131–4); to W. C. Macready (Hood, pp. 63–4); to Fanny Haworth (Hood, pp. 64–5); to John Forster (DeVane, pp. 137–40); to George Barrett, July 2 [1861] (Illinois); Story's letter to Charles Eliot Norton (James, 2, 60–71).
27. For example, *La Gazzetta del Popolo* (Florence, July 1, 1861) in an article on her life and writings spoke of her classical learning and the elegance and nobility of her poems and declared that when she died, "L'Inghilterra perdeva in lei la più celebrata poetessa vivente; l'Italia perdeva una delle più fervide, più calde, più costanti sostenitrici della sua causa; gli amici uno degli animi più generosi che palpitassero mai in cuore di donna." For similar comments see also *La Nuova Europa*, Florence, July 1, 1861.
28. The ceremonies of EBB's baptism, marriage, and burial were all performed by the Church of England. She had no choice, of course, in any of the three. The Marylebone Church was selected for the marriage ceremony because of its proximity to the Barretts' house on Wimpole Street. She was throughout her life a Congregationalist, although she did not believe in narrow sectarianism. When her strength permitted, she occasionally attended the services of the Church of Scotland in Florence.

CHAPTER 20. Epilogue: a Century of Criticism

1. Vol. *12* (1861), 41–2.
2. I have seen the notice in the *Spectator* only as it was reproduced in *Littell's Living Age*, ser. 3, *14* (1861), 489–90.
3. Vol. *114* (1861), 513–34.
4. July 6, 1861, pp. 19–20.
5. Vol. *8* (1861), 368–76.
6. Vol. *23* (1861), 555–6.
7. See Samuel B. Holcombe, "Death of Mrs. Browning," *33* (1861), 412–17.
8. Advertised for March 20, in the *Athenaeum* (March 15, 1862), p. 370.
9. Vol. *60* (1862), 157–62.
10. March 29, 1862, pp. 421–2. The article, though anonymous, appears to have been written by Chorley.
11. Vol. *13* (1862), 472–4. The reviewer wrote that she had a feverish style, a humorless point of view, and little sense of reality.
12. Vol. *72* (1862), 65–88.

13. Vol. *94* (1862), 338–56. By C. B. Conant, according to the marked copy at Harvard.
14. Vol. *36* (1862), 514–34.
15. New ser. 2 (1862), 189–212.
16. American ed., Vol. *91* (1862), 449–51.
17. March 28, 1863, p. 425.
18. Vol. *1* (1863), 311–12.
19. Vol. *62* (1863), 212–16.
20. Vol. *75* (1863), 24–43. By Kate Field, according to the marked copy at Harvard.
21. Vol. *24* (1877), 105–6. By Henry James, according to the marked copy at Harvard.
22. Vol. *8* (1877), 22–3.
23. Vol. *21* (1878), 747–53. By Marion Couthouy.
24. William T. Herridge, "Elizabeth Barrett Browning," *Andover Review*, 7 (1887), 607–23.
25. "A Study of Mrs. Browning," 7 (1896), 496–506.
26. By Thomas Bradfield, *146* (1896), 174–84.
27. Vol. *16* (1885), 153–4.
28. Ingram (p. 193) gave the date March 4, 1809, but he did not know that he was referring to the birth of Henrietta Barrett.
29. Vol. *72* (1889), 22–42; reprinted in *Littell's Living Age*, *181* (1889), 643–52.
30. See the review, which appeared originally in *Macmillan's Magazine*, *59* (1888), 138–45, as reprinted, with many changes and additions, in *Essays* (London, 1896), pp. 205–37.
31. Vol. *79* (1897), 685–6.
32. Vol. *66* (1898), 112–13.
33. See the portion of the review quoted in *Book Reviews*, 5 (1897), 176–7.
34. Feb. 18, 1899, pp. 201–2.
35. See "The Browning Letters," *Studies of a Biographer* (second series, London, 1902), *3*, 1–35.
36. Vol. *30* (1899), 99–100.
37. Vol. *82* (1899), 308–10.
38. Vol. *189* (1899), 420–39.
39. See esp. the review of EBB's *Poetical Works* in *TLS* (Feb. 5, 1904), pp. 33–4.
40. For a full and sympathetic review of Merlette see L. E. Tiddeman's article in the *Westminster Review*, *167* (1907), 82–92.
41. "A Great Poet in Her Prime," *Book News*, *24* (1906), 457–9.
42. "Mrs. Browning in Poetry To-day," *op. cit.*, pp. 464–6.
43. Vol. *23* (1906), 590–2.
44. Osbert Burdett, *The Brownings*, London, 1928; Irene Cooper Willis, *Elizabeth Barrett Browning*, London, 1928; Isabel C. Clarke, *Elizabeth Barrett Browning, a Portrait*, London, 1929; Dormer Creston, *Andromeda in Wimpole Street*, London, 1929; Carola Lenanton, *Miss Barrett's Elopement*, London, 1929; David G. Loth, *The Brownings; a Victorian Idyll*, London, 1929; Louise Schutz Boas, *Elizabeth Barrett Browning*, London, 1930; Harriet Gaylord, *Pompilia and Her Poet*, New York, 1931.
45. Vol. *21* (1930), 278–9.
46. Vol. *94* (1930), 931–40.

47. See esp. the reviews in *TLS* (Nov. 7, 1929), p. 893; *Nation and Athenaeum, 46* (1929), 319; *Spectator, 143* (1929), 724–5; *New Statesman, 34* (1929), 304.

48. Aug. 29, 1930, p. 10. The letter was signed by E. A. Altham (Henrietta's son), H. P. Moulton-Barrett (Henry's son), and E. M. Moulton-Barrett (Octavius' son).

49. See the *Yale Review,* new ser. *20* (1931), 677–90; *TLS* (July 2, 1931), pp. 517–18.

50. *Victorian Poets* (Boston, 1876), p. 137.

51. *Critical Kit-Kats* (London, 1896), p. 10.

52. *The Sonnet in England and Other Essays* (London, 1893), pp. 52, 54–5.

53. Colophon: "This book has been printed and illuminated by me, and finished in January 1897. Phoebe Anna Traquair (born Moss)."

54. Designed and executed by Andrew Vargish, Boston, 1930–31.

55. Edited by Fannie Ratchford and with notes by Deoch Fulton.

56. *Sonetos del portugues,* versión y prólogo de Julieta Gomez Paz, Adonais, CX, Ediciones Rialp, Madrid, 1954.

57. *Sonnets from the Portuguese,* printed for W. A. Clark, Jr., by J. H. Nash, pp. xii, xiv.

58. See the Bibliography, below.

BIBLIOGRAPHY

I

Principal Manuscript Sources

Wellesley College Library

About 240 letters to H. S. Boyd; 21 letters to B. R. Haydon; about 79 letters to Mrs. Jameson; about 66 letters to John Kenyon; about 94 letters to Mrs. Martin; about 434 letters to Miss Mitford; letters between RB and EBB, 1845–46 (all the "love letters"); and letters to EBB from various correspondents. Also poems, diaries, and memorandum books.

Berg Collection, NYPL

One hundred thirteen letters to Arabella Barrett; 121 letters to Mrs. Eckley; and letters to other correspondents. Poems, sketches, notes, and translations.

Huntington Library

Letters to H. S. Boyd and other correspondents. Poems, translations, commonplace book, copybook, and notebooks.

British Museum

Letters to various correspondents. F. G. Kenyon's transcriptions (Add. MSS. 42,228–31) of EBB's letters which he used in preparation for her *Letters* (1897). They include many omitted letters and portions of letters.

Collection of Arthur A. Houghton, Jr., New York

One hundred seven letters to Henrietta Barrett; 22 letters from RB and EBB to Henrietta Barrett; and letters to other correspondents. Poems, translations, and prose sketches.

Library of the University of Illinois

Fifty-six letters to George Barrett and letters to various correspondents; and letters to EBB from R. H. Horne and others.

Folger Library

Fragments of about 37 letters to Miss Mitford. Poems, prose sketches, and school exercises.

Important collections of letters and poems by EBB are also at the Harvard College Library, the Yale University Library, the Pierpont Morgan Library, the Boston Public Library, the Library of the University of Texas, and the Armstrong-Browning Library at Baylor University.

II

BIBLIOGRAPHIES

Thomas J. Wise, *A Bibliography of the Writings in Prose and Verse of Elizabeth Barrett Browning,* London, 1918.

Theodore G. Ehrsam, Robert H. Deily, and Robert M. Smith, *Bibliographies of Twelve Victorian Authors,* New York, 1936.

Gardner B. Taplin, "Mrs. Browning's Contributions to Periodicals: Addenda," *Papers of the Bibliographical Society of America, 44* (1950), 275-6.

III

PRINCIPAL RECENT BIOGRAPHIES

Frances Winwar, *The Immortal Lovers,* New York, 1950.

Dorothy Hewlett, *Elizabeth Barrett Browning, a Life,* New York, 1952.

Betty Miller, *Robert Browning, a Portrait,* London, 1952.

The following also provides useful biographical materials: Jeannette Marks, *The Family of the Barrett,* New York, 1938.

IV

EBB's WRITINGS PUBLISHED IN BOOKS AND PERIODICALS *

Books by EBB

The Battle of Marathon. A Poem, by E. B. Barrett, London, printed for W. Lindsell, 87 Wimpole Street, Cavendish-Square, 1820.

* The wording of the title pages, as well as the style of each title, has been retained.

An Essay on Mind, with Other Poems, London, James Duncan, Paternoster-Row, 1826.

Prometheus Bound. Translated from the Greek of Æschylus. And Miscellaneous Poems, by the translator, author of "An Essay on Mind," with other poems, London, printed and published by A. J. Valpy, M.A., Red Lion Court, Fleet Street, 1833.

The Seraphim, and Other Poems, by Elizabeth B. Barrett, London, Saunders and Otley, Conduit Street, 1838.

Poems, by Elizabeth Barrett Barrett, 2 vols. London, Edward Moxon, Dover Street, 1844.

Poems, by Elizabeth Barrett Browning, new ed. 2 vols. London, Chapman and Hall, 193 Piccadilly (late 186 Strand), 1850.

Casa Guidi Windows. A Poem, by Elizabeth Barrett Browning, London, Chapman and Hall, 193 Piccadilly, 1851.

Poems, by Elizabeth Barrett Browning, 3d ed. 2 vols. London, Chapman and Hall, 193 Piccadilly, 1853.

Poems, by Elizabeth Barrett Browning, 4th ed. 3 vols. London, Chapman and Hall, 193 Piccadilly, 1856.

Aurora Leigh, by Elizabeth Barrett Browning, London, Chapman and Hall, 193 Piccadilly, 1857.

Poems before Congress, by Elizabeth Barrett Browning, London, Chapman and Hall, 193 Piccadilly, 1860.

Books Written Partly by EBB, or with Short Contributions by Her

The Poems of Geoffrey Chaucer, Modernized [with an introduction by R. H. Horne], London, Whittaker and Co., 1841. "Queen Annelida and False Arcite," pp. 237-47; "The Complaint of Annelida to False Arcite," pp. 248-57.

A New Spirit of the Age, ed. R. H. Horne, 2 vols. London, Smith, Elder, and Co., 1844. Many contributions by EBB.

Memoirs and Essays Illustrative of Art, Literature, and Social Morals, by Mrs. [Anna] Jameson, London, Richard Bentley, 1846. Two versions of "The Daughters of Pandarus," translated from the Odyssey, pp. 137-8. Reprinted in *Last Poems,* pp. 132-4.

Two Poems, by Elizabeth Barrett and Robert Browning, London, Chapman and Hall, 193 Piccadilly, 1854. "A Plea for the Ragged Schools of London," pp. 3–11.

Books Issued Posthumously

Poems, by Elizabeth Barrett Browning, 5th ed. 3 vols. London, Chapman and Hall, 193 Piccadilly, 1862 [actually a reprint of the fourth edition].

Last Poems, by Elizabeth Barrett Browning, London, Chapman and Hall, 193 Piccadilly, 1862.

The Greek Christian Poets and the English Poets, by Elizabeth Barrett Browning, London, Chapman and Hall, 193 Piccadilly, 1863.

The Poetical Works of Elizabeth Barrett Browning, 6 vols. London, Smith, Elder, and Co., 15 Waterloo Place, 1889–90.

The Poetical Works of Elizabeth Barrett Browning, ed. Frederic G. Kenyon, London, Smith, Elder, and Co., 15 Waterloo Place, 1897.

New Poems, by Robert Browning and Elizabeth Barrett Browning, ed. Frederic G. Kenyon, London, Smith, Elder, and Co., 15 Waterloo Place, 1914.

The Poets' Enchiridion, by Elizabeth Barrett Barrett, ed. H. Buxton Forman, Boston, the Bibliophile Society, 1914.

Elizabeth Barrett Browning. Hitherto Unpublished Poems and Stories, ed. H. Buxton Forman, 2 vols. Boston, the Bibliophile Society, 1914.

Contributions to Annuals, Almanacs, Periodicals, and Series

"Stanzas, Excited by Some Reflections on the Present State of Greece," *New Monthly Magazine, 1* (1821), 523. Reprinted in *Notes and Queries, 195* (1950), 253.

"Thoughts Awakened by Contemplating a Piece of the Palm Which Grows on the Summit of the Acropolis at Athens," *New Monthly Magazine, 2* (1821), 59. There is a somewhat different version in *HUP,* 2, 31–33.

"Stanzas on the Death of Lord Byron," London *Globe and Traveller,* June 30, 1824. Reprinted with minor alterations in *An Essay on Mind, with Other Poems,* pp. 117–19.

Bibliography

"The Rose and Zephyr," *Literary Gazette, and Journal of the Belles Lettres* (Nov. 19, 1825), p. 750. Reprinted in *HUP*, 2, 50–3.

"Irregular Stanzas," *Literary Gazette, and Journal of the Belles Lettres* (May 6, 1826), p. 284. Reprinted in *HUP*, 2, 53–5.

"Who Art Thou of the Veilëd Countenance," *Jewish Expositor, and Friend of Israel, 12* (Jan. 1827), 14–16. Reprinted in *HUP*, 2, 71–4.

"Kings," *The Times* (London), May 31, 1831. Reprinted in *Notes and Queries, 196* (1951), 410.

"The Pestilence," *The Times* (London), Jan. 13, 1832. There is a slightly different version in *HUP*, 2, 176–8.

"Stanzas Addressed to Miss Landon, and Suggested by Her 'Stanzas on the Death of Mrs. Hemans,'" *New Monthly Magazine, 45* (Sept. 1835), 82. Reprinted in an altered form in *The Seraphim, and Other Poems*, pp. 271–5.

"Man and Nature," *Athenaeum* (March 19, 1836), p. 208. Reprinted in an altered form in *The Seraphim, and Other Poems*, pp. 287–9.

"The Romaunt of Margret," *New Monthly Magazine, 47* (July 1836), 316–20. Reprinted with alterations in *The Seraphim, and Other Poems*, pp. 119–35.

"The Seaside Walk," *Athenaeum* (July 2, 1836), p. 468. Reprinted in *The Seraphim, and Other Poems*, pp. 290–2.

"A Thought on Thoughts," *Athenaeum* (July 23, 1836), pp. 522–3. Prose essay. Reprinted in *HUP*, 2, 157–65.

"The Poet's Vow," *New Monthly Magazine, 48* (Oct. 1836), 209–18. Reprinted with alterations in *The Seraphim, and Other Poems*, pp. 79–118.

"The Island," *New Monthly Magazine, 49* (Jan. 1837), 22–5. Reprinted with alterations in *The Seraphim, and Other Poems*, pp. 185–98.

"The Young Queen," *Athenaeum* (July 1, 1837), p. 483. Reprinted in *The Seraphim, and Other Poems*, pp. 323–7.

"Victoria's Tears," *Athenaeum* (July 8, 1837), p. 506. Reprinted in *The Seraphim, and Other Poems*, pp. 328–31.

"A Romance of the Ganges," *Findens' Tableaux: a Series of Picturesque Scenes of National Character, Beauty, and Costume*, ed. Mary

Russell Mitford (London, 1838), pp. 29–31. Reprinted in *The Seraphim, and Other Poems,* pp. 171–84.

"The Romaunt of the Page," *Findens' Tableaux of the Affections: a Series of Picturesque Illustrations of the Womanly Virtues,* ed. Mary Russell Mitford (London, 1839), pp. 1–5. Reprinted with alterations in *Poems* (1844), *1*, 151–70.

"A Sabbath on the Sea," *The Amaranth: a Miscellany of Original Prose and Verse,* ed. T. K. Hervey (London, 1839), pp. 73–5. Reprinted in a revised form as "A Sabbath Morning at Sea" in *Poems* (1850), *2*, 325–8.

"L.E.L.'s Last Question," *Athenaeum* (Jan. 26, 1839), p. 69. Reprinted in *Poems* (1844), *2*, 219–22.

"The Crowned and Wedded Queen," *Athenaeum* (Feb. 15, 1840), p. 131. Reprinted as "Crowned and Wedded" in *Poems* (1844), *2*, 136–41.

"The Dream," *Findens' Tableaux: the Iris of Prose, Poetry, and Art for 1840,* ed. Mary Russell Mitford (London, 1840), pp. 7–8. Reprinted with many alterations as "A Child Asleep," in *Poems* (1844), *2*, 123–6.

"The Legend of the Brown Rosarie," *Findens' Tableaux,* pp. 15–21. Reprinted in the New York *Ladies' Companion and Literary Expositor,* new ser. *1* (May 1844), 31–5; and, with many alterations, as "The Lay of the Brown Rosary" in *Poems* (1844), *1*, 171–201.

"A Night-Watch by the Sea," *Monthly Chronicle, 5* (April 1840), 297.

"The Lay of the Rose," *Monthly Chronicle, 6* (July 1840), 13–17. Reprinted as "A Lay of the Early Rose" in *Poems* (1844), *2*, 180–90.

"Napoleon's Return," *Athenaeum* (July 4, 1840), p. 532. Reprinted as "Crowned and Buried" in *Poems* (1844), *2*, 142–51.

"The House of Clouds," *Athenaeum* (Aug. 21, 1841), p. 643. Reprinted with some changes in *Poems* (1844), *2*, 223–8.

"Lessons from the Gorse," *Athenaeum* (Oct. 23, 1841), p. 810. Reprinted in *Poems* (1844), *2*, 260–1.

"Three Hymns, Translated from the Greek of Gregory Nazianzen," *Athenaeum* (Jan. 8, 1842), pp. 39–40. Reprinted in *HUP, 2,* 222–8.

"Some Account of the Greek Christian Poets," *Athenaeum* (Feb. 26, 1842), pp. 189–90; (March 5), pp. 210–12; (March 12), pp. 229–31;

Bibliography

(March 19), pp. 249–52. Reprinted in *The Greek Christian Poets and the English Poets,* pp. 1–103.

"The Book of the Poets," *Athenaeum* (June 4, 1842), pp. 497–9; (June 11), pp. 520–3; (June 25), pp. 558–60; (Aug. 6), pp. 706–8; (Aug. 13), pp. 728–9. Reprinted in *The Greek Christian Poets and the English Poets,* pp. 105–93.

Review of Wordsworth's *Poems, Chiefly of Early and Late Years; Including The Borderers, a Tragedy,* in the *Athenaeum* (Aug. 27, 1842), pp. 757–9. Reprinted in *The Greek Christian Poets and the English Poets,* pp. 193–211.

"A Claim in an Allegory," *Athenaeum* (Sept. 17, 1842), p. 818. Reprinted with alterations as "The Claim" in *Poems* (1850), 2, 355–6.

"Sonnet on Mr. Haydon's Portrait of Mr. Wordsworth," *Athenaeum* (Oct. 29, 1842), p. 932. Reprinted with slight alterations in *Poems* (1844), *1,* 125.

"The Cry of the Human," *Boston Miscellany of Literature and Fashion,* 2 (Nov. 1842), 197–9. Reprinted with alterations and additions in *Poems* (1844), 2, 173–9.

"Sonnets" [four sonnets with no titles], *Graham's Magazine,* 21 (Dec. 1842), 303. Reprinted, with revisions, under the titles "Grief," "Substitution," "Work," and "Work and Contemplation" in *Poems* (1844), *1,* 129, 130, 133, 139.

"Introductory Stanzas," *Schloss's English Bijou Almanack for 1843, Poetically Illustrated by Miss* [Mary Russell] *Mitford.* [Appeared in London, Dec. 1842.]

"The Prince of Wales," *ibid.*

"Duchess of Orleans," *ibid.*

"Rogers," *ibid.*

"The King of Prussia," *ibid.*

"The Maiden's Death," *Pioneer, 1* (March 1843), 112. Different versions were reprinted in *Cornhill Magazine* (Dec. 1913), pp. 721–2; *HUP,* 2, 175–6, 229–31; and *New Poems,* pp. 132–3.

Review of R. H. Horne's *Orion: an Epic Poem, Athenaeum* (June 24, 1843), pp. 583–4.

"The Soul's Expression," *Graham's Magazine*, 23 (July 1843), 34. Reprinted in *Poems* (1844), *1*, 123.

"To Flush, My Dog," *Athenaeum* (July 22, 1843), pp. 670-1. Reprinted in *Poems* (1844), 2, 152-8.

"Seraph and Poet," *Graham's Magazine*, 23 (Aug. 1843), 71. Reprinted in *Poems* (1844), *1*, 124.

"The Cry of the Children," *Blackwood's Edinburgh Magazine*, 54 (Aug. 1843), 260-2. Reprinted in *Poems* (1844), 2, 127-35.

"The Child and the Watcher," *Graham's Magazine*, *24* (Sept. 1843), 158. Reprinted with some changes as "Sleeping and Watching" in *Poems* (1844), 2, 241-3.

"Caterina to Camoens," *Graham's Magazine*, *24* (Oct. 1843), 208-9. Reprinted with many revisions as "Catarina to Camoëns" in *Poems* (1844), 2, 229-36. There is a different version in *The Poets' Enchiridion*, pp. 47-9, and in *HUP*, 2, 185-6.

"The Lady's Yes. A Song," *Graham's Magazine*, 25 (Jan. 1844), 18. Reprinted with revisions and additions in *Poems* (1844), 2, 96-7.

"Loved Once," *Graham's Magazine*, 25 (March 1844), 100. Reprinted with many revisions in *Poems* (1844), 2, 205-8.

"Pain in Pleasure," *Graham's Magazine*, 26 (Aug. 1844), 65. Reprinted in *Poems* (1844), *1*, 140.

"Insufficiency," *United States Magazine and Democratic Review*, new ser. *15* (Aug. 1844), 194. Reprinted in *Poems* (1844), *1*, 150.

"Sonnet: A Sketch," *Christian Mother's Magazine*, 2 (Oct. 1845), 635. Reprinted in *Poems* (1850), *1*, 351.

"Wisdom Unapplied," *ibid.*, p. 645. Reprinted in *Poems* (1850), 2, 343-6. There is a different version in *HUP*, 2, 180-2.

"A Woman's Shortcomings," *Blackwood's Edinburgh Magazine*, 60 (Oct. 1846), 488-9. Reprinted in *Poems* (1850), 2, 398-9.

"A Man's Requirements," *ibid.*, pp. 489-90. Reprinted in *Poems* (1850), 2, 400-2.

"Maud's Spinning," *ibid.*, pp. 490-1. Reprinted as "A Year's Spinning" in *Poems* (1850), 2, 403-4.

Bibliography

"A Dead Rose," *ibid.*, pp. 491-2. Reprinted in *Poems* (1850), *2*, 361-2.

"Change on Change," *ibid.*, p. 492. Reprinted as "Change upon Change" in *Poems* (1850), *2*, 405-6.

"A Reed," *ibid.*, pp. 492-3. Reprinted in *Poems* (1850), *2*, 409.

"Hector in the Garden," *ibid.*, pp. 493-5. Reprinted with some alterations in *Poems* (1850), *2*, 265-9.

"Life," *Blackwood's Edinburgh Magazine, 61* (May 1847), 555. Reprinted in *Poems* (1850), *1*, 355.

"Love," *ibid.*, pp. 555-6. Reprinted in *Poems* (1850), *1*, 356.

"Heaven and Earth. 1845," *ibid.*, p. 556. Reprinted in *Poems* (1850), *1*, 357.

"The Prospect. 1845," *ibid.*, p. 556. Reprinted in *Poems* (1850), *1*, 358.

"Two Sketches," *Blackwood's Edinburgh Magazine, 61* (June 1847), 683-4. "Sketch II" had already been published in the *Christian Mother's Magazine*, Oct. 1845. Both sonnets were reprinted in *Poems* (1850), *1*, 350-1.

"Mountaineer and Poet," *ibid.*, p. 684. Reprinted in *Poems* (1850), *1*, 352.

"The Poet," *ibid.*, p. 684. Reprinted in *Poems* (1850), *1*, 353.

"The Runaway Slave at Pilgrim's Point," *Liberty Bell* (Boston, 1848), pp. 29-44. Reprinted with some revisions in *Poems* (1850), *2*, 129-41.

"A Child's Grave at Florence," *Athenaeum* (Dec. 22, 1849), p. 1304. Reprinted in *Poems* (1850), *2*, 424-30.

"My Kate," *Keepsake*, ed. Miss [Marguerite A.] Power (London, 1855), pp. 16-17. Reprinted in *Last Poems*, pp. 24-5.

"A Curse for a Nation," *Liberty Bell* (Boston, 1856), pp. 1-9. Reprinted with some alterations in *Poems before Congress*, pp. 59-65.

"Amy's Cruelty," *Keepsake*, ed. Miss [Marguerite A.] Power (London, 1857), pp. 75-6. Reprinted in *Last Poems*, pp. 34-6.

"A Tale of Villafranca," *Athenaeum* (Sept. 24, 1859), pp. 397-8. Reprinted in *Poems before Congress*, pp. 26-31.

"First News from Villafranca," New York *Independent, 12*, June 7, 1860. Reprinted in *Last Poems*, pp. 57-8.

"A Musical Instrument," *Cornhill Magazine, 2* (July 1860), 84–5. Reprinted in *Last Poems,* pp. 55–6.

"King Victor Emmanuel Entering Florence, April, 1860," *Independent, 12,* Aug. 16, 1860. Reprinted in *Last Poems,* pp. 59–61.

"The Sword of Castruccio Castracani," *Independent, 12,* Aug. 30, 1860. Reprinted in *Last Poems,* pp. 62–4.

"Summing Up in Italy," *Independent, 12,* Sept. 27, 1860. Reprinted in *Last Poems,* pp. 65–8.

"A Forced Recruit at Solferino," *Cornhill Magazine, 2* (Oct. 1860), 419–20. Reprinted in *Last Poems,* pp. 72–4.

"Garibaldi," *Independent, 12,* Oct. 11, 1860. Reprinted in *Last Poems,* pp. 75–7.

"De Profundis," *Independent, 12,* Dec. 6, 1860. Reprinted in *Last Poems,* pp. 48–54.

"Parting Lovers," *Independent, 13,* March 21, 1861. Reprinted in *Last Poems,* pp. 87–90.

A letter in prose to the editors of the *Independent,* mostly on the Italian situation, *Independent, 13,* March 21, 1861.

"Mother and Poet," *Independent, 13,* May 2, 1861. Reprinted in *Last Poems,* pp. 91–6.

A letter in prose to one of the editors of the *Independent,* partly on Italian politics, *Independent, 13,* May 2, 1861.

"Only a Curl," *Independent, 13,* May 16, 1861. Reprinted in *Last Poems,* pp. 78–81.

"Little Mattie," *Cornhill Magazine, 3* (June 1861), 736–7. Reprinted in *Last Poems,* pp. 1–4.

"The King's Gift," *Independent, 13,* July 18, 1861. Reprinted in *Last Poems,* pp. 85–6.

"A View across the Roman Campagna," *Independent, 13,* July 25, 1861. Reprinted in *Last Poems,* pp. 82–4.

V
Principal Publications of EBB's Letters *

Thomas Powell, *The Living Authors of England* (New York, 1849), pp. 146–52.

Letters of Elizabeth Barrett Browning Addressed to Richard Hengist Horne, ed. S. R. Townshend Mayer, 2 vols. London, 1877.

The Collector: an Historical Magazine for Autograph Collectors, 5 (Nov. 1891), 34–6; (Dec. 1891), 51–3; (Jan. 1892), 74–6; (Feb. 1892), 89–90; (March 1892), 105–7.

The Letters of Elizabeth Barrett Browning, ed. Frederic G. Kenyon, 2 vols. London and New York, 1897.

The Letters of Robert Browning and Elizabeth Barrett Barrett, 1845–1846, 2 vols. London and New York, 1899.

Letters to Robert Browning and Other Correspondents, by Elizabeth Barrett Browning, ed. Thomas J. Wise, London, 1916.

Elizabeth Barrett Browning: Letters to Her Sister, 1846–1859, ed. Leonard Huxley, London, 1929.

Twenty-two Unpublished Letters of Elizabeth Barrett Browning and Robert Browning Addressed to Henrietta and Arabella Moulton-Barrett, New York, 1935.

Letters from Elizabeth Barrett to B. R. Haydon, ed. Martha Hale Shackford, New York, London, and Toronto, 1939.

"Twenty Unpublished Letters of Elizabeth Barrett to Hugh Stuart Boyd," ed. Bennett Weaver, *PMLA,* 65 (1950), 397–418.

"New Letters from Mrs. Browning to Isa Blagden," ed. Edward C. McAleer, *PMLA,* 66 (1951), 594–612.

Elizabeth Barrett to Miss Mitford. The Unpublished Letters of Elizabeth Barrett Barrett to Mary Russell Mitford, ed. Betty Miller, London, 1954.

"Unpublished Letters of Thomas De Quincey and Elizabeth Barrett Browning, Edited from the Originals in the Grey Collection, Auckland Public Library," ed. S. Musgrove, *Auckland University College Bulletin, 44,* English Series, 7, 1954.

* Dates are for first eds. only.

Elizabeth Barrett to Mr. Boyd. Unpublished Letters of Elizabeth Barrett Browning to Hugh Stuart Boyd, ed. Barbara P. McCarthy, New Haven, 1955.

VI

Principal Publications of RB's Letters

Robert Browning and Alfred Domett, ed. Frederic G. Kenyon, London, 1906.

Letters of Robert Browning, Collected by Thomas J. Wise, ed. Thurman L. Hood, New Haven, 1933.

Robert Browning and Julia Wedgwood. A Broken Friendship as Revealed in Their Letters, ed. Richard Curle, London, 1937.

New Letters of Robert Browning, ed. William Clyde DeVane and Kenneth Leslie Knickerbocker, New Haven, 1950.

Dearest Isa. Robert Browning's Letters to Isabella Blagden, ed. Edward C. McAleer, Austin, Texas, 1951.

INDEX

Abrantès, Duchess de, 96
Adriatic coast, the Brownings' trip to, 212–13
Aeschylus, 26, 30, 43, 48, 68, 232; *Agamemnon*, 29, 431; *Prometheus vinctus*, 431; *Septem contra Thebas*, 431
Ainsworth's Magazine, 133; reviews *A New Spirit of the Age*, 120
Akenside, Mark, 11
Alessandro (Browning's servant), 222, 224
Alford, Henry, 100
Allingham, William, 371
Amaranth, 73
American Whig Review, 136 f., 240
Anacreon, 10
Andersen, Hans Christian, visits EBB, 398
Andover Review, 411
"Annuals," popularity of, 62–3
Annunziata (EBB's maid), 353, 370, 402
Arcturus, 71, 108
Aristophanes, 76
Aristotle, EBB's reading of, 76
Arnould, Joseph, 152, 189
Ashley, Lord, 118
Athenaeum, 48, 58, 61, 63 f., 67 ff., 76, 84, 90, 94 f., 100, 102 f., 105 f., 107, 113, 120, 142, 211, 228, 237, 240, 259, 263, 300, 319, 338, 347, 373, 378 f., 406 f., 409 f., 415; recommends EBB for poet laureateship, 226; Miss Mitford's *Recollections* quoted in, 259
Atlantic Monthly, 406
Atlas, 69–70, 132, 380
Aytoun, W. E., 347
Azeglio, Massimo, Marchese de, 389; calls on the Brownings, 360

Bagni di Lucca: description of, 223; the Brownings' places of residence at, 223, 272, 353
Bailey, Philip James, 95, 117, 292

Balzac, Honoré de, 97
Barker, Edmund Henry, 31, 48
Barrett, Alfred Price Barrett Moulton (EBB's brother), 56, 93, 129, 177, 350 f.; with the Brownings in Marseilles, 290; marriage, 290
Barrett, Arabel Moulton (EBB's sister), 8, 55, 73, 81, 87, 168, 173, 179, 187, 248, 357, 414; activities of, 93; description of, by EBB, 194; with EBB in London, 262; asks EBB and RB to help "ragged schools," 279; resents being sent to Eastbourne, 297; depressed spirits, 306; acquires home after EMB's death, 350–1; with EBB at Le Havre and Paris, 357
Barrett, Charles John Barrett Moulton (EBB's brother, "Stormie"), 8, 47, 56, 73, 93, 247, 248, 351; protests Pen's decision to publish the love letters, 188
Barrett, Edward, of Cinnamon Hill (EBB's great-grandfather), 1 ff., 33 f.
Barrett, Edward Barrett Moulton (EBB's father, abbreviated EMB), 290; leaves Jamaica, 1; heir to Jamaica plantations, 3; changes name to Moulton Barrett, 3; at Harrow, 3; has James Scarlett for guardian, 4; enters Trinity College, Cambridge, 4; marries Mary Graham-Clarke, 5; purchases Hope End, 6; country occupations, 8; EBB's first book is dedicated to, 11; pride in EBB's early poetry, 12 f.; contemptuous attitude toward EBB's verses, 24; financial losses, 33, 35 f., 46; in London for business reasons, 35, 46; loses possession of Hope End, 35; moves family to Sidmouth, 43; appears restless in Sidmouth, 46–7; moves family to London, 54; early dislike of London, 55; moves to Wimpole Street, 71; EBB dedicates *Poems* (1844) to, 123–4; EBB's

467

Barrett, Edward Moulton (*continued*) love for, 146; loses EBB's confidence after "the Pisa affair," 159; increasing displeasure in EBB, 173 ff.; disinherits EBB, 183-4; attitude after EBB's marriage, 187-8, 248, 297; sees Pen Browning, 297; orders family to Eastbourne, 297; sends family to Ventnor, 305; "forgives" his three married children, 350; death, 349; representation of, in Besier's play, 420-1. Character and personality: 4, 19-20, 33, 36 f., 81, 90-3

Barrett, Edward Barrett Moulton (EBB's brother, "Bro"), 39, 58, 80 f., 91; birth, 5; acts in plays at Hope End, 10; leaves Hope End for Charterhouse, 10, 15; career at Charterhouse, 16, 35; EBB's verses addressed to, 15; visits Mrs. Moulton at Hastings, 16, 18, 432; withdrawn from Charterhouse, 16, 35; in Jamaica, 47; activities in London, 56; with EBB at Torquay, 73 ff.; death, 79

Barrett, Elizabeth Barrett Moulton. *See* Browning, Elizabeth Barrett

Barrett, George Goodin Barrett Moulton (EBB's brother), 47, 56, 81, 156 f., 188, 262, 298, 312, 357, 391 f.; EBB's description of, 93; reconciled to RB and EBB, 248; retires from the law after EMB's death, 351

Barrett, Georgina Elizabeth (Mrs. Alfred P. B. Moulton Barrett, "Lizzie"), 129, 290

Barrett, Henrietta Barrett Moulton. *See* Cook, Henrietta

Barrett, Henry Barrett Moulton (EBB's brother), 56, 93, 177, 357

Barrett, Mary Clementina (Cay-Adams) Moulton (wife of Samuel Barrett Moulton Barrett, uncle of EBB), 34 f., 48, 431

Barrett, Mary (Graham-Clarke) Moulton (EBB's mother), marriage, 5; birth of children, 5 f., 8; pride in EBB's early poetry, 12 f.; description of, by EBB, 18; death, 32

Barrett, Mary Moulton (EBB's sister), 8

Barrett, Octavius Butler Barrett Moulton (EBB's brother "Occy"), 56, 73, 93, 351

Barrett, Richard (EMB's cousin), 34, 194

Barrett, Samuel Barrett Moulton (EBB's brother), 8, 35, 56, 73; career at Charterhouse, 16, 35; death, 78-9

Barrett, Samuel Barrett Moulton (EBB's uncle), 1 ff., 17, 34, 48, 157, 211, 431; description of, by EBB, 35; leaves for Jamaica, 35

Barrett, Septimus James Barrett Moulton (EBB's brother, "Sette"), 56, 93, 188, 351

Barretts of Wimpole Street, by Rudolf Besier, 420-1

Basil, St. *See* St. Basil

Beattie, James, 102 f.

Beaumont, Francis, 98, 230

Beethoven, Ludwig van, 96, 254, 279

Bell, Robert, 83, 117

Benson, Arthur Christopher, 413

Bentham, Jeremy, 111, 120, 397

Bentley, Richard, 23

Berkeley, George, 21, 23

Besier, Rudolf. *See The Barretts of Wimpole Street*

Bethune, George W., 227

Bevan, James Johnstone, 173

Bible, 30, 41, 43, 99, 410

Bigland, John, 10

Bion, 10, 154, 228

Blackwood's Edinburgh Magazine, 68, 70, 94, 126, 129, 132, 150, 193 f., 206, 228, 233, 339 ff., 343, 345, 347, 376-7, 409

Blagden, Isabella ("Isa"), 303, 331, 353 ff., 359-60, 391, 413; life and literary career, 283; friendship with the Brownings, 283; visits Casa Guidi during EBB's last illness, 400-2; helps RB after EBB's death, 402, 404; to Paris with RB and Pen, 404

Blanc, Louis, 320

Blanchard, Laman, 96

Blaquière, Edward, 429

Blessington, Marguerite, Countess of, 59, 62 f., 75, 113, 118

Blithedale Romance, by Hawthorne, 343

Blomfield, C. J., 48, 431

Boaden, James, 20

Bonheur, Rosa, EBB on, 292

Index

Book News, 417–18
Bookman (New York), 418
Boott, Francis, 355
Bordman, Nelly, 90
Borrow, George, 97
Boston Miscellany of Literature and Fashion, 85, 108, 110, 226
Boston Museum of Fine Arts, 24
Bowring, Sir John, visits EBB, 397–8
Boyd, Ann Henrietta (daughter of HSB), 25, 37 f., 40, 45 f., 51
Boyd, Ann Lowry (wife of HSB), 25, 37 f., 45 f.; death, 50
Boyd, Hugh M. (father of HSB), 25 f.
Boyd, Hugh Stuart (abbreviated HSB), 7, 10, 20, 23, 43, 101, 129, 156, 413 f.; moves to Great Malvern, 25; character of EBB's letters to, 25; enters Pembroke College, Cambridge, 26; early literary career, 26; moves to Malvern Wells, 26; interest in the Greek Christian Fathers, 26; description of his character and ability by EBB, 26–7; first meeting with EBB, 28; description of his appearance by EBB, 28; reads Greek with EBB, 28–9; commends EBB's translations from Greek, 29; moves to Bathampton, 40, to Sidmouth, 45; association with EBB, 50; moves to London, 50; increasing loneliness, 51; decline of friendship with EBB, 61, 146–7; approves of EBB's engagement, 155; receives visits from EBB in *1846*, 168; EBB's visit to, immediately after wedding, 178–9
Boyle, Mary, 205
Bracken, Annette, 353
Braun, Madame Emil (formerly Miss Thomson), 154, 279
Bridell-Fox, Mrs., 143
British Museum, 106, 235, 422
British Quarterly Review, 132 f.
Broadway Journal, 126, 137
Brontë, Emily, 417, 424
Brougham, Henry Peter, 1st Baron, 51
Browning, Elizabeth Barrett (Elizabeth Barrett Moulton Barrett): birth, 5; daily activities at Hope End, 8; attends services at Congregational Church, 8; takes part in drama at Hope End, 10; distress at temporary separation from Bro, 15; sojourn at Boulogne, 16; trip to Paris, 16; trip to Carlton Hall and Fenham Hall, 17; trip to Worthing, 17; her year at Hastings, 17; friendship with Uvedale Price, 24; first meeting with Boyd, 28; rapid growth of friendship with Boyd, 28 f.; early contributions of verse to periodicals, 30, 61; corresponds with E. H. Barker, 31; grief over mother's death, 33; anxiety due to threatened loss of Hope End, 36 ff.; distressed at prospect of separation from Boyd, 37 f.; interest in proposed Reform Bill, 39; depressed in spirits after Boyd's departure, 40 f.; further depression because of loss of Hope End, 42; leaves Hope End for Sidmouth, 43; activities in Sidmouth, 44; reads with and assists Boyd, 50; friendship with G. B. Hunter, 52–3; moves to London, 54; friendship with Kenyon, 56; meets Mary Russell Mitford, 57–8; course of friendship with Miss Mitford, 59–60; descriptions of appearance and personality, 61, 185, 205 f., 211, 239, 249, 264 ff., 292, 305; sent to Torquay, 72; moves to Beacon Terrace, 74; depressed spirits at Torquay, 85–6; grief over Bro's death, 79–82; leaves Torquay for home in London, 86–7; begins correspondence with RB, 150; RB's first visit to, 151; refused permission by EMB for trip to Pisa, 154–9; income, 157–8, 193 f., 245–6, 282, 348; engagement to RB, 159–60; increasing physical activity in *1846*, 167–8; shocked at Haydon's death, 171; marriage, 178; depressed because of father's attitude after her marriage, 184, 187–8, 203, 212, 248–9, 263, 297–8; anger because of brothers' coldness, 184, 188–9, 203, 212, 247; opinions on Italian art, 201, 212, 245; birth of only child, 222; mentioned for poet laureateship, 226; distressed at Miss Mitford's reference to Bro's death, 258–60;

Browning, Elizabeth Barrett *(continued)* grief over EMB's death, 349; fame after publication of *Aurora Leigh*, 351; attends masked ball, 352-3; stricken after treaty of Villafranca, 367; grief over Henrietta's illness and death, 392; receives severe blow from death of Cavour, 399; last illness and death, 400-3; interment service, 403. *See also* Browning, Robert, and Elizabeth Barrett

READING: early interest in metaphysics, 9; studies ancient and modern languages with Bro, 10; wide acquaintance with literature, 10; criticisms of books read, *1823-25*, 20 ff.; criticism of Milton's *Prose Works*, 22; comments on A. W. Schlegel, *Cours de littérature dramatique,* 23; encouraged by Boyd to read Greek, especially the Greek Fathers, 28 f.; reads classics and modern literature, 29 ff., 41; reads Old Testament in Hebrew, 41; Boyd's influence on her reading, 51; interest in philosophy and religion, 51-2; reading tastes, 94; reads Greek at Torquay, 76; books and periodicals read before her marriage, 94-100

WORKS

"Amy's Cruelty," 280
Anacreon, paraphrase on, 154
"Appeal," 49
Apuleius, paraphrase on, 154
"August Voice," 373
Aurora Leigh, 408 f.; composition of, 271, 274, 279, 285, 303 ff.; dedication, 307; correction of proof sheets, 306 f.; date of publication, 308; sensational popular success of, 310-12; alleged immorality of, 312-13; main theme, 313; plot and sources, 313-37; reviews of, 337-47; Virginia Woolf on, 421
Battle of Marathon, 10, 64, 141
"Bertha in the Lane," 128, 237, 411
"Book of the Poets," 102-3
on Boyd, Hugh Stuart: "His Blindness," 232; "His Death," 232; "Legacies," 232-3

Casa Guidi Windows ("Meditation in Tuscany"), 206-9, 217-19, 230 f., 251 f., 282, 304, 443; reviews of, 240-1
"Catarina to Camoëns," 237; RB affected by, 128, 234
"Child's Grave at Florence," 211
"Christmas Gifts," 372
"Claim," 228
"Court Lady," 372
"Cowper's Grave," 67, 69, 409
"Crowned and Wedded Queen," 77
"Cry of the Children," 113, 114-16, 194, 237, 409
"Cry of the Human," 85, 108, 436
"Curse for a Nation," 372, 376, 378-9
"Dance," 372
"Daughters of Pandarus," 154
"De Profundis," 82, 407
"Dead Pan," 113, 122
"Denial," 304, 444
"Deserted Garden," 66, 69, 121
"Development of Genius," 24
"Drama of Exile," 103, 121, 124-7, 130 f., 134 ff., 252, 271
"Dream," 77
"Epistle to Dearest Papa in London," 20
Essay on Mind, with Other Poems, 13, 24 f., 71, 141
"Essay on Mind," 14, 23
Euripides, paraphrase on, 154
"First News from Villafranca," quoted, 366
"Flower in a Letter," 436
"Forced Recruit," 389
"Greek Christian Poets, Some Account of the," 94, 100-2, 147
Greek Christian Poets and the English Poets: published by RB, 409; reviews of, 409-10
"Hector in the Garden," 233
Hesiod, paraphrase on, 154
"Hiram Powers' Greek Slave," 202
Homer, paraphrase on, 154
"House of Clouds," 137
"Hymn," 49
"Idols," 49
"Inclusions," 228, 444

470 *The Life of Elizabeth Barrett Browning*

Index

"Insufficiency," 111, 228, 444
"Introductory Stanzas," 106
"Isobel's Child," 66, 68 f., 128–9, 411
"Italy and the World," 374–5
"King Victor Emmanuel Entering Florence, April, 1860," 389
"Lady Geraldine's Courtship," 123, 127, 131, 134, 139, 237 f., 312, 411, 417
"Lament for Adonis" (translated from Bion), 154, 228
Last Poems, 154, 384, 388; reviewed, 407–8
"Lay of the Rose," 77
"Legend of the Brown Rosarie," 77, 127, 417
"Leila," 15
"L.E.L.'s Last Question," 76
Letters (ed. Kenyon), 413–15
Letters (the love letters), 415–17
Letters to Her Sister, 419–20
Letters . . . to . . . Horne, 410–11
"Life and Love," 228, 444
"Little Friend," 66, 228
"Lost Bower," 113–14, 137
"Maiden's Death," 110 f.
"Measure," 67
"Mother and Poet," 397
"Mournful Mother," 128
"Musical Instrument," 388, 407
"My Doves," 67, 69
"My Kate," 280
"Name," 66
"Napoleon III in Italy," 373, 376 f.
"Napoleon's Return," 77
"Night-Watch by the Sea," 77
Nonnus, paraphrases on, 154
"North and the South," 398
"Notes on a Trip to Paris," 16
"Pain in Pleasure," 135
"Parting Lovers," 397
"Past and Future," 130, 234
"Picture Gallery at Penshurst," 48
"Plea for the Ragged Schools of London," 279
Poems (1844), 122–38; reviewed, 132–8
Poems (1850), 228–36; reviewed, 236–9
Poems (1853), 235, 271, 282
Poems (1856), 235, 304

Poems (1862), 408–9
Poems before Congress, 371–5, 388; meaning of title, 371; preface quoted, 371–2; reviewed, 375–81
"Poet's Vow," 62, 69
"Portrait," 129
Prometheus Bound . . . and Miscellaneous Poems, 47; reviewed, 48
"Prometheus Bound" (earlier translation), 48, 59, 72
"Prometheus Bound" (later translation), 94, 150, 153, 228, 230–2, 240, 271, 443; reviewed, 238
"Proof and Disproof," 304, 444
"Psyche Apocalypté," 84–5
"Queen Annelida and False Arcite," 82 ff.
"Question and Answer," 304, 444
"Regulus," 10
"Rhyme of the Duchess May," 127–8, 131
"Ring," 444
"Romance of the Ganges," 63
"Romance of the Swan's Nest," 129–30
"Romaunt of Margret," 61 f., 121, 135, 406
"Romaunt of the Page," 63, 127, 238
"Rose and Zephyr," 14
"Runaway Slave at Pilgrim's Point," 111, 194
"Sabbath on the Sea," 73, 228
"Sea-Mew," 66, 69
Seraphim, and Other Poems, 11, 59, 61, 64 f., 124, 130, 143, 229, 381; reviewed, 67–71
"Seraphim," 65–6, 69, 71, 103, 130, 271
"Sleep," 69
"Song against Singing," 67
"Sonnets from the Portuguese," 228, 251, 271, 304, 407 ff., 412 f.; composition of, 154; first shown to RB, 233–4; meaning of title, 234; revisions, 235–6; reviews of, 238; continued popularity of, 422–3; quoted, 160, 233, 235
"Stanzas to Bettine," 230
"Stanzas on the Death of Lord Byron," 12, 14

Browning, Elizabeth Barrett (*continued*)
"Stanzas Occasioned by a Passage in Mr. Emerson's Journal . . . ," 14
"Summing up in Italy," 389
"Tale of Villafranca," 372-3
"That Day," 111
Theocritus, paraphrase on, 154
"Thought on Thoughts," 61
"To Flush, My Dog," 113
"To G.B.H.," 52
"To the Memory of Sir Uvedale Price, Bart.," 49
"To Miss Mitford in Her Garden," 67
"To Victoire, on Her Marriage," 48
Two Poems, 193, 279-80
"Two Sketches," 194
"Verses to My Brother," 15
"Victoria's Tears," 67, 228
"Vision of Poets," 113, 127, 136
"Weeping Saviour," 67, 228
"Where's Agnes?" 384
"Wine of Cyprus," 129
Browning, Robert (the poet): ancestry, birth, and boyhood, 139-42; early trips to Italy, 144 f.; first reads EBB's *Poems* (1844), 139, 145; begins correspondence with EBB, 139, 145; descriptions of appearance and personality, 143-4, 152, 182 f., 186-7, 211, 239-40, 264, 355; RB and EBB compared and contrasted, 149-50; first meeting with EBB, 151; rapid growth of friendship with EBB, 153; engagement, 159-60; warns EBB against delaying marriage, 166, 169 ff.; marriage, 178; grief over mother's death, 222; prepares to leave Florence after EBB's death, 404; in France with father and sister, 404-5; settles in London, 405; later career and fame, 405; death, 405. *See also* Browning, Robert, and Elizabeth Barrett
WORKS
Agamemnon of Aeschylus (translation), 231
"Andrea del Sarto," 300
Bells and Pomegranates, 95, 110, 144, 157, 163, 194, 240
"Bishop Orders His Tomb at St. Praxed's Church," 163

Blot in the 'Scutcheon, 144, 408
"By the Fire-Side," 274-5, 298
"Christmas-Eve and Easter-Day," 225, 228
"Cleon," 300
Colombe's Birthday, 144, 271
Dramatic Romances and Lyrics, 110, 153, 163, 299
"Englishman in Italy," 163
"Fra Lippo Lippi," 293, 300
"Grammarian's Funeral," 300
"Guardian-Angel," 213, 298
King Victor and King Charles, 144
Luria, 154, 163
Men and Women, 298 f., 304; EBB on, 300; reviewed, 300
"Old Pictures in Florence," 300
"One Word More. To E.B.B.," 298-9
Paracelsus, 49, 95, 142-3, 144
Pauline, 141; reviewed, 142
"Pictor Ignotus," 163
Pippa Passes, 95
Return of the Druses, 144
Sordello, 144, 240, 304
Soul's Tragedy, 148, 154, 163
"Statue and the Bust," 300
Strafford, 143
"Twins," 279
Browning, Robert, and Elizabeth Barrett: departure from London after marriage, 180; visit to Vaucluse, 185; arrival in Pisa, 186; leave Pisa for Florence, 195; first stay in Casa Guidi, 204-5; return to Casa Guidi, 210; leave Florence for Venice, Paris, and London, 242; return to Florence, 268; to Rome, 275, to Paris and London, 288-9; return to Florence, 308, to France, 356, to Rome with Mr. and Mrs. Eckley, 358; return to Florence with the Eckleys, 364; later trips to Rome, 370, 392; last return to Florence, 399
Browning, Robert (the poet's father), 158, 248, 290, 357; birth, 139; at St. Kitts, 140; marriage, 140; secures post in Bank of England, 140; characteristics of, 140; sued by Mrs. Von Müller, 261; moves to Paris, 262
Browning, Robert Wiedeman Barrett

Index 473

(son of EBB and RB, "Pen"), 272, 280 f., 353 f., 402, 419-20; birth, 222; origin of name "Pen," 244; dress and appearance, 244-5, 388, 404; delicate health, 254; idolized by EBB, 254-5, 266, 285-6, 387-8; Italian appearance and manner, 286; education and career, 405; on EBB's belief in spiritualism, 393; publishes RB's and EBB's letters, 415; death, 418

Browning, Sarah Anna (Wiedemann) (the poet's mother), 140; death, 222

Browning, Sarianna (the poet's sister), 169, 248, 290, 357, 413; birth, 140; EBB's comments on, 260; moves to Paris with father, 262

Bryant, William Cullen, visits the Brownings, 354

Brydges, Samuel Egerton, 20, 22

Bulwer-Lytton, Sir Edward, 52, 95, 118; EBB on, 302; describes séance conducted by Home, 302

Burke, Edmund, 23

Burne-Jones, Edward, 305

Burney, Fanny (Madame d'Arblay), 96

Burns, Robert, 22, 102 f.

Burton, Robert, 230

Butler, Samuel, 102

Butler, Samuel (editor of Aeschylus), 48

Byron, George Gordon, 6th Baron, 10 f., 15, 20, 64, 113, 117, 244; EBB's critical estimate of, 103

Byron, Lady, 162

Campan, Madame, 20
Campbell, George, 21
Campbell, Thomas, 11 ff., 64, 117
Card, Henry, 39
Carden, Dr., 32
Carleton, William, 117
Carlyle, Jane Welsh: calls on the Brownings, 264-5; her opinions of RB and EBB, 264
Carlyle, Thomas, 88, 117 f., 130 f., 143, 184, 210, 249, 282, 292, 300; to Paris with the Brownings, 249-50
Cartwright, W. C., 358
Casa Guidi: description of, 204-5; description of the Brownings' apartment in, 210

Catalani, Madame Angelica, 17
Catullus, 31
Cavour, Camillo Benso, Conte di, 220, 360 f., 389, 401; early career of, 209-10; sends troops to the Crimea, 287; triumph of his policy of war against Austria, 362; policy of unification of Italy, 384 ff., 394 ff.; EBB's admiration of, 396-7; death, 399
Cellini, Benvenuto, 20
Chambers, Robert, 99
Chambers, Dr. William Frederick, 72, 155
Chapman and Hall, 225, 228, 240, 271, 279, 282, 304 f., 371, 407, 409
Charles Albert, King of Piedmont: declares war against Austria, 214; defeat at Custoza, 213 f.; defeat at Novara and abdication, 216; death, 220
Chasles, Philarète, 259; lectures on EBB, 260
Chaucer, Geoffrey, 88, 98, 102, 113. *See also* Horne, R. H., *Poems of Geoffrey Chaucer, Modernized*
Child, Lydia Maria, on *Aurora Leigh*, 312
Childe Harold's Pilgrimage, by Byron, 10
Chorley, Henry Fothergill, 59, 69, 90, 94, 96, 126, 132, 184, 189, 226, 237, 249, 263, 371, 378 f., 406 f.; *Authors of England,* 118; reviews *A New Spirit of the Age,* 120-1; course of friendship with EBB, 131; his review of *Poems before Congress* angers the Brownings, 378-9
Christian Examiner, 211, 236, 408, 410
Christian Mother's Magazine, 194, 228
"Christopher North." *See* Wilson, John
Chrysostom, St. John. *See* St. John Chrysostom
Cicero, 14, 31
Cinnamon Hill, Jamaica, 1, 92, 179
Clark, William Andrews, Jr., 423
Clarke, Adam, 31, 43, 50 f., 100
Claudian, 10
Cliffe, Eliza, 39
Cliffes, 42
Clive, Mrs. Archer, receives visit from the Brownings, 279

Cobbe, Frances Power, 284; on RB, 351–2
Cocks, Lady Margaret, 42
Coker, Dr. William, 17
Coleridge, Samuel Taylor, 57, 64, 103, 143, 249
Coleridge, Sara, 249
Collins, Anthony, 52
Commelines, 42
Condillac, Etienne Bonnot de, 14, 23
Considérant, Victor, 320
Cook, Henrietta (Barret Moulton Barrett) (EBB's sister), 32, 37, 42, 55, 73, 81, 91, 173, 248, 262, 297 f., 350, 391, 414; birth, 5; early activities and interests at Hope End, 8, 10; friendship with William Cook, 93; engagement to Cook, 165; description of, by EBB, 194; marriage, 247; the Brownings' last visit with, 307; death, 392
Cook, William Surtees, 93, 165, 247
Cooper, James Fenimore, 21
Corkran, Henriette, impressions of EBB and Pen, 266
Corkran, Mr. and Mrs. John Frazer, 292, 301; receive visits from the Brownings, 266–7
Cornhill Magazine, 388
Cottrell, Count Henry, 211; on "the spirits," 308
Cottrell, Sophia, 211; on "the spirits," 308
Cousin, Victor, 292
Cowley, Abraham, 103
Cowper, William, 96, 102
Coxhoe Hall, 2 ff.
Crawford, Thomas, 277
Crébillon *fils*, 98
Crimean War, 287–8
Critic, 133
Crosland, Mrs. Newton, calls on EBB, 263
Crosse, Mrs. Andrew, her impressions of EBB, 265
Crow, Miss (EBB's maid), 74, 87, 90
Curtis, George William, 204, 406
Curzon, Mr., 37
Cushman, Charlotte, 283, 346, 358; with EBB in Paris, 267; portrait of, by Page, 278

Daily News (London), 211, 345, 380
Dante, 10, 210, 213, 215
Darley, George, 95
Darwin, Erasmus, 14
De Barry, Dr. Robert Fitzwilliam, 75 f.; death, 78
Descartes, René, 23
Dicey, Edward, visits EBB, 398
Dickens, Charles, 94, 97, 118, 211
Dilke, Charles Wentworth, 61, 93 f., 102, 105
Disraeli, Benjamin, 85, 95
Disraeli, Isaac, 23
Domett, Alfred, 144
Douglas, Frederic S. N., 10
Dowglass, Fanny, 205; letter to EBB reproduced, 199
Dryden, John, 102 f.
Dublin University Magazine, 312, 341, 345, 347, 407
Dumas, Alexandre, the Elder, 97 f., 198
Dumas, Alexandre, the Younger, 253
Duncan, James, 13
Dunlop, John, 21
Du Potet de Sennevoy, Jules, Baron, 99
Duyckinck, Evert A., 71, 108

Ealing, séance at. *See* Home, Daniel Dunglas; Spiritualism
Eckley, David, EBB on, 356
Eckley, Mr. and Mrs. David, 354; friendship with the Brownings, 355–6; take the Brownings to Rome, 358
Eckley, Sophia May (Mrs. David), 359 f., 393; EBB on, 355–6; friendship with EBB ends suddenly, 382–4
Eclectic Review, 14, 133, 237 f., 241, 409
Edgeworth, Richard, 20
Edinburgh Review, 406, 416–17
Elgin, Lady, 251, 255; EBB's opinion of, 252
EMB. *See* Barrett, Edward Barrett Moulton
Emerson, Ralph Waldo, 136, 224
English Bijou Almanack, 106
English Review, 237 f.
Epictetus, 30
Erasmus, 31

Index 475

Euripides, 30, 43; *Rhesus*, 29; *Bacchae*, 29, 430; *Heraclidae*, 29, 430; *Hercules furens*, 29, 430; *Alcestis*, 41; *Troades*, 41, 430; *Cyclops*, 430; *Ion*, 430
Examiner, 69 f., 94, 129, 135, 142, 237 f.

Faucit, Helen, 143 f., 271
Field, Kate, 210, 283, 400, 406, 410; her impressions of EBB, 265
Fields, James T., 251, 311
Findens' Tableaux, 63, 77, 436
Fletcher, John, 98, 230
Florence, EBB's first view of, 195; description of, 196–7; the Brownings' everyday activities in, 198–200; EBB's description of chariot races in, 200; the Brownings' apartments in, 195, 204–5, 210; EBB's fondness of, 269, 281–2
Flower, Eliza, 145
Flower, Sarah, 145
Flush (EBB's dog), 60, 87, 168, 180; stolen and held for ransom, 176–7; death, 282
Fonblanque, Albany, 117
Ford, John, 102
Forster, John, 135, 142 f., 171, 249, 264, 292, 371
Fourier, Charles, 320, 326; opinions of, 327
Fox, Charles James, 20, 22, 24
Fox, William Johnson, 142 f., 145, 249, 263, 292, 371
Francis, C. S., 236, 240, 251, 305, 371
Fraser's Magazine, 237 f., 377–8
Fuller, Margaret (Marchesa d'Ossoli), 136; life and literary career of, 224–5; description of, by EBB, 224–5; death, 225

Garibaldi, Giuseppe, 218, 220, 240, 389, 394, 396; EBB on, 386–7, 395; EBB on his expedition to Sicily, 391
Garrick, David, 20
Garrow, Theodosia (later Mrs. T. A. Trollope), 74
Gascoigne, George, 230
Gellius, Aulus, 31
Genlis, Countess de, 20, 96

George Pisida, 100 f.
Gibson, John, 277
Gilfillan, George, 226
Gladstone, William Ewart, 366
Globe (London), 133, 345, 378
Globe and Traveller (London), 12
Goethe, 9
Gordigiani, Michele, portrait of EBB by, 355, 359
Gore, Catherine, 94, 117
Gosse, Sir Edmund, 419, 422
Graham-Clarke, Arabella (Altham) (EBB's grandmother), 12 f., 17
Graham-Clarke, Arabella (EBB's aunt, "Bummy"), 12, 17, 32, 37 ff., 43, 74, 173, 189, 248
Graham-Clarke, John (EBB's grandfather), 2 f., 5, 17
Graham-Clarke, John Altham (EBB's uncle), 17
Graham's Magazine, 108 f., 135, 137
Greek Christian poets. *See under* EBB's Works
Gregory Nazianzen, St. *See* St. Gregory Nazianzen
Grey, Charles, 2d Earl, 39
Grisanowsky, E. G. F., 367
Griswold, Rufus W., 135
Guardian, 237, 239 ff
Guerrazzi, Francesco Domenico, 215, 240; made dictator of Tuscany, 216; EBB's opinion of, 218
Guizot, François, 254

Habington, William, 230
Hale, Nathan, Jr., 108, 110
Hall, Robert, 51
Hall, Samuel Carter, 61
Hall, Mrs. S. C., 94, 117
Harding, Dr., 227
Harper's Magazine, 237, 406
Harvard College Library, 422
Hawes, Stephen, 230
Hawkins, Laetitia Matilda, 20
Haworth, Euphrasia Fanny, 145, 354, 359, 413
Hawthorne, Nathaniel, 283 f.; on Hiram Powers, 202; on W. W. Story, 273; on Harriet Hosmer, 277; meets EBB in

Hawthorne, Nathaniel (*continued*)
London, 305; on EBB, 305, 355; on Pen, 354; visits the Brownings in Florence, 354-5; on RB, 355. *See also Blithedale Romance*
Haydon, Benjamin Robert, 169, 284; EBB's correspondence with, 106-8; death, 170-1
Hayley, William, 96
Hazlitt, William, 107, 117 f., 120
Heaton, Ellen, 359
Hedley, Arabella (EBB's cousin), 173
Hedley, Jane (Graham-Clarke) (EBB's aunt), 73, 156, 173, 175, 189, 349
Hedley, John ("Uncle Hedley"), 73, 173, 175
Heliodorus (author of the *Aethiopica*), 30, 100
Hemans, Felicia, 21, 49, 63, 96, 118
Hephaestion, 30
Heraud, John A., 95
Herodotus, 14
Higginson, Thomas Wentworth, 417
Hillard, George Stillman, 57, 71, 205-6
Holland, Henry Richard, 3d Baron, 20
Home, Daniel Dunglas, 284; T. A. Trollope on, 293; conducts séance at Ealing, 293-4; EBB on, 294-5; RB on, 295; RB angry with, 295-6; Bulwer-Lytton on, 302; Robert Lytton on, 302; séances in Florence, 308
Homer, 9 ff., 15, 25, 30, 88, 230; *Iliad*, 43; *Odyssey*, 43
Hood, Thomas, 114, 136
Hooker, Richard, 9
Hope End, 5, 8, 114; description of, 6 f.; seized to satisfy EMB's creditors, 35; the Barrett family's departure from, 43
Hoppner, Mr. and Mrs. R. B., 200
Horace, 10, 22, 31
Horne, Richard Hengist, 88, 93, 95, 143, 249, 436; helps EBB, 77; life and literary career, 83; edits *Poems of Geoffrey Chaucer, Modernized*, 82-3, 227; collaborates with EBB in writing "Psyche Apocalypté," 84-5; *Orion* reviewed by EBB, 104-5; report on children's employment, 114-15; later career of friendship with EBB, 121, 148-9; publication of EBB's letters to, 410-11; edits *A New Spirit of the Age*, 116-19; collaborates with EBB in writing *A New Spirit*, 116-17; critique on EBB in *A New Spirit*, 118-19; *A New Spirit* reviewed, 119-21; *A New Spirit* referred to, 16, 88
Hosmer, Harriet, 282 f., 358; life and artistic career, 277
Howitt, Mary, 63, 95; visits EBB, 305
Howitt, William, 97, 451
HSB. *See* Boyd, Hugh Stuart
Hudibras, by Butler, 102
Hugo, Victor, 97 f.
Hume, David, 9, 21
Hunt, Leigh, 83, 107, 117 f., 130, 226; letter to RB praising *Aurora Leigh*, 310-11
Hunt, Theodore W., 411
Hunter, George Barrett, 74, 90; close friendship with EBB, 52-3; early description of, by EBB, 52; later career, 53; characteristics of, 53; decline of fortunes, 147; quarrels with EBB, 147-8; violence toward RB, 148; breaks friendship with EBB, 148; death, 348-9
Hunter, Mary (daughter of G. B. Hunter), 52, 66, 147
Huxley, Leonard, 419

Independent (New York), 82, 388, 397, 408
Ingram, John H., 412-13
Irving, Washington, 11, 118
Isocrates, 30
Italy, EBB's disenchantment with Italian literature and the Catholic Church in, 192-3; further disillusionment, 215, 217; EBB's delight in, 198, 353

James, G. P. R., 94, 117
James, Henry, 211, 273
Jameson, Anna (Murphy), 21, 97, 117, 143, 154, 156, 170, 249, 263, 292 f., 360, 413; course of friendship with EBB, 162; with EBB at Rogers' art gallery, 168-9; encourages EBB to go to Italy, 174; accompanies the Brownings from

Index

Paris to Pisa, 181–7; visits the Brownings in Florence, 202–3; with EBB in Paris, 254; death, 382
Jane Eyre, by Charlotte Brontë, 316–17, 337, 343
Janin, Jules, 97
Jarves, James Jackson, 256, 393; life and literary career, 283; interest in spiritualism, 284, 302
Jerdan, William, 14
Jerrold, Douglas, 117
Jewish Expositor and Friend of Israel, 30
John Bull, 134, 379–80
John Chrysostom. *See* St. John Chrysostom
John Mauropus, 100
Johnson, Samuel, 20, 102
Jung-Stilling, Johann Heinrich, 96, 99

Kant, Immanuel, 21
Keats, John, 64, 70, 99, 102, 107, 123, 136, 210, 398
Keepsake, 280
Kemble, Adelaide (Mrs. Edward Sartoris), 282, 292, 303; the Brownings' friendship with, 278–9
Kemble, Fanny (Mrs. Pierce Butler), 249; the Brownings' friendship with, 278–9
Kemble, John Philip, 20
Kenyon, John, 14, 72, 74, 90 f., 93, 113, 123, 130, 139, 143, 156, 159, 162 f., 170 f., 175, 210, 246, 249, 264, 279, 282, 305 f.; influence on EBB, 56; kindness toward EBB, 146; relationship to the Barrett family, 56, 433; life and writings, 56–7; introduces EBB to M. R. Mitford, 57–8; helps EBB with *Poems* (1844), 122, 124; approves of the Brownings' marriage, 184; manages EBB's funds, 189; serious illness, 306; receives the Brownings at West Cowes, 306; *Aurora Leigh* dedicated to, 307; death, 348; his legacy to the Brownings, 348
Kenyon, Sir Frederic George, 7, 413
Kinglake, Alexander W., 97, 292
Kingsley, Charles, 327; EBB's opinion of, 264

Kinney, Elizabeth Clementine (Dodge) Stedman, 360; EBB on, 270–1; on "the spirits," 308
Kinney, William Burnet, 283; friendship with the Brownings, 270
Kirkup, Seymour, 283, 368; life and interests, 284–5
Knickerbocker Magazine, 137, 410
Knowles, James Sheridan, 118
Kock, Paul de, 97 f.

Lafarge, Madame Marie Pouch-, 96
Lamb, Lady Caroline, 63
Lamb, Charles, 57, 107
Landon, Letitia Elizabeth, 21, 63, 65, 77, 95 f.
Landor, Walter Savage, 56, 59, 62, 64, 117, 130, 143, 283, 369, 391; EBB's first impression of, 58; on *Aurora Leigh*, 311; befriended by RB, 368; placed by RB in Wilson's lodging house, 369–70; quarrels with Wilson, 390
Las Cases, Emmanuel, 20
Lawrence, Sir Thomas, 2, 24
Ledbury, 6
Le Havre, EBB's dislike of, 357
Leighton, Sir Frederick, 358
Leopold II, Grand Duke of Tuscany, 205, 207, 240; EBB's approval of, 208; flees from Florence, 216, 364; return to Florence, 216; EBB's low opinion of, 217 f.
Lever, Charles, 117, 197, 223
Lewis, Matthew G., 96
Liberty Bell, 111, 194, 228, 372
Library of Congress, 422
Lindsell, W., 11
Lippincott's Magazine, 411
Literary Gazette, 14, 22, 30, 63, 70, 241, 346
Literary Souvenir, 21
Literary World (Boston), 411 f., 416
Livy, 31
Locke, John, 9, 21, 23
Locker (afterward Locker-Lampson), Frederick, on EBB, 292
Lockhart, John G., 21; his comment on RB, 278
London, the Barrett family moves to, 54; the Barretts' homes in, 55, 71–2; the

London (continued)
  Brownings' places of residence in, 247, 260, 292, 305
London Mercury, 420
London Quarterly Review, 413
Longinus, 29; De sublimitate, 30
Lover, Samuel, 117
Lowell, James Russell, 108, 131, 136, 264, 273, 417; EBB's friendship with, 110–11
Lowell, Maria (White), 111, 264, 417, 438
Lubbock, Percy, 418
Lucan, Pharsalia, 31
Lucretius, De rerum natura, 31, 113
Luther, Martin, 52, 280
Lytton, Robert (Owen Meredith), 272, 283, 331, 353; friendship with the Brownings, 269; EBB's opinion of, 269–70; on "the spirits," 302; praises Aurora Leigh, 311

Macaulay, Thomas Babington, 95, 117
Macpherson, Gerardine (Bate), 174, 183, 186 f.
Macready, William Charles, 59, 118, 143; RB quarrels with, 144; visits the Brownings in Paris, 303
MacSwiney, Mr., 10
Mahony, Francis Sylvester (Father Prout), 211–12, 371
Malmesbury, Earl of, tries to maintain peace, 361
Malthus, Thomas Robert, 111, 120
Marryat, Captain Frederick, 94, 117
Marsh, George Perkins, 270
Martin, Mrs. James, 47, 349–50, 413
Martin, Mr. and Mrs. James, 6, 42, 189
Martineau, Harriet, 88, 97, 117 f., 130 f., 143; course of friendship with EBB, 111–12
Massinger, Philip, 98, 102
Mathews, Cornelius, 13, 71, 113, 121, 225; EBB's friendship with, 108–10; reviews Poems (1844), 136
Maurice, Frederick Denison, 327
Mauropus. See John Mauropus
Mazzini, Giuseppe, 218, 220, 252; sees the Brownings, 264; EBB's disapproval of, 395

Mérimée, Prosper, 292
Merlette, Germaine-Marie, 417
Methodist Quarterly Review, 136
Metropolitan Magazine, 68, 70, 132
Mignet, François Auguste, 292
Mill, John Stuart, 142
Milnes, Richard Monckton, 95, 99, 117, 123, 184, 305, 355, 371
Milnes, Mr. and Mrs. Richard Monckton, 264
Milsand, Joseph, 259, 292, 300, 357; EBB's opinion of, 252
Milton, John, 103, 230; Paradise Lost, 9, 169; Prose Works, 22
Mimnermus, 48
Mitford, Mary Russell, 25, 59, 90, 106, 118, 131, 155, 162, 184, 249, 410, 413 f.; beginning of friendship with EBB, 57–8; course of friendship with EBB, 59–60; describes EBB, 61; edits Findens' Tableaux, 63, 77, 436; disapproval of RB, 95, 190; fears that EBB is forgetting her, 189–90; opinion of Casa Guidi Windows, 241; offends EBB by referring to Bro's death, 258–60; death, 292
Mohl, Madame Julius, 254, 292, 303; EBB's opinion of, 252
Molière, 10
Montgomery, Robert, 95
Monthly Chronicle, 69, 77, 436
Monthly Repository, 142
Monthly Review, 68 f., 133
Montpensier, Duchess of, 96
Moore, Thomas, 11, 64, 120
Morgan, Lady Sydney, 58, 118
Morphine (or opium), EBB's use of, 75, 89, 190
Morris, William, 300, 305
Motley, John Lothrop, 359
Moulton, Charles (EBB's grandfather), 2, 92
Moulton, Elizabeth (Barrett) (EBB's grandmother), 1 ff., 5, 13, 16 f., 157; death, 36
Moulton, Sarah Goodin ("Pinkie") (EMB's sister), 1 f.
Moxon, Edward, 76, 103, 122 f., 194, 225, 251, 282

Index

Müller, Mrs. Von, sues Robert Browning, Sr., 261
Mulock, Dinah (later Mrs. Craik), calls on EBB, 263
Murphy, Francis, 2
Musset, Alfred de, 254
Mystères de Paris, by Sue, 98, 251, 322–3, 330, 335

Napoleon III (formerly Louis Napoleon), 251, 256, 287, 301, 361 f., 369, 384, 389, 394, 396 f., 414; destroys the republic of Rome, 218; *coup d'état*, 256–7; EBB on, 257 f., 360, 363–4, 366 f., 373–4, 386; RB's attitude toward, 258; EBB observes his entrance into Paris, 266–7; agreement with Cavour at Plombières, 360–1; leads army against Austrian troops in Italy, 362; asks for armistice at Villafranca, 362; reasons for armistice, 363; his policy toward Italy, 371, 394; seizes Savoy and Nice, 385
Nation (New York), 410, 415
National Quarterly Review, 346
National Review, 340, 342, 345, 420
New Monthly Magazine, 11, 15, 49, 61, 94, 133, 142, 406, 436
New Quarterly Review, 126
New Spirit of the Age. See Horne, Richard Hengist
New York Daily Tribune, 135, 224
Newnham, William, 99
Newton, Sir Isaac, 23
Nightingale, Florence, 376 f., 424; calls on EBB, 263; EBB on, 288
Noble, James Ashcroft, 422
North American Review, 71, 346, 409
North British Review, 347, 409
Norton, Mr. and Mrs. Brinsley, 287
Norton, Caroline, 63, 65, 95, 117
Norton, Charles Eliot, 273; visits the Brownings in Florence, 239–40; visits the Brownings in London, 305
Nuttall, Dr. G. B., 17

Ogilvy, Mrs. David, 243
Ogilvy, Mr. and Mrs. David, 243
Opie, Amelia, 9
Orme, Mrs. (EBB's governess), 8, 83, 436

Orr, Mrs. Sutherland, 140 f., 414
Ossian, 25
Ovid, 10

Page, William, 201, 256, 276, 281; EBB's opinion of, 277–8; artistic career, 277–8
Paine, Thomas, 9, 141
Palmerston, Lord, 366, 377, 391; helps Italian cause, 219–20, 367
Pancoast, Henry S., 418
Pantaleoni, Diomede, 398
Paris, EBB's childhood trip to, 16; EBB's fondness of, 182–3, 246, 301; the Brownings' apartments in, 246, 250, 301, 303
Parker, Theodore, visits EBB, 387
Parkhurst, John, 41
Parr, Samuel, 22, 32, 51
Patmore, Coventry, 95, 123, 347
Paul Silentiarius, 100 f.
Percy, Thomas, 22, 103
Perkins, Charles Callahan, 359
Petrarch, 127, 185, 245
Peytons (of Barton Court), 7, 42
Pierpont Morgan Library, 235
Pindar, 30, 43
Pioneer, 110
Pisa, the Brownings' arrival at, 186; their home in, 187; EBB's description of, 190; the Brownings' domestic routine in, 191; social life in, 192; the Brownings' departure from, 195
Pisida. See George Pisida
Pitt, William, the Younger, 20
Pius IX, 214, 217, 240; early liberalism of, 206–7; EBB on, 209; flees from Rome to Gaeta, 215; his power restored by Louis Napoleon, 218; refuses to yield in *1861*, 396
Plato, 10, 230; *Phaedo*, 30; EBB's reading of, 76
Plutarch, 14
Poe, Edgar Allan, reviews EBB's works, 126, 137–8
Pope, Alexander, 9 f., 13 f., 102
Powell, Thomas, 227
Power, Marguerite A., 280
Powers, Hiram, 255 f., 272; life and career, 201–2

Presbyterian and Reformed Review, 411
Press (London), 343, 347
Price, Sir Uvedale, 23 f., 27, 36
Procter, Adelaide, 166, 292
Procter, Bryan Waller (Barry Cornwall), 95, 143, 166, 184, 249, 280, 292, 305; on *Aurora Leigh*, 311
Prospective Review, 133, 240
Proudhon, Pierre Joseph, 320
Prout, William, 52
Pusey, Edward Bouverie, 118
Putnam's Monthly Magazine, 346

Quarterly Review, 68 f.

Racine, 10
Radetzky, Marshal von, 213 f., 216
Reade, John Edmund, 95, 445
Reader, 410
Revue des Deux Mondes, 252, 259, 300
Ricardo, David, 111
Ricasoli, Bettino, 364, 389, 401
Richardson, Samuel, 96
Risorgimento:
  FIRST PHASE: popular demonstration in Florence, EBB's description of, 207–8; Charles Albert declares war against Austria, 214; is defeated at Custoza, 214; declares war again, 216; is defeated at Novara, 216; all Italy, except Piedmont, again dominated by Austria, 220; reasons for failure of uprising, 220–1
  SECOND PHASE: outbreak of war against Austria, 362; battles of Magenta and Solferino, 362; armistice at Villafranca, 362–3; northern and central Italy united, 385; Sicily and southern Italy added to new Kingdom of Italy, 395
  ENGLISH HELP TO THE ITALIAN CAUSE: 219–20, 366–7, 384, 395
Ristori, Adelaide, 292
Ritchie, Lady Anne (Thackeray), impressions of EBB in Rome, 265–6
Robinson, Henry Crabb, 56, 264
Rogers, Samuel, 24, 64, 123, 249; EBB visits art collection of, 168–9

Romagnoli, Ferdinando, 301, 353; EBB on, 290–1
Rome: the Brownings' apartments in, 275–6, 358, 370, 392; EBB's opinion of, 280, 359; RB's dislike of, 280; RB's gay social life in, 280–1, 359, 393
Rossetti, Christina, 417, 420, 424
Rossetti, Dante Gabriel, 131, 293, 300, 303 f., 371; on *Aurora Leigh*, 312
Rossetti, William Michael, 131, 293, 371; on *Aurora Leigh*, 312; on Napoleon III, 381
Rossi, Pellegrino, 214 f.
Rousseau, Jean-Jacques, 9
Rowton, Frederick, 227
Ruskin, John, 300, 371; receives the Brownings, 263; EBB's opinion of, 263; praises *Aurora Leigh*, 311
Russell, Lord John, 366, 377, 384, 391, 395
Russell, Odo, 358
Ruth (Mrs. Gaskell), 336, 343
Rymer, Mr. and Mrs., 293, 302
Rymer, Mrs., 295

St. Basil, 26, 29 f., 50 f.
St. Gregory Nazianzen, 25 f., 29 f., 43, 50 f., 232; EBB translates three hymns of, 100
St. John Chrysostom, 25 f., 29 f., 43, 50 f., 100, 230
St. Synesius, 26, 30, 51, 100; EBB's translation of, 101–2
Saint-Pierre, Jacques de, 21
Saint-Simon, Duke of, 96
Sand, George (Madame Dudevant), 97 f., 198, 313; EBB's sonnets addressed to, 130; the Brownings visit her in Paris, 252–3
Saturday Review, 338, 375–6, 406, 408
Saunders and Otley, 64
Scarlett, James (later Lord Abinger), 4
Scheffer, Ary, 254
Schindler, Anton F., 96
Schlegel, A. W., 23
Scholefield, James, 48
Scott, Sir Walter, 11, 107
Scully, Dr., 75, 78, 85
Sedgwick, Catharine M., 97

Index

Severn, Joseph, 398
Sévigné, Madame de, 10
Seward, Anna, 96
Shakespeare, William, 9, 98, 102, 197, 202, 411
Shaw, Mrs. Francis George, 276 f., 280, 438
Shelley, Mary Wollstonecraft (Godwin), 117
Shelley, Percy Bysshe, 11, 64, 68, 76, 99, 102, 107, 118, 123, 141, 143, 200, 223, 251
Shirley, James, 102
Sidmouth: description of, 44; the Barretts' homes in, 44, 54
Siena, the Brownings' places of residence in, 227–8, 367, 369, 390
Sigourney, Lydia, 97, 131
Silentiarius. *See* Paul Silentiarius
Silverthorne, James, 178, 260
Smith, Sydney, 117 f.
Smith, Thomas Southwood, 118
Sophocles, 30 f., 43; *Ajax*, 20; *Oedipus Tyrannus*, 28
Soulié, Frédéric, 97 f., 191, 198
Southern Literary Messenger, 137, 407
Southey, Caroline, 65
Southey, Robert, 21, 56, 64, 96, 117
Spectator, 126, 238, 241, 339 f., 343, 406, 414, 416
Spence, Joseph, 23
Spenser, Edmund, 102, 127, 230
Spicer, Henry, 255
Spiritualism, manifestations of, 255; EBB's interest in, 255–6, 294 ff., 303, 393; EBB talks about, with Hawthorne, 305, 355; referred to, in *Aurora Leigh*, 326. *See also* Eckley, Sophia M.; Home, D. D.; Jarves, J. J.; Kirkup, Seymour; Stowe, H. B.
Staël, Madame de, 20; *Corinne*, 41, 318–19
Stanhope, Leicester, 429
Stedman, Edmund Clarence, 270, 419, 422
Stendhal (Henri Beyle), 97, 191
Stephen, Sir Leslie, 416
Sterling, John, 123, 136
Stewart, Dugald, 23

Stoddard, Richard Henry, 410
Story, Edith, 272, 276, 281, 369
Story, Emelyn (Mrs. W. W.), 360, 369, 438; EBB's opinion of, 272
Story, Joe, 272; death, 276
Story, William Wetmore, 256, 272, 277, 368, 399; life and artistic career, 273; asks RB to come to Velletri, 281; RB models in studio of, 393
Story, Mr. and Mrs., 275, 358, 390–1, 400, 402; become acquainted with the Brownings, 211; friendship with the Brownings, 272; trip to Prato Fiorito with the Brownings, 274; at Siena with the Brownings, 368–9; help the Brownings at Rome, 370
Stowe, Harriet Beecher: visits EBB, 352; on spiritualism, 393
Stuart, James Montgomery, 197, 223
Stuart-Wortley, Lady Emmeline, 63
Sue, Eugène, 97, 198. *See also Mystères de Paris*
Sumner, Charles, 273; visits the Brownings in Paris, 357
Sunbeam, 67–8
Swedenborg, Emanuel, 99
Swinburne, Algernon Charles, on *Aurora Leigh*, 310
Synesius, St. *See* St. Synesius

Tablet (Dublin), 341, 347
Tait's Edinburgh Magazine, 94, 132, 226
Talfourd, Field, his portrait of EBB, 359
Talfourd, Sir Thomas Noon (Serjeant), 95, 97, 117 f., 131, 143, 171
Taylor, Bayard, 249
Taylor, Sir Henry, 95, 117, 445
Taylor, Tom, 171
Tennyson, Alfred, 49, 65, 70, 88, 117 f., 120, 123, 138, 210, 264, 332, 408; EBB's early admiration of, 95, 104; description of portrait of, 118; EBB compared with, by reviewers, 68, 136; EBB on his claim to poet laureateship, 226; sees the Brownings in Paris, 246–7; visits the Brownings in London, 292–3; EBB distressed at his "Riflemen Form!" 365
Tennyson, Mrs. Alfred, 264; EBB on, 247

Tennyson, Frederick, 272, 286; friendship with the Brownings, 270
Terence, 31
Thackeray, William Makepeace, 95, 291, 388; meets EBB in Rome, 279
Theognis, 48
Ticknor, George, 72, 110
Tilton, Theodore, 388, 408
Times (London), 30, 64, 179, 258, 262, 364, 375, 393, 421
Times Literary Supplement, 421
Torquay: EBB sent to, 72; EBB's homes in, 73–4; EBB departs from, 86–7
Transcript (Boston), 415
Trant, Mrs., 27 f.
Trepsack, Mary, 1 f., 5, 17, 168
Trollope, Frances, 94, 97, 117, 192, 197, 283; on D. D. Home in Florence, 302
Trollope, Thomas Adolphus, 75, 283 ff., 355; on D. D. Home, 293
Tuckerman, Henry Theodore, 226
Turnbull Library, 22
Twisleton, Mrs. Edward, visits EBB in London and Florence, 265
Tyrtaeus, 14

United States Magazine and Democratic Review, 109; reviews *A New Spirit of the Age*, 121

Vallombrosa, the Brownings' trip to, 203–4
Valpy, A. J., 48
Vasari, Georgio, 187, 191, 198
Vaudoncourt, F. G. de, 429
Venables, G. S., 375
Victor Emmanuel II (King of Sardinia and later King of Italy), 216, 220, 361, 364, 386, 389, 394
Villari, Pasquale, 272

Virgil, 11; *Aeneid*, 10, 31, 41; *Eclogues*, 31; *Georgics*, 31
Voltaire, 9, 142

Walpole, Horace, 20
Wardlaw, Ralph, 51
Ware, William, 211
Warton, Thomas, 102
Wedgwood, Julia, 234
Wellesley College Library, 20, 413
Werther, by Goethe, 9
Westminster Review, 134, 342, 344, 347, 397, 412; reviews *A New Spirit of the Age*, 120
Westwood, Thomas, 106
Whipple, Edwin Percy, 136
Wilson, Dr., 400 ff.
Wilson, Elizabeth (Madame Romagnoli), 180, 197, 200, 353, 391, 401; at EBB's wedding, 178; engagement and marriage, 290–1; appears to be insane, 365–6; difficulties with Landor, 390
Wilson, John (Christopher North), 68 ff.
Wimpole Street (Barretts' home at No. 50): purchased by EMB, 71–2; description of EBB's room, 88
Wither, George, 230
Wolf, F. A., 43
Wollstonecraft, Mary (Mrs. William Godwin), 9
Woolf, Virginia, on *Aurora Leigh*, 421
Woolner, Thomas, 371; on *Aurora Leigh*, 311
Wordsworth, William, 24, 56 ff., 64, 83 f., 88, 90, 99, 117 f., 120, 123, 130, 143, 311; EBB describes her first conversation with, 58–9; EBB reviews *Poems* of, 103–4; writes EBB, 107; death, 226

Xenophon, 10, 30

Yale Review, 421